THE LIFE OF RICHARD WAGNER
1866-1883

ERNEST NEWMAN

The Life of
RICHARD
WAGNER

VOLUME FOUR : 1866–1883

CASSELL

LONDON

CASSELL & COMPANY LIMITED
35 Red Lion Square, London WC1R 4SG
and at Sydney, Auckland, Toronto, Johannesburg,
an affiliate of
Macmillan Publishing Co., Inc.,
New York

First published in Great Britain 1947
This edition 1976

ISBN 0 304 29763 1

Printed in Great Britain
at the
University Printing House, Cambridge
(Euan Phillips, University Printer)

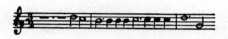

FOREWORD

THIS FINAL volume of the Life of Wagner has taken me longer than I had anticipated: I can only plead in extenuation that the past four years of war have not been exactly ideal for sustained intellectual work.

The severance of communications with the Continent since 1939 has perhaps meant my missing some new material, though I hardly think that much of first-rate significance will have come to light during that time. No Life of Wagner, of course, can be considered as anything like final until Wahnfried has opened many more of its treasures to our examination; it is probable, indeed, that more than one of our present facts and judgments will call for correction or modification when certain eagerly awaited documents, such as Cosima's diaries, Wagner's "Red Book" and "Annals" and "Brown Book", and the correspondence of Wagner and Cosima, are published in full, when certain letters to and from Liszt, Bülow, Cornelius and others are released from quarantine, and when a number of passages that have obviously been suppressed in letters already published have been restored.

Errors in my earlier volumes there are bound to be; no work on this scale that has occupied an author for many years can possibly be free of them. I have derived some consolation in this connection from the study of the five volumes of Wagner-Ludwig documents issued in recent years by Dr. Otto Strobel, the archivist of Wahnfried. Dr. Strobel is by far the ablest, the best-informed, and the most conscientious of the long line of Wagnerian editors; yet his later volumes contain several self-corrections, further corrections, and even corrections of previous corrections. All in all, however, I feel I can plead, as Sydney Smith once did, that if I have sometimes blundered it was "not in consequence of neglect but in spite of attention". *Feci quod potui; faciant majora potentes.*

The reader may perhaps be surprised at the amount of space

allotted to Nietzsche in this volume. I had been accumulating for many years material for a book on Nietzsche. But I had become increasingly conscious latterly that even if I could ever find time to write that book — which is unlikely — my interest in it had faded; so I decided to incorporate in the present volume most of the material I had collected bearing on the relations of Nietzsche and Wagner. After all, Wagner-biography and Nietzsche-biography will for ever be inseparable. So far the subject of the personal relations of the two men has been superficially treated because it was no one's province in particular to go into it minutely: the Nietzscheans, inheriting their idol's hatred of Wagner, were too glad of any stick to beat the latter with to question the truth of some of the statements of the philosopher and his sister, while the Wagnerians with no particular interest in Nietzsche merely turned with a contemptuous shrug of the shoulders from the stupidities and vulgarities of *Der Fall Wagner* and dismissed that brochure and its author from their minds. What we may call the Nietzsche-Wagner legend has consequently had a long and almost unchallenged run.

That it *is* largely a legend I have tried to show in the present book, a legend deliberately imposed on the world by Elisabeth Förster-Nietzsche, who took it over from her brother's talk and from *Ecce Homo*. Nearly forty years ago Bernouilli and others drew on themselves the enmity of the Nietzscheans by their frank criticism not only of Elisabeth's lack of intellectual qualifications for the task she had assumed but of the way she went about it. Later research leads us to the conclusion that they under- rather than overstated the case against her. My own conviction, after long and intensive work at the much-admired Life of Nietzsche, is that it is one of the major impostures of literary biography.

In these pages, of course, I am not concerned with Nietzsche's philosophy as such. My concern has been purely and simply with Nietzsche-Wagner *biography* at the points where the orbits of the two men crossed — to find out just what happened, and why. For some of the plain facts of the affair have obviously been falsified by Elisabeth, while her interpretations of them, merely taken over as they were from her brother in the last poisoned years of his sane life, are not to be accepted as blindly as they have hitherto been at their face value. The world is familiar with Nietzsche's jibe at official Wagner-biography — it was *"fable convenue,* or worse", he said. But that description applies equally well to official Nie-tzsche-biography; it is high time, indeed, that Elisabeth's work went the way of those of Glasenapp and Chamberlain on Wagner and that of Lina Ramann on Liszt, to be replaced by something more objective in its presentation of the facts and more scrupulous in its purpose and methods.

E. N.

Tadworth, January 1945.

THE LIFE OF RICHARD WAGNER

CONTENTS

ADDITIONAL SOURCES AND REFERENCES

English translations exist of the works marked with an asterisk.

A

ANVP = CHARLES ANDLER: *Nietzsche, sa vie et sa pensée.* 6 vols. Paris, 1920 ff.

B

BON = C. A. BERNOUILLI: *Franz Overbeck und Friedrich Nietzsche: eine Freundschaft.* 2 vols. Jena, 1908.

BWG = LOUIS BARTHOU: *Richard Wagner et Judith Gautier, documents inédits.* (In *Revue de Paris*, 1 and 15 August, 1932).

C

CER = O. CRUSIUS: *Erwin Rohde: ein biographischer Versuch.* Tübingen, 1902.

CNU = PAUL COHN: *Um Nietzsches Untergang.* Hanover, 1931.

CRWD = HOUSTON S. CHAMBERLAIN: *Richard Wagner der Deutsche als Künstler, Denker und Politiker.* Leipzig, n.d.

CWBD = *Cosima Wagners Briefe an ihre Tochter Daniela von Bülow, 1866–1885: herausgegeben von Max Freiherr von Waldberg.* Stuttgart and Berlin, 1933.

CWFN = *Die Briefe Cosima Wagners an Friedrich Nietzsche, herausgegeben von Erhart Thierbach.* I Teil. Weimar, 1938.

E

EJ = CARL EULER: *Friedrich Ludwig Jahn, sein Leben und Wirken.* Stuttgart, 1881.

EP = WALTHER EGGERT: *Parsifal vor 50 Jahren: ein Bayreuther Zeitbild.* Bayreuth, 1932.

F

FBDJ = RICHARD FRICKE: *Bayreuth vor dreissig Jahren. Erinnerungen an Wahnfried und aus dem Festspielhause.* Dresden, 1906.

FNEN* = ELISABETH FÖRSTER-NIETZSCHE: *Der einsame Nietzsche.* Leipzig, 1914.

SOURCES AND REFERENCES

FNJN* = ELISABETH FÖRSTER-NIETZSCHE: *Der junge Nietzsche.* Leipzig, 1912.

FNLN = ELISABETH FÖRSTER-NIETZSCHE: *Das Leben Friedrich Nietzsches.* 3 vols. Leipzig, 1895–1904.

G

GAWM = ALBERT GUTMANN: *Aus dem Wiener Musikleben: Künstler-Erinnerungen 1873–1908.* Vol. I. Vienna, 1914.

J

JRW = ADOLPHE JULLIEN: *Richard Wagner, sa vie et ses œuvres.* Paris, 1886.

K

KB = FRIEDRICH KLOSE: *Bayreuth: Eindrücke und Erlebnisse.* Regensburg, 1929.

KGSB = JULIUS KAPP: *Geschichte der Staatsoper Berlin.* Berlin, 1937.

L

LMW* = LILLI LEHMANN: *Mein Weg.* 2nd ed. Leipzig, 1920.

M

MEW = RICHARD GRAF DU MOULIN ECKART: *Wahnfried.* Leipzig, 1925.

N

NBO = *Friedrich Nietzsches Briefwechsel mit Franz Overbeck, herausgegeben von Richard Oehler und C. A. Bernouilli.* Leipzig, 1916.

NEH* = NIETZSCHE: *Ecce Homo.* [Edited by Raoul Richter, n.d. 1908].

NERW* = ANGELO NEUMANN: *Erinnerungen an Richard Wagner.* 3rd ed. Leipzig, 1907.

NGB = NIETZSCHE: *Gesammelte Briefe.* 6 vols. Leipzig, 1900–1909.

NNS = LUDWIG NOHL: *Neues Skizzenbuch.* Munich, 1868.

NW* = NIETZSCHE: *Werke.* 20 vols. Leipzig, 1895 ff.

P

PRWV = HENRY PERL: *Richard Wagner in Venedig: Musikbilder aus seinen letzten Lebenstagen.* Augsburg, 1883.

R

RB = LEOPOLD REICHWEIN: *Bayreuth: Werden und Wesen der Bayreuther Bühnenfestspiele.* Bielefeld and Leipzig, 1934.

RKS = ERWIN ROHDE: *Kleine Schriften.* 2 vols. Tübingen, 1901.

RWBB* = *Bayreuther Briefe von Richard Wagner, 1871–1883.* Leipzig, 1911.

RWBH* = *Briefe Richard Wagners an Emil Heckel, herausgegeben von Karl Heckel.* Berlin, 1899.

RWJG = *Die Briefe Richard Wagners an Judith Gautier, herausgegeben von Willi Schuh.* Zürich, 1936.

RWLD = *Fünf unveröffentlichte Briefe Richard Wagners an Lorenz von Düfflipp, mitgeteilt von Sebastian Röckl:* in *Die Musik*, XXV Jahrgang, 1932/3.

RWSP = SEBASTIAN RÖCKL: *Richard Wagner und die "Süddeutsche Presse".* (In *Zeitschrift für Musik*, July, 1933).

S

SERW = LUDWIG SCHEMANN: *Meine Erinnerungen an Richard Wagner.* Stuttgart, 1902.

SNWR = ERNEST SEILLIÈRE: *Nietzsches Waffenbruder, Erwin Rohde.* Berlin, 1911.

V

VM = PETER VIERECK: *Metapolitics. From the Romantics to Wagner.* New York, 1941.

W

WL = HANS VON WOLZOGEN: *Lebensbilder.* Regensburg, 1923.

WMZP = ULRICH VON WILAMOWITZ-MÖLLENDORFF: *Zukunftsphilologie! Eine Erwiderung auf Friedrich Nietzsches "Geburt der Tragödie".* Berlin, 1872.

WMZZS = ULRICH VON WILAMOWITZ-MÖLLENDORFF: *Zukunftsphilologie! Zweites Stück: Eine Erwiderung auf die Rettungsversuche für Fr. Nietzsches "Geburt der Tragödie".* Berlin, 1873.

THE LIFE OF RICHARD WAGNER
1866-1883

CHAPTER I

THE MALVINA SCHNORR
EPISODE: ♀

1

THE ATMOSPHERE at Triebschen meanwhile had not always been so "optimistic" as Bülow made it out to be.[1] War had broken out on the 14th June. On the 18th Wagner gave the King the sound advice to make a tour of various towns and visit his troops in the field: Ludwig did so, and was everywhere greeted with an enthusiasm that showed how far the country as a whole was from siding with the politicians and the Press against him. But throughout it all the old hunger for Wagner gnawed at his heart. "Ah, my dear Friend", he wrote to him on the 2nd July, after his return, "you are my only solace in grief and affliction. Would that we were united once more! No longer can I endure it!" On the 14th Wagner told him of the peace of soul that had come to him through his absorption in the *Meistersinger*. The mysterious chemistry of the artistic mind had brought it about that precisely at the moment when the real Germany seemed to many people to be going down in ruins, the ideal Germany of his dreams sprang into vigorous life before him in his poem and his score. He compared his situation with that of 1849, when, after the crashing of his political illusions, he steadied himself inwardly by working out the plan of the *Ring*; now he finds his consolation in the closing words of his *Meistersinger*:

> Though should depart
> the might of holy Rome,
> no harm will come
> to holy German art!

"And so I have hope", he wrote to the King, "because I trust only in us twain. That is the meaning of my gladness." Ludwig was glad with him for his own sake: "The times are very serious", he wrote;

---

[1] See Vol. III, p. 552.

"I have to go through many cloudy days. But there is one thing that always strengthens me and marvellously uplifts me in pain and sorrow — my love for you, my adored one, my firm faith, my boundless trust in you, my unique one, my life's star on which my existence depends, and with whose passing my mission also will be at an end."

But the clouds are gathering round him: [2] he can see nothing in the world but treachery and deceit, the breaking of oaths, the disregard of treaties.

"God grant that Bavaria's independence can be preserved! If not, if mediation fails, if we are to come under the hegemony of Prussia, then, away! a phantom king without power I will not be!"

Before Wagner could reply to this, Ludwig had addressed to Cosima, on the 21st, the most moving letter that ever came from his pen:

"I earnestly beg you not to be alarmed at the contents of this letter. It is not written, as you might perhaps imagine, in a mood of lamentable desperation. No, I am serious, and withal cheerful. . . . I am driven to tell you that it is *utterly impossible* for me to remain separated any longer from him who is everything to me. . . . Fate has intended us for each other: only for him am I on earth: every day I see and feel this more clearly. . . . O, dear Friend, I assure you that here they do not and never will understand me: hope abandons me . . . nothing will ever be achieved here by the removal of Ministers or Cabinet officials. So long as I am King I cannot be united with him: the stars are against us. . . . We must be united for ever. The world does not understand us: and what concern of ours is the world? Dearest Friend, I implore you, prepare the beloved one for my resolution to lay down my crown. He must be pitiful, he must not ask it of me any longer to endure these torments of hell. My *true, God-given* vocation is this — with him to abide as faithful, loving friend, never to leave him. Tell him this, I beg you: put it to him that in this way we can carry out our plans, that I shall die if I have to live without him. . . . Then shall I be able to do more than I can now, as King; then shall we be potent, living and working for future generations.

"My brother is of full age: to him I will hand over the government: I will come with my faithful Friedrich,[3] and stay there whither I am drawn, where I belong. There with him is felicity: we shall have the illusion that here on earth we are in heaven. We shall not be idle: no, I hope to be of use to him, to serve him in many things. . . . I conjure you, write to me quickly, send me the joyous news that the unique one,

---

[2] The Bavarians had been defeated by the Prussians at Kissingen on the 10th July.
[3] Count Paul von Taxis.

the adored one understands that there are higher crowns, nobler king-doms than the unhappy ones of this earth, that he approves of my plan, that he realises the power of my love for him, that he knows that with him alone can I live. O my Friend, then only will I begin to live: rescue me from this sham existence. . . . Do not call my design extravagant or quixotic. By heaven, it is not; some day mankind will comprehend the power of this love, this predestination. . . It is not the difficult po-litical situation that has driven me to this resolution — that would be cowardice, — but the thought that my true destiny is never to be ac-complished in that field. Here, under these conditions, I can be nothing to him, the dear one: that I see clearly. My place is with him; destiny calls me to his side. . . ." [4]

2

The letter, not only the tone but the feverish reiterations of which reveal the agitation in which it was written, was addressed to Cosima in order that she might prepare Wagner for its contents before let-ting him read it in full. Cosima, perplexed and distressed, wrote Ludwig at once a long, non-committal and eminently tactful letter, for which, as the King's reply shows, he was deeply grateful and by which he felt himself consoled and strengthened. She had to admit that he was right, that in his place, subject to his trials, she would have acted as he had done; but while administering the balm of her sympathy she subtly prepared him for an answer from Wagner that would dissolve his dream. This letter of hers is one of her diplomatic masterpieces; she approves and justifies the King's resolution, and at the same time — without saying so in so many words — impresses it on him that his plan is impracticable. "The Friend will send you the word for which you long, and fortify you both in the grandeur of your intention and in the patience with which to await the hour for it."

Wagner's lengthy reply was sent off on the 24th. It too is a mas-terpiece in its appeal to the basic elements of Ludwig's psychology — his proud sense of his kingly office, and his vision of a Germany regenerated through that religion of art of which Wagner was the prophet. Wagner points out to him that as the head of the largest German state outside Prussia he has a political duty to Germany; while as for his plans for culture, how can he ever realise these

[4] KLRWB, II, 74–5, where for the first time the letter is given in full: as printed in MECW I, 293 ff it is not only incomplete but sometimes untrue to the original.

except *as* King? When he is older he will see not only what must be done to bring his dreams to fruition but how to do it. But when that time comes it will be too late, if he abdicates now; and then he will reproach himself for having thrown away his power. Let him learn now what he will assuredly discover later — that Munich is not Bavaria: it is, and always will be, a hot-bed of priestly-political intrigue which the politicians in part manœuvre, are in part controlled by. Let the King turn his back on Munich and look towards the real Bavaria, the centre and the symbol of which is ancient Nuremberg. Ludwig, like himself, builds high hopes on the message to the German world which the *Meistersinger* is to bring; and the fitting birthplace of the *Meistersinger*, German in its blood and bones, is Nuremberg. He exhorts him, therefore, to bear his burden patiently for another year. The Nuremberg production of the *Meistersinger* will draw the eyes of all Germany to that town. The Music School on which each of them has set his heart can be transferred there from Munich — from Munich, with its thick-blooded, priest-ridden mob, to the old town that is the true heart of Bavaria. Nuremberg can even be made the political centre of the country, with Bayreuth as the royal Residenz.

From this we surmise that already, if as yet only in the dimmest outline, some conception of Bayreuth as a goal was defining itself within Wagner. Five months before the date of this letter — on the 20th February, 1866 — he had written to Bülow, from Geneva,

"Nuremberg comes ever more clearly into my line of vision. . . . That this genuine and unique *German* seat of the arts, Protestant Nuremberg, has come to belong to the Bavarian throne, and thus form part of the domain of my fervently Catholic royal Friend, is wonderfully significant. That is the proper place for the future 'German Academy', for everything that cannot thrive in the rotten, un-German Residenzes of our little Louis the Fourteenths . . . for our School also, and in due course for a general School of Art and Science, that shall be German and non-Jewish. I could wish that the King would grant me a pavilion of the Bayreuth Schloss as a country seat — Nuremberg close by, Germany all around me. But for heaven's sake not a word about all this; even the King would not understand it just yet. I must bring the thing home to him — indeed to the world — gradually and purely empirically. Hans Sachs's place is in Nuremberg. . . ."

It was a few weeks after this — about the middle of March — that Wagner dictated the well-known passage in *Mein Leben* in which he describes that first view of his little Bayreuth glowing in the evening light, on his journey from Karlsbad to Nuremberg in July, 1835; a happy memory, he added, "that remains with me to this day".

The upshot of his advice to Ludwig was — Do not abandon the field to the enemy just yet, for your own sake, for mine, for Bavaria's.

"While Germany, as seems likely to be the case, sinks politically into a long winter sleep under the guardianship of Prussia, let *us* prepare quietly and tranquilly the noble hearth at which the German fire can some day re-kindle itself. . . . I ask you to have one whole year's patience. If this is impossible, I shall understand. But if I am to accompany you in constant fidelity you must stand forth, both during and after your abdication, in fullest glory. If it were your desire to sacrifice yourself merely to me, you would sacrifice me also; for I should have to vanish wholly from your life were I to fear that you would ever have reason to regret your resolve."

Two days later he sent a brief note to the King, urging him to summon Prince Hohenlohe at once, go into the political situation exhaustively with him, and ask his counsel. To this, we learn from a letter of the 29th July from Paul von Taxis to Wagner, the King could not consent: Hohenlohe, besides being too Prussian in his leanings, had displeased him by his attitude in the recent sittings of the Chamber.[5] On the matter of his abdication, however, he took Wagner's advice to heart, sending him a telegram of thanks on the 26th in which he assured the Friend that he felt marvellously strengthened and would endure. To Cosima he replied at greater length, assuring her that Wagner's peace of mind took precedence of everything else in his eyes; he would set himself to break the powers of evil that encompassed him in Munich, so that he and his idol might some day be reunited and together carry out their great plans for the German world of the spirit.

3

The autumn of 1866, however, brought all three of them a burden of fresh troubles of the commoner kind. A storm of unparalleled ferocity broke over Triebschen from a quarter in which everything till then had seemed set fair.

[5] It was not until the 31st December that Ludwig made Hohenlohe Minister of the Royal House and for Foreign Affairs, as well as President of the Ministerial Council.

Wagner's enemies in Munich had shown cunning strategy in concentrating their attack on his private life, and especially on his relations with Cosima; this latter was to prove the weakest point in his armour for a long while yet. His influence with the King in artistic matters was apparently unshakeable: even the revelations Ludwig had had of his passion for luxury at other people's expense do not seem to have made the slightest impression on his regard for him — a striking tribute to the magic of Wagner's personality. The King was curiously right when he insisted that the world had no understanding of them and of the true nature of the bond between them; he himself was one of the few people great enough to see that, dubious as Wagner's personal conduct had often been, the grandeur of his aims and the purity of his idealism entitled him to a consideration that would have been excessive in connection with any other man. The Cosima complication, however, was a priori likely to prove a rather different matter. Wagner and Cosima had all along deceived Ludwig as to the true nature of their association, and they had latterly gone to the audacious length of making him responsible for a public expression of his belief in the innocence of it. What would happen if some day he were to learn the sorry truth about it all?

That knowledge, or at any rate the dawning of it, was to come to him in the winter of 1866–7, from a quarter and after a fashion that could never have entered into the calculations of either Wagner, Cosima or Bülow. The Malvina Schnorr episode is one of the strangest in all Wagner's career. Its interest today is twofold — it shows the complications and frustrations, public as well as private, in which Wagner became enmeshed through his association with Cosima, and it throws into the highest relief the demonic quality in him that often, through no fault of his own, drew weaker spirits into his orbit, to his own great discomfort and their destruction.[6]

After the death of her husband in the summer of 1865, Malvina Schnorr's grief brought her to believe that she could communicate with him by means of spiritualism. Wagner, when danger threatened him later from Malvina, tried to make out that her mind was

---

[6] Our knowledge of the Malvina Schnorr episode has been greatly increased during the last two or three years by the many documents published for the first time in KLRWB and GIS. Herr Garrigues' book contains a number of obvious minor factual errors; these have been faithfully dealt with by Dr. Otto Strobel in an *Auseinandersetzung mit C.H.N. Garrigues*, in KLRWB, Vol. V.

fundamentally unhinged. There is no proof at all of that, however: she was undoubtedly febrile and sometimes a trifle abnormal, but no more than any other sensitive person is, man or woman, whose thoughts are turned by the loss of some dear one to the possibility of communication with the dead. Her father, Jean Antoine Henri Garrigues, came of a Huguenot family that had fled from Languedoc to Germany at the time of the revocation of the Edict of Nantes. Her mother was Nannette Palmié, of mixed Huguenot and German blood, in whose heredity there seems to have been a strain of mental unbalance due to too close interbreeding.[7] In 1896, at the age of seventy-one, Malvina was persuaded to undergo a "magnetic" treatment for her nerves, in the course of which the quack played shrewdly on the old lady's inveterate obsession with the memory of her dead husband and her desire for reunion with him.[8] Through the medium of this "magnetopath" she received, as she thought, spirit-messages from the long-dead Schnorr. After these séances she became noticeably more introspective and religiously "exalted"; and in March, 1897 the doctors, solemnly diagnosing her case as one of "paranoia exaltiva auf seniler Basis", recommended her removal to a mental institution in Obersendling, near Munich. It may be technically correct to say, as Dr. Strobel does, that she remained there "three-quarters of a year". The fact is, however, that as early as October the head of the institution had seen no reason to detain her any longer as a patient, and she had stayed on voluntarily until mid-December merely because for the moment she had no home of her own to go to. Her brother had doubted from the first whether the doctors had had any valid reason for sequestrating her; and to us today his doubt seems justified.

While the reader will take facts of this kind into consideration when studying the Malvina-Wagner episode of 1866–7, it must be insisted on that she was in no scientific sense of the word "insane" at that or any other time.

The King had granted her an annuity after Schnorr's death, and shown her other signs of favour. It was understood that she was to join the staff of the new Music School — a proof of Wagner's belief in her as an artist. The relations between Cosima and Malvina in

[7] GIS, pp. 32-3, 67.
[8] GIS, p. 439 ff. Garrigues' account of the affair is based on Malvina's diary of the forty-one séances.

the spring and summer of 1866 appear to have been of the friendliest description. Cosima — along with Wagner — had been active in securing the royal pension for Malvina; while the latter nursed Cosima devotedly during an illness in Munich in the following September.[9] Malvina was no doubt in a highly nervous state all this time; but no one saw the smallest reason to question her "sanity". Bülow put her down to sing Ortrud in some performances of *Lohengrin* that were contemplated for May and June of that year in Munich. In November Wagner was considering a proposed production of *Lohengrin* under Bülow in Paris during the World Exhibition to be held there in 1867, with Roger as Lohengrin; the Ortrud was to be Malvina. During that summer and autumn both Wagner and Cosima had entrusted Malvina with various friendly commissions in Munich. As late as November, 1866 there was no cloud on the horizon.

4

Having heard that Bülow was still in Basel, and presuming his wife and family to have joined him there, it occurred to Malvina to go to Lucerne and try to dispel Wagner's melancholy by giving him a detailed account, which she had not yet had an opportunity of doing, of Schnorr's last hours. Unfortunately she took with her a pupil, one Isidore von Reutter, by all accounts a neurotic young woman of small intelligence and less education, who claimed mediumistic gifts that enabled her to communicate with Schnorr. The pair arrived at Triebschen on the 10th November.[10] They returned to Munich two days later.

On the 22nd Wagner addressed an agitated letter to King Ludwig. Malvina's behaviour at Triebschen, he told him, had been of a kind which made him fear that his old and revered friend had completely lost her reason. Frau von Bülow, acting as the guardian of his peace, had kept Malvina from him as well as she could, and thereby drawn on her devoted head "the hatred of the eccentric Frau Schnorr" to so alarming a degree that "the most frantic explosions" are now to

---

[9] See her letter of the 19th September, 1866 to Bülow, who was in Basel at the time. She assures him that she will do everything for Cosima that "true friendship" can suggest: "she is as dear to me as my own soul: I cannot say more than that." KLRWB, V, 37. In a letter from Cosima to her little daughter Daniela of the 12th September Malvina is "Auntie Malvina Schnorr." CWBD, p. 5.

[10] Garrigues (GIS, p. 326) wrongly gives the date of their arrival as "the 14th or 15th".

be feared: he will have to take precautionary measures, partly of a medical kind, partly in the form of police protection, against the danger threatening him and Cosima. The trouble, he adds, is obviously a matter of "the punishable intrigues of an impostor" [Reutter], in whose machinations he sees the hand of his and the King's enemies.

Eight days before that, Cosima had written to the King in much the same strain. She had long suspected, she said, from Malvina's letters that something was wrong with the poor lady; now, to her sorrow, she sees only too clearly that the blow of Schnorr's death has affected her mind. She and Fräulein von Reutter had distressed Wagner greatly. Manifestly something had happened at Triebschen that had alarmed Cosima and Richard to such an extent that they felt it necessary for them to secure in advance, by hook or by crook, a disposition of the King's mind in their favour.

Wagner's fright is shown still more clearly in his long letter of the 23rd to Röckel,[11] who was living at that time in Munich. Poor Malvina, it appears, is as good as mad; he has gathered, from "some mysterious hints" of hers about Schnorr's death, and from "a certain look of hers [!] when I was in Dresden for the funeral", that she expected him to marry her. Under the influence of Isidore von Reutter she writes to her dead husband every night, and receives answers from him in her dreams. On the arrival of the pair at Triebschen,[12] says Wagner, they had been received by Cosima. Before seeing Wagner they sent up to him for his perusal a long document in which Reutter's supernatural visitations were set forth: the climax of them was that Schnorr's spirit had told Fräulein Reutter that she was to be the King's wife, and that Wagner, having

---

[11] KLRWB, V, 46 ff.

[12] His story to Röckel was that he had heard from Malvina on the 2nd November that she "must" see him to tell him of "the revelations made to her by her guardian angel" through the medium of Isidore von Reutter; and that "without waiting for a letter in reply from me, a few days later she telegraphed me from Lindau that she was coming to see me. My first impulse was to take instant flight, so as to escape the crazy·woman": Cosima, however, had dissuaded him from this.

After this, it is a trifle astonishing to discover that on the *5th* November he had entrusted Malvina with a rather delicate commission with regard to the servants he had left in Munich. His letter to her (KLRWB, IV, 167) is of the friendliest description: there is not the barest hint in it that he regarded her as a "crazy woman" from whom he would have to flee. Dr. Strobel suggests that Malvina's letter did not *reach* Wagner on the 2nd November, as he tells Röckel, but was *dated* the 2nd, and that it did not arrive until after the despatch of his letter of the 5th. The suggestion seems to be made, however, merely to save Wagner's face.

unlimited influence with the King, was to arrange a meeting between them. Going down to the three women he saw at once, he says, that Malvina was on the verge of complete insanity; accordingly he humoured and conciliated her. Later she gave him "an indescribably insane amorous look". The next day Cosima called at the Lucerne hotel at which the two ladies were staying, and handed Malvina a letter in which Wagner told her that he would have no further communication with her until she had dismissed the impostor Reutter.[13] Thereupon, he says, Malvina broke out into threats against Cosima; [14] later she called again at Triebschen, saw Wagner alone, and treated him gently as a sadly misguided man whom it was her mission to save. Retiring to his own room after an awkward mid-day meal, and coming to the conclusion that he was "not there to be the playball of any kind of lunacy", he sent Malvina a few lines by a servant [15] and went out for a walk to steady his nerves.

5

On his way back, calmed by the fresh air, he fell in with Malvina; she walked about with him for an hour, giving him some details

[13] The actual letter, dated 10 P.M., 10th November, is now available in KLRWB, IV, 169.

[14] As it happens, Malvina's letter of the morning of the 11th to Cosima has recently come to light: it bears a jotting in Cosima's writing — "Letter from Frau von Schnorr after I had declined to discuss Fräulein von Reutter's visions." "O Cosima!" it runs: "your heart will be the best judge whether *I* am the one who ought to ask for forgiveness. If it answers you 'Yes', then from the bottom of my heart I plead 'Forgive!' The frightful wound dealt me when parting from you was healed by God's hand in the night: not even a scar remains, and the hand I stretch out to you is pure and honest. Dear one, be warned! Do not fight against a power that will crush you if you try to hinder it! Do not oppose the will of God, for he alone prescribes our path for us. . . . Do not deprive me of faith in your love and loyalty: the loss would grieve me too much! Farewell, and remain mine! Your true Malvina." (KLRWB, V, 41). Wagner must have been either very agitated or very unscrupulous to convert Malvina's appeal to Cosima not to struggle vainly against "the will of God" and the "power" of the spirit world into a threat on *her* part to "smash" Cosima. There is nothing in Malvina's letter about Cosima's offence having consisted, in "coming between" Malvina and Wagner, and so far from Malvina turning the full torrent of her "fury" on Cosima, as he informs Röckel, her letter is not only friendly but affectionate towards her.

[15] This must be the short note of the 11th November given in KLRWB, IV, 169. "I feel incapable, dear friend", it runs, "of listening to your promised disclosures. . . . I leave you in order to preserve my peace. . . . May the true spirit of your dead one help to rescue you from the snares of a derangement which, as I see clearly, is fostered by a wretched creature who deserves punishment." This letter is now in the Wahnfried archives: from a note on it in Cosima's handwriting we learn that Malvina returned it to Wagner after her talk with him that afternoon.

of her husband's death that moved him deeply. The fact that she did *not,* as he appears to have expected, make him a proposal of marriage — indeed, she told him that it was the desire of Schnorr's spirit that she should not marry again — he put down to what is known in alienist circles as "the cunning of the insane", the serio-comic principle of which is that if a person suspected of being insane does something indubitably insane, that proves his insanity; while if he defeats our expectation by behaving in a wholly rational manner, this, so far from proving his sanity, is a yet more convincing proof that he is insane; for he is practising on us the notorious "cunning of the insane", which enables them to simulate sanity to perfection. It is an ingenious theory, which, from the alienist's point of view, has the advantage of making every spin of the coin show heads for him and tails for the "subject".[16]

The next day — the 12th — Wagner received a letter from Malvina in which she expressed the calm certainty that, having recognised in her the true friend whom heaven had destined for him, he would visit her in Munich, to hear from her what he had refused to listen to at Triebschen.[17] Cosima is neither mentioned nor hinted at in this letter, the burden of which is that it is Malvina's mission, guided by the spirit of her dead husband, to help Wagner to complete his great artistic work. He is at liberty to call her a false prophetess, she says, if what she now tells him does not come true; when he has regained composure he will come to her in Munich; the scales will fall from his eyes, and he will no longer spurn, as he had done in Triebschen, the document of Isidore von Reutter's "Dream", — of which more will be said later. Wagner tells Röckel that Malvina had said he would soon recognise the true friend [herself] appointed him by heaven, and, though he had repulsed her because a false friend [*Freundin,* meaning Cosima] had come between them, he would hasten to her in Munich and beg for all the communications he had scorned. There is no mention of any such "false" friend in the original letter, nor is there the faintest hint in it of a threat to "smash Cosima to pieces". It may perhaps be pleaded, on Wagner's behalf, that these and similar allegations against Malvina in his letter to Röckel may be based on *verbal* remarks of hers. But this

---

[16] "Tell me, in mercy tell me, have you a strawberry mark on your left arm?" "No." "Then you are my long-lost brother." *Cox and Box.*

[17] KLRWB, V, 43–4.

[13]

plea is ruled out by his own words, from which it is perfectly clear that he is purporting to give Röckel a summary of Malvina's letter of the 12th.

According to Wagner's story to Röckel, he replied "gently" to this letter of Malvina's,[18] telling her, however, that he had decided not to have any further communication with her for six months. "And now the mad woman gave vent to furious maledictions — once more [sic!] she threatened Frau von Bülow with life-and-death persecution." In the light of what we now know of Wagner's misrepresentations of Malvina in his letter to Röckel, we hesitate to accept this statement of his literally until we have better evidence for the truth of it than his mere word. It is clear, however, that at some time or other during the next few days Malvina had turned on Cosima, and that this had made Wagner break his resolution not to communicate with her again for some time. His letter to her of the 19th November [19] is summarised accurately enough in one of the 23rd to Röckel.[20] He writes to her in a tone that is half appeal, half threat. He regards Reutter as being the tool of his Munich enemies. (This seems to have been all along either mere distracted guess-work or pure invention on his part. All the evidence goes to show that Reutter was a mere half-wit; there is nothing whatever to indicate that she was being used as a tool by anyone). What was really at the back of Wagner's mind, and the prime cause of all his apprehensions, is plain enough from this letter of his. Finding herself unable to persuade him, as she had managed to persuade herself, that his artistic mission could be accomplished only with her aid and that of the protecting spirit of Schnorr, Malvina had managed to convince herself that it was the evil influence of Cosima that was keeping them apart.

The line she now took, in order to "save" him from this "evil influence", was the eminently feminine one of threatening to inform Bülow that Wagner and Cosima were lovers. He told her loftily that if she did so she would merely receive from Bülow the reproof she deserved — in saying which he was sure of his ground, in view of the peculiar constitution of the triangle. But manifestly he was scared at the prospect that Malvina's "calumnies" might reach the

---

[18] She was by this time in Munich.
[19] It will be found in full in KLRWB, IV, 169–171.
[20] KLWRB, V, 46–51.

King's ear; and, as the sequel was to prove, in his fright he took precisely the wrong line in threatening her with his vengeance if she did not at once recognise the error of her ways, dismiss Reutter, and cease to play into the hands of his enemies. He goes so far as to ask Röckel to see Malvina and warn her of what he will do if she "makes a scandal" and does not get rid of Reutter: the latest he has heard about Malvina is that she is determined to "go to the maddest lengths" to rid herself of her "rival" [Cosima]. He suggests that Röckel shall see the lawyer Gotthelf, as it is a matter for both a doctor and the police. Precisely what, if anything, Röckel did in the matter we do not know: Wagner's letter to him of the 27th November [21] contains merely a brief sentence or two of thanks for having permitted himself to be plagued by him.

As for the real attitude of Malvina towards Cosima at this time we have at present nothing first-hand to go upon but her letter — recently discovered — of the 22nd November,[22] which is evidently a reply to Wagner's of the 19th. The tone of this letter is one of reasoned unreason; that is to say, while immovably convinced of the genuineness of her own "mission" where Wagner is concerned, she has no feeling against Cosima except in so far as she seems, to Malvina, to be working against Wagner's higher interests as an artist. This letter of the 22nd November is one of the most illuminative of the documents bearing on the case.

6

"Frau Schnorr", says Kapp,

"was not at all 'mad', as Wagner maintained, but simply crazy with jealousy; and her passion, under the influence of her cunning friend, drove her to employ the romantic methods described by Wagner. These failed because her story found no credence in the one quarter that mattered, namely, with the King. For the time being, therefore, Malvina had to deny herself revenge. But when Cosima came to live in Munich again in the following winter her hatred of her favoured rival flamed up once more, and she launched into insults which caused Wagner, in a letter to the Cabinet Secretariat of the 18th November, 1867, to demand that she be turned out of Munich. As this was not

---

[21] KLRWB, IV, 172–3. Kapp's versions of all these letters (in JKWF, p. 254 ff) are now superseded by the more accurate ones in KLRWB.
[22] KLRWB, V, 45–6.

done he repeated his demand on the 30th, threatening that he would not set foot in the town again until the guilty one was removed. This time his wish was granted: Frau Schnorr was told to leave Munich, under the threat of the loss of her pension. She went to live in Hamburg." [23]

This is the somewhat naive story that has hitherto found credence. It is quite true that Malvina was not "mad"; but there is just as little foundation for the theory that she behaved as she did *because,* being "in love with" Wagner, she became "crazy with jealousy" at the sight of Cosima in the position at Triebschen she desired for herself. Both terms, "love" and "jealousy", call, in the present instance, for a rather different interpretation from the conventional ones.

Malvina had not, as the legend has it, gone to Triebschen possessed by a "passion" for Wagner and resolved to force him into matrimony, and then, finding Cosima living there as his "mistress", gone "crazy with jealousy". As we have already seen, her attitude towards Cosima was quite friendly even for some time after the first conversation with Wagner on the 10th November. It only changed when she became convinced that it was owing to Cosima's influence that Wagner would not take her "spirit" revelations at her valuation and regulate his future conduct as an artist by them. Her "love" for Wagner was primarily the after-glow in her of her immense love for Schnorr, and of her grief — a grief that never left her to the end of her days — for the loss of him. And the root cause of all the trouble, we can now see, was *Tristan.* Had Schnorr died a year or two earlier or later the situation of the winter of 1866–7 would never have arisen; nor would it have arisen if the opera with which Schnorr was so closely associated in the last weeks of his life had been *Tannhäuser* or *Lohengrin.* But the whole atmosphere of *Tristan* was a peculiar one, and the circumstances in which Schnorr and Malvina had become involved in the destiny of the work were without parallel in the theatrical career of either of them. *Tristan* has become so much an everyday matter with us that it is hard for us to realise the terrific emotional impact it had upon its own generation. Wagner himself, when the performances of May, 1865 were over, remained for a long time in a state of dazed incredulity that such a thing could have been possible — that human beings could go through such shattering emotional experiences and still be

---

[23] JKWF, p. 264.

alive and normal. He had never been able to open the score of the work without feeling that in the music of it there was something that only the soundest natures could admit into themselves with safety. "Child!" he had written to Frau Wesendonk in April, 1859, while he was engaged upon the third Act, "this *Tristan* is becoming something *terrible!* This last act! ! ! I fear the opera will be forbidden — unless the whole thing becomes a mere parody by bad performance. Nothing but middling performances can save me; completely good ones will certainly drive people crazy — I can see nothing else for it!" [24]

All the circumstances attendant upon the floating of *Tristan* had been calculated to raise both Schnorr and Malvina to the highest pitch of nervous tension. For five years they had been fascinated by the work, at once dismayed and attracted by its difficulties, which they set themselves to overcome. At last they found themselves entrusted with the task of imposing the "impossible" work on the world, a task which by this time had taken on for each of them the character of an almost religious mission. There followed two or three months of superhuman effort; and then, his task accomplished, Schnorr's light sputtered out like a candle that has burnt itself to its socket. "O Siegfried, Siegfried, farewell! Console Richard!" he had cried when the first torturing pain of his malady struck through him. Already he divined that his hours were numbered; and his thoughts were not for himself but for the Master whom he worshipped. "My Richard loved me!" he cried in his delirium. "I die happy: *He* loved me!" Wagner was in his mind incessantly: in what was almost the final paroxysm he sang, to notes of his own, passages from the *Götterdämmerung* text which Wagner himself had not yet set to music. Then he cried out pathetically again for Richard: they must urge him to come quickly; he *must* see him once more; "Richard, do you not hear me?" [25]

This was the distressing story that Malvina had poured into Wag-

[24] Bülow conducted the opera again in Munich in 1869. "It is a fatalistic, ominous work," he wrote to Pohl. "Our solo-repetitor Eberle is now in a madhouse as the result of the excitement of the rehearsals." He seems to have recovered fairly quickly, for in the autumn of 1869 the theatre management half-thought of entrusting the first *Rhinegold* performance to him: his breakdown over *Tristan*, however, was still remembered against him. See Düfflipp's letter of the 20th February, 1870 to Bülow, in BB, IV, 365.

[25] See Wagner's moving account of Schnorr's last hours in his letter of the 26th July, 1865 to King Ludwig, in KLRWB, I, 134–5.

ner's ears during the hour or two that he spent in the house of desolation on the day of Schnorr's funeral. "He exhorted his wife", says Wagner, "to go to us [i.e. Wagner and the King]: there [in Munich], with us, she was to help to complete what we had begun with him."

The effect of all this on a woman of the nervous diathesis of Malvina was just what might have been expected; it hardly needed the "visions" of Fräulein von Reutter to set up in her the obsession that she was now called upon by the Fates to play a responsible part in Wagner's future life as an artist. She felt she had more claim on him than anyone else, for through him she had lost the man she loved and adored. This latter point is one that now calls for consideration in some detail.

CHAPTER II

THE MALVINA SCHNORR
EPISODE: II

1

THERE CAN be little doubt today that Schnorr himself attributed his fatal illness not simply to the draught from the wings at the last *Tristan* performance but to the physical and mental exhaustion to which his long preoccupation with the nerve-racking part had reduced him. Malvina regarded him as having, in a sense, sacrificed his life to the man for whose art they both had so profound a reverence. Wagner, in the *Recollections of Ludwig Schnorr von Carolsfeld* which he wrote in May, 1868, is manifestly anxious to negate that impression: he says that Schnorr himself had assured him — while still in Munich, of course — that it was not "the singing and acting that took it out of him" but his lying still, bathed in perspiration, in an icy draught from the wings in the third act. Schnorr may certainly have insisted on that: it would have been perfectly in keeping with his noble character and his immense regard for Wagner to have done so. But there is evidence that at Triebschen Malvina told Wagner the whole truth about Schnorr's death; and the passage cited above from the *Recollections* was probably designed to salve his own grieved conscience.

An entry in his "Brown Book" on the 24th August, 1865 points strongly to the fact that he felt *Tristan* to have been, indirectly, the cause of Schnorr's death. "My Tristan! My Beloved!" he confides to this secret page.

"I drove you to the abyss! I was used to standing there: my head does not swim. But I cannot see anyone else standing on the brink: that fills me with frantic sympathy. I lay hold of him to check him, to draw him back, and I push him over, just as we kill the somnambulist when we cry out to him in our alarm. Thus I pushed him over. And myself? My head does not swim. I look down: it even delights me. But — the friend? Him I lose! Mein Tristan! Mein Trauter!"

(These are the dying Kurvenal's words as he drags himself to the feet of Tristan:

> Tristan! Beloved!
> Chide me not
> that the true one comes to thee!).

Wagner's obsession by this image of himself and his martyred friend on the edge of an abyss is shown by his trying to cast it into poetical form: the first three lines of the projected poem are still in the Wahnfried archives.[1]

Even more significant than this is a passage in Wagner's letter to the King of the 22nd July, immediately after the news had reached him of Schnorr's death on the preceding day. "Mein Tristan! Mein Trauter!" he cries out in his anguish. "For me he lived, for me he died." In Dresden, on the day of the funeral, so he had written to the King on the 26th, they told him that the principal concern of the dying man had been to correct the impression that his death was due to overstrain in connection with *Tristan*. In spite of that comforting assurance, Wagner, in the "Brown Book" entry of a month later, could still reproach himself with having driven Schnorr over the abyss.

More significance must be granted to these self-reproachings on Wagner's part immediately after the catastrophe than to the *Recollections* of nearly three years later, which were written when his heart was still hot with resentment against Malvina for the trouble she had given him in the winter of 1866–7, and it had become necessary for him to correct publicly the now widespread impression that Schnorr had been killed by *Tristan*. The precise nature of the tenor's last illness is difficult to decide today. Malvina's nephew, Dr. Franz Schnorr von Carolsfeld, assured Herr Garrigues that he "now knew definitely" that the singer had died of typhus;[2] and though this confident professional diagnosis came a trifle late — forty-nine years after Schnorr's death — it may be correct. But what we are concerned with here is not so much the cold scientific fact as the opinion current at the time. Schnorr would certainly not have called the world to witness, on his deathbed, that it was *not* Wagner's

---

[1] See KLRWB, I, lix.
[2] GIS, p. 288 *note*, quoting from a letter from Dr. Franz Schnorr of the 1st June, 1914.

opera that had killed him, if the superhuman strain that *Tristan* had put on him had not been a matter of comment already.

That public opinion in general regarded the great tenor as a sacrifice to his devotion to Wagner is beyond dispute. Malvina herself says so frankly in her letter of the 22nd November, 1866, in which she makes a last desperate attempt to induce Wagner to believe in her "mission". It is her desire, she tells him, to reconcile him not with heaven alone but with the world, for the world, including the doctors themselves, accuses him of being the cause of Schnorr's death, and is set against him in consequence; and she, who has suffered so much, would fain stretch out her "protecting hand" over his head, forgive him and pray for him.

2

The precise degree of truth in the belief at that time that Schnorr had laid down his life for Wagner is of minor importance in the present connection: all that concerns us is that Malvina believed he had, and that now, in one of those attacks of "exaltation" that seem to have been periodic with her, she had come to Wagner to fulfil her Ludwig's dying wish by helping the great composer in her own way. The word "love" occurs more than once in her letter of the 22nd November; but it obviously has a peculiar meaning for her, and we must not be misled by her employment of it. Wagner, in his fright, saw "matrimony" written in the "Liebesblick" she gave him — or he imagines her to have given him — on one or two occasions. But he himself admits, in his letter to Röckel, that she had told him, during their walk on the 11th, that it was the "spirit's" wish that she should not marry again, though he rather fatuously assumed that this was merely a cunning move on the "mad woman's" part to allay the suspicion she had sensed in him. Nothing in the documents we possess can be said to justify that assumption. Knowing something of his chequered life, she saw him as a Tannhäuser still enslaved to the flesh and vainly seeking the path that would lead him into a purer atmosphere. He has only to give heed to the revelations that have come to her from another world, she assures him in her letter of the 12th November, for the scales to fall from his eyes; then he will discover what he has been groping towards all his life, "that the pure divine womanliness you have celebrated in your works can alone bring a man redemption", and that she has been called by Fate to bring him to the perception of this. When he does perceive it he will write his most glorious work; "and perhaps we and all who have striven and suffered as we have done will enter at about the same time with Ludwig [Schnorr] into that world in which all human misery has its end."

The emotional tension becomes still greater in her letter of the 22nd, which concludes thus:

> "See, this it is [her forgiveness and protection of him] that I will and must, that my and *your* Ludwig implored of me when dying. Therefore do not repulse me; recognise the purest, most self-sacrificing love! And believe me, even if you *would* tear yourself away from me you *cannot*. My spirit holds you firmly fast; and even were the frail body to succumb in the fearful combat, before God's throne, to the last day of all, my soul will entreat the All-merciful to save yours! I impeach only the infernal spirit [Cosima] that deludes yours: God's chastisement on her guilty head: vengeance is *His!* If you yet wish to hear words of consoling love from my lips, then come, come soon, for I am dying, dying for you. Your true Friend, beyond death, Malvina." [3]

These words, all the attendant circumstances being taken into consideration, hardly justify the crude literal interpretation the scared Wagner put upon them; apparently what Malvina had in mind was a union of souls, in which, by serving the artist Wagner and helping him to live entirely and worthily for his ideal, she would also be serving the memory of her Ludwig, who alone had meant, and forever would mean, anything to her as a man. The old theory that she had gone to Triebschen in a flutter of "love" for Wagner, had unexpectedly found Cosima there, had realised for the first time the "guilty" nature of their association, and at once gone "crazy with jealousy", is not only crude in its psychology but at variance with the facts. Malvina was already as fully aware as scores of other people in Bavaria were of the irregular relations between Cosima and Wagner.[4] There was no "crazy jealousy" at all on her part during the first few days of her visit to Lucerne. This is clear enough from the concluding passage of her letter of the 11th November to Cosima: after exhorting her not to struggle against the spirit powers

---

[3] KLRWB, V, 46.
[4] See the passage in her letter of the 12th January, 1867 to the King (quoted *infra*, p. 28), in which she makes it perfectly clear that she knew how Ludwig had been tricked, in June, 1866, into giving Cosima a public certificate of "honour".

and the will of God [5] she adds, "Recognise the almighty power, and, with your wonderful gifts, help to achieve, instead of trying to frustrate, what you *cannot* overcome. Do not deprive me of belief in your love and loyalty." Malvina was thus not only willing, but anxious, to have Cosima's co-operation in the task of "redeeming" Wagner; "jealousy" of her "rival's" success did not come into play at all. It was only during the next few days, when it became evident that Cosima was confirming Wagner in his scepticism towards the spirit messages, that Malvina turned against her and upon her — not because Cosima was occupying the place on the Triebschen hearth which she desired for herself, but because, as Malvina saw the matter, she was encouraging Wagner to reject the messages from Schnorr and thus flout the will of heaven.

And so, in her letter to Wagner of the 22nd, she concentrates her rage on Cosima, but not, be it stressed, on Cosima as an unfaithful wife and a woman no better in general than she ought to be, but as an evil spirit, working against the light. "O, I know it full well", she writes,

"the unclean spirit that speaks through your words. It is not *you! Your* spirit is noble and true, your heart is great and warm! Woe to that devilish being that has put ignominious fetters upon your noble spirit: the judgment of the eternal God will fall upon it. . . . You try to frighten me with worldly persecution, *me*, who do not recoil in fear and trembling from the terror of *death*. No, the world has no power over me; *you* have no right in me! Your miserable letter — through which another speaks — has not affected me because my mind is pure and true, and what I do is right and good." [6]

This is surely the language not of a woman consumed with jealousy, of the common female kind, of an enthroned "rival", but of a febrile creature exaltedly convinced of her artistic mission and her divine guidance, and only at second remove furious with her "rival" for standing in the way of these. What happened afterwards was just what might have been foretold: the spasm of exaltation having spent itself, the sense of grievance over the frustration of her "mission" faded into the background and was replaced by the ignobler feeling of purely personal resentment against Cosima as Wagner's "evil spirit". And as they were both women, Malvina

[5] See *supra*, p. 12, *note* 14.
[6] KLRWB, V, 45.

naturally now declared war to the knife on Cosima *qua* Cosima, and made relentless use of what she knew to be the irreparable weakness in her defences — the long association with Wagner and the deceit that had been practised on the unsuspecting King. It was fear of exposure in *that* quarter that made Wagner move heaven and earth to have Malvina discredited or suppressed.

3

To Wagner's agitated letter of the 22nd November, 1866 [7] the King replied with a mere couple of lines in his letter of the 6th December, "I hope to God that peace has descended upon Triebschen again, and that there will be no recurrence of that wretched disturbance of tranquillity." Evidently, while seeing no reason to doubt Wagner's version of what had occurred, he did not attach great importance to the matter; and the immediate sequel of events was calculated to confirm him in this easy-going attitude. On his return to Munich he had found awaiting him a letter from Malvina, which he sent to Cosima on the 11th December, adding merely that "it will not be without interest for you; it is a strange mixture of clarity and error, truth and fiction." We gather from Wagner's reply to Ludwig, on the 15th, that this letter of Malvina's had contained "calumnies" about himself and Cosima; she had moreover described him as "characterless and weak". For the moment, however, his and Cosima's joint diplomacy was equal to the emergency. Brushing aside, as not worth serious consideration, Malvina's charges against himself, he actually professes the deepest concern at *the King's* position in the matter. [8] He sends Ludwig the document, containing Reutter's "Dream", that had been left at Triebschen — a silly story of how the young woman had seen, in a forest, a noble lion [the King] attacked by tigers and hyaenas; how she drove the fell beasts away and laid her hands upon the lion's wounds, which were healed at once by her touch; how the lion, with a grateful look, flung himself at her feet; how, in two later dreams, the spirit of Schnorr had revealed to Reutter that it was her mission to marry the King and guide him in the right path — the spirit

---

[7] See *supra*, p. 10.
[8] This was a technique he employed over and over again in his letters of this period to Ludwig.

adding, somewhat incongruously for Schnorr, that "Richard Wagner must make smaller demands on the human voice, and write more songs, so that he will become more popular and make everything easier." [9]

The "Dream" is so childishly foolish that one wonders, at first sight, why it should have roused Wagner to such fury and made him fulminate as he did against the "impostor Reutter". The explanation of his anger is no doubt in part, as Malvina's nephew suggests, that the passage in it in which Schnorr is made to say "Malvina is right — out of love for Richard I became a sacrifice to art", "touched him on his Achilles heel". Apart from that, he must have resented the passage in which Schnorr is represented as advising him to make Reutter his intermediary, for his own [Wagner's] sake, with the King: "You [10] have understood me rightly", Schnorr's "spirit" had said to Reutter,

> "for you yourself shall be Siegfried's [the King's] wife when your task is fulfilled. Only thus can the great work succeed; for his character is too weak to carry it through without help. You must sacrifice your plans in order to take your place by his side as protectress of art, to work with and for him. Richard must for my sake do all he can to learn to love you, for his obstinacy and pride will militate against his happiness. If you [10] succeed, then you [10] will win a great victory, and I have one step less to climb; if you [10] fail, then all is lost and I must still wander restlessly hither and thither for a long time."

Wagner advised the King to take stern measures against Frau Schnorr, as "it is time to deal in the most drastic fashion with the consequences of the beer-house conversations with ministerial and Cabinet Councillors that have become the impudent practice in Munich, about the most intimate matters affecting the royal person." Ludwig is to have Malvina informed that unless she keeps quiet "and leaves you and others unmolested", and removes herself as far as possible from Munich to enjoy the pension that has graciously been granted her, this will be withdrawn. He has been assured by Malvina's doctor that she is perfectly sound in health: he therefore has no hesitation in suggesting to the King what he be-

---

[9] The "Dream", the original of which is still at Wahnfried, is given, in part, in KLRWB, II, 117. It has more recently been printed in full (in GIS, p. 351 ff), from a copy in Copenhagen.

[10] The plural *ihr* or *euch* in each case, meaning Malvina and herself; elsewhere "you" is *du*, signifying Isidore.

lieves to be the best cure for the temporarily overwrought condition of the poor dear lady's nerves.

The whole letter is a masterpiece of tactics. It and its accompanying "Dream" could be trusted to touch the King upon his most sensitive spot — his sense of his royal dignity, on which the silly Reutter was laying her vulgar hands. He would be particularly annoyed by the reference to his "weak character". It was craftily suggested to him that the two women were hand-in-glove with the King's enemies in Munich; and he was left to infer for himself that insinuations about Wagner's and Cosima's honour, coming from such a quarter, were necessarily false and worthy of condign punishment.

4

Malvina, however, was not to be disposed of so easily. On the 20th December we find the King forwarding to Cosima another letter which she had sent to his adjutant, Captain von Sauer: "its contents are shocking", he added, "but I regard it as my duty, as your sincere and true-to-death friend, to send it to you." [11] "In this letter, which was dictated by revenge and jealousy", says Dr. Strobel in a footnote to this passage, "Frau Schnorr had tried to enlighten the King as to the *real* relations of Cosima and Wagner." On the 30th Wagner tells Ludwig that he has written to Captain von Sauer, who, he hopes, "will behave discreetly and chivalrously". He has asked himself what the significance can be of "this quite groundless, insane disturbance of the painfully-won peace of certain noble, magnanimous people" — meaning, presumably, Cosima, Bülow and himself — and has found the answer to be that Fate intends it for a test of *the King*, who, he hopes, has thwarted the intentions of "the criminal" by dealing as severely with her as she deserves.

---

[11] There has recently been published (KLRWB, V, 53–4) a letter of the 25th December from Cosima to Malvina, evidently written after the former had received from the King Malvina's letter of the 20th. The tone of Cosima's letter, in which she offers Malvina her hand in friendship and forgiveness, is admirably conciliatory; but reading between the lines we can see that her approach is largely dictated by fear, and that it must have given Malvina herself that impression.

The King's covering lines show that as yet he saw no reason to question the account of the matter that Wagner and Cosima had given him. "You can imagine", he wrote to Cosima, "how agitated I am, the righteous anger I feel towards that worthless, accursed woman, who has dared to revile my dearest friends in this fashion."

Malice and crookedness could hardly go further than that. Not daring to give the King a categorical assurance that there was nothing whatever in Malvina's charges, he craftily makes it appear that the offence is even more against the King than against himself, and advises him not merely to condemn Malvina on *his* assurance of her vileness but to refuse her any opportunity of appeal against his judgment. To these depths of turpitude had he and Cosima been gradually reduced by the circumstances of their attachment to each other, which had been born of their souls' need of each other; they were now desperate hunted animals, ready to fall with tooth and claw on anyone who stood in the way of their escape. On the 2nd January, 1867 he lays another trap for the young King's emotions: he paints in moving colours the sufferings of Bülow, whom he has just seen; not only is his career ruined but he "sees his own honour dragged once more through the mire with that of his wife", and all through his fidelity to Wagner. Cosima herself has gone down under the strain: she cannot sleep, and is nearing a confinement for which her husband, unable to offer her the proper domestic care, has to rely upon the friend [Wagner] who happens to be better circumstanced to supply it. Since Malvina's existence in Munich depends on the King's grace, he is to impose silence on her by threatening her with the loss of her pension.

Ludwig's letters to both Wagner and Cosima at this time show no diminution of his confidence in them or his affection for them; and the foolish Reutter played directly into Wagner's hands with a letter (to Captain Sauer) which the King dutifully passed on to Triebschen on the 8th January (1867). The letter is now at Wahnfried; according to Dr. Strobel, "Isidore von Reutter coolly makes herself out to be a 'defenceless girl' whose 'honour' has been deeply wounded by Wagner and Frau von Bülow." "I have had Frau Schnorr informed", says the King, "that if she does not leave Munich within a fortnight she will forfeit her pension. Perhaps this will be effective." As a matter of fact the royal letter, a copy of which is now in the Sächsische Landesbibliothek in Dresden, requires her to leave not merely Munich but Bavaria. It expressly adds, however — a point which Ludwig does not mention to Wagner — that the pension may continue to be paid as usual if she goes away.[12] Was the King, who seems to have remained loyal to his

---

[12] GIS, p. 339.

memories of the part Malvina had played in the unforgettable *Tristan* days, beginning to suspect that after all there may have been something in her charges? Did he perchance do what it had been Wagner's object all along to prevent him from doing — distinguish between the angry but perfectly rational fulminations of Malvina and the obviously half-witted rantings of Fräulein von Reutter? Was he prepared to resign himself to making the best of a bad business — to leave things as they were and hope that with Malvina outside Bavaria there would be limits placed to the spread of the scandal?

5

Whatever may have been in his mind he must have been considerably surprised by the long letter, running to nearly seven pages in print, which she addressed to him on the 12th January, 1867, after having received on the 9th the official command to leave Bavaria: perhaps it was the plainest speaking to which Ludwig ever had to submit in the whole course of his existence.[13] What the King has given, she says, the King can take away. Her crime is simply that she has told him the *truth* about a couple who are unworthy of a friendship such as his, a couple who have duped him and lied to him.

> "Last summer, when he *dictated* to you the letter to Herr von Bülow, he made you perpetrate a piece of folly that damaged only *you*, since the relation in which W. stood towards the wife of the gentleman in question was already known to the world; and now he is the motive force in the injustice done to me, which, if a syllable of it becomes known, will cost you thousands of hearts."

Knowing that her foes at Triebschen would try to persuade him that she was mad, she had sent the King a number of Schnorr's letters to her, to enlighten him as to the true character of both of them. She had been unmoved by Wagner's threats. She asks only to be confronted with "the guilty ones". She advises Ludwig to make private enquiries about the Wagner-Cosima-Bülow matter; there are plenty of people who will be able to supply him with information. "Your royal ermine is to cover their shame; but consider well, my King, that the royal ermine itself will be soiled." She repudiates

---

[13] It is given in full in GIS, p. 340 ff, from a copy in Malvina's own handwriting now in the Dresden Library.

any malign influence over her on the part of Reutter, whom she now regards, or professes to regard, more or less as a young simpleton with a touch of the "psychic" about her. To the "Dream" about which Wagner made such a to-do she attaches no importance at all, and she cannot understand how it could have "so perturbed the irrational man that he read God knows what *lèse majesté* into it." [14] The document had been left by accident at Triebschen — it had fallen from her bag: [15] Wagner had improperly kept it and as improperly sent it to the King for his own purposes. Her purpose in going to Triebschen had been to speak to Wagner of Schnorr's last hours, tell him the true cause of his death, and assure him that she was still the devoted servant of Wagner's art. She found him in the toils of a "conscienceless woman", from whom she wished to rescue him: she had given him a medallion portrait of Schnorr with a lock of his hair, in the hope that it would be a talisman for him now that he is "in the toils of the evil demon". Wagner had so far misunderstood her anxiety about him that he had the absurd presumption to imagine she was in love with him — she, the widow of Ludwig Schnorr! She rejects the unclean notion with contempt. She felt that she had been entrusted by Schnorr with a mission to "save" Wagner. She had done her duty; but the wretched man had refused to listen to the voice of true friendship.

"Unless you come to recognise that only Wagner's *mind* is worthy of admiration, and that a sharp distinction must be drawn between this and his *person*, then I know that unspeakable grief and misfortune await you, that you will never find peace, and that a new and frightful danger threatens you, which fills me with horror and terror." [16]

---

[14] She had evidently forgotten that two months earlier she herself had taken Reutter and her visions very seriously. She seems also, at first sight, to contradict herself as regards her knowledge of Wagner's liaison with Cosima. In one place in this letter to the King, defending Reutter from the charge of having "instigated" her against "the guilty pair", she says that "the Fräulein knew as little about the culpable bond as I did. What I perceived, what I unfortunately saw to be *true*, my own sense showed me." Compare this with the sentence already quoted from another part of the letter, to the effect that Wagner's relations with Cosima were known to everyone in the summer of 1866. Perhaps what Malvina means in the former of the two passages just cited is that it was only at Triebschen, at the sight of the pregnant Cosima, that she realised the *full* extent of the association, and that Isidore von Reutter had nothing to do with opening her eyes in that respect.

[15] This seems to be untrue.

[16] Peter Cornelius, who had a great regard for Malvina, found his position between her and Wagner a difficult one. In February, 1867 Wagner accused him of a "veritable crime" in having, as he had heard, "placed faith even for a moment in Frau Schnorr". A day or two later Cornelius met Malvina in Munich. "She said", he writes to his

She will *not* leave Munich, she tells him: she will remain there as a witness to the truth of what she has said, whatever the consequences may be.

6

"Frau Schnorr", the King wrote to Wagner on the 14th January, after receipt of her letter of the 12th,

> "to whom I sent word that she would lose her allowance if she did not leave the country within a fortnight, replies that she *will not*. I think in the end she will have to yield to necessity."

These three or four calm lines are the only reference to the matter in his lengthy letter, which is mostly concerned with his longing to hear the *Meistersinger* and his unquenchable hope that Wagner will give up Triebschen and settle down again in his Briennerstrasse house. Manifestly the artist Wagner was impregnably entrenched in his soul; how, indeed, could he lose faith in *this* Wagner without the centre-pin of his own existence being withdrawn? But about the man Wagner he was probably doing some quiet thinking. "I cannot and will not believe", he is reported to have said, "that Wagner's relations with Frau von Bülow go beyond the limits of friendship. That would be frightful." He is also said to have sent for Wagner's former servant Franz, who was at that time in charge of the Briennerstrasse house, and questioned him: the shrewd fellow, however, professed ignorance of the Cosima matter. Ludwig must have been asking himself seriously whether after all there was not some fire to account for the vast amount of smoke that had been blowing up so long from the Munich Press and elsewhere, and to which Malvina was now adding her fuliginous contribution.

---

fiancée, 'Well, Papageno, I haven't seen you for some time'. I replied, 'Starry Queen, I'm sorry, but Sarastro [Wagner] is my older friend, who has always acted well by me'. 'Well, trust him only till you are in a fix yourself'. [Thus in the official edition of the letters: in the later and more candid biography of Cornelius by his son it reads "Trust the liar only", etc. (CPC, II, 105)]. 'Starry Queen, we mustn't attach so much importance to personalities. Sarastro is the builder of our whole temple; all the priests sound the horn he hands to them. The letter to Tamino [the King] was much too strong'. 'O, Tamino is well-disposed towards me: he has sent me his compliments. But Sarastro is a villain'. On this, I turned on my heels and said, 'Starry Queen, I have the honour!'" Cornelius recurs to the subject the next day: he feels, he says, that out of loyalty to Wagner, to whom he owes everything, he cannot range himself on Malvina's side. CABT, II, 483–5.

It has to be borne in mind that Cornelius had been shown Wagner's letters to Röckel; he consequently accepted as gospel Wagner's version of what had happened during Malvina's visits to Triebschen.

On the 17th February she wrote to someone who cannot be positively identified, but was probably the Leipzig Kapellmeister, Julius Rietz, saying she wished to take up her public career again, and asking for his assistance and advice. In this letter her recollection of what had happened at Triebschen in the preceding November is obviously at fault here and there: she attributes sentiments to herself at that time that perhaps only came to her later. She says, for example, that at her first entry into "the luxurious house" and her first sight of "Frau von Bülow, dressed up and in an advanced state of pregnancy (her husband lives in Basel)" her eyes were "suddenly opened" as to the company she was in.[17] She laughs at the "ludicrous" notion that she wanted to marry Wagner, and accuses him of being the source of paragraphs to that effect that had appeared in certain papers. Cosima, in her placatory letter to her of the 25th December, 1866, tries to make it appear that Malvina's own conduct had given birth to these rumours. But Malvina blames Wagner also for certain journalistic reports that the doctors had declared her to be mentally affected beyond hope of recovery; and one asks oneself whether it may not have been Röckel who was responsible for all this publicity. In his letter of the 23rd November, it will be remembered, Wagner had categorically assured Röckel both that Malvina was "on the verge of complete insanity" and that she had it in her mind to marry him.

Wagner spent the second week of March, 1867 in Munich, and Malvina seems to have feared that while there he might do something to her injury. On the 24th her brother-in-law Karl Schnorr von Carolsfeld, who was living at that time in Munich, wrote to his father in Dresden:

"He [Wagner] sent Röckel to me, to invite me to a conference with him; but I did not go. Röckel told me a number of things, from which I saw that W. had woven a pretty tissue of lies about Malvina. For all that he graciously offered to take steps to induce the King to restore her pension; and he was very much astonished and annoyed to learn that all this had been arranged already."[18]

The King, in fact, had relented: face had been saved by the restoration of the pension on condition that Malvina retired for a while to Tegernsee or some similar place *within* his dominions.

---

[17] KLRWB, V, xlvi.
[18] GIS, p. 357.

That was of itself something of a victory for her; and it is perhaps an indication that Ludwig had already come to believe that the truth in this wretched matter was not entirely on Wagner's side.

All this while Cosima and Wagner must have been given furiously to think. The King had taken his own course with regard to Malvina, without consulting or even informing them. It was a sign of strength in him that he never wasted words over minor things: in the present instance he seems to have decided for himself that Wagner and Cosima were not wholly correct about Malvina, and having so decided he first of all put things right with regard to her, so far as lay in his power, and then dropped, for as long as he could, an iron shutter between himself and Triebschen on the matter. That it was revived towards the end of 1867 was the fault of Wagner himself.

In September, 1867 Cosima and Bülow returned to Munich. In mid-November Wagner, apparently as the result of communications made to him by Cosima, urged Court Secretary Düfflipp to have Malvina removed from Munich; hearing of which, Cosima wrote to Düfflipp making light of the matter. Wagner returned to the assault on the 30th with an angry letter to the King, in which he enlarged once more on the disturbance to his own, Cosima's and Bülow's peace that Malvina constitutes. The latter has "provoked" Cosima, either in the street or in the theatre. Resorting to his usual technique, he suggests to the King that Malvina had deceived *him*; she had ostensibly bowed to the royal will only in order that she might remain in Munich, where she could carry out her schemes of "vengeance" against Cosima. The King is invited to imagine the effect of it all on

> "this poor man [Bülow], morbidly sensitive and already sufficiently harassed as he is, and not less on his wife, who in complete innocence conferred nothing but benefactions on the worthless woman!"

He has reason to believe that Malvina is only awaiting his [Wagner's] return to Munich to put into execution her vow of vengeance. He wants the King to order her to ask Cosima's pardon, either verbally or by letter, and to confess that she has been led into these evil ways of hers by an "impostor". If Malvina will do this, Wagner will raise no objection to her remaining in Munich, on condition that she never again crosses his path or Bülow's. There can be no question,

[32]

of course, of Malvina now being employed in Munich for artistic purposes: moreover Wagner suggests that her pension, which, he says, was raised from 1,200 florins to 2,000 by the good offices of Cosima, should be reduced to the lower figure, which is large enough for such services as Malvina had rendered. He proposes this not merely on the grounds of "what is right", but for the remarkable reason — remarkable as coming from Richard Wagner — that he wishes "to protect himself from the reproach of being the cause of quite useless and unmerited expense to the Civil List."

7

To these depths of subterfuge, shabbiness and malice had Wagner and Cosima step by step been forced to descend by their desperate need to save themselves. Well may Lucretius say that to see a man as he really is we must observe him in danger and adversity; for then the mask falls from him, the man as he is remains, and the very words of truth come up from the heart itself. We are reminded of Edouard Schuré's observation that "to keep looking at Wagner's head was to see at one moment the front face of Faust and at the next the profile of Mephistopheles."

The next letter from the King to Wagner is dated the 9th March, 1868; so that unless some letters between the pair have been lost we must conclude that he did not reply at all to Wagner's letter of the 30th November. His patience was by that time evidently exhausted; he saw no reason why he should waste his time on matters of this miserable kind, which had nothing to do with Wagner's art. On the 9th December, 1867 he sent to Düfflipp an extract from Wagner's letter with a covering note of his own:

"I recently received a letter from Richard Wagner, in which he asks me to punish Frau Schnorr — in what fashion you will see from the passage in the letter which I enclose herewith. Return it to me quickly; I await your suggestion with regard to this matter. The eternal wrangles and complaints on the part of Wagner, Porges, Fröbel and the rest of them have become thoroughly repugnant to me. I have shown these people so much indulgence and patience, conferred so many benefits on them, that they ought to have every reason to be satisfied and grateful; the thread of my patience is at last beginning to break." [19]

---

[19] BLKB, p. 197.

Did he already believe, and at the same time shrink from believing, that the main, if not the whole, truth was on Malvina's side? The political history of those days, and the fluctuations of Ludwig's feelings towards Wagner and Cosima, will come up for discussion in another chapter. Meanwhile we have to note that on the 13th December (1867) the King wrote thus to Düfflipp, from Hohenschwangau:

"I received your letter this evening. It is as if I had fallen from the clouds. This refined, intelligent Frau von Bülow occupies herself with scribbling for the Press! [20] She writes these dreadful articles! Really I should not have thought the cultivated Cosima capable of a piece of knavery of this sort! But I am still more surprised that you believe the situation as regards Wagner, Frau von Bülow and Frau Schnorr is not koscher [free from suspicion]: if it should turn out that the miserable rumour is true — which I was never able to bring myself to believe — should it after all be really a case of adultery — then alas!" [21]

In the light of this last sentence we can see clearly enough why Wagner and Cosima were so desperately anxious to conceal, by hook or by crook, the real facts of the matter from the King.[22]

In 1870 we find Wagner writing to Pusinelli à propos of certain "false and evil things" that were being said about him in Dresden, and placing them to the credit of Isidore von Reutter, "a friend of Frau Schnorr, who absolutely wanted to marry me." [23] Wagner — or was it Cosima? — seems to have been obsessed with the idea that plans were afoot to end his widowerhood willy-nilly. We actually find him telling the King, on the 16th July, 1868, that he suspected Röckel of trying to plant one of his daughters on him! — an insinuation for which, as Dr. Strobel says, there is no supporting evidence whatever.

8

Neither Cosima nor the later Wahnfried bodyguard ever forgave Malvina for the part she played in enlightening the King as to the true relations of Cosima and Wagner. Houston Stewart Chamberlain, in his Wagner biography of 1896, told his readers that in con-

---

[20] For the meaning of this see *infra*, p. 120.
[21] BLKB, p. 198.
[22] The subsequent history of Malvina does not concern us here. The reader will find the full story in Garrigues's pages. She died in 1904, at the age of seventy-eight.
[23] RWAP, p. 224.

nection with the *Tristan* performances of 1865 "two names deserve special mention, those of Hans von Bülow and Ludwig Schnorr von Carolsfeld". Malvina, whose Isolde neither Wagner nor the King could praise too highly at the time, he ignores. But the limit of the ungenerous is achieved by Glasenapp in his treatment of Malvina, treatment in which the hand of Cosima is everywhere apparent. He indulges in every possible disparagement of Malvina's work in connection with *Tristan*, even going so far as to say that

"we know that ever since his settling in Munich Wagner had in his mind's eye, for Isolde, not Frau von Schnorr but solely and exclusively Fräulein Tietjens (at that time in London), whose voice was in the plenitude of its youthful power."

Compare this with Wagner's own declaration in his Open Letter of the 18th April, 1865 to the Vienna *Botschafter*, in which, after referring to the frustration of his plans for giving the opera in Karlsruhe in 1859, he said that there he "would have had the same singers [Schnorr and Malvina] for the principal parts who now, six years later, when I have obtained perfect freedom of choice", are the only ones "among the numerous personnel of the German theatre" who are "qualified for the solution of my problems". That this passage was perfectly well known to Glasenapp is shown by his close paraphrase of it on page 266 of his third volume. That volume, however, had been issued in 1899, before he had come under Cosima's influence to the extent that he did later. In his fourth volume (1904), in which he has to deal with the Munich *Tristan* performances of 1865, and during his labours on which he lived for some time at Bayreuth, he had manifestly become the mouthpiece of Cosima's resentment against Malvina, a resentment still implacable after nearly forty years.[24]

It is true that for a moment, in the summer of 1864, Wagner had thought of Therese Tietjens for his Isolde. On the 16th May he had asked Karl Klindworth, who was at that time living in London, to see this singer — about whom Wagner could have known nothing at first hand but whose voice was world-famous, — and sound her, if he thought she would be suitable for the part, as to the possibility of her taking the rôle of Isolde in Munich next year; if she were willing, Klindworth was to coach her in it. Apparently the latter's

---

[24] See, on the Cosima-Glasenapp point in general, GIS, pp. 459–466.

report upon her was favourable, for Wagner, in his next letter to Klindworth, on the 8th June, says he has written to her direct, but so far has had no answer.[25] But by the 25th June, 1864 he had dismissed the lady from his thoughts, as is shown by his brief and impolite note to Klindworth — "The Tietjens can. . . ." Meanwhile some of the German papers had announced that she was to sing Isolde. This seems to have drawn a protest from Schnorr, whom Wagner pacifies in a letter of the 31st October in which he advises him not to attach any importance to "the Tietjens canard": "I desire nothing more ardently than that your dear wife may maintain the will, the joy and the strength for the great task she has undertaken, which can be carried out only by a soul in friendly alliance." [26] Nearly two months before that, indeed, he had told Frau Wille that he was going to give *Tristan* next May, "with the Schnorrs"; while in the plan for the future which he drew up for the King in January, 1865 "Schnorr and wife" are cast for *Tristan*. This of itself puts in its proper perspective Glasenapp's assertion that Wagner had had "not Frau Schnorr but solely and exclusively Fräulein Tietjens" for Isolde "ever since his settling in Munich".

It is thus clear that while Glasenapp was technically correct in saying that Wagner had thought of Tietjens for his Munich Isolde, he had done so merely because he surmised, from what he had been told about her voice, that she might be able to sing the difficult part — not at all because he was acquainted with her capabilities in general and ranked her above Malvina, which is the impression the unwary reader gets from the story as told by Glasenapp.

Wagner's contemporary letters prove conclusively that in 1865 there was no singer on the Continent but Malvina to whom he could think of entrusting the part of Isolde. Perhaps at forty her voice was no longer at its best, a fact that may have led him to consider for a moment the younger Tietjens. But Malvina, as he assured the King in March, 1865, was a "true artist", who was thoroughly devoted to him and had lived in the part for several years: he was certain in advance that she would "surprise the world". A few weeks later, during the rehearsals, he told the King that "Frau Schnorr

---

[25] RWFZ (where the two letters have been printed in the wrong order), pp. 396, 399. See also Wagner's letter of the 1st June, 1864, to Bülow, in which he tells him of his plan for the summer of 1865 — "*Tristan and Isolde* with Schnorr and Tietjens."
[26] GIS, p. 212.

overtops everything I could have expected: there is *nobody* I could compare with her in this part: she reminds me of my youthful model, the famous Wilhelmine Schröder-Devrient" — which was the highest praise he could have bestowed on any singer. Still later he calls her "perfect", above and beyond comparison with any other living female artist. On the 26th September, 1865 he told Frau Wille that for *Tristan* he had had "a wonderful pair of artists, sent me from heaven . . . astoundingly gifted." In a letter of October, 1866, just before the trouble began at Triebschen, he had addressed her as "dear, good Malvina, unforgettable Isolde!" and described her as an "incomparable artist". But if he could perhaps never really forget his "unforgettable Isolde" he could at any rate let his resentment carry him later to the point of ignoring her and her great services to him in the *Tristan* days. As has been seen, in his detailed *Recollections of Ludwig Schnorr von Carolsfeld*, written and published in the summer of 1868, he does not so much as mention Malvina's name. If anything could have made the spirit of the noble Schnorr turn against him, it would have been that. All in all, few things in Wagner's career reflect so much discredit on him as his treatment of Malvina Schnorr.

CHAPTER III

MOVES IN MUNICH

1

W<small>E MUST</small> now take up again the chronological sequence of events at the point at which it had to be interrupted in order to present the full Malvina story in continuous form.

For the King, the year 1867 seemed to open under the happiest auspices. There appeared to be little difficulty now in the way of the realisation of his passionate desire to have Wagner in Munich again. "Pfo" and "Pfi", whom Wagner regarded as his arch-enemies, had both quitted the scene, Pfistermeister having given up his post as Cabinet Secretary on the 1st December, 1866,[1] Pfordten having resigned on the 19th of the same month. He was succeeded on the last day of the year by Prince Hohenlohe, whom Wagner looked upon as sympathetic towards him and his "cause".

The complex character of the young King is nowhere more apparent than in the contrast between his letters to Wagner regarding all these personages and his contemporary letters to other people about them. When he writes to Wagner, "Pfo" and "Pfi" are "Alberich" and "Mime", who must be removed at the first opportunity because they stand in the way of his and Wagner's plans for the regeneration of the German world through the theatre: we almost expect to hear the appropriate *Ring* motives at the bare mention of their names. But to his grandfather, the one-time Ludwig I, who often counselled him in political matters, he writes about them with the most objective sense imaginable of Real-Politik. Pfordten simply *had* to go, he says in a letter of the 13th January. "His politics last year enjoyed, it is true, not only my own full assent but that of the country. But he just had not the expected success." Bavaria had lost the war and been forced to submit to onerous peace terms,

---

[1] Pfistermeister told Böhm in later years that he had surrendered his post, though it meant the sacrifice of 9,000 florins of his income, because Wagner's interference in affairs of state had become intolerable. BLKB, p. 137.

with the "natural result" that the men who had the destinies of the country in their hands at that time, Prime Minister von der Pfordten and Feldmarschal Prince Karl (the King's great-uncle), had been held responsible by the whole nation for the catastrophe.

"To govern with such a Minister is a pure impossibility, let his inclinations be of the best and his knowledge of the widest. So it comes about that Pfordten is the innocent sacrifice to the catastrophe of 1866."

The Minister himself, he continues, had been among the first to recognise how matters stood. At first the King had hoped to persuade him to reconsider his resignation, but in the bitterness of his anger he had stipulated for such conditions in a purely personal matter — the reference is obviously to Wagner — as would have involved a humiliation for the King. Ludwig had therefore no option but to part with him; and his only possible successor seems to be Hohenlohe, whose programme meets with the royal approval.[2]

In the autumn of 1866 Wagner had given Ludwig to understand that he had been driven out of Munich by the machinations of certain enemies whom the King had been too irresolute to stand up to as he should have done. Ludwig, he contended, was in no less danger than himself from the politicians; and no thought of returning to Munich would he entertain until these "criminals" had received the punishment they deserved. At the commencement of 1867 it seemed to the King that he had done everything required of him by his exacting Friend. He had parted with Pfordten and Pfistermeister, installed Hohenlohe, and made other changes in the governmental personnel. In the early days of January Semper had shown him the model of the proposed festival theatre, and received a handshake and the royal assurance that the building would begin at once. Wagner's scheme of 1864 for the founding of a Music School in *his* sense, with Bülow as director, was also to be realised, Ludwig agreeing with him that without such a school the theatre would be merely "a costly toy" — though he urged, quite reasonably, that as Semper's splendid building could not be completed in much less than five years, work on it should commence at once. "We will bid the age of Pericles arise once more", he wrote to Cosima in January.

"The German nation, whose spirit has sunk so low, will at last recover confidence in itself, and the other peoples of the earth will pay homage

[2] BLKB, p. 152; Michael Doeberl, *Entwickelungsgeschichte Bayerns*, III, 458.

to ours and bow before its spirit. . . . I am so happy and sure of victory: great things must happen this year: the foundation stone of the great festival theatre will be laid", and so on.

Thus the King; and thus, no doubt, it would have all turned out had Wagner's views and interests coincided at every point with his. But Wagner had interests and plans of his own.

Except, perhaps, during the first few feverish weeks after his banishment he had never been really anxious to return to Munich. He had thrown himself as energetically as he did into the business of getting Pfordten and certain others removed partly because his fury with them for having worsted him in December, 1865 made peace of mind impossible for him until he had avenged that "crime", partly because he honestly saw in Ludwig the destined "redeemer" of the German nation and thought him to be in danger from his own servants. The sybilline spirit of Frau Dangl [3] must have been hovering about him when he wrote to his sister Klara Wolfram, on the 15th January, 1867, that he had saved from "ruin" "the last and only hope among the German princes", who was "being betrayed and enmeshed by his own most confidential officials". To his sister Luise Brockhaus he wrote in a similar vein a couple of days later. We need not take too literally his statement that his own cares had oppressed him *only* in so far as they concerned "my ardent love and sympathy for the young King of Bavaria". That was merely the usual Wagnerian "literature", and Luise, who knew her brother's capacity for self-dramatisation, no doubt smiled as she read it. But he was sincere enough in his belief that it was owing to *his* efforts that the King had been able to "rouse himself" and summon the strength to "free himself and his country from the direst shame".

2

It looks today as if, for lack of certain documents only recently made available, neither the older school of Wagnerians nor the purely political historians of Bavaria have given us a wholly true picture of the state of affairs between May, 1864, when Wagner first went to Munich, and December, 1865, when he was driven out of it. For the partisan Wagnerians, of course, he was from beginning to end the incarnation of all the unselfish virtues, and "Pfo"

---

[3] See Vol. III, pp. 359–60.

and "Pfi" and the rest of them the double-distilled essence of all
the vices. But the matter can now be seen to have been far more
complex than was formerly imagined. The King, in his passion for
Wagner and all that Wagner stood for as an artist, was undoubtedly
given at times to thinking affairs of state a bit of a bore, and it is
clear enough that now and then during the critical months preceding
the war of 1866 he was disinclined to face up to the full seriousness
of the situation. His great-uncle Prince Karl told the ex-King Ludwig I that he himself was racked with anxiety over Bavaria's future:
the King, he said, seemed to take no interest in military matters,
and, indeed, to be indifferent to everything but night rides to the
Roseninsel [4] and games with the young Prince Taxis. There is a vein
of peevish exaggeration in all this, but it is undeniable that the
King's Ministers more than once had difficulty in establishing contact with him during that critical time. And all his sins of omission
and commission in this regard were mistakenly charged to the account of Wagner, who, it was generally believed in Court circles and
political quarters, was craftily using the inexperienced boy for his
own personal, and especially financial, ends. These people were
incapable of distinguishing between the man and the artist. They
saw Wagner only in the light of his personal failings and his record
— his insatiable passion for luxury at the expense of others, his
lack of conscience where debts were concerned, his notorious ingratitude towards benefactors, his ruthless egoism in the pursuit of
his ends, — and were convinced that having found a heaven-sent
dupe in the innocent young Wittelsbacher the crafty "Musikant"
meant to exploit him to the full and achieve the ruin of everyone
who stood in his way. Thus we find the Prussian Ambassador in
Munich informing Berlin in October, 1866 that the reasons for the
disgrace then threatening Pfordten all led back to Richard Wagner:
this intriguing musician, he said, would not rest until he had resumed his comfortable existence in the capital and was able to do
what he liked with the royal purse. "He knows that Pfordten brought
about his banishment, and he is now using his incredible influence
over the young monarch to undermine Pfordten's position." [5]

---

[4] The "Island of Roses", in the Starnberg Lake, to which the King was in the
habit of retiring every now and then.
[5] Doeberl, III, 457, quoting from a document in the archives of the Prussian
Foreign Office, Berlin.

The Ambassador's informant was Pfordten himself, who told him that he had bluntly refused to make any concessions where Wagner was concerned —

"a man whose morals and dispositions are in every respect dubious, and who has made it his object to feed the King's mind with not merely useless but positively dangerous stuff in order to subject him to his will";

while Wagner tries on the one hand to lure the boy into political Utopias, on the other hand he confirms him in the notion that a King must not be gainsaid in anything, and seduces him into the most nonsensical expenditure. Pfordten, it appears, has done his best to open the King's eyes to the real character of the man, and Wagner can never forget or forgive the statesman's share in the events that led to his expulsion from Munich.

3

But were the hands of the officials quite clean? Wagner always maintained that his one object in plunging into Bavarian politics was to save the King from his own Ministers, who were plotting to get complete power into their own hands. That view of the situation finds some confirmation in the diaries of Hohenlohe, who knew everything that went on not only above but below the surface in Munich political circles. On the 3rd June, 1866 he records that some brawls that had just occurred between the mob and the police had been without doubt the work of "paid agents".

"Who is at the bottom of it all is not quite clear. The Liberals say it is the Ultramontanes [the clerical party] who are trying to get up a revolution and drive the young King out. . . ."

Four months later he describes in some detail the intrigues of the politicians against the King. Hohenlohe had just had a conversation with Dr. Oscar von Schanzenbach, his personal physician, whose practice brought him into close touch with the highest society of the capital.

"He told me that for the last fortnight he had met the King almost every evening at the house of Paul Taxis. His judgment of the King was very favourable, and it becomes more and more obvious that the neglect and the mistakes of which the King has been accused are really due to the Cabinet. My instincts were not deceived; it is really true that Pfistermeister and Lutz purposely képt the king in isolation that they might pursue their protection policy undisturbed in conjunction with Pfordten and Bomhard [the Minister of Justice].[6] In consequence the King knew nothing of the military memorial service. It was Pfistermeister who induced the King not to attend the funeral of General Zoller, not to visit the hospitals, etc. It appears that Schanzenbach has helped to open the King's eyes."

Wagner was therefore not alone in his conviction that Ludwig was being "betrayed and enmeshed", as he put it in his letter to Klara Wolfram: there were undoubtedly many in the Court party and among the clericals and the professional politicians in general who were working, even at this early stage of his reign, to have the King removed from the throne for the easier furtherance of their own personal or party ends.[7] In doing all he could to open Ludwig's

---

[6] That is to say, they deliberately edged him out of public affairs and then spread the report that he could not be induced to concern himself with them. The "service" mentioned in Hohenlohe's next sentence was for General von Zoller, who had been killed in the battle of Kissingen (10th July). Public feeling in Munich at the time had run high against the King, who was charged with refusing to receive the officer who had brought the body back, and, in general, of showing only a languid interest in the war. "A 'high war lord' who refuses to receive an officer returned from the battlefield!" Hohenlohe had noted in his diary on the 13th July. "Is it not enough to make people rail?"

Böhm (BLKB, p. 115) comments unfavourably on what he calls the "credulity" with which Hohenlohe, in his entry of the 11th October, accepts "the improbable *fable convenue* of the Wagner party", told him by "Wagner's friend Dr. Schanzenbach", of the machinations of Pfistermeister, Pfordten and Bomhard. To this it may be replied that if the story had been as utterly "improbable" as Böhm tries to make out it is not likely that so shrewd a practical politician as Hohenlohe, who knew all the highways and byways of Bavarian politics, would have given it the consideration he did. "My instincts were not deceived" are his words; they imply that he himself had suspected manœuvres of the sort *before* Schanzenbach told him his story. The point is not whether the story was true in all its details: the suspicion of Bomhard in particular was probably unjustified. The point is that Hohenlohe regarded such an explanation of recent events as Schanzenbach had given him as wholly consistent with his own observations.

There is no evidence, by the way, that Schanzenbach was a "friend" of Wagner's at this time: his name does not come into the story until the 6th January, 1867, when he wrote to Wagner on behalf of Hohenlohe. Furthermore, the Court circles in which the fashionable physician moved were, in general, the last that could be described as belonging to a "Wagner party". Hohenlohe himself never met Wagner until March, 1867, nor did he particularly want to ḿeet him even then.

[7] See, for instance, Wagner's letter of the 5th February, 1867 to Röckel: "My influence on Bavarian politics consists simply in this, that during the time when, as everyone knows, the authority and dignity of the King were so besmirched that his removal from the throne was manifestly being plotted, I gave emphatic expression to the ardent desire to see an independent and honest man by the King's side, in place of diplomatic lackeys." KLRWB, IV, 180.

eyes to the danger threatening him Wagner was not thinking solely
of his own interests; he was honestly concerned also for the young
King. It may have been through an excess of self-esteem that he
imagined *he* was competent to steer the Bavarian ship of state
through the troubled waters then beginning to beat against it, or at
all events to select the ideal captain and crew and give them their
sailing orders. In practical politics he was never more than the
veriest amateur, as is shown not only by his naive belief that in the
mid-nineteenth century the solution of the age-long German problem depended on "the princes" identifying themselves with "their
folk" in a way more operatic than realistic, but by his inability,
then as at all times, to grasp the elementary fact that the life of a
nation depends upon many more things than its theatrical and operatic "culture" or its naive reactions of hatred for Jews, or Jesuits,
or Prussia, or Austria, or whatever the catchword or the bogy of
the time and the place may be. In January, 1867 he was confidently
assuring Röckel that "external politics" did not concern and never
had concerned Bavaria! It is not surprising that the practical
politicians, who had to deal with such very unoperatic problems as
foreign relations, taxation, armaments, codes of justice, education,
tariffs, excise and so on, should have kicked hard against the intrusion of this self-confident amateur from Saxony into the affairs of
Bavaria. But whatever we may think of Wagner as a politician there
can be no question that he believed everything he did politically
to be in the King's and all Germany's interest no less than in his own.

4

But, he goes on to say to Luise Brockhaus in his letter of the 17th
January, 1867, he and the King are now to some small extent at
cross-purposes. For himself, his sole desire is to remain in the
heavenly seclusion of Triebschen and get on with his creative work,
whereas for Ludwig the hard-won victory over the politicians loses
all its meaning "unless I soon return to him for good". Still, he
continues complacently, he is hoping to bring his young friend
round to his way of thinking, "since he is equal to any sacrifice for
me". He was to discover, before long, that there were sacrifices
which the King was not prepared to make even for Richard Wagner's sake.

His letters to his other friends about this time show that he had made up his mind not to live in Munich again on any conditions. But he did not put it quite so baldly as that to the King. He did, it is true, tell him frankly that he would not occupy the Briennerstrasse house again. But he still thought it prudent to hold out to the suffering young man, whose heart was aching with love for him — or at all events for what he represented in the sphere of the ideal — the hope of seeing him from time to time in Munich or elsewhere. To his other correspondents he saw no reason to be anything but outspoken. Ludwig, he tells Mathilde Maier, is absolutely bent on his returning in the spring. To dissuade him he will have to see him again and talk to him. To Röckel he is franker still. He is appalled, he says, at the King's impulsive decision to embark at once on the festival theatre scheme, for he himself has other things in his mind just now than "Wagner-Theatres and Wagner-Strassen." For the present, however, all he can do is to let events take their own course and trust to the young man's fire dying down. Nothing on earth will ever tempt him back to his Munich house, though he will revisit the town occasionally for the King's sake, staying with the Bülows.

It is doubtful whether Wagner knew, just then, precisely what he wanted or how he was most likely to get it. A few months' experience of Triebschen had convinced him of the folly of ever plunging again into the stormy, muddy waters of Munich public life. He had recommenced work on the *Meistersinger,* and once more realised that true happiness, for him, was to be found only in poetising and composing. In all sincerity he could assure the King of this and beg him, in the interests of the ideal they had in common, to allow him to remain in his Asyl. In a letter of the 21st March he even gave Ludwig a hint that he no longer desired even to take any part in the production of his works in Munich: experience had taught him, he said, that to throw himself in person into "the carrying-out of our art-plans" — which obviously included not only rehearsing his works but superintending the schemes for the festival theatre and the Music School — would mean his being worn out physically in a few years, to the ruin of his creative faculty. Other people might be able to produce his operas, he said; he alone could write them.

Obviously what was in his mind just then was henceforth to leave the main business of production of his new works in Munich, and of "model" performances of the older ones, to Bülow, he him-

[45]

self looking in at the last moment, perhaps, to make sure that everything on the stage was as he would have wished it to be. This meant that Bülow would have to be impregnably entrenched in Munich. Yet if Bülow were to settle there permanently Cosima would either have to rejoin her husband or run the risk of another bespattering by the Press; and Wagner knew well enough by this time that life for him was impossible without her. If ever he sat down to sort out all the pieces of his puzzle he must have been dismayed by the number and the confusion of them. If only Bülow had been accommodating enough to die, as Minna had done, one at any rate of Wagner's two main problems would soon have found its own solution: he and Cosima would then have been able to marry without scandal. But their "illicit" relations were by this time known to quite a number of people in Munich, especially since Malvina had returned there and given rein to her tongue. Another journalistic campaign against himself and Cosima was to be avoided at all costs; while it was more essential than ever that the truth should be concealed from the King after he had been tricked into a public declaration of his own confidence in the innocence of their relations. Yet if another public scandal could be avoided only by his giving up Cosima, of what final use was his Triebschen haven going to be to him?

5

With problems of this sort doing their unceasing devils' dance in his brain, and with the echoes of the Malvina affair still making themselves heard occasionally, it is not surprising that his health suffered so much in the early months of 1867 that he himself wondered at his being able to make the headway he did with the music of the *Meistersinger*. Nor was Cosima his only worry. His most immediate concern was to safeguard his artistic interests in Munich by ensuring Bülow's official standing there; and before he could do that he had a good deal of trouble not only with the King and the officials but with Hans.

As we have seen, Bülow, after the scandal hunt led by the Press against him and Cosima in the autumn of 1866, had settled in Basel. For his own sake as well as Wagner's it was vital that he should return to Munich as soon as possible — for Wagner's sake, because if Hans, in a fit of discouragement or of temper, should elect to settle in Berlin again Cosima would either have to go with him or bring the yelping pack on her traces once more by openly making her home in Triebschen; for Bülow's sake, because he was still completely the slave of the higher genius and more powerful personality of Wagner, to serve whose art seemed to him the one thing that justified his own existence. Accordingly in the early weeks of 1867 we find Wagner putting continuous pressure on the King to show some public favour to Bülow. Hans, as was so often the case with him, was behaving like a fractious child. He knew he was not popular in Munich, not merely because he was known to be a Prussian and thought in some quarters to be a Prussian spy but because, as he himself frankly recognised, he had an unexampled gift for getting on the wrong side of everybody. The orchestral players mostly respected him, but few of them really liked him. He had enemies everywhere, at Court, in the Intendanz, among the politicians, in the beerhouses, among the Munich musicians in general, his arrogant contempt for whom, from Lachner downwards, he never had the tact to conceal, and above all in the scandal-loving Press, for which he was always the easiest of game. He could hope to carry on again in Munich, then, only if guaranteed special powers by the King.

On the 18th January (1867) Wagner tabled his terms for Bülow's return in somewhat peremptory fashion. Hans was to be appointed director of the projected Music School, with full authority to staff and run it on the lines laid down in Wagner's Report of the spring of 1865; [8] he was to be authorised to reorganise the Theatre orchestra and to engage whatever singers from abroad might be necessary for the production of the *Meistersinger;* he was to be given supreme control of the operatic side of the Theatre; it was to be left to him to decide which, if any, of the pupils being trained for Wagner by Friedrich Schmitt were coming up to expectation; and he was to be given a Bavarian decoration.

This last stipulation may have been Bülow's own. He had apparently mounted his high horse, talking angrily about the consideration due to him as "a Prussian nobleman"; and though, when he got into this vein, he tried Wagner's patience almost to breaking-point, it was still necessary to humour him. Pfistermeister, on his retirement, had been raised by the King to the hereditary nobility;

- [8] See Vol. III, p. 319.

[47]

this sign of the royal good will had rankled in Wagner, who would have preferred his defeated enemy to be hanged, drawn and quartered, and he actually complained to Ludwig that a mere Pfistermeister should have been publicly favoured in this way while a Bülow was passed over. Bülow himself may possibly have attached no particular value to the order that was being sought for him beyond that of a fresh public guarantee, on the King's part, of that "honour" of himself and Cosima the Press attacks on which had galled him beyond endurance. The plain and simple solution of this part of the problem — to divorce Cosima there and then and let her go to Wagner — he could not bring himself to face up to squarely.

6

In the early days of 1867 Wagner was anxious not only to confer with Ludwig on the Bülow and related matters but also to meet the new Premier, whose appointment he flattered himself had been mainly his work, and whose co-operation, therefore, he felt he had a right to count on in his own plans. But many other forces besides Wagner's advice to the King had been behind Hohenlohe's advancement to the highest post in Bavarian politics. He had obviously been in the running for some time, though it was not until after the war and the resulting fall in Pfordten's stock that the attention of the political world in general was centred in him. He had been offered, on the 1st November, 1866, as he records in his diary, "the Ministry of Domestic and Foreign Affairs and the post of Prime Minister", with the further post of Chief Royal Chamberlain in the offing — "un honneur que je gôute fort médiocrement", he drily remarks. Cautious enquiries on his part had led to the discovery that

"at the moment there was no sufficient reason for a change of Ministers, and that I could not calculate upon a specially favourable reception by public opinion. My entry to the Ministry would be generally approved, but there is no great anxiety for my appointment. Parties were not yet organised, and the anti-Prussian feeling is not yet sufficiently pacified.[9] At the same time I cannot conceal from myself that the King's

---

[9] Hohenlohe's North German bias was notorious. See Prince Paul Taxis' letter of the 29th July, 1866 to Wagner (KLRWB, IV, 156–7), voicing the King's doubts at that time about Hohenlohe. Later, when his opinion of Hohenlohe's capacity and trustworthiness had begun to decline somewhat, he could not act as decisively as he

desire to have me as a Minister . . . proceeds from his passion for Wagner. The King remembers that I formerly characterised the removal of Wagner as an unnecessary measure, and hopes that I will be able to secure his return. I have no desire to form a Wagner Ministry, though I also consider that Wagner's return *later* would be by no means a misfortune."

Hohenlohe, of course, as a practical politician, had a great many more matters to think about than the fortunes or misfortunes of an opera composer. Naturally his first concern was to consolidate his parliamentary position; so he did not take kindly to the suggestion that he should meet Wagner within a bare week or so of his appointment to the premiership. On the 6th January the King passed on to Wagner the Prince's pressing desire that he would defer his projected visit to Munich from the 8th to the 18th. "A considerable number of people", Ludwig wrote, "closely associate Hohenlohe's appointment with the question of your return here; and he thinks that if you were to come now it would be impossible for him to maintain his position." One of Hohenlohe's first cares, it appears, is to secure the good will of the Press, which will be difficult if the impression gets abroad that he is working for Wagner's return.

Hohenlohe himself, though too wary to communicate with Wagner direct, got into indirect touch with him through the trusty Schanzenbach. The latter wrote to Wagner on the 6th, to the effect that the Prince had not the least criticism to make of Wagner's position with regard to the King, but only hoped that he would delay his return until the new régime was firmly in the saddle. Hohenlohe was of course in error in imagining that Wagner was consumed with longing to settle in Munich again. He was proposing to revisit the town now simply to confer with the King about the steps to be taken to further their artistic plans, and to impress on him the urgent necessity of holding Bülow. But as Ludwig had still not abandoned the hope of persuading Wagner to return to the Briennerstrasse it is not to be wondered at that Hohenlohe and others should believe that a scheme of that sort was at the back of Wagner's mind also. Schanzenbach discussed the local situation at full length in a fur-

would have liked to do for fear of offending Bismarck, who knew what an asset the Bavarian Minister was to him in his far-reaching schemes for Prussian hegemony in Germany. Already in March, 1867 the King had arrived at the point where he could describe Hohenlohe to Bomhard as a *filou* who had traduced the latter.

ther letter of the 13th January to Wagner, the gist of which is once more that Hohenlohe sees no danger, and indeed never had seen any, in Wagner's close association with the King, but that he deems it prudent to wait until he has firmly established his Ministry before he takes a public line in this matter.[10]

7

As there seemed to be no hurry in Munich to comply with Wagner's wishes with regard to Bülow, and as the tone of his letters to the King was becoming more and more uncompromising, indeed peremptory, Ludwig sent his Court Secretary Düfflipp [11] to Triebschen on the 23rd January: on his way back to Munich he had a talk with Bülow on the 25th, in Zürich, where Hans had a professional engagement that day. The fact that instead of replying direct to Wagner's latest urgent appeal the King sent Düfflipp to try a little personal diplomacy with him suggests of itself that the Bülow problem did not look so simple to him as it did to Wagner.

Apparently neither the King nor the officials were willing to go quite as far as Hans desired. "Prussian nobleman", Wagner notes in his "Annals" on the 13th February, putting the words in inverted commas, perhaps with a derisive intention, but at any rate indicating that the inflated expression had been Bülow's own. "Bülow is giving

---

[10] Schanzenbach blandly assures Wagner that Hohenlohe does not know he is writing to him, and that he himself wants to avoid the appearance of mixing himself up with matters that do not concern him. We may probably take the first of these statements with a grain of salt.

A fortnight later Schanzenbach went to Triebschen, at the Prince's request, to discuss the situation with Wagner. Gottfried von Böhm (BLKB, p. 157) casts doubt on Sebastian Röckl's statement that at "the end of January 1866" — the actual date was perhaps the 1st February — Hohenlohe had sent his physician to Triebschen "to set forth his political plans and assure himself of Wagner's powerful support". "There is no confirmation of this", says Böhm, "in Hohenlohe's diaries." That is true; but we now know for certain, from a letter of Wagner's of the 8th February to August Röckel (KLRWB, IV, 180) that Schanzenbach *had* been in Triebschen a week before, and that he *had* been "sent there" by Hohenlohe. That the latter thought it prudent not to confide these facts to his journal is a proof that even diaries cannot always be relied upon to reveal the whole truth, and that the diarist sometimes throws more light on himself, for posterity, by what he omits than by what he puts in. This is not the only instance in which Hohenlohe's journal prefers the gold of silence to the silver of speech.

[11] Düfflipp was Court Secretary, not, as some writers appear to imagine, Cabinet Secretary. Pfistermeister had been succeeded in the latter post by Neumayr, who made way a little later for Lutz.

an immense amount of trouble", Wagner had written to the King on the 20th.

"It was extremely indulgent and gracious of you not to let yourself be misled in the first place by his crazy behaviour. For me it was not so easy; indeed, I had already made up my mind to break with him entirely, a course which would naturally have had serious consequences. He arrived here, at last, on Sunday [the 17th], in order to come to an understanding with his wife, who, it goes without saying, was no less exasperated by the 'Prussian nobleman'." [12]

Wagner goes on to tell the King that Hans had arrived at Triebschen on the very day when Cosima was delivered of her daughter Eva. She is doing well, Wagner is happy to say.

"The poor unhappy Hans also seems to be a little calmer. The powerful influence of his wife, always clarifying and illuminating, has too long been lacking to him. . . . Bülow is possessed by a positive abhorrence of Munich just now: if we can overcome this, the marvel can be achieved only by our love for the wonderful lord of our lives."

On the 13th February Bülow had written to Düfflipp to this effect:

"The royal command conveyed to me in your esteemed letter of the 11th, to come to a speedy and definite decision with regard to the propositions made to me by his Majesty, unfortunately leaves no course open to me but to return a simple refusal to the propositions, at the same time thanking him humbly for his kindly intentions. [My reasons for this refusal I will set forth publicly.]" [13]

To Raff, three days later, Bülow wrote that having rejected the "insufficient" propositions made to him from Munich he now intended to settle down for good in Basel.

"Is it not sad that for the last six months I have had to do without my family and vegetate like an old bachelor? Now, thank heaven, I have my fate in my own hands: an individual existence becomes possible for me. That this is no longer bound up with Richard Wagner's plans will mean no injury to our old friendship, as we shall be living so close to Lucerne and Wagner will not return to Munich without me. Next autumn I will go to America, to win a little material independence."

---

[12] Bülow had evidently used the expression in his talk with Düfflipp.
[13] KLRWB, II, 145, *note*. The document is printed there from Bülow's own draft, now in the Wahnfried archives; evidently Hans had forwarded it to Wagner. In the draft the final sentence is enclosed in blue-pencil brackets: presumably it was omitted from the actual letter sent to Düfflipp.

The "we" obviously means himself and Cosima; Bülow seems to have imagined that "face" could still be saved in the eyes of the world by Cosima officially occupying his establishment but spending most of her time with Wagner. The daughter born to Cosima on the 17th he knew perfectly well was not his. Yet the unhappy man could still stoop to try to inveigle the King into some sort of public demonstration of his faith in the "honour" of the triangle.

He refused to accept the offers made him by Düfflipp until the King had redeemed his incautious promise, given in too naive a reliance on the word of Wagner, Hans and Cosima, to punish the "criminals" who had dared, in the summer of 1866, to hint at the plain truth about the relations of the trio. This point, and this alone, appears to have constituted the bar just then to Bülow's acceptance of the King's proposals, for matters relating merely to his work in connection with the School and the Theatre could have been arranged without much difficulty, nor indeed were there any "criminals" in *these* quarters to be publicly "punished" for Bülow's gratification. In the preceding December he had been made a supplementary Bavarian Court Kapellmeister. "The King of Bavaria", he tells Raff in his letter of the 16th February,

"will no doubt be very angry with me and deprive me of my Kapellmeister title. This I am expecting; but although I am no republican I would find it impossible to serve any King who does not think and act as a King should but merely has a feeling for art."

Like Wagner, he could hardly conceive the Munich political and artistic world as having any raison d'être except in relation to his own concerns. "The political developments in Bavaria", he wrote to Raff a few days later,

"will have a very important bearing on my future. This seems crazy, but so it is. If Hohenlohe falls — and the Jesuits are doing their utmost to bring him down — then *we* are impossible for Munich, or Munich for us."

That Munich in particular, and Bavaria in general, might have other and perhaps even more engrossing things to concern themselves with than a composer and a conductor does not seem to have entered Bülow's head.

8

But as he was essential to the Wagner cause in Munich, and that cause, in turn, was vital to the King's happiness, and as, moreover, it was vital to Wagner's and Cosima's happiness that the new Bülow ménage should not be located too far away from Lucerne, the fretful, resentful Hans had to be pacified in some way or other. Wagner, manifestly worried by the turn events were taking, determined to see the King at the first opportunity. He had finished the Orchestral Sketch of the second act of the *Meistersinger* on the 23rd September, 1866, and begun the Composition Sketch of the third act on the following 2nd October. By the 7th February, 1867, this too was completed: at the end of the Sketch he wrote, "7 Febr. 1867, St. Richard's day, completed expressly for Cosima." Little more remained to be done now but the formal lay-out of the music in full score, a protracted process enough, to be sure, but, in view of the comprehensive nature of the Sketches, a matter of patient elaboration rather than of creation. The orchestral score, he told the King, would run to some three hundred pages, which ought not to occupy him more than about a hundred days. With the *Meistersinger* now virtually off his hands he could endure to tear himself away from Triebschen for a few days to talk matters over with the King and Hohenlohe.

Bülow had returned to Basel on the 24th February, a week after the birth of Eva. On the 2nd March the two elder children — Bülow's own — were sent with their governess to Hans's mother in Berlin; the other two remained at Triebschen. On the 9th Wagner went to Munich, where he remained until the 18th, putting up at the Bayerischer Hof Hotel. He was met at the station by Röckel and other friends, including Cornelius, whom he had not seen since his flight from the town in December, 1865. Wagner's health being bad, his moods and his manners varied considerably from hour to hour. At one time he would be cordiality itself with Peter; at another, something less than amiable. Cornelius wrote to his fiancée, a couple of days after the Master had left Munich again, that Wagner would hardly make a good impression on anyone meeting him just now for the first time. He had wounded Peter by his coolness towards the libretto of the new opera — *Gunlöd* — on which Cornelius was then at work; and his manner in general had been too egoistic and his temper too capricious. He held, it appears, a "court" every evening, monopolising most of the conversation, as was his habit, laying down the law on every subject under the sun, favouring the company with long readings from his autobiography — the manuscript of which he seems to have carried about with him everywhere for his own satisfaction and the delectation of his friends, — indulging himself in the usual tantrums when crossed, and, as always, alienating and hypnotising by turns everyone who came in contact with him.

Peter, for all his affection and admiration for him, refused to see him otherwise than exactly as he was, nor was his vision any less clear where some of the Master's friends and acquaintances were concerned. He had no illusions about Röckel, for instance, whom he respected as a man, while seeing that this new association of his with Wagner in political matters would most likely "upset the apple cart once more", as he put it. He was amused at Wagner's psychological naiveté where Schanzenbach was concerned. Wagner, obviously gratified by the fashionable physician's *empressement* towards him, had misconceived the source and object of it, taking it for granted that here was yet another influential person who could be useful to him. He told his friends that he hoped to find in Schanzenbach "another Standhartner".[14] "I could not help smiling to myself", says Cornelius. "O genius! O reader of men!" Standhartner, he says, is a noble, gentle, amiable character, a lover of music for its own sake, whose unselfish friendship for Wagner has survived all trials, all disillusionments; he has done everything for Wagner and seeks nothing in return. And now Wagner is simple enough to think he has found a second Standhartner in this Herr Schanzenbach, who has obviously something very different at the back of his mind from merely serving Wagner's ends!

On the 10th Wagner had an audience with the King in the Residenz. They discussed, among other matters, the production of the *Meistersinger* and the appointment as Theatre Intendant of a certain Baron Gustav von Putlitz, formerly of the Schwerin Court Theatre, whom Cosima seems to have thought likely to be a docile instrument for Wagnerian purposes.[15] Wagner gratified Ludwig by prom-

[14] See Vol. III, Chap. 8, etc.
[15] See her letter to the King in MECW, I, 338. Cosima, in days gone by, had translated one of Putlitz's works into French. She did not rank him very high as a poet, she told the King, though she credited him with a *flair* for the theatre. His chief

ising to settle in Starnberg for a little while in the summer, when *Lohengrin* was to be given at the Court Theatre, but pleaded once more that his health and his work depended on his not entering Munich again except for a brief visit now and then.

On the evening of the 12th he called on Prince Hohenlohe. He came away innocently pleased with the interview, feeling, as Cosima expressed it afterwards in a letter to the King, that in the new Premier he had "a real support". Hohenlohe himself has left us a fairly detailed account of the meeting in his diary. Wagner appears to have been somewhat embarrassed at first, but the seasoned diplomatist and aristocratic man of the world put him at his ease by the tactful remark that they had two points in common — "we were both hated by the same party, and we were united in equal veneration for the King". "Thereupon", continues Hohenlohe, a faintly ironic smile seeming to play on his lips as he writes,

"he became more communicative, spoke about the way in which the King had been treated and so tormented that he had twice written to him that he would abdicate; and told me, amid protestations of not wishing to take credit to himself, that it was *he* who had recommended me to the King as Minister. Then he came to the task of Bavaria as a German State whose population united the versatility of Franconia with the imagination of Swabia and the native strength of Bavaria; said that the King was just the man to rule this German State and to realise the ideal of the German spirit (*Deutschtum*); went on to speak of his artistic aims, of his experiences in this country, of his plans for the establishment of a school of art, of the obstacles that had been put in his way, and came finally to the Cabinet. Among other things he spoke of the necessity of my remaining in the Ministry. To which I replied that this did not depend upon myself; and that I could not guarantee that attempts would not be made to undermine the King's confidence in me, and that I was the less sure of retaining this since the King, following the tradition of the Royal House, did not treat with me direct but only through the Cabinet.[16] He then said that this could not continue so; whereupon I drew his attention to the danger of engaging in a conflict with the Cabinet, a danger of which he must be well aware. He mentioned my political programme, into a few details of which I entered. Finally he expressed the hope that the King would never lose confidence in me."

---

recommendation in her eyes and Wagner's would be his complete ignorance of music; they evidently hoped that this would result in his leaving operatic matters mostly in Bülow's hands. Nothing came of their suggestion, however: it seems to have been unacceptable to the King.

[16] For the meaning of this see Vol. III, p. 220.

And with that, Wagner virtually disappears from the pages of Hohenlohe's diary. The hard-bitten parliamentarian must have seen at a glance that he had to do with an amateur, a visionary who need not be taken seriously except in so far as he might be able to influence the King occasionally through the young man's passion for art. As soon as it became manifest to Hohenlohe that he had been wrong in supposing that Wagner was yearning to return to Munich, and that consequently his own parliamentary task need not be complicated now by his having to consider the attitude of this party or that towards Wagner, the "Musikant" ceased to be of any pressing importance to him. He could give his whole attention to such urgent practical matters as his diary, his letters and his speeches show him to have been concerned with at this time — the sorely-needed reorganisation of the army; the upkeep of fortresses; Bavaria's relations with the other South German States; Prussia; Austria; the Ultramontanes; German union; the North German Confederation; the Zollverein; national finance, weights, measures and coinage; banking laws; railways, posts and telegraphs; the maintenance of European peace; and so on — leaving the musician to dream to his heart's content of a new Germany making its finale-to-the-third-act entry into Valhalla under the banner of a King of grand opera.

9

Hohenlohe was not the only distinguished individual whom Wagner met during his visit to Munich: on the 16th March he paid his respects to no less a person than the King's fiancée.

Ludwig had caused a flutter among his subjects in the third week of January by becoming engaged to his cousin Sophie, a daughter of Duke Maximilian of Bavaria and sister of the beautiful Empress Elisabeth of Austria. She was two years younger than the King. The reason for this strange step on Ludwig's part was never very clear until his own letters of a later period threw some light on it. Sophie's enthusiasm for Wagner seems to have influenced him, though we cannot be sure that there was not some calculation in her enthusiasm. Ludwig appears also to have seen in her, for a while, a being as lonely as himself. "Sophie is an honest, sympathetic soul, full of intelligence", he had written to Cosima on the 5th January. "Her fate has a certain similarity with mine: each of us lives in an environment that misunderstands and misjudges us: we exist, as it were, on an oasis in a sandy desert." Wagner was probably the first to whom (on the 22nd), Ludwig telegraphed the news of the engagement, in appropriately Wagnerian terms — "Walther informs the dear Sachs that he has found his faithful Eva, Siegfried his Brynhilde." His courtship seems mostly to have taken the odd form of impressing it on Sophie that the one being on earth he really loved was Wagner. "You know the nature of my destiny", he wrote to her:

> "about my mission I wrote to you once from Berg. You know that I have not many years to live, that I will quit this earth when the terrible thing happens, when my Star is extinguished, when *He*, the true and beloved Friend, is no more; this will be my end too, for I could not go on living. . . . You will agree with me that the essence of our [his and Sophie's] association was Wagner's strangely moving fate."

Wagner warmly approved of the engagement, partly out of genuine affection for the King and a desire for his happiness, partly, it is permissible to think, because a married Ludwig would presumably have less time and less inclination to devote to Wagner's affairs an attention which was now becoming irksome to him. But as the months went on, the King obviously became less and less keen about selling himself into matrimonial servitude. The prime reason, perhaps, was that he had come to look with rather different eyes at Sophie, whose conversation and devotion to needlework had begun to bore him; but he resented also the hectoring tone of her father's letters to him and jibbed at the attempts of his own mother and his prospective mother-in-law to shape his life for him. On the 11th October came the official public announcement of the dissolution of the engagement by mutual consent, "it having become evident that there was lacking the true inclination of heart to heart that guarantees a happy marriage". By this time the country in general had come round to Ludwig's way of thinking; many people did not like the idea of a marriage between such near relations, while the King's congenital preference for his own sex may have already begun to be surmised.[17]

---

[17] Catulle Mendès' *roman à clé*, *Le Roi Vierge*, was not published until 1881, but it is of course based on the facts and gossip of an earlier period. "Take from me my throne if you like", he makes the young man say to his mother when she urges him to marry, "but I will not give up my bed!"

In less than a year after the end of her romance Sophie became the wife of Duke Ferdinand d'Alençon, a grandson of Louis Philippe. Like Ludwig, her sister Elisabeth,

But in March, 1867, when Wagner went to Munich, there was no cloud on the horizon. Sophie was all girlish curiosity to see the great Master to whom her betrothed had dedicated his own life and, by all indications, was likely to dedicate hers. Her recently published letters to Wagner throw an interesting light on the state of things in Munich just then. She sent him her cordial greetings in a letter of the 13th, begging him to exercise the utmost caution with regard to his call on her. It was absolutely impossible, she said, for her to see him in "our house", for her mostly anti-Wagnerian family were doing all they could to prevent their meeting. She would receive him at the house of her married brother Duke Ludwig, on whose good will and that of his wife she could rely. "Parzival [the King] can unfortunately not be present; that would cause too much sensation, which must be avoided at any cost." The next day she sends Wagner detailed strategic instructions. On Saturday the 16th, punctually at one o'clock, he is to present himself at Kanalstrasse No. 33. Her sister-in-law will meet him at the door: Sophie will arrive at the house just after him. He is not to come in a carriage belonging to the hotel, but to pick up a cab in the street, dismissing it when he arrives; her brother-in-law will arrange for him to be taken back. Next day she alters the time to half-past twelve; the vital

---

and the latter's son the Crown Prince Rudolf, she came to a tragic end; she perished in the appalling Charity Bazaar fire in Paris in May 1897.

Le Roi Vierge, by the way, is to a great extent mere fantastic flummery, but it is still worth reading as a means to reconstructing to some extent several of the leading personalities of the third quarter of the nineteenth century. There is an excellent picture, drawn from life, of Wagner in one of his tantrums: Catulle must often have seen him behaving like that when he was crossed.

Everyone can see at a glance that King Frederick II of Thuringia in the novel is King Ludwig, that the composer Hans Hammer is Wagner, and that the Abbé Glinck is Liszt. One or two other identifications may help the ordinary reader who is perhaps not well acquainted with the milieu of the book. The mysterious queen whom the King is supposed to have worshipped from afar is the French Empress Eugènie. Her confidante, the Countess Soïnoff, is an admirably drawn portrait of Princess Pauline Metternich. The Russian countess who makes so much trouble for the Abbé Glinck is Liszt's notorious Olga Janina. The opera *Floris et Blancheflor* is *Tristan and Isolde*. Madame Dzalergy, the white lady whom Théophile Gautier had celebrated in his "Symphonie en blanc majeur", and who, in the novel, marries a Count Loukhanof and is suspected in more than one European chancellery of being a political spy, is Wagner's friend and Liszt's former love Mme Kalergis, by her second marriage Mme Mouchanoff. Countess Sternistz (*sic*), wife of the Prussian Minister of the interior, is Cosima's Berlin friend Countess von Schleinitz. Mona Kharis is Lola Montez. A novel like *Le Roi Vierge* would in these days involve the author of it in at least half-a-dozen libel actions. Because of its treatment of King Ludwig it was banned in Bavaria.

thing, she insists, is to keep strictly to the time-table so that they shall not be seen together at the street door.[18]

Wagner was deeply moved by his interview with the artless young bride on the 16th; for the first time, he said afterwards, he had looked into eyes out of which shone anxious love for the King.

10

He returned to Triebschen on the 18th: Bülow, who had been in Munich for a few days, travelled back with him as far as Augsburg, where he had to give a recital. They felt they could congratulate themselves on the result of their visit to the capital. It had been agreed with the King and the Theatre Intendanz that Hans was to settle for good in Munich on the 15th April as a regular Kapellmeister and director of the Music School, to conduct *Lohengrin* in June and the *Meistersinger* on the 12th October (the day appointed for the royal wedding), and to receive the order of the Knight's Cross of St. Michael, first class. But apparently there was some ambiguity about these terms when put in writing, for on the 5th April Bülow wrote to Draeseke that the fat was in the fire once more: "the weakness of the one man whose command alone would have sufficed for our protection, the vileness" — everyone who did not instantly do what Wagner and Bülow wanted them to do was "vile" — "of the faithless servants who lord it over him — *n'en parlons plus*. I remain in Basel. . . . Wagner went to Munich yesterday to say definitive good-bye for both of us."

The prime trouble was perhaps in connection with the projected change in the Intendanz; Wagner, after his return to Triebschen, had urged the King, if opposed by his officials, to settle the Putlitz matter in true operatic fashion by "once more wielding Siegfried's sword". But things were not quite so easy as that, as even a man so unteachable by experience as Wagner was might have realised by this time. In the first days of April Cosima received from Röckel a letter the contents of which were to be passed on to Wagner only if he were likely to be calm enough to endure them! Röckel, a born mischief-maker if ever there was one, accused Düfflipp of having organised a new "revolt" against Wagner. The King's Secretary,

[18] KLRWB, IV, 183–4.

it was alleged, had said that Wagner and Bülow were troublesome people to handle; that they would not obey orders; that Wagner, instead of devoting himself to the fulfilment of his contract as regarded his new works, persisted in meddling in things that were no concern of his, such as the Intendanz and the Music School; that nothing would come of all his schemes; and that if he did not cease putting pressure on the King to do things he did not want to do, such as summoning Putlitz and giving Bülow the sweeping powers he demanded at the School, it would go ill with him. Röckel had further learned (or surmised) that interested parties were trying to inflame the King against Wagner through his pride, insinuating that the musician was well on the way to becoming his overlord. The other active members of "the Düfflipp cabal" were said to be Lachner and Schmitt,[19] with Lutz and "the whole Austrian party" as willing helpers. This party, says Röckel, cares nothing one way or the other about the art-plans of the King, and would even be prepared to further them were not Wagner personally such a menace. Intrigues against Hohenlohe are in full blast, and King Ludwig has actually had Pfistermeister to dinner! And so *ad infinitum;* Röckel was in his element in this world of gossip, wire-pulling and chicanery, and never so happy as when he was setting other people by the ears.

We need not take seriously all he says against Düfflipp, who seems to have been consistently well-disposed towards Wagner. Being the King's servant, not Wagner's, his first duty was to his royal master. He was talking simple common sense when he hinted that it would be better for the composer himself, in the long run, if he would just get on with his music and not keep meddling with matters outside his province. Though Wagner was inclined to forget the fact,

---

[19] I.e., Intendanzrat (Theatre Councillor) Wilhelm Schmitt. There is considerable confusion regarding this gentleman in Wagner literature. He is sometimes called Friedrich, and, as such, confused with the singing teacher of that name whom Wagner had brought to Munich. (He even figures as "Friedrich Schmitt" in the indices to volumes 4 and 5 of KLRWB). Röckel himself does not improve matters by referring to him as "Schmi*d*t", as do also Wagner, Bülow and Cornelius in their correspondence. Stemplinger (SWM, p. 143), unaware that "der treue Friedrich" was the King's and Wagner's private name for Paul von Taxis, takes a passage in a letter of the King of the 13th September, 1866 to Cosima — "From the 1st January the faithful Friedrich will be the Theatre Intendant" — to apply to this "Friedrich" Schmitt, whose first name, anyhow, was Wilhelm! Dr. Strobel, correcting Stemplinger's error, still calls Wilhelm "Friedrich". Seldom can the great Smith clan have caused such confusion in literary history.

the Munich Court Theatre had other functions to perform in the national life besides the production of Wagner operas. The situation as the ordinary Münchener saw it at that time must have been something like this. One German "foreigner", a Saxon composer, had descended on the town as the King's "favourite". He was moving heaven and earth to have the operatic side of the Theatre and the new Conservatoire placed under the supreme command of his own chief henchman, another foreigner — and, worse still, a Prussian. Yet another of his henchmen had been imported from Leipzig to teach the local professors of singing their business. Still others, such as Porges and Cornelius, had been brought from Vienna, and Nohl from Heidelberg. If Wagner were allowed to have his way, the local Court Theatre and the national Conservatoire would exist merely to serve him. Only a pair of egoists so short-sighted as Wagner and Bülow could have failed to see that, human nature being what it is, the granting of their demands would sooner or later mean friction in the Theatre. More level-headed people, such as Düfflipp and the King, saw this quite plainly and were doing all they could to steer clear of trouble. But Wagner, as usual, could see no side but his own, admit the validity of no claims but his own; and towards the achievement of his ends he now drove with characteristic energy and ruthlessness. He got what he wanted, but at a cost that made the victory finally not worth while.

11

After reading Röckel's letter Wagner acted swiftly. On the 4th April he was back again in the Bayerischer Hof Hotel, whence he sent a request to the Residenz for an audience with the King; recent experiences, he said, had shown him clearly what decisions, especially with regard to Bülow, would have to be taken if "peace" was to be obtained. He saw Ludwig at ten o'clock the next morning. In a letter to him later in the day he speaks of his being unable to carry out the resolution that had brought him back to Munich — by which, apparently, he meant saying that "definitive farewell" of which Bülow had spoken in his letter to Raff. Wagner may have actually tried that abortive bluff; for this letter of his shows his hand plainly enough to anyone familiar with his technique. He begins by drawing one of his favourite organ stops on these occasions, the pathetic-sentimental vox humana. The "dream of youth", it appears, may yet be realised if the right solution of the present problem is found. That solution is simplicity itself: the King is to order Düfflipp to come at once to a complete understanding with him as to Bülow, and to have the royal decree put into execution immediately. If, he insinuates, the King by any chance feels ill-disposed towards Düfflipp — "and God knows you would be justi-fied in that" — Wagner suggests replacing him by one of his sub-ordinate secretaries, Eisenhart, who will be "thoroughly loyal". Neither he nor Bülow, of course, really wants anything at all — not Wagner, because for him the King's "wonderful" love is ample compensation for all he has suffered in his life as an artist, and not Bülow, who, thanks to his reputation, can maintain himself and his family anywhere. No; all they want is to attain their lofty goal.

Wagner met Düfflipp on the 6th, and seems to have realised that the Court Secretary was not the snake in the grass he had assumed him to be on the strength of Röckel's letter. On the 7th he saw Bülow in Basel. (He had hoped for a further meeting with the King before leaving Munich. Ludwig obviously shrank from the nervous wear and tear of another harangue from him; so he pleaded ill health and pressure of public business as an excuse for being unable to grant his request. He assured him, however, of his undying affection and his confidence in the triumph of their cause). Hans had already received the official intimation of his appointment as Royal Kapell-meister in ordinary service, with the promise of "a further post with a fixed salary" when the Music School should materialise. Suspicious as to what might lie behind this phrasing, Wagner sent Düfflipp, from Basel, a long telegram that was in effect an ulti-matum: Bülow must receive at once a contract ensuring him the directorship of the School. The Court Secretary's reply was to the effect that this was precisely what the phrase meant and what had been intended all along.

It was an easy victory, for the King had set his heart on model performances of *Tannhäuser* and *Lohengrin* during the summer, and for these Bülow was indispensable.

CHAPTER IV

SHADOWS FALLING

1

THE INNER relations of the triangle are something of a mystery during this period. Cosima, who had been flitting about for some time between Wagner and Bülow, went on the 16th April to Basel, whence she and Hans moved on to Munich two days later: on the 1st May they were joined there by Daniela and Blandine. Hans rented in the Arcostrasse, No. 11, a larger apartment than was necessary merely for himself and his family; two rooms in it, furnished from the Briennerstrasse house, were reserved for Wagner's occupation whenever he might visit the town. It is little wonder that the puzzled Cornelius admitted himself unable to make head or tail of the new situation. According to his son and biographer, both Peter and Bülow really believed just then that the "affair" between Cosima and Wagner was at an end.[1] "For Cornelius", says the son,

"it was all a huge mystery beyond his solving. In the end he went by the *appearance* of things and let himself be deceived, just as poor Hans von Bülow was also deceived:[2] for we cannot believe that Bülow was still acting a part before the world's eyes. There is no doubt about it — *he was led by the nose*. They made him believe what he wanted to believe, and what, in view of Wagner's changeableness in matters of passion, was not altogether incredible — that the affair had cooled down and Cosima was now prepared to return to her husband. . . . Enough that Cornelius was convinced of the re-establishment of the Bülow union and was content to leave it at that, without further enquiry into the why and wherefore."[3]

[1] But even to say that Cornelius and Bülow "believed the affair to be at an end" implies, of course, that both of them knew there *had* been an "affair".

[2] I.e., not "deceived" by Wagner and Cosima as to their relations since the summer of 1864 — the evidence against that is decisive, — but gulled into believing that these relations were now ended. Carl Cornelius's remark that "we cannot believe that Bülow was *still* [italics mine] acting a part before the world's eyes" is equivalent to saying that so far Bülow *had been* doing so.

[3] CPC, II, 113. Carl Maria Cornelius tells us, in the omitted passage represented by dots in the above quotation, that he "cannot here go into the grounds for this supposition". That is a great pity.

It may possibly have been so, though in the light of our latest information it is difficult to believe that this is the full story. What is beyond question is that both Wagner and Cosima were so devastatingly unhappy at this new separation that they would have had to be actors of the most consummate and calculating kind to conceal their misery from Bülow and make him believe that all that had so far happened between them was just an "affair" that was now over. Cosima had hardly left Triebschen for Basel on the 16th when she telegraphed to Wagner, from Olten:

> "Es ist bestimmt in Gottes Rath,
> Dass man vom Liebsten, das man hat,
> Muss scheiden": [4]

whereupon Wagner confided to the pages of his "Brown Book",

"I have never been so unhappy in my life as I am now. . . . I went home on foot and collapsed through weariness. A short leaden sleep . . . brought up within me all the misery of my life as it were from the profoundest depths of my soul. I long for a serious illness and death. I can do no more, want to do nothing more. If only it would end! Today she left me. What this parting means! What good are later meetings? The parting remains. It is pitiable!" [5]

That the King expected a certain amount of trouble as the result of Bülow's return to Munich is shown by the terms in which he informed the Intendanz of the new appointment. *Lohengrin* and *Tannhäuser*, he said, were to be put into rehearsal at once, for production in June and July. Bülow would be subject, as Kapellmeister, to the usual disciplinary regulations vis-à-vis the Intendanz, and conformably thereto would not encroach on the rights and privileges of others: per contra, the King confidently expected the whole of the theatre personnel to co-operate amicably with him and to avoid anything likely to cause misunderstanding. Ludwig's heart was set on hearing *Lohengrin* and *Tannhäuser* under "model" conditions. It was perhaps only because Bülow was the one conductor who enjoyed Wagner's confidence that the King and his advisers had agreed to his and the composer's terms. Having done so, though the common sense in which Ludwig was anything but deficient

---

[4] "It is God's decree that we must part from the one we love most."

[5] KLRWB, II, xxi, xxii. On the 17th Cosima telegraphed to him again, this time from Basel; she was manifestly as wretched as he was. By that time she had rejoined Bülow.

warned him that all would not be plain sailing in the theatre with Bülow in a position of authority there, he followed his usual line of procedure in awkward situations — he shut his eyes, as well as he could, to tiresome reality and hoped for the best. The fact that Lachner had asked for and been granted, under the pretext of ill-health, "leave of absence" from the 3rd June to the 13th July — the period during which the theatre would be wanted for the Wagner performances — of itself indicated a desire on the part of the theatre authorities to steer clear of trouble so far as that would be possible.

2

For the moment the future seemed to be full of good omens for the Wagner-Bülow cause. Bülow at once began to arrange for a staff after his own heart for the Music School; Cornelius and Rheinberger were engaged as teachers, and Franz Wüllner, of whom we shall hear more later, was commissioned to organise a department of choral singing. Wires were pulled to get *Gunlöd* accepted by the theatre, but the King was none too well-disposed just then towards Cornelius; it still rankled in him that Peter had preferred Weimar to Munich in the summer of 1865, and consequently had not been present at the production of *Tristan*.[6] On the 25th April, in a letter

---

[6] Light on Cornelius's state of mind at that time is thrown by a letter of his to Carl Gille, of Jena, which was omitted from the official edition of his correspondence. It was printed for the first time in an article by Georg Kinsky in the *Almanach der deutschen Musikbücherei* for 1924–5, pp. 316–324.

The *Cid* had disappeared from the Weimar stage after only two performances in May, 1865. On the 17th June Cornelius, still in Weimar, wrote to Gille asking if he could oblige him with a loan of 500 thalers for three years. He was evidently in utter poverty: to pay his fare from Munich to Weimar he had had to pawn his watch, while in order to transplant himself from Vienna to Munich in 1864, at Wagner's pressing request, he had had to borrow 30 florins from Standhartner. Wagner, he says, had at that time asked Pfistermeister for a grant of 200 florins to cover Peter's removal expenses, but had later "calmly accepted" the Cabinet Secretary's refusal. Peter's salary in Munich was a miserable 1,000 gulden per annum. Surely Wagner must have seen the dire straits in which Cornelius constantly was for money; and surely, out of the large sums he was extracting from the King for the luxurious adornment of his Munich house he could have spared something to ease the burden of the poor brother artist whom he had tempted to Munich solely to serve his ends. As Peter puts it in his letter to Gille, Wagner could get thousands, but not even hundreds could be found for "us poor appendages". After the production of the *Cid* he had written to Wagner, explaining why, to his regret, he could not be in Munich for the *Tristan* performances, it being impossible for him to leave Weimar just then; but Wagner had not vouchsafed a reply to his letter.

It was not because of any personal resentment towards Wagner the man, however, that Cornelius had kept aloof from *Tristan*. The reason was that he felt the mighty

to Mathilde Maier, Wagner plumed himself on his latest victory in Munich, a victory due, he opined, to the vastitude of the King's love for him. He would never settle in Munich again, he said, as his young adorer's proximity brought with it too many agitations; besides, in the capital he would be pestered by the politicians again, and contacts of that sort went against the grain with him. But he would gratify the King by celebrating his next birthday with him in Berg, and in October the *Meistersinger* would be produced. He would attend only the final rehearsal of this, he said, as he had vowed never again to expose himself to an ovation from the public.

As for the ardent young idealist on the throne, he was more pathetically convinced than ever that 1867 would be the year of years, with the *Meistersinger* as the crown of all his efforts in the great cause. "We shall achieve everything!" he telegraphed to Wagner on the 4th May, the anniversary of their first meeting, signing himself "Walther von Stolzing".

As the date of his birthday grew nearer, however, Wagner became more and more reluctant to carry out his promise to spend it in the neighbourhood of Berg. To the King he pleaded, on the 15th May, that not only his peace of mind but his very health depended on his not being interrupted in the scoring of the *Meistersinger*, which work, he said, he hoped to lay at his benefactor's feet on the King's birthday, the 25th August: but we may surmise also that he shrank from raising another storm just then in political and journalistic quarters. Ludwig's reply was that while he fully recognised how essential the quiet of Triebschen was to Wagner in his creative mood, he could not surrender without a pang the hope of seeing him

---

work to be a hindrance to the development of his own modest talent. "I must be free", he wrote to Gille . . . "Wagner is a Venus, I a Tannhäuser". . . . "This much is certain—my entirely different nature prescribes for me an entirely different ideal, which must evolve steadily work by work, uninfluenced, in freedom, along a path of my own. I felt this long ago: I ought never to have gone to Munich. . . .[where] I realised only too clearly that the hazel-bush cannot grow up in the shade of the oak, that it must get its sunlight far away from that."

As a matter of fact, Cornelius, for all his care, had not been able to prevent the *Tristan* influence from showing itself here and there in the second act of *Der Cid*.

It was not until he had obtained, at the end of July, a loan of 100 thalers from his brother Franz that he was able to return to Munich; and he went only because, wretched as his salary there was, it was all that stood between him and starvation.

It should be recorded that early in 1864 Wagner had written to the Weimar Intendant, Dingelstedt, offering to conduct *Der Cid*. The offer was declined, obviously, as Heinrich Porges, who disclosed this fact for the first time in 1895 in a letter to Richard Batka, surmises, because Dingelstedt knew that Wagner would tolerate no slackness on the part of anyone in the theatre. See Batka, *Kranz* (1903), p. 177.

again on the 22nd. Cosima, cooler and clearer-sighted than the ailing, fretful Wagner, and justly dreading the consequences of his going too far in his opposition to the King, made a rather desperate attempt, in a telegram of the 19th, to induce him to change his mind. He replied in a brief wire the wording of which shows how ready he was to vent his ill-temper even on Cosima when she displeased him. Within little more than an hour of the receipt of this reply she wired him again, curtly informing him that if he did not come there would be a "complete rupture": [7] "Weigh carefully this last wish: I will not write again", she added. The King's answer to her letter was to the effect that he hoped Wagner would spend at least his birthday with him, returning immediately afterwards to Triebschen if he so desired. As for himself, a total refusal on the Friend's part would wound him grievously, but *"his* will be done": the hero [Siegfried] he said, would bow to the will of the god [Wotan].

The uncompromising terms of Cosima's telegram must have opened Wagner's eyes to the risks he would be running in flouting the King's wishes, for on the 19th he wired to Düfflipp that if his presence on the 22nd were still desired he would arrive on "Tuesday evening" (the 21st). The tone of Düfflipp's telegraphic reply proved that Cosima had been right in regarding the situation as serious: "If the journey not too troublesome for you, your arrival on the 21st most desirable. Speedy return granted for completion of your work in peace. Please reply immediately whether you are setting out tomorrow or not." [8] After that, it would have been imprudent of Wagner not to comply. It might have been better in the long run for both him and Ludwig had he not done so. For their personal relations now took a slight turn for the worse that was to continue for some time.

---

[7] Cosima's anxiety in the matter is shown by her writing to the King about it on the 19th, and further talking it over with Düfflipp.

The telegrams ostensibly passed between "Stocker" (Wagner's manservant, now Vreneli's husband) in Triebschen and "Mrazeck" (the former servant who was still minding the Briennerstrasse house). Cosima and Wagner were perpetually being compelled to resort to little subterfuges of this kind in their wires to each other.

[8] In KLRWB, IV, 189 Düfflipp's wire is printed first, so that Wagner's appears to be the answer to it. But there is practically no doubt that the true chronological order is as above. In his fifth volume (KLRWB, V, 141), Dr. Strobel himself inclines to this view, and suggests that Wagner's wire should be dated the 19th, not, as in IV, 189, the 20th. It appears that while all the other telegrams relating to this matter are quoted in KLRWB from the actual documents, this of Wagner's has survived only in a draft scribbled on the back of Cosima's first wire to him of the 19th; it is consequently undated.

3

He left Triebschen for Munich on the 21st. The King had rented for him the Villa Prestele at Starnberg, a fact which suggests a confident hope on his part that he and Wagner would enjoy each other's company for some weeks at least. On the morning of the 22nd Cosima went to Starnberg to put the house in order and lay out the birthday gifts; among these was the famous "composition piano" — a convenient combination of piano and writing desk — which the King had had specially constructed for Wagner by Bechstein. Wagner arrived a little later, and by one o'clock was with Ludwig in Berg. Cosima was not at the meeting, though it seems that the King had desired her company also: her excuse was that she wished to avoid giving her enemies any further pretext for attacking her, the "calumnies" of Malvina — that wicked woman, as she calls her — having left her in a highly nervous state. The house being still not quite fit for occupation, Wagner returned after the interview to Munich. It was not until the 30th that he settled down in Starnberg — and on the next day Ludwig set out with his brother Otto and his adjutant, Captain von Sauer, on a visit to Eisenach, to see the Wartburg and the Hörselberg and get some hints for the coming production of *Tannhäuser!* Röckl opines that he went at Wagner's request. That is doubtful: the King seems, indeed, to have absented himself rather more continuously than Wagner liked, judging from an entry in his "Annals" — "König verreitend und verreisend". Ludwig returned on the 2nd June, but must have gone away again almost immediately to the Aachensee and the Zillerthal. But on the 6th he was back in Berg once more, and late that night he paid Wagner a surprise visit in the Villa Prestele: this was the first time they had met since the 22nd May. But his letter of the 5th is so full of the usual protestations of love for Wagner and confidence in the triumph of their cause that we can only ask once more why, having attached so much importance to having Wagner near him during these weeks, he should not only receive him so rarely but actually remove himself from the Master's neighbourhood as often and for as long at a time as he did.

That something had gone wrong is suggested by Wagner's letter to him of the 29th May from Munich, saying that things had turned out precisely as he had foreseen:

"I cannot stay here any longer at present. I am not yet in a condition in which I can renounce complete quiet and seclusion. I am ill and wretched, and frittering my days away to no purpose."

He would like, he says, at any cost to see the King again, to thank him for his love. Shall he come tomorrow, or wait until the day after? The next day he went to Starnberg, and on the 31st Ludwig left for the Wartburg without having seen him! Was there already at the back of the King's mind a slight reluctance to meet him in the flesh? Did he suspect that the true, or at all events the main, reason for Wagner's preferring Munich to Starnberg during the preceding week or so had been the fact that in Munich he could be constantly with Cosima while in Starnberg he could not? Did Ludwig already sense at times, however dimly, that their earthly ways were destined some day to part, and that wherever the great ideal they had in common might in the end be realised it would be elsewhere than in Munich?

4

It must be admitted that it is anything but easy, at first sight, to reconcile the surmise that the King was reluctant just then to meet Wagner very often in the flesh with his persistent appeals to him to settle near him. But the mentality of the King abounds in paradoxes of this kind; they were the result, in part, of his tendency to abandon himself wholly to the mood of the moment. Perhaps a partial explanation of the inconsistency with which we are dealing here is to be sought in Wagner's obstinacy in forcing his political opinions on him: we can well understand that his long-distance ardour for Wagner as the high priest of their religion of the regeneration of mankind through the theatre was somewhat cooled when the musician snatched, as he manifestly did, at each opportunity of personal intercourse with the young King to try to direct his political policy for him.

Wagner's motives and moods are sometimes as difficult to unravel as those of Ludwig; but it is clear that while his purely artistic aims were all that mattered to him on the long and broad view, the circumstances of his time and place conspired to convince him that these aims would be realised only in a new world in general and a new Germany in particular — a Germany in which Bavaria, and a young King brought up on the pure milk of the Wagnerian doctrine, were to play a determining part. He had been so eager for the appointment of Hohenlohe because he thought he would be more likely to attain his artistic ends through him than through any other Bavarian politician of the day. "Reflect!" he had written to the King on the 11th January; "we can and will achieve everything, but only on the condition that your land is secure and tranquil. Otherwise we are just suspended in the air, powerless." With opinions of that kind Ludwig would no doubt agree, at all events in the early stages of their association; but it is obvious that he could not stomach Wagner's persistent attempts to dictate to him the practical means by which the "security and tranquillity" of Bavaria were to be achieved. For all his relative inexperience, Ludwig seems to have realised fairly soon that the less reliance he placed on Wagner's advice in purely political matters the better it would be in the long run for both of them — to say nothing of Bavaria. Let us try to assemble the evidence on these points.

5

In the early part of 1867 Wagner had launched a fresh attack in force. Declaring himself to be deeply concerned about not only his own interests but those of the child of his spirit, the King, he drew up an elaborate programme for him to follow. He had been assured by Schanzenbach that Hohenlohe was not one of those who scented danger to Ludwig in his personal association with the "Musikant", or even in the latter's return to Munich. The astute Hohenlohe was of course only handling him tactfully until he could be sure just how much or how little the "Musikant's" influence counted politically with the King, and until he had built up round himself a party strong enough to carry his own programme through parliament. All that Wagner could see, all that interested him, indeed, was that if there was a single influential politician in Bavaria through whom he might now achieve his own ends it was Hohenlohe. In his letter of the 18th January, therefore, he had urged Ludwig to support the Prince at all costs. On the 21st February he repeats and underlines his advice: if the King must sacrifice someone let it be Bomhard — who can go to where Pfordten is — and Lutz. The King's only answer to all this is two or three lines in pencil, acknowledging Wagner's letter, saying he will reflect upon it, and promising to write to him shortly. But it is not until the 5th March that he does so; and though the letter is a fairly long one, covering such matters, among others, as his love for Wagner, his enthusiasm for their cause, the founding of the Music School, Bülow, Porges, Semper, a performance he had recently seen of Spohr's *Jessonda*, illustrations for *Tristan*, and his hopes for the production of the *Meistersinger* in the summer, all he has to say about politics is this; "My dear Friend, don't worry on Hohenlohe's account. He has my confidence, and I am glad that the portfolio is in his hands; nor is anyone trying to shake my confidence in him."

As we have seen, Wagner had been in Munich from the 9th to the 18th March, during which period he was admitted to an audience with the King only twice, on the 10th and the 17th. He was in the capital again between the 4th and the 7th April, and saw the King for a little while on the morning of the 6th, to discuss the question of Bülow's appointment. He could hardly have returned to his hotel before he was writing to Ludwig, as we have already seen, suggesting that if he had as much reason to be dissatisfied with his Court Secretary Düfflipp as *he* had, he might replace him by Eisenhart — a hint of which the King evidently did not take the slightest notice. On the 25th April, feeling, no doubt, that his personal influence on the young man was beginning to weaken, he had sent him a long letter containing what he professed to be his last political will and testament. He makes it clear that in his opinion the question of the realisation of their cultural ideal is inseparably bound up with Bavarian politics, though of course he protests, as usual, that the anxiety that is racking him is all on the young King's account, not on his own. He will now, for positively the last time, give him in brief the benefit of his experience of the last few years with regard to the King's personal situation and that of his land.

After reminding him of the conspiracy on foot in the summer of 1866 to have him deposed, he insists that Ludwig must now surround himself with new men of the right kind. Where changes of personnel are for the moment impracticable the King himself must take the political initiative: nothing can save Bavaria but his choice of the right means and his resolute pursuit of them. Wagner proceeds to tell him in much detail what the right means are. The disastrous war of 1866, he says, was the consequence of Bavaria's

not having taken vigorous action in favour of the German Bund.
Bavaria is now in equal danger from Prussia on the one side and
from Austria and the Jesuits on the other, instead of being able to
act as arbiter between them as her position and her power entitle
her to do. Bavaria's only hope of safety lies in an alliance with
Prussia, which can never "annex" her, whereas Austria can and
will do so as soon as she recovers from the war. In the long run a
Bavarian-Prussian alliance would force Austria also to link up with
all the other German States. Bavaria could be the cement, the
heart of this confederation.

> "And then Germany *will* be something, will be powerful: the German
> will be conscious of himself; and what 'German' means, what the 'Ger-
> man spirit' means, *we* will show the world. . . . From Munich let the
> banner of the noble German spirit wave over Germany, the banner I am
> weaving, which my glorious Siegfried [the King] will then wave high
> over the lands."

But to accomplish this the King must not wait to be driven by events:
he must take the initiative. When lately Wagner had seen Prince
Hohenlohe in Munich he had put these views before him. "The dry
gentleman became aflare: something shone out of him that pleased
me greatly."

> "He will give you sagacious help; but you, *you*, my august Friend, must
> will, clearly and definitely *will*. Take up the alliance with Prussia with
> the utmost energy: [9] let Bavaria's help and co-operation be recognised
> as of the greatest value. . . . Now or never! Call up your vigorous
> Bavaria: push on the preparations for war with the greatest energy!
> Give the order for one thing, and always just one thing — the utmost
> expansion of the Bavarian military power, and at once, with all pos-
> sible speed. In heaven's name do not let yourself be driven by Prussia!
> Forward! Forward! Now is the time to throw Bavaria's weight into the
> scales against the Prussians: thus you will make yourself the leader
> of South Germany, and Austria must follow you, *must!*"

To which long tirade the King's only reply was a two-line telegram nine days later, reminding him that it was on that day three
years ago that they had first met. It was the long-distance equivalent
of the whistle and the upturned eyes with which, as Wagner com-

---

[9] Perhaps at this point the King, who had an excellent memory, recalled that a
year or eighteen months earlier Wagner had been cursing Prussia up hill and down
dale as a semi-barbarian un-German state, and Bismarck as "an ambitious Junker,
deceiving his weak-minded King in the most shameless fashion."

plained to François Wille, the King used to greet his *viva voce* lucubrations on politics.[10]

6

It was because he sometimes felt the King to be slipping out of his hands that Wagner urged that they ought to meet oftener in the flesh. He had the gift of words in abundance, and Ludwig had not; in conversation the younger man could always be swept off his feet. And it was no doubt because he was aware of this rhetorical advantage on Wagner's part that more than once the King, after imploring him with tears in his eyes to settle near him, contrived to see as little as possible of him after he had come. It probably chilled and exasperated him to find that, in spite of all the warnings he had had, Wagner was still not cured of his bad habit of trying to give him lessons in governing a kingdom. Ludwig, at the centre of things, had soon discovered how immensely more complicated political practice is than political theory. To talk, as Wagner did, about the necessity for a confederation of the German States was easy enough; he was only one of many million Germans who saw that this would have to come about some day, somehow. But the King and the politicians knew the immense distance that can lie between an ideal and the realisation of it. There had constantly to be taken into consideration the mutual jealousies and animosities of the South German States; the general feeling in them against the mentality and the Protestantism of the North; the dislike and mistrust of them all for Prussia, combined with the prudent desire of each of them to stand in her good books in the event of her resorting to violence against any one of their number; the personal and hereditary pride of the sovereigns who, like Ludwig, strongly objected to becoming merely the mediatised puppets of Prussia; the rivalries and suspicions of the military heads of the various States; the conflicting commercial interests that would somehow have to be either recon-

---

[10] In the summer of 1866, Frau Wille has told us, her husband called on Wagner in Triebschen and tried to induce him to get the King to remain neutral and offer himself as mediator in the dispute between Austria and Prussia. "Wagner, who at that time loathed Bismarck and Prussia, refused, saying that in *political* matters he had no influence at all with the King, who, 'when he (Wagner) tried anything of the kind, used to look up at the ceiling and whistle'". RWEW, p. 118.

Ludwig seems also to have been offended at times by Wagner's lack of decorum. "I can't associate with him", he is said to have confided to the actor Kainz in later years: "it is too difficult. Just imagine, when he speaks of his enemies he hammers on the table with his fist." BLKB, p. 559.

ciled or overridden; ticklish questions of diplomatic powers and foreign representation; and so ad infinitum.

The King, who, however much he might loathe politics and despise politicians, was no fool, knew only too well that problems of this kind were not to be settled by his riding in shining armour into the midst of the other German monarchs and their parliaments and Ministers, rising in his stirrups, flourishing Siegfried's sword, and proclaiming himself the heaven-appointed saviour of the German race. Even if he had had any desire to play that star part he knew perfectly well that the other leading members of the company would never consent to his appropriating it; and he objected to being cast for it willy-nilly by an amateur producer away in Triebschen, whose conception of practical politics had always been ludicrously infantile. It must have irritated him to find that no number of silent snubs had the least effect on the self-complacent amateur who seemed to imagine that practical politics were as simple as his own theories about them.[11] It was no doubt considerations of this sort that were at the back of the King's mind when he told Düfflipp, as he obviously had done, that he wished Wagner would not persist in trying to get him to do things he had no inclination to do, and that it would be better for all of them if the musician were to stick to his trade. The suspicion that he was being politely snubbed seems after a while to have penetrated even Wagner's self-esteem; and this, combined with the misery of being separated from Cosima and the irritations inseparable from even the shortest stay in Munich, would be quite enough to account not only for his going back to Triebschen to sulk and pose but for the resolve forming within him to edge the King out of his artistic life, so far as would be possible. The dim perception he already had that the national theatre of his dreams would have to spring up elsewhere than in Munich began about this time to crystallise into a conviction.

---

[11] "But who is there with such clearness or confidence that he can take upon him to write skilfully and accurately of the proper and relative duty of every several vocation and place?" asks the wise Bacon, who was both a philosopher and a man versed in practical affairs. "But treatises on matters of this kind which do not savour of experience, but are only drawn from a general scholastic knowledge of the subject, are for the most part empty and unprofitable. For although sometimes a looker-on may see more than a player . . . yet it were much to be wished that only men of most practice and experience should meddle with such arguments; for the writing of speculative men on active matter for the most part seems to men of experience, as Phormio's arguments of the wars seemed to Hannibal, to be but dreams and dotage." *De Augmentis Scientiarum*, Book VII, Chapter 2.

Wagner never made any secret of his opinion that although Bülow could be trusted to make the music of an opera of his speak very much as he had meant it to do, only he himself could weld all the factors of the work into a dramatic unity. This being so, he might reasonably have been expected to co-operate heartily in the "model" performance of *Lohengrin* which the King so ardently desired. All he did, however, was to exercise, at Bülow's wish, a more or less grudging supervision of the final rehearsals. It probably mattered very little to him now whether Munich had model performances of his earlier works or not; from his present point of view they would not be worth his wearing himself out in yet another struggle with the customary opera house inertia. But it was a foregone conclusion that if he did not throw himself energetically into the work of tuning the singers, machinists and others up to their full tension much would be left undone and much done badly, for Bülow, though as usual doing three men's work, had his hands full with the music alone. So it is not surprising to find Wagner already hinting to the King on the 4th June that things are going none too well, owing to "slacknesses" of various sorts in the theatre; still, he "earnestly hopes" that the performance will give Ludwig "some small rewarding joy". The King, writing from Aachensee on the 5th, was in the seventh heaven of happiness in anticipation of the performance on the 10th; once more he assured Wagner of his eternal love and fidelity. He hoped he would co-operate in the production of *Tannhäuser* that was to follow that of *Lohengrin;* while in October the building of the new theatre would begin.

Albert Niemann, whom the King had heard as Lohengrin shortly before his accession to the throne, had already, in February, 1866, been invited, in an enthusiastic personal letter from Ludwig, to sing as "guest" in some performances of *Tannhäuser* and *Lohengrin* planned for the summer of that year. These were to be "wholly in accordance with the intentions of the composer". Niemann was willing, but the war of 1866 prevented the carrying out of the scheme. Apparently Ludwig hoped to obtain him for the performances of 1867, but as the tenor refused to sing the rôles without the cuts to which he had grown accustomed, Wagner suggested the engagement of Tichatschek. Perhaps, with Schnorr dead and Niemann ruled out, he had not a very wide choice in the matter; but it certainly looks as if he had succumbed to an attack of sentiment quite unusual with him where the performance of his own works was concerned. The King is said to have acquiesced unwillingly, for Tichatschek was then nearing the completion of his sixtieth year.[12] He appears to have retained even at that age something of his old silvern splendour of voice, though not even Wagner dared credit him with a superfluity of intelligence; he confined himself to saying that *Lohengrin* was the one really good thing the tenor had ever managed to do. After hearing his old Dresden colleague at a rehearsal he assured the King that while in his singing and declamation of the part he suggested a painting by Dürer, in his appearance and gestures he was like a Holbein. "Have confidence in me", he wrote to Ludwig on the 6th June; "forget all preconceived opinions, and, like me, you will be amply rewarded." The colour is perhaps laid on just a trifle too thick; one gets the impression that he was trying to persuade not only the King but himself that a serious mistake had not been made.

On the evening of the 7th June he is obviously a trifle perturbed about the prospect in general. He sees all kinds of faults in the production — faults which, surely, he himself ought to have taken in hand earlier. The Telramund (Franz Betz, from Berlin) having suddenly become hoarse, the final full rehearsal, at which the King was to be present, had to be postponed for a day or two.

For the young King, this *Lohengrin* production was to have been the greatest event in his life since the *Tristan* performances in 1865. It had been a torment to him, he wrote to Wagner, to have to wait three years for this work which had been the source of his love for the Master and faith in his art; while for Wagner the production was

---

[12] As Tichatschek is not mentioned in the Wagner-Ludwig correspondence of the spring of 1867, the inference is that Wagner had raised the question of his engagement *viva voce* during his visit to Munich in March. Erich Engel (EWLW, p. 373) gives in facsimile a letter from Wagner to the tenor dated "Bayerischer Hof, 14 March, 1867", in which he expresses his joy over the revival of *Lohengrin* in Dresden with his old friend in his old part. He had thought of attending one of the performances "secretly", but this had proved impracticable. "Now my young King ardently desires to hear *Lohengrin* soon; so it occurs to me that if you were to come here we could both hear you in it. Now decide quickly: will you come and sing Lohengrin a few times, say in June or July?. . . . Will you? Can you? Telegraph me Yes or No. Then details by letter."

Wagner had an audience with the King on the 17th, and it was presumably then that he told Ludwig what he had done and received his assent to the engagement of Tichatschek.

to be "a festival of the triumph of our friendship", a festival which, he hoped, Ludwig would remember to the end of his days. It was all to turn out very differently.

The final rehearsal had been called for ten A.M. on the 8th June. At eleven it was announced from the stage that it would have to be postponed "owing to unforeseen circumstances": the fact was that the King had refused to be present when he heard that the theatre was to be occupied by a considerable company. To the actual final rehearsal three days later only a few privileged guests were invited. Wagner was so delighted, or tried to persuade himself and others that he was, with Tichatschek's performance that he embraced him on the stage. But the King had seen and heard it all with the pitiless eyes and ears of the disappointed idealist. He was annoyed by the old tenor's tremolo. Through his opera glass he saw not the poetic Knight of the Grail of his boyhood's dreams but a sagging face painted and plastered into a simulacrum of youth, and an ancient body maintaining its uncertain equilibrium in the boat only by clinging to a pole let into the deck for that charitable purpose. He saw nothing he could call acting, only a succession of "grimaces", as he complained afterwards. Shattered was his dream of the spirituality of the Middle Ages; he had been fobbed off with the poorest theatrical make-believe. Even this was not the worst: Tichatschek, who no doubt brought, as tenors love to do, his own favourite costume with him, was not wearing the blue cloak in which Ludwig had expressed a wish to see him; nor could the King endure the raw acting and unmelodious singing of the Ortrud, Frau Bertram-Meyer, an importation from Nuremberg. Wagner, for his part, had been against entrusting the part of Elsa to the nineteen-years-old Mathilde Mallinger. He and Ludwig, indeed, were now very much at cross-purposes.

8

The King went back to Berg in a bad temper not only with the unfortunate tenor but with Wagner. His ironic description of the would-be Knight of the Grail was "the Knight of the Rueful Countenance": he might come to Munich next year for the foot-washing if he liked, but *he* never wished to see him again. On the 12th Wagner sent a querulous letter to Berg. Ludwig, he complained, should not have turned his opera glass on the ruin. Wagner had expressly warned him against this: "You disregarded my warning . . . he cannot stand this test, and the inevitable disillusionment followed." After the catastrophic rehearsal the King had peremptorily ordered the engagement of another singer for the actual performance. This, of course, put Wagner in an awkward situation with regard not only to the tenor but to the rest of the company and the public: Ludwig's unceremonious dismissal of Tichatschek was obviously a criticism of Wagner's choice of him. So we soon find him trying the old technique once more on the King. Ludwig, he hints, should be careful what he is about, for he is playing straight into the hands of their enemies: already there is talk in some of the papers of a "new disgrace", and the public will have no doubts about this if either the performance of Lohengrin is cancelled or it takes place without the King being present. They both know, from sad experience, what further consequences will follow; Wagner's power to reform the Munich theatre will be paralysed, the vilest theatrical cabal will have triumphed, — and so on in the old familiar style. If all this is to happen there is only one thing left for him to do, to return, like another Lohengrin, to his Monsalvat, bequeathing his sword and horn to the King and trusting to the faithful Hans to go on fighting the heathen for him. This time, however, his pathos fell on unresponsive ears; Ludwig was immovable.

He desired the performance to take place on the 16th, he wrote to Düfflipp. "But on no account will I listen to Tichatschek, or Nachbaur, or Vogl. I was very dissatisfied also with Frau Bertram-Meyer. Schmitt [13] [the acting Intendant] is to allot the part of Ortrud to Dietz,[14] or to telegraph for some other singer who is equal

---

[13] The King calls him "Schmidt"! (See note on the Schmitts and the Schmidts, *supra*, p. 60, *note* 19).

[14] Franz Nachbaur was a young man of twenty-two, at that time located at Darmstadt. He was destined to be the first Walther in the *Meistersinger*. Sophie Dietz was a member of the Munich company.

Heinrich Vogl (1845–1900), a native of Munich, had joined the Munich theatre in 1865. Hearing good reports of him, the King recommended him to Wagner in November of that year as a possible future Siegmund, and suggested that he should be put in Friedrich Schmitt's hands to be trained on Wagnerian lines. Wagner accordingly asked the young man to call on him. Apparently Vogl declined the invitation at the prompting of the theatre management, which in the first place did not want to hurt Lachner's feelings by transferring the young tenor to Schmitt (Lachner was Vogl's teacher), and in the second place had no desire to be deprived of the general services of so promising an artist for the sole benefit of the Wagner repertory. It was a long time before either Wagner or the King could forgive Vogl for placing his own interests before theirs.

to the rôle to come to Munich. . . . Schmidt (*sic*) has raised fresh difficulties with regard to *Tannhäuser*." But Ludwig insists on this work being given in July: it means a very great deal to him. Only when these two works have been perfectly performed is the *Meistersinger* to be taken in hand.

A letter from Düfflipp to Wagner showed the latter how things now stood between him and the King. Wagner's amour-propre was badly hurt. He thought that Ludwig's wishes with regard to the *Lohengrin* performance might have taken the form of the expression of a friendly wish rather than a blunt royal command; but he had either forgotten or had all along been unaware how sorely he had been trying the King's patience of late. His bluff had been unexpectedly called, and for a moment he did not know what card to play. He went back to Triebschen on the 15th in a vile temper,[15] leaving it to others, as was often the way with him, to do the disagreeable donkey-work in the world of rough realities while he sulked majestically in his tent, dramatising himself, as usual, as the most injured and most innocent man on earth. Cosima sent the King a long letter in her best diplomatic vein, not denying that he had been justified in what he had done, but pleading with him to try to see it all from Wagner's point of view also. It is clear from this letter that Ludwig's uncompromising assertion of his royal authority, with its consequent rough reminder to Wagner of the unbridgeable distance between their stations, had taken both Cosima and Wagner completely by surprise.

To Bülow, who assuredly was no diplomatist, fell the difficult task of soothing the wounded susceptibilities of the two cashiered singers. Tichatschek had demanded from Wagner, no doubt for purposes of publicity, a letter expressing his satisfaction with the tenor's performance at the rehearsal; but Wagner had the sense to decline to do just then what would certainly have been resented by the King as a public reflection on himself. He shifted his responsibility on to Düfflipp, whom he commissioned to say something mollifying to the tenor, though he himself wrote soothingly to Tichatschek later. Bülow had some trouble with Frau Bertram-Meyer, who appears to have been behaving temperamentally. In a letter to her of the 15th June he expressed his own appreciation of

---

[15] The King seems to have ruled out all possibility of a personal discussion of the matter by the simple process of leaving Berg.

her "eminent dramatic talent", but protests that as a mere servant of the Intendanz he has no choice but to obey orders. He warned her of the imprudence of ventilating her grievance in the Press and "demanding satisfaction"; after all, he blandly pointed out to her, her case was not so bad as that of her colleague Herr Tichatschek, who had had this set-back in the evening of his career, while hers was still in its noontide.

The performance duly took place on the 16th, the King being present. The Lohengrin was Vogl, the Ortrud Therese Thoma, who married Vogl in the following year. With both these singers Bülow had achieved miracles of coaching in a few days. The King voiced his gratitude in a personal letter to him after the performance.

9

As for Wagner, not even the fact that the dogs at Triebschen were delighted to see him again and the peahen started laying in honour of his return could console him for his rebuffs in Munich. He was sorry now that he had ever allowed himself to be persuaded to go there, he wrote to Cosima. He cannot bring himself to write to "his Parzifal", he tells her, for what he would have to say would read like a reproach; his one desire now is for peace. Cosima passed it all on to the King, as, of course, she was expected to do, Wagner thus achieving his triple object of giving vent to his annoyance, of conveying to Ludwig that *he* was the one to blame for everything that had happened, and getting credit for swallowing his grief in saint-like fashion and suffering martyrdom in dignified silence. This time the technique worked, as it had done so often before. Ludwig wrote him an affectionate, penitent letter from the Hochkopf, whither he had fled to forget, in the divine solitude of the mountains, the world "that perpetually misjudges me and with which I never can nor will be on terms of friendship." He kissed, he said, the hand that had so grievously chastised him; he longed for nothing but closer communion with the beloved one; he regretted that it was *Lohengrin* of all things, the work that had meant so much to him since his boyhood, that had caused the recent misunderstanding between them; he lived now on the hope of seeing the *Meistersinger* and then the *Ring*.

Confident now that he had the King, so to speak, where he wanted him, Wagner turned the whole battery of his sophistical rhetoric on him in a long letter of the 25th June. As often happened with him, he dramatised himself in such masterly fashion as to believe in the end that he was the part he was acting. But through all his astute attempts to put the King dialectically in the wrong we hear booming the leit-motif of his annoyance with him for having, in the first place, sought his company so seldom during those three weeks in Munich and Starnberg, and for having acted so imperiously after the disastrous production on the 11th, instead of discussing the situation confidentially with him. This had been the greatest blow dealt to his pride since he and the King had first met three years ago.

We see also from his letter how "impossible" he must have been in the Munich theatre, how utterly incapable he was of seeing anything whatever from anyone else's point of view. He tells Ludwig of a little scene between the Acting Intendant Schmitt and himself. Schmitt had told him that he knew perfectly well that he [Wagner] and his associates were trying to bring about his overthrow, but that the King had assured him that he would not discharge him, nor would he appoint Putlitz. Wagner protests angrily against the bare notion of his being engaged in a conflict with "this Herr Schmitt". Here is the King bent on the most far-reaching plans for a new theatre, the production of the *Ring*, and so on; and all that has been happening lately is to be looked upon as just "a personal *rancune* between me and Herr Schmitt". The unspeakable Schmitt actually talks of having "triumphed over my machinations". Could there be a crazier misunderstanding than this? And — we might have been sure that this was coming — it was a misunderstanding in which the King's Majesty was involved, for had not Düfflipp complained to Wagner that it was wrong to try to influence the King in favour of persons and courses against his inclination? The plain fact was, of course, that for some time past Wagner and Cosima had been doing everything in their power to have Putlitz made Intendant in the Wagnerian interest, a step which, within a very little while, would have resulted in either the dismissal of Schmitt or his reduction to a nullity in the theatre. Wagner, presumably, was to be at liberty to intrigue against anyone whom he regarded as standing in his way, but for them to resent his machinations and try to

[81]

defend themselves against them was an impermissible descent into the crudely personal.[16] Nobody except himself and Cosima wanted Putlitz in Munich; yet he was too blindly Wagner-centric to see that Düfflipp was really doing him a service in warning him against trying to push the King into courses repugnant to him. There was hardly anything Wagner did in connection with the Munich theatre that was not calculated to make those responsible for running it dislike him; yet he was always frankly astonished at being disliked. He could put it all down to nothing but the incurable vileness of non-Wagnerian human nature.

10

As was his diplomatic custom, the King, in his reply, tried to soothe the angry man by agreeing with him in broad principle, without, however, accepting his version of the details of the matter or even discussing them with him. His general correspondence shows again and again how little he allowed Wagner to influence him in matters other than those of art pure and simple. He would listen to what he had to say for or against this politician, this official, or that, and then take his own line of action for reasons entirely unconnected with Wagner. Readers whose acquaintance with him has been confined to a superficial and more or less cynical reading of his effusive letters to Wagner have no conception of the hard core of the man. As has already been pointed out, he was capable of taking two diametrically opposed views of one and the same person in his entourage according to whether he was considering him in his relation to Wagnerian affairs or his relation to Bavarian affairs in general. He could with equal sincerity at one moment vie with Wagner in the application of derogatory epithets to a Pfistermeister or a Pfordten, and in the next recognise objectively the man's good qualities in his own sphere: Böhm, who, as we have seen, was associated for many years with Pfistermeister in the Bavarian government service, tells us that after the one-time Cabinet Secretary's

---

[16] I am reminded of an anonymous letter sent by some Irish patriots some years ago to a highly-placed English official, informing him that they meant to assassinate him at the first convenient moment. (I believe they did so in the end). "Of course you will understand", they added, "that there is nothing personal in this." There was "nothing personal" in Wagner's underground activities against Schmitt and others; he merely wished to plug them with lead.

resignation in 1866 he was invited no less than twelve times by the King to take up his office again.[17] Wagner, Bülow and the rest of them regarded conduct of this sort on the King's part as evidence of weakness of character. Rather do they point to a basic toughness of intellectual and moral fibre in him. It is observable again and again that however humble and penitent he may be in his replies to Wagner's paternal chastisements of him he hardly budges an inch from the position he had taken up over this matter or that. He sincerely regretted that the *Lohengrin* affair had turned out so badly, because he saw that Wagner was hurt and angry over it; but he took back nothing of what he had done and said during and after the crisis, and he made it clear both to Wagner and to the people in the theatre that he now intended to have *Tannhäuser* as soon as might be practicable. On the 1st July Wagner wrote to Málwida von Meysenbug congratulating himself on having, as he seems to have imagined, re-established his ascendancy over the young man by his superior dialectic. "I have rescued him", he said, "and now hope I have preserved for the world, in him, one of my best works." His mistake was in imagining that the King, devoted as he was to him, saw himself only as one of Wagner's works.

---

[17] "You know", Ludwig wrote in reply to Wagner's letter of the 25th June, ". . . . that there could be no question whatever of my being the victim, even for a moment, of the nonsensical notion that it was a mere matter of a *rancune* between you and Schmitt, the wretched booby. You know me, yes, you love your ever-faithful Parcifal, and you can rest assured that our relationship, the like of which the earth has never seen, is so sublime and divine that never can so much as a shadow of the meaner world pollute it with its venom." But all the same he retained the "wretched booby" in his post, though he knew how eagerly Wagner desired to have him superseded by his own nominee, Putlitz.

CHAPTER V

FRÖBEL AND THE
SÜDDEUTSCHE PRESSE

1

FOR ALL his resentment over the events of the last few weeks, Wagner was happy enough as soon as he had fairly settled down again to his work on the *Meistersinger*. The full score of the second act of this he finished on the 22nd June (1867); and he seemed so full of energy that Cosima blithely assured him that, like Titian, he would be doing his best work at ninety — a forecast that might have come almost literally true but for the heavy burden laid on him by Bayreuth. Meanwhile they were busy in Munich with preparations for the *Tannhäuser* production so ardently desired by the King — a production incorporating the changes made in the work for the Paris performances of 1861. Bülow was soon complaining to the Intendanz of the sloth and stupidity of some of the theatre officials; apparently it had not dawned on any of them that the scores in general use, dating from 1845, were not valid for the present purpose. In addition to all this there were the usual misunderstandings about rehearsal times and places and all the other matters about which misunderstanding is *de rigueur* in an opera house.

Things were not improved by Bülow's having to go to Paris on the 18th July to act as one of the adjudicators in an international competition of army bands: one of his fellow-judges was Hanslick, whom the Paris officials appear to have regarded as an authority on music. Bülow returned to Munich a week later to find matters in the opera house a stage or two nearer chaos than when he had left. By dint, however, of the most incredible labours on his part he managed to bring *Tannhäuser* to performance on the 1st August. The King was not present, the Court being in mourning for his uncle King Otto of Greece, who had died a few days before; but Ludwig attended a private performance on the 3rd, to which only a handful

[84]

of people, mostly officials, had been invited. Cosima, in spite of Bülow's veto, had managed to smuggle herself in. She had been very active in spying out the land for Wagner all through the rehearsals, reporting gratuitously to the King on the "disorder and lack of discipline" in his theatre, and especially the lack of understanding and good will on the part of Intendanzrat Schmitt — all with that innocent air of disinterested devotion to higher aims under which she knew so well how to cloak her own and Wagner's relentless pursuit of their ends.

The Tannhäuser in these performances was a local singer named Hacker: Mathilde Mallinger was the Elisabeth. After the second performance the utterly exhausted Bülow was given six weeks' leave: he paid a flying visit to Triebschen on the 5th, and on the 7th went to St. Moritz. On the 11th Cosima arrived at Triebschen from Munich with Blandine: Daniela and Isolde had preceded her there on the 6th.

Wagner, in his fear that his personal influence on Ludwig was not what it had been, had more than once complained that they met too rarely now for a heart-to-heart talk; but he declined to grasp the opportunity for such talks by accepting the royal invitation to *Tannhäuser*. He made out, of course, that his refusal was prompted by the sad conviction that he could not "help" the King by so doing, his servants in the theatre being the knaves and fools they were. But to Bülow he showed his real mind: he had no interest in the *Tannhäuser* affair, he said, except in so far as Hans was affected by it; for his part he was "absolutely dead to these undertakings". So once again he turned a deaf ear to the King's poetic rhapsodies on the theme of their great mission for the salvation of Germany, and, by once more withholding his co-operation in Munich, threw away yet another opportunity of repairing the damage done during these last few months to the bond between them. For damage there undoubtedly had been, for all the protestations of undying love and devotion on both sides.

2

The King, travelling as Count Berg, had visited the Paris Exhibition towards the end of July. He went, it appears, somewhat unwillingly. He knew nothing whatever about the town at first hand, of course, but he "hated" it, he told Wagner, as the stronghold of "materialism, low sensuality and godless frivolity": the mere thought of this "modern Babylon" brought home to him all the more forcibly the need to oppose to this "accursed Sodom and Gomorrah of our epoch" a citadel of the spirit, "where everything noble and beautiful can find its home", and in which Wagner should sit en-throned as high-priest-and-monarch-in-one of the kingdom of the ideal.

Wagner's reply to all this must have been written on one of his good days. He advised the King to go, and to go without prejudice, for the sensible reason, among others, that it would enlarge his knowledge of the world. He sang the praises of Paris as the centre of civilisation, possessed of a culture solidly sure of itself which the other European capitals envied and imitated in vain. He told Ludwig how much he himself had owed to Paris as an artist, to the models of acting and of production it had set before him in the theatre. Then he turned to more personal matters. He embarked upon a long sermon the gist of which was that no one could do good work with poor tools, that those with which the King had hitherto tried to work were hopelessly bad, and that it pained him to see his exalted Friend in "this fearful situation" yet be able to do no more than grieve over him from afar. But Ludwig ignored the obvious hint. He wanted, if he could avoid them, no more upheavals either in his theatre or in his Government. He saw, no doubt, that Wagner was at his old tactics again: he would not take any personal share in trying to improve matters in the Munich theatre, yet he and Cosima tried indefatigably by roundabout means to undermine the position of everyone there whom they disliked. The burden of his latest complaints to Düfflipp had been that the preparations for the *Meistersinger* production were in other hands than his. About the recent performances of *Tannhäuser* and *Lohengrin*, he said, he could maintain silence. But a new work like the *Meistersinger* would be another affair altogether; only he was capable of seeing to that. In Paris in 1860, he said, the Opéra and everyone and everything in it had been placed at his disposal; the best singers had been assembled from all quarters, and not a costume, not a piece of scenery had been decided upon without his previous approval of it; yet here in Munich, with an art-loving monarch interested in Wagner's ideal and keen to secure model performances of his operas, preparations for the new work are being made without the creator of it being consulted.

All which was true enough; what Wagner forgot to mention was that in Paris he had flung himself bodily and wholeheartedly into the daily life of the opera house, whereas in the present instance he virtually refused to cross the threshold of the theatre while at the same time pulling all sorts of underground wires from the safe seclusion of his Swiss retreat. In the circumstances he was hardly entitled to complain that the general feeling towards him in the Munich theatre was something less than cordial. Nor, we may surmise, did he improve matters by trying what was virtually a bit of blackmail on the King. In any other German theatre, he said — conveniently forgetting for the moment the difficulties he had had in the past with practically all the German theatres and his low opinion of nearly everyone in charge of them — he would be surer of a punctilious attention to his wishes as regards the staging of the *Meistersinger* than he is in Munich. "Should I", he asked Düfflipp, "beseech our gracious King's permission not to give my new work at all, or shall I beg him to allow me to produce it first in model style in some foreign theatre . . . ?" [1] But the days when he could carry off a bluff of that sort were nearing their end. Another two years were to go by before the bluff was finally called by the King; but, as events before the close of this very year 1867 were to show, the sorely-tried young man was beginning to see that many, perhaps most, of Wagner's troubles in every phase of his career had been of his own making, the consequences of angularities in his personal character, and to resent the addition to his own grievous cares of the petty troubles perpetually arising from these angularities.

For the King's birthday on the 25th August Wagner could send him this year only a short poem in which he hailed him as "Germany's most kingly son". He hoped, however, soon to send him the *Meistersinger* manuscript in celebration of a still happier occasion, the wedding with Sophie on the 11th October. Ludwig's reply was heavy with present pain and sick with apprehension. "Could I but spirit myself away", he sighed, "to you and the Freundin in dear, quiet Triebschen, were it only for a few hours!" As for his wedding, he would prefer it to take place privately, if that were possible; he shudders at the thought of a pompous public ceremony in

---

[1] RWSP, p. 704.

his capital. He apologises for unloading "these small cares" on to Wagner. The latter, however, could read between the lines: he sensed that Ludwig was racked with doubts as to the wisdom of going through with the marriage. His reply of the 22nd September is full of affectionate concern. He reaches out his hand to him, he says, looks in Ludwig's eyes, and asks whether he has not need of the Friend. The pain, sorrow and anxiety in his heart does he not yearn to pour out to him? To whom should Ludwig open his soul if not to the only being who understands him?

> "I live only for you; and I know for sure that no counsel can avail you so much as that of a sympathy that is all yours and yours alone. Tell me, my dear and kind one, my beloved Friend, my adored lord and treasure, what it is that oppresses you. An inner voice gives me the answer, but I can reply to it only if it comes to me from you."

On the 11th October, as we have seen, the annulment of the engagement was publicly announced, and then the King could tell his Triebschen friends what a load had been lifted from his heart. He felt, he said, as if he had recovered from an illness that had menaced his very life; for he had realised that Sophie had only the most superficial understanding of him as he really was, and it was only her youthful charm that had blinded him for a while to that fact. It is probable that Sophie had really been in love with him, and out of that girlish love had entered, as best she could, into his passion for Wagner. Her calculating mother had chosen to regard his enthusiastic letters to Sophie as "ordinary love-letters". Seeing his unhappiness, Sophie herself became unhappy; and then, out of sympathy and pity for her, he had allowed himself to drift into a betrothal. By the autumn he had become so desperate at the thought of the impending ruin of his life that had it not been possible to withdraw becomingly from the engagement he had determined to take prussic acid.[2]

Meanwhile, during the late summer and autumn, a new development was in process in Munich on which Wagner based the highest hopes for the success of his and the King's cause.

---

[2] See his eminently sensible letters to Cosima in MECW, I, 379–81, 392.

3

In the *Report to His Majesty King Ludwig II of Bavaria upon a German School to be founded in Munich* (1865), Wagner had suggested the creation of a weekly journal to be devoted to furthering the ultimate aim of the School — the redemption of German culture through the drama in general and the Wagnerian music drama in particular. He had in mind, as joint editors, Heinrich Porges and a Munich musical journalist, Dr. Franz Grandaur. The contributors were to be drawn from the teaching staff of the School, with occasional articles by Richard Pohl, who was at that time living in Baden-Baden. According to Bülow's letter of the 2nd June, 1865 to Pohl, the journal was to be "didactic, critical, polemical; no 'correspondence', except in a few exceptional cases; no advertisements; no so-called 'intelligencer' [announcements]; prodigiously distinguished!" Grandaur's name had been suggested by Bülow, who thought it would be smart diplomacy to have a native Münchener as at least a nominal leading light of the journal. But Wagner soon withdrew his favour from Grandaur, who showed too little enthusiasm for the project or faith in the success of it. Wagner's next choice of a co-editor with Porges seems to have been Pohl. We gather from his letter of the 27th July, 1867 to Düfflipp that Court Secretary Hofmann had actually been instructed by the King to take the necessary steps for launching the paper in 1865; with Wagner's exile from Munich in December of that year, however, the scheme had fallen through. But as regards the new Music School he had been for a while triumphant all along the line. The Conservatoire, which dated from 1846, was closed by a royal order at the end of July, 1865. There were many difficulties to be overcome before the new School that was to take its place could be got into working order: some of these difficulties were created by Wagner himself, who, as always, was at the mercy of his mood of the moment. The King had done everything he could to meet his wishes. The decree establishing the School was issued on the 16th July, 1867, the 1st October being fixed for the opening. Bülow was appointed artistic director of the institution, which was to be staffed in accordance with his wishes; the administrative control was vested in the Court-Music-Intendanz.

But the music journal had been only a part of the grandiose

scheme outlined by Wagner in the spring of 1865. "Along with this specific journal, which was intended less for the public than for those interested in art", said Wagner in his letter to Düfflipp just mentioned,[3] "there was to have been established a great political paper in which our aims in connection with the founding of a genuinely German musical and dramatic style were to be set forth and treated as intimately bound up with the higher interests of the nation." (There is nothing to this effect, however, in the published *Report*. Perhaps both Wagner and the King felt that it would be impolitic to make this part of the plan public just then). Wagner had suggested "an enlargement and reinforcement" of the official Government paper, the *Bayerische Zeitung*, with Julius Fröbel as editor.[4] This scheme had apparently been cold-shouldered by some of the King's Ministers, for the double reason that they were suspicious of everything that might add to Wagner's power and that Fröbel's record as a federalist made him less than *persona grata* to them. The King too, who regarded a "German Parliament" as a threat to his own sovereignty, was at first reluctant to summon Fröbel to Munich, though he was so little prejudiced against him personally that he subsidised to the extent of 1,500 gulden the publication of two volumes of his political essays.

In November, 1865 the King had suggested that Fröbel should submit to him a *précis* of his principles and objects in relation to Bavarian politics and the German question; but Wagner, while passing on the suggestion to his friend, hinted that it was not worth while doing anything at the moment, the attitude of the politicians being what it was. In his memoirs, however, Fröbel tells us that he sent Wagner, on the 4th December, a letter on the subject which was intended to be passed on to the King. But six days later Wagner had to flee from Munich: he took the letter with him, and Fröbel did not receive it back until the following April. It is doubtful whether he himself was very keen just then to exchange Vienna for Munich. He

---

[3] RWSP, pp. 701–3.

[4] Fröbel was the son of the famous educational reformer Friedrich Wilhelm August Fröbel. He and Wagner had been acquainted in Dresden in 1847–8. For his share in the Austrian political troubles of 1848 Fröbel had narrowly escaped execution: he fled to America, where his experience of the federal system convinced him that it was along some such lines as these that the solution of the problem of German unity would have to be sought. Wagner had met him again in 1863–4 in Vienna, where he was part-editor of Uhl's *Botschafter* and doing odd political and diplomatic jobs for the Austrian Government.

knew several of the Bavarian politicians personally and had an extensive knowledge of the intrigue going on behind the façade. He was speaking from first-hand acquaintance with the subject when he said [5] that the Munich politicians were playing false with the young King for their own purposes, secretly encouraging him in his "Kindereien" — as they called his enthusiasm for art — and then craftily feeding the public with stories, greatly exaggerated, of his indulgence in these "Kindereien", the object of it all, of course, being to discredit him as an unpractical visionary and so seize power for themselves: which goes to confirm Wagner's contention that Ludwig was being "betrayed and enmeshed" by his own officials, and that it was his duty to save the boy from them. [6]

4

Towards the end of May, 1867 Fröbel happened to be in Munich at the same time as Wagner; he had come to discuss various matters with one of Hohenlohe's henchmen, Count Tauffkirchen, among them a project for settling him in the capital as Professor of Politics at the University. Wagner took him to Bülow's house, where, according to Fröbel, Wagner revealed an old scheme of his for having the latter made Cabinet Secretary, with the editorship of the new paper as the best route to that goal. It was apparently Hohenlohe who, recognising the use this kindred spirit could be to him, took the decisive step towards fixing Fröbel in Munich, though Wagner's influence must certainly have counted in the matter: according to him, Hohenlohe's invitation to Fröbel was to found a journal for the furthering of "the same noble and salutary tendencies" in politics as those of Wagner in the sphere of art: the feuilleton of the journal was to be at the disposal of Wagner and "other exponents of my art-tendencies." [7] By the end of July, 1867 negotiations had

---

[5] FEL, II, 467.

[6] It is interesting to note that in his memoirs (1891) Fröbel, though he obviously has the poorest opinion of Wagner's capacity for realistic politics, small understanding of him as an artist, and little liking for him as a man, avers his belief in the honesty of his "romantic" intentions where the King was concerned. In this respect, he says, Wagner differed from certain other people who were playing fast and loose with the King for their own ends, who would have been glad enough to make use of Wagner for those ends had he proved sufficiently pliable, and who declared war on him when he refused to aid and abet them.

[7] Wagner's letter of the 27th July, 1867 to Düfflipp, in RWSP, p. 701 ff.

progressed so far that Hohenlohe could ask Fröbel to submit a "programme" for the paper. This programme having met with the approval of the King, his Ministers, Wagner and Cosima, it was decided to replace the *Bayerische Zeitung* by a new journal with the title of the *Süddeutsche Presse:* for the five quarters extending from the 1st October, 1867 to the end of 1868 it was to receive a State subvention of 20,000 gulden in all, to which the King added another 10,000 gulden from the Cabinet funds to meet the expenses of the daily Wagner feuilleton.

No sooner had the publication of the new paper been decided upon than Wagner began to bombard Fröbel with advice as to the form and the tone the feuilleton should take. Though he himself would contribute to it occasionally, in the main he wished it to be in the hands of Porges and Pohl. Semper should also be invited to contribute. Notices of ordinary musical and theatrical events could be entrusted to Grandaur. Virtually all the articles were to be anonymous, but the general tone of the writing about art and literature was to be serious, at the furthest remove imaginable from the "trivial Jewish tone" that had lately become so popular — an obvious side-blow at the flash-Harry journalism of Hanslick and his confrères. Probably Fröbel did not at first resent Wagner's hints as to the conduct of the art page: after all, it was specifically for the preaching of the gospel according to Wagner that the King was subsidising the feuilleton. But even so he must have felt, as responsible editor of the paper, that he would prefer to do his own thinking about the matter and the manner of even the art pages.

We can have little doubt, however, as to his reaction to certain other passages in Wagner's letters. Wagner seemed to be possessed by the notion that the function not merely of the feuilleton but of the new paper as a whole was to serve *him* as a mouthpiece. More than ever now he identified the German cause in general with himself: nowhere but in a new Germany could his ideal of art be achieved, while conversely without that ideal the Germany of his dreams could never come into being.

"I would briefly define my position in relation to your journal thus", he wrote to Fröbel. "I desired a political paper, of a quality hitherto unknown, for several reasons — (1) for its own sake; (2) because of the great influence it could exert; and (3) to have a paper in which I could discuss my art-tendencies at length without any fear that by doing so I would be descending to a plane on which a serious, honest man only courts defeat. Consequently I suggested to the King two years ago that he should invite you to found a paper of this sort. Now you have received the invitation through another quarter, and the King sanctions a participation in the production of your journal for the specific advocacy of my art-tendencies."

To all which, in the abstract, Fröbel could perhaps assent. But when Wagner further made manifest his belief that Providence had laid on *him* the task of saving Bavaria and its King from the priests and bureaucrats, and his assumption that *his* aims and methods would as a matter of course be those of Fröbel also, the latter must already have sensed that sooner or later he and Wagner would arrive at a parting of their ways. For Fröbel had no sentimental illusions about Wagner as a practical politician. The plan for a new Munich journal had been discussed between them during Wagner's visit to Vienna in October, 1865. As Fröbel listened to his excited talk he recognised, he tells us, that the musician's aims were of the noblest kind, "but he saw politics too poetically, I might say theatrically or operatically." He had obviously got it into his head that his confidential relations with the King imposed enormous responsibilities on him; and as Fröbel had been given to understand that Wagner had considerable influence with the King and would not hesitate to use it, he already saw the likelihood of a clash some time or other between himself and "the gifted but unpolitical artist." [8]

5

The two men, the one ideological but realistic, the other so purely imaginative as to have only the loosest hold on political reality, were assuredly not fitted to work together for long. Fröbel tells us of a talk he had with Liszt and others in Bülow's house in September, 1867. Wagner, he had then argued, might be right in wishing the theatre to be once more what it had been in the public life of ancient Greece. But Fröbel could not agree that the necessary conditions for this existed in their day: to realise his ideal Wagner would need to found a new religion from which would spring new social conditions. Liszt assented. Moreover, Fröbel went on, although Wagner had not yet founded this new religion of his in which the theatre

---

[8] FEL, II, 397–8.

was to take the place of the Church, some of his partisans behaved as if he had, and so provoked opposition.[9]

But for a little while all went well, or at any rate not too badly, in the editorial office of the *Süddeutsche Presse*. The political "programme" of the new journal, defining the future Bavarian attitude towards the German question as a whole, had been given to the world at the end of August. With the programme itself we are not concerned at the moment; we have only to record that it not only satisfied the King — no doubt because of the determining rôle it allotted to Bavaria in the German-Austrian and general European situation — but received the august approval of Wagner, Cosima, Bülow and Liszt. Evidently for Wagner and Cosima the main *raison d'être* of the paper was to assist in bringing the Wagnerian golden age into being. The programme, Cosima assured the King, had "made a great sensation. I believe that in the foundation of this paper resides the possibility of a renaissance of the German spirit, and so I hail it with sincerely uplifted joy." "You know, my valued friend", Wagner himself wrote to Fröbel,

"... the considerations that made me suggest the founding of a political journal: everything stands or falls with — Germany. Thanks for your excellent programme. [An advance copy of it had evidently been sent to him.] I am with it heart and soul."

He thoroughly approves of Fröbel's view of the "quite unparalleled importance of Bavaria", which fortunate land is now to be stimulated to great decisions. "Our chief task must be to rescue this so vigorous and capable Folk from the neglected condition into which education by priests and bureaucrats has brought it." A strong, independent Bavaria must be the envy of all the German lands; and so forth. Reading which, Fröbel probably asked himself whether it was he or Wagner who was supposed to be directing the *Süddeutsche Presse*.

In the first *Abendblatt* of the paper Wagner began a series of anonymous articles on *German Art and German Politics* [10] which

---

[9] FEL, II, 486.

[10] Issued in book form early in 1868: they will be found in Vol. VIII of RWGS. His other contributions to the *Presse* were an article on W. H. Riehl's *Neues Novellenbuch* and one on Ferdinand Hiller, *à propos* of his book *Aus dem Tonleben unserer Zeit*. These were reprinted in the *Musikalisches Wochenblatt* of the 22nd March, 1872 and 3rd May, 1872 respectively, and later in Vol. VIII of RWGS.

are of peculiar interest today. He begins with the thesis, now so familiar to the world and always so grateful to German ears, that the Germans are God's own people.[11] He quotes approvingly the dictum of Konstantin Frantz, his latest mentor in matters political, that the French influence, which is wholly "materialistic", must be destroyed if civilisation is to be saved:

> "and this precisely is the mission of Germany, because of all Continental countries Germany alone possesses the needful capacity and strength to bring about a nobler culture against which French civilisation will no longer have any power." [12]

France, Wagner continues, although "at the head of European civilisation", is "spiritually bankrupt". True, there is much that is rotten in German life also; but that, of course, is due to French and other bad foreign influences having temporarily submerged the sounder native instincts of the Teutons. As the ancient Roman world stood in need of "a total regeneration of the European Folk-blood", so now there is required "a re-birth of the Folk-spirit" — a "mission" allotted to the Germans. The trouble in the past has been that the German princes have betrayed and frustrated the true German spirit. The Germans, it seems, are fundamentally the kinsmen of "the godlike Hellenes", as Winckelmann and Lessing had perceived; Goethe had symbolised the same great truth in the marriage of Helen and Faust in the Second Part of his poem — the wedding of "the Greek ideal" to "the German spirit". German Youth, when uncorrupted by foreign influences, is the flower of humanity.

> "Strictly speaking, ever since the regeneration of the European Folk-blood [13] the German has been the creator and inventor, the Latin the shaper and exploiter: the German nature has remained the true fountain of continuous renovation."

---

[11] "The German people are the Chosen of God", the last of the German Kaisers assured his army on the 4th August, 1914.

[12] The quotation is from Frantz's *Untersuchungen über das europäische Gleichgewicht* (*Inquiry into the European Balance of Power*).

[13] It would have been as unkind to ask Wagner just what he meant by this as it would be today to try to read a definite meaning into a rhapsody of this sort: "Blood and soil, as fundamental forces of life, are the symbols of the national-political point of view and the heroic style of life. . . . What does blood mean to us? We cannot rest satisfied with the teachings of physics, chemistry or medicine. From the earliest dawn of the race this blood, this shadowy stream of life, has had a symbolic significance, and leads us into the realms of metaphysics. Blood is the builder of the body and the source of the spirit of the race. In blood is embodied the race, from blood arises the character and destiny of man; blood is to man the hidden under-current, the

The re-birth of the German spirit will not only "ennoble the public spiritual life of the German Folk" but "found a new and truly German civilisation, extending its benefits even beyond our own frontiers." That has been "the universal mission of the German Folk since its entry into history."

6

These views were not original or even peculiar to Wagner: they had been slowly taking shape and gathering strength in the German mind for more than half a century before his time. The seed of all of them is to be found in the writings and speechifyings of "Father Jahn". [14] For this ignorant, arrogant, clamorous boor, the son of a Prussian parson, even the Prussianised historian Treitschke could find no more flattering description than "a blustering barbarian, a loud-mouthed ranter." [15] Jahn anticipated the Nazi mentality and the Nazi régime in more ways than one. He was an antisemite. He approved of the public burning of books not sufficiently "German" in tone. He yearned prophetically for a Führer who should heal Germany by "iron and fire", a man whom the Folk would honour as a saviour, forgiving him all his sins.[16] Germany was first of all to achieve internal unity, then take in the Danes, the Netherlanders and the Swiss; on the other side of Europe it had a "mission" to subdue and Christianise the Balts and Slavs, for the Germans shared with the ancient Greeks the distinction of being "humanity's holy people". Individual ideas and individual rights were all to be subject to the will of the State as the expression of "aggressive nationalism": there was to be "One God, One Fatherland, One House, One Love." [17] No German should marry an unnaturalised alien.

---

symbol of the stream of life from which man can arise and ascend to the regions of light, of spirit and of knowledge." (From a speech by Rector Krieck, of Frankfort University, in 1935; quoted in Joseph Needham's *The Nazi Attack on International Science*, 1941, pp. 11–12.)

From this it was a natural and easy transition, for Germans, to the later wild talk about "the dark destiny incarnated in the blood of the master-race" — meaning, of course, their godlike selves.

[14] Friedrich Ludwig Jahn (1778–1852), the celebrated founder of the "Turnvereine" (gymnastic clubs).

[15] Heine called Jahn a "mattoid".

[16] Carl Euler, *Friedrich Ludwig Jahn, Sein Leben und Wirken* (1881), p. 368. This and the following citations are from Jahn's *Deutsches Volksthum* (1810).

[17] Euler, p. 122.

Jahn's hatred of the French knew no bounds. Good Germans should not even speak the immoral tongue of their neighbours; "there is nothing to choose between the father who lets his daughter learn French and the man who apprentices his daughter to whoredom", he declared. "Germany needs a war of her own in order to feel her power", he laid it down after the fall of Napoleon;

"she needs a feud with Frenchdom to develop her national way of life in all its fullness. This occasion will not fail to come."

He believed in the virtues of "blood and soil" as fervently as Wagner or Alfred Rosenberg or any other German phantast of yesterday and today. Already in 1810 he was hymning the virtues of "racial purity". "The purer a people the better; the more mixed, the worse": "just as animal cross-breeds have no genuine power of propagation, so cross-bred peoples have no real continuity of life." [18]

If Jahn did not actually coin the word *Volksthum* (Folkdom), as he is credited in some quarters with having done, he at any rate started it off on its present currency with his books *Deutsches Volksthum* (1810) and *Merke zum deutschen Volksthum* (1833). According to him, only so far as a nation is a Folk, and thinks and behaves as one, can it play any decisive part in history; for Folkdom is

"that which the Folk has in common, its inner being, its life and soul, its power of propagation and capacity for expansion . . . a folkic thinking and feeling, loving and hating, joying and sorrowing, hoping and longing . . . intuition and faith."

This is essentially the same definition as Wagner's — the Folk is all those who feel a need in common.

7

The German nation as a whole was not yet quite as drunk with self-glorification as it was to become later; the final phase of that

---

[18] Euler, p. 117. Compare the following words of wisdom from the mouth of a living German "scientist": "The only differences that exist between the human and the animal world are between Nordic man on the one hand and animals in general, including non-Nordic or sub-men." From Dr. Gauch's *Neue Grundlagen der Rassenforschung* (*New Foundations of Race-Research*), quoted in C. E. M. Joad's *Liberty Today* (1938), p. 117.

degenerative process was not to set in until after 1870. But the agreeable cup had been constantly at its lips for long before then; and we can see the potent stuff beginning really to go to Wagner's head about this time. The success of the war of 1870 with France, if it did not make Germans in the mass love the Prussians any more than of old, did at any rate set by far the greater part of the nation adoring and imitating Prussian "efficiency". We have seen Wagner, in 1865, emptying the vials of his hatred and contempt on Prussia in the "Journal" he kept for the private guidance of King Ludwig, and then suppressing every passage in that now inconvenient key when he published these lucubrations under the title of *What is German?* in 1878.[19] By 1867 Prussia had not yet shown itself quite so "efficient" as to fill Wagner with Germanic pride at the thought of it; but already here and there in these *Süddeutsche Presse* articles we see him beginning to cast admiring glances at the rising bully of the North. In 1865 he had seen in Prussia's predominantly military organisation only a source of weakness to Germany and of danger to other nations: the Prussian (and in a lesser degree the Austrian) system of being "continually under arms against all Europe" had resulted, he said, in

"a military caste that is absolutely non-German and useless, imitated as it is from the warrior-castes of purely conquering peoples, and inapplicable to our conditions."

But even by 1867 he had come round to the point of view that Prussia's victory over Austria and Bavaria in the preceding year had been due to "the last remnant of the German spirit, extirpated everywhere else", i.e., "the military organisation retained by Prussia" from the days of the struggle against the first Napoleon. The French, Wagner hints, will henceforth have to be careful what they are about: "one word from the victor of Königgratz,[20] and a new power emerges in history before which French civilisation will pale for ever."

The feeling that it was Prussia's mission to "save" and glorify a greater Germany had long ago been expressed in Jahn's *Deutsches Volksthum*. Jahn looked to Prussia for "a revival, in due season, of the ancient German Reich", with a *Grossvolk* in that Reich which

---

[19] See Vol. III, Chapter xix.
[20] 3rd April, 1866.

would accomplish great things in world history.[21] "Germany", he continues,

"if it is one with itself, if it develops, as a German commonwealth, its prodigious and as yet unexplored forces, can some day be the establisher of eternal peace in Europe, the guardian angel of humanity"

— the creator, in fact, of a "New Order".

8

So long as Wagner confined himself to laudations of the "German spirit" in general and of Bavaria in particular his *Süddeutsche Presse* articles were tolerably sure to meet with approval. Certainly the King was delighted with the earlier ones: it would be of the highest benefit to everyone, he told Cosima in a letter of the 10th November, if the Friend could be persuaded to voice his opinions oftener in public. Would that other German princes would give these articles their attention, for all that Wagner has to say about the estrangement of the princes from their Folk, and the duty incumbent on them to atone for their past sins against the Folk, is only too true! To the gratified author himself the King swore, eleven days later, that *he* would do everything in his power to make good the failings of the German princes —

"these servile imitators of French fashions, these worshippers of that glittering civilisation which has an eye only for the sleek surface of things, instead of penetrating into the soul of them. . . ."

He builds high hopes on the effect of Wagner's articles:

"By heaven! anyone who is not enchanted with them and convinced and converted by the magic of their speech and the profundity of thought revealed in them, does not deserve to live!"

Ludwig's next letter to Wagner is dated three months and a half later, and much had happened in the interval. On the 9th December the King, as we have seen,[22] told Düfflipp that he was tired of "the eternal wrangles and complaints on the part of Wagner, Porges, Fröbel and the rest of them", and that "the thread of his patience" was beginning to break. Apparently the last straw, so far as Wagner

---

[21] Euler, p. 116.
[22] See *supra*, p. 33.

was concerned, had been the latter's pestering him once more to punish Malvina Schnorr for having dared to cast doubts on his and Cosima's "honour". The realisation that he had not only been grossly deceived and lied to but tricked into giving a public assurance of his own belief in the "honour" of the pair would of itself, perhaps, account for a temporary revulsion of feeling towards Wagner: he always reacted sharply to anything that might lower the royal dignity. But something more than this must have happened just then to explain, at least in part, his drastic action on the 19th of the same month with regard to Wagner's articles.

The thirteenth article appeared in the issue of the 17th December. Two days later a Government official descended on the office with an order from the King that the publication of the articles, which he described as "suicidal", was to be suspended for the present. The fourteenth article was actually in proof by that time: the type was at once broken up. The discontinuance of the articles was announced editorially on the 19th December in this wise:

"We ask our readers' indulgence for the late appearance of today's *Abendblatt*. A series of articles under the title of *German Art and German Politics* has been appearing in that sheet: these the editor, however little he agreed with the opinions expressed therein, would have allowed to run on to their conclusion, since at the end of this year . . . the relation hitherto existing between the political and the artistic direction of the paper — a relation which conceded a certain freedom to the latter — was to have ceased. The contents of the last published article of the series, however, and the similar character of that intended for today's issue, were of such a nature that the editor regards it as his duty not to permit the publication of any more of these articles."

What had caused this astonishing right-about-face on the part of the King? It is difficult to be sure, but a survey of all the known facts may authorise a tentative explanation. When the King wrote so enthusiastically to Wagner about the articles on the 21st November some eight of them had appeared. In these the writer had sung the praises of the two preceding Kings of Bavaria, hinted broadly that the mission of the present occupant of the throne was to set an example to the other German princes, and laid it down that the theatre is "the spiritual seed and kernel of all national-poetic and national-ethical culture", no genuine Folk-culture being possible until the lofty rôle of the theatre had been fully recognised. With all this the King would be in warm agreement. Thereafter Wagner had launched into a number of high-sounding if somewhat empty generalisations about the history of the arts in general from the time of the Greeks, the nature and function of the actor, the differences between the French mind and the German, between the French drama and that of Schiller, the mistakes made by the German princes and their theatre Intendants, and the superiority of the German, with his bent towards "the ideal", to the more "material" Frenchman. With practically all this, again, the King could be expected to agree. But in his twelfth and thirteenth articles Wagner had wandered off into a variety of matters which Ludwig no doubt felt to be outside the legitimate province of the musician — schoolmasterish reproofs of, and admonitions to, Church and State, criticisms of the growing bias of the State towards the utilitarian, an exposition of the supposed function of the monarch in the correction of this bias and of the good the King might do by conferring orders on the right people for the right things, and so forth. It was perhaps because Wagner himself had no very clear idea what he was talking about that his style in these two articles is seen at its worst, the cloudy verbiage serving as a sort of smoke-screen to cover the strategic withdrawal of the intelligence.

The fourteenth article — the one vetoed by the King — went on in much the same vein. It was not until the fifteenth (and last) article, which, like its immediate predecessor, never saw the light in the columns of the *Süddeutsche Presse,* that Wagner began once more to get into touch with realities and talk about them something like a practician. His thesis here was that if the theatre was to exert a good influence on culture it could only be by model performances of a few great works. That would of necessity mean closing the State theatre every now and then to allow due preparation of these masterpieces: either that, or a special theatre would have to be built for such productions exclusively. He hoped that, however addicted the ordinary citizen might be to the normal fare served up to him by the commercial entrepreneurs for his relaxation after his day's work, he would still be willing to come to the better things in order to find his own soul again, sink himself in it, and go home a better man, "forgetting, in the noblest sense, the toil and trouble of life for the sake of its loftiest ends." In a word, as we can now see, — Bayreuth, the ecstatic vision of which had long been perfectly clear

[101]

to Wagner's inner eye but was as yet hidden from all his readers. How to reconcile the devotee of the ordinary theatrical "entertainment" to the frequent closing of the State theatre for long periods, in order that some work or other in which he perhaps did not take the smallest interest might be rehearsed again and again, was a problem beyond Wagner's or any other man's solving. The only possible solution of it was, so to speak, the evasion of it — the creation of a purely Wagnerian theatre that should be under no obligation to the State or the municipality and free of the necessity to make concessions to the taste of the average tired business man.

9

It was a pity that the King should have imposed his veto on the articles just when the author was approaching a sphere truly his own and beginning to talk something like sense. Fröbel, for his part, was no doubt glad that the tension between himself and Wagner had at last reached its climax. He had disagreed, he tells us, with several things in the articles, while Wagner had further annoyed him with complaints that the paper had not been severe enough in its criticism of certain actors. He must particularly have resented Cosima's lecturing him on Wagner's behalf, as she was indiscreet enough to do on the 12th December. Fröbel had objected to a campaign being conducted against some actress or other — recommended to the King by the Grand Duke of Mecklenburg-Schwerin — before she had even made her début in Munich. In this he thought he traced the hand of Wagner and Cosima, and he assured the latter that it was only out of regard for her that he had not dismissed the writer summarily. Wagner, as always when he was crossed, began to be rude, while Cosima, in her attempts to placate Fröbel, irritated him still further by her reverential assumption that in everything connected with art Wagner was the "Meister" whose judgment was to be accepted as infallible. On the 13th Wagner wrote Fröbel that it had never been his desire to have anything to do with a political paper, and he would prefer now to revert to his original plan for an independent journal devoted solely to artistic interests. He accordingly suggested that the residue for 1868 (8,000 florins) of the King's subsidy of 10,000 florins should be returned by Fröbel to the Treasury for the founding of "a specific [weekly] art journal": that hav-

ing been done, Fröbel would be free to run the art section of the
Süddeutsche Presse according to his own notions.

Cosima's attempts to pour oil on the troubled waters — accompanied, it goes without saying, by pious protestations, with meekly
folded hands, that the last thing she would wish to do would be to
"mix herself up with things that did not concern her and were beyond her understanding" — probably only succeeded in intensifying Fröbel's exasperation. To penetrate the hard hide of her and
Wagner's belief in themselves, he must have seen, was quite impossible. "Wagner can do no otherwise",[23] she complacently told
Fröbel: "this is his strength against the world, but also a danger."
As for herself, his word was law: "you know that I always refrain
from expressing any opinion as against the Meister, whose ideas
about art have become our faith." [24] It apparently did not occur to
either her or Wagner that other people, in matters of deep concern
to them and strong conviction, might also feel that they "could do
no otherwise". Merely as editor of a paper — any paper — to
which Wagner happened to be contributing, Fröbel was entitled to
stand up for the rights of his position. In the present instance he was
doubly entitled to do so because Wagner had evidently been giving

---

[23] "Kann nicht anders" — Luther's famous reply to the Diet of Worms when invited to recant.

[24] An early example of the fanatic-romantic *Führerprincip* so dear to the German
mind and so incomprehensible to more critical and more politically developed
peoples. "The ideas of Adolf Hitler", said Reichsminister Frank, a leading German
jurist, in 1936, "contain the final truths of every possible scientific knowledge."
"The Führer", said the *National Socialist Landpost* in May, 1940, "prepares and
builds a new world in which life will enter upon a new spring": Hitler had been
"selected by an eternal Spirit in order that it might manifest its creative power
through him."

The true founders of Wagnerism as a "faith", a religion, were Cosima and Houston Stewart Chamberlain; the latter not only prostrated his own intellect before
Wagner's but regarded it as the bounden duty of the rest of humanity to prostrate
theirs. See, for instance, CRWD, p. 72 ff.

Of course the great artist, or great creator or innovator of any kind, "kann nicht
anders": he must make for his goal regardless of everybody and everything. Posterity,
surveying what he has achieved, freely grants him this; but posterity is a bad psychologist and a biased holder of the scales if it does not also see matters in detail
from the point of view of the contemporaries whose windows he broke and whose
toes he trod on. "Such demoniac personalities [as Wagner]", said Heinrich Porges
some years after the Master's death, "cannot be judged by ordinary standards.
They are egoists of the first water, and must be so, or they could never fulfil their
mission." But Porges, who knew Wagner as few men did at that time, saw also that
other people often had a good case against him. While he objected to the bad taste
of some of the naggings at Wagner in Weissheimer's memoirs, he was honest enough
also to say that "Glasenapp's blind idolatry" was equally repugnant to him. See his
letter of the 15th May, 1898, to Richard Batka, in the latter's *Kranz* (1903), p. 172.

vent, in a journal that was regarded all over Europe as the official organ of the Bavarian Government, to opinions *on politics* with which the people responsible for the conduct of Bavarian affairs might not care to be publicly associated.

Wagner's letter to Cosima of the 18th December [25]— written, that is to say, before the King put a stop to the articles — makes it tolerably clear that one of the difficulties had been Wagner's quarrelsome references to the French. "My German tendency", he said, "is not only something inborn in the depths of me but the result of a life rich in experience and based on a fairly exact knowledge of the French nature." Compromise is impossible for him. If, however, Fröbel prefers to believe that the salvation of the world lies in "the Americanisation of Europe", and that each "political power-nuance", such as that of Louis Napoleon, is to be a matter of bargaining,[26] then he and Wagner are not likely to understand each other in future. As usual, he can admit no virtue whatever in any opinion but his own. He is entirely possessed by the conviction that the very breath and being of his art is "the German spirit": as Cosima put it in her letter to Fröbel, "his Germandom [Deutschtum] he will never disown or even so much as water down. . . ."

To which Fröbel probably felt like replying: "Nobody concerned with the running of the *Süddeutsche Presse* is anxious in any way to water down your *Deutschtum*, to dilute your conviction that at bottom *your* cause and that of Germany are one and indivisible. But you really must permit other people to do their own thinking about these things. 'Germany' and 'Germandom' are abstract terms, capable, in the practical sphere, of an infinite variety of connotations; and you are not entitled to take it for granted that it is everyone's duty, at your bidding, to interpret them solely in your sense. No one disputes your right, as an artist, to work in the way that seems to you best for an ideal which you regard as the only one worth pursuing. But it is another matter altogether when, in the process of identifying your artistic ideal with 'Germany', you choose to give 'Germany' a particular range of application that does not commend itself to those responsible for the founding and the running

---

[25] It was intended, of course, to be passed on to Fröbel.
[26] The reader will bear in mind that at that period a collaboration of the South German States with Napoleon against Prussia was always within the range of possibility.

of the *Süddeutsche Presse*. By all means put every ounce of your remarkable gifts into the business of converting the world to your view of the salvation of Germany and the world through the theatre. But opera is one thing, politics another; and you must not expect those to whom the latter is the first concern to behave as if they believed the former to be the only thing that really matters."

10

The gist of Fröbel's "programme", given to a keenly expectant European world in the autumn of 1867, had been that the new German situation created by the war of 1866 and the failure to form a South German Bund had laid a new responsibility upon Bavaria as the strongest South German power; for the peace of Europe depended now upon the South being able to throw itself decisively into the scales in support either of Austria against Prussia, or of Prussia against France, or of France against Prussia. The ideal to be striven for was the welding of North Germany, South Germany and Austria into one great German entity which should play a decisive rôle in European politics. It was significant that while the programme met with a cool reception in some Germanic quarters it was warmly welcomed by the French Press. The Paris correspondent of the *Allgemeine Zeitung* had telegraphed that

"the French Government would very much like to see a solution of the German problem in the sense indicated by Fröbel; meanwhile it welcomes the mere fact that the thesis of a perpetuation of the line of the river Main, and the establishment of Bavarian hegemony south of this, should have been put forward for discussion. . . . Should Fröbel's programme find approval in Germany, and Prussia place no obstacles in the way of its realisation, France would henceforth have no occasion to concern herself with German affairs."

Fröbel's ideas, added the same correspondent a few days later, were in complete agreement with French views, especially on the question of the frontier, which,

"even for the most pacific-minded Frenchman, constituted a *casus belli*. Never, perhaps, in the whole of his active career has Fröbel had so great a success as in Paris during the last few days, particularly among those Frenchmen who do not feel the least jealousy towards a free and great Germany." [27]

---

[27] BLKB, 193 ff.

In view of all this, and the delicacy of the international situation, Fröbel, Hohenlohe and the Bavarian politicians in general might reasonably jib at the markedly unfriendly tone of Wagner's references to France,[28] for which, appearing as they did in the official journal, they themselves would be held responsible.[29] The King had described the articles as "suicidal". Fröbel, writing some twenty years later, takes this expression to mean that "by continuing these articles Wagner would make the relation between himself and the King impossible." But this still leaves us asking *why* that would be their probable result. Manifestly Ludwig would not have taken such drastic and openly unfriendly action against Wagner without what seemed to him and his advisers very good reason. But Wagner, in the blindness of his egoism, could see no justification for the universe existing at all except for the realisation of his dream of the regeneration of mankind through the drama; and if the glorification of "the German spirit" that was inseparably bound up with this had as its necessary obverse the vilification of the French civilisation in the presence of which so many a German, in his heart of hearts, suffered from an inferiority complex, he cared nothing for the possible political results of the spitting of a venom that was in about equal parts personal and national.[30] He was entitled to

---

[28] The King, during his visit to Paris, had had a talk with the Emperor in Compiègne, when the latter warned him against engaging himself too closely with Prussia. The pair met again on the occasion of Napoleon's visit to Augsburg in the following August, when they travelled to Munich together. One of the subjects of their conversation may be surmised from a passage in Ludwig's letter of the 22nd August to his grandfather: "Thank God the prospect in general seems pacific; perhaps we shall yet succeed in bringing about a tolerable state of affairs in Europe without the dreaded catastrophe."

[29] Let us recall that Wagner, in his letter of the 19th December to Cosima, had asked her to tell Fröbel that he meant his fifteenth article to be his last utterance on the subject of art and politics in the pages of the *Presse* — also that "the French will be mentioned only with recognition of their good qualities". The significance of this sentence seems to have been overlooked by the historians. It appears to me to indicate beyond question that the root of the King's and Fröbel's sudden objection to the articles was Wagner's aggressive attitude towards the French.

[30] The sort of comic despair to which he must have reduced the practical politicians by his fanatical harpings on the theme of salvation through the theatre is illustrated in some remarks of Baron Otto von Völderndorff in his account of that interview with Wagner to which reference has already been made. (See Vol. III, p. 440). He had asked Wagner for a résumé of his views and aims. "And then there was poured out on me the 'endless melody' of a fluent rigmarole delivered with an unvarying nasal twang, without any rise or fall of the voice: there recurred time after time such expressions as 'my royal Friend', 'German art', 'ideal moulding of public life', 'ossified bureaucracy', 'mist-clouds of malevolent enemies', 'Jewish gnawing at German Folkdom', and so forth. It was all ingenious, but unclear, confused, and above all

hold any opinions he liked on any subject under the sun; what he was not entitled to was to express dubious political opinions of his own *anonymously* in the columns of the official Bavarian political journal. The only possible solution of the problem of his need for self-propaganda was one along the same lines as the ultimate solution of his problem of the theatre — to found a journal of his own, countenancing no point of view but his own, wholly under his control, and identified by the world with himself and himself alone. His bitter experiences with the *Süddeutsche Presse* must have played a determining part in the foundation of the *Bayreuther Blätter* in 1878.

Fröbel's dissatisfaction with him towards the end of 1867 was a matter not merely of a difference of opinion on certain points of politics. Wagner's demands for space for the elaboration of his own and his henchmen's views upon art had expanded in the course of time, and this expansion necessarily meant an increase in the paper's working costs — to say nothing of the frequent clashes of opinion between Fröbel and these henchmen; as he puts it in his memoirs, through the medium of the royal subsidy Wagner exerted an influencé on the pages devoted to art criticism which sometimes came into collision not merely with Fröbel's personal views but with his conception of his responsibility as editor of the paper. On the 27th August, 1868 the Government gave him notice that the subsidy of 20,000 gulden would cease at the end of that year; and when the final accounts came to be made up it was found that this amount had failed to cover the expenses of the *Presse* by some 4,000 gulden. For this unsatisfactory state of affairs Fröbel blamed the uneconomic way in which he had been compelled to run the art feuilleton in Wagner's interest.

To complete the record it may be added that when his contract with the Government expired, Fröbel took over the paper as his private property and ran it for a few years as his own political mouthpiece. In 1873 he sold it to a Munich banking house and entered the German consular service.

---

unpractical. . . . No less unserviceable was his exposition of what I was to aim at in conformity with the royal instructions — 'to bring the theatre and music into intimate union with the political life of the people'."

CHAPTER VI

THE SHADOWS DEEPEN

1

W E MUST now retrace our steps a little way in order to make a rapid survey of events in general during the autumn of 1867. That it was in Wagner's mind at this time to make Triebschen his home for the rest of his life is shown by a letter of the 13th September to Düfflipp, in which he suggests that the King shall grant him an immediate 6,000 florins to meet his expenses in connection with the place. The grant was duly made on the 14th October. This was not a fresh draft on the King's purse but merely a final regularisation of the matter of the Briennerstrasse house, which had cost the King 20,000 florins and had been placed at Wagner's disposal for life. The rental of Triebschen was 3,000 florins a year, and Wagner had originally taken the place for three years certain. Between April, 1866 and March, 1867 the King had authorised the payment to him of 17,000 florins in all. Thus the 6,000 florins now granted brought the total payment to him in respect of Triebschen up to 23,000 florins, a sum as near as makes no matter to the original cost of the Briennerstrasse house, which he had formally returned to the King on the 1st September, 1866.[1] He wanted the 6,000 florins now, he explained to Düfflipp, not merely to complete the furnishing and altering of Triebschen but also to clinch the right to renew the lease for the rest of his life on very favourable terms.

But Triebschen meant, of course, for him, Cosima as well, and of that happy consummation there was at present sadly little prospect. When she left him on the 16th September to rejoin Hans in Munich, Wagner confided his misery to the pages of the Brown Book. "What love is", he wrote, "a man can learn only at my age — the grave of life. How weary I am!" He likens Cosima's brief visit to him to the reappearance of Christ to the faithful after his death;

[1] See Vol. III, p. 466 ff.

"So camest thou to me once more: two nights and a day my house har-
boured thee. And now gone, quite gone. Whither? — Where I myself
am I know: in the grave."

The pain was genuine enough, even if his self-pity, as usual, acquired an additional zest through self-dramatisation. "Greetings
from the Wanderer to the Rester. Soul like sky mournful yet conscious of bliss", Cosima wired to him from Zürich that same evening, addressing the telegram to "Stocker" at Triebschen and signing it "Vorstel"; to which Wagner at once replied,

"Greeting from dream and grief in Tollheim. May it hearten the *Vorstellung* that the *Wille* is in sore need of cheer. The Brown Book slips
from his hand. Eva greets Loldi. Tears and blessings to the vic-
tors . . ." [2]

Even in their sincerest moments there was something of the stage
player in each of them at this time: Wagner in particular rejoiced
and sorrowed over himself on paper as luxuriantly as the dramatist
or novelist does over one of his favourite characters, while the most
ordinary occurrences of domestic life, when they happened to *him*,
became charged with cosmic significance. To most human beings, a
child of theirs is just a child of theirs. To Wagner, his little Eva was
a sign and a portent. "Each day increases the touching awe with
which I draw near to Eva", he wrote in the Brown Book on the
27th. "There lies, lives and laughs [observe the alliteration à la
Ring [3]] the bright token that 'I too was born in Arcadia'. Dear,
dear wife!" [4]

2

But before the "Liebes, liebes Weib!" could be taken literally
there was Bülow to be reckoned with. He seems to have come back
from his holiday in St. Moritz not much better in health than when
he went there; and matters were not improved by his forced labours
on *Lohengrin*, which was given, at the urgent desire of the King, on
the 29th September, with Nachbaur — apparently Ludwig's own
choice — taking the place of Vogl. Liszt was present both at this

---

[2] On the use by Wagner and Cosima of "Wille" and "Vorstel" as confidential
names for each other see Vol. III, p. 513. "Tollheim" — literally "Mad Home" — is
a Wagnerian construction on the model of the "Nibelheim" of the *Ring*.
[3] "Da oben ihr lebt, lacht und liebt . . . .". Alberich in the *Rhinegold*.
[4] KLRWB, V, 69.

performance and at one of *Tannhäuser* on the 22nd. He had left his Rome retreat towards the end of August to attend the Musical Festival at Meiningen and conduct his *St. Elisabeth* at the Wartburg; after which he made his way by slow stages to Munich, where he arrived in the third week of September. There can be no doubt that his prime object in going there had been to discuss the Wagner problem with Cosima and Bülow.[5] Hans was even more debilitated than usual, not only in the last stage of exhaustion but suffering from a tumour in the throat that made talking almost impossible for him, yet doing half-a-dozen men's work in connection with the theatre and the Music School. The Abbé Liszt made Munich his base, off and on, until the end of October, paying the customary round of visits, enjoying the fleshpots of this frivolous world to the full, writing to his pious Princess, in his best Franciscan vein, that ever since he was a child he had conceived life as sad and death as sweet, assuring her that "ma véritable nature, c'est la passion du martyre", and proving his saintly contempt for this miserable world and its profane values by moving heaven and earth to get himself presented to the King, though without success.

There were news-hawks even in those days, and the movements of the Abbé Liszt were a matter of journalistic interest if not of national importance. So he had to resort to strategy in order to keep his projected visit to Triebschen a secret. On the 3rd October he

---

[5] I have suggested (Vol. III, p. 266 etc.) that Cosima may have told her husband at Starnberg in July, 1864 the true state of affairs between her and Wagner, and that it was simply to discuss the grave new situation with her father that she had gone on the 19th August to Karlsruhe, where Liszt was to attend the festival of the Allgemeiner Deutscher Musikverein. This conjecture has since been amply confirmed by a letter of Liszt's offered for sale in Otto Haas's catalogue No. 7 of Autograph Letters and Manuscripts. I was unfortunately too late to acquire the document; but the summary of it given in the Catalogue, imperfect as it is, is sufficient to establish the truth of the theory I had put forward in my third volume.

The letter, which is described as being "in French, to an unknown lady", is dated Karlsruhe, 17th August, 1864. Liszt tells his correspondent that "he has bad news from [of?] Hans v. Bülow, who is retained (*sic*) with fever at Wagner" [*sic.*] The next citation is given in the Catalogue in the original French. It may be translated thus: "My daughter has not breathed a word to me for more than a month: I know only that she is with her husband at Wagner's house on the Starnberg Lake." This, as I had conjectured on other grounds, proves conclusively both that Cosima *had* written to her father in the early days of July, and that her journey to Karlsruhe on the 19th was not in accordance with any previous arrangement to attend the festival with him but was due to a sudden impulse on her part. It is observed that Liszt tells both this correspondent (on the 17th August) and Princess Wittgenstein (on the 21st) that he has not replied to Cosima's letter, as he *does not wish to influence her.*

had an engagement in Stuttgart, where he was joined by Richard Pohl from the near-by Baden-Baden. On Sunday, the 6th, the pair were in Basel. On the evening of Tuesday Liszt sprang it on the astonished Pohl that he was returning the next day to Munich, but intended to call at Triebschen on the way to see Wagner. Pohl, like everyone else, must have suspected for some time that there had been a cooling off in the friendship of the two great men: Liszt's absence from the *Tristan* production of 1865 seemed to suggest that.[6] But if he speculated on the matter at all it was without the smallest illumination from Liszt, though Pohl was wideawake enough to see later that the détour via Basel had only been a device to throw inquisitive outsiders off the scent, the true reason for the trip having been all along the call on Wagner.

At three o'clock on Wednesday Liszt was in Triebschen. He went there alone, Pohl having been packed off on an excursion to Flüelen; on his return to his Lucerne hotel in the evening he found Wagner's carriage waiting to take him to join the others in the house by the Lake. Wagner and Liszt having managed to say all they had to say to each other on the subject of Hans and Cosima in a six-hours' talk, the rest of the evening could be devoted to more easeful matters. Liszt played at sight long stretches from the manuscript full score of the *Meistersinger*, Wagner taking all the vocal parts: "I have never heard a finer performance of the *Meistersinger*", said Pohl nineteen years later, "such ravishing truth of expression, such beauty of phrasing, such clarity in every detail." Under the wings of song the two old friends were warmed again into something like their old affection for each other. Liszt had been to see him, Wagner wrote to the King a few days later, and they had found their way back to the old golden days again; "he is a dear, great, unique creature". To the Princess Wittgenstein Liszt briefly reported that while Wagner had changed outwardly — his face was pinched and lined — his genius was as powerful as ever.

---

[6] Pohl, though in such close touch with the personalities of the Wagner-Bülow circle, appears to have been all his life unaware of the meeting between Liszt and Wagner at Starnberg at the end of August, 1864, for he says that until this meeting of October, 1867, the pair had not seen each other for six years, i.e., since the Weimar festival of 1861.

Liszt never visited Triebschen again. The next occasion when he and Wagner met was in Weimar in 1872.

Pohl's interesting account of the excursion to Lucerne with Liszt will be found in RWJK (1886), pp. 78–84.

"I was amazed by the incomparable sap, audacity, vigour, abundance, verve and maestria of the *Meistersinger*. No one but he could have produced such a masterpiece."

Liszt had evidently confided to his old friend his consuming desire to be received by the King, for we find Wagner begging Ludwig, out of love for *him*, to invite Liszt to Hohenschwangau, were it only for an hour. But the King pleaded that with his tiresome mother at the castle he would be unable to find an opportunity to talk to the Abbé as he would like to do; so after all his wire-pulling the indefatigable tuft-hunter had to return to Rome with his desire to add one more name to the long list of royalties he had met still ungratified.

Of what was said between Liszt and Wagner during those six hours in Triebschen we know nothing, though obviously they had arrived at some sort of understanding as to the immediate future, at any rate, of the triangle. For all the secrecy in which the affair was enveloped, it is clear enough that the visit to Lucerne had been a matter of previous planning between all the parties concerned. "Liszt's visit", Wagner recorded in his "Annals" after his visitor had gone: "Dreaded, yet agreeable." Liszt had left for Munich in the early hours of the 10th, feeling, as he said later, that he had seen Napoleon at St. Helena. While he was still in the train, "Stocker" wired from Lucerne to "Mrazeck, 21 Briennerstrasse, Munich", "beautiful, peaceful visit; left early this morning. No sleep, but full of hope." There was no need to specify the visitor. Cosima would know that already; all that Wagner had to do was to comfort her with the news that the dreaded conference had passed off "peacefully". When further documents relating to the episode become available it may be found that by October, 1867 a crisis had been reached in the inter-relations of the triangle. A variety of evidence points in that direction — the fretful misery of all three of them; the difficulty Bülow had in making up his mind whether to leave Munich or stay in it, and, if the latter, on what face-saving terms superficially consistent with his "honour"; Wagner's despair over the eternal problem of how to make Triebschen his haven from the world and yet not be separated from Cosima; and, finally, this sudden intervention of Liszt. Du Moulin Eckart, who had access to many documents that have not yet been published, assures us not only that Liszt's visit to Triebschen was paid in "a singular frame of mind", he having gone there to discuss at length with Wagner "those deep and vital questions which affected him quite as profoundly as they did his daughter and the Meister",[7] but that the purpose of a party at the house of the painter Kaulbach in Munich on Cosima's name-day (the 27th September), at which Liszt was present, had been to give a *démenti* to all rumours that he was not "on his daughter's side".

Even Bülow seems to have been pleased and heartened, for a while, by the recent turn of events. On the 20th October we find him telling the Berliner Carl Bechstein that he thinks of de-Prussianising himself and becoming a Swiss national. Not that he admires Bismarck any less than of old, but that he wants to be "quite free politically": Munich is going to become an "art-town", and Bavaria will not let herself be gobbled up by Prussia and condemned to waste on military fripperies the money that would be better spent on nobler ends. But, as might have been expected, this "yea-saying" mood did not last long with him. By mid-November Wagner was complaining to Mathilde Maier that Hans's "unfortunate disposition" was once more giving him a lot of trouble. Apparently things in Munich had not been going to Bülow's satisfaction: he had been indulging himself in "outbursts of rage" against the town, and "reproaching us for once again having persuaded him to his ruin, which is pure nonsense." Wagner's patience with him was almost at breaking-point: evidently the sickly, peevish Bülow was a difficult man to handle. Wagner himself, it appears, what with work and worry, is often at the end of his physical resources. Still, he assures Mathilde, things are not going too badly with him at Triebschen and with his cause in Munich. His mental powers are in first-rate shape: it is only disturbances in his emotional life that get him under. The *Meistersinger* score is nearly finished. The Music School and the new journal are both going well; Liszt and Semper are to be invited to settle in Munich; the King is beginning to assert himself; and all that is needed now in the theatre is a change in the Intendanz.

---

[7] Liszt and Cosima were Roman Catholics.

4

For the spasm of energy shown by the King during the last few weeks Wagner took a good deal of credit to himself. In a long letter of the 25th October he had warned the young man of political dangers ahead and given him some sensible advice. Ludwig, he says, has mortally offended certain powerful interests — by which are meant Sophie's family — by breaking off his engagement. These interests will now be out for revenge. The familiar technique will be put in operation again: rumours about the King's political incapacity will be set going once more as preliminaries to a demand for a regency. The public will be fed with stories of how he neglects affairs of state in order to follow his "fantastic inclinations", how he "thinks of nothing but Wagnerian operas and leaves the weightiest matters concerning the crown to be dealt with by his Cabinet Secretary as the latter chooses." Wagner passionately urges him to recognise the danger and brace himself to meet it. He must show his people, and indeed the world, what they can expect from him: he must decide upon "eine grosse Politik" and plunge in person into the fight. Wagner wants to see Bavaria great and independent; and the fact that he goes on to say that "only a strong and energetic King of Bavaria can create the conditions for realising my art-ideal" does not detract in the least from the sincerity of his exhortations to the King. He was in no way answerable for Ludwig's proneness at times to believe that the interests of art came before those of the State — this was rooted in the boy's nature before Wagner came on the scene, — and he should be given full credit for never having used his influence over the King, as thoughtless people have so long imagined he did, solely to attain his own selfish end regardless of all interests but his own. Far from craftily encouraging the enthusiastic boy in operatic "Kindereien" to the neglect of everything else, as his enemies averred, he never ceased urging him to take the duties of his office seriously, to fight against his inclination to solitude and move about more freely among his people, and so on.

Later in his letter Wagner turns to more personal affairs. He is having much trouble again, he says, with the "uncommonly gifted" but "ailing and fretful" Bülow, though he feels considerable sympathy with him in his complaints that his efforts for the "new" in

the theatre are perpetually frustrated by the partisans of the "old",
who see the personal danger they are in if the "new" should triumph.
Wagner gives a couple of concrete instances. The disposition of
the players in the orchestral pit at Munich is as irrational as that of
Dresden had been in days gone by.[8] Bülow had insisted on a fresh
arrangement: the management complies with his wishes whenever
he has to conduct, but reverts to the old senseless seating as soon as
his back is turned — merely that Lachner's face may be saved by a
show of authority. The orchestra is needlessly harried and confused by all this chopping and changing. Again, Wagner had for the
past year been training a young musician in his own methods, with
a view to placing him at some time or other in the Munich theatre.
An opportunity for this had recently presented itself; but when
Bülow broached the matter he learned that, without his having been
consulted, the post had been filled for a term of ten years. And
Wagner, as always when he could not get his own way, was very
much annoyed.

5

The young man with the recommendation from Triebschen was
Hans Richter. It is a fair conjecture that Wagner was already looking forward secretly to the time when the *Ring* would have to be
produced elsewhere than in Munich and under another conductor
than Bülow. For one thing, before *Siegfried* was finished and the
Götterdämmerung written there would inevitably be a complete
breach with Bülow over Cosima. For another thing, no one knew
better than Wagner that Bülow's gift was a purely musical one; he
had little more sense of the dramatic side of opera than Liszt had.
Weingartner said of him in later years that from the moment he
began a rehearsal

"only the orchestra seemed to exist for him; he gave no more attention to the stage than was necessary to correct musical errors. . . .
He conducted an opera as if it were a symphonic work in which the
singers' voices were merely instruments. . . . There was entirely lacking that feeling between stage and orchestra that constitutes the link
between the actuality of drama and the transcendentalism of music.

---

[8] See Vol. I, pp. 367, 467 ff.

. . . Under Bülow's baton everything proceeded on the purely musical plane. Even the most necessary interruptions by the producer made him angry." [9]

Wagner no doubt thought that in the young Richter, whose musical qualifications, he already saw, were out of the common, and whose dog-like worship of him made him promisingly plastic material, there was the making of the genuine Wagner conductor he had always longed for. (He and Cosima became a trifle disillusioned about him later at Bayreuth, but that is another story). The manuscript of the earlier pages of the full score of the first act of the *Meistersinger* had been returned to him by the engravers in such a soiled condition that he was reluctant to entrust the remainder to them, as his autograph was to go to the King. It occurred to him to keep a copyist on the premises for about six months, and he asked Schott if he could suggest a likely person for the post. Schott could not help him, but Kapellmeister Esser of Vienna recommended a young man of twenty-three — Hans Richter by name, son of a Raab conductor (already deceased) and an opera soprano who had lately taken to teaching — who had begun his musical career as a hornist in the orchestra of the Kärntherthor Theatre.

The young man arrived in Triebschen on the 30th October, 1866. (In his letter of the next day to his mother he says that Wagner half-remembered him: this suggests that they had met in Vienna). He was given a room on the second floor, with an enchanting view over the Lake; and those of us who happen to have known the lusty trencherman that was the Richter of later years are relieved to learn from his first Triebschen letter to his mother that he had been told he was free to eat and drink as much as he liked. Wagner and Cosima showed the somewhat over-awed young man every possible kindness. The size and style of the ménage impressed him; it consisted, according to his diary, of "Wagner, Baroness Bülow and the

---

[9] WL, I, 303. He once said to Albert Gutmann, "The *Meistersinger* and *Tristan*, those two master-works, will always be admired, but don't talk to me about the 'Götter-Meschpoche'. Besides, the truth that Wagner aspires to he has not attained in the music-drama. Fundamentally the sung drama will always be a great lie. The recitative drama in combination with music, the task of the latter being to illustrate the soul-states of the characters, — that is purer truth. The future belongs to melodrama." GAWM, p. 16. Gutmann explains that "Meschpoche" is Jewish for "Sippschaft" (clan, crew). Wagner's instinct had probably warned him already in the 1860's that Bülow would never do for the *Ring*.

children, Lulu, Boni, Loldi; [10] the housekeeper Vreneli; her niece Marie; the children's governess; Agnes, the nursemaid; Marie, the cook; Steffen, valet; the boots, Jost; and myself. In addition two peacocks, two cats, one horse; friends Russ and Koss [the dogs]; also a lot of mice." [11]

The "Triebschen Jean Paul", as Wagner used to call him, soon made himself *persona grata* in the house by his docility and inexhaustible willingness to oblige: he was equally ready to make music with Cosima, to amuse her and Wagner with jokes such as playing the tenor songs from the *Meistersinger* on the horn, to romp with the children and exercise the dogs, and to execute little domestic commissions in Lucerne and the neighbourhood. He worked with a will at his copying, proud to be the chosen one for such a task, and well aware that he was receiving the best initiation into practical music of any young man in Europe. By Christmas he had ingratiated himself with them all to such an extent that instead of being restricted, as at first, very much to his own quarters at the top of the house he was made one of the family. He accompanied Wagner and Cosima to Zürich on the first day of the new year to see Semper's model of the festival theatre; and when Wagner and Cosima went to Starnberg in May, Richter followed them with the two-years-old Isolde and the nursemaid. Wagner had quickly realised the musical capabilities of his young secretary, who, he further discovered, had refused a small opera post to take on the Triebschen work; and before Richter had been there a month Wagner had promised him that when the copying was finished he himself would see to it that he would not have to "go back to his horn-playing". In February, 1867 he definitely assured him that when the *Meistersinger* came to rehearsal he would be given a job in connection with it in which he would have a chance to "distinguish himself". (At that time it was planned to give the first performance of the new work in October, 1867, in honour of the King's wedding). Richter, for his part, realised from the beginning how marvellously kind the Fates had been to him in sending him to Triebschen. "Nowhere else", he wrote to his mother,

---

[10] Eva was not born until the following February.
[11] KLRWB, V, 153.

"could I have learned what I can here, under the eyes of this genius. What I have learned here will open a way for me through the whole world. . . . I am happy in the consciousness of being really liked by the greatest man of all time: my gratitude and reverence are boundless." [12]

6

Having completed the full score of the *Meistersinger* on the 24th October (1867) Wagner felt he was entitled to a little holiday. As it was too late in the year for a "cure", he decided to go to Paris for the closing days of the Exhibition. He left for France on the 28th October and returned to Triebschen on the 4th November, having seen none of his former Paris friends except Nuitter. "At the Exhibition", Glasenapp tells us,

"he was filled with pity for a poor stall-keeper who had been unable all the time to sell a splendid collection of brilliantly-coloured tropical butterflies: this Wagner bought, and it is still one of the ornaments of the big drawing-room in Wahnfried."

Such consideration for the poor exhibitor is indeed touching. We find, however, from Richter's letters *of the preceding December* to his mother, that Cosima had just commissioned him to enquire in Vienna for a collection of butterflies suitable for presentation to Wagner on his name-day, the 7th February. She would not mind going to as much as 20–30 florins for it: the case, however, would have to be handsome, as it was to stand in the drawing-room, where it would have to face the competition of costly vases and things of that sort. The collection arrived early in February; and Cosima and Wagner were so pleased with it, Richter told his mother, that they wanted, by May or June, another to balance it. The Paris purchase of the following October, then, was not quite the purely spontaneous act of pity for the poor tradesman that Glasenapp would fain make it out to be. [13]

On the 23rd December Wagner descended on Munich once more, partly to spend Christmas with Bülow and Cosima, partly to discuss with Hans the preparations for the *Meistersinger* production. His heart must have been sore within him over the drastic action of the King with regard to the *Süddeutsche Presse* articles, though on

[12] Extracts from Richter's letters of this period to his mother are given in BFF, 1938, p. 53 ff: others, from the diary kept during a second residence in Triebschen, between September, 1869 and April, 1871, will be found in KLRWB, V, 163–6.
[13] See Richter's letters to his mother, in BFF, 1938, pp. 56–58.

the 22nd Ludwig gave him a welcome proof of the continuance of his personal regard. The reader will recall that under one of the clauses of the agreement of 1864 with the Treasury for the completion of the *Ring*, Wagner was to receive an extra payment of 1,000 florins per annum for the three years ending the 1st October, 1867. The automatic cessation of this payment on that date would have reduced his yearly pension from 8,000 to 7,000 florins; but on the 22nd December the King ordered it to remain at the larger figure. After this, and in spite of his annoyance over the *Süddeutsche Presse* contretemps, it must have been with genuine gratitude in his heart that Wagner sent over to the Residenz, on the 24th, the manuscript score of the *Meistersinger* as his Christmas gift to the King.

It was on the 27th, apparently, that he had his next shock. "Düff:" we read in his "Annals": "royal warning to C. with regard to legations, etc. Next day to the King: $2\frac{1}{2}$ hours. Propitiation and apology to C." The circumstances attending this audience with the King are set forth by Cosima in a letter to him of the 29th. The 28th, she said, had been a dark day for her and for Wagner: "contrary to my habit I had lost my self-composure, and that morning I had spoken disconsolately about having to do with people like Fröbel." Wagner had tried to put heart into her, but in vain: then, sick and depressed, he had gone for a walk, choosing side streets in which he would be unlikely to meet anyone he knew; he had kept asking himself why he went on living, and had returned in poor spirits. But in the evening Düfflipp had called and carried him off to the Residenz — to a better world, as Cosima puts it. He came home again so "transfigured" that all Cosima's depression vanished into thin air. Immediately on the receipt of this letter the King wrote to her to tell her what joy and uplifting this meeting with "the dearly loved Friend" had brought him also. He begged her to "forget the recent talk with Düfflipp", to regard what the latter had said to her as unsaid. "I gladly take it all back; it was just a passing cloud that must not overcast our sun."

Dr. Strobel's comment on all this is that

"after the royal veto on the continuance of *German Art and German Policy* in the *Süddeutsche Presse*, Fröbel . . . had been at odds with Wagner, and in his long-developing antagonism to him had at last gone so far as to denounce Cosima to the King, accusing her of political machinations."

In the absence at present of positive evidence that Fröbel was the cause of the trouble it may be prudent to suspend judgment on that point. But whoever the mischief-maker may have been — and Cosima had many enemies besides Fröbel — it is clear enough that she was suspected, rightly or wrongly, of indiscreet talk about politics with some members of the various foreign legations in Munich. The chief interest of the episode, however, lies in the fact that it perhaps justifies our taking a different view from the one that has hitherto prevailed as to the meaning of the word *Pressschmiererei* in the King's letter of the 13th December to Düfflipp.[14]

7

Let us look again at the wording of that letter of Ludwig's. "Your letter reached me this evening. It is as if I had fallen from the clouds. This refined, intelligent Frau von Bülow occupies herself with scribbling for the Press! She writes these dreadful articles! Really, I should not have thought the cultivated Cosima capable of a piece of knavery of this sort." Wagner biographers and historians of Bavaria alike have always assumed that these words applied to the *German Art and German Policy* articles. But they were ignorant of the passage quoted above from Wagner's "Annals" and from the King's letter to Cosima of the 29th December, which between them put a different complexion on the matter now. To Düfflipp the King speaks of Cosima's devoting herself to *Pressschmiererei*. Now how, we may ask, could Ludwig possibly have applied that description to the *Süddeutsche Presse* articles, even in a fit of exasperation with Cosima and Wagner? How could he possibly describe as "dreadful" the very articles he had been praising so warmly week by week until, for some reason or other, he thought it impolitic to allow the fourteenth of the series to be printed? Let us recall that in his rescript to the editor of the paper the criticism of the articles had not been that they were contemptible "journalistic scribblings" but that they were "suicidal". The historians may well have felt themselves to be up against an insoluble problem when they tried to account for so amazing a volte-face on the King's

---

[14] See *supra*, p. 34.

part.[15] But the difficulty vanishes if, guided by the fresh documents now available, we apply the King's contemptuous words *not to Wagner's Süddeutsche Presse articles at all*, but to certain others of the baser sort which must have recently appeared in the German Press — not necessarily in Munich, or even in Bavaria — and which local gossip not merely traced to Cosima's contacts with the diplomatic world — hence the sentence in the "Annals" about the "royal admonition to Cosima with regard to legations, etc." — but actually attributed to her pen. Not only is there no mention, or even a hint, of his *German Art and German Politics* articles in Wagner's note in the "Annals" but there is no hint of these either in the King's letter to Cosima of the 29th or in her reply of the same day. If an apology were due to Cosima for the ascription of these articles to her and for the King's plain expression of contempt for them, surely one was equally due to Wagner?

What had happened on the 28th December is evident enough: for the moment, though perhaps only for the moment, Ludwig had been, as usual, reduced to helplessness by Wagner's personal magnetism. Always, he told Cosima directly after the meeting at the Residenz, after "the Dear One" left him he felt as if a god had been with him, blessing him with his magic power. And finding him in this melting mood, Cosima, with, of course, Wagner looking over her shoulder as she wrote, tried to make the most of her momentary

[15] Ludwig's latest biographer, Werner Richter (*Ludwig II. König von Bayern* (1939), pp. 192–3), after remarking that the King's "sudden change of opinion" with regard to Wagner's articles has never been explained, asks, "Was it Wagner's glorification of Prussia — scarcely a year after the war, and in the subsidised Bavarian journal — that revolted Ludwig, or his discussion of what France 'owed' to the Revolution? Or was it his generally pungent criticism of the German princes?" The first and third of these hypotheses are negatived by the King's letters to Wagner and Cosima of mid-November. It is evident from these that he was delighted with the criticism of the German rulers. Again, such "glorification" of Prussia as Wagner had indulged in had appeared in the second and fourth articles, both of which had been published in October; yet as late as near the end of November the King has nothing but praise for Wagner. The dissertation on the French Revolution — which, according to Wagner, had so disciplined the French that they had become the first military power in Europe, — would presumably have been in the King's hands before his enthusiastic letter of the 21st November to Wagner. If he was outraged by opinions such as these, why did he wait another month before taking action?

Glasenapp misleadingly assures his readers that the King's "real" view of the articles was that expressed in his glowing letter of the 21st November to Wagner. Apparently Glasenapp was reluctant to face squarely the plain unpalatable fact that between that date and the 19th December the King had for some reason or other arrived at quite another "real" view.

tactical advantage. She sent Ludwig the two suppressed *Süddeutsche Presse* articles (Nos. 14 and 15), which he had not yet seen. She enclosed with them what she described as the "base" paragraph in which Fröbel — assuming, according to her, that Wagner was in "disgrace" — had announced the suspension of the articles. It would have been so simple, she contended, for him merely to have stopped publication, without "publicly insulting" the friend whom he had hitherto flattered; in saying which she conveniently forgot her own and Wagner's previous lavish flattery of Fröbel to his face when he had looked like being their docile tool. She now suggests that Hohenlohe shall tell Fröbel, "in the King's name", that the series is to be completed. Fröbel "will naturally decline", for he has committed himself publicly too deeply; "and this will furnish a plausible excuse for getting rid of a man whose miserable nature petrifies me." It would give her the greatest pleasure to see him punished, she confesses. And she urges the King to read the two new articles, though, reverting to her usual technique of flattery and calculated humility where he is concerned, she protests that all this advice of hers is offered "in childlike, artless fashion", "always with the reservation that the King's will is invariably mine." That Fröbel, as she conjectures, has made accusations against *her* she can easily forgive; "but what he has done to the Friend [Wagner] is of a sort that makes all other basenesses seem negligible."

8

Cornelius (now happily married) saw Wagner more than once during his stay in Munich, and found him generally in good humour, though he seemed to tire quickly. On the whole, things seemed to be going well with him and his cause. He had consolidated his financial position. The King had promised to establish Semper and Liszt in Munich, the latter as a sort of director of Catholic church music. (Neither plan, as it happened, was realised). Wilhelm Schmitt had been pensioned off in November, and Baron Perfall, till then Intendant of the Court Music, was made provisional Intendant of the Theatre.[16] Wagner, Cosima and Bülow all sang Perfall's praises at that time: Wagner and Cosima became much less enthusiastic about him later. January, 1868 saw the end of Lach-

---

[16] See Vol. III, p. 315 *note*.

ner's long connection with the Munich theatre. Hans Richter, who, his work on the *Meistersinger* score finished, had said good-bye to Triebschen at the beginning of December, by the end of that month had been made chorus and solo coach at the Opera, no doubt as the result of Wagner's personal intervention with the King at their meeting on the 28th. When Wagner left Munich for Triebschen on the 8th February, 1868, then, he had a good deal on which to congratulate himself. But it rankled in him that Ludwig would not yield to him in the Fröbel matter: and this, one conjectures, was the prime cause of the estrangement that manifestly sprang up between them at this time. There is a gap of more than three months in their correspondence — from the end of November, 1867 to the second week of the following March, — while during Wagner's seven weeks' stay in Munich he and his royal Friend had met only once.

That something had gone wrong between them is clear both from the letter of the 9th March (1868), in which the King at last breaks the silence, and from Wagner's reply of the 12th. Ludwig begs for news of him. It is "martyrdom" not to see him or hear from him. Would that he himself could spend a few days in Triebschen in the coming summer, or Wagner visit him in Hohenschwangau in the autumn! Above all he is longing for the *Meistersinger,* and he still has not given up hope as regards the Semper festival theatre. His heart aches for the consolation and support that only his idol can give him: his burden is not a light one, "alone in the loveless, empty, desolate world". This was a dangerous tone in which to address Wagner; it gave him an all too confident feeling of the weakness of the defences through which he had to make his way. His reply is one of his literary masterpieces. He poetises and dramatises them both; and in his opening sentence —

"O my King, my wondrous Friend, Wherefore this to me? Why waken the old hopeful chords of my soul, that should have died into silence? 'Once upon a time' — that is the troubled song that alone can resound within me now"

—he lays upon the suffering young man the whole burden of the guilt for the present coolness between them.

His letter is one long reproach, none the less hard for the King to bear for the artfully-conveyed suggestion throughout that it is Wagner whose spirit is really broken beyond repair, though his capacity for patient endurance and for extending forgiveness to those who have injured him is still without limit. The end of all things has come for him; nothing remains to him on this weary earthly pilgrimage of his but "the last renunciation". His world, such as it ever was, lies in ruins about him; and the ruin has been wrought by the failure of his hopes for the King. What avails all that Ludwig has done to make his mere worldly existence tolerable for him? His will to create has been lamed; and if he does not complete his work, not for much longer will he need the fine things with which the King's generosity has embellished his useless existence: "a cottage will suffice to house the wrecked remnants of my life". Not, of course, that he is reproaching the young man in any way: on the contrary, he will bless his name to his last breath. What grieves him to the depths of his soul is the revelation that his blessing can no longer save the King, that he must abandon all hope for him since he himself destroys his own salvation, Wagner's warning voice being projected only into a vacuum. His self-pity knows no bounds: "why", he asks, spinning a denser and denser web of words about himself, and luxuriating, like the artist he is, in the poetic ring of them,

> "why do you now break in upon my silence, wakening in me again the old intoxicating hopeful chords which I would fain hear no more, since if I am to hope, my hope could have no other reason than that I hope *for you*, for whom I must hope no more."

The root cause of the tragedy is, he contends, that Ludwig could never see the world through *his* eyes. The King has disappointed him. Wagner's dream had been of his mission to help "the German world-ash-tree, the marvellous tree of the Norns", to spread its vast leafage "over all feeling human hearts". The god had seemed to send him the youthful hero who should bring the new sap of spring into that ancient tree. And it would have been so easy for the hero! He was young, he was a King, everything lay in his power, everybody was at his feet. A child could have told him what to do — to show the whole world what he is and bend it to his magic. But the potential hero *would* not; and the old serpent, taking new heart, has gnawed at the roots of the tree. And so on. It is Wotan reproving Brynhilde for having dared to flout his will.

The peccant Valkyrie in the opera had at least the spirit to question the wisdom of the god and the justice of her punishment:

Was it so shameful,
what I have done,
that my offence must so shamefully be scourged?
Was it so base,
this deed that I wrought,
that such debasement for me thou dost shape?
Was what I did
so full of dishonour
that it robs me of honour for aye?
O say, father!
Look in my eyes then:
silence thy rage,
master thy wrath,
make clearer to me
the hidden guilt,
that thou setst thy face like a stone,
and dost turn from thy favourite child.

Poor Ludwig took his chiding and his chastisement more humbly. There was a time, he says sorrowfully, when his words could heal Wagner's wounds: have they now lost their old power? But he knows that what he was in the beginning he still is — chosen for Wagner by God.

"Could I only convince you of the real condition of things! I know this infamous Press, through which you hear these detestable lies and calumnies about me. Woe to me if at the time I had let myself be misled by what I heard about you. I merely followed the inward voice that led me to salvation. My faith remains firm: O God, it is impossible that you should despair of me!"

He is humble enough to admit that he *had* been weak, had not asserted himself as he should have done. But, he pleads, in words that show that the old heartache is now perilously near becoming heartbreak, the Friend does not realise the difficulties of his position.

"O my Friend, rosy appeared the world to me in those days: I thought men noble. Since then I have endured such unspeakably bitter experiences that it became impossible for me to embrace this utterly wretched world in love. I could only feel myself repelled by those devilish souls when I came to know them. Well-founded was my hatred and contempt for humanity: only in myself, and above all by sinking myself in our ideals, could I find solace and elevation. I shrank within myself,

[125]

for the horrible outside world filled me with loathing and shame. Now all this is over: it was a cleansing process, an episode in my life. I am strengthened; I will forget and forgive the horrible things done to me, will throw myself bravely into life, earnestly do my duty, go the right road, which I know full well; for clearly do I recognise my great task, which, believe me, I will faithfully and conscientiously perform. . . . I will tear fiercely at the Friend's heart until the wall that separates us falls down, the gloomy veil drifts away from between us. I know you will forgive the dark way of thinking into which I fell, for God knows there was reason for it."

But Wagner must believe again in his chosen one, and take heart afresh and not let his great work collapse in ruin. That would be something the King could not endure and live.

9

There can be little doubt that the head and front of Ludwig's latest offending had been his refusal to rehabilitate Wagner publicly after the loss of "face" he had undergone by the suppression of the last two *German Art and German Policy* articles. We have seen Cosima taking advantage of the King's apology to her at the end of December to send him the manuscript of these two articles, suggesting that Hohenlohe should command "in the King's name" the printing of them in the *Süddeutsche Presse*, and that if Fröbel refused to do so he should be dismissed. This would be "a just and salutary punishment". But Ludwig was deaf to her blandishments. He took a fortnight to reply to Cosima's letter; and when he did, on the 12th January, he merely said that he had read the articles "with lively interest" and now returned them to her "with cordial thanks". Thereupon Wagner himself must have sent them to Hohenlohe, for in one of his *Bayreuther Blätter* articles of 1879 — *Shall we hope?* — he informed his readers, à propos of his hopes in 1867 that the German aristocracy would play their part in the regeneration of the German folk-spirit, that

"a former head of the Bavarian Government, Prince Chlodwig Hohenlohe, who was very well disposed towards me, told me that he would not have been able to find ten members of that class to enter into my ideas." [17]

---

[17] RWGS, X, 120. The ironic tinge in Hohenlohe's words had evidently escaped Wagner: it would never occur to one so possessed with a sense of his political mission as he was that other people could take him something less than seriously. From first

As it was in the fourteenth and fifteenth articles that these ideas were set forth, it was obviously these he had sent to Hohenlohe in the hope of enlisting his support against Fröbel.

His assault had thus failed all along the line; and, as usual when he was frustrated, he saw red and thirsted for vengeance. It never occurred to him even as a remote possibility that the King might have had excellent reasons of state for not taking the same view of the articles as he did. In the blindness of his egocentricism he could see no reason for any institution continuing to exist except as an instrument for furthering his own ends of German regeneration through the theatre; while the last weakness of which he would have been capable would be to doubt his own plenipotential capacity to give monarchs and ministers lessons in statecraft. In his view the King's failure to rehabilitate him and crush Fröbel was due to "weakness". In this he deceived himself. It was because of the King's strength of mind and character that he quietly insisted on seeing matters political through purely political eyes: the weaker side of him came into evidence only whenever, out of his passion for his and Wagner's ideal, he abased himself before the Master in an agony of grief for having hurt him. But it has to be noted that for all his pain at having had to cross him frequently in practical matters he very rarely gives way to him.[18] Wagner had reached the point at which he sincerely believed that Bavaria and the Wittelsbach monarchy between them had produced Ludwig II solely that he might do *his* work: a Queen, he once said grandiloquently, had to bear this wonder for him — for *him!* It was a point of view in which Ludwig himself, in his moonshine moments, was inclined to encourage him; but it was not a point of view which Bavaria as a whole could be expected to share.

10

The interchange of letters cleared the air for the time being. But the old clash between idealism and reality soon began again. The

to last it never seemed to have dawned on him that political and social problems are primarily matters not of words but of hard realities. Every German social and political problem could be solved in the twinkling of an eye, he thought, if only the "princes" could be got to do their historic duty to the "Folk".

[18] It was just at this time that Hohenlohe told the Prussian General von Stosch that the King was "the strangest blend of complete ignorance of real life and very great intellectual capacity." BLKB, p. 257.

plan for bringing Liszt to Munich had come to nothing. Towards
the end of March the trouble with Semper came to a head: tired of
being chivvied from pillar to post, the great architect threatened
legal proceedings if his claim for payment for the work he had
done was not met.[19] And about the same time Wagner was called
upon by a Munich court of justice to settle at once his twenty-one-
years-old debt to Frau Klepperbein of Dresden or undergo arrest.[20]
As Wagner was in Munich just then, arrest would have been easy.[21]
He arrived there on the evening of the 17th March; and on the next
day Frau Klepperbein's lawyer, in default of payment, applied to
the court for an order for his apprehension. Wagner had to send in
hot haste to Düfflipp to help him out of his difficulty. The secretarial
office apparently being closed, Düfflipp advanced Wagner the 2,200
florins required out of his own funds. Thanking him on the 21st,
Wagner suggests repayment by the withholding of his allowance on
the three quarter-days November 1st, February 1st (1869) and
May 1st; and he hopes it will not be necessary to trouble the King
with any knowledge of "this disagreeable experience". It had been
only a few days before that he had been reproaching Ludwig, in
his best Wotan style, for having brought their ideal down in ruins:
it would never have done for Brynhilde, bowing her head to take
her chastisement for having flouted the god's will, to have raised
her reverent eyes and seen Fafner and Fasolt presenting a warrant
for Wotan's arrest in connection with that little matter of payment
for the building of Valhalla. But Wagner was not spared that crown-
ing humiliation. As it was not within Düfflipp's official competence
to order payment of the sum by the Treasury he had no alternative
but to inform the King of the circumstances and get his sanction for
what had been done. On the 27th Ludwig formally authorised an
advance to "the tone-poet Richard Wagner" of 2,200 florins against
his stipend.[22]

The precise reason for Wagner's visit to Munich at this time is
not clear: it may possibly have had something to do with the triangle. Judging from the brief reference to it in the "Annals", the

---

[19] See Vol. III, p. 435.
[20] See Vol. III, p. 437.
[21] This perhaps gives us the key to an entry in the "Annals": "C. warns against
return to Munich."
[22] Since the account of the matter in Vol. III of the present Life was written,
further details have been given in the fifth volume of KLRWB, p. 260.

King regarded this fresh appearance of the composer in Munich as less a visit than a visitation; "My coming seems to surprise the King. I neither see him nor hear from him" — this although it had been only on the 16th that Ludwig had written his sorrowful, penitent letter in response to Wagner's chiding of him. From Munich Wagner wrote him on the 21st, promising that *Siegfried* would be completed before the year's end, again on the 30th, saying that owing to difficulties of casting it would be impossible to produce the *Meistersinger* that spring as had been planned, and once more on the 17th April, on which evening *Lohengrin* was to be given. The King, owing to a sickness that confined him to his bed, was unable to be present at the performance, — a gala one in honour of the Crown Prince Friedrich of Prussia, who was spending a couple of days in Munich en route to Italy. (Ludwig's illness may have been, in part at any rate, of the diplomatic order: he had no great liking for the Prussian soldier-prince, who stood for everything in life and in politics that was repugnant to him).[23] Wagner suggested that he should run over to the Residenz that evening, to celebrate *Lohengrin* with his royal Friend and bring him a gift from Cosima. The King, however, briefly excused himself, sent him the usual affectionate greetings, expressed a hope that the difficulties in the way of the *Meistersinger* would soon be overcome, and wished him goodnight. It looks as though, having only just recovered from one exhausting attack of Wagner fever, he did not wish to run the risk of another.

In a letter of a month or so later, written after Wagner's return to Triebschen, the King casually mentions that he has it in mind to reconstruct the ancient castle ruins by the Pollat gorge. "The situation is one of the finest to be found anywhere", he says, "inaccessible, inviolable." There will be several guest chambers, one of them for Wagner. The new castle will be "a temple worthy of the godlike Friend" who alone can bring salvation and blessing to

[23] The Crown Prince had several talks with the bed-ridden King. He has left it on record that these conversations touched on every subject under the sun — except Bavaria, Prussia and Germany, which, of course, were the topics the Crown Prince really wanted to talk about! We see the young King, who is generally written down as a nincompoop, once more using the technique he so often drew upon to get him out of a difficulty with Wagner — retiring into his shell, letting the other man do the talking, wearing discussion down by evasion or killing it by downright mutism, and emerging from his shell again, as if nothing had happened, when the discouraged assailant had retired.

mankind; it will be in every way finer and more commodious than Hohenschwangau, "which is profaned every year by my mother's prose". Though neither he nor Wagner knew it at the time, this was an omen. It is the foreshadowing of the passion for building that was to bring Ludwig to ruin less than twenty years later; and it clearly links up on the one hand with the recognition that his heart's desire of a magnificent festival theatre in Munich would never be realised now, and on the other hand with the feeling that as he and the world would never understand each other his only hope of making existence tolerable for himself was by creating not merely a spiritual but a physical solitude about him, through which the world's coarse voice and clumsy fingers would be unable to reach. It was always dangerous to drive him too far, as even Wagner was to discover to his cost before long: there invariably came a point where, tired of yielding ground, and flaming with anger against those who thought they could play illimitably upon his ardours or his weaknesses, he took a stand from which no power on earth could move him.

CHAPTER VII

THE *MEISTERSINGER* YEAR

1

THE ENGRAVING of the orchestral and vocal scores of the *Meister-singer* had been completed by the spring of 1868, not before Franz Schott had passed through many anxious hours. He had contracted with Wagner for the work as long ago as 1862, and had made him substantial payments in advance of delivery of the manuscript. He was reluctant to start printing before the whole manuscript was in his hands; apart from the possibility of Wagner's dying before he had finished the work, there was no knowing when the final page of the huge score would be delivered to him. Wagner characteristically told the worried publisher that he had no one to blame for his troubles but himself: had Schott financed him for another ten or twelve months in the Biebrich days, as Wagner had suggested in 1862, the score would have been finished three years ago, he wrote the poor man in 1867! "It was unfortunate, God knows, that you didn't do the right thing!" Schott could only cross himself and hope that Wagner's confidence that this would be the most successful of all his works would be justified by events.

Wagner certainly took the most businesslike pains to give the opera a good start. He had an idea for two piano scores — one that would show something like the real texture of the music so far as the piano could reproduce it, the other a much simplified one — "musically superficial", as he put it — for the use of "singers, conductors, choir trainers, stage managers and so on", which throws an interesting light on his opinion of the musical capacity of some of these people. In the end this benevolent scheme was dropped, only the "real" piano score, made by Tausig, being published. Wagner further suggested the issue of a number of "morceaux detachés" from the opera, for which he would provide suitable introductions and endings where necessary: fourteen of these actually appeared, and no doubt did a good deal towards lightening Schott's enormous expenses in connection with the engraving of what was unquestionably the biggest operatic score yet issued.

The casting of the work for Munich was not accomplished without considerable difficulty. Wagner had set his heart on obtaining Johann Beck [1] from Vienna for the part of Sachs; his other first selections were Swoboda (Vienna) for David, and Gustav Hölzel (also of Vienna) for Beckmesser. As he could not visualise Vogl as the "aristocratic, ardent, poetic" Walther von Stolzing [2] he was forced to look outside Munich for a player of the part. For a while he thought he had found his man in Bachmann, of Dresden, but the Intendant of the Dresden Opera refused to release him for the weeks when Munich would need him. In the end the choice fell upon Franz Nachbaur, of Darmstadt. Negotiations with most of the other singers fell through for this reason or that; but the cast finally chosen was about as good as any other that Germany could have offered Wagner just then. Franz Betz, of Berlin, who had sung Kurvenal in the Munich performance of *Tristan* in 1867, became the Sachs; Nachbaur the Walther; Schlosser, of Augsburg, the David; Hölzel the Beckmesser; Bausewein the Pogner; Mathilde Mallinger the Eva; and Frau Dietz, a veteran of the Munich Theatre, the Magdalena. Richter spent some time in Darmstadt coaching Nachbaur. Franz Seitz, the costume designer of the Munich Theatre, took infinite pains, under Wagner's direction, to secure historical accuracy in the costumes. The designing of the scenery was shared between the Court Theatre painters Quaglio, Jank and Döll. The ballet mistress, Lucille Grahn, of whom Wagner appears to have thought highly, was entrusted with the working out of the complicated movements of the crowd at the end of the second act. The machinist of the

---

[1] It was in connection with Beck that Wagner used, apparently for the only time in his life, the expression "creating the part". (See Vol. III, p. 6).

[2] See Wagner's letter of the 30th March to the King. He calls Vogl "a thoroughly incompetent singer". In NNS will be found an unsparing exposure of the early Vogl's shortcomings. Nohl, writing in 1867, is discussing the *Lohengrin* performances of that year in which Vogl had been substituted for Tichatschek. According to Nohl, the young tenor's only asset was a powerful voice. Vogl, a man of plebeian origin, had been an elementary school teacher; and Nohl is rudely contemptuous of his intellectual quality, such as it was. He blames "an exceedingly incompetent Theatre Intendanz" for pandering as it has done to the self-esteem of a beginner who has everything to learn in the matter of acting, psychological characterisation, and so forth. "The lack of culture characteristic of his former environment has unfortunately continued in the new sphere in which the Herr Schoolmaster has arrived after so sudden a success; indeed, it almost seems to have increased." NNS, p. 262. This tallies with what Wagner has to say about the impossibility of Vogl as Walther.

Darmstadt Theatre, Karl Brandt, was called in to deal with the formidable new problems presented by the opera; and the general stage management was entrusted to Dr. Reinhard Hallwachs, imported from Stuttgart. All in all, the Munich Theatre provided little of the personnel for the production apart from the orchestra and the chorus. Each of these was enlarged for the occasion, the orchestra numbering ninety.

2

Because Wagner himself was often there to initiate the singers into the psychology of their parts the acting rose to something like the level of his desires; and as early as the beginning of June he could assure Franz Schott that the production would be "masterly in every respect". For himself he never had the least doubt that the new work was going to be a great success. "Remember this", he had written the anxious Schott in December, 1866;

> "against me I have the professional musicians and journalists, for reasons that are quite obvious to me; what I have for me is the genuine public, and, happily, the biggest public, that of the theatre,"

— an ironic comment on the absurd doctrine that has been too long current, that "Wagner, like every other great composer, was not appreciated during his lifetime".[3] Even before the *Meistersinger* saw the light some of the other German theatres were competing for the honour and profit of the first production after that in Munich: Vienna proposed to open its new opera house with it. It lay in the nature of the case that none of the theatres proved able to produce the difficult work as quickly as they had hoped. For one thing, its length was against it; only a month after the first performance in Munich we find Wagner telling Schott, à propos of some recent experiences of his with Dresden, that he has decided not to insist on performances without cuts in the German theatres in general, "for reasons that are not flattering to the theatres, principally be-

---

[3] It is true that in the Foreword to the second edition of *Opera and Drama* he indulges himself in the luxury of a lament over "the little inward worth of my successes with the theatrical public". But that merely means that the public had not taken his *ideological* intentions as seriously as he thought it should have done. By the very fact of saying that his successes were "grounded on a misconception" he admits, at any rate, the successes.

cause my refusal to give way would necessarily involve me in personal labours which I must carefully avoid." [4]

3

The preparations for the *Meistersinger*, arduous as they were, did not represent the whole of Wagner's activities during the spring and early summer of 1868. In March he wrote a Foreword to his *German Art and German Politics* articles, which he was about to reprint in book form. A month later he drafted a dedication to Konstantin Frantz of a new edition of *Opera and Drama* which had at last been called for after some seventeen years. It appears from this dedicatory epistle that at the very time when Wagner was making the acquaintance of Frantz's writings on Germany, the famous political publicist in his turn was beginning to take an interest in Wagner the artist-thinker. "Who", the latter writes,

"can measure the significance of my joyful amazement when, with full understanding, you cried out to me from the so grievously misunderstood central point of my book, '*Your* Downfall of the State is the Founding of *my* German Empire!' . . . And in this *German Spirit* which has so surprisingly brought us two together, starting as we did from the uttermost opposites of the ordinary view, in the deeply-felt recognition of the grand vocation of our Folk, we may now well believe with strengthened courage."

The reader will recall that the first of the *Süddeutsche Presse* articles had opened with a quotation from Frantz's *Inquiry into the European Balance of Power* (1859) in which the "mission" of Germany to substitute a "nobler culture" for the "materialistic civilisa-

---

[4] The following are the dates of some of the first productions of the work after that of Munich:

Dresden:	21 January,	1869.
Dessau:	29 January,	1869.
Karlsruhe:	5 February,	1869.
Mannheim:	5 March,	1869.
Weimar:	28 November,	1869.
Hanover:	26 February,	1870.
Vienna:	27 February,	1870.
Berlin:	1 April,	1870.
Leipzig:	6 December,	1870.
Prague:	26 April,	1871.

For the projected Hanover, Leipzig and Prague performances the theatres, in 1868, could think of no one for the part of Walther but the indefatigable, undiscourageable Tichatschek!

tion" of the French was declared. During recent years Wagner had been growing more and more nationalistic in his thinking, partly, no doubt, through his preoccupation with the *Meistersinger*.

The *Recollections of Ludwig Schnorr von Carolsfeld*, written in May 1868,[5] were a more purely personal matter. It was in April that he told the King of his plan to re-issue all his poems and prose writings in ten volumes. He was contemplating also, he said, a book in which the profounder philosophic problems bearing upon music, tentatively discussed by Schopenhauer, were to be investigated. This, we can now see, was the germ of the *Beethoven* of two years later. From the sketch in the "Brown Book" of the plan for a complete edition of his works we gather that at that time he intended the tenth volume to consist of extracts from his autobiography.

4

From his visit to Munich in March he had returned to Triebschen in the third week of April. A month later he was in the capital again, this time to take seriously in hand the preparations for the *Meistersinger*. The 22nd May, his fifty-fifth birthday, he spent with the King on the Roseninsel. Apparently he found the young man's *Schwärmerei* something more than he could digest just then in anything but small doses; for on the 28th we find him begging, for all their sakes, that he shall be left to devote all his energies to his work in the theatre. He had once more that strange feeling, familiar to him since at least the *Tannhäuser* period, and seemingly recurring whenever he had either the composition or the production of a new work in hand, that death would overtake him before the task was done. For the rest, he promises the King a practically perfect performance of the *Meistersinger*. Now that he has seen Betz at close quarters he realises that he was predestined for Sachs and Wotan. Nachbaur pleases him more and more each day. The Mallinger will be an enchanting Eva: she is talented and unspoiled. Nothing can be found in all Germany to equal the Beckmesser of Hölzel in originality.

"Everything, everything is as it should be; there won't be the smallest thing that jars. And everyone concerned is filled with such zeal, yea, enthusiasm, that each rehearsal is a festival."

[5] See *supra*, p. 19.

Seldom, he says in a further letter, can the creator of a new and difficult work have been lucky enough to meet with such competent performers and so much good will. He is pleased with everyone and everything — with the scenery, with the highly intelligent and zealous Hallwachs, whose services he hopes to enlist again at some future date, and with Richter, for whom he suggests a higher appointment after the performance. (Richter became a "Musikdirektor" on the following 1st September). All that is necessary now is for the amiable and willing but not particularly gifted new Intendant, Perfall, to be stimulated by a talking to from the King himself.

Wagner does not mention Bülow, probably because *his* competence and industry and his admiration of what he called the fine Cellini-like craftsmanship of the *Meistersinger* score were never for a moment in doubt. But he would not have been Hans von Bülow had he not had an occasional attack of nerves or fit of depression. It seems to have been during the earlier stages of the preparation of the work that during a rehearsal in his house, happening to turn the pages of the composer's manuscript score, he came upon a photograph of Wagner with the little Eva. He left the room to conceal his emotion. It was after one of the later rehearsals with piano that Wagner noted in his "Annals", "Depressing sense of profound hostility and alienation on the part of Hans"; followed, in June, by "Orchestral rehearsals: great trouble with H." He and Hans and Cosima must have often felt at this time that the final solution of their problem could hardly be delayed much longer; and matters were probably not improved by Bülow's mother, who detested Cosima, choosing just this time to come and stay with her son.

5

They were a nervy crew at the best of times, and it is little wonder that all of them, Wagner in particular, sometimes found the strain rather more than they could stand. Judging from the "Annals", Wagner seems to have found cause for exasperation in something Cornelius had done or had not done. Another trial to him was Weissheimer — now a conductor in Würzburg — who had come to Munich partly to hear the *Meistersinger*, partly to get an opera of his, *Theodor Körner*, accepted by the Munich management. Even the fact that he had received financial favours at this young man's hands in the days of his need might not of itself have been sufficient to prejudice Wagner against him. But he had other reasons than resentment over benefits conferred for being annoyed with Weissheimer just then. Like all composers of the second to the twenty-second order, Weissheimer was passionately anxious to confer the fruits of his inspiration on a world reluctant to deprive him of the exclusive enjoyment of them, and he firmly believed in the duty of other composers, who happened to have had the luck to "arrive", to "do something for him". Unfortunately Wagner never took very much interest even in good contemporary composers, and was utterly indifferent, if not positively inimical, to the mediocre ones. He was incapable of Liszt's facile insincerity in these matters; it was torture to him to have to listen to the music of these people, and he saw no particular reason why he should undergo that torture.

But in days gone by he had irresponsibly recommended Weissheimer here and there, with the benevolent intention of doing the young man a good turn without having to undergo the ordeal of becoming intimately acquainted with his music. When, therefore, Weissheimer found it impossible to get him to listen to the *Körner* score in Munich, he was not unnaturally puzzled and hurt; as he plaintively put it, if Wagner could speak well of his music without having heard it, why should it be so difficult to get him to listen to it now he had the chance to do so? Moreover, when Wagner heard that Weissheimer had been manœuvring for an audience of the King in order to beg him to command the production of his opera in the Court Theatre, he not only warned the young composer against tactless moves of this kind but offered himself as intermediary in the matter. And so, when it turned out that he himself had no real intention of doing anything as regards either the King or the Theatre — and obviously he was right in refraining from interfering in an affair in which neither Ludwig nor Perfall would have welcomed his interference — once more Weissheimer felt, not altogether without reason, that he had a grievance against him.

Weissheimer was not one of Germany's leading intellects, and he undoubtedly took himself too seriously as a composer. A man quicker in the uptake would have seen that it was unreasonable to expect the composer of a *Meistersinger*, at present engaged several hours a day in the rehearsal of the glorious work, to take a passionate interest in a *Theodor Körner*. Only a saint would have been capable of that, and even he would probably have been only pretending. But all the same Weissheimer does not quite deserve the malicious handling — prompted, one suspects, by Cosima — he receives in the pages of Glasenapp. It is true that some of the statements in his memoirs are erroneous and others doubtful; few men's memories can be trusted with regard to events that happened thirty years or more before the time when they sit down to record them, and Weissheimer's memory was no better than the average in this respect. But for our knowledge of this particular episode we are not dependent upon the caprices of his memory: the story is told in full in his contemporary letters to his wife. He certainly had some sort of a case against Wagner, who should either have done something for him or told him outright that he could do nothing, instead of leading him to expect his friendly co-operation and then side-stepping him. But anyone less self-absorbed than Weissheimer was would have seen that Wagner was ill, fretted and overworked, and would have forborne to press his own claim to consideration just then.

The main trouble, as always, was that it was virtually impossible for Wagner to do a disagreeable but necessary thing tactfully; his practice when pushed a bit too far was to lose his temper and become rude. The result was that all Weissheimer's friends thought him rather badly treated. Heinrich Porges, who certainly could not be accused of lack of loyalty to Wagner, told Weissheimer that he would never have believed that Wagner could behave in such off-hand fashion towards him. Cornelius, meeting the composer on his way to lunch at Bülow's house (where Wagner was staying), warned him solemnly that he was "going to his *Henkersmahl*" (the last meal of a man condemned to death). When the other asked him what he meant, Cornelius merely replied, "You'll see!" Weissheimer was present when Bülow was indiscreet enough to show Wagner the score of his own music to *Julius Caesar*, and heard poor Hans take a vow afterwards that he would never do anything of the sort again. One day he and Bülow, at the latter's suggestion, were going through the score of *Körner* together when the maidservant came in with a request that they would stop playing the piano, as "the Meister wanted to sleep". "It was eleven in the morning!" says Weissheimer. "Bülow closed the piano and jumped up in exasperation, saying,

'It is a high honour to me to live with the great Meister, but sometimes it is more than one can put up with!' "

Weissheimer himself, writing to his wife on the 7th June, said that everyone agreed that during the last three years Wagner had "changed for the worse"; he himself "hardly recognised him this year". Draeseke, who had come to Munich for the *Meistersinger*, seems to have expressed the general opinion when he said,

> "It isn't exactly pleasant to have anything to do with him at present; but later, say in thirty or forty years, the whole world will envy us, for he is a gigantic phenomenon that will loom larger and larger after his death, more especially as the great image cannot be disfigured then by any more perverse traits."

It all ended with Weissheimer going back to Würzburg in a huff, convinced, according to Bülow (in a letter to Pohl), that "Wagner was jealous of him and had intrigued against his *Körner*. What do you think of that?"

6

The favoured few who attended the *Meistersinger* rehearsals saw clearly that a new era was being inaugurated not only in operatic creation but in operatic production. The work differed from all Wagner's previous ones in its rapid succession of stage incidents of the most varied kind, for each of which an appropriate movement or gesture had to be taught the actors, and the correspondence brought out between word and tone and miming on the stage and the lines and colours of the orchestra. Wagner alone could solve the thousand problems of this sort that presented themselves. Fortunately, in spite of his fatigue, he was almost invariably in the best of moods in the theatre, often obtaining his end not only by the most extraordinary patience but by irresistible charm of manner. Contemporary evidence unanimously agrees that had he chosen to take to the stage — a career for which his voice and stature unfitted him — he would have been the greatest actor in Europe. One incident in particular seems to have remained vivid for a long time after in the minds of those who witnessed it. Hölzel did not satisfy him in the episode in the second act in which Beckmesser, exasperated beyond endurance by Sachs's interruptions of his serenade,

turns on the cobbler "with the utmost fury", as the stage direction
has it:

Oh, you vile child of the devil!
This trick's the last I'll stand from you!
Silence, or by all that's evil
I swear I'll beat you black and blue.

To show Hölzel what he wanted here, Wagner sprang at Sachs "like
a tiger", says Nohl; and Hölzel, a man of the same age as Wagner,
could come nowhere near reproducing that convulsive leap.

He seems to have met with the utmost devotion from everyone in
the company with the exception of two or three members of the
orchestra, of whom the most offensive was the boorish hornist
Strauss,[6] taking advantage, as usual, of his economic independence
to insult his intellectual betters. There is a good deal in the German
journalism of that epoch of which one cannot approve, but the licence allowed it at all events permitted it to call a spade a spade
when occasion required; and it is comforting to find Nohl, in his
report upon the *Meistersinger* rehearsals, indulging in the plainest
speaking about the "brutality" of this charming specimen of Munich
beer-culture towards the Meister — this "musician of the old school,
destitute of anything approaching refinement", who arrogantly pre-
sumes upon his "purse-proud connections" [7].

7

After the last dress rehearsal, on the 19th June, Wagner
thanked from the stage the whole [8] of the personnel for the zeal with
which they had given themselves up for so long to the study of "an
exceedingly complex work", the miming of which had bristled with
difficulties of a type new to them. To the orchestra his words were,

---

[6] See Vol. III, pp. 377–8.
[7] NNS, p. 361. What Bülow must have suffered at the hands of some of the
players we can surmise from a letter of his two years later to Düfflipp. "Even in connection with the Court Theatre orchestra", he writes, "the great majority of which
was well-disposed towards me, I recall only too sorrowfully how some of the players —
Herren C.M.W., S.'[Sandelbach], Str. [Strauss] and others — by their unceasing
assiduity in spiting and provoking me by their malice, rudeness and laziness, used
to poison for me all pleasure in the success of this or that performance in the concert
room or the opera house."
[8] With the exception of Fräulein Mallinger, who was absent on that occasion
through indisposition.

"To you I need say nothing more. You are German musicians: we understand each other without words." The central theme of his short discourse was that necessity for the regeneration of German national art that was his very heart's desire. Schiller, he reminded them, had said that whenever art has declined the guilt for this has lain on the artists themselves, and whatever other factors might have contributed to the present abasement of the German stage one thing was certain — that if ever it was to rise again it could only be through the artists. That decisive point had now been reached with the *Meistersinger*. The blame for the decay of the German stage had often been laid at the door of opera, and not altogether unjustly.

> "But not only the German opera is to blame — rather that we have found a place in our theatres for foreign products having their origin in quite other conditions than ours, and that we have imitated those products. One thing only will restore our ruined stage to health — the creation of a truly German musical-dramatic art, and above all the most perfect production possible of it, which can be achieved only by the whole of the forces concerned being animated by a common conception. This has happened here."

The little speech, which had been delivered in a quiet, heartfelt tone, profoundly moved those who heard it: there could have been few among them who did not realise at last that with Wagner a new day had dawned for German art.

To the King, on the morning (the 19th) of the final rehearsal, which was a performance in everything but name, Wagner sent a brief note expressing his confidence that Ludwig would perceive, under the popular humour that played upon the surface of the new work, "the profound melancholy, the lamentation, the cry of distress of poetry in chains, and its re-incarnation, its new birth, its magic power triumphing over the common and base." The rehearsal was attended by some five or six hundred people, among them the King.

The first performance proper, on the 21st, at which, of course, Ludwig was present, was attended by friends and enemies of Wagner from all parts of Europe. The performance, it is interesting to note, was frequently broken in upon by applause after this or that "number", so far were the audiences of that epoch from appreciating the unbroken continuity of texture in a Wagner music drama. Wagner would have preferred not to be present, but that would have not only hurt the King but discouraged the singers. He meant, however, to watch the performance unseen by the audience. But when, as etiquette prescribed, he presented himself to the King immediately after the latter's arrival, Ludwig insisted on his seating himself by him in the royal box. Though called for by the audience at the end of the first act, Wagner did not appear on the stage; but at the conclusion of the second and third acts he bowed his acknowledgments from the box at the request of the King.[9] A remark generally attributed to Bülow, "Horace by the side of Augustus", spread over Europe in a few days. For a mere musician to behave in this fashion in a royal box was regarded as an outrage upon German etiquette by the more aristocratic members of the audience; while even the plain people present were so astounded that, as one awed newspaper reporter expressed it, they instinctively looked up to see if the ceiling of the theatre were not tumbling down. "Wagner", he wrote,

> "the branded, exiled heretic, whom not much more than two years ago even the King's grace could not shield from the malignity of the upper and lower rabble of our art-metropolis, now rehabilitated in expressible fashion in the selfsame royal box in which, till then, only royalties and their descendants had ever been seen!"

8

It was the highest light yet in Wagner's life. The incident was insignificant in itself, but as a symbol it was tremendous. The fight seemed definitely won at last. There was still much opposition, of course, especially on the part of Wagner's political enemies and of the stupider and baser journalists such as Hanslick; but in the main the reception of the *Meistersinger* by the German public was not only cordial but affectionate, for in the splendid work it saw itself as in a mirror. Some of the coolness, if not actual enmity, was of course plain honest philistinism, as in the case of Fröbel,

---

[9] That, at any rate, is the story as Glasenapp tells it: according to him, after the singers had taken numerous calls, the audience turned towards the royal box and clamoured for the composer until at last the King persuaded Wagner to show himself. Ludwig Nohl, however, who was present, tells us, in his virtually contemporary account of the performance, that the King "hastily left the box as soon as each act was finished." This is more credible than Glasenapp's story. Ludwig always did his best to conceal himself from public view in the theatre, and to escape from his loyal subjects as quickly as he could when the curtain fell.

who his whole life long regarded the *Meistersinger* as Wagner's worst work, and who refused to print in the *Süddeutsche Presse* an article dealing with the recent production of the opera because he thought the tone of it too enthusiastic: how, he naively asks in his memoirs, could words have been found to do justice to a great *political* achievement after language had been strained in this fashion over a merely *artistic* one?

Not all the opposition was as relatively harmless as this. Wagner's old friend Laube distinguished himself by a frontal attack on the *Meistersinger* in an article in early September in — appropriately enough — Hanslick's paper, the *Neue Freie Presse*. As we have seen, Wagner and Laube had to some extent renewed their old-time friendship in the Vienna days of 1861.[10] In the autumn of 1867 Laube, anxious to give up his post as Director of the Burg Theatre, had cast longing eyes on the Intendantship at Munich, which, he surmised, would soon be vacant. He appealed to Wagner's good offices in the matter. Wagner apparently did not regard him as wholly suitable for the post, but, as his letter of the 3rd October, 1867 to Bülow shows, thought that in the event of Perfall becoming Intendant he could find no better regisseur or technical director than Laube: "he is a sound practician", he wrote, "knows a great deal, is enormously energetic, and strict." Wagner's attitude is understandable: he could not have done personally with Laube as official head of the Munich Theatre, but honestly thought he might be of real service to the institution in the department — the purely dramatic — for which his talents and his experience certainly qualified him. But Laube seems to have set his heart on the Intendantship, and to have regarded Wagner as directly responsible for the disappointment of his hopes. In this he was mistaken, for many other factors had come into play.[11] He took his revenge in his *Presse* article, which, so far as we can gather from the extracts from it that have survived, was distinguished more by abuse of the *Meistersinger* than by anything that could be called criticism; but Laube's prominent position in the German theatrical world led to its being quoted far and wide.

---

[10] See Vol. III, p. 151.

[11] Possart, who was a member of the Munich company at that time, tells us that the real obstacle was the King, who did not wish to have a commoner as Intendant of his Court Theatre. PEE, pp. 219–220.

On the 8th September the Leipzig musical journal, *Die Tonhalle*, published the first part of a long article by Cornelius on the new work. The anti-Wagnerian editor of the paper, Dr. Oskar Paul, who is chiefly known to scholars today by his translation of, and commentary on, the *De Musica* of Boethius, saw fit to accompany Cornelius's article with what he called a "counterpart", in the shape of a reprint of Laube's *Neue Freie Presse* article. Cornelius's reaction to this was swift and decisive: he told Paul what he thought of him and forbade publication of another word of his own essay.[12]

Wagner, for his part, behaved in characteristic fashion. He dashed off three acid sonnets to Laube [13] (who had by then become director of the Leipzig Town Theatre), in which he ironically congratulated that town on its latest acquisition, and Laube on his acquisition, so to speak, of such a town. The sonnets were signed "An enthusiastic Leipzig Patriot", and, according to Glasenapp,

> "sent with an accompanying letter of Wagner's of the 10th September to an Austrian political journal, which, however, had not the pluck to print them! So well-accredited was Laube's name at that time, and so unequal the measuring-rod for what could be said against him and against Wagner!"

But that, as we now know, is not the whole story, which in its totality does not reflect much credit on the composer of the *Meistersinger*. It is with regret that we see Wagner, as on certain other occasions, resorting to anonymity in order to strike at someone or something he dislikes without incurring any personal responsibility for what he is doing. The reader will probably ask himself why any Vienna journal should have jibbed at printing three piquant poems on the subject of Laube which, openly emanating from Richard Wagner, would have been first-rate "copy". He will understand the situation better when he reads Wagner's letter of the 10th September to Richter, who was at that time in Munich.[14]

> "I do not know Porges' address, street or number. Be so good as to copy out the accompanying sonnets clearly and correctly and give the transcript to Porges in my name. I want him to use his connections to

---

[12] The complete article, together with Cornelius's letter to Paul, will be found in CAMK, pp. 173–187.
[13] RWGS, XII, 370–1.
[14] RWHR, pp. 9–10.

get the poems printed in some approachable Vienna political journal — naturally one inimical to the *Neue Freie Presse,* such as the *Wanderer.* My name must not be disclosed."

That Glasenapp was aware of this letter seems to be proved by his giving the 10th September as the date on which the sonnets were "sent with an accompanying letter of Wagner's to an Austrian political journal", which is an inaccurate statement of the facts. Not only was there no letter *of Wagner's* to any paper, but he was insistent that his authorship of the poems should not be revealed: he sent them to Richter, who was to copy them and pass them on to Porges, who was to try to plant them on one of his journalistic connections in Vienna. As it happened, the *Wanderer* had ceased publication some months before this time, though Wagner appears not to have been aware of this; but as the editor of that journal was his old friend Friedrich Uhl, to whom, as the then editor of the *Botschafter,* he had addressed the open letter of the 18th April, 1865 on the coming performance of *Tristan* in Munich,[15] there could have been only one motive on his part in proceeding as he did — to assault Laube in the dark with no danger to himself. One likes him better when he fought in the open, as he did when, in the following March, he sent Laube a curt note to the effect that the latter would be doing him a great favour if he would use his position at the Leipzig Theatre "to see that my operas are never given there again". This Laube affair, by the way, was not the only one in which Wagner tried to use Richter as his own little private quisling.

One further example of the enmity towards him in certain German circles may be given here. Some years after the events just recorded, an article by Cornelius with the title of *German Art and Richard Wagner,* in which a survey was made of what Germany owed to the new impulse given to its art by the composer of *Tristan* and the *Meistersinger,* appeared in the Vienna *Deutsche Zeitung.*[16] The editor accompanied it with a remark that "henceforth the Wagner matter is inseparable from the German matter". Thereupon Brahms's crony Dr. Billroth, who was a shareholder in the *Deutsche Zeitung,* not merely wrote to another well-known anti-Wagnerian, the famous art-historian Lübke, expressing his anger over the article and the editorial note, but protested directly to the editor.

---

[15] See Vol. III, p. 369.
[16] It will be found in CAMK, pp. 187–200.

10

On the whole, however, Wagner had little to complain of in the reception of his latest work; and what must have gratified him more than anything else was the feeling that the *national* importance of the *Meistersinger* in particular and of his work in general was now fairly on the way towards recognition by his fellow-countrymen. Even the Berlin comic paper *Kladderadatsch* broke into enthusiastic verse on the "national" theme. By its very subject and nature the new work was calculated to appeal as no previous creation of Wagner's had done to the fast-accumulating German national consciousness of itself and of what the Germans were coming to regard as their world mission. The most definite and most detailed expression of this point of view is to be found in the articles of Ludwig Nohl that followed the production. By a curious coincidence, that production took place within a few days of the celebrations at Worms of the great deed of Luther which, as Nohl puts it, "first truly made us Germans Germans", the deed that was a demonstration of "the German truth of conviction". "It was *one* thought, *one* feeling", he says, that animated both celebrations in 1868, the thought, the feeling, that the German Folk had found its real soul in Luther and in Wagner. Each had not only freed the German spirit from foreign fetters but had endowed it with the strength and independence to realise the future "world-dominion" of that spirit.

> "Herein resided the deep inwardness of the relation of these two festival events to each other; both were signs that at last we are beginning to possess and enjoy in every sphere of life our pure, unalloyed individuality of being. Both events, considered in their final essence and in the wealth of their effects on our life, were the deed of *the fully-awakened spirit of the German nation.*"

Only today, "after, indeed, an epoch of servitude to a foreign pseudo-civilisation [presumably the French]", is this German spirit, at long last, emerging from "a merely instinctive feeling" to "clear consciousness of itself", and achieving its mission not only in "ideal wishes and hopes" but in "the realistic force of a firm will and a sure laying hold of things, a force which henceforth will fill all our thinking and all our doing and bring to final completion the lofty edifice of our national existence." [17]

[17] NNS, p. 309 ff.

It is not only in the sprawl and muddle of his clumsy prose, the thought stumbling and spluttering its way through the involved syntax like a hippopotamus ploughing through a mud-flat, that Nohl shows himself truly of the tribe of Richard. Even more striking is the similarity of ideas. For Nohl, as for Wagner, not only is Germany at last beginning to find itself but it is on German culture that the future salvation of the whole world is going to depend; as he says, the *Meistersinger* production filled all Germany with a presentiment of the renewal of the national life, and it could almost be taken as a sign of the times that from many a mouth, in many a journal, a parallel had been drawn between

"the recent successful achievement in the political sphere [the humbling of Austria by Prussia?] and this latest decisive battle within the sphere of art . . . proof enough that there is a general instinctive conviction of the inner connection of the two things." [18]

11

A second performance of the *Meistersinger* should have been given on the 24th June, but indisposition on Hölzel's part necessitated a postponement to the 28th. The remaining performances before the closing of the theatre for the summer took place on the 2nd, 7th, 12th and 16th July. On the last evening of all, Fischer having become hoarse, Richter sang the part of Kothner at very short notice.[19]

Wagner went back to Triebschen on the 24th June. Immediately after the first performance the King had written him a deeply-felt letter, proclaiming once more his belief in him and in the triumph of their ideal. "Fate has called us to a great work", he said; "we came into the world that we might testify to the truth. . . . To you I owe everything, everything! Hail German art! In this sign will we conquer!" In his reply, after thanking the King for all the grace he had bestowed on him and the happiness he had brought him, Wagner said he had resolved that in order not to add to his difficulties again he would forever refrain from any contact with actual affairs in Munich. To the world he would be as one dead: more withdrawn

---

[18] See the series of articles in NNS, pp. 309–460.
[19] The *extra* expense of the *Meistersinger* production, i.e., the cost of the "guest" singers, the new scenery, and so on, amounted to 48,000 florins.

from it than ever, he would live henceforth only to create: soon *Siegfried* would be in the King's hands. More clearly than ever before he sees with how great a King the Fates have linked his own life. "You are the rescuer, the redeemer! See me here speechless at your feet!"

In all this there is perhaps a touch of the physical exhaustion and depression that were bound to follow upon a month of such work and excitement as Wagner had just been through in Munich. But there was something else. That month had been sufficient to convince him that only in a theatre of his own could he hope to achieve what he regarded as his mission. It has been the fashion among biographers to blame the "stupidity" and "ill-will" of Perfall and some of his associates for the many unpleasantnesses that Wagner had to undergo at this time and later in Munich. But that is a prejudiced view. Perfall and the others would have been either less or more than human had they slavishly submitted to being cancelled out by Wagner in their own theatre. An impossible situation had gradually defined itself there: some of the outsiders or new-comers, in particular Betz, Hallwachs and Richter, had arrived at a point where they could bluntly declare that when it came to a difference of opinion or procedure between Wagner and the Intendanz, they would take orders only from Wagner. In his heart of hearts Wagner must have known that no theatre could be run permanently as the Munich institution was being run just then on his account, with the more important performances mainly in the hands of "guests" only nominally under the control of the local Intendanz, and with their adoration of Wagner collaborating with their sense of their own indispensability for the job in hand to make them scornful of any authority but his.

Wagner would not have the slightest feeling for Perfall in these things, convinced as he was that nothing in Munich, or indeed in the world, mattered but his own work for the redemption of German culture through the theatre. But he could always feel very acutely for himself; and he must have realised by now that it would be a sheer impossibility for him to go through this kind of thing in connection with each new production of his. Moreover the Cosima matter was bound to come to a head before long, and when it did, not only was there likely to be unpleasantness between himself and the King but Bülow would almost certainly have to sever his connection with Munich. So it is without surprise that we find him writing to Perfall, the day before the first performance of the *Meistersinger*,

"Since, thanks to the happy assembly of talents and the intelligent zeal of the regisseur [Hallwachs] granted me,[20] everything has turned out excellently, it is with all the greater satisfaction that I take this opportunity of informing you that I now gladly cease all connection with the Royal Court Theatre."

12

He certainly had not Bülow on his side in the general matter of the Munich Opera. For all his devotion to Wagner, nothing was further from Bülow's thoughts than to regard his Munich Kapell-meistership as solely a Wagnerian function. He was ready and willing to conduct operas of all schools if only they had some good in them; and whatever he put his hand to he carried through with the conscientiousness that never deserted him as an artist. "My principle as a practical artist", he wrote to Emil Bock in October,

"is bonapartish — destruction of the old parties *and* of the new. The party for which I make propaganda is that of the people who can and do. Here in Munich my immediate aim is primarily to give model performances of all classical masterworks";

and "masterworks", in this connection, meant anything, in any genre, that had a note unmistakably its own. For his part he found Perfall intelligent and willing, and he must often have sympathised with him in his complaints about Wagner's "groundless suspicions".

We shall do well not to take as seriously as the Wahnfried satellites have done the theory that in every conflict of Wagner with the German theatres he was in the right and they in the wrong. The directors of those theatres were perfectly justified, for example, in asking for cuts in the *Meistersinger*, the work being decidedly too long for performance intact under ordinary theatrical conditions. Wagner's contention was, of course, that these conditions should be set aside. His simple explanation of the matter was that Intendants, singers and the rest of them wanted the opera shortened because they were "lazy and incompetent"; and he refused at first to let any theatre have the keenly-desired work unless it would guarantee a performance without cuts. In the end, as we have seen, he

---

[20] Not a word of recognition, be it observed, of Perfall and his staff!

had to withdraw from this position, partly out of consideration for his publisher's interests.

Nor was the question of cuts the only source of friction with some of the larger theatres. The reader will recall that in 1852 Wagner himself had wrecked the plan of the Berlin Intendant to give *Tannhäuser* by stipulating that as he himself was banned from German soil just then, Liszt should be given authority to act for him in the Berlin Theatre. Liszt, being a man of the world, had had the good sense to point out that he could go to Berlin only in response to a direct and definite invitation from the local Intendant; for obviously his presence there as Wagner's plenipotentiary would have been taken as an insult by the people whose business it was to produce opera in the Prussian capital. Untaught and unteachable by experience, and with his usual scant understanding of the psychology of others, Wagner now took the same wrong line with regard to the *Meistersinger*.

His naïveté as a psychologist is revealed in a letter of his to Herbeck, *à propos* of a plan to give his new work in Dresden.

"As none of the official Kapellmeisters there is capable of a true understanding and reproduction of my work, and as it is impossible for myself to take any part in the rehearsing of it, I suggest the private co-operation of the young Music Director Hans Richter, who is at present in Munich. Being intimately acquainted with all my intentions, he succeeded in training both the Munich singers and the chorus to the most admirable accuracy in an astonishingly short space of time. He would do the same thing in Dresden, but of course strictly *privatim*, and consequently without any offence to the Kapellmeisters: in addition he would teach the singers the right tempi down to the last shade, as well as the correct expression, so that when it came to the official theatre rehearsals the Kapellmeisters would, as it were, have the right conception forced on them by the singers. By this means I could be fairly sure of a performance of the only kind that has any value in my eyes, and that would redound to the credit of the Dresden Theatre."

The pathetic, incredible innocence of it! And of Glasenapp too, who is honestly astonished that

"to this protective measure the Dresden directorate objected that they could not possibly consent to having their Kapellmeisters placed under the superintendence of a young musician."

But what else could Wagner have expected? Rietz and the others were no doubt as dull as Wagner said they were; but would any man with the smallest understanding of human nature have expected them to acquiesce for a moment in such an arrangement as he suggested? And of course he lost his temper and sulked as he generally did when he could not get his own way at once. He was sick and tired of the lot of them, he wrote to Tichatschek: he had made up his mind to have nothing more to do with any theatre, so stupid were the administrators of them all.

His own management of his own affairs, however, was not always ideally intelligent. In mid-September, 1868 he received a letter from Hülsen, the Berlin Intendant, pointing out that while the Berlin Opera, by its payment of 100 ducats to Wagner for the *Flying Dutchman* in January, 1844 had legally acquired the right of performance of that work in perpetuity, the Berlin system of paying royalties not having been established until the following March, he regarded it as a moral obligation on his part to let the *Dutchman* now rank on a royalty basis as soon as enough performances had been given to cover the original lump payment. To this letter, which, considering how much Hülsen disliked Wagner, can only be considered rather handsome of him, Wagner did not at the time vouchsafe any reply.[21]

13

In the theatres, as everywhere else, Wagner was his own worst enemy, and we may reasonably decline to believe, without confirmation from less prejudiced quarters, all the bad he has to say about the Intendants and Directors. Bülow, at any rate, could get on well enough with Perfall, as his letters show. Nor can we always be quite sure that Wagner was not deceiving himself not only as to the defects of those whom he took to be his enemies but as to the virtues of those who were anxious to show themselves his friends. In August, 1868 he gave Hallwachs a glowing testimonial: he pronounced him the best opera producer he had ever known, on the strength of what he had seen of him at close quarters during the rehearsals and performances of the *Meistersinger*. Hallwachs, he said, understood every one of his directions at once, and carried it out intelligently to the smallest detail. Perfall took a different view

---

[21] KGSB, pp. 84–5. The opera was given in Berlin about this time with Betz as the Dutchman, but with scant success.

of the matter. "The staging of the *Meistersinger*", he told a correspondent in July,

"cannot be taken as a test of Hallwachs's capacity. Not he but Wagner was the producer. Hallwachs's awkwardness and slowness made him a joke among the personnel. He showed that he had no idea of the business of a regisseur. . . . In Wagner's presence he knew how to cloak all his failings and to put the blame on Director Franz Seitz, who was not in Wagner's good books. If Wagner praises Hallwachs it may be because *he* recommended him and because Hallwachs is a foreigner; for everything native [to Bavaria] is to this gentleman [Wagner] *eo ipso* bad and reprehensible. Hallwachs's behaviour towards the Munich Intendanz generates a strong suspicion that with his entry into the theatre the spy system was firmly established, that every one of my steps was watched, and that in his heart of hearts Herr Hallwachs regards Herr Wagner as his real chief, with the duty of constantly reporting to him regarding my own doings. Furthermore, he would be well cast here for the rôle already taken upon himself by another of Wagner's recommendations, Richter, brought by him into the theatre as solo-repetitor — the rôle of inciting the personnel against their chief whenever he tries to restore order by means of his own subordinates."

Allowing for a little error on both sides, it looks as if the main truth might be with Perfall. Wagner's belief in himself and his passion for dominance would certainly be played up to by clever people bent on advancing their own interests: flattery and unquestioning obedience would go a very long way towards securing his good opinion. And nothing is clearer than that some of his yes-men, modelling themselves on him, behaved with a rudeness equal to his own towards the Intendanz, trusting to his protection, which they thought all-powerful, to save them from what would have been anywhere else the logical consequences of their insolence and insubordination. One of them at any rate, Richter, was to discover before he was much older that he had taken too much for granted as regards Wagner's power in Munich, and trusted rather too blindly to his protecting hand.

It is certain that when Wagner left Munich after the first performances of the *Meistersinger* it was already in his mind never again to take part in the production of one of his works there — a course which even he must have sensed would be bound to affect for the worse his relations with the King. But both of them would have been astonished and shocked had they been told then that it would be eight years before they were to set eyes on each other again.

CHAPTER VIII

THE BÜLOW–COSIMA CRISIS

1

O N THE 10th July the King loyally informed Cosima that he had heard on good authority that Röckel had been repeating the old Malvina "calumnies" about her and Wagner: it grieves him, he says, to have to tell her this, but he cannot reconcile it with his conscience to hide it from her.[1] Cosima, of course, sent the note on to Wagner, who, in his letter of the 16th to Ludwig, tells him she has been so grievously wounded by his news and the depth of human depravity it discloses that she will leave Munich at once, perhaps never to return there.[2] Her physicians have ordered her to a milder climate. She will probably spend the coming winter in Italy, in the neighbourhood of her father or of other relations; and this step may of necessity lead to a request from Bülow that the King shall accept his resignation of his Kappellmeistership. Wagner still tries to keep up the old bluff that the whole trouble has its roots in the "machinations" of evil-minded people who have unfortunately been permitted to go "unpunished"; but at any rate, he says, the King and himself and Cosima can now hope for peace.

He reminds Ludwig of a vow he had long ago taken not to be present at the production of the *Meistersinger,* a vow he had been compelled to break out of consideration for his performers.

---

[1] KLRWB, II, 235 *note*.

[2] To his credit he stands up for the loyalty of Röckel. It may be added that Cosima told Röckel what she had heard about him, without, however, disclosing the name of her informant. Röckel, after promising that he would deal with the person whom he suspected of being responsible for the trouble, seems to have satisfied himself that the "gossip" was hardly worth bothering about any further, and to have quietly let the matter drop. This apparently angered Wagner, who, in the following November, reproached him bitterly for not having "justified himself" in the proper quarter: no doubt, he snapped, "political affairs left you with no time to occupy yourself with trifles of this sort". Röckel replied placably that he was no longer young enough to get worked up over slanders and misunderstandings.

This was the last interchange of letters between the two old friends.

"Yet my vow I did not break; my declaration that I would not be present at the first performance of any of my works was prompted mainly by my aversion from the spectacle of the public of an ordinary theatre performance and immediate association with it."

He reminds the King of another vow of his, that if ever the great scheme for the festival theatre should be realised he would make a "sacrifice" of the joy of seeing the *Ring* produced in it, being content to pay in complete retirement his ardent homage to the benefactor who had made that result possible. His life belongs to the King alone: he will nurse his broken health in order to find the strength to serve him by completing his great work. As for Cosima, the King shall have news of her from him now and then. She is "so profound, so rare a being" that she does not belong to this world: therefore she will disappear from it, as every noble creature has to do who is working for the world.

Once more we can only say that he is merely writing "literature". He is not being completely honest with the King.

He had left Munich in June virtually resolved never to visit the town again. By mid-July his mind was made up on this matter. We find him assuring Richter that if his efforts to plant him as a Music Director in the Munich Theatre at a salary of 1,200 florins a year should not succeed he will take care of him in some other way. "For your further information", he continued,

"I may say that whether you get a post in Munich or not, you will *never* come into contact with me there again, for I am firmly resolved never to return there and never again to have anything to do with the Munich Theatre. This unshakeable resolution of mine has its root in certain happenings of decisive weight."

The date of this letter is the 21st July. Now it was on the 16th that Wagner had told the King that as the result of the latest "calumnies" about himself and Cosima the latter had determined to leave Munich for good. These were obviously the "recent happenings" to which he refers in his letter to Richter as putting an end to his own association with Munich.

Why should he think that severance necessary? By his own admission to one friend after another, he ranked the recent *Meistersinger* production as the best that any of his works had ever had. He still had the love and confidence of the King, and could count with certainty on the best material Germany could provide being assembled

for his next production, that of the *Ring*, on having as many rehearsals as he liked, on the subservience of everyone concerned to
his will. Why then should he set fire to the bridge between Munich
and himself in this fashion? His dislike of Perfall and other officials cannot possibly be looked upon as the really determining factor. Let us accept, for argument's sake, his theory that the Munich
officials, instead of co-operating with him, had done their utmost to
frustrate him. In that case, surely, there was less reason than ever
before for him to cut loose from Munich: for if the "criminals" had
done their worst and failed so abjectly on the occasion of the
Meistersinger, what had he to fear in connection with his next production there?

Nor can we be satisfied with the traditional story that Wagner
broke with the King because his artistic conscience had been outraged by Ludwig's determination to bring out the *Rhinegold* before
the *Ring* was ready in its entirety. Wagner at that time not only had
no objection to the piecemeal floating of the *Ring* operas but actually contemplated it himself. In February, 1868 the Munich management had it in mind to reconstruct the stage during the coming
summer vacation. In a letter to Düfflipp of the 5th of that month
Wagner approved of this scheme, which, he said, would not only
raise the Munich Theatre at last to the level of the best theatres in
Germany but would make it, as he expressed it, fairly well able to
cope with such scenic demands as his Nibelungen drama would
make on it.

> "It would consequently not be impossible, in the event of his Majesty
> so desiring, to give anticipatory performances of the separate mem-
> bers of this cycle, at intervals, say, of a year: thus a beginning might
> be made next year with the *Rhinegold*, to be followed by the *Valkyrie*
> in the year after that, the whole work being thus produced in succes-
> sive stages." [3]

This rules out for good the notion that the breach between himself
and the King in 1869 was due to his anger over Ludwig's insistence
on producing the *Rhinegold*. He *was* angry with him; but it was for
other reasons than a supposed assault on the artistic unity of the
Ring.

The trouble really dates from the summer of 1868, when the Malvina episode raised its ugly head once more, this time more threat-

---

[3] RWBA, II, 300–1.

eningly than ever. By the trickery he had practised on the generous-hearted young King in the summer of 1866, a piece of trickery for which not only Cosima but Bülow must share the odium with him, he had put a weapon in the hands of the Fates which they could be counted on to use against him with deadly effect sooner or later. Nemesis came in the July of 1868. Munich was evidently seething with gossip about the triangle: Cosima's further stay there had by now become impossible, and if her flight should bring the scandal much further into the open how could Bülow remain at his post in the town? Then, with Bülow gone, what was going to become not merely of the plans for the *Ring* and other "model" performances but of the Music School, into the work of which Bülow had thrown himself with such splendid energy and enthusiasm?

2

The sensible and honest thing would have been to make a clean breast of the matter to the King long ago; but how could he do that now, after having deceived and publicly degraded the unsuspecting boy as he had done two years before? The measure of his perplexity is given by his desperate attempt still to maintain the old façade of lies and bluff. The most recent trouble, he desperately tries to make out in a letter of the 19th July to the King, began with Ludwig's absence from a recent performance of the *Meistersinger:* this had started malicious rumours of a fresh "disgrace"; next, "it was learned, from people in the know", that

"very evil reports about my relations with Frau von Bülow had aroused an ungracious mood in his Majesty. That suffices: the object is attained. The happiness and peace of mind of three honourable people [himself, Cosima and Bülow] are once more undermined, perhaps permanently; for I ask just one question of any human being with any delicate feeling at all — what is likely to be the effect on the mind of a being so irritable, so excessively sensitive as Bülow, when now, after three years — after an utterly unprincipled intriguer such as your former Cabinet Chief, stopping at nothing to attain his ends, to satisfy his thirst for revenge had publicly besmirched Bülow's marriage, — it is still believed that the surest way for anyone to prejudice you against me is to rake up some more of this filth? What reaction do they think this perpetual fouling of his honour will have on the unhappy husband, what clouds it must ultimately bring down upon this marriage, what unendurable torments it must call forth?"

[156]

The King's reply to this wild talk was grave and sensible. The person who had told him of the revival of the "calumnies", he said, was not one of Wagner's enemies, as the latter imagines, but a good and upright man [4] whom it had pained deeply to have to listen to them. Making, perhaps, a last brave effort to persuade himself that he still believes in Wagner's protestations, he assures him that "the children of darkness and wickedness" will not achieve very much with their "gross inventions". But he gives Wagner the sound advice to dissuade Frau von Bülow from leaving Munich; to do that would simply be bringing grist to the mill of the evil-minded. He apologises for having, with the best intentions, told Cosima what was being said about her, and hopes she will continue to write to him. He wants to dismiss it all from his mind and to lose himself in ecstatic memories of the divine *Meistersinger* days — which will give him strength, he hopes, to endure "the horrible unpoetic turmoil of the coming days in Kissingen", where he will have to entertain their Majesties of Russia, — and in dreams equally ecstatic of the completion of the *Ring*.

For the moment, then, Wagner might be able to soothe himself with the thought that the day of reckoning had at any rate been postponed. That it would inevitably arrive he must have been well aware; but his strategy when it did would have to be determined by the lie of the land and the quality of his resources at the time.

3

Feeling, after the King's letter, that he could breathe freely again for a while, he sent him, on the 22nd August, as a birthday gift, a finely-bound engraved score of the *Meistersinger*, together with a dedicatory poem of four stanzas in which he sang the joy of the bond between the King and the artist, and the *Meistersinger* as the living symbol of it. He followed this up on the 25th with a letter in which he besought the King's grace and help for one Ludwig van Beethoven, son of the notorious nephew Carl who had so distressed the composer during the last years of his life. For detailed information about the son, and the dignity with which he was bearing the most unmerited blows of fate, he referred his patron to Beethoven's biographer Nohl. It seems that the newest Ludwig van Beethoven, who

---

[4] Presumably Düfflipp.

had been at one time employed in the record office of the Teutonic Order but had lately taken up his abode in Munich, where he was living in dire need, was anxious for a post of much the same sort as his old one: Wagner suggests that the King might find him work in his Cabinet Secretariat. But seemingly the man was indelibly tarred with the paternal brush. It turned out that he had had to leave Vienna in a hurry because of a little trouble with the police; and it was not long before a warrant for his arrest had to be issued in Munich. History seems to contain no further record of him.

The King, in his grateful acknowledgment of the *Meistersinger* score, spoke of the solace it had brought him in a period made wretched for him by such bores as his mother, the Austrian Emperor, and Sophie and her husband, the latter couple constituting the greatest trial of all for him. As some sort of compensation can he have a production of *Tristan* in the autumn? he asks. And when will *Siegfried* be ready? For his soul hungers for the manna that only the god of his life can send him. And he implores Wagner to try to placate the angry Semper, now all out on the war path: evidently Ludwig cherished a faint hope that the scheme for the festival theatre in Munich might yet go through.

On the 22nd July Cosima had fled from Munich to Triebschen. On the 10th August Cornelius joined them there for a few days, during which he read his *Gunlöd* text to them: Wagner advised him *not* to compose it, while Cosima, rather surprisingly, was of the opposite opinion. Poor Peter, who had hardly ever known what comfort and good living were, was enchanted with Triebschen and its surroundings, above all with its heavenly quiet. "To look out over water, mountains and country like this and not hear a sound of man and his activities! This is the place to dream in, to compose in!" One gets the impression that, accustomed though he was to Wagner's regal way of living, he was rather overwhelmed by the splendour of his present ménage. "God grant", he said to him, "that nothing ever drives you away from here!" What worried Cornelius was to see so much money being spent on the place when Wagner had it only on a six years' lease.[5] "He has sunk a pile of money in it", he wrote to his friend Carl Hestermann,

---

[5] But, as we have seen, he contemplated extending the lease.

"reconstructed and furnished it; and when you see an aviary with golden pheasants and other rare birds, you can't help saying to yourself, 'God bless us, what must all this be costing the man!' In addition, the laying out of a few acres of park and kitchen garden, some eight servants at least, and a horse and carriage."

Wagner can have no capital to fall back on, continues Cornelius, "and at a mere turn of fortune's wheel he will have to leave his retreat and go on his wanderings again."

Peter noted, though, signs not only of prosperity present but of still greater prosperity to come. While he was at Triebschen the Paris impresario Pasdeloup called on Wagner. "They are absolutely swarming round Wagner now", Peter wrote to his wife,

"trying to get contracts from him for the rights of performance of his operas in Paris and Italy. *Lohengrin* is wanted in five quarters in Paris. And as Wagner could not dispose of *Lohengrin* to M. Pasdeloup the latter said, 'Well then, the *Meistersinger, Les Maîtres Chanteurs!'* "

At the same time the Milan music publisher Francesco Lucca was negotiating with Wagner regarding possible performances of *Rienzi* and the *Flying Dutchman* in Italy, for which purpose the good Pusinelli was asked to rouse the somnolent Dresden publisher of the scores, Müller, and get him to send copies to Milan. Madame Lucca had called at Triebschen and offered him 50,000 francs down for the Italian publishing rights in his works. Wagner's star was certainly rising. However, he assured Pusinelli, as he did practically all his correspondents at this time except the King, "nowhere, especially in Germany, can anything entice me to come forth from my retirement."

4

There was no doubt a good deal more which he thought it wise not to disclose to the King just yet. His jottings in the "Annals" hint at fateful resolutions with regard to Cosima and Bülow; but the hour had not yet struck for the final decisive step. And in spite of all his personal griefs and annoyances and his business preoccupations he could still bend his faculties to creative work. During the last days of August he made a sketch in the "Brown Book" for a comedy in one act on the subject of Luther — apparently as an antidote to depression. He seems to have gone no further with his scheme, however, which may have been merely a stray vibration caught *en passant* from the Luther celebrations of that summer. Du Moulin Eckart is at pains to discredit the theory that it was "the parallel between Luther's bride and Cosima [then living in Trieb-schen] that prompted him." [6] Dr. Strobel, however, disagrees with Du Moulin on this point; and the portions of Wagner's sketch which he prints support his view that the drama had at any rate some of its roots in his communion with Cosima at that time. The sketch shows Luther very much as Wagner saw himself just then — looking out from the Wartburg upon the beautiful world outside his window, troubled within himself, doubtful of himself and of all things, but strengthened in soul by the glance of a woman's eye and the glint of her golden hair. But this was not all: the play was to be concerned also with "the German 'rebirth' through philosophy, poetry and music" — the very thesis, in fact, of the articles by Nohl from which extracts have been given above. Whatever the dramatic world may or may not have lost through the shelving of the scheme, we may be permitted a regret over the loss of the scene of Luther's wedding, for which "music" is specified in the sketch, on the joyous theme of "Who loves not wine, woman and song. . . ." [7]

Bülow, towards the end of August, went on a fortnight's visit to Raff in Wiesbaden, what time Cosima was at Triebschen with Wagner. What arrangement had been come to between the members of the triangle we do not know, but one surmises that Bülow still believed it possible to avoid, or at least postpone, the unpleasant publicity of a divorce. Cosima he could do without; he was well aware, indeed, that she was no longer in the smallest degree his. But he had found a sphere of activity in Munich that suited him, and he did not like the idea of having to leave it. He came back from Wiesbaden, so Cornelius told Hestermann, looking very well, and evidently not fretting at all over his grass widowership. Cornelius felt moved to quote ironically a few lines from Heine in which Pluto consoles himself for the prospect of having to spend six months in the underworld without Proserpine:

> Aber ich will mich verschnaufen
> Hier im Orkus unterdessen;
> Punsch mit Lethe will ich saufen,
> Um die Gattin zu vergessen;

---

[6] MECW, I, 438.
[7] The sketch will be found in BFF, 1937, pp. 159–160,

(But meanwhile I will recover my breath here in Hades, drinking punch-cum-Lethe to help me to forget my spouse).[8] The accent, perhaps, for both Cornelius and Bülow was more on the punch than on the waters of oblivion: after all, for a sensible man there are compensations in this world for the absence even of a Cosima from the domestic hearth. Cornelius apologises humorously to his wife, who is very fond of Bülow and is, so to speak, looking over his shoulder as he writes, for what she may regard as a piece of poor wit at Hans's expense. Yet she is right, he adds. Wagner and Cosima look upon themselves as the sole touchstone for noblemindedness, and woe to anyone who dares apply mere ordinary tests to them and their union! It looks as if Peter for the life of him could not dramatise Wagner and Cosima as they so loved to dramatise themselves — he had seen them too often at too close quarters for that, — nor could he persuade himself that on purely sentimental grounds alone Bülow would find the loss of Cosima an irreparable misfortune.

5

Apologising to the King for not having replied to his letter of the 14th September until the 14th October,[9] Wagner tells him that on the former date he had gone for a change of air over the St. Gotthardt to the Borromean Islands and Genoa (where Ludwig's letter had caught up with him) accompanied by the Freundin:[10] the object of the excursion, he says, had been to rid her of her depression by the sight once more of the land of her birth. They had been delayed a full week on their homeward journey by the terrible floods in the Ticino Valley; it had cost them "unheard-of exertions", including a six-hours' walk over boulders deep in flood, in an unceasing thunderstorm. They thought their last hour had come, and by the lightning flashes, says Wagner, they saw life in all its terrible seriousness. "Illusion could no longer prevail! To look death in the face is to know the whole truth: to save what is eternal in one means turning one's back on all false appearance."

---

[8] The stanza is taken from the fourth of the poems entitled *Unterwelt*. In Heine, by the way, the first line runs thus: "Süsse Ruh! Ich kann verschnaufen". No doubt Cornelius's misquotation of it is intentional. The whole poem should be read to get the full savour of the subtle irony of Peter's application of it to the triangle.

[9] Or perhaps the 16th. His letter appears to be misdated.

[10] They returned to Triebschen on the 6th October.

Two days ago,[11] Wagner continues, Cosima, accompanied by the children, had gone to Munich to put her affairs in order and "in dignified fashion carry out her unshakeable resolves". His blessing had gone with her: he had good reason to honour her as the purest witness to sincerity, the most consummate being, he had ever encountered.

> "She belongs to another world-order than this. There is nothing for me to do but stand by her: may you, kind and noble one, range yourself faithfully by my side in this matter!"

From the hints thus given him the King will realise that Wagner has reached a grave crisis in his life, the hour for weighty decisions. It will be difficult for him to make all this, and the origins of it, perfectly clear to Ludwig. Much he must leave for the future, perhaps for posterity; for the present he can only provide his benefactor with material sufficient to base a true judgment upon, though much in his life-story will become fully clear to him only later. There is a good deal more to the same effect in this long letter of mid-October. Even the *Meistersinger* evening, the dazzling climax of his life in its outward aspect, is now for him merely *Wahn*: "nobody understands me; many marvel; the majority scoff at me." Even during those exacting but wonderful rehearsals of the work he suffered greatly in a way about which he cannot speak to the King, who lacks the inner clue to his emotions at that time. (He is no doubt referring to the consciousness of that "profound enmity and estrangement of Hans" which he had noted in the "Annals").[12] "Never again will I attend a performance of my work."

The letter sounds a new note in his correspondence with the King, a desire to tell all, and yet a fear — a fear to be fought down only by so patheticising himself that criticism and possible resentment on Ludwig's part will be swept away in a warm flood of pity for him.

He follows up this letter a few days later with one in which he urges the King not on any account to part with "the poor, yet so excellent Bülow". Certain "necessary resolutions", the causes of which do not concern "the shallow world", will in all probability soon place Hans in a position in which he will be able to find his life's mission and his inner satisfaction solely in the most faithful

---

[11] Actually on the 14th.
[12] See *supra*, p. 136.

performance of his official duties. May it not be made harder for him to do this, for he has had much to endure, and his only armour against the slings and arrows of outrageous fortune has been a frenzied plunging into work. Wagner is afraid that Bülow will soon find himself very solitary and will need the protection and encouragement of the King.

Wagner's next two letters and a telegram are dated the 4th November, the 29th December, and the 1st January; but there is no letter from the King to him between the 14th September, 1868 and the 10th February, 1869. This constituted the greatest gap in their correspondence until then.[13] To the letter that broke the long silence we shall return in due course. Meanwhile it is necessary to unravel the new tangle of events hinted at in Wagner's letters.

6

The great crisis had come that autumn. From the story as told by Du Moulin Eckart one gets the impression that once more Bülow had been "deceived", that he had unmasked the "deception" by accident, and that in his rage he had seriously contemplated making an end of Wagner. The journey of Cosima and Wagner to Italy had been wrapped in a "veil of mystery", and when the veil was torn aside Bülow saw "nothing but treachery and lies".

> "When, having opened a letter in the most innocent way,[14] he became aware of this journey and of the full extent of the Meister's relations with Frau Cosima, which were known to all the world and hidden only from him, he laid aside the baton which he had wielded on Richard Wagner's behalf and took up the pistol."

He had already been practising pistol-shooting during his stay in Wiesbaden; and now, says Du Moulin portentously, it becomes clear that this pistol-practice of his "had more than a merely symbolic significance". After the reading of the mysterious letter his one thought was to demand "satisfaction" of Wagner in the manner

---

[13] On the 27th December Cosima had also written to Ludwig, hinting in her own way at the new orientation her life had taken. To this letter he did not reply, as is evident from his letter of the 10th February to Wagner.

[14] One's first impression on reading this is that Providence showed a certain poverty of technique in resorting once more to its device of putting a vital letter in Bülow's way and whispering in his ear, "Open! Read!" The simple truth appears to be, however, that Du Moulin is confusedly thinking of the opened letter of May, *1866*.

"traditional among gentlemen"; but the friend whom he consulted about the matter replied, "You cannot fight a duel with the Meister", whereupon Bülow "fell back into his chair and burst into a fit of hysterical sobbing". When restored to reason he told all his friends what his wife and Wagner had told *him* — that for reasons of health Cosima had gone to stay for some time with her step-sister, the Countess de Charnacé, in Versailles. To this lady he "poured out his soul": his letter to her is "heartrending". In it "he revealed his knowledge of that journey to Italy", and spoke pathetically of his ruined health, his broken career, his "more than problematic future". It would be difficult to imagine a tissue of greater muddle or greater absurdity than this. It is not merely that a year or two one way or the other means, as usual, nothing to Du Moulin. His facts are even more inaccurate than his figures. Let us try to piece events together in their natural order and see what conclusions may be drawn from them.[15]

7

Cosima, as we have seen, had shaken off the dust of Munich on the 22nd July, after the King's revelation of a new campaign of gossip against her. That she had consciously cut herself off for good not only from Munich but from Bülow is shown by the fact that as soon as she arrived in Triebschen she began to keep a diary — [16] a symbolic act, as Du Moulin might say, indicating that a new life had begun for her. In the beautiful and moving sentences with which the diary opens she tells, for the future enlightenment of her children, whom, she says, she wishes some day to know her as she really was,[17] how 1868 has marked the turning-point in her outward life, for in this year it has been granted to her to realise in action what had been the inspiration of her soul for five years past — from the

---

[15] Guy de Pourtalès's account of the matter (PW, p. 334 ff) is also confused in its chronology.

[16] Or does Du Moulin's "from the very moment of her arrival in Triebschen" refer to her *final* settling there on the 16th November? As always, he is maddeningly vague: he flits backwards and forwards from fact to fact, from date to date, with as little sense of design as a fly zigzagging across a window-pane.

For our present purpose, however, it makes no difference whether Cosima's diary was begun in July or in November: all that we are concerned with is the light it throws on her attitude towards Bülow.

[17] Daniela was at that time in her eighth year, Blandine in her sixth, Isolde just entering on her fourth, Eva in her second.

day when she first knew that till then her life had been only "a desolate, unlovely dream". "I did not seek this realisation, nor try to
bring it about: it was destiny that imposed it on me." Within her,
all had been "waste and desolate" until the One came through whom
it was made clear to her that she "had never really lived at all".

> "My love was a new birth, a redemption, the death of all that was futile
> and bad in me; and I vowed to myself to seal it by death, by the holiest
> renunciation, or else by complete devotion, proving myself worthy of
> the work of love that has fallen to me, if ever I am able to requite it."

When she had seen her "only friend, the guardian spirit of my soul,
the revealer of all that is noble and true, driven out into solitude
alone, forsaken, loveless, friendless", she had been irresistibly
driven to brave everything and take his burden on her.

Whether Bülow had been "deceived" or not as to the Italian journey of Cosima — and as we shall see presently, there is no reason
to assume even that — he was certainly not ignorant of the state of
affairs during the last few years. To say, as Du Moulin does at this
point, that it was only when he opened "in the most innocent way"
that [hypothetical] letter in the autumn of 1868 that he became
aware of the full extent of "the Meister's relations with Frau Cosima,
which were known to all the world and hidden from him alone", is
to fly in the face of common sense. We have seen that there is every
reason to believe that Cosima had told him the truth as early as the
summer of 1864. Liszt's brief visit to Triebschen in October, 1867
had had no other object than to talk the matter over with Wagner.
And Bülow himself, in his angry letter of the 15th September, 1869
to the Countess de Charnacé, said that he had submitted to "a life
of incessant torture for more than three years" — which may be
taken to mean from the time when it became evident that Cosima
was about to bear Wagner a second child. The decisive turn taken
by events in the autumn of 1868 could therefore have been no surprise to him.

There are grounds for thinking that it had already been agreed
between them all at the time of the *Meistersinger* production that
a decision could not be much longer delayed, and the incident of
the "Röckel" letter merely accelerated matters. We have seen how
miserable Wagner was at that time because of the strained relations
between himself and Hans. "Cosima promises to follow [to Trieb-

schen] in a week", he notes in the "Annals". Then, immediately after his return to Lucerne,

> "In serious, grievous mood. After a few days, caught cold. Ill. Doctor every day: nerves, sweating, weakness. Beginning to be very clear about my situation and the state of things. Profoundest disinclination to any sort of movement: recognised in the destiny of my relation to Cos. and Hans the cause of my incapacity to will anything. Everything no use: the Munich attempts abortive: see it to be indispensable never to return there."

These last words seem to mean that no such external shoring-up of the rickety triangle as that of the last few weeks would be possible again. In another ten days or so his bodily health was restored, but the other wound bleeds afresh.

> "Apparent necessity of resignation to the most pitiable fate: precisely foreseen by Cos. since our separation last year: she had no faith in anything, and consequently doubted of me."

Next comes a reference to the King's letter to Cosima and Röckel's "scandal-mongering about my relations with Cosima"; and then,

> "Wrote to the King [16th July]. Immediately formed resolution that C. must leave Munich. Delay in her coming. Anxiety. She arrives 20 July [actually the 22nd] . . . Difficult communications about resolution. Plutonic and Neptunic solutions! Agreed upon the main matter."

Is it reasonable to suppose that all this painful time Cosima never once opened her mind to Hans on the vital subject of her leaving him for good?

8

But if Bülow, by the summer of 1868, had been well aware for a full four years of Cosima's conviction that her mission in life was to serve and save Wagner, why, it may be asked, could not a divorce have been amicably arranged long ago? The obstacle to that course seems to have been all along, in the main, Bülow himself, and more now than ever before. There were other complications, of course. Liszt, a deeply religious man himself, and with his still more religious Princess always at his elbow, shrank in true Catholic fashion from the idea of divorce. A further religious complication was that while Cosima was a Catholic, Wagner was, if anything at all, a Protestant. But on Bülow's side the cardinal objection to a divorce had been all along threefold, his chivalrous desire to spare Cosima the horror of the world's prying eyes and foul fingers, his reluctance to do anything that would start a fresh hue-and-cry, as he put it, against the Meister, and his natural objection to being driven out of the Munich Theatre.

It was the third of these considerations which in all probability weighed most with him in the autumn of 1868. He had come to like Munich and to enjoy his work there. Unlike Wagner, he got on well enough with Perfall: on one occasion when, in a spasm of bad health and bad temper, he had disparaged him to Bronsart, he was honest enough to admit in his next letter that he had been hasty and unjust. He saw himself at Munich on a rising tide of useful activity. In July, 1868 efforts had been made to attract him to Paris — by Pasdeloup, who offered him the musical direction of the Théâtre-Lyrique, and by the impresario Ullmann, who wanted him to take charge of the projected performances of *Lohengrin* at the Théâtre-Italien. Bülow refused both invitations: his sole ambition, he told Ullmann, was to perform his duties in Munich in such a way as to make the Opera and the Music School model institutions of their kind in Germany. "It matters nothing to me", he wrote gaily,

"whether the operas of Wagner are given badly or not given at all in Paris or London, in the Italian tongue or the Roman or the Abyssinian, whether Tamberlik sings Lohengrin in or out of tune, whether the jockeys hiss or the *biches* applaud."

And to Raff he wrote, "I concern myself solely with music, not politics, or aesthetics, or literature, and still less intrigue" — all of which is not only a statement of his own faith but a glancing blow at Wagner's mistakes. He had, in fact, become for the time being thoroughly satisfied with Munich and keen about his work there, so much so that we can understand his reluctance to be forced out of the town by Wagner and Cosima.[18] For that, in plain language, was what a divorce would have meant so far as he was concerned. Wagner and Cosima stood to lose little or nothing: indeed, their part in the transaction would be almost all pure gain, for they could

---

[18] Kapp holds that Bülow acted as he did in the Cosima-Wagner affair in 1868 and 1869 because he "hoped in this way to damp down the public scandal and so make it possible for himself to carry on through the winter his artistic activity in Munich — the fight for Wagner's works." (JKWF, p. 273). But Bülow's letters make it abundantly clear that he conceived his "artistic activity in Munich" in a much wider sense than simply "the fight for Wagner's works".

entrench themselves in Triebschen and let the foul winds of the world rage about their fortress as they would. But for Bülow it all meant that Munich would suddenly be made impossible for him. Already he had suffered much there on Cosima and Wagner's account, but he was now living that down, as he thought. The publicity of a divorce would have given his own enemies, Wagner's, and the more blackguardly journalists the chance they were longing for — to proclaim it from the housetops that he owed all the good fortune that had come to him in Munich to his complaisance as a husband. Can we wonder that both now and later he fought obstinately, desperately, against the idea of a divorce? [19]

The story of the pistol-practice, with Wagner as the destinaire some day of an avenging bullet, lacks confirmation from any reliable quarter. Du Moulin attributes the story to "a friend who appreciated equally both Wagner and Bülow": presumably this "friend" was his own father.[20] It is quite true that Bülow did some pistol-shooting at Wiesbaden, but there is no reason to see anything "symbolic" in that. Hans had gone to stay with Raff in order to rest and enjoy himself. In those days there was a Casino in Wiesbaden as in certain other towns of the Rhineland; and Bülow, who liked gambling, spent a good deal of his time playing roulette. Pistol-shooting was no doubt just one more of the amenities provided by the benevolent entrepreneurs, and there is no more reason to attach even a "symbolic" significance to Bülow's toying with pistols in Wiesbaden than to the pigeon-shooting of a discarded husband of today at Monte-Carlo.[21]

9

Bülow had no need of a second accidentally opened letter to make the situation clear to him as it was in the autumn of 1868. After the long list in the "Annals" of the places Wagner and Cosima had visited in north Italy come the entries, "Faido, Hotel de Poste. . . . Three bad but profound days. 3rd October (Saturday): deepest

---

[19] A quiet dissolution of the marriage was impossible, as under Prussian law desertion did not constitute grounds for divorce. There was no course open to him, if he wished to release Cosima, but full publicity.

[20] See Vol. III, p. 295, *note* 35.

[21] Albert Gutmann tells an amusing story *à propos* of Bülow's passion for gambling. See GAWM, pp. 27–28.

mood. Cosima writes." This letter of hers to Hans, says Dr. Strobel, does not appear to have been preserved; but he has no more doubt than anyone else can have that in it Cosima informed Bülow of her and Wagner's resolution never to be separated again. According to one legend, Hans had been kept in ignorance of the excursion to Italy, but the hands of Wagner and Cosima had been forced by their accidental meeting there with some people who knew them.[22] Dr. Strobel puts the matter in this way:

> "Wagner and Frau Cosima agreed to go to northern Italy together, in order, as Du Moulin believes, 'to clear up the whole situation'. On the 14th September, four days after Bülow's return to Munich [from Wiesbaden] they set out on their journey, as to which Bülow was at first hoodwinked, Cosima, out of consideration for him, having told him that she must go to her step-sister Countess Charnacé, in Versailles, there to look after her sorely damaged health for a while and eventually go to Italy with her." [23]

But is there any evidence to support Du Moulin's statement? The only reference in Bülow's correspondence at this time to anything of the kind is in a letter of his to Carl Bechstein, in which, after a reference to his "gloomy mood", he says,

> "my dear wife's health is very uncertain. . . . The doctors advise a change of climate, Munich being too inclement for her; and it is probable that I shall have to be separated from her for some time: she is going either to her step-sister in the south of France or to Italy."

But the date of that letter is the *16th October* — thirteen days after Cosima had written to him from Faido, eight days after her return to Triebschen with Wagner. The passage therefore cannot relate in any way to the journey to Italy. But that is not all. When that passage was written she was actually in Bülow's house. On the 14th October she had left Triebschen for Munich with her four children, for the express purpose of imploring Hans to put an end to the intolerable situation by giving her a legal release. (She no doubt took the children with her because Wagner intended to pay a visit shortly to his relations in Leipzig). The events of the four weeks spent by Cosima in Munich can be traced with entire certainty by

---

[22] "17th, Genoa", we read in the "Annals" . . . . "Liphort junior and senior. Annoying." The Liphorts were friends of the Bülows.

[23] See the article *Flucht nach Triebschen, ein Beitrag zur Lebensgeschichte Cosima Wagners*, in BFF, 1937, p. 77 ff.

the help of Wagner's "Annals", the telegrams that passed between him and Cosima, and his own letter of the 24th August of the following year to Madame Mouchanoff-Kalergis.[24] Let us note, *en passant,* that there was not a word of truth in Bülow's statement to Bechstein — made immediately after Cosima's arrival in Munich — that she was going to leave the town on the doctor's advice, and that she intended to settle down for some time with Claire Charnacé either in the south of France or in Italy. Cosima never had the smallest intention of doing anything of the sort, and could not have given Bülow any reason whatever to think she would. He was deliberately fibbing.

Wagner had accompanied Cosima as far as Augsburg on her journey to Munich on the 14th. He returned to Triebschen the next day, and the first entries in the "Annals" are,

"Anxious expectations. Only letters. . . . Cosima's news — promise to change her faith. . . . To Rome? Bewilderment and passionate concern: to [25] Cl. Charnacé — to Munich. Cosima beside herself. Greatly disheartened: decide on journey and call at Arcostrasse. C. more composed."

10

In his long account of the matter to Madame Mouchanoff-Kalergis in the following year, Wagner said that it was in July, 1868, after he had told Cosima that he would never return to Munich, that she decided she must have a "definitive separation" from Bülow. It was not merely that she felt it to be her mission to come to him and help him to complete his life's work. It had become clear beyond question to all three of them that it was impossible to carry on in the old style any longer — it meant the ruin not merely of their happiness and their work but of health itself. The Italian excursion could therefore have had for its object merely to think out in new surroundings the best way to achieve an end long desired and resolved upon. Since the question of divorce had been mooted long ago, why, we may ask, should Cosima have written Hans, on the 3rd October, a letter which was presumably meant to force a decision? A quite simple explanation suggests itself: by that time Cosima had

---

[24] KLRWB, II, 12–13, V, 79 ff, 93 ff. See also Otto Strobel's article in BFF, 1934.

[25] I.e., "wrote to": Wagner had written the Countess urging her to go to Munich to try to dissuade Cosima from going to Rome to see Liszt.

realised that she was pregnant by Wagner for the third time. For a dozen reasons it was unthinkable that in these circumstances she should occupy Bülow's house during the coming months: apart from the unpleasantness to be expected, and not without excuse, from Bülow himself and his mother, her condition would soon have made her once more the butt of her enemies in Munich.

Let us turn now to Bülow's letter of the 15th September of the following year (1869) to Claire de Charnacé.[26] "Last November", he says,

> "when I asked her an almost indelicate question about the motives for her brusque departure [27] — I had begged her in vain to await the coming of Liszt, in January — Cosima saw fit to reply to me with a false oath."

That falsehood, one surmises, was a denial of her pregnancy, as becomes fairly evident when we continue with Bülow's letter. He discovered the falsity, he says, a few months ago from the *newspapers* (the underlining is his own),

> "which bluntly announced the Meister's happiness at having been at last presented by his mistress [28] — name in full! — with a son, which had been given the name of Siegfried. . . ."

It must have been in a mood of utter desperation that Cosima arrived in Munich on the late 14th or early 15th October. It will be remembered that Bülow, in his letter of the 16th to Carl Bechstein, spoke of the probability of her going to live for some time either in Italy or in the south of France. The one word in that communication that has even the smallest hint of a contact with truth is "Italy", though not at all in the way that Bülow intended to suggest. Cosima, in sheer despair at being unable to make Hans see sense, had determined to sweep out of her path one main obstacle to the divorce and remarriage — the fact that she was a Catholic. This is the meaning of the "To Rome?" in the "Annals": Cosima planned to go thither and ask her father's approval of a change of faith on her part. Wagner, when he heard of this, saw the danger of the move: nothing could seem better calculated to wound Liszt to the depths

---

[26] It will be found in PW, pp. 336–339, where it was printed for the first time (in 1932).
[27] She had left him, for absolutely the last time, on the 16th November, 1868, and gone to Triebschen.
[28] On the 6th June, 1869.

of his soul and to destroy the last remains of whatever sympathy he may have had for Wagner and Cosima in the Bülow matter,[29] which was never much. In his agitation Wagner could think of no better means of dissuading Cosima from her purpose than sending her step-sister to Munich to reason with her. Cosima, bitterly resenting this move on his part, turned on him with an exasperation one would never have expected of her: this unasked-for interference, she wired to him, made existence intolerable for her. Claire's coming, she told him in her next telegram, had been in the highest degree offensive to her, and the refusal as regards Rome most painful.[30]

So strained was the situation by now that Wagner himself had to go to Munich on the 1st November. An entry in the "Annals" suggests that he called on Bülow, but nothing is known of what was said between them. He left for Leipzig the next day. On the 4th he addressed to the King a request for an audience, preferably in Hohenschwangau. It was refused. The Cabinet Secretary seems to have given as the reason for the refusal the coming visit of the Empress of Russia to Munich, but this was merely official eyewash: the true reason was the King's resentment over the long deception which he now saw to have been practised on him. In a letter of the 7th November to Düfflipp, Wagner tries to make out that he had merely wished to discuss a matter of his art with Ludwig; but the "Annals" suggest pretty conclusively that his real object had been to make a clean breast of his relations with Cosima, and perhaps he thought he would have more chance of winning his cause in a personal interview than by a letter. But the King was running no risks of that kind with him. He was hurt and annoyed, and as he could not write to Wagner in the old affectionate, devoted terms he preferred not to write at all. When he did resume the correspondence, three months later, it was clearly in another key, whatever pains he might be giving himself to reestablish the old one. In two people alone had he believed, Wagner and Cosima. These two had lied to him and tricked him as no politician had ever done; and, knowing

---

[29] Liszt had apparently ceased to correspond with Wagner long ago, and did not begin again till 1872. Their published correspondence contains no letter on either side between Liszt's of the 7th July, 1861 and Wagner's of the 18th May, 1872, in which the latter invited his old friend to the ceremony of the inauguration of the Bayreuth undertaking.

[30] She was by now no longer even staying with Bülow in the Arcostrasse; she had taken up her abode at 74 Türkenstrasse with Wagner's former servant, Franz Mrazeck, and his wife.

him as we now do, we have no difficulty in believing that his inner life was affected for some time by the revelation of their duplicity.

It could have been in no cheerful mood that Wagner went to Leipzig on the 2nd November, with the question of the divorce no nearer settlement than it had ever been, and with the suspicion that he had lost, perhaps, more ground with the King than he would ever be able to recover.

CHAPTER IX

COSIMA DECIDES

1

W AGNER'S VISIT to Leipzig seems to have been the outcome of a weakness rather rare with him — the desire to see some of his relations again. That in turn may have come from the feeling that, as events were turning out, he was not likely to see very much of the outer world in general for some time. In a letter to his sister Klara of the October of this year he indulges in yet another of his bouts of self-pity. His life, he says, is becoming more and more isolated: on the one hand there is his growing soreness towards a world that always misunderstands him, on the other there is his "lack of family", — which, in view of his recent achievements in paternity, is a somewhat surprising statement on his part. However, on the principle of any port in a storm, to a man in his frame of mind just then even relations may seem better than nothing; and his week's stay in Leipzig, from the 2nd to the 9th November, seems to have done him considerable good. He stayed with his sister Ottilie, the wife of the orientalist Professor Hermann Brockhaus, in their house in the Querstrasse. He had come, he insisted, to see *them*, not his native town of Leipzig, which had always behaved so badly to him; the Brockhaus servants were therefore told to be careful that no word of his visit got abroad in the town, and only a few trusted intimates of the family were allowed to see him.

One of these was Frau Ritschl, the wife of one of the most eminent classical scholars of the day. Until recently Friedrich Ritschl had been a professor of classical philology at the University of Bonn, where one of his most promising students had been a certain Friedrich Nietzsche, who had gone there from the famous old school at Pforta. In 1865 there had been a disagreement, of a type not uncommon in the German academic world, between Ritschl and another professor, Otto Jahn,[1] in consequence of which the former had removed himself to the University of Leipzig; thither he had been

---

[1] Author of the famous Life of Mozart.

followed by several of his students, among them Nietzsche, who, at the time of Wagner's visit to Leipzig, had just completed his twenty-fourth year.

The story of his first meeting with Wagner may be read in full in his own long and glowing letter of the 9th November to his friend Erwin Rohde. One evening, after Wagner had played what Nietzsche describes as "the Meistersingerlied" to the Brockhaus circle, Frau Ritschl happened to mention that she already knew the piece quite well through a certain student of the name of Nietzsche, who was notorious in scholastic circles for his passion for Wagner's music. Surprised at this evidence of interest in him in Leipzig, the Meister expressed a desire to make the acquaintance of the young man. Nietzsche was accordingly invited for the evening of Sunday, the 8th. He felt himself, he told Rohde, suddenly transported into a fairy tale, his only worry being how to array himself as became so great an occasion. A local tailor, as it happened, had promised to deliver his new evening suit that very day. He descended on the man in the afternoon, found the suit still not ready, and extracted from him a promise that it would be delivered before the hour was out; then he bought a copy of *Kladderadatsch* and chuckled as he read that Richard Wagner was in Switzerland but was having a fine new house built for him in Munich. By seven o'clock the clothes had still not arrived, and Nietzsche was getting desperate, for he lived some distance from the Querstrasse. When at last an old man brought them, a new complication arose — the tailor required cash on delivery. Arguments and promises of future liquidation being of no avail, the student and the messenger broke off diplomatic relations and plunged into total warfare. Nietzsche, with a truly German sense of the importance, in war, of securing a good strategic position at the outset, tries to get into the trousers. The old man holds on to them, and Nietzsche, fighting in his shirt, is worsted: the callous myrmidon of a sordid commercial system packs up the suit again and disappears with it, leaving Nietzsche, still in his shirt, breathless on the sofa, looking at his everyday black coat and wondering if that is "good enough for Richard". In the end it had to be.

In the Brockhaus drawing-room he found only the family and Wagner. "I am presented to Richard", he writes,

"and say a few reverential words. He wants to know exactly how I came to be so well up in his music, abuses horribly all performances of his operas with the exception of the famous Munich ones, and makes fun of the Kapellmeisters who call out amiably to their orchestras, 'Gentlemen, now some passion! My dear fellows, now a bit more passion!' Wagner imitates the Leipzig dialect very well. . . . Before and after dinner he played all the most important parts of the *Meistersinger*, taking the various voices; he was very exuberant. He is, indeed, extraordinarily lively and fervid: he speaks very rapidly, is very facetious, and makes a company of this entirely private kind very gay."

And truly Wagner was always at his best in small select companies of this kind, where he could do most of the talking and was listened to with respectful admiration, free from interruption by pestilent people, such as the professors and Pfistermeisters and Pfordtens and Fröbels and Perfalls of this wicked world, who presumptuously advanced opinions of their own instead of humbly taking down the tables of the law as they came straight from Sinai. It goes without saying that he regaled the gathering with a reading from the manuscript of his autobiography; according to Nietzsche, the passage chosen for this occasion was "an exceedingly entertaining scene from his student days in Leipzig", which he read in a style at the mere recollection of which Nietzsche once more dissolved in laughter.

The man of fifty-five and his thirty-one-years junior found another point of contact in their common admiration for Schopenhauer, upon whom, says Nietzsche, Wagner discoursed enthusiastically and at length, saying how much he himself owed to him, and that he was the only philosopher who had understood the nature of music. At the end of the evening Wagner shook hands warmly with the young man, invited him to pay him a visit in Triebschen some day for a chat about music and philosophy, and commissioned him to make his sister Ottilie and his other relations acquainted with his music.

Such was Wagner's first meeting with one who was destined to be before long, and for a few years, his closest friend, and, after his death, one of his foulest enemies.

2

Leaving Leipzig on the evening of the 9th November, Wagner spent the next day in Augsburg, where, in response to a wire to Cosima, Daniela, Blandine and Isolde were brought to see him by their nurse Hermine. On the 11th the children returned to Munich and Wagner to Triebschen, where Cosima joined him five days later with Isolde and Eva. This was the end of all pretence on her part of keeping up appearances so far as Bülow was concerned. He knew perfectly well that she had gone to rejoin Wagner with the fixed intention of never leaving him again. By this time Wagner had managed to persuade himself that he was the most unhappy and most ill-used man in the world. No one who saw his life merely from the outside, he moaned to Konstantin Frantz on the 14th, could measure the extent of his misery. He was living in a complete desert, which he could not endure much longer were it not that a domestic change of the profoundest importance was impending. Life was inexpressively hard and bitter for him, he said, as it had been ever since his imprudent youthful marriage. That his own coming happiness, for which he was fighting so desperately, was being purchased at the cost of Bülow's never seems to have weighed in the least with him.

And it was true, in a sense, that his world was at the moment crumbling about him. He could doubt no longer that the King was offended with him. His dreams of influencing Bavarian politics were at an end; it is noticeable that from this time onwards he practically ceases to try to direct Ludwig's thinking on these matters. Munich was virtually closed to him and Cosima from now onwards. The record was a sad one, but the last thing he could have been brought to admit was that every link in this long chain of frustration had been forged by his own hands.

Cosima had hardly left the Arcostrasse before Bülow was mendaciously telling his friends that she had gone to stay with her stepsister in Versailles because of the calumnies to which she was exposed in Munich. How this deception was to be kept up indefinitely he probably never dared ask himself; for to allow that question to rear its menacing head was to evoke also the yet more menacing problem of how long he would be able to maintain his position in Munich. His only escape from the cares incessantly gnawing him was by plunging more frantically than ever into work. The *Meistersinger* had been taken in hand again after the summer recess, and had been proved to be well within the powers of the local personnel; indeed, Kindermann, the new Sachs, was in some respects superior to Betz.

To the last days of November belongs the curious history of one Fräulein Vollmann. On the 20th of the month Wagner forwarded to Düfflipp a letter he had received from this young lady, who was quite unknown to him — a letter the pathos of which, it appears, tore at his heart. One of the most admirable features of his character was his compassion for, and eagerness to help, anyone possessed of less of this world's goods than he — unless, of course, the person in question had put himself or herself unforgiveably in the wrong by becoming a creditor. He now felt bound to relax for once his rule of not making use of that "influence" over the King with which the world wrongly credited him. Düfflipp was asked to make the necessary enquiries about Fräulein Vollmann, and, if the result of these should warrant her being helped as she desired, to put the facts before his Majesty.

Wagner's innocent eyes were opened by Düfflipp's realistic reply of the 3rd December. It seems that a certain Vollmann, treasurer of the Munich University, a man with private means and in receipt of a good salary, had become involved in speculations and not only lost all his own money but embezzled University funds to the extent of some 15,000 florins. He was now in gaol, awaiting trial and likely to get a sentence of several years' imprisonment. His daughter, the Fräulein Vollmann who had appealed to Wagner for help, seems to have inherited all the paternal resource. Finding herself enceinte as the result of an association with some person or persons unknown, she had not only assured her father that the child was the King's and that she was confident of a handsome grant from the royal treasury for it — enough to restore the fallen fortunes of the University official — but that her amatory relations with his Majesty had been arranged by no less a person than Richard Wagner. She had already applied to the King for help; failing in this, and the unlawful activities of her father having come to light, she had fled to Switzerland, there, as Düfflipp drily put it, to try to impose on the man she had so grossly slandered. "What do you say to this edifying story?" he asked. What Wagner had to say to it was that it confirmed him in his opinion that the world was so wicked a place that the less he had to do with it henceforth the better.

3

His literary activities during the last months of 1868 were confined to a resumption of the dictation of *Mein Leben*, the writing of the *Reminiscences of Rossini* [2] that were published in the *Allgemeine Zeitung* of the 17th December, the preparation of a new edition in brochure form of his pseudonymous *Judaism in Music* articles of 1850, and, as we have already seen, the composition of three sonnets to Laube. These vitriolic poems had by no means purged his soul of its rancour against his former friend. In December he happened to light once more on Laube's article on the *Meistersinger*, and his anger flamed up afresh not only at the outrage itself but at the knowledge that the criminal responsible for it was being received socially in the Brockhaus home! He could not refrain from pointing out to Ottilie how offensive this unpardonable tolerance was to him. He hopes that if Laube ever mentions *his* name in the Querstrasse he will be at once put in his place: and if an appeal to the man's sense of decency should be ineffective, he is to be asked whether he would like Wagner to publish his letters of this year to Frau von Bülow and himself. Wagner has the less scruple in making this suggestion in that Laube is well aware that "even with his consent I am incapable of dirty tricks of this sort". So exquisite a feeling for the decencies of controversy does him infinite honour; but one would like to know how he could square that feeling with his scheme to lampoon Laube in a Vienna paper under the safe shield of anonymity. Perhaps, however, it would never occur to him that some people might regard this as coming under the rubric of a dirty trick: the elastic Wagnerian conscience never had any difficulty in reconciling little antinomies of that kind.

The new edition of *Judaism in Music*, which was dedicated to Frau Mouchanoff, appeared in early March. His best friends shook their heads over his folly in thus needlessly creating fresh hatreds for himself.

"I have just received from the publisher Weber the brochure of Wagner's Judaism articles (considerably enlarged). [3] Lord in Heaven, what a shindy there'll be!",

---

[2] Rossini had died on the 21st November.
[3] This was an exaggeration.

wrote Bülow to Pohl on the 6th March; and again, ironically, to Raff, whose quintet had just been performed in Munich,

"Your quintet went very well . . . and had a huge success. You are popular here with all musicians and cultivated music-lovers. Rubinstein's quartet,[4] on the other hand, was a failure, in spite of the sympathy for Jewish music aroused by Wagner's pamphlet."

Even Cosima, as venomous an antisemite as Germany could show at that time, seems to have been doubtful of the wisdom of this step on Wagner's part. Esser told Schott that he could not understand how Wagner could have committed such an indiscretion. If "P. . ." in Wagner's letter of the 6th April, 1869 to Bülow stands for either Pohl or Porges it is fairly evident that yet another of his closest friends regretted the step. Pauline Viardot Garcia wrote him from Paris in strong protest. Bülow told him that the brochure was making things increasingly difficult in Munich, not only for its author but for himself.[5]

According to Wagner, the main object in republishing the long-forgotten articles was to answer a question put to him by Madame Mouchanoff — why was the Press so unrelaxingly hostile to him? The only explanation he could give was that most of it was in the hands of the Jews. The possibility that quite a number of people everywhere might dislike him because of notorious defects in his own character would not, of course, occur to him. He was, in fact, in a state just then of constant irritation with everything and everybody, a mood in which he seemed to be always on the look-out for a pretext for a quarrel. It was so, for instance — to run a little ahead of our story — in the case of his one-time friend Eduard Devrient, who had the misfortune to publish, in the spring of 1869, a book of *Recollections of Felix Mendelssohn-Bartholdy*. Wagner, in a fit of ill temper, seized upon the occasion to publish first of all an article and then a pamphlet entitled *Herr Eduard Devrient and his Style*, the greater part of which was devoted to an attack on the bad writing of the book, though he managed to find a little space also for some sneers at Devrient's relations with Mendelssohn and his direction of the Karlsruhe Theatre. If there was any need at all in Germany for a brochure of this sort there was certainly no

---

[4] Rubinstein was a Jew.
[5] Bülow himself, however, could be antisemitic enough when it suited him to be so.

reason why Richard Wagner should have wasted his time in writing it — except the desire to find a personal victim for the rancour against the German world in general that filled his soul just then. Knowing well that he was doing something that hardly presented him in the most favourable light imaginable, he issued the Devrient pamphlet under the pseudonym of "Wilhelm Drach" — [6] one more instance of his preferring to fire at someone he disliked from behind a hedge rather than in the open. The true authorship of the pamphlet could hardly have been a secret for long; and Bülow was right when he said to Jessie Laussot, in April, 1869, that by his latest brochures the Meister had himself made "fraternisation with the world" impossible. But Wagner, of course, was as blind as ever to the fact, so plain to everyone else, that if he persisted in going out of his way to make enemies he could hardly complain if enemies he had: his own view of all such matters was that a world incurably evil had entered into a conspiracy of hatred against the one truly righteous man in it.

4

Notwithstanding his consciousness that the King was not very pleased with him, and for an excellent reason, Wagner had not hesitated to approach him towards the end of November, 1868, through Düfflipp, with a new financial suggestion. This time, however, it was a request not so much for a fresh benefaction as for a rearrangement of the terms of an older one. With his accumulating responsibilities as the father of a family he appears to have seen the necessity of making some provision for the future. His idea was to insure, with a French company, for a capital sum to accrue in the event of his death, earmarking for this purpose future incidental receipts from his works. To secure the policy, however, he would have to make a substantial first payment; so he wants the King to advance him a capital sum against which will be set the aforesaid receipts as they come in. He begs the favour (in addition to the already existing grant, in respect of which a final payment of 2,000 florins is to be deducted from his allowance on the 1st December

---

[6] The reader will remember that his attack of 1836 on Rellstab had been sent to the *Neue Zeitschrift für Musik* under the same pseudonym. See Vol. I, p. 383. The article on Devrient's book (in the *Norddeutsche Allgemeine Zeitung*) had been anonymous.

next), of a new advance of 10,000 gulden, the whole to be redeemed by deductions of 2,000 gulden per annum from his pension, in monthly payments beginning the 1st January; i.e., his allowance for the next six years will be 6,000 florins a year instead of 8,000. This arrangement will secure him the necessary tranquillity of mind to carry on his work — which, he points out, has been the express desire of his royal benefactor all along. As nothing seemed to have been done in the matter by the following February he raised it once more in a personal letter to the King; and on the 2nd March he was granted the desired loan of 10,000 florins.

For his Christmas gift of 1868 to the King — who had still not broken his silence — he sent the original manuscript, in four volumes, of the full score of *Rienzi*.[7] On the 29th December he addressed a long letter to Ludwig, thanking him for all he had done for him during the past four-and-a-half years, and lamenting that he has been so long denied the light of the sun of his life, though he still basks in its warmth. He believes, however, he is fulfilling the King's will in devoting himself now and henceforth in peace and quiet to the completion of his tasks. He is in regular communication with Bülow about the Theatre and the School, offering advice whenever he can. His cause is going well in France and Italy, especially the latter, where intelligent people are hoping for a regeneration of Italian taste through his works. One of the leading Italian men of letters, Boïto, has made a verse translation of the *Rienzi* text. So far has the enthusiasm for him in Italy gone that the young Crown Princess hopes to attract him to Florence, there to superintend in person the re-birth of Italian taste in music; but of course he will be careful to collaborate only with his counsel. If, as seems highly probable, he was simple enough to think that all this would bring the King back to him at once in a flutter of fear at the prospect of losing him, he was mistaken. Ludwig's sole reply was a brief telegram on the 1st January, sending him all good wishes for himself and his work in the new year, and promising to write "as soon as possible".

It was not until the 10th February (1869) that Ludwig broke his five months' silence, and his doing so may have been due, to some small degree, to yet another imposture, of no great importance in

---

[7] Not of *Lohengrin*, as the biographers state, though in his letter of the 20th December to Düfflipp Wagner himself, by a slip of the pen, calls it *Lohengrin*.

itself and more comic than anything else, practised on him by Wagner and Cosima. In a postscript to his letter to the King of the 29th
December Wagner said he was enclosing a letter from the Freundin
that had just reached him, addressed to his Majesty; and the letter
in question is indeed duly dated by Cosima the 27th! The object
of this rather childish little ruse was to conceal from Ludwig the
fact that she was all the time with Wagner at Triebschen, where,
indeed, she had been for the past six weeks. Her letter had contained a hint, for anyone who could read between the lines, that her
life had now taken a new orientation: she thanked the King for
having "loved *him* to whom my life is dedicated, and fostered the
faith that has transfigured my soul".

There is just a possibility that the assurance, as on the surface
it seemed to be, that the pair were not actually living together went
some way towards reconciling Ludwig to their now manifest deception of him in the past. He wanted so much to be able to believe
in the man Wagner again, less for Wagner's sake than for his own;
for the greatest of his griefs had been the feeling that an end was
coming to his hopes of "saving" German culture and so Germany
and the world. His first anger had burned itself out, and now he
was back again in the old ardent, affectionate, devoted mood, desiring only the re-building of the ideal world that had been in danger
of collapsing about him. Once more it is to Wagner that he looks
for solace and encouragement in his uncongenial task as King. He
will write soon to the Freundin, he says; meanwhile he begs her and
Wagner not to believe that his long silence has been due to any
cooling of his friendship and love for them. He is hungry for more
pages of the autobiography. In the coming summer the Theatre will
produce *Tristan* again, and after that, he trusts, the *Rhinegold:* he
implores Wagner to do all he can to make the latter possible, for
he needs pure joys of this kind if he is to go on bearing the heavy
burden of his duties. And he is trying to persuade himself once
more that "our ideal" will surely be realised to the full.

Wagner's immensely long reply to this must have occupied him
for the major part of the 23rd and 24th February. Much of it is
taken up with a description of his life at Triebschen, to which we
shall return later. It is only towards the end that he addresses himself to the question of his attitude towards the proposed *Rhinegold*
production, and with that also we shall deal in a moment. It is first

of all necessary to run an eye over certain events at Triebschen during the first two or three months of 1869.

5

On the 13th April Bülow wrote to his old friend Jessie Laussot, now living in Florence, that he was all alone in Munich, having sent his children to Lucerne, where his wife had also arrived from Versailles. He no doubt told the same story to all his friends. It is quite true that on the 8th he had sent Daniela and Blandine to Zürich, and that Cosima had met them there and taken them to Triebschen, where Isolde and Eva already were. The remainder of Bülow's story is false: no one was better aware than he that Cosima had never been to Versailles. To the charge of deliberate untruth on Bülow's part there can be no defence now. Cosima's contemporary letters to the little Daniela (published in 1933) are obviously written from Triebschen; and no one in his senses will contend that letters from a mother to a child of eight-and-a-half, living in her father's house, were not read, and intended to be read, by him.[8] Details about "Uncle Richard", such as his telling Cosima of an accident to one of the pheasants, make it perfectly clear that she was in Triebschen. In a couple of the letters — those of the 28th November and the 21st January — there are references to "Aunt Claire"; and the faintest possibility that what Cosima is saying to Daniela about Countess Charnacé may be based merely on letters from her is ruled out by the entry in Wagner's "Annals" showing that her step-sister had been staying in Triebschen.[9]

But this is by no means all the evidence that Bülow was perfectly well aware from the moment Cosima left Munich on the 16th November, 1868 that she was going not to Versailles but to Triebschen. Du Moulin's record of the next three or four months, which is based on Cosima's diary, leaves us in no doubt as to this. Her position, he says,

"was by no means an easy one. In accordance with a wish of her husband's — a rather doctrinaire and formal wish — she was to live in

---

[8] Bülow's mother was also living with him at this time.

[9] "Fair copy of *Siegfried* Act I finished. Took up again idea of *Judaism*. Claire Charnacé: somewhat Mathildish" — i.e., resembling Frau Wesendonk. The environing entries establish the date of the Countess's arrival as the end of November.

concealment in Triebschen. She had complied with this, and now had to recognise that it was not so easy. The servants of the Bassenheim family,[10] which was otherwise very friendly, spied on her, and there was a danger of the secret of her whereabouts being revealed in Munich."

That Bülow, in spite of the story about Versailles that he had put about in November, knew that Cosima was at Triebschen is further proved by his suggesting that she should leave it. "But now came a new disturbance on Hans's part", says Du Moulin. "He wrote to the Meister asking that his wife should visit Versailles and await there the further course of events." As usual, Du Moulin gives no date, but from a number of little pointers in the text [11] it is clear that the passage relates to somewhere near the end of February.[12]

Precisely what motivated this move on Bülow's part we do not know: all that Du Moulin has to say on the subject is that it came from "a certain narrowness of understanding as well as from the difficulty of the matter in its State aspect." Whatever Bülow's motive may have been, however, the relevant passage in Cosima's diary demonstrates beyond all question the falsehood of the story that Hans imagined his wife to be at that time with her step-sister in Versailles. It appears that Cosima "at once grasped what Hans meant by this last communication of his" — in which she was rather more fortunate than we are — and that for a time she was strongly in favour of doing what he had suggested. Perhaps what Bülow had in mind was some more or less formal step preliminary to the divorce, which all three of them must have known to be inevitable before very long. His mother was, as usual, making mischief between him and the woman she hated so much, and Cosima's diary shows that, as Du Moulin puts it, Liszt "kept himself at a distance", his attitude being "almost hostile". Cosima's letters to Daniela show that Liszt had been visiting Bülow in Munich, so that it is probable that the old tormenting question of a divorce had come up again. Reference by Du Moulin to the arrival of a letter from the King to Wagner which had been forwarded to the latter through Bülow gives us at least one chronological clue in this maze of inference

---

[10] Count Bassenheim and his wife were neighbours living on the opposite side of the Lake.

[11] For instance, a casual mention of "St. Richard's day" — the 7th February.

[12] It is a great pity that as yet no extracts from Wagner's "Annals" after 1868 have been published.

and conjecture. We know that the letter in question was dated the 25th February [13] — about the time when, as seems probable on other grounds, Bülow threw his bombshell into the peace of Triebschen; and the supposition may perhaps be permitted that Liszt had again been raising difficulties. "Your father", said Wagner to Cosima about this time, as appears from her diary, "would certainly make objections to our union if I were to become a Catholic in order to facilitate it", — which, whatever else it may prove, shows at any rate that one of the obstacles to the divorce had all along been the opposition, on confessional grounds, of Liszt and the Princess Wittgenstein.[14]

6

As Cosima's chief desires at this time were to be divorced and to be re-united to her two eldest children, it looks as if Bülow's suggestion that she should leave Triebschen for a couple of months had had some bearing on these matters; otherwise it would be difficult to account for her thinking the suggestion perhaps worth acting upon. That she did think so is evident from the passage in her diary in which she says she did not "persist" in her idea of telling Hans that she would "go to Munich to the children for two months, and then return with all four of them to Triebschen at the beginning of May"; her object being "to avoid a scandal, on account of the children as well as of the King". The full meaning of it all evades us; but perhaps what was in her mind was that while she would have to be at Triebschen for her confinement in June — as in the case of Eva, — by spending a couple of months in Munich in Bülow's house she might give check to the gossip which must already have been circulating in the capital as to her long absence and the reason for it. Her scheme, however, broke down in face of the passionate protests of Wagner, who declared that if she were to leave him for even two months it would be the end of him and of his work.

Two plain facts emerge from this tangle of evidence. One is that

---

[13] It will be found in KLRWB, II, 265 ff.

[14] Cosima goes on to say that she asked Richard if, in case of necessity, he would have turned Catholic in order to marry her. That, he answered, was "the devil of a question", as he could not imagine the contingency arising. Cosima was a little taken aback at first, but saw the matter from his point of view later, a change from Catholicism to Protestantism being easier, it is said, than the reverse process, inasmuch as it does not involve an acknowledgment of previous heresy.

Bülow was lying, and knew he was lying, when he told everyone that Cosima was in Versailles; and the demonstration of this is of itself sufficient to undermine our faith in all the other legends that have passed into history of his having been "deceived" for years by Wagner and Cosima. The second is that while the question of divorce was now more urgent than it had ever been, a solution of the problem that would at the same time commend itself to all parties (including Liszt), avoid public scandal, and not add fuel to the fire of the King's displeasure, was as far from attainment as ever.

This uncertainty it was that cast a shadow over the happiness of the pair in Triebschen in the winter of 1868–9. Most painful of all to them must have been the recognition that it was they themselves who had created the main difficulty, so far as the King was concerned, by their public trickery of him in 1866.

"They were both perturbed about their relations with the King", says Du Moulin, on the evidence of Cosima's diary, "and they could not shut out the thought that the Meister's pension might be stopped. But what affected him more deeply were his spiritual experiences with the King, which made him more afraid of the possibility of his having to decline the pension than of a hostile step on Ludwig's part. But they weighed the consequences. 'We talked over the possibility of a future in a Paris garret. One living room and two bedrooms for us and the children! God knows what Fate has in store for us!'"

Wagner in a garret, in Paris or anywhere else, at this stage of his life is of course inconceivable. For one thing he would have fought heroically against such a fate to the last gulden of his last friend; for another, as even Cosima saw, "his already completed works would surely secure them against want, even without the King". But that they should have discussed the possibility of the King's abandonment of Wagner gives us a partial measure of their perception of what they had been guilty of with regard to him. As it happened, they were perturbing themselves unnecessarily. Ludwig would have been incapable of a shabby stroke of that sort — a reflection that was no doubt at the back of Wagner's mind when he indulged in his easy heroics about the garret in Paris.[15]

---

[15] It is true that in a moment of flaming anger against Wagner at a later date he did indeed talk about withdrawing the pension. (See *infra*, p. 223). But the remark was made to Düfflipp only, and we hear no more of the subject. Ludwig was far too high-minded to injure Wagner in that way.

7

The petty prevarications to which they were now committed — irrevocably committed so long as they held back from making a clean breast of the matter to the King — must have been exceedingly galling to them: at any moment a fresh strain might be imposed, by the sheer pressure of events, upon some weak spot or other in the complicated tissue of their pretence. It was so, for instance, with the autobiography. This had been throughout in Cosima's handwriting, she taking down from Wagner's dictation. When therefore the King became eager for a further instalment of the manuscript Wagner was reduced to further fibbing. He had "heard from" the Freundin,[16] he tells Ludwig in February — the impression intended to be conveyed is that he had heard from her by post — that her bad health made writing difficult for her; her physician, indeed, had strictly forbidden anything of that kind. Consequently he would have to look round for a suitable copyist. Enquiries in the neighbourhood having proved fruitless, he has commissioned Richter to look for what he requires in Munich. The copyist will have to settle in Lucerne for some time,[17] "for it is quite impossible for me to part with this dictation: the copyist must do his work under my own eyes." The truth is that he and Cosima had begun work once more on the autobiography in the preceding November. A jotting in the "Annals" at Christmas indicated that the section relating to Scho-

---

[16] The childish fiction was kept up by Cosima also. On the 25th March (1869) she began a long letter to the King which she continued on the 7th, 8th and 9th April. The second instalment begins thus: "Nearly a fortnight has passed since the foregoing lines, and now I am in Triebschen." The impression she wished to convey to the King is that she has just arrived there, whereas she had been there continuously since the 22nd July, 1868, apart from the trip to Italy with Wagner in September and October and the four weeks, from mid-October to mid-November, which she had spent in Munich discussing matters with Bülow.

In this long letter, by the way, she says a great deal that is obviously intended to prepare the King for the news of the final throwing-in of her lot with that of Wagner. (An extract from the letter is given in KLRWB, II, 267 *note*). She must have been sick in every fibre of her being of the net of duplicity in which she and Wagner had gradually become entangled, and anxious to cut through it now at any cost. As Bülow put it in his letter to Countess Charnacé, "When your step-sister [Cosima] is free — perhaps the proceedings in the matter of a separation cannot be completed in less than a year from now, — when her liaison with her lover has been legitimised before 'public opinion', she will become herself again, and will no longer have to lie from morning to night." Nor, we may add, would he.

[17] The man he had in mind was one Waschmitzius, who, under Richter's supervision, was occupied just then in copying out for Wagner the articles of his youth that had appeared in various periodicals no longer obtainable.

penhauer was taken in hand about that time, and by the following February they had arrived at the Zürich period. Cosima seems to have paid scant attention to the prohibitions of her doctor!

On the 1st March Wagner began the Composition Sketch of the third act of *Siegfried:* he had been greatly pleased, he wrote to the King, to find he could recapture without difficulty the mood and the idiom of the work he had laid aside twelve years before. He hoped to have the whole score ready for presentation to his benefactor by the end of the year. Before that time came, however, he and the King were thoroughly at cross-purposes over the production of the *Rhinegold* in Munich, the story of which will be told in full in the next chapter. Meanwhile there are one or two loose ends of biography and history to be disposed of.

8

That profound philosopher Albert Eustace Peasemarch could have desired no better demonstration of the part played in human history by "the inscrutable workings of Fate, or, as some call it, Destiny", than the record of the friendship of Wagner and Nietzsche. Fate had manifestly made up its mind to throw them together in spite of the geographical distance between them. Had Ritschl not quarrelled with Jahn, Nietzsche would not have followed the former to Leipzig in 1865. Had he and Rohde carried out their plan for studying a year or two in Paris he would not have been in Leipzig in 1868. Had Wagner's daemon not driven him to Leipzig in the November of that same year on no better pretext than that it was time he saw something of his relations, he would not have met the young friend of Frau Brockhaus and Frau Ritschl who had already attracted attention by his knowledge of the *Meistersinger*. The more than three hundred miles between Leipzig and Lucerne would probably have reduced to a mere conventional *politesse* the older man's invitation to the younger one to call on him. But the Fates were not going to be thrown out of their stride by a trifle of this last sort. They arranged before many weeks were over that a professor of classical philology should be required by the University of Basel, and that the authorities there should ask Ritschl if he could tell them something about a young man named Nietzsche whose recent articles in the *Rheinisches Museum* had attracted some attention in the philological world, that Ritschl should reply that the young man in question was a genius, and that consequently Nietzsche should find himself, in February, 1869, at the age of twenty-four, appointed to an academic chair in a Swiss town some fifty miles from Lucerne. Did the thought of being not far from Richard Wagner influence him, one wonders, in making a decision against which he felt certain vague inner promptings? Certain it is that the card on which he announced the astonishing news to Rohde ended with the words, "Long live free Switzerland, Richard Wagner and our friendship!"

He settled in Basel in the third week of April. Less than a month later, while on an excursion to the Lucerne neighbourhood with some friends, he broke away from the others on the morning of Saturday, the 15th May, and walked to Triebschen. Pausing diffidently at the gate, wondering whether he had not perhaps taken the general invitation of the preceding November too literally, he heard some anguished harmonies being reiterated on the piano; he recognised them at a later date as belonging to the phrase that accompanies Brynhilde's words

> Verwundet hat mich
> der mich erweckt,

("He who awakened me has dealt me this wound"), in the third act of *Siegfried*. It was an omen!

The servant told him that Herr Wagner could not be disturbed at his work, which would occupy him until two o'clock. Nietzsche left his card, and was turning away when the servant came back with the query from Wagner whether this was the Herr Nietzsche whom he had met in Leipzig. Discovering that it was, he invited the young man to return and have lunch with him. This, however, Nietzsche could not do, as he had to rejoin his party; but he accepted an invitation to call at Triebschen again on the following Monday (Whit Monday). So excellent was the impression he made on that occasion that he was asked to spend the following Saturday, the 22nd — Wagner's birthday — in the quiet house by the Lake. His professorial duties made it impossible for him to accept, whereupon a further invitation followed, this time for the week-end of the 5th–7th June. Nietzsche had to leave early on the Monday for Basel; and it was only later that he learned that at four o'clock that morning Frau von Bülow had given birth to a son, on whom the name of Siegfried had been bestowed. Vreneli announced the world-shaking event to Wagner in the words "Ein Sohn ist da!" words which he was to repeat ecstatically in the poem of two stanzas in which he dedicated the *Siegfried Idyll* to Cosima:

> Erscholl ein Ruf da froh in meine Weisen:
> "Ein Sohn ist da!" — der musste Siegfried heissen.

It is pleasing to be able to record that the cosmos realised the greatness of the event and behaved with becoming solemnity. According to an entry in Cosima's diary, the sun, which, with a fine sense of stage lighting, had chosen this as the most appropriate moment to rise above the Rigi, cast its first rays right into Richard's room, surprising him with "an incredibly beautiful fire-glow" which lit up the orange wall-paper and was reflected on "the blue casket with my portrait on it", thus "transfiguring the picture with an unearthly splendour." [18]

9

Wagner and Cosima had quickly taken to the young man. It was evident at a glance that intellectually he was of superior calibre to anyone of his sex who had so far swum into Wagner's orbit; and the latter was agreeably surprised to find a member of the professorial class, his relations with which had hitherto never been very cordial, so obviously prepared not only to think with him but to learn from him. As for Nietzsche, he was in the seventh heaven of happiness. Wagner, he wrote to his friend Rohde, was everything that could have been hoped,

> "a prodigally rich and great spirit, an energetic character, a lovable, fascinating man with a vast passion for knowledge. I must end my letter, or I shall be singing a paean."

And a little later,

> "He realises everything we could have wished: the world really does not know the human greatness and singularity of his nature. I learn a great deal in his company: this is my practical course in the Schopenhauerian philosophy."

So the happy double fugue went on in the weeks and months that followed, during which time the young professor spent many an ecstatic hour in Triebschen the mere memory of which in later years, when he had sundered himself irrevocably from Wagner, could

---

[18] MECW, pp. 450–1.

move him almost to the tears of a Peri for a lost paradise. Wagner must have been enchanted to be told that his young disciple — for such he seemed to be at that time — admired him for his deep and concentrated ethical impulse, his earnest spiritual conception of the world, and his profound Germanism, every note in which great symphony set a responsive chord vibrating in Nietzsche's heart. Wagner, on his side, could assure the young man's sister Elisabeth that her brother and his friends "belong to an absolutely new and wonderful order of men, the possibility of which I never believed in before." [19] The only fly in the ointment was Nietzsche's obstinacy in the matter of his vegetarianism. "Nietzsche was a vegetarian on principle", says Du Moulin gravely.

> "The Meister reproved him for this, holding that the contest of all against all ran through the whole of creation, so that it was necessary for man to get strength through his food in order to accomplish great things. Nietzsche agreed with him absolutely, but persisted in his abstinence, which made the Meister really cross." [20]

It is piquant to find Wagner, the fanatical vegetarian of a few years later, trying to set Nietzsche against vegetarianism, and impressing it on the future philosopher of the "Will to Power" that "the contest of all against all ran through the whole of creation".

10

On the 15th June, nine days after the birth of her and Wagner's third child, Cosima, in a letter from which some extracts have already been given,[21] implored Bülow to make an end of the intolerable situation between them. On the 9th Hans had sent in his definitive resignation as Kapellmeister: he was morally and physically at the end of his tether, he told Karl Klindworth. He still had some obligations to fulfil in Munich, among them the conducting of some performances of *Tristan* that had been commanded by the King for the closing week of the month. Wagner would have liked Hans to make these a pretext for resigning: naturally it would have been much more agreeable to him to have it said that Bülow was leaving Munich because of an offence on the part of the King to his "honour as an artist" than that the true reasons should be known. By the end

---

[19] FNJN, p. 250.
[20] MECW, p. 459.
[21] See Vol. III, p. 295 *note*. The letter will be found in full in KLRWB, V, 115 ff.

of May the matter of the divorce had clearly arrived at its climax. Wagner wanted a personal talk with Bülow: the latter was at first agreeable to this, for he found writing, he said, "horribly difficult", there being so much that could not be said in that form; but after the interchange of the decisive letters of the 15th and 17th June between Cosima and himself he begged to be excused from going to Triebschen, for the reasons, among others, that the meeting would be painful for Wagner, that he himself would find it a "dangerous" emotional strain, and that he had gone into everything fully in his letter to Cosima. "So it seems to me that a meeting of us two is superfluous. It is better that at my really definitive departure from Munich I should say my last farewell to you in writing." [22] They never saw each other again.

11

Cosima, in her letter of the 15th, had expressed the hope that his real reason for leaving Munich was his feeling that he could no longer serve his art there as he could have wished. Bülow's view of the matter will be found in his letter of the 15th September to Claire Charnacé. After saying that it was *from the newspapers* that he, like everyone else, had heard that Cosima had presented Wagner with a son nine days before, he continues thus:

"The hell I endured during the last period of my activity [in Munich] is beyond imagination. In constant contact as I was with a host of musicians, professors and pupils, and in face of a publicity that showed small consideration for me — the most widely-read paper praised me for the devotion I had brought to the study of the work of my wife's friend, — I had only one of two alternatives, either to be regarded with the most insulting pity as a man ignorant of what everyone else knew or to be covered with infamy for having concluded a most shameful deal as the favourite of the King's favourite. At the same time the papers announced that the divorce was imminent — this before I had taken the first step towards it!"

It is little wonder that he told Cosima and Wagner that he was tired of "simulating and dissimulating". Against this she protested: so far as his relations with her were concerned no blame, she said, could be fastened on him, no shame be visited on him: his character was too well known for that — which must have brought a wry

---

[22] See his letter of the 21st June in BNB, pp. 470 ff.

smile to his lips. She would prefer him to remain at his post in Munich, in the first place because by doing so he would be able to put something aside for his children, in the second place because he was not fitted for the life of a wandering artist. She had kept on hoping against hope that matters might be so arranged between them that he would not have to uproot himself in Munich. She glances for a moment at the sad failure of their marriage through fundamental incompatibility, and then continues,

"You will never know how I have struggled and what I have suffered, and it is impossible for me to describe the consternation I felt when it became clear that the project of a life *à trois* was unrealisable"

— yet another proof that Bülow had not been "deceived" all this time.[23]

It was not that she herself shrank from suffering, of which she had had her share; it was "the presentiment that things could not go on like this, and that you yourself were hastening the catastrophe." Her affection for him remains unchanged; and it is in the name of that affection that she asks him, if he can find the strength to separate publicly from her, to let her have the education of the children, for she fears for their happiness if they should pass into the charge of his mother. She knows what the verdict of his family and of the world will be upon her, but she believes he can rise superior to thoughts of that kind. The small allowance of 6,000 francs which she receives from her own father and mother she begs him to put aside for the future of the children.

Bülow's long reply of the 17th June [24] is in his loftiest vein. He takes the blame on himself for having "poisoned her life", acknowledges how much he had constantly owed to her patience, her friendship, her good feeling, her indulgence, her sympathy, her encouragement, her counsels. He has lost her, and now he is bankrupt in body and soul. She has chosen to consecrate her life and all her fine qualities to another; he admits she is justified in doing so, and says his sole consolation in his torments has always been the thought that "over there Cosima is happy". He has given out as the reason for the resignation of his post the deplorable state of his health, as to which no one can have any doubt: the gradually increasing load

---

[23] Du Moulin quotes an entry in her diary on the 8th January, 1869 (Hans's birthday), which shows that the difficult problem of a life *à trois*, which Bülow had evidently wished to continue, was racking her soul beyond endurance.

[24] BNB, p. 477 ff.

of work, intrigues, calumnies and obstacles of all kinds has combined with the loss of Cosima's support to break him. Economically he is not sacrificing much, his salary as Kapellmeister being a mere 4,000 florins a year. His grief is that while he feels he can no longer accomplish very much in Munich he knows it is being said of him that he owes his position to the favour of the King and to his "complaisance de mari". So it is better that he should go; and he finds a melancholy satisfaction in the fact that his career in Munich is ending, as it had begun, with *Tristan,* "that gigantic but fatal work".[25] Yes, without reproach to the great creator of it, *Tristan* has dealt him the *coup de grâce:* it has drained him, as it had drained others, of the last ounce of strength. He must leave the town that has become a hell for him since Cosima departed, and try to build up a new life elsewhere.

He sees now that he must separate his lot entirely from hers and Wagner's, "even in thought, so far as that is humanly possible". But he still shrinks from the publicity and the vexations of a divorce, though should Liszt think that her association with Wagner ought to have that "official affirmation" he will drop his opposition to the step. In any case he entrusts the children to her. The 6,000 francs of income which she receives from Liszt and her mother he asks her to devote to the expenses of his daughters' education.[26] He will turn over to Cosima and the children, when he leaves Munich, the whole of the contents of his house there: he will take away with him only his clothes, his books and his music. Whither he will flee he does not at present know; his one desire is to break radically with everything that might remind him of the past and so cripple him in his effort to begin afresh. Only one memory does he wish to take with him — that of his gratitude for all that Cosima has done for his development as an artist. "May God protect and bless", the generous letter ends, "the mother of the fortunate children to whom she wishes to continue to devote herself."

---

[25] "It was with *Tristan*", he had written to Carl Bechstein a few days before this, "that my activities here began four years ago. There lies more meaning than you can as yet fathom in the fact that it is with *Tristan,* too, that my activities are ending." The reader will remember that "four years ago" (in April, 1865) on the day of the first orchestral rehearsal of *Tristan,* Cosima had presented him with Wagner's child Isolde.

[26] "The money of your own which you brought to our unfortunate marriage", he says, "was it not for me, ashamed as I was of my poverty, the first stumbling-block, the first disturbing factor?"

CHAPTER X

THE BREACH WITH THE KING

1

WE HAVE seen, in the summer of 1868, the dawning of an interest in Wagner in Italy. In Paris, too, there was a demand for his works about this time which would certainly have increased steadily but for the war of 1870. Pasdeloup had produced *Rienzi* in the *Théâtre-Lyrique* on the 6th April, 1869; by June it had run to no fewer than twenty-five performances, to the great enrichment of Pasdeloup, as Wagner remarked rather wistfully to Richter. The impresario planned to put *Lohengrin* into rehearsal immediately, and to follow this in February, 1870 with the *Meistersinger*. On the same day that *Rienzi* had been first given in Paris *Lohengrin* had been produced in Berlin under the new Kapellmeister, Karl Eckert, who had recently replaced the slow-witted Taubert and Dorn as musical head of the Opera. "Terrific success, Jews all reconciled", Tausig, himself a Jew, telegraphed Wagner, in ironic reference to *Judaism in Music*, thereby drawing on himself the displeasure of the Meister and Cosima for treating so solemn a subject as themselves with such levity. The Jews were supposed to be everywhere trying to take their revenge for *Judaism in Music;* and Glasenapp regarded it as quite an encouraging sign of the times that in spite of them Wagner should now be making some headway in the traditional stronghold of Mendelssohn and Meyerbeer. One of these signs was his election, on the 9th May, 1869, as a foreign associate of the musical section of the Prussian Royal Academy of Arts. Though in general he placed little store by these gewgaws it no doubt gave him a peculiar sly pleasure to accept this one. In accordance with routine, the Academy, when notifying him of the proposed honour, had asked him for "an outline of his life and a statement of his present position and titles". He replied, with appropriate gravity, that in the matter of his biography he had nothing to add to the article on him in the Brockhaus *Konversationslexikon,* while his position and titles consisted in his having no position and no title. Thanks to the beneficence of the King of Bavaria, he continued, he was assured permanently of the priceless privilege of not having to enter into any personal relation with any German musical or theatrical institute of art. The last "official title" awarded him would be found in the document in which the Saxon Ministry of Justice had given him permission to enter Saxony again: it ran thus, "To the former Royal Saxon Kapellmeister Richard Wagner". Since then no titles have come his way except that of honorary membership of various German singing clubs and musical societies. Some five years ago, he continued, the Capitular of the Maximilian Order had nominated him for that Bavarian honour. But he had declined it because of a misunderstanding; [1] on which account he had later had to decline, for diplomatic reasons, the St. Mauritius and St. Lazarus Order which the King of Italy had wished to bestow on him. [2]

2

Had it not been for the ever-present annoyance of Bülow's refusal to come to heel in the matter of the divorce, indeed, Wagner would have found life enjoyable enough at this time. The old cordial relations seemed to have been gradually established with the King once more, though reading between the lines we can see that Wagner was handling him with special wariness just then. He knew full well that Ludwig was eager now not only for revivals of his older works but for a hearing of so much of the *Ring* as was already practicable for performance; and Wagner must have had a foreboding that this desire would lead before long to trouble between them. Formerly his grievance had been that the King seemed to avoid personal contact with him; but now we find *him* pleading, as the 22nd May once more draws nigh, for permission to spend his birthday undisturbed in Triebschen. He will regard as his real natal day this year, he casuistically assures the King, the day on which he can lay the completed score of *Siegfried* at his protector's feet. Till then, "No birthday! No celebration! Even in Triebschen no

[1] See Vol. III, p. 316.
[2] See Vol. III, p. 518 *note*. It is not clear from his letters of 1866 whether he had actually refused the Italian decoration, or merely surmised that the Saxon Government, prejudiced as it had always been against him, might be offended by his wearing it.

notice shall be taken of it!" He forbore to mention to the King that less than a week earlier Cosima had invited Nietzsche to come to Triebschen on the festal 22nd — an invitation which, as we have seen, the young professor was unable to accept. Cosima, of course, had her own views as to how the great day should be spent. Richter came expressly from Munich for it, travelling two nights in order to have half a day in Triebschen; and he surprised Wagner, on the morning of the day, by waking him with Siegfried's horn call blown lustily outside his bedroom. When Wagner came down to breakfast he found his room turned into a flower garden, he told the King in his letter of the 26th. Four pretty little creatures — "the daughters of our Freundin", as he tactfully describes them — made up as the Messengers of Peace in *Rienzi*, approached him with palm branches in their hands, and "the two eldest recited old Greek poems in celebration of spring". The presents were laid out, including, of course, those from the King. After this naïve sort of mummery, in which he seems to have taken a childishly solemn delight on each of the birthdays he celebrated under Cosima's aegis, came the climax of her delicate forethought for him. At what must have been considerable expense she had secretly arranged for the visit to Triebschen of the Maurin-Chevillard String Quartet, the only one in Europe, according to Wagner, that could play the last quartets of Beethoven as they should be played.[3] Wagner, who had come down in his dressing-gown, had the surprise of his life when he saw the players, among whom he recognised Maurin as an acquaintance of the Paris period. They treated him, according to Glasenapp, to the posthumous quartets in A minor and C sharp minor and the one in E minor.[4]

He was further flattered that day by the visit of his young Alsatian admirer Edouard Schuré, who had heard the Munich performances of *Tristan* in 1865 and the *Meistersinger* in 1868, and had re-

---

[3] The members of this famous quartet were Jean Maurin, Chevillard, Mas and Colbain. As Chevillard (the 'cellist) was unable to leave Paris just then his place at Triebschen was taken by Jacquart.

Röckl and others say that the Quartet was sent to Triebschen by the King. This is a mistake, as is shown, for one thing, by Cosima's letter of the 26th April to the Quartet, given in TLFW, p. 289.

[4] The only E minor quartet of Beethoven is the Op. 59, No. 2. Is "E minor", one wonders, a slip of the pen for E flat — i.e., the great posthumous work in that key? The official title of the Maurin-Chevillard organisation, by the way, was "Société des *Derniers* Quatuors de Beethoven".

cently written a very appreciative article on him in the *Revue des deux Mondes*. And so, Wagner nonchalantly informs Ludwig, his stoical plans for a birthday without celebrations had come to nothing. He had, however, salved his conscience by insisting that only one toast should be drunk — that of the King.

For a few weeks after that, all seemed to be going well with him. Ludwig, always ready to forgive and forget, apologised in his customary humble fashion for having insisted on the *Tristan* revival against Wagner's wish, pleading the intensity of his desire to hear again this work that had always meant so much to him, and which he needed more than ever now to compensate him for the greyness of his mundane life. He has resolved once more, he says, to devote himself earnestly to his duties as King and show himself oftener to his people; and he is overflowing with gratitude to Wagner for all he owes to him.

3

Finding him in this melting mood, Wagner thought the opportunity to work upon him for his own immediate end too good to be missed. He knew that the King had set his heart on productions of the *Rhinegold* and the *Valkyrie* that year. He knew also that the *Rhinegold* in particular, with its many new problems of mise en scène, was likely to fare ill unless he co-operated personally in the production. But as he was determined never to enter the Munich theatre again the only course left open to him was so to work upon Ludwig that he would countermand the production. This he set himself to do, in characteristically sophistical fashion, in a long letter on the 1st July. He does not say outright what is obviously in his mind: he prefers a more indirect tactical approach, which, knowing the King as he did, he might hope would succeed. He told him that lately Dresden had asked him for the *Valkyrie;* he had replied that the *Ring* belonged to the King of Bavaria, to whom he advised the Dresden Intendant to apply, confident, however, that Ludwig's answer would be that "these works are not for the ordinary repertory theatre", and that the whole object of the King's beneficence to him had been "to preserve these noble works from the profane contact of our opera houses". The artful implication was, of course, that having laid this down with regard to other German theatres the King would be bound to recognise that it applied equally to his own.

No one acquainted with Wagner's strategy on occasions of this kind is likely to be taken in by him in the present instance. He is at his favourite game of trying to get what he wants from the King by representing it as something not desired by Wagner himself for its own sake and his but something vital to the larger design of Providence for the cosmos. *Agnoscis eloquentiam Reguli.* We of today, with all the new documentary evidence of the last few years in our hands, can see clearly enough that he was not playing quite straight with the King at this time. To what extent he had already worked out in detail in his own mind his plan for a theatre of his own we cannot at present be sure; but it is certain that, without telling the King so in so many words, he was already resolved not merely to shake the dust of Munich off his feet but to close down on all the young man's dreams of making the Munich Court Theatre the focus of the Wagnerian regeneration of German culture. What else could have been in his mind when he discussed with Cosima the possibility of his having to surrender the royal pension? He was even considering, in the early months of 1869, throwing out feelers in the direction of Bismarck. It was barely three years since he had been emptying the vials of his hate and scorn on Prussia in general and Berlin in particular,[5] and describing Bismarck to Ludwig as "an ambitious Junker, deceiving his weak-minded King in the most shameless fashion". Now, in the early weeks of 1869, it is to the ambitious Junker and his weak-minded King that he half-thinks of turning for the speedier achievement of his own ends.

"It is noteworthy", Du Moulin tells us on the authority of Cosima's diary,

> "how the greatness of Bismarck forced itself into the solitude of Triebschen, how Wagner saw no one else but Bismarck who could help Germany and art, and how he proposed to write in this sense to the statesman's wife to induce her to get her husband to become a protector of art."

Cosima, we learn, "warned him against such a step and such a letter." She did the sensible thing, even if the reason she gave —

---

[5] In his "Journal" of 1865, written for the political education of King Ludwig. See Vol. III, p. 475 ff. The reader will recall that Wagner omitted every anti-Prussian and anti-Bismarckian passage of this sort from the *public* imprint of the "Journal" in 1878.

that such a letter would not have met in Berlin with the understanding it deserved — was not the one calculated to do her and Wagner most credit. For what Wagner contemplated doing was nothing less than treachery towards Ludwig, treachery which, had he heard of it, would have dealt the young idealist a mortal blow; nothing would have been so certain to break him as the knowledge that the man for whom he had done so much, for whose ideal he had made such sacrifices and borne such calumny, was now proposing to brush him aside and turn to the real head of that Prussia which Ludwig so hated and mistrusted, as the only man who could "help Germany and art" — which meant, of course, in Wagner's mouth, directing Germany and art into Wagnerian channels. Wagner, of course, does not breathe so much as a hint of this to Ludwig; but we, who now know so much that was carefully concealed from him, do not find our respect for Wagner's character heightened by the discovery that he could even contemplate so cold-blooded a piece of treachery. His whole character, indeed, with its plentiful littlenesses and meannesses, is seen at its worst between about 1865, when he was driven out of Munich, and 1870, when at last, with the Cosima complication finally cleared up and the plan for Bayreuth beginning to take clear shape in his mind, his ship won clear of the muddy waters that had so long clogged and befouled it, and set sail on the great voyage of adventure that gives a legendary dignity and splendour to his closing years.

The King, who was anything but the mere gushing half-wit he is popularly supposed to have been, was not in the least taken in by Wagner's casuistry over the *Rhinegold*. He knew perfectly well by now that the root of the whole trouble as regards Wagner and Munich could be expressed in a single word — Cosima. His respect for her great qualities of soul and will remained unchanged, then and afterwards; but it must have become crystal clear to him by now that, let Wagner juggle with words as he would, the *fons et origo* of his turning his back so inexorably on Munich was the impossibility of his facing publicity there again by reason of his appropriation of Bülow's wife; and he saw no reason why everything that had been agreed upon between him and Wagner for making the Munich Theatre the temple of the new German religion of art should be cast into the melting-pot for so shabby a reason as that. He did not reply to Wagner's letter of the 1st July by so much as a line. His own next letter, indeed, is dated the 22nd October; and by then a great deal had happened which neither of them had foreseen.

4

For the moment there were no open signs of the coming storm. For the King's birthday on the 25th August Wagner sent him a fair copy made by himself of the Orchestral Sketch of the third act of *Siegfried,* along with a dedicatory poem. Whether Ludwig personally acknowledged the gift and the compliment we do not know: if he did not, Wagner must have had his first real warning of the seriousness of the situation in which he had landed himself by his attitude towards the *Rhinegold* production, the true story of which can at last be reconstructed in full from the wealth of new documents lately made available.

Of the King's legal right to command a performance of this work, the full score of which had long been in his hands under the agreement of 1864, there could be no question; nor had Wagner, as has already been pointed out, the smallest objection to a production of each section of the *Ring* as it became ready, irrespective of the tetralogy as a whole, which was to come later. Nor again, when the King's order was issued to put the *Rhinegold* in hand for the 25th August in Munich did he make the slightest protest; he actually co-operated in the scheme, indeed, so far as this was consistent with his not leaving his Triebschen refuge. His concern, as he told Ludwig in his letter of the 1st July, was not so much about the fact of a production as about the form it was likely to take, that is to say, the degree to which it would correspond with his intentions. He even admitted by implication, though reluctantly, that the work would be possible even without his personal collaboration. The recent production of *Tristan,* he grudgingly allowed, had proved better than he had expected, and had certainly given the King pleasure; and he prayed God that the *Rhinegold* also might turn out "to some degree intelligently" even in his absence. He had tried, employing his customary technique, to persuade Ludwig that he would be playing into his enemies' hands by giving the work; here he was, they would say, once more spending a great deal of money on a big new "opera production", and in times so difficult as these. What Ludwig ought to say was "No! the performances of the *Ring* should be national festivals, offered by the King to his people and the whole German race". Wagner has no doubt that his works will have an enduring life and exercise "an increasing influence on the development of humanity". But if the King does not choose to act as Wagner has suggested it is his duty to do, he will send him an exact statement of his wishes as regards the *Rhinegold* production.

5

On the 25th June Bülow had promised the King to take three months' leave for his health's sake when the Music School closed (at the end of July), and during that time to reconsider his application to be allowed to resign his post as Kapellmeister. He had given as his reasons for that step the increasing burden of his duties in Munich, the opposition he was meeting with from some members of the orchestra, the campaign against him in the Press as "the favourite of a royal favourite", and

> "the joylessness of my private existence, which has received a heavy blow through the definitive separation from my wife, who prefers to devote her life to the loftier consideration of the creator of immortal masterworks in your Majesty's service." [6]

With Bülow thus removed from the scene, Richter, as the new Music Director and the accredited representative of Wagner's interests in the theatre, came into the forefront as the conductor-to-be of the *Rhinegold*. He spent some days at Triebschen in the first week of July, when Wagner gave him his instructions with regard to the production. Almost at once misunderstandings with the Intendanz began, as was only to be expected, the relations between it and the far-off composer being what they were. On the 5th we find Wagner telegraphing petulantly to Richter and the theatre people in general, "Do what you like, any way you like; I cannot be of help." (This seems to have related to a difficulty that had arisen in the allocation of the rôle of Alberich).

On the 14th, Angelo Jank, scenic artist of the Munich Theatre, was in Triebschen, where he submitted to Wagner his proposed de-

---

[6] He definitely tendered his resignation on the 7th August, as from the 10th September, and left Munich on the 19th. The King allowed him to retain the rank of royal Kapellmeister, and granted him, in recognition of his great services, an honorarium of 2,000 florins a year, which Bülow, however, did not accept.

signs for the *Rhinegold*. Wagner was "not particularly pleased" with these, as he informed Richter on the 17th. He complained that the instructions he had previously given to the imported Brandt and Hallwachs had not been passed on by them to Jank, their excuse being that "out of spite" they had not received an official authorisation to do so. Consequently Wagner had had to start all over again from the beginning, he said. "The usual experience!" he added angrily. But he was still very far from repudiating the Munich proceedings or dissociating himself from them. A few days later he is asking Richter to see that the rehearsals are open to the Russian composer and Wagner-admirer Serov, who, with his wife, was at Triebschen at various times in July. Wagner sends Richter a few interesting hints for the guidance of Schlosser, who is to play Loge. He is to be careful, in such episodes as the calling up of the flames, not to do anything that will have a comic effect. His costume has been agreed upon with Seitz, the theatre costumier. His face is to be pale and shining, his eyes large and black and intensified by silver foil; his hair a light red, and erect like twisted flames. "God bless him; he will do his work quite well." Betz, the Wotan, is to pay particular attention to his hat, which must be of very original design, as this is the god's characteristic mark. He must *never* remove it: it must seem to be part and parcel of him. The gods in general are never to change their outward appearance in any way.

On the 25th July Wagner is again asking Richter to see that certain people are "discreetly" admitted to rehearsals: this refers, among others, to Catulle Mendès and his young wife, the former Judith Gautier, and Villiers de l'Isle-Adam; the trio had been staying in Lucerne for some time, had paid several visits to Triebschen, and was now on its way to Munich.[7]

A little later we get the first hint of trouble brewing. Richter has evidently had it in his mind to resign his post; Wagner encourages him in this, but advises him to be firm with the theatre authorities and insist on being guaranteed an independent position, for only in that way will he get anywhere.

The date of this letter — the 25th July — is of the first importance in our investigation of the *Rhinegold* episode. The biographers have told us that when Richter sent in his resignation on the 28th

---

[7] See Chapter XII.

August it was because his conscience would not allow him to have anything to do with a production that did not do justice to Wagner's wishes as regards the scenery and machinery. The letter just cited, however, makes it clear that at least five weeks before the 28th August, — long before the difficulties arose in the theatre which were supposed to have been the honourable motive for Richter's resignation, — he and Wagner had already been hatching a plot for putting pressure on the King and the Intendant in the new Music Director's interest. There is no hint whatever, in Wagner's letter of the 25th July, of Richter's resigning because of the badness of the *Rhinegold* situation.[8] He contemplated doing so purely and simply in order to extort from the Intendant a guarantee of greater power for himself in the Munich Theatre. This guarantee, says Wagner, will not be obtained by "good-natured methods". In plainer language, blackmail alone will succeed: therefore Richter is to "abide firmly" by his demand to be released from his engagement. If he does this, they will

"perhaps consult me, and only then will it become possible for me to secure for you a position without which it would only be hell for you to remain in Munich."

By the 13th August the plot has advanced to the stage at which Wagner can advise his protégé to send his resignation direct to the King in writing.

"Do this with an air of just wanting to tell him the plain truth — that you had hoped to serve the King by an exact carrying-out of my [verbal] instructions and [written] directions with regard to my art; instead of which you have found it impossible to obey the instructions of an Intendant whose utter ignorance amounts to opposition to everything that emanates from *me*. *Lay the whole emphasis on this.* My hope is that in the end the King will see fit to retain you: if this should prove not to be the case, you would have a bad time in Munich. Beg of him the grace of being allowed, as a recognition of your exceptional and very responsible achievement with the *Rhinegold,* to remain on the royal pay-list until the piano score of *Siegfried* is completed. Perhaps, though, a better course will be to say nothing about this for the present, but to leave it to me to bring up this point personally according to the King's reply."

---

[8] The orchestral rehearsals did not begin until the 11th August.

Then comes a postscript: "I open this letter in order to bring it into line with the telegram I decided later to send you.[9] I think you should send your application for resignation to the King quickly *before* you come here: it cannot be handed in too promptly if possibly good results are to follow from it."

It is crystal-clear that, long before matters with regard to the *Rhinegold* reached the point at which Richter tendered his "honour-saving" resignation, Wagner had been plotting to instal the almost unknown young man, for his own ends, in supreme power in the Munich Theatre. He thought he had only to disparage Perfall for Ludwig to discard him; but he was to discover, before long, that he had grossly over-estimated his influence over the King and his capacity to throw dust in the young man's eyes.

6

It could not have tended to improve matters that when Wagner had anything to say to the Intendanz he generally said it not directly but through Richter and others. The Intendanz sends Wagner the designs for the *Rhinegold* costumes: he returns them, with his comments, not to Perfall but to the employees concerned. He complains that insufficient thought has been given to the question of the costumes, and that he should have been consulted about the matter long ago: that is to say, after having belligerently assured the Intendanz more than once that he meant to have nothing more to do at any time with the Munich Court Theatre, he makes it a grievance against it that it does not consult him before it moves a single step. The best painters and archaeologists, he says, ought to have been set to work at the problems of the costumes. They have turned out "too Greek" for his "Germanic gods". He wants them to be "more clothed", and each god to be characterized by his special attribute — Froh, for instance, by the sickle, Fricka by the distaff, Freia to be shown as the goddess of flowers and fruits, and so on. Above all, there is to be no gold about any of them, as self-evidently gold is not yet known to the gods.

---

[9] That telegram ran thus: "Meeting with the singers here indispensable. Arrange this. Await today's letter. Resignation-request conformable to this." The reference is to a visit of Betz, Schlosser and Schelper to Triebschen on the 18th August. See *infra*, p. 207.

By the 11th August it was possible to begin the rehearsals in the theatre. Richter must have at once reported unfavourably about them to Wagner, for the latter, as we have just seen, wires him on the 13th that it is indispensable that some of the singers shall confer with him at Triebschen. There is still no suggestion whatever that the artistic soul of him regarded the mere fact of a *Rhinegold* production as a moral outrage, or that he looks upon the present attempt as foredoomed to failure. On the contrary, in this letter of the 13th August he makes it clear that while he does not hope for very much in the way of acting or staging, he will be satisfied with a good *musical* performance — "that the score shall be rendered correctly and animatedly". The rest he can give up, but

> "the music must be beyond reproach; in which case the main thing is saved. It would have suited me best to have the whole performance without scenery and costumes."

However, he attaches great importance to a conference with the singers. Accordingly Betz (Wotan), Schelper (Alberich), and Schlosser (Loge) [10] went to Triebschen on the 18th.

A few days later he sends Richter instructions as to the play-bills: the new work is to be described as *"Das Rheingold, Prelude to the Trilogy The Nibelung's Ring,* by Richard Wagner".

Wagner had no reason to complain of parsimonious treatment on the part of the Intendanz. He was given his choice of singers from all the German opera houses.[11] He was allowed his own machinist, Karl Brandt (Court Theatre machinist to the Grand Duke of Hesse), and his own regisseur, Hallwachs. The orchestra, increased for the occasion by the engagement of several players from abroad, consisted of 68 strings, 3 flutes (and piccolo), 3 oboes (and cor anglais), 3 clarinets (and bass clarinet), 3 bassoons, 8 horns, 3

---

[10] Röckl says that Heinrich (Mime) was also there; but a letter of Cosima's to Nietzsche shows that this is an error. The letter in question is dated "Thursday", and in it Cosima speaks of the singers having been at Triebschen "yesterday". Thierbach, the editor of CWFN, makes "Thursday" out to be the 5th August. But this is impossible: it must have been the 19th. In this letter Cosima says, *à propos* of the *Rhinegold* production, "The whole thing is a great worry to me; but it is perhaps as well that the public shall be initiated bit by bit and obscurely (*verhüllt*) into a conception which it is not wholly disposed and ordained to grasp." This is yet another indication that Wagner was not, as has always been supposed, set against the Munich *Rhinegold* because he objected to the tetralogy being produced piecemeal.

[11] "At Wagner's request, Hans Richter went to Stuttgart, Darmstadt, Mainz, Kassel, Brunswick, Berlin, Schwerin and Hanover to look for the right singers for the *Rhinegold* and the *Valkyrie*." RLW, II, 84.

trumpets (and bass trumpet), 3 trombones (and bass trombone), 1 bass tuba, 2 harps, the usual percussion, and 18 tuned anvils. Wagner had asked that the stage should be reconstructed and the orchestra lowered: this task was entrusted to Brandt, and the theatre was closed from the 28th June to the 10th August to carry out the work. It seems, indeed, as if the very thoroughness with which Wagner's demands were met accounted, in part, for the confusion that developed as the time for the production drew nigh: for a long while the technical staff were hindered in their work by being deprived of the use of the stage, and when at last they could really get down in practice to the difficult new problems of machinery with which the opera confronted them they found the time allotted them too short and their ideas still unclear; so that it was little wonder that the closing rehearsals revealed various technical shortcomings and filled almost everyone with a sense of fear.

The text-book had been given by Perfall to the scenic designers and the machinists as long ago as mid-March — a fact of which Wagner must have been perfectly well aware — and, as we have seen, Karl Brandt had waited on him in Triebschen early in April for his instructions. Röckl records that Wagner gave passionate expression to Brandt of his displeasure: if the King was bent on having the *Rhinegold*, he said, he ought to have it performed in the concert room; he himself did not want it to be given in an ordinary theatre — forgetting that at the time of the contract of 1864 with the King he himself had sketched a plan for the performance of the work in the Munich Court Theatre in 1867–8,[12] and that such a performance was implicit in the contract that gave the King the property in the work in return for the three-years' stipend granted to Wagner. He furthermore told Brandt that the Munich Theatre would be incapable of producing the opera properly without his collaboration. Clearly he thought he had only to sulk enough for the King, for peace's sake, to countermand the production: [13] then, when he real-

---

[12] See Vol. III, p. 228.

[13] A passage in his (undated) letter inviting Judith Gautier and Catulle Mendès to Triebschen, which must have been written in the early July of 1869, is of significance in this connection. The Mendès are thinking of visiting the Munich Exhibition of Art. In case they should wish also to hear one of his works, Wagner informs them that *Tannhäuser, Lohengrin, Tristan* and the *Meistersinger* have been given in June, "and the *Rhinegold* will not be given before the 25th August at the earliest, if at all". Evidently he thought at that time that his mere opposition to the scheme would lead to the King's abandoning it.

ised there was no hope of this gambit succeeding, he tried to find a working compromise between helping with his counsels and refusing to budge from his lair in Triebschen. It was hardly to be expected that the Intendanz, to which he had behaved with such open unfriendliness for more than a year, would work for him with the same ardour as it would have done for a composer who had shown himself better mannered and more accommodating. Given, then, the combination of a certain slackness in some of the officials, Perfall's knowledge that Wagner was all the time goading his own creatures, especially Richter, Brandt and Hallwachs, to rebellion against the Intendanz, the technical difficulties that began to pile up as soon as the scenery was tried out on the stage, and the relentless pressure put upon the management by the King, who, fully aware of all that was going on, was by now thoroughly angry with Wagner and determined not to be frustrated by him, it cannot be wondered at that things ran less and less smoothly the nearer they came to the day appointed for the production, the 25th August.

7

Wagner was certainly co-operating now to some degree, but his co-operation at so great a distance was bound to be ineffectual, and much of it had come too late. Evidently, however, he had persuaded himself, by mid-August, that he could count on a performance which, though falling short of his ideal in some respects, would at any rate do *musical* justice to his score. On the 21st August he tells Otto Wesendonk that if he should think of coming to Munich to see and hear the *Rhinegold* he will not find *him* there. But, he continues,

"although these performances will take place in quite another fashion than the one I had in my mind some time ago, yet I could not forbid them to the King of Bavaria, to whom, of course, I am so vastly indebted for my artistic freedom. However, everything is being done according to my directions: the singers, conductors, painters and machinists had all to come to me and take my instructions; but I have refused most emphatically to go and take a personal part in the all too familiar and often very vexatious commotion. So if you feel inclined to go to the *Rhinegold* I think you will experience something at all events very respectable as a whole. Nothing has been spared to comply with all my technical requirements: that my singers are not precisely gods you will probably see for yourself, without my drawing your attention to their human quality."

This is not at all the language of a man whose artistic conscience has been mortally insulted by the King's command and the Intendanz's method of carrying it out.

Half the musical celebrities and notorieties in Europe had flocked to Munich for the *Rhinegold* — Liszt, Serov, Saint-Saëns, Joachim, Pasdeloup, Hanslick, Klindworth (from Moscow), Pohl, Hermann Levi (from Karlsruhe), Manuel Garcia and Chorley (from London), Tourgeniev and Pauline Viardot-Garcia (from Paris), together with social notabilities such as Liszt's old friend Mme Mouchanoff. Never since opera began could any event have created such eager anticipation. And it was quite on the cards that the performance might have taken place, if not on the 25th, at any rate not long after, without much real harm being done to the work or any intolerable grievance being felt by the composer of it. But everything was brought crashing to the ground by Richter, who, one suspects, had latterly got a bit above himself. Bülow's connection with the Munich theatre being now at an end, and Wagner's opinion of German conductors in general being what it was, there was nothing surprising in Richter's deciding that now or never was his chance to stake out a claim to step, before long, into Bülow's shoes. After all, calculations of this sort are not unknown in opera houses. But it was a different matter, perhaps, when this virtually unknown young man, who, but for his fortunate connection with Wagner, would have had to begin as a conductor at the bottom of the ladder in some minor German theatre or other and work his way up slowly, took it on himself to behave in a way that led to the stoppage of the great machine that had taken so many months, so great labours, to get going.

To the annoyance of the King, it had been found necessary to postpone the production for a few days. The theatre did indeed re-open on the 25th, but it was with Spohr's *Jessonda*. The final rehearsal of the *Rhinegold* before an invited audience numbering some five hundred was fixed for the 27th, and the first public performance for the 29th. The King was present at the rehearsal. It opened with a request by Hallwachs, from the stage, that the audience would overlook certain imperfections in the machinery which all their zeal had not yet been able to overcome, that it would not regard this as the real final rehearsal, and would consequently refrain from public discussion of it. The work was gone through, under Richter, without a single stoppage. The reception of it seems to have been cool, even Wagner's most faithful adherents being puzzled by it. It is said that this fact of itself justifies Wagner's attitude all along towards the venture. But can we be sure that even if he had taken a larger part than he did in the production the result that evening would have been very different? Many of the stage problems of the work are still unsolved today. We have become indulgent in these matters, however; we take in the action and the scenery with our imagination as much as with our bodily eyes, and see such things as the practicable rainbow from the mountain top to Valhalla,[14] the swimming Rhine maidens, the episode in which Alberich changes himself first into a serpent and then into a toad, and others that need not be specified, not as they are actually put before us but as Wagner intended us to see them. To the audience at that rehearsal in 1869 no such accommodation of the judgment of the eye to the inner vision of the imagination was possible, and could not be expected, even had the machinery worked with perfect smoothness throughout, which, unfortunately, it did not.[15]

---

[14] When it is attempted in the theatre, which is not often!

[15] Each of the Rhine Maidens should have been placed in a trolley, the wheels being hidden by her garment. The tossing they got as the trolleys moved up and down and round about had made one of the Rhine Maidens sea-sick at a rehearsal, whereupon the others refused to have anything to do with the sinister contraptions. In the end the cars were occupied by three intrepid ballet girls — a species apparently not subject to stage sea-sickness — while the characters sang their parts from the wings. Well might the comic paper parody their song in local dialect in this fashion:

> Wigala wogala weia,
> Bleib i ɑuf der Schaukel, so muss i speia.
> Wigala wogala wack,
> Fall i abi, so brich i's Gnack.

> (If I stay on the see-saw I shall vomit:
> If I fall off I shall break my neck).

But either the device must have been Wagner's own — he had gone over all these things with Brandt — or he had left the problem to the machinist to solve as best he could because at that time he did not quite know how to solve it himself. And in either case would the apparatus have worked any better, or the stomachs of the daughters of the deep been any more resistant, had he been in the theatre in person? We seem to remember that even at Bayreuth in 1876, where Wagner saw to everything himself and had unlimited authority, there were occasional difficulties with the *Ring* scenery. The complete dragon for *Siegfried*, for instance, failed to arrive in time.

Agitations now descended on Wagner not as single spies but in battalions, and the telegraph wires and letter posts between Munich and Berg and Triebschen were kept very busy.

Already on the 24th Betz, who was hand in glove with Richter, had written to Wagner that he could not reconcile it with his conscience to conceal from him that the *Rhinegold* production looked like turning out a ludicrous affair. He suggested that Wagner ought to come to Munich and see for himself. As, however, the many strangers who had flocked to the town for the great event were entitled to some consideration, Betz proposed a concert performance of the work for them in the theatre. He showed the letter to Richter, who advised him not to send it just then. But on the morning of the 27th Betz could contain himself no longer. Everyone concerned, it appeared, looked forward with dread to the general rehearsal appointed for that evening: Hallwachs had even suggested that it should be postponed — a proposal to which, it went without saying, the King would have turned a deaf ear. From what Betz had heard, he imagined that the confusion had all come about through a lack of understanding and co-operation between Brandt and the local costumier (Seitz) and machinist (Penkmayr). Wagner, he concluded, had only to come and see the chaos for himself and he would assuredly veto the performance.

Betz's letter would presumably have reached Triebschen on the morning of the 28th. In the early afternoon came a wire from Richter. The "main object", he said, had been attained in that the "true friends" of the composer had had "the musical part" put before them in as perfect a form as possible.

> "But I cannot refrain from saying that a performance before a public audience is impossible, because of the scenery. Orchestra very good; Liszt himself and others have expressed their satisfaction. Prevent performance at any cost":

the many friends who had come to Munich for the *Rhinegold* could be compensated by "a rapid succession of performances of *Meistersinger, Lohengrin, Tannhäuser* and possibly *Tristan.*" This was evidently meant to be the decisive stroke in the carrying out of the plot hatched weeks before. Richter's "main object" had been achieved:

he had proved himself competent to rehearse and conduct the work. Wagner was now to veto the public performance on the grounds that the mise en scène was inadequate, and three or four other Wagner operas were to be given in its stead. Since 1864 the Wagner works had been entirely in the hands of Bülow. Now that he was no longer there, there was no conductor in the Munich Theatre to whom the Wagner works could be entrusted but Richter. He, therefore, would come full into the limelight and be appointed Bülow's successor with plenipotentiary powers; while Perfall, held answerable for the *Rhinegold* fiasco, would be, if not formally superseded, at any rate discredited in the eyes both of the King and of the public.

The next move was obviously Wagner's. The plot seemed to be shaping beautifully. Richter's telegram was sent from Munich at 9.30 on the morning of the 28th. It was received in Lucerne at 1.40, and would no doubt arrive at Triebschen shortly after two o'clock. At 2.25 Wagner telegraphed to the King asking him to postpone the public performance (planned for the 29th) until such time as "the difficulties as yet not overcome can be given further thought", and to order the production of "my older works for the benefit of the numerous friends".

The mine had long been laid, and now the fuse was lighted. There came in due time an explosion, but not the one expected by Wagner and Richter. For a moment, indeed, there was silence. As the King was at Berg, the telegram did not reach him until 6.15 that evening. No reply seems to have been vouchsafed.

9

The next day, the 29th, Wagner wrote to Ludwig *in modo patetico*, harping, as usual, on the suffering he was patiently undergoing, and, again as usual, blaming the Intendanz for having brought about this catastrophe by its slackness in obeying the royal orders. He enclosed Betz's letter with his own. Once more the King, who must have seen clearly enough by this time that the root cause of the whole trouble was Wagner's persistent refusal to co-operate amicably with the theatre authorities, ignored him. His blood was up, as Wagner must have realised the same day. At mid-day he received a wire from Richter to the effect that the performance had been postponed to Thursday, the 2nd September, but that he, Richter, having "saved his musical honour", had positively refused to conduct. As his "musical honour" had never been in the smallest danger since he had first set foot in the Munich Theatre, the pretext lacked validity, not to say plausibility. He had tendered his definitive resignation on the 28th. The letter to the King [16] in which he had asked to be relieved of his duties runs to some fourteen lines of print without so much as a semi-colon between its opening words and the final full-stop. It calls for a literal point-by-point translation, regardless of the feelings of the English reader:

"Most submissive and respectful request of the undersigned to be graciously relieved of his post as Music Director of the Court Theatre after the production of the *Rhinegold* has taken place, since a truly successful artistic activity, such as the humble undersigned has set before himself as his highest life-task, especially with regard to the production of the works of the great Meister Richard Wagner and their interpretation in the true spirit of the poet-composer, will, if not perhaps by reason of the lack of good will, at any rate through the absence of any kind of higher comprehension of these tasks on the part of the present Intendant Herr Baron von Perfall, be absolutely impossible so long as this at present sole-determining authority is not opposed. by a factor with equal sovereignty in certain musical questions."

This to the King and the Munich Theatre Intendanz.from a young employee from nowhere!

The literal rendering into English of the cumbersome German text is justified in order to demonstrate the true authorship of the document. It must have been as clear to the King and Perfall as it is to any present-day student of Wagner's style that *he* had had a hand in the drafting of it. All that Richter had to do was to sign on the dotted line.

In a communication to the *Neueste Nachrichten* of the 1st September, and again in a letter of the 14th September to the Leipzig *Signale*,[17] Richter says that this resignation of his had been handed in on the 21st August. If so, it was perhaps not taken quite literally. He had simply asked to be relieved of his duties *after* the production of the *Rhinegold*, the general rehearsal of which was fixed for

---

[16] It will be found in RLW, II, 224.
[17] See *infra*, p. 230.

the 27th, and the public performance for the 29th; and no doubt hopes were entertained at that time that the storm would blow over. What is certain is that it was on the evening of the 28th that Richter definitely told the Intendanz that he would have nothing to do with the performance on the 29th. After the rehearsal on the 27th a meeting of the Intendanz had been called, and to an enquiry from the King whether a performance on the 29th were possible it was replied that there was now no obstacle so far as the scenery was concerned. Hearing of this, there was no course open to Richter but to refuse to conduct with that scenery, for he had gone too far now to extricate himself in any other way from a pit of his own and Wagner's digging: the stage apparatus was no concern of his. His decision was at once communicated to the Cabinet Secretariat. The King was furious. Summoned to a meeting of the Intendanz, at which Düfflipp was present in the King's name, Richter reiterated his refusal to conduct. Perfall reminded him of his obligations under his contract with the Theatre. Richter's reply was that the only chief he recognised was Wagner: [18] him he would obey, but no one else. The gesture, meant to be heroic, was hardly distinguishable from impudence. His engagement was not with Richard Wagner but with the Intendanz of the Munich Theatre: Richard Wagner had no more of a controlling voice in the direction and discipline of that Court institution than any other composer had. So the Intendanz did what it was perfectly justified in doing, and what any management of any theatre would have done in the circumstances: it suspended its insubordinate employee there and then.

The angry King now had the bit between his teeth, and there was no holding him. On the afternoon of the 29th a telegram was delivered at Triebschen. It was from Baron von Loën, the Intendant of the Weimar Theatre; it informed Wagner that as the King of Bavaria was set on having the *Rhinegold,* Perfall wished to engage

---

[18] On the night of the 28th Wagner had telegraphed to Richter asking him to wire him whether the performance (on the 29th) was going to be given "in spite of my counter-action" — i.e., his telegram to the King on the afternoon of the 28th. One surmises that Richter, in his blind self-confidence, had timed his ultimatum of that evening without consulting Wagner. In his telegram to Wagner on the morning of the 28th (see *supra*, p. 212) he had merely suggested that the performance should be "prevented at any cost". It was the meeting of the Intendanz on the morning of the 28th — a meeting at which Düfflipp represented the King and at which Perfall had said that so far as the mise-en-scène 'was concerned there was no obstacle to a performance — that forced Richter's hand and made a quick decision necessary. He made the wrong one.

Lassen, the Weimar Kapellmeister, to conduct the work: Lassen would await Wagner's opinion on the matter in the Hotel Vier Jahreszeiten, Munich. Wagner's angry reply to Loën was to the effect that he could not be expected to endure an outrage because of the incompetence and ill-will of the Munich Intendanz, that he trusted to Lassen's sense of honour to refuse, and that "Richter is my conductor, and will conduct as soon as the conditions outlined in my telegram of today to Hofrath Dürflipp are complied with".

Later in the afternoon of the 29th came a telegram from Richter saying that he had been suspended by the Intendanz because of his refusal to conduct "with the present scenery": "[they are] looking for another conductor." "Liszt of my opinion", he added. It was presumably in reply to this that Wagner wired to Richter approving his action, and saying that he had telegraphed Dürflipp his "conditions for next Sunday: if these fulfilled, conduct." In this wire to the Court Secretary Wagner blamed the Intendanz for the imperfections of the mise en scène, and asked for a private performance without scenery, or at any rate the giving of full powers to Brandt and Frau Grahn with a view to ensuring the performance on Sunday being of a kind that would protect his work against "absurdity". He himself is too unwell to go to Munich, for the latest news from there has upset him grievously.

The next day came a telegram to Triebschen from Dürflipp, whose intervention in the matter was an unmistakable sign that the King had now made the conduct of affairs at the Court Theatre his personal concern. The trouble with the scenery, said Dürflipp, would soon be put right by Brandt: Frau Grahn (the ballet mistress) was also helping. Things were not so bad as Wagner feared; but "Richter has gone too far and has spoiled the situation." The King is bent on having a production soon; so Dürflipp asks Wagner to "make a sacrifice to love and sanction the performance". He asks for a speedy and assenting reply, for he would sincerely regret it if Wagner should bring about an irremediable rupture, as he will assuredly do by refusing. It will be observed that Wagner had said nothing to Dürflipp about Richter conducting; this, indeed, he seems to have complacently taken for granted, in spite of Richter's suspension. But on this point the King, Dürflipp and the Intendanz were all agreed: they had finished with the young subordinate who had put forward the impudent claim to govern the whole Munich Court

Theatre in the name of Richard Wagner. Simultaneously with Düfflipp's wire to Wagner went off one to Bülow (in Berlin). It was his Majesty's "absolute will", Düfflipp told him, to have the *Rhinegold* performed as soon as "the obvious defects in the inscenation are remedied"; and the King earnestly hopes that Bülow can see his way to conduct. "In my opinion", Düfflipp continued,

> "Herr Wagner has not been correctly informed as to the matter, and I do not think you will be acting contrary to his views if you stand fast loyally and comply with the King's desire."

This was obviously true, on Wagner's own showing: if he would have been satisfied with the inscenation as it would be after a little more work on the part of Brandt and Frau Grahn, so long as a good performance of the music was guaranteed by Richter being at the conductor's desk, he could have no logical objection to the same result being obtained under a conductor of Bülow's superior calibre. But Bülow, who was on the point of leaving Berlin for a rest in Wiesbaden, declined the King's invitation, as was natural in all the circumstances. He had no desire, and was in no condition, to be dragged back into "the Munich hell".

10

By this time Wagner could no longer doubt that the situation as between himself and the King had become one of the utmost gravity. On the 30th he sent him a long letter in his usual vein of self-justification in face of a wicked world. Richter's action, it appears, has saved his work from a ridiculous scenic production. Even Liszt, who in general has no eye for such things, his interest in opera extending no further than the music, agrees that the scenery will not do, though the performance of the *music* at the rehearsal had been faultless.[19] Wagner reproaches the King for having broken his promise of old to him in ordering the production of the *Rhinegold*.[20]

---

[19] This again shows how little Richter's "musical honour" was at stake. The position, so far as the Intendanz and he were mutually concerned, was simply this — that an employee engaged solely to take charge of the musical side of a performance was refusing to conduct unless the scenery, the machinery and the stage management met with his approval. To have given in to him would have been to make him the master of the body that employed him. No Intendant in Germany could have been expected to submit to that. Richter's suspension for insubordination was not only technically justifiable but morally necessary if discipline was to be maintained.

[20] "See in particular", says Dr. Strobel in a note on this passage, "the King's letter

Seeing himself compelled to assent to this, he had tried to secure at any rate a good *musical* performance by means of a conductor devoted to him. For the rest, he had been given the machinist Brandt, who had absorbed all his instructions so intelligently that Wagner believed he could feel quite easy about the inscenation also. But when, four weeks ago, the painter Jank had come to Triebschen, Wagner had discovered that none of his instructions to Brandt had been passed on to the other people concerned; and he had learned later that the Intendant had declined to treat with Brandt and Hallwachs as Wagner's plenipotentiaries. (In this Perfall was technically correct: since he was responsible to the King and to the public for the Theatre, he had a right to insist that any instructions emanating from Wagner should be communicated to him direct, so that he in turn might pass them on to the people concerned. Obviously the line taken by Wagner, if successful, would have reduced the Intendanz to a pure nullity in its own theatre. When things went right, Wagner and Brandt and Hallwachs would get all the credit for them; when things went wrong, the blame would be thrown on Perfall. And in view of Wagner's previous rudeness to him at a time when he thought he could safely be rude as he would never have need of him again, Perfall could be pardoned for giving a slight pressure to the screw whenever he was lucky enough to find Wagner's thumb beneath it).

Perfall, Wagner continues, had set Penkmayr and Brandt at loggerheads, and, whenever they came to a deadlock, decided in favour of the former. Finally, preparations in general had begun

---

of the 7th December, 1864, first paragraph." The paragraph in question runs thus: "Now we shall see the fulfilment of our wish; the work you scarcely dared to hope would come to life shall be produced, and wholly according to your will. That I on my side will do, be the trouble what it may; this wondrous work we will bring as a gift to the German nation, and thus show other nations what 'German art' can do."

But obviously the King was merely promising that when the time should come for producing the work Wagner could count on the fullest assistance on his part. It was implicitly understood that the production should take place *at the King's Court Theatre in Munich*. Ludwig never envisaged such a situation as that of four years later — Wagner, having by his own public and private conduct made Munich impossible for him, trying to deprive the King of both his legal and moral rights as regards the work. Wagner had imagined that by the simple device of saying that the *Rhinegold* bristled with new problems of stagecraft which only he could solve he could discourage the Court Theatre from attempting it without him. But since he had made it clear beyond all possibility of misunderstanding that he had finished for good with both Munich and its theatre, was it not evident that it was he who was trying to make the agreement virtually null and void by passive default on his part?

too late; and he admits that much that had gone wrong at the rehearsal will come right with a little more perseverance.

If the performance now set down for the 2nd September is postponed, and the scenic arrangements are improved as Düfflipp had
promised in his telegram, Wagner makes bold to guarantee the
King a performance "next Sunday" (the 5th) which will redeem
the work and give his Majesty some pleasure. But for this one thing
is indispensable — Richter must conduct. He knows that the Intendant is looking around for another conductor; but he hopes the
name of Richard Wagner is sufficiently respected everywhere among
artists for them to be horrified at the idea of lending themselves
to such an outrage. He ends by a tearful appeal to Ludwig not to
take sides against him with the incompetent, the ill-disposed, the
small-minded, yes, the malignant people who are trying their best
to make his work ridiculous(.!). He hopes that this time the King, so
often silent of late, will grant him the grace of a reply, so that he
may at once put into execution his plans for redeeming his promise
for "next Sunday".

11

Three reflections spring to the mind on reading all this. First,
that if what was wrong with the inscenation could have been put
right with a few hours' more rehearsal there could not have been
so very much wrong with it after all. Second, that the King, listening
to yet another of Wagner's whimperings about his own perfect innocence and the vileness and incompetence of everyone who did not
bow the knee to him, must have felt inclined to answer him as Siegfried answered Mime in somewhat similar circumstances:

> Still mit dem alten
> Starenlied!
> Soll ich der Kunde glauben,
> hast du mir nichts gelogen,
> so lass mich Zeichen sehn!

> (Cease with that endless
> starling-song!
> If I may trust thy story,
> if nought but truth thou'st spoken,
> let me a sign behold!)

[219]

Third, that only a man so fundamentally incapable as Wagner was of seeing anything from anyone else's point of view could have imagined for a moment that the King and the Intendanz would agree to his terms so far as Richter was concerned. That young man had claimed an authority that was neither in the letter nor in the spirit of his agreement as a second-rank conductor, and he had refused to obey his employers' orders, saying he recognised no master but Wagner. After that, his reinstatement at the bidding of Wagner would have been tantamount to suicide on the part of the Intendanz.

If we try to visualise conditions as they were in the Munich Theatre at this time we can hardly come to any conclusion but that the people there were justified in practically everything they did in the long-drawn-out tragi-comedy. As they saw the matter, an institution designed for the benefit of the whole community was being periodically turned upside down by an alien musician and a crew of his alien helpers, who had no interest in the Munich Theatre for its own sake, who had descended upon it for their own purposes and would depart from it as soon as those purposes had been accomplished, and who had vast privileges but no responsibilities.[21] The ringleaders in the present trouble all came from afar. Betz was from Berlin, Brandt from Darmstadt, Hallwachs from Stuttgart; Richter was a young man from nowhere who had been planted upon the opera house by Wagner not merely for the ends of Wagnerian art but to keep an eye on Perfall, as the latter had excellent reason to believe, and to send secret reports to Triebschen, as the documents now in our possession amply prove to have been the case. What the King and the Intendanz felt like saying to Wagner was probably something like this: "Either come into the Munich Theatre or keep out of it; but if you elect, for domestic reasons of your own that are no secret to anyone, to keep out of it, for heaven's sake make your abstention a reality, not a hypocritical pretence; do not say in one breath that you wash your hands of the institution and in the next claim to govern it through your minions. For heaven's sake, if you want either to fight or to be friendly come out into the open to do it; but do not ask us to acquiesce eternally

---

[21] This commonsense view of the matter was expressed in an article in the *Allgemeine Zeitung:* "The general opinion is that so important an art-institution as the Munich Court Theatre should not be any longer the arena for unrestrained licence, intriguing presumption and juvenile arrogance [meaning Richter!] which the satellites of the new Archimagus are making of it."

in a game in which all the aces are to be up your sleeve and only the common cards are ours, every one of our moves being reported to you by your spies within our citadel, while *we* never know what trick *you* are up to until it has been played on us."

To Wagner's long performance on the vox humana and tremulant in his letter of the 30th August the King maintained a stony silence. But to Düfflipp, on the 29th, he had sent a letter which it would not have pleased Wagner to know about. He is furious, he says, at Richter's insolence. Düfflipp is to try to induce Bülow to return to the conductor's desk for this one production. If Richter or anyone else in the theatre refuses to obey plain orders, then "the weeds must be pitilessly uprooted"; Düfflipp is empowered to take the strongest measures with "these worthless creatures". He insists on the performance taking place on Wednesday, the 1st September, and he mentions some particulars in which the general rehearsal can and must be improved upon. The scene in which the gods suddenly grow old had been very badly managed: the desired effect, he says, can be obtained by the simplest means — by burning a mixture of salt and alcohol. Schlosser's conception of Loge had been completely wrong: there must be an improvement here, or the performance will be a faulty one, which is the exact opposite of what the King wants.

12

On the 30th he rushes into the fray again. He sends Düfflipp the letter from Betz enclosed in Wagner's letter to him of the previous day. He fears, he says, that things are as described by Betz, and that the mistake has been to let matters go as far as they have done. "For this", he says, with an impartial distribution of the guilt,

"Richter, Hallwachs, Penkmayr and Seitz are to blame. Frustrate the intrigues of Wagner and Liszt. Let me know at once how matters now stand, as my patience is coming to an end."

Having thought things over, Wagner seems to have come to the conclusion that after all he was not too unwell to go to Munich, and that he had better do so at once in a last desperate hope of saving the situation. On the evening of the 30th he telegraphed to Düfflipp that, in accordance with his letter of that day to the King, he would guarantee a good performance on the 5th if Richter were reinstated, and that he himself would now take a hand. In a telegram to Richter later that evening he asks him to inform Düfflipp that he [Wagner] will attend a private rehearsal next Wednesday (the) 1st September) to decide whether a performance is possible on *Thursday*. But it must be under no one but Richter, whom he asks to join him in an effort to appease the King.

On that same day Ludwig sent Düfflipp a second letter that shows how pitifully mistaken Wagner had been in supposing he could work on the young man as he had been accustomed to doing. "Wagner and the theatre rabble", he says, are both of them behaving shamelessly and criminally. They are openly revolting against his orders, and he will not tolerate it. Richter is to be dismissed at once and not allowed to conduct again. The people in the Court Theatre owe obedience to *him*, the King, not to Wagner's whims. He sees it stated in several journals that he has countermanded the production. Düfflipp is to see that the truth is made known: the production is to be pressed on with the utmost energy,

> "for if these abominable intrigues of Wagner are permitted the whole rabble will become more and more shameless and presumptuous and in the end get quite out of control; so the evil must be pulled up by the roots."

Not only is Richter to be sent away, but Betz and the others are to be brought to heel. He has never known such insolence. But he has every confidence in Düfflipp. "Vivat Düfflipp! Pereat theatre rabble!" In other words, he meant to be master in his own house, and the sooner the Wagners and the Richters and the rest of the troublemakers realised it the better for them. And having unburdened himself of all this, he prepared to leave Berg for the almost inaccessible Hochkopf, thus making communication with him difficult and forestalling any move of Wagner's to descend on Munich and try his blandishments on him.[22]

---

[22] A letter of the King's to Düfflipp, evidently dashed off in Berg, just before leaving for the Hochkopf, shows that he was by no means unreasonable. The performance, he insists, *must* take place on Sunday. "Wagner's wishes must be given all possible consideration, for in the main they are reasonable." He continues, however, "Read his letter to me, which I enclose [i.e., Wagner's of the 30th], and do all you can to stop him from coming here [i.e., to Munich]. But he need not know that this is *my* wish, otherwise there will be the devil to pay, and we shall not get anywhere, now or later."

Sure enough Wagner, blissfully ignorant of what a sorry figure he cut just then in Ludwig's eyes, arrived in Munich in the early morning of Wednesday, the 1st.[23] Before he left Triebschen, on the 31st August, he telegraphed Richter to ask Düfflipp for a scenery, lighting and costume rehearsal with piano at ten o'clock, and another at mid-day with the full orchestra. Apparently he took it for granted that Richter had only to present himself at the theatre, armed with *his* authority, to be allowed to conduct. Düfflipp, one surmises, must have given the King, who had not yet left Berg, a hint of what was impending; for we find Ludwig telegraphing him, at 12.15 on the 31st, that an immediate end must be made of the "miserable and quite unpardonable intrigues of Wagner and company", that there positively must be a production next Sunday, and that Richter is to be discharged at once. And at the end — and this, *nota bene,* in a telegram that would be bound to come under many curious eyes: "If W. dares to offer any more opposition his allowance is to be taken from him for ever, and not another work of his is to be produced on the Munich stage."

Evidently Richter had not realised even yet that the Intendanz meant what it said when it refused to be dictated to by him; both Wagner and he were still blindly confident that their *Putsch* would succeed. On the 31st, relying on Wagner's telegram to him of the 29th to see him through,[24] Richter wrote to Düfflipp thus:

"I have read an article — apparently inspired by the Intendanz — in the *Neueste Nachrichten* (with reference to my refusal to conduct the *Rhinegold*), which can easily be taken to imply that I would persist in my refusal *in any circumstances.* I therefore permit myself the liberty of reminding you of our yesterday's discussion, during which I made it clear to you, à propos of Herr Wagner's telegram, that I would place myself at your disposal with the greatest pleasure as conductor of the *Rhinegold* when the composer's conditions are fulfilled";

and he repeats and underlines this last clause, with a "take-it-or-leave-it" air that does more credit to his self-assurance than to his perception of his real standing as regards his employers.

---

[23] As he did not want his presence to be known in the town, Richter found a lodging for him with a friend of his own, Reinhard Schäfer, at 6½ Neue Pferdestrasse.

[24] "If my conditions to Düfflipp for next Sunday are fulfilled you can conduct."

It is easy to see why Wagner insisted as he did on the point of Richter's reinstatement; if, after the conductor's defiance of King and Intendanz in the composer's name, he were not taken into favour again, it would be a public defeat for Wagner himself. So 'in the telegram he sent to Ludwig as soon as he arrived in Munich in the early hours of the 1st September he again placed the ultimate emphasis on Richter: without him, he said, it would be impossible for him to keep his promise of a good performance of the *Rhinegold*. But he was rebuffed on every side. Perfall refused to have Richter,[25] and the King, who was now at the Hochkopf, ignored Wagner's telegram. To Pfistermeister, indeed, he wrote from the Hochkopf on the 2nd,

"The wretched development of the *Rhinegold* affair, which has now grown intolerable to me, has reached its climax in R. Wagner's coming to Munich entirely against my will. It would serve him perfectly right if there is a nasty demonstration against him, now that the Bülow scandal is *au comble. J'en ai assez.*"[26]

Perfall, quick to see his tactical advantage, and with the certainty of having Düfflipp and the King to back him up, declined to allow Wagner the rehearsals he had asked for — on his own conditions, — thus concentrating his main force at his strongest point, Richter's over-stepping of his authority. This, indeed, had been Wagner's fatal mistake — to urge Richter to send in his resignation if the scenic arrangements were not to his liking. He had thereby played what he thought was the winning ace: it was promptly trumped, and the game was irretrievably lost. As we have seen, he had asked Richter, in his telegram of the 31st August, to arrange a scenery rehearsal with the piano at one o'clock on the 1st September, and a full orchestral rehearsal at mid-day. Both requests were refused by Düfflipp and Perfall at their meeting with him; and one senses a touch of panic in his letter to Düfflipp of seven o'clock the same

---

[25] "Situation doubtful", Wagner wired to Cosima. "No rehearsal held. Trouble over Richter. Way out under discussion." Röckl (RLW, II. 95) gives a slightly different version: "No rehearsal because of Richter trouble. Perhaps tomorrow evening. Way out under discussion." The discrepancy arises from the fact that Röckl is quoting from a pencil draft in Wagner's handwriting, and Dr. Strobel from Wagner's fair copy, now in possession of the Richter family: this was evidently the actual wording of the telegram sent off by Richter.

[26] SWM, p. 72. The letter was found by Stemplinger among Pfistermeister's papers, and printed by him for the first time in an article on *Die Wagnerlegende* in the *Süddeutsche Monatshefte*, June, 1932, p. 631.

evening. Since they left him, he says, he has come to the firm resolve to supervise the rehearsals himself, under the conditions he
had laid down. Perfall can resort to any publicity he likes in order
to save his official honour, without either Richter or himself con-
tradicting him. But let him rather prove that he means what he
says — that he is interested in the success of the *Rhinegold* — and
help Wagner by "a good ordering of the rehearsals". It would be
gratifying to Wagner if a scenery-and-piano rehearsal for that same
evening could even now be arranged; in any case, such a rehearsal
is absolutely necessary tomorrow morning, in which case the orchestral rehearsal could be dispensed with. To all this, we may be sure,
Düfflipp and Perfall would have assented, had not Wagner linked
his request with the impossible demand for Richter's reinstatement.
And so his final assault on the entrenched position was hurled back
with heavy loss. A rehearsal of the scenery *was* held that evening,[27]
but without either Wagner or Richter.

Wagner's complete defeat now being apparent to him, it was
time for him to strike a noble attitude. This he did in a telegram to
the King of the 3rd from Triebschen, where he had returned, with
his tail between his legs, on the morning of the previous day. The
good Düfflipp, he says, will tell the King what has made it necessary
for him, Wagner, to desist from the attempt to redeem his promise
to secure a good performance. Nothing remains to him now but solemnly to adjure the King to countermand the production, but solely
on the ground of its incurable imperfection, of which he has been
unfortunately able to assure himself. For all time, the world-weary,
disillusioned god declares, with a magnificent fling of his Wotan-
cloak over his shoulders, is the undertaking that had been so high-
mindedly planned brought down in ruins if it makes such a beginning as this. This is his last word: only after he has been able to
obtain some sort of calm will he try to explain himself in more
detail.

But again no reply: it is not until the 22nd October, indeed, a
month to the day after the production of the *Rhinegold*, that the
King breaks a silence that had by then lasted four months. Wagner's
defeat in the eyes of the Munich musical world was complete. But,
as usual, he was unteachable. He could explain opposition to his

---

[27] This is evident from Betz's letter to Düfflipp, written at midnight. See *infra*,
p. 227.

will on only one hypothesis, that a whole wicked world was engaged in a conspiracy to crucify its one heaven-appointed saviour. And, again as usual when he was brought to bay, he resorted to the most palpable sophistry to save his face. The *Rhinegold* affair had been commented upon everywhere in the German Press, mostly, one gathers, in terms uncomplimentary to himself. When, after the production had actually taken place, he felt called upon to say something in his defence, the best he could achieve was this, in a letter to the *Allgemeine Zeitung:*

> "The fact that my abstention from personal co-operation in no wise implied a long-spun intrigue against the Intendant was proved by my going to Munich, as soon as the evil results of the leaderless undertaking had become apparent, not indeed to obtain a satisfactory production of my work but simply to assist in getting a production that would redeem the honour of the Intendanz."

Candour compels one to say that there is not a word of truth in all this casuistry. The whole trouble had arisen from his obstinately refusing from the beginning to co-operate with Perfall, in the belief that he occupied an impregnable position with regard to the Theatre and the King. He had consented to come in and help only at the very last moment, and then not out of any altruistic concern for "the honour of the Intendanz" but simply to save his own face when his bluff in the matter of Richter had been called. And called it had been, not only by Düfflipp and Perfall but by the King himself.

CHAPTER XI

THE *RHINEGOLD* AFTERMATH

1

THE REST of the story will not take very long in the telling. For lack of a conductor the production could not take place, as the King had insisted, on the 5th September, a fact which would not help to improve his temper; application had been made to Lassen (Weimar), Herbeck (Vienna), Levi (Karlsruhe), and Saint-Saëns (Paris), but naturally all of them had declined; in part out of consideration for Wagner, in part because they hesitated to undertake so fearsome a responsibility at such short notice. A further complication was that a new Wotan would now have to be found, Betz having gone back to Berlin. He left Munich on the 2nd September, after having written Düfflipp, at midnight on the preceding day, a letter the peacock strut and petulance of which were almost worthy of a prima donna or a tenor. Perfall, in a conversation with Betz, had shown that he was well aware of the contents of the singer's letter of the 24–27th August to Wagner, which the latter had forwarded to the King, and the King had passed on to his Secretary. Betz seems to have been naively astonished that this letter should have confirmed the Intendant's suspicion and dislike of him as one of Wagner's "spies". Like Wagner, he railed against Perfall's lukewarmness and ill-will; and, again like Wagner, he did not see that an Intendant who had been treated with such marked discourtesy as he had been by Wagner and certain others was hardly likely to be bubbling over with friendly feeling towards them.

A conductor willing to undertake the *Rhinegold* task was at last found in Franz Wüllner, a capable if not brilliant musician who had been associated with Munich since 1864, first of all as conductor of the Royal Church Choir, then as head of the choral singing classes at the Music School. He had had comparatively little experience of large-scale conducting, and no doubt he saw in this sudden turn of fortune, in spite of all the risks attending it, an opportunity to carve out a career for himself.[1] His task was anything but an easy one, for some of the rôles had had to be redistributed and therefore much of the work begun all over again. When at last the *Rhinegold* came to performance, on the 22nd September, it was with the following cast:

Wotan	Kindermann.
Fricka	Fräulein Stehle.
Loge	Vogl.
Donner	Heinrich.
Froh	Nachbaur.
Alberich	Fischer.
Mime	Schlosser.
Fasolt	Petzer.
Fafner	Bausewein.
Erda	Fräulein Seehofer.
Woglinde	Fräulein Kaufmann.
Wellgunde	Frau Vogl.
Flosshilde	Fräulein Ritter.

Meanwhile the main result of the indiscreet moves on the part of Wagner and Richter had been a fresh outburst in the Press on very much the same lines as that of 1865. Düfflipp had been perfectly clear-sighted when he warned Wagner, in his own interests, to keep out of the business, for if once he set foot in Munich he would have the whole pack of journalists at him again. In the forefront of the fray was the *Allgemeine Zeitung,* the Munich correspondent [2] of which was undoubtedly in the counsels of the Intendanz. In an anonymous article on the 11th September he spoke openly of Perfall's "victory" over "intrigues", of Wagner's ambition to play the part of "Jupiter tonans", of the impossibility of carrying on the ordinary work of the Theatre if his lust for mastery were pandered to. Perfall was commended for having issued an ultimatum — "Either this influence must be broken for ever, or I go." Then fol-

---

[1] He was thirty-seven at this time. In the next year he was made first Court Kapellmeister. In 1877 he removed to Dresden, where he succeeded Rietz as Kapellmeister at the Opera and Director of the Conservatoire. In 1882 he was supplanted by Schuch at the Dresden Opera. After a good deal of miscellaneous conducting he followed Hiller as Director of the Cologne Conservatoire and conductor of the Gürzenich Concerts. He died in 1902. He was the father of the well-known singer Ludwig Wüllner.

[2] Julius Grosse.

lows the passage about the "Archimagus" already quoted on page 220.

The attempt, the scribe continues, to turn the Court and National Theatre into a Wagner Theatre pure and simple must be resisted, especially when the "famous Magus" takes it upon himself to assume sovereign powers and give orders about matters that have already been decided by the proper authorities and the Cabinet.

"Are we really living under a dynasty, the plain common sense of the Müncheners asks, that hurls its lightnings from Lucerne and claims authority to lay down new laws not only for art but for public morals?"

— a plain reference to the Wagner-Cosima scandal.

It was well known, so the article goes on, that Wagner had been from the beginning against a public production of his work, no doubt for good reasons of his own. Then, finding his aim of stopping the performance unattainable by direct means, the composer had tried indirect, — prompting Richter to refuse to conduct, although the small defects in the inscenation revealed at the general rehearsal could easily have been put right in a couple of days. "There followed the suspension of the refractory vassal." Thereupon Wagner, finding himself cornered, had changed his tactics. Formerly he had been root and branch against the production; now he suddenly intervenes in person and decides to push the production through, but still under Richter. His object clearly had been to set the Intendanz aside, but in this he had failed: his royal protector had refused to see him, to the great satisfaction of his people, as it showed

"a recognition of the true character of this musical autocrat, who, with the unconcern of genius, has carried his poetic morals into the sphere of real life and staged a Wagner-Tristan Cosima-Isolde vis-à-vis Bülow-Marke."

It was not all in the best of taste, but most of it was from the point of view of the time and the place unanswerable. And of course the less intelligent of the journalists saw in Wagner's recent conduct a piece of pure political opportunism: the cry went up that he was deserting his former Liberal principles and throwing in his lot with the Court clerical party, by way of retaliation upon the King.

2

Wagner had no difficulty in disposing publicly of sheer nonsense of this latter kind, but the *Allgemeine Zeitung* attack was less easy to deal with. He replied at great length in the issue of the 16th. On the whole it was a poor effort. He discanted upon his ideals; he fell foul of Perfall; he blustered about his "honour". What he did not do was, of course, to rebut charges and insinuations to which he had no real answer — that he had virtually claimed to govern the Munich Theatre from Triebschen, that he had imagined he could show the most marked unfriendliness towards the Intendanz and still count on its good will, that he had tried to coerce it in the matter of the *Rhinegold* production through his tool Richter, and that his political activities and his private life had made him *persona non grata* in many quarters.

Richter also had joined in the fray, in a long communication to the Leipzig *Signale* bearing the date 14th September. For the most part it is merely rude to Perfall in the way by that time customary in the Wagner circle. It is also notable, however, for an occasionally elastic handling of the truth. He speaks, for instance, of an obvious desire on the part of certain people in the theatre that the production should be a failure — which is decidedly overstepping the bounds not only of fact but of probability; Perfall, whose position depended on the King's favour, and who knew full well that Ludwig's whole heart and soul were in the enterprise, would never have been so stupid as to work directly against it.[3] Again, Richter says that after the general rehearsal on the 27th August "the most disquieting reports reached Lucerne from various quarters", as a result of which Wagner no doubt persuaded the King to postpone the production for a few days. The only "disquieting reports" of which we have any authentic record, the only ones, indeed, likely to have reached Triebschen on the following day, were firstly Richter's telegram on the morning of the 28th, exhorting Wagner to "stop the performance", and Betz's letter written on the 24th and posted on the 27th.[4]

---

[3] What the King thought of all this mud-flinging at Perfall is to be deduced from the fact that on the day of the performance of the opera he raised him from the rank of Acting to that of actual Intendant.

[4] Possibly Judith Mendès, who had been in Munich and in close touch with Richter for the last month or so, also telegraphed to Wagner: she would of course

Richter says there is no truth in the story that at the conference that followed this rehearsal he declared that he would not conduct the performance even if the King were to order him to do so. But that disclaimer on a purely verbal point merely diverts attention from the admitted fact that he had refused to obey the orders of his employers (of whom the King was one) unless he had his way in a department that was not his province. He tries to make it appear that it was only after the failure of the conference with the Intendanz and his request to be allowed to resign that he telegraphed to Wagner. This was quite untrue, as the facts already set forth prove beyond question. There is the same lack of candour in his statement that "the telegram cited by the inspired journals in which Wagner urged him to refractoriness" [5] is an invention with a purpose, as is also the supposed dispatch reading "I am coming: you will conduct." This is mere verbal jugglery: on the 29th August Wagner had wired to him that he had put his "conditions" before

be heart and soul with him, and with Richter as his accredited mouthpiece. According to her own story in later years she was waiting outside Schäfer's house in the Alte Pferdestrasse when Düfflipp and Perfall called on Wagner on the 1st September, and she saw the couple leave: from their faces, she says, it was apparent to her that the conversation inside had been heated. When the coast was clear she entered the house: she found Wagner bitter and ironical, but calmer than might have been expected.

Judith's reminiscences, however, recorded as they were forty years after the events, hardly rank as historical documents. She gives us, for instance, a dramatic picture of the perfidious Perfall coming before the curtain at the general rehearsal of the 27th August, bowing and scraping and making insincere apologies for the defects of the scenery, and Richter "striking angrily on his desk, as if hitting the back of the traitor." As a matter of fact it was Wagner's partisan Hallwachs who made that speech.

[5] Both Wagner and Cosima certainly encouraged this refractoriness, and, in the case of Betz, who was as essential to the performance as Richter, positively appealed for it. "In the Meister's name", Cosima wrote to Richter on the 29th August, "try to get Betz to say that he will not sing." And sure enough, on the night of the 1st September Betz told Düfflipp that "he would leave Munich first thing tomorrow morning." Wagner must have heard of this, for in a letter of the 3rd — after having had time for second thoughts on the matter — he tells Düfflipp that he has asked Betz *not* to do what he had threatened, for the practical reason that while he entirely approves of Richter's action, a withdrawal on Betz's part means a total end to all hopes of the situation being redeemed. Throughout it is evident that he had never had a thought of going to Munich with the intention of being placable for the sake of carrying the thing through, as is hypocritically claimed in the *Signale* article. What he was really aiming at was to make the Intendanz publicly climb down by taking Richter back. And this happened to be the one point on which neither the King nor the Intendanz could or would give way. On the 20th February of the following year Düfflipp wrote to Bülow, "I will permit myself to say only this, that I still maintain that the removal of Music Director Richter was a disciplinary measure absolutely necessary in the circumstances."

Düfflipp, and *if* they were fulfilled, Richter could conduct, and again on the 30th that he is coming to Munich to see if there is any way out of the difficulty, but "in no case with any other conductor but you."

There is the same kind of legerdemain with words in the statement that Wagner had gone to Munich with "the most pacific intentions", desirous only to "mediate", to "conciliate", with the intention now of tolerating anything that might be done to his work which he could no longer avert. The simple and central truth was that he had made his sanction of the production dependent upon the impossible condition of the reinstatement of the mutinous Richter. Wagner went back in disgust to Lucerne, the statement continues, because he had now become convinced of the "intrigue" against him. This again concealed from the readers of the *Signale* the fact that the refusal of the Intendanz to have Wagner in the theatre was the direct consequence of the fundamental inadmissibility of his claim with regard to Richter.[6] Finally the writer of the letter scores a trifling debating point when he says that Wagner could not have been refused an audience of the King for the reason that he had not asked for one. The casual reader of 1869 could hardly have guessed from this that the reason why Wagner had not requested an audience was that he realised from the long silence of the King how deeply offended he was with him, and how useless it would be to try to see him.

All in all, the *Signale* letter is an unpleasantly crooked piece of casuistry. And what makes it still more unpleasant is that although it is signed "Hans Richter" it emanated from Richard Wagner. It was dated, as has already been said, the 14th September, and purported to come from "Pasing, near Munich". Richter had left Munich on the 7th, and after a couple of days in Zürich had arrived at Triebschen on the 10th. There he remained until the 14th, when he went to Paris, which he did not leave until the 26th October. The document had been put together while he was at Triebschen. It was Wagner who sent what he calls "Richter's article" on the 14th to the latter's Munich friend Schäfer, asking him to post it to the *Signale* in Leipzig: it would never have done, of course, for it to

---

6 In his telegram of the 1st September (from Munich) to the King, Wagner says that unless he is assured of "my pupil's co-operation" he must "at once withdraw entirely". He insists on this on one occasion after another.

bear the Lucerne postmark! The whole fabric of Wagner's life at this time seems to be shot with petty dissimulation and subterfuge.

The only other document that needs to be mentioned in connection with the case is a piquant one. It is the draft, still among Wagner's papers, of a letter to Wüllner in which we get a hint of the sort of language he was addicted to when he was really annoyed. "Hands off my score!" it begins. "That is my advice to you: if not, to the devil with you!" He advises Wüllner to confine his activities to conducting singing clubs; if he must try his hand at opera scores, let him get them from his friend Perfall.[7] To that gentleman he is to say that if he does not confess to the King his personal incapacity to produce Wagner's work, Wagner will set such a fire blazing round him that not all the hole-and-corner scribblers who are financed out of the pickings from the *Rhinegold* costs will be able to blow out. And so forth in his best Billingsgate style. And so saying he gave a few more people — for one may be sure that the letter had more readers than Wüllner — occasion and excuse to leer and jeer and jape at him for his bad temper and worse manners. In the *Rhinegold* affair he was once more his own worst enemy.[8]

3

The King attained his object in the end with three performances of the *Rhinegold*, on the 22nd, 24th and 26th September. The opera was as great a "success" as any musical work can be that breaks with tradition at so many points: the listeners least accessible to what was new in it were particularly distressed by its long stretches of "recitative" — the only name they could find for Wagner's continuous flow of vocal melody free of all formal schematism. It was these worthies, no doubt, who broke into applause, in the old-fash-

---

[7] The reader will recall that Perfall dabbled in opera composition himself. See Vol. III, p. 316 *note*.

[8] He reminds us in more than one respect of that sadly misjudged man the great and good King Gama:

> If you give me your attention I will tell you what I am:
> I'm a genuine philanthropist — all other kinds are sham.
> Each little fault of temper and each social defect
> In my erring fellow creatures I endeavour to correct.
>
> . . . .
>
> I love my fellow creatures — I do all the good I can —
> Yet everybody says I'm such a disagreeable man!
> And I can't think why!

ioned style, after Loge's lyrical narration: here at any rate was something they could recognise as "melody"! The absence of "ensembles" — for the Rhine Maidens' trios can hardly be called by that term — was another grievance among the upholders of operatic tradition. Cornelius no doubt summed up the general opinion of cultivated musicians in his article on the production in the *Neue Zeitschrift für Musik*.[9] Peter, who was never an out-and-out Wagnerian, could not reconcile himself to some features of the work: he thought the composer stuck rather too doggedly to his "principles" at times. But the musician in him was sensitive to most that was new and characteristic in the idiom of the opera.

All this, however, is a matter of small moment today. More relevant to our present subject are Cornelius's remarks on the production. The scenic changes, he said, about which there had been so much excited discussion, worked on the whole "with such precision that they conveyed absolutely no impression of being associated with such extraordinary difficulties"; and if one or two things, such as the too solid rainbow, could have been improved upon, the question still arose, "Is it possible that these things had created such a commotion and had such prodigious consequences?" Peter's words suggest that he thought the hullabaloo of the last few weeks, on the whole, simply much ado about nothing. The principal trouble, he opined, was that Wagner had not attended at least the final rehearsals. Quite so, we may comment; but would it not have been better still if he had shown some willingness to attend the rehearsals at a much earlier stage? For all the trouble there had been he himself was mainly responsible. Richard Fricke, whom Wagner called in in 1876 to help him in various matters connected with the staging of the *Ring* at Bayreuth, has described in detail the difficulties attending the realisation of the opening scene of the *Rhinegold*. Even when the machinery for the swimming Rhine Maidens was at last ready — which was not until the final rehearsals for the festival were well under way — an elaborate scheme for control and synchronisation had to be worked out.[10] Richard Fricke, who solved the problem in the end, was himself for a long time doubtful whether the scene would be possible. It is evident that in 1869 Wagner had not given sufficient thought to

[9] This is not reprinted in his *Literarische Werke*.
[10] See *infra*, Chapter XXIII.

the mechanical and other difficulties involved; it was hardly likely, therefore, that the Theatre Intendanz could find the perfect solutions. Had Wagner, however, chosen to co-operate from the beginning the King would have seen to it that no pains were spared to solve the problem. In any case it was unreasonable of Wagner to blame the Intendanz for not being able to do what he himself obviously had no notion how to do at that time.

The most crushing comment of all upon his conduct throughout the affair and on his wild protestations that the Munich production would damage the prospects of the *Ring* beyond repair, and also the confirmation of Cornelius's hint that the tumult and the shouting had been mostly much ado about nothing, are unconsciously supplied, however, by Wagner himself in his letters of the 21st September and 22nd October of that same year to Schott. Herbeck, the Vienna Kapellmeister, had been to Triebschen seeking permission to give the *Rhinegold* in 1870, and after that the remaining operas of the cycle in successive years. Dresden had been throwing out similar feelers. Wagner gives no hint of being set on principle against the concession: he merely suggests that the Dresden theatre is not all he could wish it to be, and that his relations with the King look like being clouded over. In the second of the two letters he refuses permission to the Darmstadt theatre to give the *Rhinegold*, not absolutely and for ever, but only "for the present", until after it has produced the *Meistersinger*. "On the other hand", he continues, "I would have no objection to raise if the Vienna people should still wish to give next year a model performance of the *Rhinegold*, as they propose." [11] Manifestly he did not think the prospects of the work ruined, or even seriously damaged, by the Munich production. But being still sore over his defeat there he worked off his ill temper in a little poem,[12] the gist of which is that while the stupid dwarfs might play as they liked with the Ring it would merely bring them gold, and the curse will one day overtake them and all the other robbers who forget that the work will succeed only in the hands of him who fearlessly guards the Rhine gold. It is a pity he was not oftener content to work off his tantrums in a bit of harmless doggerel.

We have seen that in his telegram of the 31st August to Düfflipp

---

[11] Neither of these productions materialised.
[12] *Rheingold*, in RWGS, VIII, 338.

the King had threatened to withdraw Wagner's allowance. There was never, of course, the least likelihood of this. The words escaped him in a moment of irritation, and were probably forgotten before sundown. But it looks as if Düfflipp had given Wagner a hint of the King's outburst when he saw him in Munich on the 1st September, for on the 4th we find Wagner anxiously asking Schäfer to see his former servant Franz Mrazeck, who still attended to some of his affairs in Munich, and find out whether he had come upon any snag when applying on the first of the month, as usual, for the instalment of the allowance then due, as so far he has not yet received the remittance and he is becoming very much worried about it. Schäfer is to send the information by letter, not by telegram — a side-light on Wagner's constant anxiety at this time with regard to public "indiscretions" in connection with his private affairs.

4

It has been necessary to insist again and again in the foregoing pages that the root cause of all his troubles with the Munich theatre at this time was his relations with Cosima, because this aspect of the matter is one which the Wahnfried school of biographers, inspired as they were by Cosima herself, were at great pains to conceal. We have just seen Wagner taking up in his private correspondence a quite different attitude towards the *Rhinegold* production from the one he saw fit to adopt in public and *vis-à-vis* the King. Further light on what was really in his mind is thrown by his letter of the 19th September to Mathilde Maier. She is not to distress herself too much about the affair, he tells her. It was just a spiteful trick on the part of the Fates — a "childish indelicacy" of the King's in insisting on having the *Rhinegold* just now: he himself had foreseen the disagreeable consequences, but had been "too proud" to want to do anything in the matter — which, one is bound to say, is an account of the affair very wide of the truth. In a few weeks, he continues, the divorce will probably be carried through, and certain other difficulties will gradually disappear.

> "The most difficult thing will be to persuade the King to withdraw entirely from the wretched, horrible Theatre for about three years. If I can succeed in this I may be able to indulge myself in the hope that later on — but of course in wholly different circumstances — I can help him to realise his fondest wishes."

The inner meaning of all this is obvious — first the divorce, with its inevitable consequence, the complete fading out of Bülow from Munich musical life; then two or three uneventful years in which both to live down the contumely that Munich would visit on him and Cosima at first and to bring Richter back in a position of authority there. One has one's doubts, however, as to whether he was wholly sincere even in this. His correspondence makes it clear enough that in his heart he knew he had finished with Munich for good. For what could the town mean to him now? He had no ties of real friendship there, and socially, indeed, it would always be more or less impossible to him. In the Theatre he had just had a sharp reminder that his power was not so great as he had imagined it to be. And by this time he had been forced to recognise that the days of his self-assumed guardianship of Bavarian politics were over. The King had cut the leading strings that Wagner had tried to fasten on him as a ruler; and, even worse than that, he had shown him that in the artistic sphere too he meant to insist on what he regarded as his rights in the partnership between the musician and himself. We shall perhaps not be doing Wagner much injustice if we assume that already he was thinking hard about his old plan for a theatre of his own. In any case his real opinion with regard to Munich was that expressed in a letter to Porges written within a few days of that to Mathilde Maier:

> "the unheard-of baseness of which I have once more been the victim there in connection with the *Rhinegold* has naturally alienated me absolutely from it for all conceivable time."

And on the 12th October we find him telling Eduard Avenarius of his resolution never again to take part in the performances of his works.

5

It must soon have seemed to him, however, that he once more had the King in the hollow of his hand. For the relations between them began to follow, to some extent, the now familiar course: Ludwig's anger having burnt itself out, he was filled with remorse for having hurt Wagner and with grief at the thought that their common ideal might be endangered; and in the excess of his contrition he abased himself in a way that must have made Wagner believe his ascendancy over him would soon be as great as ever. On the 22nd October the King broke his long silence with a letter that shows how atrociously he had suffered. He has had a conversation with Brandt, he says, and it has heartened him to talk with someone so devoted to Wagner.[13] "The age is not yet ripe for our ideal", he cries; "it is only too true that we are simply the sureties for the age to come." Then he gives us a glimpse into the abyss of his suffering.

"If I may say so, I think you imagine my position to be easier than it is. To be so completely, absolutely alone in this bleak, cheerless world, alone with my own thoughts, misunderstood, mistrusted, this is no small thing. In the first days of my ascension to the throne it was, in a way, by the charm of novelty that I appealed to the people. But alas for those who have to do with the mass, and well for those who, like yourself, can operate through individuals. Believe me, I have come to know men. I went towards them with genuine love, and felt myself repulsed; and wounds like these heal slowly, so slowly!"

And he wants to know if Wagner is now working at the *Götterdämmerung* and if the poem of *Parsifal* will soon be begun.

Wagner was too skilled a tactician to betray any eagerness to grasp at once the hand thus held out to him in love and longing. He must first of all take advantage of the King's access of weakness, first of all play upon the boy's repentance, put him thoroughly in the wrong, and then, by a feigned withdrawal, engineer him into making a further advance. His letter of the 1st November, the gist of which is that, although he feels no bitterness, his heart is too full for him to speak with all the sincerity he would like, is one of his masterpieces of dialectic. Their mutual love endures, he says; but for himself there remains nothing now but complete renunciation of any hope of joy through his works. Henceforth he must sink himself in creation, trying to forget that there are forces that would deliver these works up to the base assoilment of the common world.

[13] Ludwig had sent for Brandt to discuss with him a production of the *Valkyrie* in December, 1869. Brandt and the scene painters told him that they could not possibly be ready in so short a time. The musical authorities, for their part, pointed out that at least two months and a half would be necessary for the copying of the score and the making of the parts, so that even the orchestral rehearsals could not begin before January, 1870. On the 11th of that month the King issued a new order: the *Valkyrie* must be given with the least possible delay, and followed, also in the coming summer, by *Siegfried*. He was evidently not *au fait* with all the practical difficulties of the opera house.

As Düfflipp explained to Bülow in a letter of the 20th February, 1870, all this had gone on without Wagner being informed, because correspondence with Triebschen had ceased.

The technique worked, as it always did with the King. Ludwig at once protests that people delude themselves if they think they twain have parted: were that to happen it would be the end of him! The desire to hear Wagner's divine work, he pleads, had been overwhelming; if he erred, he begs forgiveness. His surrender is complete.

> "I abhor a lie. I will not try to excuse myself. I will say frankly that I recognise my fault and repent of it. I ought to have communicated my wishes to you personally and have felt a not unjustified resentment towards those who . . . thought themselves qualified to carry out your intentions."

His devotion to Wagner is as great as ever.

> "Your ideals are mine; to serve you is the mission of my life. No human being is capable of hurting me; but when *you* are angry with me you deal me a deathblow."

Wagner is to write to him and assure him that he forgives him: separation would cut his very life's-nerve: he would not be far from suicide.

> "What is the dazzling possession of a throne in comparison with a friendly letter from you? . . . Yes, Parcival knows his duty, believe me, and, purified, will endure any test."

The garrison having surrendered unconditionally, as it seemed, the conqueror could afford to show a little magnanimity, though still taking care to underline the enormity of the King's offence. He hopes the bond between them will indeed endure unimpaired; but never again will he submit himself to what he has recently gone through in Munich. So he asks Ludwig to say frankly whether he really wishes to carry out the great plan they had agreed upon for the production of the *Ring* in such a way as to present it to the German world as "the monumental starting-point for a new and noble epoch of art". The King's behaviour during the last two years [14] had convinced him that he did not really wish that plan to be consummated; and Wagner tries to make out that it was the perception of this that had made him retire into his Triebschen solitude. What

---

[14] "Yes, now exactly two years", he adds pointedly. The reference is obviously to the suppression of the final *Süddeutsche Presse* articles in December, 1867. It is an indication of how this rebuff still rankled in Wagner.

he could not forget, and could hardly forgive, was the King's having produced the *Rhinegold* as part of the ordinary wretched opera repertory, before an audience of subscribers and even journalists! And he puts to Ludwig the plain question — Do you want my work as I wish it to be, or do you not? If he does, Wagner stipulates that Ludwig shall withdraw entirely from all concern with the Court Theatre for a few years, for it is unworthy alike of the royal Friend and of Richard Wagner; and, carried away by his own casuistry, he urges that the King ought even to take this resolution in the interests of his country, the political situation calling for his personal care. As compensation for this withdrawal Wagner would be willing to give the whole work before *the King alone* as often as he liked, though provisionally without the stage setting; and during that time they could be planning a production in the fullest sense of the term. But Ludwig will only be making life harder for Wagner if he continues to order his Intendant to give further performances of the *Ring*, performances which it will be impossible for him, the creator of the work, to attend — to say nothing of the fact that such performances can convey only a false impression of it.

6

To this letter of Wagner's of the 20th November the King does not appear to have replied. His native common sense must have told him that Wagner was laying down impossible conditions for him as regards the Court Theatre; and perhaps he had a suspicion also that there was more behind it all than was visible on the façade — that Wagner was merely manoeuvring for position, trying to put the Munich Theatre once for all out of the reckoning by barring all performances of the *Ring* there until his plans were ripe for a production elsewhere. As usual when he could not at once see his way through a difficulty, the King wisely remained silent.

He sent Wagner, however, the customary gifts at Christmas, and this gave the latter an opportunity for writing again at some length on the 30th December. He had hoped, he says, to make his own Christmas offering the manuscript of the complete prelude to the *Götterdämmerung*,[15] but ill health had held him up in his work.

---

[15] He means the Orchestral Sketch. He had begun the first stage of the prelude, the Composition Sketch, on the 2nd October, and apparently completed it in a very

He is in excellent vein now, however, and full of confidence in his creative powers; and it is interesting to find him, as on more than one other occasion, discussing his musical procedure with the supposedly unmusical King as he rarely did with any other correspondent. In this new score of his, he says in effect, there is no padding, no reliance on a routine scheme of composition; each fragment of the music has to be as full of essential matter as only the main portions are in a long poem. This necessitates unceasing invention, genuine inspiration in every bar. One appreciates the point when one remembers Coleridge's dictum that no long poem can be poetry throughout.

Wagner seizes the opening given him by a kind reference on the King's part to Cosima, in the note accompanying the Christmas gifts, to prepare him, in roundabout fashion, for the further developments impending at Triebschen. Death and life, he says, had been hanging in the balance; great resolutions had had to be taken; but some day all will be clear to everyone and success will justify him.

The King replied on the 6th January (1870). Wagner's letter, he says, has been a great refreshment to him in his heavy duties as ruler. He will be faithful to the end to Wagner and to the dreams of his youth, and victory will be theirs. He has recently been alone in his beloved mountains again, heartening himself for his leaden cares of state; and there his thoughts have been with the great artist who means everything to him, the creator who gives form and impetus to the dreams of his own youth for the betterment of mankind. Parcival is as ardent as ever to seek out the Holy Grail through all the ends of the world until it is found. Once more he protests that Wagner is his king and his god, the lord of his life, the very reason for his being, and that when Wagner's light dies out his day too will be done. But his next sentence or two must have warned Wagner that new dangers were ahead.

"It is for you that I wear my crown: tell me what your will is and I will obey. But do not deprive me of the very atmosphere of my exist-

---

short time. It was not until the 11th January, 1870 that he started work on the Orchestral Sketch. The last stage of all would be the complete orchestral score, from which alone, of course, a performance could be given. By delaying the completion of the full scores of *Siegfried* and the *Götterdämmerung* Wagner could put it out of the power of the Munich Theatre to produce these works.

Wagner's letter of the 30th December, 1869, by the way, refers to the Norns scene: this, according to his nomenclature, was the "prelude" to Act I.

ence by forbidding me the production of your works, in which I delight, and which are indispensable to me in this horrible world of my duties, which sometimes becomes intolerable to me."

Then, after a kindly reference to Cosima and the children,

"O how I envy you, able as you are to live in the ideal in dear, beautiful Triebschen! Think with compassion of the poor distant Friend who is being perpetually dragged down from the higher world to this futile earth on which he is condemned to live and labour."

If Wagner could have felt that the King was merely pleading to be allowed to console himself from time to time with the works already in the Munich repertory he might have let this pass. But he sensed that more was involved than that: the King was consumed with the desire to see the *Valkyrie* on the stage, and the score was in his possession. So Wagner braces himself now for the final assault. Ludwig has asked to know his will, to be given commands which he will obey. Here, then, is Wagner's will, set forth in a long letter of the 12th January, 1870.

7

Dialectically he has the boy at his mercy. He has gathered from talk in the papers that Ludwig means to order the production of the *Valkyrie* this year. What "commands", then, can the composer give? Let it be as the King wishes. Wagner feels that this is not in accordance with the plans they two had drawn up long ago for the production of the *Ring*. He stipulates now only for the same favours that had been granted him in the cases of *Tristan* and the *Meistersinger:* but without his continued personal co-operation his new works cannot possibly be given in accordance with his intentions. This is the first point on which he must insist — "Command the production of my works, but not without me." He contrasts the *Tristan* production with that of the *Meistersinger*. In the former case he had had, he says, the devoted co-operation of the faithful Pfistermeister, to whom he now gives a handsome testimonial, which is obviously motivated, however, less by regard for "Pfi" than by detestation of Perfall, on whom he pours out his wrath. He forgets or ignores what must have been as obvious to the King as to everyone else, that between 1865 and 1869 his relations with Munich had changed for the worst almost entirely through his own fault,

[242]

and that he had no right to expect exuberant cordiality from the Theatre officials whom he had lost no opportunity of insulting and impeding.

With Perfall he refuses point-blank to have anything to do, now or in the future. If the King wants a new work of Wagner's, he must commit it wholly to Wagner's charge. Four conditions are peremptorily laid down:

1. The King is to command him to give within a stated time model performances of the *Rhinegold* and the *Valkyrie,* and to confer on him absolute power to take whatever measures he sees fit to that end, which measures he [Wagner] is to communicate only to the Court Secretariat. (That is to say, the Intendanz is to be sidetracked).

2. The Theatre is to be closed for six weeks — four weeks for rehearsals, two for the performances.

3. Simultaneously Perfall is to be given a six weeks' "rest", all his duties and powers during that period being transferred to the secretary of the theatre. A special secretary is to be allotted to Wagner for negotiations with the artists and so on; and this secretary is to deal only with the Court Secretariat.

4. The performers and assistants chosen are to be entirely at Wagner's disposal during the whole of the six weeks, and for whatever he may do with regard to them he is to be responsible solely to the Court Secretariat. Wagner alone is to decide which collaborators are to be called in from abroad.

With the Court Theatre in its other activities he renounces all desire of connection; but as regards his own exceptional works the King is to do as the Romans did for exceptional State ends — suspend all legalities and appoint a dictator. And, playing for time, he stipulates that these model performances shall not be put in hand until 1871, for three reasons — it will take time to find his ideal interpreters; his health and the composition of the *Götterdämmerung* demand a long period of retirement from the world; and he does not wish to resume contact with that world until after his position with regard to Cosima is finally cleared up by a marriage. But if Ludwig is really resolved on giving the *Valkyrie* this present year, no time is to be lost in endowing Wagner with whatever absolute powers may be necessary. He suggests that Porges shall be granted him as secretary and plenipotentiary.

[243]

As on many another occasion, we can get the measure of Wagner's sincerity by comparing one document with another. We have already seen that the legend that he was irreconcilably opposed to separate productions of the four sections of the *Ring* will not hold today. To the King he tried to make out that another production such as that of the *Rhinegold* would ruin the chances of the total work "for all time". But that he really did not think so is proved by a passage in Cosima's diary. When he learned that Ludwig was planning a production of the *Valkyrie*, says Cosima, he was "startled". "It is really terrible", she goes on.

> "But Richard says, 'He cannot kill the work [i.e., the whole *Ring*]. I alone can do that, by breaking off and not completing it. The fact of his spoiling the thing now [i.e. the *Valkyrie*] will not diminish the effect if once the works [plural] are given in accordance with my intentions.' " [16]

And in a letter to Pusinelli of the 12th January — the very day on which he had sent his ultimatum, with its stern conditions, to the King — we find him making light of the whole matter. "My young King" is causing him some distress, he says.

> "Last summer things went badly with the *Rhinegold;* but he would not be dissuaded from it. Now the command is: Everything! Everything! Only not to postpone any longer the performance of my new works I should command, everyone will obey me. There, that all makes me worried again. God knows how I shall succeed in bringing myself to a position something of that sort — to have any desire myself for this. Still, I'll try, and — perhaps — it's possible that I may produce the *Rhinegold* and *Valkyrie* next summer." [17]

---

[16] MECW, I, 465. The excellent English version of Du Moulin's book by Mrs. Alison Phillips does not quite reproduce Wagner's meaning here. She makes him say, "I only can ruin it, if I am interrupted and cannot complete it." The German reads, "Ich kann es allein umbringen, wenn ich mich unterbreche [if I *interrupt myself*] und es nicht vollende." What Wagner means is that only one thing can "kill" the *Ring* — his own refusal to finish it. It was actually by a variant of this very technique that he made any other productions than those of the *Rhinegold* and the *Valkyrie* impossible in Munich: he simply refrained from sending the King the orchestral score of *Siegfried* on completion, as he had contracted to do in 1864.

[17] This whole passage, like many others, was suppressed in the official edition of the letter (in RWFZ). I quote from Mr. Elbert Lenrow's English version (RWAP, p. 226), made from the original manuscript, which, together with those of all Wagner's other letters to Pusinelli, passed into the possession of the American owner of the Burrell Collection. Mr. Lenrow's remarks, in the Introduction to his book, on the unscrupulousness with which these letters were manipulated in the official edition are very instructive as to the ways of Wahnfried in these matters. They were subjected, he says, to "systematic suppressions and manipulations calculated to con-

This, be it observed, relates to the summer of 1870: Wagner was quite willing to produce, if the King insisted on it, both the *Rhinegold* and the *Valkyrie* in Munich in some six months from the date of his writing, although he must have known better than anyone else the tremendous amount of preparation that would be necessary for the second of these works alone. He would hardly have consented to do this had he really believed that productions of this sort would be fatal to the prospects of the *Ring* as a whole.

8

What then was at the back of his mind when he wrote as he did to the King on the 12th January, suggesting that Ludwig should either keep out of the Theatre altogether for a few years or, alternatively, postpone the *Valkyrie* to the summer of 1871 and then give Wagner *carte blanche* with regard to the production, the theatre to be closed entirely for six weeks, and Perfall to be sent on "leave"? The conclusion seems irresistible that he was merely jockeying for position. A passage in Cosima's diary throws some light on the subject. When, in January, 1870, it became clear that the King was bent on having the *Valkyrie* that year, both she and Wagner were "seriously alarmed".

> "When I told him that I should not be able to attend it, he declared, 'Then on no account!' And yet again he returned to the point that it was unthinkable to him that one of his works should be given without my being present."

Cosima could not bring herself to face Munich just then, when the German Press was doing its foulest with her over her association with Wagner. The main object of his attempt to induce the King to postpone almost indefinitely the production of any further portions of the *Ring* was undoubtedly to gain time: the divorce was to be carried through as rapidly as possible, the pair were to marry, and then, after a long interval in which, it might be hoped, the venom of her assailants would have spent itself, Cosima could once more show herself in Munich should Wagner at that time seriously think

---

ceal certain facts regarding Wagner's actions and views. Entire paragraphs were omitted, whole sentences and parts of sentences were pruned out, phrases were re-written, and in one instance, even, a less compromising word was substituted for the one which Wagner himself wrote."

of co-operating in the Court Theatre. We are perhaps justified in thinking that he never had any real intention of doing so; having got the King to consent that nothing should be done until the summer of 1871 it would have been the easiest of matters for him to raise fresh objections then, and bit by bit postpone the day until he could go to the King with the scores of all four operas and arrange for a production of the *Ring* in its entirety, or, alternatively, produce it himself elsewhere.

Further light on what was really in his mind is thrown by another passage in Cosima's diary. "People will always be indebted to me", Wagner told her,

> "for at any rate *Tannhäuser* and *Lohengrin*. But this whole production [the *Ring*] calls for a higher general level of culture. If this does not come about, then the most perfect performance in Munich will be of no avail."

He could hardly have expected "a higher general level of culture" in the course of a year or two! What point would there be, then, in giving any more of the work in Munich so soon, even under the conditions he had laid down to the King? Evidently what he had in mind was a postponement of the production until he had succeeded in bringing about this raising of the culture-level in Germany as a whole, or, if that were not possible, at any rate in producing the *Ring* only before an audience of select spirits drawn from all quarters for that one purpose. In a word, he was already pre-visioning a Bayreuth. Once more, he was merely playing for time with the King — time to think as well as act.

The conditions he laid down in his letter of the 12th January, 1870 may actually have been put forward with the design of having them rejected by the King as impossible. Ludwig's common sense, as well as the counsels of Düfflipp and Perfall, would make it clear to him that the Munich public simply would not tolerate the handing of the State Theatre over for six weeks of the year, lock, stock and barrel, to this dictator and his forces from abroad: nor would Perfall have submitted tamely to being elbowed aside in the way Wagner had suggested. The whole Theatre would have been turned upside down; and the King had had enough of that already. Both he and his advisers, moreover, must have seen at a glance a weakness in Wagner's scheme for a production of the *Valkyrie* in that same year under his own supervision, a weakness of which Wagner himself must have been fully conscious, though he carefully refrained from drawing attention to it. The only conductor he could possibly have had in mind was Richter. But on that point the King and the Intendanz could not and would not give way. It was no doubt the sober recognition of the radical impracticability of Wagner's scheme that made Ludwig refrain from replying personally to his ultimatum by so much as a single word.[18] He commissioned Düfflipp, however, to inform him that his proposal to postpone the *Valkyrie* until 1871 was unacceptable and to say that he would be glad to hear if he had any alternative suggestions to make. To this Cosima replied, on Wagner's behalf, that he had none: "in particular he could not suggest a conductor, as those who enjoyed his confidence had been driven out of Munich."

This was a bad exposure of the central weakness of his case. No one but himself had driven Bülow out of Munich, as a direct consequence of the Cosima scandal; while Richter had rightly been dismissed because he had refused to obey any orders but Wagner's. Reading between the lines, continued Düfflipp in the letter to Bülow just mentioned, it was evident that they would have to leave Wagner in peace and proceed without him until matters were simplified by the clearing up of his "relations". Düfflipp had tried to persuade the King to wait a while, but he was immovable. In what he calls this "calamity" he appeals to Bülow for a "helping hand". He himself is reluctant to entrust the *Valkyrie* to Wüllner, out of respectful consideration for Wagner, who is set against the man. Eberle, who might have undertaken the task, is engaged for some months in Berlin.

> "But the King says that it is Wagner himself who is answerable for all these unpleasantnesses, and that he must bear the consequences. It was because of Wagner that you were compelled to resign: it was Wagner's outbursts of temper that drove Richter to behave so improperly and thus made his retirement from his office inevitable."

For these sins of Wagner the King declines to pay; and he insists that the production is to take place as soon as possible. Consequently

---

[18] Düfflipp, in his letter of the 20th February to Bülow, points out another obstacle: it was a pure impossibility, he said, for the King to summon Wagner to Munich while the latter's "unfortunate relations" [with Cosima] remained as at present.

Düfflipp begs Bülow to do the generous and forgiving thing and serve at once the King and art by coming to the rescue.

Bülow, who was recuperating in Italy, found it impossible to accept the invitation, but suggested Klindworth — at that time in Moscow — as an excellent substitute. Thereupon Düfflipp, with the full approval of the King, asked Hans to consider whether he could not see his way to return in full service to Munich, where every day they missed him more and more. Bülow, in a long letter of the 8th March, regretted his inability to fall in with this new suggestion. He sorely needed rest of body and mind: "in Munich you need a sound man, not a sick one." The sound man is Klindworth; for himself, he must for a long time avoid the excitement of Wagner's music. He has formed this resolution with deep regret, but he has no choice. For this and other reasons, "to return to Munich seems to me suicide pure and simple": even one half-year there under the conditions he has described to Düfflipp — to say nothing of the infamy of the Press and the personal malice of the Müncheners — and he will be an old man, fit only for the hospital ward.[19]

The deadlock was complete. But the King's will remained unshakeable: at all costs he meant to have the *Valkyrie* in the summer of 1870.[20]

---

[19] In a later letter he tells Düfflipp that in his opinion the personal co-operation of Wagner is a prime necessity for the model performances desired by the King. But as Ludwig could not countenance Wagner's return in a position of supreme authority in the Theatre until the Cosima situation had been legalised, they were all of them back in the old vicious circle once more. Throughout all these negotiations with Wagner and Bülow the Court Secretary stands out as a man of tact and honour and unfailing good will towards Wagner.

[20] Bülow's correspondence with Düfflipp and Klindworth will be found in BB and BNB.

CHAPTER XII

SUNSHINE AND CLOUD IN
TRIEBSCHEN

1

APART FROM the annoyance accompanying the *Valkyrie* plans of the King, Wagner could have had few grievances against the world during the period we have just been covering — the autumn of 1869 and the spring of 1870. However much he might rail against the theatres and the public, he could hardly help being gratified by the production of the *Meistersinger* in Vienna (27th February, 1870) and in Berlin (17th April, with Niemann as Walther), and *Lohengrin* in Brussels (22nd March, under Richter). In a letter of the 5th May to the King he could speak with pleasure of the growing enthusiasm of the German youth for him and his work, and of the dawning of a general recognition that his ideals were unrealisable in the German theatre as it then was.

His domestic happiness was almost unclouded. He was bathed in the atmosphere always most congenial to him — one of fanatical love, unwearying devotion, illimitable self-sacrifice, and unquestioning agreement with everything he said and did. Cosima played four-hands arrangements of the Haydn and Mozart symphonies with him, and was even able to please him with her Beethoven playing. They read their favourite literature together, and vied with each other in the naïveté of their critical comments on it. Now and then Wagner would be irritably jealous of the affection she lavished on the children; but he would always repent quickly of any harsh word to her, and raise her to the seventh heaven of happiness again by fresh praise of her and protestations of gratitude to her. She was skilled in the elaboration of the solemn little mummeries that so pleased him at Christmas and on his birthdays. All in all, but for an occasional annoyance over the self-will of the King or the delay in the coming of the divorce, his life at Triebschen may be said to have been one of ideal felicity.

Cosima too would have been entirely happy could she have dismissed from her mind all thought of Bülow. But the wreck that she and Wagner had made of his life haunted her conscience, especially in the sleepless hours of the night, as the numerous references to him in her diary show. It may be that she was inclined to dramatise herself and her mental tortures to some extent: it was almost too easy for her to see herself as another hapless Gretchen pouring out her contrite soul at the feet of the image of the Mater Dolorosa. But that she was really suffering is beyond question. The business of doing so, indeed, fell entirely on her shoulders, for Wagner was always too sorry for himself to have much leisure to break his heart over Bülow.

As for Hans, he was perhaps less in need of pity than Cosima found a voluptuous misery in believing. Grievous as his wounds had been, Italy healed them rapidly. He had settled in Florence, where he could enjoy the company of an old friend of his boyhood, Jessie Laussot. She was now a trifle deaf, but living an energetic life in the musical and intellectual circles of Florence, which were thrown open to Bülow through her. Did these two victims of Wagner's devouring egoism, one wonders, compare notes about the past and present? Hans, a born linguist, set himself to perfect his Italian and took a great liking to the Italians, whom he declared to be a sounder branch of the Latin stock than the French. He soon surrounded himself with friends and pupils, and almost managed to persuade himself that Italy would be a better terrain for him as a musician than Germany.[1] His elasticity of spirit soon enabled him to take life again with much of the old sardonic humour: it was the genuine Bülow, for instance, who, during a visit to Berlin in April, inserted an advertisement in the Leipzig *Signale* that during his absence from Florence all communications on matters of art were to be addressed to "my friend and secretary, Cavaliere Cesare Rosso, Via Santo Spirito, 31". The said "Cavaliere" was Jessie Laussot's house porter's cat, one Rosso (Red), with whom Bülow had struck up a warm friendship.[2]

And now that Germany seemed so far away and his jangled

---

[1] To Raff he wrote gaily, "What do all the Br's matter to me — Brahms, Brahmüller, Brambach, Bruch, Bragiel [Bargiel], Breinecke [Reinecke], Brietz [Rietz]? Don't talk about them. . . . The only one of them who interests me is Braff [Raff]."

[2] Also with a kitten of the Cavaliere, whom Bülow had adopted and to whom he gave the name of Rossino.

nerves were beginning to steady themselves he could take a cooler view of the question of the divorce. He wisely kept as clear as possible of Liszt, whose repugnance towards that step seems to have been almost as fundamental as ever, though he too was gradually yielding to the sheer pressure of events; and in March Hans could tell his mother that he had promised his Berlin lawyer to make the journey thither to carry out the formalities prescribed by Prussian law. He did so early in April, and was told that if he would return about the beginning of June he would find everything in order in another month or so. The lawyer was as good as his word: the marriage was dissolved on the 18th July (1870).

In this connection a passage in a letter of the 31st July from Klindworth to Bülow that was suppressed in the official edition of the Bülow correspondence (BB IV, 429) is of interest, as showing what Hans's closest friends thought about the whole matter. Klindworth had been spending some days in Triebschen, where Cosima, weeping passionately, had asked him to implore Bülow to forgive her for the terrible wrong she had done him: she would reproach herself to her dying day, and only his pardon could bring some alleviation of her sufferings. "She will never see her father again, for she is incensed over his scant sympathy in the matter." Wagner too had been full of protestations of undying love and respect for "his dear Bülow" and his "noble heart". "It is enough to drive one frantic", says Klindworth.

> "Indeed they had to do with one of the noblest and most self-sacrificing of men, and their disgraceful perfidy would have deserved to have met with one who would have shown them no consideration, but paid them back in their own coin. No doubt they felt rather humiliated and embarrassed with me, knowing me to be an old friend of yours." [3]

[3] BBLW, p. 119. On his way to Triebschen Klindworth had had a talk with Düfflipp in Munich. "Düfflipp," he wrote to Bülow, "hopes that after the marriage in Lucerne he will be able to induce Wagner to visit Munich again; but in this he deceives himself. Wagner is very angry, and swears that rather than have anything more to do with the Munich Theatre he will let everything go, break completely with the King, and give up Triebschen." Yet he wanted to place Klindworth in the Theatre, because he thought he "could rely on him". There would *not*, he said, be a production of the whole *Ring* there under his own supervision; but he had in his mind "another grand plan" — evidently meaning in a theatre of his own. When that had been accomplished, Klindworth, having been installed in the conductor's desk at Munich, was to reproduce the "model" performance there.

2

For all Wagner's pose as a lone Prometheus doomed to unceasing torture as a punishment for having brought a priceless gift to men, his health just now was good and his energy immense. Often ailing, as he put it in a letter to Pusinelli, he was never really ill; the mere removal of a worry was enough to make a new man of him physically. In February, 1869 he had given the King a pleasant picture of his daily round. Rising early, he washed in cold water, made a light breakfast, and ran a rapid eye over the headlines in the newspaper. Sometimes he would read *in toto* an article on some subject that particularly interested him; but generally speaking, he said, the less he heard of the outer world the happier he was. Letters were written, and at ten o'clock he settled down to work at the copy of the orchestral score of *Siegfried* which he was making for the King. At one o'clock his servant Jacob Stocker — Vreneli's husband — summoned him to lunch; this was followed by another glance at letters and the papers over his coffee, and this by a short sleep or a little interlude at the piano, according to his mood at the moment. At three o'clock, donning his "Wotan hat", he went out with the two dogs, generally walking to Lucerne, where he called at the post office or pottered about in an antiquarian book shop. By five o'clock he was back in Triebschen; after a quarter of an hour's rest he would start work again on his score, or perhaps write more letters. At eight o'clock came a light supper, then a couple of hours or so of reading; and by eleven he was in bed, though sleep often eluded him.

In the late autumn of 1866 Cosima had sent the King a description of the house as it was just after Wagner had altered it to his fancy.

"By the closing up of the two windows the drawing-room has acquired a long wall, on which the *Tannhäuser* picture and the *Rhinegold* cartoons show up splendidly: it terminates with the bust of the protecting spirit [King Ludwig] of this home and that of the spirit protected [Wagner]. A fireplace, on which stands the clock with the Minnesingers (your first Christmas present), has enticed Loge to it. Opposite the long wall, between the two doors, in a well-lit position, hangs the oil portrait of Wagner, the [King's] first birthday gift; and underneath this are arranged all the splendid things he has received during his life, silver bowls and wreaths, with two statues — of Tannhäuser and Lohengrin — showing up magnificently among them. Between the two windows is the piano, over which hang the medallions of Liszt and Bülow. The small room adjoining the drawing-room has become the library, delightfully alive with Hohenschwangau and the photograph of the protector. It is exceedingly quiet and pleasant down there: we call it 'Stolzing', and we haven't driven a nail or set a chair in place without looking at each other and imagining 'Parzival' to be here."

(Most of the objects mentioned were birthday or Christmas gifts from the King).

The picture is expanded in Wagner's letter to Ludwig of February, 1869. His work-room, he said, was the newly-made "green room", in which had been incorporated part of the room in which Ludwig had slept during his visit of May, 1866. Here were his books: on the walls hung a large photograph of the King and an aquarelle of Hohenschwangau, sent him by the King in November, 1865. (This is still at Wahnfried). In the drawing-room were portraits in oil of the King, of "my father" (Geyer), of Goethe (made for Wagner by Lenbach from an engraving), and of Schiller (a copy of Tischbein's painting of 1803), as well as another picture or two and "our busts". From this room two doors led into what he called his "gallery", which contained a collection of engravings and photographs of scenes from his operas, a Buddha given him years ago by Cosima's mother, the Countess d'Agoult, and souvenirs of various kinds. The dining-room was another of his reconstructions. His tea he took in a smaller drawing-room on an upper floor. This room, he tells the King, is for the use of the Freundin when she visits him in the summer — one of his little mystifications, this, for Cosima had been permanently settled in Triebschen since November, 1868.

About the furnishing of the house Wagner says nothing to the King; but we who are familiar with the somewhat baroque decoration of his Munich home cannot have any doubt that Triebschen exhibited the same peculiar taste. Nietzsche's sister has left us a sketch of the place as it was when she stayed there in the spring of 1871. The house, she tells us, which blended so harmoniously with its surroundings,

"was not furnished in a manner befitting its style, but in accordance with the taste of a Paris furnishing firm, which had been disagreeably lavish with its pink satin and Cupids. [The 'taste', however, was Wag-

ner's own: the Paris firm had merely obeyed instructions.] Thus I
have preserved a very unpleasant memory of the furnishing of the
simple old house. But its inmates and the scenery reconciled one to
the decorations and made them seem picturesque."

The costumes of the occupants struck her as being no less incon-
gruous with the scenery. She describes a walk she and her brother
took with them along the lakeside. Cosima was dressed in

"a pink cashmere gown with broad revers of real lace which reached
down to the hem of the garment; on her arm there hung a large Flor-
entine hat trimmed with a garland of pink roses."

Wagner followed her in

"a Flemish painter's costume — a black velvet coat, black satin knee-
breeches, black silk stockings, a light-blue satin cravat tied in many
folds, showing his fine linen and lace shirt, and a painter's beret on
his head, which at that time was covered with luxuriant brown hair." [4]

This was the costume in which the musician of the German sagas
discoursed to Nietzsche that afternoon on Greek tragedy.

3

It must have been an ideal life for a creative artist, one for which
Bach or Beethoven or Mozart or Wolf would have thought the sufferings of his earlier years almost worth while. Triebschen combined most of the privacy of a desert island with all the amenities
and luxuries of civilisation. Practically all the visitors to the house
were worshippers happy to sun themselves in the presence of the
great man; and the few who did not behave becomingly were soon
put in their place by Cosima. It was so, for example, with their
neighbour on the other side of the Lake, Countess Bassenheim, who,
presuming on the fact that she was the daughter of a Prince Ottin-
gen, was inclined to put on the airs of a *grande dame* condescending
to the company of commoners. Cosima had a technique that dealt
easily with that sort of thing. With people like Schuré and Mme
Mouchanoff, who had a due sense of Richard's artistic stature, there
was no trouble of any kind. To the latter lady Cosima read the
Sketch for the *Parsifal* opera, the spirituality of which gave the

[4] FNJN, p. 255 ff.

hard-cored woman of the fashionable world a new insight into Wagner's complex nature.

In the autumn of 1869 Triebschen had had a visitor who was destined to play a curious part in Wagner's life some years later. Théophile Gautier's lovely daughter Judith had written some glowing articles on Wagner in a Paris journal. These, with the enthusiasm of youth, she sent to Triebschen, receiving in reply a long letter of thanks in which Wagner gave her the psychological key to the prelude to the third act of the *Meistersinger*, which Pasdeloup had been performing at his Paris concerts.[5] In the spring of 1869, when the rumour circulated that he would be present at the coming performances of *Rienzi* in Paris, the editor of *La Liberté* thought to improve the occasion and add to his circulation by getting him to contribute a biography of himself to the paper. Wagner's reply, made *via* Judith, was that he was *not* going to Paris, the *Rienzi* production, and any others of the kind, being merely personal speculations on the part of the theatre directors, with which he had no concern. He explained why his thirty-years-old *Rienzi* seemed to him particularly adapted to the taste of the French public, but also why he could not abandon his retirement in order to assist in any theatrical enterprise whatever. This had been the sole reason for his refusal to go to Paris, he said, for he cherished no resentment against the town for its treatment of him in 1861. The letter, which was manifestly intended to be seen by other eyes besides those of the addressee, was published in the issue of the 10th March of *La Liberté*.

4

In the summer of 1869 Judith, her husband Catulle Mendès and their eccentric friend Villiers de l'Isle Adam accepted an invitation from Wagner to visit Triebschen en route to an International Art Exhibition in Munich. Wagner could not have been prepared for the dazzling beauty of the girl who introduced herself and her companions to him in the railway station at Lucerne on the 16th July. Judith was not quite nineteen; she had already been married some two years to the nine-years-older Mendès. She had one of the most sensitive artistic intelligences of her time, and much of her

---

[5] The story of the eleven-years-old Judith's interest in Wagner during the *Tannhäuser* days of 1861 is told in Vol. III, pp. 120–1.

father's distinction of style. She was only seventeen when she published *Le Livre de Jade,* a collection of translations of poems from the Chinese: she had learned that language thoroughly from a mandarin who had taken up his abode with her father. Wagner, whose intimates at this time included few really young people, must have been swept off his feet by the "Hurricane", as Judith's family used to call her. She has told us the full story of the pilgrimage in her own exuberant way in *Le Troisième Rang du Collier.*[6] Wagner turned all his charm upon the young devotees, played and expounded *Siegfried* to them, showed them all the beauties of the place and the neighbourhood, treated them liberally to the excellent champagne sent him by his old friend Chandon, told them the sad story of his life in detail, and performed all the prettiest tricks in his famous repertory, such as sending the scared Cosima sky-high in the children's swing, climbing trees (at fifty-six), and scrambling up the side of the house as far as the balcony by means of the shutters and mouldings — feats in the presence of which Cosima registered the appropriate wifely terrors. It was a very different Wagner from the one whom Mendès had met on a solitary occasion in 1861, when he was at odds with all the world: he had struck Catulle then as "an enraged tom-cat, hairs a-bristle, claws bared". In 1869 both he and Judith were impressed by Wagner's eyes, which were at once piercing and ingenuous; their expression, Catulle tells us, was childlike, virginal. He noted also the curious fact that while Wagner's body seemed to be a quivering mass of feminine nerves, the head and face always retained a splendid serenity.

The descent of the lively Parisian trio on Lucerne and Triebschen had one or two awkward consequences. Judith, who had been born with the true journalistic instinct, sent an article on "Richard Wagner at Home" to the Paris *Le Rappel:* this was reprinted in the Lucerne *Journal des Étrangers,* with the natural result that Triebschen was sometimes made intolerable for Wagner by tourists. Per contra, the little party found itself, after a few days, being treated with extraordinary respect at their Lucerne hotel. The rumour had

---

[6] This was published in 1909. It must be borne in mind that a good deal of what she sets down as the recollection of conversations in Triebschen is actually taken from letters of Wagner and Cosima to her.

Mendès touches more briefly than Judith does on these Triebschen days in his *Richard Wagner* (1886). Neither of them mentions the other by name in these reminiscences. They had separated in 1874, and Judith had resumed her maiden name.

gone round the town that King Ludwig and Adelina Patti were paying frequent calls at Triebschen, where the prima donna was studying a rôle in Wagner's next opera. Villiers had been positively identified by a well-informed local barber as the King of Bavaria, and Mendès as his adjutant, Count Paul Taxis, while Judith, of course, was Patti.[7] Another incident that amused them all was the receipt by Wagner, as a direct consequence of Judith's article, of a letter from a lady in Thonon. The story of Wagner's buffetings by fate had, it seems, convinced her that she was his sister in the spirit. For she too had had her trials. She had come down in the world, she said. She was passionately devoted to music, but had no piano; so in order to cultivate her art, as she put it, she proposed to settle with her five children at Triebschen, where "your house will be my house and your piano my piano". Wagner was no doubt grateful that she did not further propose to regard his compositions as her compositions.

When Serov and his wife, whom Wagner knew already, also presented themselves in Triebschen, the rival parties bristled at the sight of each other like dogs disputing over a toothsome bone. Judith and the others had come to regard the great man as exclusively theirs; the Serovs resented this competition in a field where they thought they had a prior claim. Judith noted with keen satisfaction that while the dogs barked at Serov they always wagged their tails when *she* appeared. But on the 25th July the French trio had to leave for Munich, where they hoped to see the *Rhinegold;* and with the departure of the "Hurricane" peace descended on Triebschen once more.[8]

5

Wagner had behaved so charmingly to his French visitors partly because they never made any attempt to conceal their adoration of

[7] According to Mendès, it was he who was taken for the King, and Villiers for Taxis. An interesting and well-informed article on Villiers — *Villiers de l'Isle Adam and Music*, by G. Jean-Aubry — will be found in *Music and Letters* for October, 1938.
[8] Wagner's letters to Judith from 1869 to 1878, now in the Paris Bibliothèque Nationale, were published by Tiersot (in TLFW) in 1935, with, however, many inaccuracies and omissions. Three years earlier, Louis Barthou had summarised the letters in two articles (BWG) in the *Revue de Paris;* he had had access also to various letters from Cosima to Judith which are today likewise in the Paris Library. Barthou's articles are not free from errors of date and of fact. In 1936 Dr. Willi Schuh published a complete German translation (RWJG) of the whole of the Wagner letters to Judith, with a long and informative introduction.

him, partly because Judith was the beautiful Judith. It was a less agreeable side of his nature that he showed to Minna's daughter Natalie. After her mother's death she had tried to make a living by letting rooms, and Wagner helped her with an allowance of 120 thalers a year. Relations between them remained fairly good for two or three years, though Wagner was not pleased with Natalie for refusing to give up his letters to her mother, of which there were some four hundred.[9] He carried on a desultory correspondence with her, and succeeded in February, 1869 in obtaining from her the little Buddha image, given him years ago by the Countess d'Agoult, which he had left for safe keeping with Minna during the years of his wanderings after 1861. A letter of November, 1867 once more demands the letters, we are told, "in almost threatening language."[10] Ultimately she sent him at least two hundred and sixty-nine letters,[11] assuring him that these were all: as a matter of fact she had kept back a large number, including some that "showed him in a somewhat unfavourable light"; apparently she was afraid that he or Cosima would destroy them.[12] (They were bought from her later by Mrs. Burrell). Wagner must have been very well aware which letters had been withheld, and why; and it was perhaps his anger at being frustrated that made him stop Natalie's small allowance soon after her marriage to one Bilz[13] — a somewhat shabby act, considering his lavish expenditure at that time on Triebschen.

It is pleasant to be able to record that he behaved more generously later. Natalie was soon left a widow and had to enter a Leisnig almshouse. (It was there that Mrs. Burrell found her and opened up negotiations with her for the sale of her papers). Through the Bayreuth banker Feustel Wagner made her a grant of 3,000 marks towards her support in the institution. Herzfeld[14] prints a letter to

---

[9] She was entitled to retain them, as Minna had left her all her possessions.
[10] CBC, No. 460 (6).
[11] That is the number published by Wahnfried.
[12] HMP, p. 351.
[13] "Natalie has just married Bilz: R. W. writes to say he can no longer pay her an allowance", runs the summary in CBC of a letter dated, according to the Catalogue, the 17th October, 1869. Perhaps the year should be 1868, for on the 31st July of that year we find him congratulating her "on her intended marriage to Mr. Bilz", and his letters of the 10th October and 27th November, 1868 are apparently addressed to "Natalie Bilz-Planer". (CBC, Nos. 460 (4), (5) and (6).)
[14] HMP, p. 352.

him of the 17th May, 1882 from Natalie that is full of affectionate gratitude. She spent ten years in the almshouse, being supported after Wagner's death by Cosima.

6

Of all the guests at Triebschen at this time the most notable and most welcome, however, was the young professor from Basel: Cosima made a point of inviting him as often as possible because he had a peculiarly beneficial effect on Wagner. The basic structure of Nietzsche's mind had not yet defined itself as clearly as it was to do some three or four years later. He was still one with Wagner in his admiration for Schopenhauer, and there was a good deal of ground common to them where music and the Greek drama were concerned. Wagner was convinced that he had acquired a disciple of a type superior to anything he had been fortunate enough to meet with before, one who could be trusted to work, under his leadership, for the regeneration of the German spirit through music and the theatre. For Nietzsche, Wagner was still a great and wholly sympathetic spirit, his Pater Seraphicus, as he called him.

Nietzsche seemed so young that Cosima could never quite see him as a university professor: she not only mothered him but patronised him in a way that must sometimes have been distasteful to one so aggressively self-centred as he.[15] She loaded him with small commissions to be executed for her in Basel; and though he attended to them all conscientiously and cheerfully he now and then lamented that she appeared to have an inadequate notion of the demands his own work made on his time. Wagner, for his part, entrusted him with what could have been the anything but easy task of arranging for the printing of his autobiography by the Basel printer Bonfantini and taking charge of the proofs. It was on the 3rd December, 1869 that Wagner sent him the first batch of manuscript.[16] It was perhaps when he read this that doubts began to steal

[15] It cannot be called a pleasant face that looks out from the photographs that show him as he was at this period: pliability is the last weakness that could be expected from a young man of that type.

[16] Fifteen copies were to be struck off: this number was afterwards changed to twelve. As everyone knows, the wily Bonfantini made a further one for himself, unknown to Wagner. It was by the acquisition of this latter copy from the printer's widow in 1892 that Mrs. Burrell was able to get on the track of many of the people

[259]

into his mind as to Wagner's complete sincerity in certain personal matters. In August of that year Wagner's sister Cäcilie Avenarius — Geyer's daughter — had visited Triebschen: it was twenty-one years since she and Wagner had last met. Some old letters of Geyer to her mother had recently come into her hands, and it is permissible to assume that she talked to him about these; for as her Christmas gift she sent him copies of them, while Cosima presented him with an almanac containing a reprint of Geyer's play *Der bethlehemitische Kindermord*. Both gifts moved Wagner deeply, especially the letters. There are good reasons to believe that they convinced him that Geyer was his father,[17] and that he had made Nietzsche, who spent that Christmas in Triebschen, his confidant.

7

But whatever Nietzsche's thoughts were on this and certain other matters he kept them to himself just then. Cosima seems to have found him at this time slightly antipathetic, in spite of her feeling of general benevolence towards him. "She had not found it as easy as the Meister", Du Moulin tells us,

"to feel at one with his nature, and she had been repelled by much that was doctrinaire in him, till he succeeded more and more in establishing himself as an intimate."

Reading between the lines, we may take this to mean that she found his superior specialist knowledge of his own subjects a chill and a check on her own and Wagner's vaporous theorising about them: Nietzsche's note books of a slightly later time indicate that he was somewhat critical of Wagner's amateurishness in the field of Greek scholarship, though as yet his own thoughts on the relations between Greek drama and Wagnerian music drama ran on much the same general lines as those of his Pater Seraphicus.

In the early weeks of 1870 Nietzsche sent Wagner the manuscripts of his Basel lectures on *The Greek Music Drama* and *Socrates and Greek Tragedy*, in the latter of which he adumbrated his

mentioned in the book who were still living. Natalie was one of them. In a letter of Wagner's to Bonfantini of the 12th January, 1873, now in the Burrell Collection, the number of copies to be printed is given as eighteen.

[17] For a full discussion of this subject see NFF, p. 240, Appendix II in Vol. II of the present Life, and Appendix I in Vol. III.

later notorious theory that the destruction of the true spirit of the ancient Greek drama had been the fell work of the "rationalising" Socrates and Euripides.[18] Wagner and Cosima read the lectures with mixed feelings. They could approve of Nietzsche's bold theses so far as they seemed to bring up reinforcements to Wagner's philosophy of art; but they no doubt sensed something in them that was not fundamentally Wagnerian, and were vaguely suspicious of it. They both exhorted him to work out his ideas on a larger scale. Wagner admitted the younger man's superiority in philology, but hinted that if he were equally versed in music he would look at certain things in another way; "remain a philologist", he complacently advised,

"but let yourself, as such, be guided by music. . . . Show what philology is really for, and help me to bring about the great renaissance in which Plato will embrace Homer, and Homer, filled with the ideas of Plato, now becomes the greatest Homer of all."

Nietzsche's letters in reply have apparently been destroyed; but his sister tells us that he smiled at Wagner's advice,[19] for the two lectures had been only feelers thrown out by him towards a larger work in which the many new ideas pullulating in the hinterland of his consciousness were to find organised expression. Wagner had not the remotest perception of where the individuality and the relentless driving force of Nietzsche's mind would some day carry him; he could assimilate the young professor's thinking only in so far as he could work it into the tissue of his own ideals.

8

He had hardly recovered from the annoyance of the *Rhinegold* production before he set to work on one of the most seminal of his prose writings, *On Conducting,* in which he defined squarely the new demands made upon a conductor's capacity by the changes in music, and the corresponding changes in the sensitive performer's attitude towards music, that had taken place during the nineteenth

---

[18] His notes for the lectures will be found in Vol. IX of his *Werke,* pp. 33–69.

[19] Suspicion attaches, however, to all these statements of Elisabeth's of what her brother "told her later" about this, that, or the other episode in his relations with Wagner. Her untrustworthiness as a biographer will be dealt with in some detail in later chapters of the present Life.

century. He began the treatise about the end of October, 1869. It ran in the *Neue Zeitschrift für Musik* in weekly instalments from the 26th November of that year to the 21st January of the following one, and was then published in pamphlet form by the Leipzig firm of C. F. Kahnt. It was prefaced by a "Motto from Goethe".

> Fliegenschnauz' und Mückennas'
> Mit euren Anverwandten,
> Frosch im Laub und Grill' im Gras,
> Ihr seid mir Musikanten! [20]

"From Munich comes another great vexation", Wagner wrote to Richter in March, 1870.[21]

"God knows what they are going to do there now! I am determined not to go there on any account. In these circumstances I foresee in the end a breach with the King."

There is rather more in this than appears on the surface.

Matters were beginning to shape badly for him again in Munich. The King's evident determination to produce the *Valkyrie* was not Wagner's only worry. A storm had blown up in Germany in the wake of the Vatican decrees asserting the infallibility of the Catholic Church. The King, with the sound political sense he so often displayed where great issues were concerned, had publicly ranged himself on the side of the Catholic Ignaz von Döllinger, who had boldly denied the validity of the Papal claims. As a consequence of Ludwig's action the Bavarian Ultramontane party was scheming once more to have him deposed; and Wagner feared they might succeed, in which case his pension would be sure to be in danger. For more than one reason, then, he had to do some hard thinking just then about his material future and that of his art. As regards the former he could reasonably hope that he could live on his receipts from the theatres, where his popularity was increasing daily: while the whole question of what he should do with regard to the *Ring* suddenly took on a new aspect from his reading of an article on Bay-

---

[20] "Flies' snouts and gnats' noses, with your kindred, frog in the leaves and cricket in the grass, ye are my performers." The quotation is from the scene of Titania's golden wedding feast in *Faust* (Scene 22). In Goethe the last line runs: "Das sind die Musikanten", and the second line is "Mit ihren Anverwandten."

Wagner was not misquoting from memory, but giving Goethe's verse an ironical turn to suit the purpose of his pamphlet.

[21] The letter is undated. Richter was at that time in Brussels.

reuth in Brockhaus's *Konversationslexikon*. At the back of his mind, perpetually preoccupied as it was at this time with the idea of a production of the *Ring* in a theatre under his own control, there must already have been some thought of Bayreuth. On the evening of the 5th March he asked Cosima to turn up the article on the place in the Brockhaus encyclopaedia; and in a flash he seemed to see the first step towards the solution of his problem. The 5th March, 1870 was always regarded by him and Cosima in later years as the "birthday of Bayreuth".

The little town, which dated from the thirteenth century, had come into prominence in the eighteenth as the "Residenz" of a sister of Frederick the Great, Wilhelmine, wife of the Markgrave Friedrich (1735–1763). This pair built the handsome "Neues Schloss" that is known to all visitors to Bayreuth today, and improved the Eremitage — a country house, a few miles from the town, that had been begun by a previous Markgrave. They did more: they built an opera house, and thereby, at long remove, made their tiny residency immortal. In 1791 Bayreuth was ceded by the then reigning Markgrave to the Prussian crown; but nineteen years later Napoleon assigned it to Bavaria. After the defeat of Bavaria in 1866 the land-hungry King Wilhelm of Prussia wished to incorporate Ansbach and Bayreuth once more in his domain; but from this he was dissuaded by Bismarck, who doubted whether these and other territories which the King desired to annex would show any loyalty towards Prussia in the event of another war. At the time, therefore, when Bayreuth began to attract the attention of Wagner it was part of the territory of his royal patron. This simplified matters considerably: while Ludwig might feel merely hurt at Wagner's sidetracking Munich, as he was now bent on doing, the founding of a Wagner theatre in any non-Bavarian German town would have been likely to alienate him utterly.

Visitors to Bayreuth who have glanced at the seemingly miniature old opera house will be as astonished as Wagner was in March, 1870 to learn that it had the largest stage in Germany. The idea that this old theatre was the very place for the *Ring* must have taken root in him at once. By June, when Richter came once more to Triebschen to resume his duties as copyist, Wagner's mind must have been practically made up on the subject. Cosima spoke to Richter of her "hopes" for the new adventure: "the only thing for which we will give up our refuge [Triebschen] will be this blossoming of art in Bayreuth", Du Moulin quotes her as saying. Wagner, of course, did not breathe a word of all this to the King. That he had been prepared to forfeit his pension, if necessary, in order to attain his goal, is shown by a letter of the 6th November, 1869 to Catulle Mendès,[22] written while he was still smarting under his experiences with the *Rhinegold* in Munich. Mendès had suggested arranging a series of concerts in France of Wagner's works, to be conducted by him. Wagner half-promises to do so in the coming year, by when, he hopes, certain difficulties will have been removed from his path — by which he means that he will then be married to Cosima and consequently able to appear in public with her. He confesses that many a time of late he has had to contemplate the unpleasant possibility of one of these days having to earn his daily bread by concert-conducting: by resigning himself to taking the world as it is, however, he may still manage to preserve the independence and leisure for creation that have been made possible for him by the King, to whom he pays tribute as the only man who knows what is due to an artist like himself.

9

But in the summer of 1870 matters once more took a bad turn in Munich. After a long silence, Wagner, fretted by Ludwig's manifest resolution to have the *Valkyrie* at any cost, had made a last appeal to him, in a poem dated the 13th April, to be true to the holy bond between them.[23] Copying the poem into the "Brown Book", under the title "To the King", he (or Cosima) added the significant comment, "dernier effort!". Ludwig thanked him warmly for it on the 2nd May, assured him that he was still heart and soul with him in pursuit of their "common ideal", swore that he would sooner throw himself from the tower of the Munich Frauenkirche than be false to their cause, but begged him not to be angry with him for being unable, in what he apologetically calls his "youthful impetuosity", to wait until 1871 for the *Valkyrie,* as

---

[22] Louis Barthou (BWG, p. 487) wrongly suggests 1867 as the date of the letter.
[23] The poem, commencing "Noch einmal mögest du die Stimme hören", will be found in RWGS, XII, 392. Wagner sent it to Ludwig in commemoration of the sixth anniversary of their first meeting.

Wagner had suggested. Wagner must not think that the King is indifferent to the manner in which his works are given, the truth being that he can get to the heart of them in spite of a few deficiencies in performance. "So now sentence me to death if you can!" And once more he gives us a glimpse into the true nature of his trouble: sick to the very depths of him with cares of state, he needs the spiritual comfort that only Wagner's works can bring him.

Against the tone of the letter and the main substance of it Wagner could have no possible complaint; but it must have been clear to him now that it was useless to struggle any longer against what had to be, the King being what he was. Their correspondence of the next few weeks is of the friendliest nature on both sides, but silent on the two really vital subjects — on the King's side the *Valkyrie*, on Wagner's, Bayreuth. For the Master's birthday (the 22nd May), Ludwig sent a groom to Triebschen with the gift of a fine carriage horse.[24] In his letter of thanks Wagner enlarges once more on the congenial theme of his complete alienation from the world, though he is gratified to discover that many people, in particular the younger generation, are beginning to perceive the true mission of his life. The King, perhaps, did not grasp at that time the full import of the remark that

"people realise that for my works, which have come only by external accident into the category of 'operas', I must have a theatre wholly my own, to which there must be invited not the lounging opera public, accustomed solely to the trivial, but only those who hitherto have remained aloof from these shallow entertainments."

With the ordinary theatre he has finished for ever. The *Meistersinger* was his last concession of that kind; "never again will the theatres get a work of mine". But of Bayreuth *per se* he does not breathe a word; his letters to Ludwig at this time do not contain the smallest hint of the definiteness of the resolution he had come to in the preceding March.[25] And so the King, in his reply, makes no ref-

---

[24] Its baptismal name was Liese, but Wagner, it goes without saying, changed this to Grane. We learn from a letter of Cosima's to Nietzsche that old Fritz, who till then had had the honour of drawing Wagner's carriage, was at first very much hurt at the coming of a rival; but peace seems to have been restored by putting them in the shafts together.

[25] Nor, by the way, did he ever mention to Ludwig a plan that seems to have occurred to him in March, 1870 for founding an international theatre — which of

erence to Wagner's talk about a theatre of his own: he merely repeats his assurance of undying loyalty to him and to "our ideals" hopes he will not give up the idea of writing *Die Sieger*, and asks for a further instalment of the autobiography.

It is only on the 15th June, when Wagner can have no further doubt as to the King's intentions with regard to the *Valkyrie*, that he presents him with what is virtually another ultimatum. He begs Ludwig, if he must have the work, to produce it for himself alone, the public being excluded on any pretext that will serve: he is to hear it as many times as he likes under the guise of *rehearsals*, and then announce that, for "inner reasons", the *performance* will have to be postponed. If this request of his is not granted, he will show no ill-humour, but for a long time the King will not hear his voice again. To Wagner's not very plausible suggestion, of course, Ludwig could not possibly accede. Public opinion would not have tolerated so obvious a piece of trickery in connection with the Court Theatre; the only practical result of it would have been to save Wagner's face at the certain cost of a fresh outcry against the monarchy. So the King made no reply.

Wagner's whole position was basically untenable, as the future was to prove. It was a priori impossible to ensure that even a theatre of his own could be run merely on the contributions of a select audience of devotees; financial considerations alone would sooner or later necessitate the admission of the general public. Again, the *Ring* had hardly been produced at Bayreuth (in 1876) before Wagner himself authorised its being given elsewhere. He no doubt meant, at the time, what he said when he told Schott on the 19th July (1870) that it would be absolutely impossible for him now to

---

course meant, for him, a Wagner theatre — in Paris. This idea seems to have been the result of the successful production of *Lohengrin* in Brussels, under Richter, on the 22nd of that month. Wagner found he had an enthusiastic admirer in Louis Brassin, a Brussels pianist, whom, apparently, he had in mind as manager of the Paris undertaking. Richter would have been the musical head of it: Wagner was anxious to redeem his promise to look after his protégé. See his letter of the 25th March, 1870 to the Mendès pair and Villiers de l'Isle Adam (in TLFW, pp. 314–5).

In October, 1869, in a letter to Richter, he had emptied the vials of his wrath on Paris. He has no great faith in Pasdeloup's capacity to serve him; and he has "simply no belief at all" in productions of his operas in the French capital. But his opinion of the French (and the Belgians) seems to have risen considerably after the warm reception of *Lohengrin* in Brussels. He talked now about a combination — in the international theatre, by the instrumentality of Brassin and Richter — of "the spirit of French initiative and action" and "German assiduity and persevering knowledge".

allow the *Ring* to be given up to the theatres as ordinary "operas".[26] But Schott must have asked himself ruefully how, in that case, he was to reimburse himself for his great expenditure on the work; for manifestly the fewer the performances the smaller would be the demand for copies of the scores. Wagner, in his usual airy way where other people's pockets were concerned, suggested that well-to-do enthusiasts would still want to buy copies of the very expensive full score for their libraries, while he himself would persuade the King to take twenty-five or thirty copies. But while he was thus indifferent to what might happen to poor Schott, he proceeds in the next breath to ask how things are going with the *Meistersinger*. He hopes orders from the theatres are coming in well, for he is in sore need of royalties, and handsome ones at that.

10

On the 24th June the final rehearsal — it was the twenty-fifth — of the *Valkyrie* took place in Munich before an invited audience. (The King was not present; he was at Hohenschwangau. Nor did he attend the first public performance on the 26th, his reason for these abstentions being that he wanted to hear the *Rhinegold* and the *Valkyrie* in succession). The second performance took place on the 29th; after which the two operas were given alternately on the 7th, 10th, 14th, 17th, 20th and 22nd July. Wüllner conducted, and the cast for the *Valkyrie* was as follows: Siegmund — Vogl; Sieglinde — Frau Vogl; Brynhilde — Sophie Stehle; Wotan — Kindermann; Hunding — Bausewein; Fricka — Anna Kaufmann; Helmwige — Anna Deinet (Frau Possart); Gerhilde — Fräulein Lenoff; Ortlinde — Fräulein Müller; Waltraute — Fräulein Hemauer; Siegrune — Fräulein Eichheim; Grimgerde — Fräulein Ritter; Schwertleite — Fräulein Seehofer; Rossweisse — Fräulein Tyroler. The Munich theatre thus supplied the whole of the personnel. The extra expenses of the production amounted to 41,500 florins. The performances, like those of the *Rhinegold* the preceding year, attracted devotees, enthusiasts and cavillers from all over Europe, among them Joachim, Brahms and Saint-Saëns: the last-named congratulated himself on being alive to hear two such great

---

[26] He had written in the same sense to Esser two months earlier: never again would he surrender one of his works to the theatres.

works. Wagner did all he could to dissuade his personal friends from going to Munich, and in some cases succeeded. But Liszt was there, and the two Mendès and Mme Mouchanoff. The *Valkyrie* made a great impression; even the journalists most hostile to Wagner had to admit that it was a work of "gigantic talent", as the Munich *Neueste Nachrichten* handsomely described it. Wagner was thus proved to be completely wrong in his forecast that the production would damage irreparably the prospects of the *Ring* as a whole: on the contrary, it whetted the public appetite for the complete work.[27] Once more one has the feeling that there had not been very much wrong with the *Rhinegold* production of 1869 except with regard to some of the machinery; and, as has been pointed out on a previous page, some of the scenic problems of the work have never really been solved from that day to this.

---

[27] In February, 1874 he felt called upon to explain publicly why he objected to concert performances — for which there was a great demand — of extracts from the *Valkyrie:* if these, he said, could give his friends a true idea of the work there was no real necessity for the tremendous efforts he was making to present the *Ring* intact in Bayreuth. "The problems of such a production only I can solve, especially as the singular success of the Munich performances of the *Valkyrie* — with which I had nothing to do — showed me how incorrectly my work has so far been understood." But to say that the *Valkyrie* had succeeded for the wrong reasons was to admit the fact of the success; and that success, so far from ruining the prospects of the *Ring* as a whole, whipped up general interest in the work.

CHAPTER XIII

THE BAYREUTH IDEA

1

THE KING had good reason to reach out wistfully to whatever consolation the works of Wagner could give him, for his heart
was heavy within him. War was approaching.

"German affairs bore me horribly", Wagner had written to
Mendès on the 25th March (1870). "God knows if I shall still be
able to prevent a new scandal in Munich. [The *Valkyrie* produc-
tion]. Everything is cracking." The glib phantast who had been
giving lessons in statecraft to German statesmen and political thinkers, who had foisted on King Ludwig his correspondence course on
"What is German?",[1] who had exasperated the practical people
beyond endurance by "seeing politics too operatically", as Fröbel
put it, was so absorbed in his own affairs at Triebschen, in finishing *Siegfried*, fuming at the delay in putting the divorce through,
and cursing everyone in Munich for their vileness towards him, that
he had no conception of the terrific storm brewing on the political
horizon. German affairs simply "bored him horribly"! Safe in his
Eden by the Lake, *he* could manage to shut out most of the sight
and sound of the unpleasant real world; while the young King who
had made this immunity possible for him, and whose political position in his own country had been made infinitely more difficult
for him by his devotion to Wagner, had to endure his complaints
and reproaches at the very time when the royal office was becoming
a burden almost more than he could carry.

War between France and Prussia broke out on the 19th July. The
position of the South German states had given them a peculiar
weight in the long dispute of the two great Continental Powers.
Public opinion in Bavaria was divided on the question of intervention: the liberal-nationalistic portion of the town population was
largely on the side of Bismarck, while for the peasants the real

[1] See Vol. III, p. 475 ff.

"enemy" was not France but Prussia — "better", they said, "a century of France than a year of Prussia." The King, who by now was rid of the too Prussian-minded Hohenlohe and had for his Minister-President the strongly Bavarian Count Bray-Steinburg, acted quickly and decisively. He had been watching the development of events closely: "it was as if his instinct told him", says his latest biographer,

"that in these days and hours he must be clear-headed and on the alert — that inherited instinct through which his ancestors spoke to him the more distinctly the more obvious it became that the existence of the kingdom they had bequeathed to him was now at stake." [2]

"Is there really no means of avoiding war?" he asked his anxious ministers on the night of the 15th July. By then it had become clear to everyone with any judgment that neutrality and action on the side of France were equally impracticable. After hours of anxious self-communion the King gave the order for the mobilisation of the Bavarian army: he had been clear-sighted enough to range himself on the side of the cause of German unity. There was some opposition in the Chamber to the Government demand on the 17th July for a vote of 27 million gulden, but the French declaration of war against Prussia that very day decided the issue: there was no more talk of neutrality.

2

On that same day the two Mendès and Villiers were once more in Triebschen, on their way home from Munich.[3] They found Wagner in a state of high excitement over the outbreak of war; and while his French visitors could not share his views as to the ultimate responsibility for it they could at any rate respect the fervour of his patriotism. But as the weeks went by, the "German spirit" of which he had so often sung the praises went more and more to his head; and on the 12th August, replying to a friendly letter from Catulle and Judith, he launched out into a tactless lecture to them on the failings of their country. He fulminated against what he called the

---

[2] Werner Richter, *Ludwig II, König von Bayern* (1939), p. 214.
[3] From Richter's diary (KLRWB, V, 164) we learn that their travelling party included Saint-Saëns and Duparc. Apparently they all went on to Triebschen on the 20th, where they were initiated into the second act of the *Valkyrie*, the Norns Scene, and portions of *Siegfried*. Wagner sang the vocal parts, and Saint-Saëns, according to Richter, "accompanied very well" at the piano.

sentimentality of the "French spirit", its "false poetry", its absorption in the "actuality" of the present, its "narrowness", which made it so difficult for others to come to an understanding with it. On the other hand, "the Germans' nurse has been history", which has at the same time consoled and fortified them. For that reason, what was now being said by the French, even by the most elevated minds among them, seemed to Germans like himself only "false logic adorned with misplaced eloquence." The "Spirit of History" had forged the instruments by which the French were to be punished for their crimes. Wagner has a fleeting perception that this is not precisely the right time to talk as he is doing to his devoted French friends; but he soon salves his conscience on that point with his usual clumsy casuistry. He feels it is his duty to say the word that will deliver them from their suffering, a word that is to "refresh their nerves like cold water". It is this: "Try to find a real statesman!", one who will "tell the French nation what the German nation is and what it wants; for it is this nation . . . not the 'Prussians', that is knocking at your doors." And so ad infinitum. His French friends are to look at things like "practical philosophers" and recognise, with him, that what is now happening is a judgment of God on the French, the profound sense of which they will do well to study. If he were in their place, and saw Paris crumbling into ruins, he would say that this should be the starting-point for the regeneration of the French people; for during the last two centuries there had been no Frenchmen, but only Parisians!

It was natural and permissible for him, as a German fanatically convinced of the superiority of the "German spirit" to all other national spirits, to hold these views; [4] but it was the very blindness

---

[4] Verdi's views on the situation are interesting. "The disaster of France", he wrote to Clarina Maffei on the 30th September, 1870, "desolates my heart as it does yours. It is true that the *blague*, the impertinence, the presumption of the French was and is, in spite of all their misfortunes, unbearable; but after all, France has given the modern world its freedom and its civilisation. And let us be under no illusion about it — if France falls, all our liberties and our civilisation fall too. Let our littérateurs and our politicians vaunt the knowledge and the science and even, God forgive them, the arts of these conquerors; but if they would only look a little below the surface they would see that in their veins still runs the old blood of the Goths, that their pride is beyond measure, they are hard, intolerant, despisers of everything that is not German, and of a boundless rapacity. Men with heads but no hearts; a strong but uncivilised race. And that King [of Prussia] of theirs who always talks about God and Providence, with whose assistance he is destroying the best part of Europe! He imagines himself predestined to reform the morals and punish the vices of the modern world!!! A fine sort of missionary! . . . Anyhow, I would have pre-

of ill-breeding for him to force them just at that moment on French friends so warmly attached to him as the Mendès had shown themselves to be. Catulle seems to have replied to it all with great self-restraint, expressing the hope that there was a higher sphere in which they could still all remain one, that of Love and Music. But there were no limits to Wagner's lack of tact. Replying to Catulle's letter, and thanking him for the tone and the matter of it, he cannot refrain from further indiscretions. What deprives him of all hope for the French, he says, is that he hears nothing from them but expressions of "patriotic courage", a resolve to "exterminate any invader of their soil".[5] He has waited in vain for a single man among them who would have the courage to declare the truth — the said truth being that the cruel would-be invaders have been themselves invaded by those who foresaw their intention. And once more Catulle, in July, 1871, after having passed through the horrors of the siege of Paris and the Commune, gives the crude ranter in Triebschen a lesson in courtesy; what had consoled him and Judith in their sufferings and privations, he said, had been the thought that Wagner was happy in his Swiss retreat.

ferred a peace concluded after our being defeated by the side of the French to this inertness of ours, that will end in our being despised. We shall not be able to avoid the European war, and we shall be devoured. It will not happen tomorrow, but it will come. A pretext will easily be found [by the Germans] — Rome, or the Mediterranean, or the Adriatic, which they have already declared a German sea." *Copialettere*, p. 604. See also his letters of the 10th August to De Sanctis and the 13th September to Arrivabene. Verdi, like many others, saw clearly that the Germanisation of Europe meant sooner or later the barbarisation of Europe.

[5] From Cosima's diary we discover that he "felt the war to be something holy and great" — for the Germans, of course; it was obviously criminal of the French to resist. When reports, admittedly false, arrived of the burning by the Turcos of two villages in Baden and of the French being reinforced by 6,000 Austrians, "the Meister demanded point-blank of his French friends that they should realise 'how we hate these characteristic qualities of the French'". Cosima, not to be outdone, was "indignant" at "the terrible effect of the French mitrailleuses": "machine-guns for our troops, their finery for our women — that is what the French have for us!" "The children and I are praying for the Germans", she piously records; but when she hears that the Empress Eugènie had been praying before the image of the Madonna in the Church of Notre Dame des Victoires — Notre Dame des Mitrailleuses, as Wagner wittily re-christened it — she found that "trivial". "Richard said that the French capital, the *femme entretenue* of the world, would be destroyed. As a young man he had not been able to understand how Blücher could have desired this, and he had disapproved of him. Now he understood him. The burning of Paris would be the symbol of the freeing of the world at last from the pressure of everything that was bad. In 1815 the Allies had refrained from doing anything to the city because they all meant to go there soon and amuse themselves. Richard wanted to write to Bismarck and beg him to bombard Paris."

3

He had every reason to be happy. Life in Triebschen, in general, had run along very pleasant lines for him during the winter of 1870–1. He entertained several times a group of musicians from Zürich (Rauchenecker, Kahl and Ruhoff), who, along with either Hegar or Richter (the latter taking the viola part), regaled him with his favourite Beethoven quartets. He visited or received some of his Swiss friends of former days, among them the Wesendonks, the Willes, Sulzer, Hagenbuch and Hermann Müller.

For the Christmas Day of 1870, which was also Cosima's thirty-third birthday, Wagner had prepared an affectionate surprise. Wholly unknown to her he had been working up some old musical material, intimately associated with her in his mind, which in 1864 he had designed for a string quartet.[6] He now re-fashioned and enlarged this material to constitute what is known today as the *Siegfried Idyll*.[7] Richter had secretly rehearsed in Zürich, then in Lucerne, a small orchestra of musicians from the former place, consisting of a few strings, a flute, an oboe, two clarinets, a trumpet, two horns and a bassoon. The trumpet part was taken by Richter himself. (The feat was not a superhuman one, as the part consists only of thirteen easy bars; but it made it clear to Cosima why Richter had been so addicted to practising the trumpet during the last few days: she had apparently begun to have her doubts whether Triebschen was as quiet a place as she had imagined). On the morning of the 25th the players grouped themselves on the stairs leading to the upper floor, where, in the presence of the astonished Cosima, the children and Nietzsche, Wagner conducted the first performance of the lovely work. Sulzer arrived from Zürich in the afternoon in

---

[6] See Vol. III, p. 271 ff.

[7] The dedicatory page of the manuscript bears the following description: "Triebschen Idyll, with Fidi's Bird-song and Orange Sunrise, presented as a Symphonic Birthday Greeting to his Cosima by her Richard, 1870." When the score was published, in 1878, Wagner prefaced it with a poem, commencing "Es war dein opfermuthig hehrer Wille", in which he sang Cosima's praises for the double service of devoting her life to him and presenting him with a son.

"Fidi" was the domestic name for Siegfried. The "Orange Sunrise" refers to nature's handsome recognition of the importance of the boy's coming into the world by picking out in glowing colours, on the morning of his birth, the orange wall-paper by the bedroom door. (See *supra*, p. 191).

time to hear a second and third performance, together with a Beethoven sextet [8] and the Wedding March from *Lohengrin*.

Purged of the passion for giving the universe lessons in practical politics, with the Cosima complication at last at an end,[9] and with his patriotic imagination stimulated by the success of the German arms, Wagner now entered upon a new and most vital period of creation, both musical and literary. The day after the outbreak of war he began his notable essay on *Beethoven*, which he finished on the following 11th September. Motived, in part, by the desire to contribute something of his own to the Beethoven centenary celebrations in the December of that year, the essay served him as an outlet for all he felt just then not only on the subject of the Schopenhauerian doctrine of the nature of music but also on that of the virtues of the German spirit. Equally important, in another way, is the paper on *The Destiny of Opera*, which he read as his "installation thesis" at a session of the Berlin Royal Academy of Arts on the 29th April, 1871. For some years now his pen was to be mainly occupied with matters concerning his own art, on which he could bring to bear the full weight of a lifetime's thought and practical experience. His prose writings from now onwards, until the time, three or four years before his death, when he once more became

---

[8] Presumably Op. 81, in E flat, for string quartet and two horns.

[9] They were married at eight in the morning of the 25th August — the King's birthday — in the Protestant Church at Lucerne. The witnesses were Richter and Malwida von Meysenbug. Nietzsche had been asked to be one of the witnesses, but he was in France at the time.

On the 20th Wagner had sent Düfflipp, for transmission to the King, Richter's copy of the Orchestral Sketch of the first act of the *Götterdämmerung*, together with a poem, commencing "Gesprochen ist das Königswort", in which Wagner congratulated Ludwig on having ordered the mobilisation of the Bavarian army on the 16th July. On the 21st he asked Düfflipp to pass on to the King the news that he and Cosima were to marry on the 25th. On the morning of that day Ludwig thanked him *by telegram* for the Sketch, and assured him that his thoughts were with him and Cosima. There is no letter of his to Wagner between the 5th June, 1870 and the 18th February, 1871.

The situation was not without its humours: the President of the Société des Amis du Divorce, 71, Rue Saint-Sauveur, Paris, having read of the marriage in the papers, sent Wagner a letter informing him that he had been made an honorary member of the Society.

It was from the papers that Liszt heard of the marriage, a week after the event. Cosima had not written to him for a year, he told Princess Wittgenstein on the 11th September. What he thought of it all is indicated by the fact that when his Paris bankers got into touch with Germany again after the war he instructed them to pay Cosima's allowance, as before, not to Frau Wagner but to Baroness von Bülow. Wagner was very angry over this "slight", and Cosima had to break her long silence and write to her father in protest.

unduly conscious of his mission as seer and prophet, are among the most suggestive documents in musical literature.

His minor works of 1870 and 1871 hardly call for mention except for the sake of completing the record. The war had made him more consciously German than he had ever been. In 1863, in a poem on *The German Fatherland,* he had asked bitterly just what the "German Fatherland" is. Is it Nibelheim, or Gotham-land? Is it where the Jew gives himself airs, where every knave laughs in his sleeve, where everyone takes himself seriously, where mediocrity thrives and spits in the face of what is noble, where one must be a hundred years old before he can hope for recognition? — and so on. Yes, he concludes, this is the Fatherland. But that was written in the days when things were going badly with him, and his natural impulse was to blame Germany for it. Now his patriotic fervour finds vent in a poem *To the German Army before Paris,* and in the *Kaisermarsch* with its choral finale, in which he sings the praises of that King of Prussia who had now become German Kaiser: "Heil, Kaiser! Heil King Wilhelm! Highest of crowned ones! . . . Through you arose the German Reich like an oak-tree putting forth new green leaves. Heil your ancestors! Heil your banners, which we carried when with you we smote the French. . . ." He was sufficiently critical of himself never to be under the illusion that the *Kaisermarsch* was one of his best musical works.[10]

To the German Army before Paris — five stanzas in which he glorified the Germans as a nation of born conquerors, insulted the French, and hailed the creation of a new Kaiserdom [11] — was not published until 1873, when Wagner used it to introduce Volume IX of his Collected Writings. He had, however, sent it in the early weeks of 1871 to Bismarck, then at Versailles, who acknowledged it in a letter of the 21st February in which he in turn complimented

---

[10] For his own disparaging comments on it see Vol. III, p. 448, *note.*

[11] I cannot deny myself the pleasure of quoting Ashton Ellis's English version of the lines:

> Das hohe Lied
> Dem Siege-Fried
> jetzt singen ängstlich Diplomaten,
> vereint mit ärgerlichen Demokraten! —

> The lofty psalm
> of triumph's-calm
> is hushed by voices diplomatic
> attuned to peevish counsels democratic.

Wagner on having won a victory of his own over the Parisians with his works.[12]

The tumid doggerel of the "People's Song" with which the *Kaisermarsch* ends was an afterthought on Wagner's part, as is sufficiently shown by the fact that the music (the main melody of the March) lies badly for all the voices.[13] It is to Wagner's credit that he himself did not take the "poem" seriously; it could have been no one but himself who parodied it at Christmas, 1871, when the children greeted Cosima with a version of it in which

> Heil! Heil dem Kaiser!
> König Wilhelm!
> aller Deutschen Hort und Freiheitswehr!
> Höchste der Kronen,
> wie ziert dein Haupt sie hehr!

became

> Heil! Heil der Mutter!
> Unserer Mama,
> Ihrer Kinder Hort und Tugendlehr'!
> Beste der Frauen,
> wie ziert Dein Lob Dich hehr!

while the praise of the Kaiser's ancestors and his victorious standards:

> Heil seinen Ahnen,
> seinen Fahnen,
> die dich führten, die wir trugen,
> als mit dir wir Frankreich schlugen!

became transmuted into praise of Cosima's little Siegfried:

> Heil Deinem Siegfried!
> Unserem Fidi! etc.

---

[12] The letter will be found in BBW, 1901, p. 220.

[13] Also by the letter of the 15th March (GRW, IV, 346) in which he offered the work to Wieprecht, the Director of Prussian military music. Wagner wrote the March in the first instance for military band, and his idea was that the German soldiers should sing the main melody at the finish in unison, "as the English do with 'God save the King'." It was only when the work was declined in Berlin that he recast it for concert orchestra and added the words, which were to be sung *unisono* by singers not placed on a platform but distributed among the audience: the latter also was to be supplied with printed copies of the words and melody.

This domestic masterpiece was *not* included by Wagner in Vol. IX of his Collected Writings: perhaps the Kaiser and Bismarck would not have been flattered by it.[14] Its build and prosody show that on the morning of Christmas Day, 1871 it must have been sung to the melody of the *Kaisermarsch*.

4

But if there is nothing much in either the words or the music of the March it at least makes a glorious sound. Towards another patriotic work of his, however, posterity finds it less easy to exercise indulgence. This is *Eine Kapitulation*, a tasteless, witless farce, the loutish Teutonic humours of which are ungraced by a single touch of literary finesse. One does not expect the emotions of the average man in any nation to be at their most delicate during a war, and as a general principle there is nothing to be said against our making the enemy of the moment the butt of our wit. But only a man of rather coarse fibre could have gone about in Wagner's deliberate way to make merry over the terrible sufferings of the beleaguered and starving Parisians. The sorry farce, though written in November, 1870, during the siege of Paris, was not published until 1873. The only result it had then on the French was to rouse an anger in them that did not die down for a whole generation. Many of his most ardent admirers there turned away in disgust from the man who could not merely perpetrate a bestiality of this sort in 1870 but could complacently think it worth publishing three years later, when it no longer had the excuse of the war-hysteria behind it. It had the consequence, among others, of ending the friendship between Wagner and Mendès. What chiefly angered Catulle was the way in which the greatest of contemporary poets, Victor Hugo, had been handled in the crude farce. For Catulle, Wagner remained to the end a great musician, but for the man Wagner he had little now but contempt. He was among those who attended the first Bayreuth festival in 1876; but while he was there he passed the gates of Wahnfried without calling.[15]

---

[14] It is given by Du Moulin in MECW, I, 593–4.

[15] Wagner had even the bad manners and the bad taste to introduce his devoted Alsatian admirer Schuré into the farce in this fashion:

Mottü: Presentez l'arme! Où est l'Alsacien pour chanter l'hymne?
Keller: (steps forward and sings in Alsatian dialect). "O Strassburg, O Strassburg, du wunderschöne Stadt" etc.

Wagner is seen in the worst possible light, again, in the manner of his attempt to float the farce. As had so often been the case with him, now that he had a shabby thing to do he preferred to do it anonymously or under a pseudonym. He sophistically tried to make out later that in publishing *Eine Kapitulation* (in 1873) he had "no thought of making the Parisians look ridiculous after the event", for the Germans, seen in the same light, were equally ridiculous, and whereas the French always showed themselves original even in their follies, the Germans, in their attempts to imitate them, became merely odious. As usual, fooling himself in true German fashion with words he naïvely believed that he was fooling other people. He had written the farce in 1870 because he hated the French and exulted in the sufferings of beleaguered Paris: he published it in 1873 because, in his incurable vanity, he thought it witty. But in 1870, though willing enough to stab, he preferred to stab in the dark. He sent the manuscript of what he called his "comedy in the antique manner" to Richter, pretending that it was from another hand than his, and asking him to set it to music in the style of "a parody of an Offenbachian parody" and then try to get it produced in Berlin.

> "If this drollery is put on the stage in the right clever style it is bound to stand out incomparably well from the mass of similar productions at this time, and consequently prove very popular."

Whether Richter ever thought of supplying the music is doubtful; and perhaps, knowing Wagner as he must have done by this time, he was never really taken in by the attempt to conceal the true authorship of the text, though it was not until the 26th December — more than a month after he had received the manuscript — that

---

Mottü: À present: jurez!
Keller: Schuré ist nicht da!
Mottü: Bête d'Alsacien! Le jurement!

Wagner had an unhappy talent for getting on the wrong side of the French. Bizet happened one day to read the *German Art and German Politics* of 1867. "According to Wagner", he wrote to his friend Paul Lacombe, "it is the destiny of Prussia to destroy France politically, and that of Bavaria, under its King, to destroy her intellectually. . . . This pasteboard republican would amuse me vastly if he did not make me sick. I would like to rub his nose in his article."

Bizet's anger goes to confirm the view I have expressed earlier (*supra*, p. 106) that it was the feeling that Wagner's animus against the French would be likely to spoil the relations between Bavaria and France at a critical time that made King Ludwig suppress the last two of the *German Art and German Politics* articles on the ground that the series was becoming "suicidal".

Wagner admitted to him his responsibility for the work.[16] But Richter submitted it anonymously to the Berlin Vorstadttheater, which had the good sense to reject it.

5

With the King also Wagner was playing somewhat less than straight about this time.

On the 28th December (1870) he wrote to Ludwig that he hoped to finish the composition of the *Götterdämmerung* in 1871. To that end, instead of completing in full score the portion already written he thinks it better, he says, to push on without intermission with the Composition Sketch of the remainder of the opera while the creative fit is on him. As for the production of the complete *Ring,* he continues, his plans are ripening, and he will lay them before the King when the latter so desires. The plan at the back of his mind at that time, of course, was to produce the work in the old opera house in Bayreuth. Of this, however, he gives Ludwig no hint as yet, though apparently he had already let some of his friends into the secret.[17] Ludwig replied affectionately on the 18th February. He is delighted to hear that the *Götterdämmerung* is well in hand. He asks for more pages of the autobiography. To Wagner he looks for his sole consolation in a world that is so full of cares for him that he has once more been thinking of abdicating. He asks for the earliest possible information about Wagner's plan for a complete production of the *Ring,* "the greatest, most comprehensive, most marvellous of all works that ever sprang from the human mind." Perhaps he thought that, now the Cosima matter had been regularised, Wagner's repugnance to Munich would be lessened, and the production could take place there.

Wagner finished the Orchestral Sketch of the *Kaisermarsch* on the 25th, and completed the full score on the 15th March. One wonders whether his laudation of the King of Prussia in the choral finale of the work was wholly unconnected with the thought that

---

[16] See Richter's diary, in KLRWB, V, 165.

[17] On the preceding 5th September he had written to Catulle Mendès half-jocularly expressing the fear that now — in consequence of the war — Pasdeloup will not venture to play any German music in Paris, and adding that he would have to "fix up Bayreuth by way of compensation for you". Evidently he had already spoken to Catulle of his Bayreuth plan.

this time Ludwig really might abdicate, and it might therefore be prudent of the composer of the German-national *Ring* to attract the benevolent attention of the German-national Kaiser. In a postscript to the issue, in 1878, of *What is German?* he disclosed how, while the German troops were returning home after their victory, he made private enquiries in Berlin as to whether, if a "grand solemnity" for the troops were being contemplated there, he would be allowed to compose the music for it. The answer was that it was not proposed to revive painful impressions by any such celebration. He then suggested, still privately, another piece of music, to accompany the entry of the troops, at the close of which, say at the march-past before the victorious monarch, the singer-corps so carefully tended in the Prussian army should strike in with a national song. The answer from Berlin was that this was impracticable, in view of arrangements already made. Thereupon, says Wagner, "I arranged my *Kaisermarsch* for the concert room: may it fit in there as best it can!" It would be interesting to have the exact dates of this correspondence.

Wagner certainly gave some of his German contemporaries the impression that round about 1870 he was doing his best to "cash in" on the newly-aroused "national" feeling. "One of his most repellent traits as the Folk's culture-apostle", Bernouilli wrote in 1908,

"is his calculated affectation of teutomania, the shrewd way in which, on occasion, he knew how to make use of this to attain his ends. The crassest example of this is his coarse anti-French satire of 1870, the would-be comedy *Eine Kapitulation*." [18]

The judgment is not only harsh but a trifle short-sighted; for fundamentally Wagner's teutomania at this time was no "affectation" but the genuine expression of his feelings. At the same time it can hardly be denied that he made the most, for the immediate ends of his artistic ideal, of this temporary harmony between his own opinions and those of the majority of his fellow-countrymen. Undoubtedly he played the *Kaisermarsch* about this time, in more senses than one, for all it was worth to him and his Bayreuth plan.

[18] BON, I, 105.

6

To return to the King. Obviously he would have to learn the real state of affairs as to the *Ring* before very long; but Wagner even yet does not see fit to tell him the whole truth straight out. He goes so far, however, in an extremely long letter of the 1st March, to admit him into the outer court of the secret. He prepares the ground with an exposition of his development as an artist; his gradual revolt, even in his Dresden days, against the ordinary opera theatre, as being incapable of realising his ideal; his intention from the first to produce the *Ring* under the special conditions he had set forth in his Foreword to the published poem; the circumstances that impelled him to break off the composition with the second act of *Siegfried* and write first *Tristan* and then the *Meistersinger;* his resumption of work on the *Ring;* his feelings, as of "a father whose child has been torn from him and delivered up to prostitution", when the *Rhinegold* and the *Valkyrie* were given in spite of him; his inability to complete the scoring of *Siegfried,* his excuse being that he felt his imaginative powers drooping when he stared at the ruled lines; his anxious pondering of this problem; his intention of reading an essay in Berlin on *The Destiny of Opera* in which he proposes to outline his scheme for the *Ring;* [19] that scheme is to take the form of "a German national undertaking" the sole direction of which is to be in his hands. He has already chosen the place for this venture, he says, though even yet he does not tell the King where it is: he excuses himself, in studiously vague terms, from doing so, on the sophistical ground that experience has taught him the danger of being too explicit in the opening stage of a new undertaking — he does not want to evoke too much opposition to his scheme right away.

Catulle and Judith Mendès, as we have seen, already knew about Bayreuth; so did Klindworth; so did Mme Mouchanoff; so, doubt-

---

[19] He did not do so on that occasion, however; but he wrote, during the weeks that followed the composition of *The Destiny of Opera,* an essay entitled *On the Production of the Stage-Festival-play 'The Nibelung's Ring': a Communication and Summons to the Friends of my Art.* This he printed in 1873 in *A Final Report on the Fates and Circumstances that attended the Execution of the Stage-Festival-Play 'The Nibelung's Ring' down to the Founding of the Wagner-Societies,* which will be found in RWGS, IX, 311 ff. In the "Communication" just referred to he outlined his scheme for a special theatre for the *Ring,* to be realised through Societies of his well-wishers. More will be said on this subject later.

less, did others of his intimates.[20] The one person whom Wagner had not seen fit to take into his confidence all this time was the King who had done so much — indeed everything — to make the completion of the *Ring* possible. He tells Ludwig this much, however, that the place is somewhere in Bavaria, and that it has the great advantage of not necessitating the building of a theatre. He asks the King to instruct Düfflipp to get into touch with him not only on this matter but on the correlative one of a change of residence; for of course he will have to make his future home where the theatre is. He concludes with some windy advice to the King in matters political: it is true, he says, that Bavaria has lost influence through recent events, but Ludwig should console himself now by trying to achieve in the "ideal" sphere what has slipped from his hands in the real; he is to set the new Germany an "example". To talk of that kind the King was soon to give his own despairing answer: disillusioned about the real world, and disappointed in his hopes of being Wagner's full partner in the achievement of "our ideal", he shrank inward upon himself and tried to realise his artistic longings in the architectural schemes that were one day to bring him down in ruin.

7

At this point it will be a convenience to the reader to have before him in tabular form the dates and details of the completion of the *Ring*, not only for convenience of future reference but because these dates throw a little light on the not quite honest game that Wagner was playing with King Ludwig.

It will be remembered that he had suspended work on *Siegfried* in 1857, after completing the composition of the first two acts. The remaining details are as follows: [21]

---

[20] The Lucerne bookseller Prell must also have been let into the secret. In October, 1870 he collected information about Bayreuth for Wagner, who was delighted to learn from him that the situation of the town was favourable and that houses could easily be rented there.

[21] C.S. = Composition Sketch, i.e., the first swift draft.

O.S. = Orchestral Sketch, i.e., a fuller lay-out of the texture in three or four staves, with suggestions of the scoring; this Sketch, of course, would convey little to anyone but Wagner himself.

F.O.S. = the full orchestral score, from which the parts would have to be copied, and without which a performance was impossible.

Siegfried

27/9/64.	Act I, Scene 2. F.O.S. begun.
22/12/64.	Act II. F.O.S. begun.
23/2/69.	do. do. finished.
1/3/69.	Act III. C.S. begun.
14/6/69.	do. do. finished.
25/6/69.	do. O.S. begun.
5/8/69.	do. do. finished.
[*25/8/69.*	*Wagner sends the King a copy of Act III, O.S.*]
25/8/69.	Act III. F.O.S. begun.
[*18/10/70.*	*Richter begins copy of Act III, F.O.S.*]
5/2/71.	Act III. F.O.S. finished.
[*8/2/71.*	*Richter finishes copy of Act III, F.O.S.*]
[*11/2/71.*	*do. begins copy of Act II, F.O.S.*]

Die Götterdämmerung.

2/10/69.	Norns Scene. C.S. begun.
11/1/70.	Prelude. O.S. begun.[22]
5/6/70.	Act I. C.S. finished.
2/7/70.	do. O.S. finished.
[*18/8/70.*	*Richter finishes copy for the King of O.S. of Act I, including Prelude.*]
[*20/8/70.*	*Wagner sends this copy to the King.*]
24/6/71.	Act II. C.S. begun.
5/7/71.	do. O.S. do.
19/11/71.	do. do. finished.
[*4/12/71.*	*Wagner sends the King a copy of Act II, O.S. (This was mostly made by a Zürich music teacher, one Spiegel).*]
4/1/72.	Act III. C.S. begun.
9/2/72.	do. O.S. do.
10/4/72.	do. C.S. finished.
22/7/72.	do. O.S. do.
21/11/74.	Acts I–III. F.O.S. finished.

---

[22] If the reader finds the first four or five of the following details a bit confusing, he has only to remember that while, for the ordinary spectator, the "first Act" of the opera extends from the opening chord to the falling of the curtain after the scene in which Siegfried has taken the Ring from Brynhilde, Wagner describes the whole of the opening scene as the "Prelude", "Act I" commencing, for him, with the scene in the Hall of the Gibichungs.

Now in his letter of the 1st March, 1871, Wagner, as we have just seen, gives the King to understand that he had tried to settle down to making the full score of "the lately composed parts of my work", but had failed, owing to his having no heart to complete the *Ring* until there was a prospect of his being able to produce it in accordance with his intentions. But reference to the tabular statement given above will show not only that the full score of the whole of *Siegfried* had been completed a month before the date of his letter to Ludwig, but that Richter had by that time finished his copy — intended for practical use, Wagner's own manuscript, of course, being the ultimate property of the King — of Act III, and had started work on the score of Act II. Wagner, therefore, was deliberately misleading the King. His motive was obvious: he feared that if he were to send Ludwig the full score of *Siegfried* there would be a repetition of his experiences with the *Rhinegold* and the *Valkyrie,* performances of which in Munich had been made possible by the fact of the King's possession of the manuscript full scores, from which the parts had only to be copied. For a whole year (since March, 1870) the idea of Bayreuth had been shaping itself in Wagner's mind; and he had been determined all along to checkmate the King by the simple move of withholding from him the remaining scores of the *Ring*.[23] There was some excuse for his resorting to that strategy; the pity is that in so doing he had also to resort to a piece of deliberate falsehood to his benefactor, whose munificence alone had made his work, and indeed his very existence, possible, and who, by the terms of the agreement of 1864, was not only the moral but the legal owner of the scores of the *Ring*. Let us refresh our memories of the circumstances relevant to the case.

---

[23] Wagner was at this time trying to place Klindworth as Kapellmeister in Munich. Klindworth had been in Triebschen in July (1870), and Wagner had obviously told him that "on no account would he deliver up the score of *Siegfried* to the King." He is "absolutely determined" never to set foot in Munich again; he is therefore more anxious than ever to establish Klindworth in the Court Theatre, as someone on whom he can rely. The complete *Ring* will *not* be given in Munich under Wagner, for he has a big plan in his mind for producing it elsewhere: Klindworth, however, can give it in Munich after that. Düfflipp was still hoping that after the marriage Wagner could be prevailed upon to go to Munich again — yet another indication that it was Wagner's association with Cosima that had been the primary cause of the town and the Court Theatre having become impossible for him. But Wagner was possessed with a fury of hatred for Munich, and was ready to break with the King rather than go there again. See Klindworth's letter of the 31st July to Bülow, in BB, IV, 427 ff.

8

Under the agreement of the 18th October, 1864 Wagner had pledged himself, in consideration of the sum to be paid to him, to deliver the scores of all four sections of the *Ring* to the Court Secretariat within not more than three years from that date. Clause 2 ran thus: "The work is to be the property of His Majesty King Ludwig II of Bavaria." Under Clause 5, Wagner was to declare in writing at the end of each contractual year what progress he had made with the composition. Under Clause 6, an extension of the period during which the whole work was to be completed would be granted only in case of a long illness on his part. Under Clause 8, if Wagner failed to fulfil the conditions as to the completion of the work within the specified time, or such conditions in that respect as might later be agreed upon, he would be required to refund the payments made to him. Under Clause 9, if Wagner died before finishing the work (within the three years), so much of it as was completed was to be delivered to the Court Secretariat. And in his instructions of the 11th October, 1864 to Hofmann, the King said that his Court Secretariat was to draw up a contract with Wagner "under which the property of the composition mentioned is to be assured to me."

No doubt Wagner was right in regarding the agreement as more or less a formality, designed to give the matter a legal status of which the King's ministers would approve. Still, there the agreement was; and while Wagner had had no scruple in availing himself of the financial benefits accruing to him under it, he had failed to fulfil his own legal obligations. Moreover, it was implicit in the contract that the rights of performance of the work would be vested in the Royal Court Theatre. Had the King been less generous than he was, he might have pointed out to Wagner that the Bayreuth plan was an infringement of this implied right; and Wagner would have been hard put to it to rebut the charge.

No defence against the accusation of duplicity can be put up for him today. On the 28th December (1870) he told Ludwig that while he hoped to complete the composition of the *Götterdämmerung* during the coming year, he had resolved — partly in order to finish the creative portion of his work while he was in the mood for it, partly because in his then bad state of health he could not face the labour of scoring the sections he had already written — to postpone this latter task until he could embark on the orchestration as a whole. That story was quite untrue, as a glance at the table given above will show. He had finished the *full score* of the second Act of *Siegfried* in February, 1869, had begun that of the third Act in the following August, and had made such progress with it that the whole task was finished within five weeks of this letter of his of the 28th December to the King.

His duplicity is further proved by letters of his to Karl Klindworth and to Schott. The former was making the piano score of *Siegfried*. From a letter to him of the 26th April, 1870 we learn that the full score of the second Act had been in Klindworth's hands for this purpose for some time. Wagner invites him to Triebschen for his summer holiday, promising to give him then a substantial portion of Act III. He has had to suspend work on the scoring for a while, he says, in order to concentrate on the *Götterdämmerung;* but by the beginning of June, when he will have completed the first Act of this, he will be able to give all his attention to the third Act of *Siegfried*. On the 25th January, 1871 he tells Klindworth that he will send him the whole of the *Siegfried* full score in about a week — this less than a month after he had solemnly assured King Ludwig, without a blush, that he did not intend to orchestrate that opera until he had finished with the composition of its successor. And to Schott, in the autumn of 1870, he had shown quite openly the hand he kept carefully concealed when his royal protector's eyes were turned in that direction. He had been so annoyed by the production of the *Valkyrie* in Munich, he says, that he had intended not to complete the orchestration of *Siegfried,* as he knew that the King was eager to have the score, and if he got it he would immediately "repeat the experiment" at his expense. While, however, still working quietly at the *Götterdämmerung* he had also, in fact, taken the full score of the last Act of *Siegfried* in hand: "The first half of it was sent to Klindworth three weeks ago, and the remainder will follow in the New Year", so that it should be possible for Schott to publish the piano score by Easter (1871).

That score was published, apparently, about July, for we find Wagner, on the 1st of that month, asking Schott for twelve free copies, together with one copy on vellum paper for the King of Bavaria. Now with the publication of this piano score, which of course implied the existence of the full score, there was necessarily an end to the pretence that he was postponing the orchestration of *Siegfried* until he had the composition of the *Götterdämmerung* off his hands.[24] If the King did not know enough about music to be aware of that, anyone in the musical department of the Court Theatre would have been able to enlighten him. But even before July his eyes must surely have been opened to the real state of affairs. Wagner had been in correspondence with Düfflipp, to whom he must have revealed his whole scheme for Bayreuth; for on the 19th April Ludwig wrote to Düfflipp, "I dislike Wagner's plan very much: it will be a pure impossibility to produce the whole Nibelungen cycle in Bayreuth next year." To Wagner himself, five weeks later, he described the scheme as magnificent, though he still thought there were too many difficulties ahead for it to be realised in 1872.

9

How are we to account for his taking the revelation of the Bayreuth plan so placidly, seeing that it not merely meant the end of all his dreams for making Munich the centre of the Wagnerian "regeneration" of art but exposed the lack of candour in Wagner's recent dealings with him personally? He may have consoled himself with the reflection that, after all, his consuming desire to hear the *Ring* would be likely, all things considered, to be appeased sooner in Bayreuth than in Munich. There can hardly be any doubt that Wagner had named 1872 to Düfflipp as the year of production. If that were so, it is hard to fight down the suspicion that once more he was not playing straight with the King, for a mere five minutes' reflection would have been sufficient to convince him that

---

[24] He kept up the deception to the end, keeping the King in play until, his own plans being ready, he could completely out-manœuvre him as regards a performance of *Siegfried* in Munich. As late as March, 1872 we find him writing to Düfflipp, "As regards the full score of *Siegfried*, it is doing me the greatest injustice to think that I am 'delaying' the delivery of it to his Majesty. This score does not exist." To which he adds, as if trying to salve his conscience, "at any rate not completely". That was quite untrue. See his letter of the 27th March, 1872, to Düfflipp.

On the 6th February, 1872 he wrote to Schott urging him to lose no time in returning to the King the manuscript of the *Valkyrie* score, which the latter had reluctantly lent to the firm. It would annoy his Majesty, he said, and make matters very difficult for himself (Wagner), if there is any delay. The King had asked for the *Siegfried* score as a *quid pro quo*, but this, says Wagner, he must withhold from him at present "for sad reasons". Not a word here about the full score of the third Act being "non-existent", or even "incomplete"!

there was no more chance of the singers and players being gathered together and trained, the scenery painted, the stage machinery constructed, the necessary funds raised, and so on — to say nothing of the fact that the first Act of the *Götterdämmerung* was as yet not completed even in the Composition Sketch — for a production in Bayreuth in 1872 than there was for the tetralogy being produced in the moon. It is just possible that he had named 1872 with a view to rushing the King into approval of his scheme.

As a matter of fact, it was practically at the very time when Ludwig was writing his letter of the 19th April to Düfflipp that Wagner realised that the Bayreuth plan was not going to work out by any means as easily as he had expected. He and Cosima had gone to Bayreuth on the 16th, where they remained until the 20th; and one glance at the little theatre had shown them that it would be useless for their purpose. It was the most fanciful rococo, he wrote to Düfflipp on the 20th, and any reconstruction would be impossible. He had accordingly dismissed it from his mind, he said, though he had been charmed by Bayreuth and its surroundings, and was more resolved than ever to make it the home for his *Ring*. On the 12th May he publicly announced his plan for a production of the work in Bayreuth, in a theatre specially built for that purpose: the date fixed for the performance was "one of the summer months of 1873".[25] Presumably the King had not seen this announcement when, on the 26th May, he expressed his doubts to Wagner whether a production would be possible in 1872. (He was in the mountains at that time, and perhaps out of touch with the course of events in the outer world).

It is permissible, however, to suggest an alternative explanation for the calm with which he seems to have accepted the new situation created by Wagner's final breach with Munich and his concentration on Bayreuth. He must have done some hard thinking about Wagner and about life in general during the last two years, and had probably resigned himself to the conclusion that his dream of being a partner in "our ideal" of the regeneration of the German world through the theatre had small hope of being converted into reality. It has been insisted on more than once in the course of this biography, for the fact needs to be constantly borne in mind, that from the first he regarded his association with Wagner not simply

[25] The story of the founding of Bayreuth will be told in connected detail later.

as the "protection" of an artist by a King but as a partnership on virtually equal terms. They were both working for the same high end, Wagner as creator, he as the means — especially in the matter of the Semper festival theatre — by which the grandiose scheme of the seemingly impossible *Ring* might be realised. From his dream of satisfying his own instincts as an artist in co-operation with Wagner he now had a rude awakening; and that native shrewdness in reading men which more than one observer noted in him from his boyhood must have made it clear to him that if Munich was now no longer possible for Wagner it was almost entirely the latter's own fault. He had accumulated enmities in the political world by his presumptuous claim to be the guiding spirit in the political evolution of Bavaria. The Theatre authorities he had set against him by his intrigues against them and his obvious intention of placing his own tools in all the key posts. On his own frequent admission, the Munich performances of *Tristan* and the *Meistersinger* had been almost everything he could have desired, and certainly far better than anything he could have attained by himself anywhere else in Germany.[26]

There was no a priori reason, then, why, given a cordial co-operation on his part, a Munich production of the *Ring* also should not have come as near his ideal as would be possible at that time. He could have had the same free choice of singers as was open to him at Bayreuth: there was no limit to what the King was prepared to do in spending his own money on the production and in making whatever alterations in the structure of the stage might have been necessary. But Wagner had first of all killed the noble scheme for the Semper festival theatre that was to have been planned from the foundation-stone upwards expressly to meet all the requirements of the *Ring*, and then, when only the Court Theatre remained to him, he had antagonised almost everyone connected with that, and retired to Triebschen to carry out a mixed policy of sulking and throwing sand into the machinery of the Theatre. And the King, as his letters show, was perfectly well aware that the root of all the trouble of the last two or three years had been, in plain language,

---

[26] When Herbeck, for instance, was contemplating giving the *Meistersinger* in Vienna, Wagner told him (in October, 1869) that he should take the Munich production as his model; there, he said, he had had "the fullest power to realise his ideas". On the 14th October of that year, again, he told the King that the Munich performances had been the most perfect that any of his works had ever had.

the Cosima complication: Wagner had turned in a rage against the town because it had become impossible for Cosima to show herself there.[27]

10

For Wagner the great artist the King could never have anything but the profoundest respect. But as regards the man Wagner the scales must have fallen from his eyes by now. He saw himself confronted by a combination of fanatical idealism and ruthless realism against which it would be hopeless to contend any longer. The partnership between Wagner and himself might still continue on the material plane, but the spiritual bond was snapped when Munich was pushed aside in favour of Bayreuth. But the artist — or the longing to be one — was too closely interwoven with every fibre of Ludwig's being for him to remain purely passive under the shock of Wagner's desertion of him. For his impulses as an artist there was now only one outlet, and one, moreover, in which he would be dependent on no one but himself. No longer able to "create", in his own way, through Wagner and the music drama, he could at least bend stubborn stone and the energies of a thousand craftsmen to his own imperious will. It was from this period onward that he threw his main energies into the creation of those architectural fancies, dream succeeding dream, each more extravagant than its predecessor, that in the end were to ruin him. A beginning had been made in 1869 with the relatively modest Linderhof — in essence no more than the substitution for a rough hunting lodge of his father of a kingly abode in which he could be at once comfortable and alone, surrendering himself to those dreams of mediaeval kinghood that had been so cruelly frustrated in real life. But it was Neuschwanstein — actually the creation of 1871, though the idea of it had first occurred to him in 1869 — that he not only first really found himself but, in a curious way, re-gathered his lost Wagner about him also. For Neuschwanstein was his peculiar realisation in stone of all the desires now predominant in him — a

---

[27] In the early weeks of 1870, we learn from her diary, Düfflipp told them how anxious he was that Bülow should be induced to hurry on the divorce, so that the King could receive Wagner in Munich and associate with him freely again. The evidence is overwhelming that the difficulties in which the Cosima affair landed him were the root-cause of Wagner's inappeasable hatred of Munich from 1868 onwards.

seemingly inaccessible quasi-mediaeval stronghold, perched on a dizzy height of rock, adorned with numberless emblems drawn from the sagas and the Wagner operas. Herrenchiemsee was the next creation of his soaring dreams. He became the loneliest man in Europe, but a man working tirelessly, feverishly, to incarnate the visions that gave his imagination no rest. And the severance in spirit from Wagner, if not the origin of his passion for building — for that was in his blood — was certainly answerable for the direction it took and the extent of its power over him. For he too, in his way, was, like Wagner, an artist to whom visions were the true reality, and the actual world only a tiresome irrelevance, a crazy discord that could not be resolved but only broken.

CHAPTER XIV

PLANNING BAYREUTH

1

WAGNER HAD much less reason to love Berlin than to love Munich, and far less reason to be grateful to it. Why then did he make the Prussian capital his starting-point in the campaign for Bayreuth? The answer seems to be that he hoped to benefit by the up-surge of national feeling in Germany after the defeat of the French and the founding of the Reich. Regarding the *Ring* as the purest manifestation of the German spirit, it was only natural that he should conceive the floating of it to be a national German obligation. And so, to achieve his aim, he turned in the first place to the political centre of that Prussia for which he had hardly been able to find a temperate epithet in days gone by.

His plans for a production of the *Ring* had been from the very first a singular mixture of audacious idealism and dubious practicality. Let us run an eye over them afresh. His original idea, as set forth in his letter to Uhlig of the 20th September, 1850, had been to raise 10,000 thalers somehow or other and erect, in a meadow near Zürich, a plain wooden theatre in which, with the irreducible minimum of machinery and scenery, he would give three performances of *Siegfried's Death* in a single week, after which he would pull down the building and burn his score, with a parting word to his audience — "Now go you and do likewise! But if you want to hear a new work of mine, then get the money together!" Uhlig, he continues, will no doubt think he is mad: nevertheless to accomplish this some day is the hope of his life, the only purpose that can stimulate him to continue creative work.

Fantastic as his talk about burning his score may sound, it is no more so than his airy outline of the practical conditions under which he hoped to carry out his plan. The problem of expense was to be solved in the simplest way imaginable. Some rich man or other was to provide 10,000 thalers for the building. The performances themselves were to cost not only himself but the audience simply nothing. For his chorus he would train a body of Zürich amateurs. The singers and orchestra, which were to be "the best to be found anywhere", would be "invited" to come to Zürich and place themselves at his disposal for six weeks. Notices would be inserted in "all the German newspapers" — presumably also on the basis of a simple "invitation" to the proprietors, without any sordid chaffering about advertisement charges — inviting all and sundry to attend the performances gratis. One ceases to wonder how inveterately Wagner's mind could inhabit a Cloud-Cuckoo-Town of its own in matters political when we see the cheerily unpractical way in which he tackled so relatively simple a matter as the production of an opera — and an opera, at that, the music of which was still unwritten! The whole thing was characteristic of him and of the Norns that shaped his life for him: he could never achieve anything but the impossible, and the more impossible, so to speak, the better, for only a fight against odds could call forth all his energy and courage.

The first public announcement of his plan for the *Ring* had been made in December, 1851 at the end of a *Communication to my Friends*. In this he does not touch at all on practical matters, does not even wave a fairy wand over them; he merely says that he "proposes" to produce the four works "at some future time" at a festival designed for that end, and that he will regard his object as fully attained when he and his "artistic comrades, the actual performers" — which looks as if he still expected their services gratis — had succeeded in conveying his purpose to "the emotional, not the critical, understanding of those who had gathered together to learn it". Anything beyond that, he said, was a matter of indifference to him. A few weeks later we find him telling Liszt that the audience he has in mind is one of friends who will have assembled solely to hear his work, preferably in some beautiful quiet spot far from the smoke of our industrial civilisation — perhaps Weimar, he adds, but certainly no bigger place.

2

He becomes rather more precise in the preface to the first public edition of the *Ring* poem (1862). The main point, it appears, is that the production of the work shall be "free of all the influences of the regular repertory of our existing theatres". To ensure this, some German town must be found which, while able to accommodate the necessary number of visitors, will have no regular theatre of the ordinary type with which the *Ring* can come into collision, and consequently no public that has been ruined by the mental habits fostered by such institutions. He asks only for a provisional building of the simplest kind, constructed perhaps of timber, with an invisible orchestra and an auditorium amphitheatric in form. In the spring of the appointed year "a company of first-rate dramatic singers, chosen from the German opera houses", and immune for the time being from the distractions of any other theatrical activity, were to be "summoned" to the scene of the experiment, there to be coached by him in their novel task. In the summer there would be three performances of the cycle, to which the German public was to be "invited". Only in this way could he count on securing a personnel with the necessary sense of style, a thing impossible for them to acquire in the routine of the ordinary theatre. Such a personnel, indeed, he says, is not to be found *en masse* in any German opera house: there are merely gifted individuals here and there, whom he will have to train afresh and weld into an artistic whole. The vital thing for them is undisturbed concentration on the task in hand. Only in these conditions of isolation from the regular theatrical world will the singers be able to acquire, for the time being, the necessary new mentality: how otherwise would it be possible for one who yesterday had been singing a bad German translation of, say, an Italian opera to think himself the next day into the part of Wotan or Siegfried?

So with the scenic settings: the best results in this line are obtainable only when, as in the great London and Paris theatres, the painters and machinists can have the stage to themselves for weeks before a new production. The scenery Wagner has in his mind's eye for the *Rhinegold*, for example, is quite unthinkable in a theatre in which the programme has to be changed daily. The sunken orchestra, again, will both refine the tone and help to intensify the dramatic illusion for the spectator. Finally the audience, which would consist of "publicly invited" guests coming to the festival for the sole purpose of hearing the *Ring*, would enjoy advantages not open to the ordinary theatre-goer in any of the large centres of industry. Instead of the spectacle being taken as simply a refreshment or distraction after a day of disagreeable work, this time it is the summer's day that will be given up to relaxation, so that towards twilight the spectator will enter the theatre with mind and body fresh and his receptivity at its keenest. Performances given and heard in these conditions would inevitably have a lasting influence not only on the audience and the performers but on the Intendants and directors of German theatres in general, who would go back to their own establishments possessed with a new ideal of opera production.

A reversion of singers and public to their old bad habits after the festival was over would be guarded against by a repetition of the performances every two or three years. Moreover, other works of merit, selected in public competition, would in time share the programme of the festival with the *Ring:* one of these, occupying a single evening, could be chosen for production each year, the *Ring* revivals taking place at longer intervals. Along these lines only would the German spirit be able to find expression for all that is best in it.

In 1862 he is still a little vague as to the finance of the scheme. The funds might possibly be provided by "an association of art-loving, well-to-do men and women" which would whip up the necessary subscriptions. In view, however, of the notorious small-mindedness of his fellow-countrymen he dares not promise himself much success in that direction. A simple plan would be for some German prince or other to divert to the festival scheme some of the money he now squanders on the upkeep of "that worst of public art-institutions, his opera house", which, as things are at present, merely serves to corrupt German musical taste. Should the patrons of his present opera house jib at this, the prince can say to them, in effect, "Have then what you have been accustomed to and what you so hanker after every night, but not at my expense; for what I have been paying for all these years is neither music nor drama but opera, which is a gross offence to the German concept both of the drama and of music." All the prince has to do is to devote henceforth the amount he now allots to opera to the establishment of biennial or triennial performances of music drama along the lines indicated by Wagner, and so found an institution that would have an incaculable influence alike on German art-taste, on the fostering of German genius, and on the cultivation of a genuine German-national spirit.

3

As will be seen, his ideal was weak only where most ideals are apt to betray weakness, on the practical and especially the financial side. By 1862 he had realised that he would have to face up more stoutly than he had done in the 1850's to the central problem of his scheme — that of money. He still talks vaguely of "summoning" the singers and "inviting" the audience for his festival; but he must have known perfectly well by that time that all this would have to be translated, in practice, into terms of cold hard cash. Nor, in his soberer moments, could he have cherished the faintest hope that any prince could be found in Germany willing, or, pre-supposing him to be that, strong enough to abolish or side-track his Court Opera and replace it by an institution giving merely a few model perform-ances of a few special works every two or three years. But there actually was a way out of even that difficulty, and King Ludwig had not only pointed it out to him but had shown his willingness to tread it with him. The Semper festival building would have pro-vided Wagner with the theatre of his dreams without any interfer-ence with the normal operatic life of Munich as represented by the Court Theatre. He could have had for the *Ring*, as he actually had in the cases of *Tristan* and the *Meistersinger*, the cream of Ger-man singing and acting talent. He could have had a stage and ma-chinery without their like in Europe, designed from the smallest nut and bolt upwards specifically for the solution of the new prob-lems of his titanic work. The scene painters and machinists could have had the stage absolutely to themselves for experimental pur-poses for as many months in the year as they liked, without the habitués of the regular theatre having to suffer a single evening's deprivation of their accustomed fare.[1]

Undoubtedly, had Wagner's interest in the Semper theatre en-dured, the ardent young King would somehow or other have car-ried the scheme through in spite of all opposition. In the foregoing

---

[1] "We [Cosima, Bülow and himself] saw the model", he wrote to Ludwig on the 2nd January, 1867, "and were unanimously of the opinion that if this building is constructed there will be nothing of its kind in modern Europe to be compared with it. It is a marvel: my idea, my instructions, my requirements have been completely comprehended by Semper's genius . . ."

pages we have seen the main reasons why Wagner turned his back on Munich. Other reasons may have been operative in a smaller degree. For one thing, he could not conquer his inborn dislike of large towns, where there were too many people who had the audacity to have opinions of their own on all sorts of subjects on which he conceived himself to be an authority by the grace of God. His ideal all along had been a small country place where he would be less likely to be subject to this inconvenience,[2] and a theatre of his own in which his word would be law, from the laying of the foundation stone to the last nuance of the public performance. He showed what was in his mind when he said to Cosima, in April, 1871, that "the three of them alone, he and she and Richter, would create Bayreuth: there would be no regisseur, only a treasurer." And again, "he wanted to be quite independent, bound by no contract, but supported and protected by subscriptions alone." Nor must we fail to take due account of one prime desideratum which even the Munich Wagner-festival theatre could not have met — that of an environment in which his ideal spectators could spend the day in quiet preparation for the serious business of the evening in the theatre. Finally, it is probable that his twenty-years' obsession with the plan for a special production of the *Ring* in a theatre of his own in some country town or other had struck deeper and deeper roots in him with each successive frustration in other spheres, and especially that of politics. There are signs of this in his letters of 1871 to the King. It was never in his nature to suffer opposition of any kind patiently; and he had been so decisively beaten in Munich that his insatiable lust for domination may well have had its full force diverted now into the one channel in which there was still some hope of its achieving complete self-expression — a combination of town, theatre and journal in which he would be undisputed dictator.

---

[2] How this peculiarity of his struck some people may be surmised from a remark, already quoted, of Bernouilli's, who, after meeting him in the flesh, saw him as "the very type of a dionysiacally-excited schoolmaster". When you were in his company, continues Bernouilli rather unkindly, "the impression he gave you of a schoolmaster was so strong that you asked yourself whether he had not become what he was only because he had modelled himself on his namesake in *Faust.* . . . What was it but his genius that enabled him to achieve his legerdemain?" BON, I, 106.

4

The preliminaries of his Bayreuth scheme had manifestly been thought out in considerable detail long before he divulged it to the world and the King in the spring of 1871. One of his anxieties, as late as April of that year, was, as we learn, from Cosima's diary, the fact that "still no word came from the King: yet his consent was the vital thing", — a clear admission that the Bayreuth plan was fundamentally an infringement of the King's and the Munich Theatre's rights in the score under the agreement of 1864; had Ludwig chosen to insist on those rights he could have made the new adventure immensely difficult for Wagner, if not impossible. It is a supreme testimony to Wagner's idealism and artistic integrity that he should have made up his mind to achieve his end even if it meant a final breach with the King and the loss of his pension. That sacrifice, it is true, might prove less fatal for him now than it would have been even a year or two earlier; for in June, 1870 a new copyright law had come into being that gave authors and composers better protection than of old and a more equitable share in the profits of their works,[3] and Wagner's vogue was now so great that he could be sure of an income from theatre royalties.

Personal sacrifices, however, he was undoubtedly prepared to make, and that not only in the financial field. It cut him to the heart to think of abandoning his dear Triebschen and plunging once more into a struggle with the world which, he must have foreseen, would bring him endless anxieties and drain him of the last ounce of his strength. Strange as it may seem, he was hardly interested at all in the performance of his works purely for his own sake. Again and again he cursed his evil fate in being condemned to work in a medium in which, unlike that of the painter, the sculptor or the man of letters, an artist can convey his message to the world only through the co-operation of hundreds of other people and by laboriously traversing the same inch or two of ground again and again. He groaned in spirit every time he thought of what the production of one of his operas meant for him in the way of struggle with more or less intractable material — the conferences with scene painters and machinists, the endless stage experiments, the drilling of singers and players in tasks largely unfamiliar to them, the dishearten-

---

[3] Including those published before the coming into operation of the new law.

ing feeling that used to come over him of the futility and the evanes-
cence of it all, the fatigue of body and disgust of soul, the weary
days and white nights inexorably in store for him. Yet he submitted
stoically to the driving of his daemon, possessed as he was with the
belief that what he was doing was not for his personal glory but
the fulfilment of a sacred mission entrusted to him by the gods.

And just now, in 1871, he shrank more than ever not merely from
plunging into this soul-and-body-destroying labour of the actual
theatre but even from completing on paper the colossal work he
had had on his desk so long. The purely creative urge in him was
so imperative, his imagination so endlessly fertile, that for him each
work was complete when he had committed the last Sketches for it
to paper. He had lived with it, lived in it, for so many years, tearing
its secrets out of it, designing it, modelling it, at once bending it to
his artistic will and obeying the subconscious urge of it, that nothing more remained to be done with it or for it so far as he was concerned. All that was left to do after the completion of the full Sketch
was the tiresome labour of putting it all down bar by bar on paper
again in full score in the detail necessary to make his vision intel-
ligible to others, and in the first place to the dull human instruments through whom he would have to transmit his own electric
current before the drama and the music could strike their heat and
light through the more or less passive audience. And more despair-
ingly than ever in his life did he feel the cruelty of fate towards
him in this respect just when he was occupied with the final stages
of the *Götterdämmerung*. Within himself this vast work that had
occupied his thoughts for more than twenty years was already virtually complete, and his whole artistic being was crying out now
for self-expression in other fields. All kinds of impulses to musical
adventure that he had had to suppress within him in order to create
the titanic structures of his operas were obstinately asserting their
claim to burgeon into a life of their own. His one desire now, he told
Cosima, was to write symphonies and quartets of a new kind, a
desire the solitary practical realisation of which he was able to
achieve in the *Sigfried Idyll*. The desire haunted him to the end of
his days; but by the time he had completed, with *Parsifal,* the great
sequence of dramatic works all of which he had previsioned in the
distant past, he had been drained dry of bodily strength by the
superhuman labours of Bayreuth. He died, if ever an artist did, a

sacrifice to his idealism, died before he had said more than a portion of what he had it in him to say in music.

5

As we have seen, on the 16th April he and Cosima set out for Bayreuth to spy out the land: they stayed at the Sonne, a hostelry made memorable by a previous distinguished inhabitant of the little town, Jean Paul Richter. Wagner announced himself to a few of the governing authorities, who gave him a hearty welcome. "The theatre", Cosima noted in her diary, "is entirely unsuited to our purpose. So we shall have to build, which is all the better." How definitely he was now resolved on the Bayreuth adventure is shown by his already looking for not only a site for his theatre but one for his future home. For the latter he had in his eye a piece of land in what was then the Rennweg and is now the Richard Wagner Strasse, and for the former a plot close to this, separated by a road from the end of the garden of the Neues Schloss. He evidently proposed to economise his energies as far as possible by living almost next door to his theatre.

Before going to Bayreuth he had met Düfflipp, by appointment, in Augsburg on the 15th. It seems that reports about Bayreuth were by this time already circulating in Munich, and the King no doubt wanted to know just where he stood. According to Du Moulin, Düfflipp had already written to Triebschen saying that the King wanted *Siegfried* and was annoyed at Wagner's attitude towards Munich. At this latest meeting of theirs Düfflipp reiterated the royal desire for a performance of at any rate the first two acts of the opera, which Wagner had given him to understand were all that had been completed; whereupon Wagner "gravely replied that he would burn it and go a-begging rather than give it up in such circumstances." Already, indeed, he had drawn up his whole plan of campaign for Bayreuth. The circular in which he was to appeal for patrons for the undertaking had been drafted, and letters had been sent to all whom he had in mind as helpers.

On the 20th he and Cosima left Bayreuth for Leipzig, where they arrived the next day. They received a royal reception in the most literal sense of the term, for the proprietor of the Hôtel de Prusse placed the royal suite at their disposal. At mid-day he attended a rehearsal of the *Kaisermarsch* by the theatre orchestra under Kapellmeister Schmidt, at which he was given a great reception. The first public performance of the March took place on the 23rd, but at this he was not present: he had left on the preceding day for the real goal of his journey, Berlin. He halted at Dresden en route, where he had the gratification of spending a couple of days in the house of his faithful Pusinelli, whom he had not seen for many years.[4]

He arrived in Berlin on the night of the 25th, putting up at the Hôtel du Parc. Here again his coming created as much sensation as that of any king: gaping crowds assembled about the hotel day after day. Once more, indeed, we realise how great a hold he already had on a large section of the German public in spite of the hostility of the Press, and how much more he could have accomplished in the practical sphere with far less trouble had the angularities of his character and the asperity of his tongue not made enemies for him in so many quarters. On the 28th he read his paper on *The Destiny of Opera* to the Royal Academy of Arts. To do this had been the ostensible object of his journey to Berlin. But the Royal Academy of Arts, for all its high-sounding title, seems to have been an institution of such minor importance that we cannot imagine his thinking it worth his consideration in any other circumstances. His audience consisted of some fifty members, among whom the musicians were represented by such none-well-wishers of his as Dorn and Joachim. He read his paper from a chair at the end of the long conference table: there was no platform for him, no desk. It is difficult to suppose that at any other juncture in his life he would have wasted an hour of his time over a hole-and-corner affair of this kind: it is fairly obvious that he had seized upon it only as a plausible excuse for visiting Berlin, conferring with the faithful there on the subject of Bayreuth, and benefiting by the wave of enthusiasm for all things "national" that was sweeping the country just then.

---

[4] The Wesendonks were settled in Dresden now; they had given up their Zürich home in consequence of the anti-German feeling in the town during and after the Franco-German War.

6

As in Leipzig, he had proofs enough of the high esteem in which
he was now held even in the Prussian capital. On the 29th he was
given a banquet at which some hundred and twenty guests were
present: in reply to the toast in his honour he made one of his usual
speeches on the theme of the long decline of German art and the
necessity of rebuilding it in harmony with the German spirit. The
next day the Union of Berlin Musicians fêted him in the hall of
the Singakademie, where an orchestra more than a hundred strong,
conducted by Julius Stern, played the *Tannhäuser* March and the
Faust Overture. Wagner himself conducted a repeat performance
of the latter work, to the great illumination not only of the audience
but of the players. On the 31st, before a packed house in the Opera
that included the Emperor and Empress and the whole of the Court,
he conducted Beethoven's fifth symphony, the *Lohengrin* Prelude
and Finale, the *Feuerzauber* from the *Valkyrie*, and, in response
to a tumultuous demand, the *Kaisermarsch*. Evidently this last, one
of his weakest works, was just now standing him in better stead
in many quarters than some of his greater ones. But apart from
that, there could be no disputing his present vogue in Berlin, which
in the past had never shown him much cordiality, at any rate in
official quarters. Hopes were cherished that he would make the
capital the home of his "national theatre"; there was even talk of
his being invited to settle in the town as General Music Director of
the Opera. Other plans for furthering his aims were set afoot; and
though it is obvious enough that they were merely the schemes of
shrewd commercial adventurers anxious to cash in on his popularity, they at any rate testify to that popularity.

Whatever the official biographers have to say on the subject, it
was manifestly with a view to obtaining Bismarck's co-operation,
or at any rate sympathy, for the Bayreuth undertaking that he
sought and obtained an interview with the Chancellor on the 3rd
May. No trustworthy records of the conversation have come down
to us, but it is clear enough that while Bismarck was duly sensible
of the greatness, in his own line, of the man before him he felt no
call to exert himself to further his artistic ends. Wagner, however,
had friends in Berlin who lacked neither enthusiasm for his cause
nor energy in the furthering of it. Tausig, undeterred by Wagner's

fulminations against the Jews, threw himself wholeheartedly into the Bayreuth scheme. He planned the formation of a Berlin Wagner-Verein which should maintain a large orchestra, to be conducted by himself, for the special purpose of spreading the knowledge of Wagner's works. At his back he had Countess Marie von Schleinitz, the wife of Count von Schleinitz, Minister of the Royal House. This lady was a close friend of Cosima's; before her marriage to Schleinitz she had been the Marie von Buch who had been from the first Cosima's confidante in the Bülow-Wagner matter.[5] In her house, on the 31st April, Wagner gave another reading of *The Destiny of Opera* to a select audience; and he had some conferences with the architect Wilhelm Neumann, to whom he proposed to entrust the erection of his new theatre. Manifestly there had been a great deal of quiet preparation on his part and on that of his Berlin friends during the months when he was so studiously concealing his intentions from King Ludwig.

By the 8th May he was in Leipzig again; then he went on to Frankfort and thence to Darmstadt, where he discussed his plan with Karl Brandt; and after a day in Heidelberg, where an enjoyable hour or two in a puppet theatre confirmed him in his low opinion of the standard of acting in the average German opera house, he and Cosima were home in Triebschen again on the 16th, well satisfied on the whole with the results of their month's tour. His birthday, the 22nd, was graced by the little domestic mummeries in which he always took such delight.[6] Cosima had risen at four in the morning to stage-manage them. There were the usual decorations round his bust when he came down to the drawing-room; and the whole family grouped itself in a Wagnerian tableau vivant, with Cosima got up as Sieglinde with the infant Siegfried in her arms (Bülow was not present to play Hunding), Daniela as Senta,

---

[5] See Vol. III, pp. 262, 304, 534. According to Bülow, Bismarck could not endure Countess von Schleinitz. (See Bülow's letter to his mother, BB, IV, 394.) But the main reason for Bismarck's reluctance to become publicly involved in the Bayreuth affair was probably political — a diplomatic hesitation to do anything that might conceivably give offence to the King of Bavaria.

[6] The Burrell Collection lists as No. 493 the Journal of one Suzanne Weinert, who was governess at Wahnfried from August, 1875 to May, 1876. According to the Catalogue "it gives a delightful picture of the pomposity of life there". This is one of the first-hand contemporary documents that positively cries out for publication: it must throw a good deal of light on Wagner's and Cosima's passion for dramatizing themselves even in private life.

Blandine as Elisabeth, and, it goes without saying, Isolde and Eva as Isolde and Eva.[7]

7

His plan for the production of the *Ring* had been made public in a pamphlet issued from Berlin on the 12th May, in which, for the first time, Bayreuth was named as the place for the adventure.

The King's reactions during the weeks just passed are of particular interest.

We have seen that Wagner met Düfflipp in Augsburg on the 15th April and laid before him his plan for the production of the *Ring* in Bayreuth. The Secretary reported the results of the interview to Ludwig, who, as Düfflipp at once wrote to Wagner, was rather doubtful about the scheme, though he was willing to take Patronatscheine (Patron's Vouchers) to the extent of 25,000 thalers.[8] Wagner replied on the 1st May. He assured Düfflipp that the plan he had in mind was no mere whim, but the accomplishment of a purpose formed years ago. He sent him, to be passed on to the King, the pamphlet on *The Destiny of Opera* and the one entitled *On the Production of the Stage-Festival-Play 'The Nibelung's Ring': a Communication and Summons to the Friends of my Art*. He is rejoiced to find now that Ludwig is on the whole well-disposed towards his venture, even though a little sceptical as to the possibility of its succeeding. Wagner sets himself to clearing up a few misunderstandings and suspicions in connection with it. He had no

---

[7] We have to remember, of course, that grave mummeries of this sort, which seem a little childish to the non-German world, were in the very blood of the Germans and Germanised non-Teutons of that epoch. See, for instance, the delicious account by Frau von Miaskowski, the wife of one of Nietzsche's colleagues at the Basel University, of the tableau vivant from the *Meistersinger* arranged by her in a "social union" composed of the professors and their wives. "The thing was got up to please Professor Nietzsche, whose friendship with Wagner was then at its height." Nietzsche having played Walther's Prize Song on the piano, the door into the adjoining room opened, revealing the tableau designed by Professor von Miaskowski. Each of the children was "characteristically dressed". "Little Eva (aged about five), in a light-blue Gretchen costume, was holding out her foot to be measured by the tiny three-years-old Meister Hans Sachs, clad in a leather apron and cap; while from an improvised elevation the little Walther von Stolzing, in a magnificent red doublet with white puffed lace sleeves, and wearing a heavy gold chain, gazed down upon the lovely picture. Everyone was delighted, and Nietzsche, indeed, quite moved. He took both my hands and pressed them again and again while he thanked me for the charming surprise." FNJN, p. 367.

[8] It was the King's wish later that Wagner should use this money for the acquisition of a plot of land and the building of Wahnfried.

intention, he says, of inviting any of the German princes to the performances: he is concerned with the various Courts only to the extent of securing their general good will, so that when the time came they would authorise their Intendants to grant the necessary leave to such singers and players as he might need for the *Ring*.

This, of course, was an understatement of the facts. He undoubtedly had it in his mind to court the favour of Berlin as the centre of the new Reich. Of all the German cities, it was with Berlin that he had the minimum of connection, either materially or spiritually: there was no town and no people he had abused so wholeheartedly as the Prussian capital and the Prussians. But now, he saw, they could both be very useful to him in the achievement of his ideal, not only because he could reasonably hope that in the capital of the Reich, of all places, the national character of his own great undertaking would be recognised, but also because in Countess von Schleinitz and her husband he had powerful allies in the innermost Court circles. To Düfflipp he would naturally not lay too much stress on Berlin: it would have been imprudent to do so, in view of Ludwig's dislike of the Prussians in general and the house of Hohenzollern in particular.

According to Du Moulin, while Wagner was in Berlin he had received "a most discouraging letter from Düfflipp" which betrayed "a certain jealousy of Berlin" and hinted that the King "would have nothing whatever to do with the Bayreuth plan but wanted everything for himself in Munich"; to which Wagner is said to have replied in earnest terms, saying that Bayreuth was his final plan, and if it were not approved he would give it up and henceforth live only for his family. Du Moulin, presumably, based this statement of his on Cosima's diary. The only first-hand documents bearing on the matter that we possess are the King's letter of the 17th April to Düfflipp, in which he says that he does not like Wagner's project at all, as it would be a pure impossibility to give the *Ring* in Bayreuth *in 1872*,[9] and his letter to Wagner of the 26th May, in which he warmly congratulates him on his decision regarding Bayreuth.[10]

Ludwig had probably resigned himself by this time to the new situation, in which both Wagner and the *Ring* would be lost to him, and generously made up his mind not to oppose the Bayreuth pro-

[9] BLKB, p. 212.
[10] KLRWB, II, 324.

ject. That he could have killed it in its cradle had he chosen to do so is beyond question. It would be dreadful, Wagner told Cosima after his return to Triebschen, if he were forced to surrender the later sections of the work to the King: "I could not do it."

"All their cares centred on this point— whether the King would ensure the existence of Bayreuth by agreeing to the production of the work there, or stand upon his rights and demand the production of both *Siegfried* and the *Götterdämmerung* in Munich. If he did, Bayreuth would naturally be impossible for the time being; though only for the time being, for what gave it its real foundation was the completion and production of *Parsifal*." [11]

There could be no more conclusive evidence than this that Wagner knew perfectly well that he was treating his contract with the King as merely a scrap of paper. His conscience gave him few qualms on that score: what worried him most was the question whether Ludwig would tamely acquiesce in the breach of faith.

8

We may doubt whether Wagner would have found him so yielding at any other time. The fact appears to be that just then his spirit had had more shocks than it could bear, and the will to fight had died down in him. His dreams of happiness far from the madding crowd were now centred in some beautiful island or other in the Greek archipelago, in Cyprus, in Crete, or even in India. Düfflipp sobered him by telling him that his project for abdication in favour of Prussia or the Reich would be at variance with the Bavarian constitution, and if he surrendered his crown he could count on receiving from his successor, at most, the 500,000 florins which his father had granted his grandfather, Ludwig I. So the King resigned himself to trying to realise his dreams in Bavaria.

How much of what was going on in the recesses of his mind at this time was known to Wagner we cannot say; but it is clear that he had made up his own mind to proceed with the Bayreuth scheme regardless of all possible consequences to himself. His main problem now was to finance the formidable undertaking. The total cost of the building and of the performances had been estimated at 300,000 thalers; and the raising of the bulk of this sum was to be

---

[11] MECW, I, 572-3.

in the first place the work of his Berlin friends. The idea was to form an association of "Patrons", on the basis of an issue of 1,000 [12] Patronatscheine of 300 thalers each: Tausig was to be in charge of all the business arrangements until a proper Patronage Committee could be appointed. Wagner's congenital optimism led him to believe that the building could be completed between the autumn of 1871 and the spring of 1873, and the performances, which were to run for two months, be given in the summer of the latter year.[13] The subscription that had gratified him most was perhaps that of Liszt, to whom the long severance from Cosima was as grievous as it had been for her. He had joined the Committee and entered his name for three Patronatscheine. The funds were to be raised by private subscription, and as the undertaking would be entirely under Wagner's control he could guarantee, he told Düfflipp, that they would be made to suffice for the purpose. The estimated cost of the Semper theatre to be erected in the Glaspalast had been 200,000 florins. But Dresden was about to put up a temporary opera house at a cost of only 70,000 thalers; while for his part he needed only a theatre of the simplest internal construction, and for this, he has been told, his estimate will be ample.

He hopes the King will give up the idea of performing the work in Munich until after he himself has shown how it should be done. All he asks for is Ludwig's permission to do this, and his presence at the festival; for without his generous protection the work could never have been completed. Bayreuth pleases him so greatly that he wishes to make it his future home: he already has the site for his house in mind, and he hopes that Düfflipp can meet him in Bayreuth to discuss details with him. He will soon have to go thoroughly into the question of the site for the theatre with Brandt and the Bayreuth architect Wölfel; and as he cannot count on receiving any

---

[12] The figure was raised to 1,300 later.

[13] We find him asking Brandt, on the 14th September, 1871, for an estimate of the funds likely to be required between October of that year and Easter, 1872 for the preliminary work on the theatre. This before the actual site had been decided upon! He was determined, he said, to lay the foundation stone in the autumn of 1871, as he thought that function would "make a good impression" on everyone inclined to support him. (RWBB, p. 10).

The architect Neumann pointed out to him, however, that it would be foolish to lay the foundation stone in the late autumn or early winter, as work on the soil would have to be broken off immediately afterwards. He suggested March, 1872 as a better date. (MECW, I, 507). Wagner agreed with him, as is shown by his letter of the 3rd November to Heckel. (RWBB, p. 19).

funds from his supporters before Easter, 1872, he begs Düfflipp to advance him what is first necessary now, the debt to be liquidated when the subscriptions come in. He asks Düfflipp also to bring with him to Bayreuth the Semper plans, which are the property of the King. He suggested the 10th May for their meeting there, at which Brandt and Wölfel would be present.

Düfflipp could not go to Bayreuth; so on the 11th May (1871) we find Wagner asking him to send the Semper plans to him in Darmstadt, where he is to confer with Brandt. (He is careful to explain that he means to make use of the plans only in so far as he can claim an intellectual property in them, embodying as they do his own instructions to Semper). Düfflipp replied, on the 12th, that the plans had already been sent to Bayreuth. He added that at present the King could not receive Wagner as the latter had wished; he was not in the best of humours, owing to the political worries that had followed in the wake of the declaration of Papal infallibility.

In the face of all this, it is a little difficult to understand why, in the summer of 1871, Wagner should write Wilhelm Tappert a "violent" letter about the King, and, when Cosima persuaded him to tear it up, burst into tears about his patron, "who had known all and sympathized in everything, and was now abandoning him like this." [14] But this and many other matters in connection with Bayreuth will only be cleared up when Cosima's diary is published in full. The extract from the diary continues thus: "He had always, he [Wagner] said, shown himself truthful in all things. He stands there in all simplicity, and would carry this one lie with him to the grave. And he wept bitterly." Was the "one lie" that Wagner regretted the pretence that he had not completed the score of *Siegfried?* Be that as it may, it strikes us as odd that he should tell Cosima that "the disgrace of being dependent on the King" was "unheard-of and intolerable".

A heavy blow to him was the death of the brilliant young Tausig on the 17th July: for the moment it must have seemed to him almost as cruel a stroke of the Fates as his loss of Schnorr in 1865. Wagner asked Carl Bechstein, who lived in Berlin, to take over Tausig's functions; Bechstein, however, felt bound to decline out of consideration for Bülow, with whom he had close personal ties. But a new enthusiast now came into the field, to whom, in company with

---

[14] MECW, I, 575–6.

Feustel and Muncker, much of the credit of the ultimate achievement of Bayreuth is due. Emil Heckel, a music dealer in Mannheim, had written to Wagner in May, in response to the latter's appeal in the *Communication,* asking what he could do to assist him in his great undertaking. Wagner had put him in touch with Tausig, to whom Heckel broached a method that had occurred to him of bringing in people of modest means, to whom an individual subscription of 300 thalers would be impossible, by the formation everywhere of Wagner-Vereine, the members of which could club together for one or more vouchers and share the performances among them. The plan received Wagner's approval; and with Countess von Schleinitz devoting all her energies and social influence to the cause of Bayreuth, and the Weimar Theatre Intendant, Baron Loën, assuming the chairmanship of the Patronat Committee, Wagner had no reason to complain of any lack of eager helpers.

9

Clouds gathered, of course, from time to time. The enthusiasm of many people cooled down as it became clear that Wagner was bent on realising his audacious scheme in the Bayreuth backwater or nowhere. Lavish promises of money from Berlin mysteriously turned out, almost in the twinkling of an eye, to be devoid of substance, the truth being that these people had expected the theatre to be built in Berlin. Other towns were equally anxious to have it, in part as a matter of local pride, in part because they foresaw that it would mean excellent business for them. Darmstadt, where the existing theatre had been burned down in October, 1871, offered to put up a new one that would answer Wagner's purposes in every respect and be at his sole disposal for some ten weeks each summer. The town council of Baden-Baden offered him an admirable site gratis. Reichenhall pointed out the unique advantages it could offer him in the matter of summer visitors and the capacity to accommodate and amuse them. But to all of them Wagner turned a deaf ear: the merely pleasure-loving crowds in popular resorts like these were not the material out of which he hoped to form his ideal audience. His mind was made up; it would be Bayreuth or nowhere.

He was fortunate in finding there, among the civic authorities of the little place, some men of the utmost disinterestedness and highest

[309]

probity who from the beginning made his cause their own. Ottilie Brockhaus had put him in touch with a distant relation of hers, the Bayreuth banker Friedrich Feustel, who was later to render great service to his cause. Wagner introduced himself to Feustel in a letter of the 1st November, 1871, in which he set forth his reasons for choosing Bayreuth as the locale for his theatre — it had no standing theatre of its own, he explained, it was not a summer resort of the ordinary kind, and it was situated not only in the centre of Germany but in Bavaria, which made it at once convenient for him to settle there for the rest of his life and to discharge a debt of honour to his patron King Ludwig. He commends his venture to the consideration of the good burghers of Bayreuth not simply on idealistic grounds but because it will bring visitors to their town. For these reasons he hopes he will be granted the necessary terrain gratis. If he is to be allowed a choice in the matter, he would like the site he has already inspected at the end of the Schloss park. Some of his supporters, it appears, are doubtful whether little Bayreuth will be able to house the opera personnel for his festivals (which he estimates at 200 people), plus some 2,000 visitors. He would like to be assured also that the place will be able to supply the number of workmen necessary for the speedy erection of the theatre, and that there is no likelihood of strikes. What he particularly wants to impress on the town council is that this is *not* a theatrical speculation on his part with the object of making money. The performances will be given only before patrons and some invited guests: there will be no public sale of tickets, though some free seats will be placed at the disposal of the citizens of Bayreuth.

Feustel's reply seems to have set his mind at rest on all these points, and on the 7th November the town council passed a resolution authorising the mayor "to place at the disposal of Richard Wagner any site which he may consider suitable for his purpose", while the municipal authorities further pledged themselves unanimously to do everything in their power to support his "great undertaking". This must have taken a load off Wagner's mind. By the beginning of December he felt sufficiently sure of his financial position [15] to go to Bayreuth and make the final decision with respect

---

[15] As usual, he was over-optimistic. By that time, it was true, the "Wagnerianer-Verein" in Berlin had decided to take sixty Patronat certificates; but there his most influential supporters had been at work. From Vienna he had had nothing but "prom-

to the site for his theatre. He left Triebschen on the 8th December, and after a few days in Munich arrived in Bayreuth on the 14th. The terrain he had had in his mind's eye on the occasion of his visit in the preceding April had proved impracticable: for the foundations of his stage and orchestral pit he would have had to excavate to a depth of some forty feet, at which level running water would be encountered. The site next suggested by the town authorities was a plot of a Tagewerk and a half near the Stuckberg, in the St. George suburb (to the south-east of the present festival theatre): they would further purchase the adjoining land to the extent of some three or four Tagewerke, to be laid out in gardens.[16]

Wagner, who was accompanied by Brandt and the architect Neumann from Berlin, approved of the site, the natural slope of which would make it possible to provide the necessary depth below floor level for stage and orchestra without much expense for excavation. At a meeting of the town council on the 15th December it was resolved to buy the ground required and place it at Wagner's disposal for his "national theatre". Wagner, well content, left Bayreuth on the 16th. He made first for Mannheim, where he was joined by Cosima and Nietzsche: there he was to have his first experience of what he had brought on himself by sanctioning Heckel's scheme for a network of Wagner-Vereine. For excellent as the idea was in itself, it had this drawback — he was certain to be asked by one town after another to give a local concert to encourage the enthusiasts and whip up the lukewarm. These concerts were to prove a great drain on his time and strength and hold him back grievously in the composition of the *Götterdämmerung;* but there was no way of escape for him.

10

The Mannheim concert had been suggested by Heckel as a means of not only working up interest in Bayreuth in his own town but encouraging others to set about the founding of Vereine. The concert took place on the 20th, the programme consisting of the *Magic Flute*

ises" to do something really generous during the winter. In Leipzig only three-fourths of one certificate had been subscribed for. Munich had done nothing. All this, of course, refers to the activities of the various Vereine. There may have been individual subscriptions apart from these, but nowhere could they have been numerous.

[16] A Tagewerk was an old Bavarian land measurement, corresponding to some 34 square metres.

overture, Beethoven's Seventh Symphony, the *Lohengrin* and *Meistersinger* preludes, the *Tristan* Prelude and Liebestod, and the now inevitable *Kaisermarsch*. What made the Mannheim visit really worth while from Wagner's point of view was that it gave him the opportunity to run through the still unpublished *Siegfried Idyll* for Cosima's benefit, his own, and that of a few friends. For this purpose he had asked Heckel to arrange for a small body of players to meet him on the morning of the concert as "a favour and special courtesy". The specification he gave Heckel was as follows — 6 to 8 first violins, 7 to 8 seconds, 4 violas, 4 'cellos, 2 to 3 basses, 1 flute, 1 oboe, 2 clarinets, 2 horns, 1 bassoon and 1 trumpet: in all 31 to 35 players.[17] The conductors of today who regard it as a pious duty towards what they call "the composer's intentions" to give the *Idyll* with some half-dozen strings are therefore labouring under a delusion: Wagner had contented himself with the bare minimum of string players at Triebschen for two excellent reasons, — the stairs would not hold more, and he could not afford more.

Nietzsche's reactions to the *Idyll* and the concert as a whole are interesting. He had been immensely impressed and elevated, he wrote to his friend Erwin Rohde. He now knows exactly what "music" means to him, and what he implies when he uses the term "music" as symbol of the Dionysiac; and when he reflects that to only a few hundred people in the present generation does music mean what it does for him, he feels he must wait for a completely new culture. After these golden days in Mannheim everything but music, he said, seemed unreal to him.[18]

Wagner had hardly settled down in Triebschen again before a new difficulty arose. One of the owners of the Stuckberg land, a business man of the name of Louis Rose, informed the council that he would not sell, as the construction of the theatre would interfere with the water supply of the neighbourhood and expose his sugar refinery to grave danger in case of fire. It soon appeared, however, that the forethoughtful Muncker already had another terrain in view — at the foot of the pleasance known as the Bürgerreuth. On the 2nd January, 1872 the council resolved to buy this much larger site, occupying more than 18 Tagewerke, and on the 8th Feustel and Muncker appeared in Triebschen to acquaint Wagner with

---

[17] According to Glasenapp, the actual number employed was 36.
[18] NGB, II, 276-7.

what had happened and seek his acquiescence in the new arrangement.[19] He was naturally perturbed at first at this latest evidence of the animosity of the Fates towards him ever since his birth; but it did not take long to convince him that the new site was in every way superior to either of the others. He was in Bayreuth again on the 31st, when a glance at the land showed him that Herr Rose had unwittingly done him the greatest service in refusing to sell his property. He was now safely over the first hurdle between him and his distant goal. A standing management committee for the festivals, consisting of Feustel, Muncker and the lawyer Käfferlein, was constituted immediately, and on the 5th February Wagner was once more back in Triebschen to rejoice Cosima with the good news.

<h2 style="text-align:center">11</h2>

But Bayreuth had absorbed only a part of his energies in recent months. Auber had died in May, 1871, and an obituary speech by the younger Dumas had seemed to Wagner to present the dead composer in so false a light that he felt it incumbent on him to explain to the world what he took to be the true significance of Auber. His article, *Reminiscences of Auber,* which appeared in November in the *Musikalisches Wochenblatt,* is rich in interesting matter, but it betrays throughout the notorious inability of the German mind to get really inside any culture but its own. For Wagner, all French art, without exception, suffers from "frigidity": the essence of any national spirit reveals itself in the dances of the nation: the French national dance, or at any rate, the Parisian dance, is the cancan, which Auber had raised to the dignity of an art of a sort: Auber's gift had been to reach down to the roots of the genuine French folk-spirit: and much more Teutonic sham-profundity of that kind. Berlioz, for Wagner, was a phenomenon much less characteristic of "the French spirit" than an Auber or an Offenbach: what he would have thought of a Debussy or a Ravel it is beyond the power of the imagination to conceive.

On the 1st November he had been gratified by a production of *Lohengrin* in Bologna: it was the first time an opera of his had been given on any Italian stage. The performances, conducted by Angelo

---

[19] Rose's letter, and the various resolutions of the Bayreuth town council relating to the site for the theatre, will be found in KLRWB, III, xvii ff.

Mariani, had been carefully prepared and created the utmost enthusiasm. The translation of the text had been made by no less a personage than Arrigo Boïto, to whom Wagner addressed a long letter — complimentary both to Boïto and to the Italian public — that was obviously intended for publication. That the Italians took as they had done to *Lohengrin* proved, it appears, that they had "an open mind and delicate sensitivity where art of any kind was concerned". He had hopes that by profiting by the example of "sublime" German music they would improve their own considerably. German mothers had shown themselves equal to the duty laid on them by Providence of producing "the loftiest geniuses of the world", though Wagner was doubtful whether the German Folk was wholly worthy of "the noble progeny of these chosen mothers"; and perhaps what was needed now was "a new marriage of the genii of the nations". Certainly for the Germans no fairer love-match could be conceived than "a wedding of the genius of Italy with that of Germany", a union in which his own *Lohengrin* had possibly proved itself as match-maker. It was all characteristically Teutonic, and, critically examined, not very tactful; but tact was never Wagner's strong suit when trying to convince the world that its only hope of cultural salvation lay in hitching itself to the German chariot. The conferment on him of the freedom of Bologna was the excuse, in the following October, for a further verbose letter to the Burgomaster of the city, in which he once more plumed himself, as a German, on having shown the world what Germany could do in the way of music drama, and exalted the "liberty" of the Italian mind to the disparagement of the French. For the Frenchman, it appears, simply "cannot comprehend whatever is not French, and the first condition for anyone who wants to please the French is to conform himself to their taste and the laws of that taste." That he himself was barely capable of comprehending whatever was not German seems never to have occurred to him, nor that there might be a flaw in his doctrine that foreign cultures could have no seed of vitality but what they could beg, borrow or steal from Germany.[20]

---

[20] Verdi was more sensible. "If the Germans, setting out from Bach and arriving at Wagner, write good German operas, well and good. But we descendants of Palestrina commit a musical crime when we imitate Wagner; we write useless, even deleterious operas." (*Copialettere*, p. 702).

12

Wagner's few days in Munich on his way to Bayreuth in mid-December were spent in arranging one or two small personal matters with Düfflipp. On the 4th of the month he had made his position with regard to Bayreuth finally clear to the King. Ludwig was to leave the theatre plan and the *Ring* production entirely to Wagner and the Vereine: Wagner pointed out to him, with his usual plausible sophistry, that a community of friends could do what One, however powerful — meaning the King — could not, for he would always be frustrated by people of a different way of thinking. It is to be observed that Ludwig did not himself reply to Wagner's letters of the autumn of 1871: he left matters in his Secretary's hands. Wagner's long letter of the 4th December was accompanied by the gift of a copy, to a small extent in his own hand, but mostly in that of a Zürich musician, one Spiegel, of the Orchestral Sketch of the second act of the *Götterdämmerung*. But by this time it must have been as clear to the King as it was to the musical heads of his theatre that he was being coolly outmanœuvred by Wagner — that no number of *sketches* would bring him an inch nearer the possession of the *scores* that were necessary for a performance, and the rights in which were his. Perfall and his staff could hardly have been for a moment the dupe of Wagner's artfulness. The date publicly announced for the *Ring* performances was the summer of 1873. That meant, in terms of Wagner's planning, that rehearsals would have to be begun in 1872; and no one in his senses would regard it as possible that in less than a year Wagner could compose about half of the *Götterdämmerung* and score not only the whole of that work but the last act of *Siegfried* in addition — supposing the latter score to be still uncompleted, as Wagner would have Ludwig believe. The authorities must have known perfectly well that he was withholding the *Siegfried* score simply and solely in order to checkmate his kingly benefactor.

The royal order to produce *Siegfried* in Munich had been given in March (1871). In September Perfall reported that the plans for the scenery were ready and the work was being rehearsed at the piano, but that any further progress was impossible without the orchestral score. (Wagner had allowed the piano score to be published, but had prevented Schott from issuing the full score).[21] In October he applied to Munich, as we have seen, for the loan of the King's manuscript of the full score of the *Valkyrie* — in order that Schott might proceed with the engraving of it. No immediate reply was sent to this request, the reason for which was obvious: Wagner would need the printed score and parts for the Bayreuth rehearsals. But during his visit to Munich in December Düfflipp tried to make a bargain with him: he could have the *Valkyrie* score if he would send the King that of *Siegfried*. Wagner seems to have refused; and the King magnanimously gave way, though not until the February of the following year. He did more. In his letter of the 4th December Wagner had expressed the hope that, although his patron was going to be ruled out once for all so far as Bayreuth and the *Ring* were concerned, he would continue his private beneficence to the point of assisting him to buy the plot of land on which he planned to build his future home. Ludwig granted that request without debate.

In a further letter of the 27th December Wagner poured out his soul in gratitude to the young King for all he had done for him from the first day of their meeting until now. He would have been blind indeed had he not been able to appreciate the magnitude of this latest of the many sacrifices that Ludwig had made for him. It is evident from the letter that the King was depressed by the thought that not only did the "national" character of Bayreuth annihilate all his long-cherished hopes of making his own capital the hearth and home of German regeneration, but at Bayreuth he would no longer be able to feast himself on the *Ring* in that quasi-seclusion that was so precious to him where Wagner's works were concerned. Moreover he was under no illusion as to the part that the hated Hohenzollerns who had humiliated him and his country in so many ways during the last few years were expected to play in this "national" glorification. Wagner accordingly addresses him-

---

[21] He showed his hand quite plainly later in a letter of the 27th October, 1875 to Schotts: "I have my *very special* reasons for wishing the publication of the full score of *Siegfried* . . . to be delayed, if possible, until the time when the *Götterdämmerung* is also issued. If you think this too difficult, or too disadvantageous, then I would ask you to postpone the public issue of *Siegfried* until about March next year. My fears in the matter are connected with the peculiar experiences I had in Munich" — i.e., the productions of the *Rhinegold* in 1869 and the *Valkyrie* in 1870. See RWBV, II, 194.

self to setting his mind at rest as best he can on both these points. He assures him that he himself has not approached "any of the German princes" for help in his undertaking: anything done in this way has been the private work of his devoted friends. The veiled reference is, of course, to the Prussian Court and his own influential adherents in Berlin; and neither the form nor the substance of Wagner's assurance of his own innocence in the matter would be likely to rid the King's mind of the poison at work in it. Wagner goes on to say that he does not think that Ludwig will be faced with the unpleasant duty of having to welcome the other royalties at Bayreuth, as these will not go there without invitations, which would naturally have to come direct from the King of Bavaria. But if, he dexterously insinuates, the latter should feel that he *must* issue these invitations, "having regard to the noble significance of the performances", it is to be understood that the whole *Ring* is first of all to be given for the benefit of the King alone, perhaps in the guise of a final rehearsal. And if he should further decide that it is necessary for him, having invited certain other princes to the festival, to extend hospitality to them as his guests, this at any rate shall not hold good as regards the theatre, where the King's box shall be reserved exclusively for him.

13

By the end of 1871, then, Ludwig could no longer be in any doubt as to what had happened. To all intents and purposes he had lost Wagner: an end had come to his dream of collaboration on equal terms with him in the great work of world-salvation through the theatre. To bring about that salvation he had not merely secured Wagner's personal well-being for the rest of his life. He had borne unspeakable miseries of many kinds for Wagner's sake and that of his cause, had antagonised his ministers and officials, had more than once imperilled his throne, had often been put to public shame and exposed to public insult, and now, at twenty-six, he was a hopelessly disappointed man, disillusioned about humanity in general and political humanity in particular, self-doomed to not only an intellectual but a physical solitude that could only become intensified as the years went on. In the circumstances he could well have been forgiven a reproach or two against the man who, even if from the most idealistic motives, had undoubtedly been in large part the cause of his miseries — or if not reproaches, at all events a frank expression of his disappointment.

Nothing, however, could show more conclusively not only the sanity but the nobility of his spirit than his grave letter of the 3rd January, 1872 to Wagner. He wishes him all happiness and good fortune in the year that is to see the completion of the great and god-like work. He gently turns aside Wagner's outpourings of gratitude towards him: it is he, he says, who is in Wagner's debt. Wagner is never to doubt that he will be with him in heart and soul, the truest of friends and helpers to the end. Wagner is the one man who has ever understood him as he really is, and that understanding has been the fruit of love and friendship.

> "In spite of every tempest that *appears* to divide us, in spite of all the cloud-racks that pile up between us, our stars will yet find each other: even when the profane eye cannot pierce through the thick veil to the radiant brightness of them we two will recognise each other; and when we have at last reached the holy goal we had set ourselves from the beginning, the central sun of the eternal godhead, that light and life of all things for which we suffered and fought undaunted, we will render an account of our doings, the meaning and the aim of which were to spread that light over the earth, to purify and perfect humanity with its sacred flames, making it the sharer in eternal joys."

He hints at the growing dissonances between the political world in which he is condemned to live and his inborn idealism, and the painful sacrifices he has to make, and from which he does not shrink, for the good of his land. But within himself, he assures Wagner, he preserves his idealism unsullied, making no concessions there to the stale and empty world; and it is perhaps because he has always done so that, he hopes, he has contributed, if only indirectly, to the completion of Wagner's great work.

> "Do not take this for vaunting on my part. The pure altar fire of noble enthusiasm can never be kept alive so long as the priest is too much concerned with the things of this world. We cannot serve God and Mammon: that is what is involved here." [22]

This was the last letter Wagner received from the King before the laying of the foundation-stone at Bayreuth. The music is thematically the same as of old, but the mood and the tempo are dif-

---

[22] KLRWB, II, 334–5. Du Moulin (CEMW, I, 602–3) gives the letter in an inaccurate form.

ferent; the *presto appassionato* of the earlier years is already broadening out into the final *moderato mesto e nobile*. His spirit was being sorely tried. He had lost Wagner, his youthful golden vision of a humanity not merely reborn through art but grateful to him for giving it the opportunity of such re-birth had faded into the murk of common day, and he was left alone to bear a multitude of miseries for many of which his fanatical devotion to the Wagner who had now deserted him was in large part responsible. His political enemies were at their foul work again, scheming to get rid of him, exaggerating some of his "eccentricities" and inventing others, and talking once more about his "madness". As Du Moulin puts it, Feustel, who had political as well as business contacts with Munich,

> "talked, like the rest of the world, far too much [to Wagner] about the King. What he had heard was at bottom nothing more than what the diplomatists, male and female, were whispering to one another to arouse feeling against the lonely man. . . . Marie von Mouchanoff too had told [Wagner and Cosima] how already there was talk among the people about his madness, and in addition there was his hatred of Prussia, though this power was his only shield." [23]

Then, when their machinations and calumnies goaded the hapless young King into withdrawing himself still further from the orbit controlled by them, seeking peace and solace for his heartbreak over mankind in the solitude and clean air of the mountains, this was trumpeted abroad as fresh proof of his "insanity". He knew that he had staked his spiritual all on Wagner, and that Wagner had in large measure failed him. Yet he indulges in no reproaches; merely a sigh for the lost Paradise of his heart's desire escapes him now and then, while he nobly does everything in his power to set Wagner's feet more safely on the hard road leading to his high goal. But within him must often have been the thought, even if unexpressed in words, that saddened the younger Pliny when his friend and mentor Corellius Rufus died: "I have lost the witness and pilot and director of my life: I fear that henceforth I shall live more heedlessly."

---

[23] MECW, I, 626, 632.

CHAPTER XV

WAGNER AND NIETZSCHE: I

1

MUCH WAS to happen at Triebschen before Wagner turned his back on it to begin the last league of his life's journey; and the most important event of all was the arrival, in the first days of 1872, of Nietzsche's *The Birth of Tragedy out of the Spirit of Music*. Few books have had a more curious history as regards either their genesis, the one-time commotion they caused, or their ultimate fate.

In the first term of 1870 Nietzsche gave two lectures at Basel, one on *The Greek Music Drama*, the other on *Socrates and Tragedy*; a few of the notes for them, found among his papers, have been printed in the supplement to his collected works.[1] In the summer of 1870 he wrote an essay on *The Dionysian Outlook* (*Weltanschauung*); this he read to Wagner and Cosima during the last days of July, before setting off to take up his self-imposed duties as a nursing orderly in the German army.[2] The general nature of it can be surmised from his later writings.

New light has recently been thrown on the relations between Nietzsche and Triebschen about this time by the extracts from Cosima's diary published by Du Moulin Eckart, though necessarily much still remains obscure. For Nietzsche, Wagner was still the idolised Master who stood for a great deal that the younger man was beginning to envisage as his own special world of the spirit, to whom he frequently came, if not confessedly for instruction, at any rate for confirmation of his own broodings upon the problems of life, philosophy and art, and from whom he undoubtedly imbibed many things that were later worked into the tissue of his own thought. One has the suspicion, however, that already the secret satisfaction of each of them with the other increased with the

---

[1] NW, IX, 34–41. He had already sent to Triebschen his inaugural lecture on *Homer and Classical Philology*, delivered on the 28th May, 1869.

[2] To become a Swiss professor he had had to give up his German citizenship. He was thus barred from entering the German service as a combatant.

square of the physical distance between them. "At his [Nietzsche's] coming", says Du Moulin, with more particular reference, apparently, to the summer of 1870, "they always felt great joy, and at his departure a slight feeling of melancholy." While he was recognised by Wagner and Cosima as the most gifted of the Master's younger friends, he was "in many respects very unsatisfactory", which Du Moulin, with Cosima's diary in front of him, attributes to "the unnatural reserve of his demeanour, as though he were trying to resist the overwhelming impression of Wagner's personality".

The reasons for Nietzsche's occasional "reserve" may perhaps have been not wholly, or even mainly, intellectual. There were several things in Wagner's personality which jarred on the rather prim young professor, especially his proneness to a rough-and-ready Saxon humour in what Beethoven would have described as his "unbuttoned" moments. Nietzsche, whose morals verged on prudery, found a good deal in Wagner's private life of which he could not approve: and for a long time he was ill at ease on account of the "irregular" relations with Frau von Bülow, because they compelled him to resort to all sorts of petty social subterfuges that were repugnant to him. No one rejoiced more sincerely than he when the union was "legalised" by marriage, for then there was an end to the necessity for these subterfuges either at Triebschen or outside it. Frau Förster-Nietzsche may be to some extent right in surmising that the reason why Wagner relieved her brother of the task of reading the proofs of *Mein Leben* was that he suspected there was much in the story of his early life that would have chilled Nietzsche. "And there were moments", she adds, "when Wagner was irritated by my brother's delicacy in the matter of chastity, and then he would suddenly indulge in the coarsest and most unpleasant expressions regarding himself and Cosima." [3] It is notorious that he had no control over his tongue when he was angry: even Cosima was often made to suffer grievously in moments such as these.

2

On the whole, however, it was for intellectual rather than personal reasons that a cloud seemed to descend now and then upon Triebschen while Nietzsche was there. The autolatrous young genius,

[3] FNWN, pp. 60–61.

who was becoming daily more conscious of his own powers, more convinced of his mission, must sometimes have had to summon up all his respect for Wagner and Cosima to endure in silence the blows dealt to his pride by their well-meant patronage of him, and more especially by Cosima. Unable as she was to see the world through any eyes but Wagner's, there would inevitably be times when she was even more royalist in her views than the king. She approved of the young man's classical lucubrations so far as they harmonised with the Master's opinions and could presumably be pressed into the service of his ideal; but she thought it incumbent on her to point out to him what she took to be his errors or his divagations, and to guide the young eagle back to the eyrie whenever, conscious of the growing strength of his wings, he showed an inclination to take a flight into the mountains on his own account. That inclination, she felt, ought to be curbed, not only in Wagner's interest but in Nietzsche's. The intensively-trained young scholar must often have been vexed by her confident criticism and complacent advice on matters on which she was even more an amateur than Wagner was.

One would have thought, for instance, that both the matter and the method of the lecture on *Homer and Classical Philology* would have been of too specialist a nature to warrant anything more than vague approval on Cosima's part. The lecture did indeed, as Du Moulin assures us, "create a deep impression" in Triebschen. Du Moulin's account, however, of Cosima's general attitude at this time towards Nietzsche's professional work — and after all, he *was* primarily a professor of philology, with highly specialised intellectual interests, not merely a Wagnerian mouthpiece — is very illuminative. While the young man was always welcome in the house by the Lake, more especially because of "his boundless devotion to Wagner's art-work", Cosima, we learn, was "conscious of the doctrinaire, the professorial in him: indeed, it was she who often gave the young scholar good advice about this", though she could not "repress some anxiety lest he might be working in too proud and haughty a spirit, plunging deep down into things instead of letting them react on him clearly and directly" — in other words, daring to have opinions of his own instead of allowing his course to be mapped out for him by Wagner and herself. In her "animated correspondence" with him she showed herself by no means "filled with respect for the philosopher and professor"; rather did she give him "a certain feminine guidance in all things, approaching the intellectual side of him in a certain critical spirit which she made no attempt to conceal from him". We who know how vast and sensitive was Nietzsche's intellectual pride can dimly imagine how trying he must sometimes have found her. Wagner too felt that his own function in the discussions between them was to diffuse light, and that of the young professor to receive it; and on the purely musical side he was justified in that opinion, for Nietzsche, musically inclined as he undoubtedly was, in that field was never much more than an amateur with flashes of genius.

His colossal self-esteem, of course, no more failed him there than it did elsewhere. He was greatly addicted to the dilettante practice of improvising at the piano; but though his efforts in this line created immense enthusiasm among his philological colleagues and other laymen there is no evidence that any impartial professional musician was ever impressed by them, and if, as seems to have been the case, he was given to indulging himself in the habit at Triebschen he must have tried Wagner sorely. But this was not the worst. He laboured under the strange delusion that he was a composer. At the end of the English translation of *Ecce Homo* will be found his *Hymn to Life* for chorus and orchestra, a composition of which he was as proud as Beethoven could ever have been of the Eroica or the Missa solennis. Other works of Nietzsche have been published by the Leipzig firm of Kistner and Siegel under the auspices of the Nietzsche-Archiv. They exhibit the rankest amateurism: and if he inflicted any of them on Wagner the latter's patience must sometimes have been strained to breaking-point.

3

When *The Birth of Tragedy* was published, Bülow was so enthusiastic over it that he carried it about with him everywhere and bought copies to present to his friends. Hearing of this, Nietzsche sent him the score of a composition of his own on the subject of Manfred, apparently in the hope that Hans would perform it at one of his concerts. Bülow's reply, dated the 24th July, 1872, was prompt and to the point. Nietzsche's letter and the accompanying score, he says, had embarrassed him to an extent he has rarely experienced before in cases of that kind. He has asked himself whether he ought to maintain silence, or reply in terms of "civilised banality", or say just what he thinks. He pays tribute to Nietzsche's gifts as a scholar, but hopes he may be allowed to speak freely about his music for two reasons — he is older than the Herr Professor, and he is a musician by profession. Anyhow, where the art of music is concerned mere politeness has no place. Here then is his frank opinion:

"Your *Manfred Meditation* is the most fantastically extravagant, the most unedifying, the most anti-musical thing I have come across for a long time in the way of notes put on paper. Several times I had to ask myself whether it is all a joke, whether, perhaps, your object was to produce a parody of the so-called music of the future. Is it by intent that you persistently defy every rule of tonal connection, from the higher syntax down to the merest spelling? Apart from its psychological interest — for your musical fever suggests, for all its aberrations, an uncommon, a distinguished mind — your *Meditation,* looked at from a musical standpoint, is the precise equivalent of a crime in the moral sphere. Of the Apollonian element I have not been able to discover the smallest trace; and as for the Dionysian, I must say frankly that I have been reminded less of this than of the 'day after' a bacchanal. If you really feel a passionate urge to express yourself in music, you should master the rudiments of the musical language: a frenzied imagination, revelling in reminiscences of Wagnerian harmonies, is no sort of foundation to build upon. Wagner's most unprecedented audacities, apart from the fact that they derive from a dramatic web and are justified by the words — for in his purely instrumental works he wisely denies himself prodigious things of that kind — are without exception grammatically correct, down to the tiniest detail of notation . . . But if you, highly esteemed Herr Professor, really take this aberration of yours into the field of music quite seriously (as to which I am still doubtful), then at least confine yourself to vocal music and surrender to the words the helm of the boat in which you rove the raging seas of tone. You yourself, not without reason, describe your music as 'terrible'. It is indeed more terrible than you think — not detrimental to the common weal, of course, but something worse than that, detrimental to yourself, seeing that you can find no worse way of killing time than raping Euterpe in this fashion." [4]

Nietzsche took his castigation with surprising humility, perhaps because the very thoroughness of it took his breath away, perhaps also because nothing could ever shake his fatuous belief in his own

---

[4] BBL, pp. 250–2.

gifts as a composer. When in 1882 the piano score of *Parsifal* appeared, he made the remarkable discovery that it was "exactly the sort of music" *he* had produced in an oratorio written in his boyhood. "The identity of mood and of expression was fabulous", he declared after he and his sister had gone through his own juvenile score together; and she dutifully agreed with him that some passages in the oratorio were "quite Parsifalesque", though more moving than anything in Wagner's opera.[5]

4

In July, 1870 Nietzsche and his Pforta friend Erwin Rohde were in Triebschen together. When Nietzsche read to the company his Basel lecture on *The Greek Music Drama*[6] Cosima graciously approved of it; it showed, she confided to her diary, that he had "a real feeling for Greek art", a subject on which she evidently regarded herself as an authority. Wagner had "certain doubts" about the lecture, which he expressed to the young professor "in clear and searching" terms. Rohde made an excellent impression on them both, Cosima going so far as to "describe him without qualification as more considerable even than Nietzsche", for the reason, perhaps, that while rather more than his friend's equal in some departments of Greek scholarship,[7] he had less confidence in himself where music was concerned, and was therefore content to adore Wagner without venturing to differ from him. Nietzsche was made of more stubborn material: almost from the beginning of the friendship with him both Wagner and Cosima seem to have had a dimly uncomfortable feeling that somehow or other he did not quite "fit in with Triebschen", as Du Moulin puts it. It is rather significant that Wagner did not think it advisable to show him *A Capitulation:* the young man's gorge would probably have risen at that, not merely because of the crudity of the thing itself but because of Wagner's complacent belief that it was in the vein of Aristophanes, for whom Nietzsche had a special liking.

Nietzsche's gift to Cosima at Christmas, 1870 was the sketch of

---

[5] See his letter of the 25th July, 1882 to Peter Gast, in NGB, IV, 110–111.

[6] A few of his notes for it are given in NW, IX, 34 ff.

[7] Nietzsche himself admitted this: see his letter to Rohde of the 23rd May, 1876 (NGB, II, 523 ff), *à propos* of the latter's recently published book on *The Greek Romance and its Forerunners.*

a work he was planning on *The Origin of the Tragic Idea* — the germ of the later *Birth of Tragedy*. Cosima was delighted with the sketch, but characteristically noted in her diary that she was "particularly pleased that Richard's ideas can find an extension in this field". As usual, she could see little reason for the young professor's existence except in so far as his Greek scholarship might be put to Wagnerian uses: so she indulgently pointed out to him that "anyone can have wise and great thoughts, but everything depended on their being put forward in a compact and developed form", which was only her way of hinting that the projected book would be incomplete if it did not centre in Wagner. "It was characteristic of her wonderful nature", says the adoring Du Moulin, "to give true and womanly advice" — even to the extent of telling scholars just how their specialist books should be written.

A glimmer of reason seems actually to visit even Du Moulin now and then in this connection. When Nietzsche went to Italy for a short holiday in February, 1871 without taking leave of Triebschen, Wagner, it appears, "drew gloomy inferences" from this unwarrantable conduct, "for Nietzsche was in a way worldly-minded, and it may well be that Frau Cosima's suggestions had rather hurt his vanity, though he followed them entirely." So blind were they both to the individuality of the young genius whom the Fates had thrown into Wagner's orbit, so blind to the despotic nature of his daemon. He was to be theirs and theirs alone, body and soul: a tight hand would have to be kept on the jesses lest the young hawk should take a flight on his own account and bring down another prey than the one they had marked out for him. No man of anything like Nietzsche's calibre had ever come into such close relation with Wagner's own intellectual life; yet towards no one else did he ever behave so imperiously. More than one passage in Nietzsche's later writings has the ring of personal vibrations still quivering in him from his experiences in the Triebschen days, when he must have had again and again the galling feeling that he was regarded by the Master as merely a heaven-sent instrument for the propagation of *his* ideas. "Oh, the rattlesnake joy of the old master", he hisses in *The Case of Wagner* (1888), "when he always saw just 'the little children' come to him!" Again, "One has not the least insight into Wagner so long as one has not divined his dominating instinct", which, in Nietzsche's view, was to be in everything what he had determined to be. And once more, "Wagner is bad for youths; he is fatal to women." Nietzsche is ostensibly discussing Wagner's art; but the purely human and personal note in it all is unmistakable. It is at Cosima that he is glancing retrospectively when he says that

"the danger for artists, of geniuses . . . lies in women: *adoring* women are their ruin. Hardly one of them has character enough not to be corrupted — 'saved' — when he finds himself being treated as a god. . . . In many cases of womanly love, and perhaps precisely in the most famous, love is merely a more refined *parasitism*, a creeping into the being of a strange soul, sometimes even of a strange body, and ah! at what expense always to the 'host'!"

5

One could easily multiply citations of this sort, in which the envenomed barb, ostensibly aimed at Wagner the musician, is really directed against Wagner the man: to the end of his days the thought of his one-time subservience to Wagner's imperious personality rankled in Nietzsche, and the memory of it poisoned his pen because the thing itself had once poisoned his soul. "Ah, this old robber!" he cries in the first Postscript to *The Case of Wagner*.

"He plunders us of our youths, even our women he seizes and drags into his cave! Ah, this old Minotaur! What he has already cost us! Every year processions of our finest maidens and youths are led into his labyrinth, that he may devour them; every year there goes up the cry from all Europe: 'Off to Crete! Off to Crete!' " [8]

Triebschen must often have seemed to him his own Crete. The trouble was that not only did the Minotaur exercise an irresistible attraction upon him in those days, but the attraction endured to the end of his life. The insults he flung later in the face of the devouring monster were merely the convulsive expression of his rage at his impotence to escape from him.

Unquestionably it was on Wagner that his eye was turned when he wrote the moving "Grave Song" in *Thus Spake Zarathustra*, that eloquent, heart-breaking lament over "the grave-island, the silent isle, where are also the graves of my youth".

---

[8] The allusion is to the ensemble "Pars pour la Crête" at the end of the first act of Offenbach's *La Belle Hélène*, an opera of which Nietzsche was very fond at the time when he was writing *The Case of Wagner*. See his letter of the 24th August, 1888 to Peter Gast, in NGB, IV, 399.

" 'All days shall be holy unto me' — so spake once to me the wisdom of my youth: verily the word of a joyous wisdom! But then did ye enemies steal my nights and sold them to sleepless pain: ah, whither did that joyous wisdom fly? Once did I long for happy auspices of birds. Then did ye send an owl-monster across my path, an adverse omen. . . . And when I performed my hardest task and celebrated the triumph of my victories, then did you make those who loved me most cry out that I was wounding them sorely. . . .[9] How did I bear it? How did I recover from such wounds and overcome them? How did my soul rise again from these graves? Yes, something invulnerable, unburiable is within me, something that can blast rocks asunder: it is *my Will*. In silence and unchanged it strides on through the years. Its course will it go on my own feet, my own Will: hard is the heart of it and invulnerable."

And once more in the chapter entitled "The Magician", where the style of the verse is obviously a jape at the Wagner manner, and the prose section as manifestly an outburst against the rankling memory of Wagner's one-time hold on him and his attempts to subjugate him to his own tyrannous will.[10]

6

The Nietzscheans-of-the-fold of thirty or forty years ago — now a somewhat dilapidated-looking band of heroes, the analogues in

---

[9] Here the reference to Wagner and Cosima becomes unmistakable in the light of the extracts Du Moulin gives from the latter's diary.

[10] So far as I know, the biographical significance of the opening sentences of *Thus Spake Zarathustra* has escaped the notice of the commentators. "When Zarathustra was thirty years old", the book begins, "he left his home and the lake of his home and went into the mountains. There he had the enjoyment of his spirit and of his solitude, and for ten years did not weary of it."

The "home" and the "lake of his home" seem to me to be symbols for Triebschen — his spiritual home for some years — and the Lake on which Triebschen stood. "Thirty" need not be taken absolutely literally; nor need the meaning of "the lake of his home" be pinned down to the literal geographical fact. Where Wagner lived was still Nietzsche's spiritual home for long after May, 1872, when Wagner exchanged Triebschen for Bayreuth: Nietzsche is writing *Dichtung*, not *Wahrheit*. In the same way, "thirty" is a poetic symbol covering the period round about 1873, when, as his notebooks reveal, his spirit was already beginning to reorientate itself *vis-à-vis* Wagner. Similarly the "ten years" in which Zarathustra enjoyed his spirit and his solitude is a poetic round number that covers sufficiently well the period that elapsed between the first great inward change in him and the date of the First Part of *Thus Spake Zarathustra* (1882). His emancipation was probably accelerated by the mere fact of Wagner's removal to Bayreuth: Basel was much further from that town than from Lucerne. For that reason alone the two men met less frequently than of old; and when they did, each seems to have been subconsciously aware that Nietzsche was not quite the Nietzsche of the Triebschen days.

their own sphere to the Glasenapps and Chamberlains and Wolzo-
gens in the Wagnerian — persuaded themselves, and tried to persuade the world, that as a philosopher Nietzsche was the heir of
all the ages. They seem to have overlooked the principle insisted
on by their Master himself, that a philosophy is less a system than
a man — a principle that holds good perhaps even more in his case
than in those of other thinkers. Nietzsche, it is becoming more
frankly recognised everywhere today except in the shrinking ranks
of the Old Guard, was capable in only a small degree of steady
thinking from premises based on observed facts to a logical conclusion. One of the latest writers on the subject does not overstate the
case when he says that

> "it can be said at the outset that he is not a logician at all, and that his
> contribution to critical philosophy is negligible. He cannot argue: he
> has no method, no mathematical or quasi-mathematical system. . . .
> He is a declaimer rather than a thinker. His whole system is built upon
> a void. He premises nothing to begin with, and it is often impossible
> to know what is to be assumed or taken for granted. . . . The later
> Nietzsche had a soul above logic if anyone ever had, and he never suc-
> ceeded in proving any contention scientifically. . . . It is clear that
> from his youth he disliked rational argument. This characterisation
> accounts for most of his value — and for most of his weaknesses." [11]

It is not with his philosophy — or philosophies — that we are concerned here, but solely with his relations to Wagner biography; and
these relations cannot be completely understood without reference
to his peculiar personality.

It was not merely by coincidence of philosophical outlook that
he was so strongly attracted to Heraclitus of Ephesus. The two self-
centred personalities had so much in common that it was almost a
foregone conclusion that they should find each other and join
hands across the ages. To read a present-day description of the

---

[11] A. H. J. Knight, *Some Aspects of the Life and Work of Nietzsche* (1933), pp. 4, 13.
Mr. Knight, of course, does not attempt to deny Nietzsche's genius, the lightning
flashes with which he often illuminates a subject, and, above all, his poetic fire and
his consummate literary artistry. But few people today outside the Old Guard will
dissent from the broad summing-up that "his faults are numerous and glaring, and
such as to put off many a would-be impartial critic at the very start. He is treacher-
ous and cruel: he is undisciplined, one-sided, intellectually lazy, and spiteful: but he
never writes better (and seldom more alluringly) than when he is exhibiting these
imperfections in their most flagrant aspect". And he ran true to the national strain
in putting the maximum of his energies into the congenial business of hating.

remarkable old Greek is to feel that it is Nietzsche's portrait that is being drawn in every line, his life-course that is being traced:

"Heraclitus is one of the most striking personalities in the history of Greek thought: this is evident in every turn of his 'style' — a wholly personal manner of expression, self-made, vehement, deriving from the extreme of self-consciousness, cast in incisive aphorisms. A man of the highest birth . . . an aristocrat of the spirit even more than in virtue of blood, who turned his back in bitterness and scorn on his native town, with its veritable orgies of the *Zeitgeist,* its radical democracy, which offered no practical scope in public life for natures such as his. . . . Disgusted with the doings of the rabble — the many-too-many — this man flies to the solitude of nature undefiled, to the mountain heights, the rivers, the eternally restless seas, to the starry skies at night"; where, "far from the hurly-burly of mankind, there come to the lonely brooder the profound cognitions that raise him far above time and space; here are revealed to him the eternal verities that shall one day lay their spell upon a Goethe, a Nietzsche, and many another distinguished spirit. . . . He holds himself entirely aloof from the social consciousness of his Ionian fellow-citizens — rejects it, indeed, more particularly as regards the popular religion, but in the ethical and political spheres also. He was sharply critical of, if not always just towards, his 'predecessors' in the narrower sense of the term, so far as one can speak of predecessors in connection with a mind so independent as his." [12]

7

It was a personality, then, singularly like that of Heraclitus that inhabited the frame of Nietzsche, a personality proud, violent, self-centred, intolerant, that was fated to be flung for a time by the wind

---

[12] Wilhelm Capelle, *Die Vorsokratiker* (1938), p. 126 ff. So also John Burnet (*Greek Philosophy: Part 1, From Thales to Plato,* p. 57 ff); once more each stroke recalls Nietzsche to us: "It is above all in dealing with Herakleitos that we are made to feel the importance of personality in shaping systems of philosophy. The very style of his fragments is something unique in Greek literature, and won for him in later times the epithet of 'the dark'. He is quite conscious himself that he writes an oracular style, and he justifies it by the example of the Sybil and the God at Delphoi, who 'neither utters nor hides his meaning but signifies it'." While it is true that Heraclitus's "aphorisms" owe their form mainly to the fact that his writings have come down to us almost entirely in fragments, it is not impossible that it was under his influence that Nietzsche, in his later works, made the aphorism his favourite mode of self-expression.

He was influenced also, of course, to some extent by writers like Rochefoucauld and Vauvenargues, but still more, I imagine, by Heine's *Gedanken und Einfälle,* which seem to me to have contributed not only to the form but to the substance of several of Nietzsche's pregnant jottings. These notes of Heine's were published posthumously in 1869; and we may be tolerably certain that, admiring Heine as he did, he fastened on the volume at once.

of the cosmos into the orbit of the equally powerful, equally self-centred personality of Wagner, and then, inevitably, to collide with this and sheer off in a direction of its own. The part played by Nietzsche's personality as determining his thought is vital to our understanding of his attitude towards Wagner, both during the latter's lifetime and after his death. So long as each seemed to the other to be just a factor in his own egoistic development their mutual attraction was stronger than their repulsion. But from the moment that this always unstable equilibrium became still more unstable by reason of Nietzsche's gradual realisation of what he was in himself, and his own illimitable self-esteem, his sense of his mission, his lust for power, his inability to suffer contradiction clashed with a similar complex of forces in Wagner, a breach between the two men was inevitable.[13]

Unfortunately the Nietzsche idolaters of the last generation missed the simple psychological facts of the case when they attempted to make out that the cause of the breach was Nietzsche's superior intellectual power, which one day revealed to him the rottenness not only of Wagner's philosophy but of his music. With all due respect, the idolaters were without exception quite unqualified to pass judgment on the latter issue. Not being musicians themselves, they took Nietzsche's verbal fireworks for deadly depth charges. They could not be expected to see that much of the criticism of Wagner as a musician in Nietzsche's note-books of the early 1870's is no more than the honest wool-gathering of an earnest young man battling with problems of music that were mostly beyond his capacity; while his final writings on Wagner are merely journalism of the cheapest, most ill-bred kind, the sort of mud-flinging that any man with a comprehensive faculty for hating, and a gift for coining malicious epithets and stabbing phrases, can in-

---

[13] They were so absolutely alike in their little faults that it was a foregone conclusion that one day they would hate each other like brothers. An amusing list of these resemblances could easily be drawn up in parallel columns. For instance, opposite Wagner's tyrannical demand that friends such as Cornelius and Tausig should cease doing whatever they happened to be doing and come to him the moment he wanted them would appear the letter in which Nietzsche fell foul of his sister for daring in the first place to marry, in the second place to marry a man who did not think as *he* thought. Her union with Förster, he said, was a clear proof that she meant to devote her life "not to *my* highest aims, but to the ideals that I have overcome and must now make war upon. You have become my antipodes! The instinct of your love ought to have preserved you from that." And much more to the same effect.

dulge in with respect to anyone or anything he hates merely because he or it is different from himself. There are many passages in Nietzsche's works and his note-books and letters that are well worth the consideration of the musical aesthetician of today, for it lay in the very nature of his genius to open out more than one new route in that field as in others, even if his fundamentally unsystematic mind could not follow them to their logical end. But very little that he has to say on the specific subject of Wagner's music calls for serious consideration today. More especially in his last years, the years of morbid hatred of the great musician who had once enslaved him, does he deliver himself of a vast amount of sheer nonsense that is not improved by the crude vulgarity of its tone. The place in musical history for the author of *The Case of Wagner* is by the side of Hanslick, *par nobile fratrum*.

CHAPTER XVI

WAGNER AND NIETZSCHE: II

1

WE NEED feel no surprise that neither Wagner nor Cosima quite understood the young professor during the winter of 1870/1, vaguely aware as they must have been of something going on in the depths of him that made him inharmonious not merely with them but with himself. It was not "worldliness", as they thought, that took him in the February of the latter year to Lugano, where he remained until Easter. He was very ill — his constitution had been hard hit by his war service — and even more in mind than in body: it is probable, indeed, that the main causes of most of his physical derangements and his insomnia at this time were mental and emotional. Rohde gave him some sensible advice — to keep away for a while from music, which was manifestly a dangerous nervous excitant for him; to abandon something of his solitude, which can be a wholesome thing for sound spirits but is an exacerbation of the dolours of the unsound; and above all not to overstrain his intellectual forces as he had been doing. The advice, of course, fell on deaf ears. The truth, as we can now see, was that Nietzsche's brain was awhirl with new impulses and intuitions that had not yet succeeded in defining themselves clearly and connectedly as ideas. He already saw himself as the saviour of European civilisation, but could not yet see how to make his evangel manifest to others. There were times when, in despair over the dis-harmonies in his nature and his increasing maladjustment not only to his professional environment but to German culture as a whole, he thought of fleeing from the world with Rohde into a cloister of their own founding, to which only another wholly kindred spirit or two was to be admitted, and in which, as he wrote to his friend, they could "raise themselves above the atmosphere of the day, and become not only wiser but, before all things, better men."

The equally unhappy but less volcanic Rohde threw doubts on

the practicability of the scheme; but he too, in his less complex way, was out of tune with the world and longing to endow it with a new harmony.[1] The basic trouble with them both was not, as they thought, simply that they were spiritually discordant with the more dry-as-dust of their philological colleagues. The Fates had plunged them in their early manhood into a world-phase full of torments and dangers for the mind of German youth. It was sadly evident to them, as to many other fine souls, that after the war of 1870/1 Germany had entered upon a period of absorption in material things that threatened the end of the older Germany of the spirit: the letters of Nietzsche and his friends are full of laments on this score. Being not merely youths but German youths, they fled to philosophy for comfort and justification, and the whirligig of time had confronted them with Schopenhauer as the philosopher who, they thought, had come nearest to laying bare the troublous secret of the world. Equally great was the influence on them of Wagner, not only through his music, which was a divine intoxicant for most of the ardent young souls of that epoch, but through his lofty ideal- ism, his fight against every form of German philistinism, and above all through his grandiose vision of Bayreuth, which they saw, in imagination, as the central sun of a new world of the spirit. They constantly lived at too high pressure; they were overworked, hu- mourless, over-intellectualised, perhaps under-sexed young hiero- phants,[2] possessed with the conviction that the destiny of the uni- verse lay on their shoulders, weary young Teutonic Titans stagger- ing under the load of the too vast orb of their fate. We feel, as we read their letters, that an occasional set at tennis, or a game of snooker at the Club, or a turn at sporting with Amaryllis in the

---

[1] Rohde was now a lecturer in philology at Kiel University: he received a full professorship there in April, 1872.

[2] Nietzsche, it is true, used to dance occasionally; but, *pace* the good Elisabeth, whose sisterly piety would fain make him out to be quite a gay young dog at the "exclusive" Basel balls and elsewhere, one suspects that he twirled the light fan- tastic toe on the soundest professorial principles, persuading himself that in doing so he was being very Dionysian. His letters show hardly a trace of the physical *joie de vivre* of the youth of other countries and periods.

The editor of the Brahms-Billroth correspondence has pointed out that the Ger- many of their young days was a "literary" one — "neither cards nor sports took up much of their time in their youth." BBBW, p. 60. It was thoroughly characteristic of Nietzsche's inability to be young like normal people of his age that when his health broke down in 1876 and he was granted a year's absence from the Basel University he went off to spend his holiday with the super-serious Malwida von Meysenbug, at that time an old lady of sixty.

shade would have done them a world of good not only physically but mentally, while the cosmos would perhaps not have run hopelessly off the rails during the brief hour or two when their anxious supervision was withdrawn from it.

2

The newest school of German Nietzscheans has been at great pains to absolve its idol of the reproach that he was capable only to a small extent of systematic thinking. Professor Alfred Baeumler in particular has argued with much earnestness that Nietzsche's philosophy, for all the changes it went through, all the recantations and re-affirmations it exhibits, was in reality one and indivisible; that the indecision and self-contradiction are merely superficial, the one fundamental driving force being traceable in him from first to last.[3] That is quite true, though perhaps, in the last resort, no more so of Nietzsche than it would prove to be of any other human being were all men to leave behind them as many documents as he did to serve as material for the constructive psychologist of a later day. That "the whole man thinks" has long been an axiom with thinkers; George Henry Lewes laid it down long ago that our philosophies, when they are not borrowed, are rarely other than the expression of our temperament. It was manifestly so in Nietzsche's case, which is complicated, however, by the fact that different temperaments, or, which amounts to the same thing, opposite poles of what was basically the one temperament, were apt to determine his mental course for him at different periods of his life.

His own method, in general, was not to collect facts and try out deductions from them but to indulge himself in intuitions and then look about for facts to support them. He himself, as was only to be expected, poured scorn on the thinkers who worked in the reverse way: a philosophy, he said, is primarily and properly the expression of a man. No doubt; but the trouble is that if we base our interpretation of the cosmos on our individual intuitions it is not long before we discover, to our annoyance, that other individuals have intuitions quite contrary but just as imperative; and then the

[3] See especially Baeumler's ably argued Foreword to *Die Unschuld des Werdens* (Nietzsche's posthumous papers), in the *Kröner Taschenausgabe* of the philosopher's works (1931), and the Introduction to his masterly epitome of Nietzsche's thinking, *Nietzsche, der Philosoph und Politiker* (1931).

only way to decide between the rival illuminations is by way of that marshalling of facts and testing them by ratiocination which might just as well have been undertaken in the first place: either that, or to perform a trumpet solo on the theme of our own "genius", to retire to the mountain tops and megaphone from there that it is only *our* intuitions that have any value, none other being genuine — which was the way of Nietzsche as it was of Wagner. And at the risk of appearing mulishly inaccessible to reason in face of a philosophical scheme as to the Sinaitic provenance and the prophetic importance of which the author of it never had any manner of doubt, we feel impelled to protest that Nietzsche was simply adopting the tactics of all publicists who are artists rather than scientists, better at intuition and assertion than at reasoning, — trying to give an inflated market value to a poor intellectual holding by the bold but simple process of transferring a liability to the other side of the balance sheet, declaring it to be an asset of incalculable value, and on the strength of it declaring a hypothetical dividend. And when some of the receivers of the dividend warrants protest that they cannot be accepted as sound currency in the world's intellectual markets, all the proud issuer of them has to do is to bespatter the malcontents with abuse for not being able to spread their earthbound wings in the rarefied atmosphere of the higher finance.

3

All Nietzsche's characteristic qualities as a writer — the suggestiveness and often penetrating insight of his aperçus, his frequent weakness in factual knowledge, his passion for generalising *in vacuo* — are already manifest in *The Birth of Tragedy out of the Spirit of Music*. It reveals also a curious dis-harmony of impulse: the one half of his mind was already feeling its way, rather blindly and *via* Dionysus — a Dionysus of his own, by the way, rather than that of Greek mythology — towards his later Zarathustra and the superman; while the other half was possessed with the notion that somehow or other he must square these impulses of his with Schopenhauerism and Wagnerism, and more particularly the latter.

The present-day editions of the book contain two prefaces, (1) a long document entitled "An Attempt at Self-Criticism" which Nietzsche added to the re-issue of 1886, (2) the short dedicatory "Foreword to Richard Wagner" which appeared in the original edition of January, 1872. This latter refers briefly to "the earnestness of the German problem that confronts us" and the necessity of solving that problem along aesthetic lines, with a proper sense of "the earnestness of existence". "I am convinced", the Foreword ends,

> "that art is the highest task and the proper metaphysical activity of life, as it is understood by him to whom, as my sublime predecessor on this path, I would now dedicate this book."

This Foreword is dated "end of the year 1871": it must therefore have been written after the book had actually gone to press, for the manuscript had been handed to the publisher in October, during a visit of Nietzsche's to Leipzig.

For light on the gestation and original purpose of the work, however, we must turn to yet another and earlier "Foreword to Richard Wagner", running to some seven pages, which Nietzsche had written in the February of 1871 but which he did not see fit to use in public.[4] In this document the word "music" does not once appear, nor is there any mention of Wagner himself except for a couple of brief references to his *Beethoven* and *On Conducting*. And each of these references relates not specifically to music but rather to the Germans and the hope for their "re-birth" after the Franco-German War. From the *Beethoven* Nietzsche quotes (not quite verbatim) the passage,

> "The German is brave. Let him now be so in peace also: let him disdain to appear to be what he is not. Nature has denied him the art of pleasing; in compensation it has made him deep-feeling and sublime."

The reference to *On Conducting* relates to the paragraph in which Wagner protests against the superficial "classicity" of most of the time-beaters of the day, the tradition of which he traces back to Mendelssohn's "cheerful-Grecian" conducting of great works. Neither of these citations has any particular bearing on music and Greek tragedy as such.

This rejected Foreword of February, 1871 shows Nietzsche's thoughts to have been concentrated at that time on something quite other than Wagner and the birth of tragedy out of the spirit of music. The main original purpose of the book he had in hand was

---

[4] It is printed among his posthumous papers, in NW, IX, 27–33.

to dispel the prevalent fallacious notion of "Greek cheerfulness", and it had been his intention to dedicate his work to Wagner because their conversations in Triebschen had convinced him that the composer was the one man in Europe, besides himself, who recognised the error of that conception and saw that it made any true insight into the origin, nature and goal of tragedy impossible. "Greek cheerfulness", Nietzsche argues, is a modern delusion due to the perfect proportions and clarity of Greek art, a delusion similar to that of the bather who, because the water is clear, imagines the bed of the sea to be so near that he can touch it with his hand, whereas the lesson of Greek art is that "there is no beautiful superficies without a terrifying depth". Nietzsche is sorely troubled about this misunderstanding of Greek art and the Greek nature,[5] because it is a symptom of a misunderstanding of the whole being of the universe, a misunderstanding that will prove fatal to — the Germans! He paints what is obviously a portrait of himself, if not as he actually was just then, at any rate as his prophetic instinct told him he might become — a proud, lofty spirit, fighter, poet and philosopher in one, a

> "future hero of tragic cognition on whose brow will fall the reflected splendour of that Greek cheerfulness, that gloriole which will inaugurate the re-birth-to-be of antiquity, the *German* re-birth of the Hellenic world."

It is the old self-flattering German fantasy, we see, of the Germans as the spiritual heirs of Greece.

---

[5] As was so often the case with him, he took to be an original discovery of his own what had long ago been said by others. No one with the smallest acquaintance with Greek literature could fail to be aware of the many passages that negate the popular notion of the Greeks as a race of cheerful children. Long before *The Birth of Tragedy* appeared Ruskin had written, ". . . . in their dealings with all these subjects [destiny and the life of man] the Greeks never shrink from horror; down to its uttermost depths, to its most appalling physical detail, they strive to sound the secret of sorrow. For them there is no passing by on the other side, no turning away the eyes to vanity from pain. . . . Whether there be consolation for them or not, neither apathy nor blindness shall be their saviour: if for them, thus knowing the facts of the grief of earth, any hope, relief or triumph may hereafter seem possible, — well; but if not, still hopeless, reliefless, eternal, the sorrow shall be met face to face." *Modern Painters*, VII, 274 ff. of the Library edition.

A host of citations bearing on the subject will be found in the essay *The Melancholy of the Greeks* in S. H. Butcher's *Some Aspects of the Greek Genius*.

4

Nietzsche goes on to say that he links up these hopes of a re-birth with "the present sanguinary glory of the German name". But he turns away with abhorrence from the delusion that either the Folk or the State is "an end in itself": the goal to be kept in sight is the great individual, the saint, the artist — "the culmination and final aim of humanity". Already, it will be seen, he is well on the way to the discovery of his hypothetical superman.

Then he voices at once his fears and his hopes for the German future; for of course, like all true Germans, neither he nor Wagner can see either the world as it is or the world as it ought to be except in terms of self-complacent Teutonism.

"The sole productive *political* power in Germany, which there is no need to specify more particularly [Prussia] has now won a prodigious victory, and henceforth will dominate the German nature down to its smallest molecule. This is a fact of the utmost importance, for before this power something will go down in ruin which we [presumably Wagner and himself] detest as the real enemy of every profounder philosophy and conception of art, that diseased condition from which the German nature has particularly suffered since the French Revolution, and which afflicts the best types of the German nature with perpetually recurring arthritic couvulsions — to say nothing of the larger mass, among whom the malady goes by the name of 'Liberalism', a vile profanation of a well-meaning word. All this Liberalism based on an imaginary dignity of the species 'man' will go down bleeding, together with its sturdier brothers, before the inflexible power of which I have spoken; and we will gladly give up the little charms and amiabilities inherent in this Liberalism if only this doctrine that is intrinsically inimical to culture is swept out of the path of genius. And to what other end should that hard power, with its centuries-old roots in force, conquest and butchery, serve, if not to prepare the path for genius?

"But which path? Perhaps our future hero of tragic cognition and Greek cheerfulness will be an anchorite; perhaps he will bid the profounder German natures go into the desert — blessed time in which the world, turned inward upon itself by fearful sorrow, will listen to the song of that Apollonian swan!"

Then comes the quotation from Wagner about the valour and the other admirable qualities of the Germans, which, Nietzsche continues, constitute the other guarantees for his hopes.

"If it be true — and this I may call my profession of faith — that all profound cognition is terrible, who but the German will be able to attain to the tragic standpoint of cognition which I demand as the preparation of the ground for the genius, the new educational aim of nobly striving youth? Who but the German youth will possess the intrepidity of glance and the heroic impulse to plunge into the terrible, turning his back on all those sickly Liberal-optimistic doctrines of comfort and resolving to 'live resolutely'?"

The juvenile rant is not precisely the last word either in lucidity or in political wisdom; but at any rate it makes one thing clear enough, that at that time what Nietzsche had in mind was a book about himself and German culture, not about Wagner and music drama.

5

According to Elisabeth, she and her brother arrived in Lugano, for a holiday, on the 12th February and stayed there three weeks. That brings us to about the end of the first week in March. They were then "invited by an Italian nobleman to Ponte Tresa"; but they evidently returned later to Lugano. "During the whole sojourn", says the sister,

"my brother was working at *The Birth of Tragedy*. . . . On the 10th April we returned to Basel, and here the writing continued, and also, more particularly, the weeding out. On the 26th the manuscript was sent to a publisher",

one Engelmann, of Leipzig.[6] It is curious that she should omit from the biography at this point a detail which she inserted in the later *Wagner und Nietzsche zur Zeit ihrer Freundschaft* (1915), — that whereas she returned direct to Basel her brother made a detour to Triebschen, because he wanted to read his manuscript to Wagner and Cosima before they left for Berlin about the middle of April. He was "rather disappointed" to find that

"Wagner had hoped that the new essay would serve in some way to glorify his own art. Enthusiastic as my brother was for Wagner and his art, his scholar's conscience bristled at the thought of combining anything so disparate as this with a book which at that time bore the title of *Greek Cheerfulness*. But consideration for his friend prevailed,

---

[6] In his letter to Engelmann, Nietzsche says the title of the book is to be *Music and Tragedy*. Apparently it was planned as a preliminary volume to a larger work.

and as soon as he returned to Basel he zealously set about a remodelling of his work, cutting out some chapters, confining himself to the problem of Greek tragedy, and linking this up with references to Wagner's art."

It is yet another demonstration of Wagner's compelling power over him whenever they met in person. The final section of the book, which is directly concerned with Wagner, was added in the following summer and autumn.

But Elisabeth's record is not quite accurate; either she had been unwilling, when writing *The Young Nietzsche,* to draw attention to her brother's visit to Triebschen *after* his holiday, with its consequences for his book, or her memory was very much at fault even when writing her later account of the friendship of the two men. In this she tells us that Nietzsche went to Triebschen immediately *before* going to Lugano, "simply to say goodbye to Wagner". There is no evidence of this visit, however. We know that he spent the Christmas of 1870 with Wagner. Then came the breakdown in health that made his doctor prescribe a holiday in the south and advise him to send for his young sister (at that time in Naumburg) to keep him company. On the 8th February he wrote to Rohde that he was leaving for Lugano "the day after tomorrow". He says nothing about calling on Wagner en route, nor, indeed, would that be possible in terms of the itinerary given by Elisabeth for their joint journey. She says nothing about herself having been at Triebschen just then, nor is there any record of a visit from either of them in the diary of Richter, who was living in the house at that time. But Richter *does* record, *on Monday, the 3rd April,* "Prof. Nietzsche arrived from Lugano", which is followed on the 8th by "Returned to Basel".[7] It was during that week, then, about which Elisabeth is so oddly reticent, that the strange destiny of *The Birth of Tragedy* was accomplished.

---

[7] On Wednesday, the 29th March, Nietzsche writes to Rohde that he is leaving Lugano at the end of the week. On the 10th April he tells his friend that he is back in Basel again after having spent some days in Triebschen. His letter of the 29th March is consistent with the entry in Richter's diary that records his arrival on the 3rd April; consequently the "6th April" cannot possibly be the correct date for a letter of Nietzsche's to his mother, saying that he is leaving Lugano that evening. One comes to the sad conclusion that Elisabeth did her editorial work in connection with the letters very carelessly. I lack the space to prove this in detail; but in a later chapter we shall see how far astray she is in the important matter of the dating of his letters from Bayreuth in 1876.

6

On the 20th December, when the work was in the press, Nietzsche told Rohde that

> "the whole of the final section, which is as yet unknown to you, will certainly surprise you: I have dared a good deal, but may be permitted to cry aloud to myself, in a large sense of the words, 'animam salvavi'."

Evidently the writing of that section had not been easy for him, though he was still heart and soul a Wagnerian. On the following 4th February (1872), when it had become clear that his book was going to have a rather bad press, he wrote to Rohde,

> "No one has any idea of the way in which such a book comes into being . . . but what people have least notion of is the colossal task that confronted me with regard to Wagner, which caused me many and painful inward qualms — the task of being independent even here, of taking up, as it were, an estranged position; and my Triebschen friends testify, with something of a shock, that I have been able to do this even in connection with the supreme problem presented by *Tristan*."

The writing of the final portion of the book must indeed have been full of difficulties for him, difficulties arising from his peculiar mentality, with its eternally unresolved dissonance between the intellectual and the emotional parts of his being. In the *Attempt at Self-Criticism* which he wrote as a preface to the reissue of 1886 he professed to regret having "spoiled the grand Hellenic problem . . . by the most modern things." But that had not been at all his opinion at the time, certainly not in so far as the connection of his Greek problem with that of modern culture was bound up with Wagner's art. After the Mannheim concert of the 20th December, 1871 he could assure Rohde that his musical perceptions had been "wonderfully strengthened" by the music of Wagner's he had just heard: his experiences had surpassed anything he had known until then: "this, exactly this and nothing else, is what I mean when I speak of 'music' in connection with my description of the Dionysian." And a month or so later, in January, 1872, he was proud to say that he "had concluded an alliance with Wagner: you can have no idea how close we now are to each other and how identical our plans are." Elisabeth informs us that "even at this time [i.e., while he was writing the final section of his book] my brother hinted to me that he had suppressed certain other views for Wagner's sake." Perhaps so; [8] but all the same he could tell Wagner, at the very time he was concluding that section, that he cherished the warmest and most affectionate memories of his latest visit to Triebschen (in the preceding April), and realised to the full what he owed to "his good geniuses" there. In his letter of the 26th April to Engelmann, in which he broaches the subject of the publication of his book, and which he accompanies, he says, by "the manuscript of the beginning of it", [9] he could even say that "the real object of the book is to throw light upon Richard Wagner, the extraordinary enigma of our age, in his relation to Greek tragedy." That had emphatically not been the "real object" of the book in its first conception, and the fact that he could not send Engelmann the whole manuscript in April, but could only give him an outline of what it was "really" about, is one proof among others that his visit to Triebschen had brought about a complete change in his original plan.

7

As Alfred Baeumler has pointed out, Nietzsche's mind never worked "one-dimensionally": always there were at least two cross-currents of thought and emotion in him at the same time, and often a given book of his represents, we may almost say, less what he believed at the moment to be the truth than what *had been* the whole truth for him the day before yesterday. Thus at the very time when he was appearing in the public eye as the champion of Wagner he was filling his note books with evidences of his growing divergence from him. Each published book of his, as Baeumler says, is therefore "an artistically stylised action; it is directed *against* someone or something, and can be comprehended only when its goal is comprehended." Nietzsche is indeed a fascinating subject for the psychologist. But when all is said, it remains true that there must have been something fundamentally wrong with the reasoning capacity of

---

[8] As I have already hinted, statements of this kind made by Elisabeth long after the event cannot always be taken at their face value today.

[9] Elisabeth is therefore wrong when she implies that the manuscript of *the whole book* was sent to Engelmann. It is evident that the specifically Wagnerian section of it had not yet been written, and that the book was radically re-cast after the visit to Triebschen.

a man whose mind worked in that way. It is clear that he was at once stubbornly self-centred, self-willed, yet extraordinarily susceptible to suggestion, and consistent only in his inability to achieve consistency at any given moment within himself.

It was not only Wagner who, partly through his music, partly through his Schopenhauerian aesthetic, partly through his fight against German philistinism, set up a complex of ideas in him to which another element in his nature was in subconscious opposition. Seillière rightly stresses that he had been strongly influenced by Rohde in his views on the bearing of Dionysianism and all the rest of it on the German culture-problem of the day. For Rohde, no less than for Nietzsche, Wagner was the heaven-appointed saviour of that culture. Wagner was for him, in the 1870's, "the only genius in the world today". For Rohde, as for Wagner and for Nietzsche at that time, the German people was "in the truest sense of the word the *nobility* of the nations": but it was unheedful of its "mission", and so a new barbarism, a kind of "Dark Age without the saving mysticism of the Dark Ages", was threatening to overwhelm it from the inside. He was appalled at the spread of materialism, of mediocrity in Germany during and after the war with France, at the prospect of the spiritual life of the nation now becoming centred in Prussia and Berlin.[10] He saw Wagner as the only possible saviour of civilisation, and looked forward to the creation of Bayreuth as "an oasis in the desert" of the materialism that was already beginning to engulf the nation.

More constant in his sympathies than Nietzsche, Rohde could declare in 1873, when his friend's thought was already beginning to veer away from some of its old positions, that after having spent a week with Wagner he was more convinced than ever that, "let people say what they like, the inmost nature of this great artist is of the noblest and purest kind. Whoever thinks otherwise does not know him."[11] He remained constant to Wagner even after Nietzsche, driven in another direction by his own daemon, had deserted him.

---

[10] "Manifestly?", says Crusius, "Rohde had a sort of second sight of an age of banausocracy which as yet was far enough away." (CER, pp. 46–7). This was written in 1902! One sometimes wonders what the German thinkers who were so concerned about the rising tide of national barbarism between about 1870 and 1900 would say of Nazi Germany could they see it.

[11] From a letter of Rohde's of the 29th April, 1873 to Professor Ribbeck, of Kiel, quoted in CER, p. 64.

Necessarily none of them could see Nietzsche at that time as we see him now, in the light of his full later evolution. His divagations of thought and of sympathy were a puzzle to them, as, indeed, they sometimes are even to us.[12] When he was reading the proofs of the second of his *Thoughts out of Season* in 1874 he already doubted at times, he told Rohde, whether it was really he who had written all this! To any other man but Nietzsche these violent changes of mental orientation would have caused some concern: he would have asked himself whether they pointed, perhaps, to some weakness in his make-up on which he would do well to keep a watchful eye, whether it would not be better to give his mind a thorough over-hauling in private for a few years. But in the way of that sensible procedure stood his inordinate self-esteem, his fanatical belief in his mission. For him each new idea that took possession of him was a revelation from on high, cancelling out not merely all the revelations of the rest of mankind but even his own previous revelations; and of course it was the duty of everyone else, including Wagner, to change when he changed. The Führer, so to speak, was always right.

8

And so it could come about, for example, that he could curse the *Ring* up hill and down dale in later years without giving so much as a thought to his declaration in 1872 that as the tetralogy began to take final shape it revealed itself to his "astounded eyes" as "something unbelievably gigantic, perfect, incomparable". It was precisely the same *Ring* ten or fifteen years later. It was merely that by then Nietzsche's personal equation had shifted its terms; and being constitutionally incapable either of self-doubt or of tackling the thorny problem of judgment in any sphere of thought from its roots up, he could only assume naïvely that at last a light had dawned on *him* that was hidden from the purblind eyes of the rest of humanity. The amazing thing is not that he should have

---

[12] Bernouilli, who knew the whole of the Nietzsche circle, tells us that Overbeck used often to be concerned about the intellectual future of his young colleague in Basel. (BON, I, 163–4.) Nietzsche had in some ways developed mentally at an astoundingly early age: but he had acquired more book-knowledge of one kind and another than he could quite assimilate and coordinate, his reasoning powers had not kept pace with his specialist learning, and the early association with the thirty-one-years-older Wagner had subjected him to all kinds of influences that drove him, for a time, in directions alien to his real course.

been mentally constructed like this — the diversity of human types is infinite — but that even the most slender-witted among his devotees of a generation ago should ever have taken him seriously as an authority on art in general and Wagnerian art in particular. We all of us change as the years go on, liking some things in art less than we used to do, some things more. But most of us have simple common sense enough to see that this change of taste, far from constituting the end of a given problem, is merely the beginning of another — the problem of ourselves. We ask ourselves through what peculiarity — perhaps defect — it is in us that we see the same thing in entirely different ways at different times. Our second view of it, of course, may possibly come nearer accuracy than our first. But it may also quite conceivably be less near; for it cannot be complacently taken for granted that all changes in the mind, any more than in the body, imply an increase of soundness in the organ.

For the thoughtful man, therefore, the variations of taste of which he is conscious from one decade to another are a challenging and sometimes disturbing phenomenon; for if the mysterious chemistry of the mind and the body, he reflects, can thus have changed him from what he once was, what guarantee has he that even his latest phase of taste will prove his final one? He becomes sadly conscious that aesthetic judgment is a much less simple affair than he had imagined it to be in his confident youth; that each of his reactions to a given work of art, ten years ago, twenty years ago, today, is a spark generated by the work upon a complex within him of knowledge, of experience, of reflection, of emotion, of soul's hunger, of soul's satiety, that is as unstable as the complex of physical atoms that make up his body. He does not on this account abandon the problem of taste and judgment as quite insoluble: but he sees it now for the baffling thing it is. He tries to find a rational explanation of not only his own present taste but the opposing taste of other people, to discover in each case what kind of a mental complex it is from which a judgment has proceeded.

But Nietzsche's whole intellectual bent co-operated with his vanity to make a dissatisfied self-probing of this kind impossible for him at any time of his life. Fickle, variable, autolatrous, he made virtues of these defects of his. Thus in *The Gay Science* [13] he tells us that he "loves short-lived habits", which he regards as "an

---

[13] Section 295.

invaluable means for getting knowledge of many things and various conditions." His own nature, he says, is wholly built for these habits, each of which gives him, for the time being, a passionate belief that it will endure everlastingly. Then comes a day when "the habit has had its time"; he and it shake hands and say farewell, and its place in his affections is taken by a new one, which he is convinced — for a while — will be "the ultimate right one". It was certainly a principle on which he acted in all matters of artistic taste. It is not a bad principle for the dilettante who wants to live solely for the moment and get the maximum of pleasure out of each of his fluctu- ations of taste. But it is a hopeless principle for the thinker in pur- suit of truth; and at any rate the ordinary dilettante has more sense and more modesty than to believe that each of *his* phases of taste is the final word of wisdom on a subject, and to maintain abusively that when *he* changes it is the duty of everyone to change with him. The trouble with Nietzsche his whole life long was that he combined the modesty of the peacock with the consistency of the weathercock.

9

Some of the German Nietzscheans of the generation immediately following their master saw clearly enough, however, something that was hidden from the eyes of the Wagner-Nietzsche partisans in 1872. To the latter, the wonderful thing about *The Birth of Trag- edy* had been the way in which art and science, philosophy and phil- ology, the Greek past and the German present, seemed all to have been focused into one cone of intense light. Later and cooler think- ers recognised that it was precisely this attempt to combine a num- ber of unrelated and disparate things that had made the book, taken as a whole, finally null and void. As Fritz Koegel, the first editor of Nietzsche's Sketches and Fragments, expressed it as early as 1896, Nietzsche's was "a polyphonic nature":

> "and so it came about that science, art and philosophy coalesced ever more intimately within him until, in *The Birth of Tragedy*, they brought forth a centaur — a work that could not have been achieved by a more one-sided endowment."

These polyphonic blendings and suffusions, he goes on to say, take place in different circumstances in all Nietzsche's later work, until they culminate in a centaur of the highest order, the *Zarathustra*.[14] True enough; but it leaves unanswered the question as to the staying power, the final value of such a centaur as *The Birth of Tragedy* of 1872.

The matter has been summed up best of all by August Horneffer, in his *Nietzsche als Moralist und Schriftsteller* (1906).[15] Anyone, he says, who can call *The Birth of Tragedy* a complete structure cannot have read Nietzsche's sketches for it and the posthumously published jottings.

"Nietzsche's first project had been a purely historical investigation of the Attic drama, the problem of whose origin, mighty development and swift decline intrigued him. Then he found, or persuaded himself that he had found, that the aesthetic ideas of Schopenhauer and Wagner shed a light on these questions; whereupon he attempted a philosophical interpretation of the historical phenomena, drifted into strange metaphysical-aesthetic byways which led him far away from his original purpose, and contemplated a work on tragedy in general, into which the historical would enter only by way of illustration: he went from the problem of the tragic to that of the tragic man, and tried to embody his thoughts on this problem in a drama: [16] but after that he turned to the historical again, with the intention of employing it as the foil for a glorification of Wagner's art. So it went on. The final result of all this experimentation and planning was nothing more than a torso. Not one of the designs is fully worked out. Even during the last redaction the author deleted some important passages: at several points we light upon traces of larger connections which, however, remain enveloped in a haze without allowing a unified configuration of the work to appear. This curious first work reached out into the colossal without succeeding in controlling and completely clarifying what lay nearest to hand."

That last sentence sums the case up very well. The theories of the book constantly outrun the facts, while the linking up of the facts, even when they are correct, is achieved by the usual German process of "evolving the camel out of the inner consciousness". The work owed from the first, and still owes, most of its attractiveness for the ordinary reader to its antithesis of the "Dionysian" and the "Apollonian." This was one of those facile generalisations that seem at

---

[14] NW, IX, 31–2.

[15] P. 72.

[16] The *Empedocles*, the two sketches for which, dating from 1870–1, will be found in NW, IX, 183–191. Charles Andler's luminous elucidation of these (ANVP, II, 194 ff.) should be read.

first sight to explain everything, while actually they explain nothing. It was a master-key that appeared to open every lock; armed with it, even people with the most limited specialist knowledge could re-write the history of the arts to suit their own prepossessions and prejudices. The Apollo and Dionysus of *The Birth of Tragedy* are as much poetic fancy as historical fact. The origin, nature and the diffusion of the two cults are still, to a large extent, a matter of debate among scholars, in spite of the great recent expansion of our knowledge of the sciences of comparative religion and ritual, sciences of which Nietzsche's generation knew comparatively little and he himself practically nothing.[17] He talks about "Greek music", again, as if he knew something about it as an art-in-practice, which no human being does or will ever be able to do. His whole argument, moreover, relies for its philosophical validity on theories of Wagner and Schopenhauer which by no means command universal assent. Finally — a point too often overlooked — the main argument, such as it is, relates not to humanity as a whole but to Germany in general and the Germany of the 1870's in particular. All in all, in spite of its numerous flashes of genius the book fails as a study of its professed central topic. It is of interest today only for the light it throws on the total Nietzsche as we now know him and on his relations with Wagner.[18]

---

[17] The reader who is interested in the Apollo-Dionysus subject will find an exhaustive treatment of it in L. R. Farnell's *The Cults of the Greek States* — Dionysus in Vol. IV, Apollo in Vol. V.

[18] It may be added that the fascinating problem of the origins of Greek drama is still unsolved, as may be seen from the varying views expressed in such recent English works as Ridgeway's *The Origin of Tragedy, with special reference to the Greek Tragedians* (1910), Pickard-Cambridge's *Dithyramb, Tragedy and Comedy* (1927), and the recent highly original work of George Thomson, *Aeschylus and Athens* (1941).

CHAPTER XVII

THE FOUNDATION-STONE

1

BY THIS time Wagner had of course given up all hope of producing the *Ring* in 1873; but, irrepressibly sanguine as usual,
he still believed it to be possible in the following year. Brandt, he
told Richter in January, 1872, had promised to have all the machinery ready by the summer of 1873. He himself will devote the
coming months to touring Germany in quest of singers; if he finds
what he wants he will need Richter to coach them from the autumn
until the following spring, so the young man will have to get leave
of absence from the Pesth Theatre for at least nine months. "Now
see what you can do about it. I know of no one who can replace you
where I am concerned."

The acquisition of the Bürgerreuth site and the formation of the
Administrative Committee having disposed satisfactorily of the
theatre question for the time being, Wagner could now turn his attention to a more personal affair. On the 1st February he acquired
from the brothers Stahlmann, at a cost of 12,000 gulden, the plot
of land, extending to more than three Tagewerke, on which he intended to build his future home. On the 10th February he sent
Muncker, who had undertaken to take charge of the preliminary
operations, the most precise instructions and a plan for the lay-
out of the ground. The place for the house was indicated exactly.
From the street to the house, with its two side-buildings, there was
to run a broad drive flanked by chestnut trees, and, on either side of
these, fruit and vegetable gardens shut off by hedges and enclosed
at the extremities by shrubberies and pine trees. The pleasure garden was to be at the rear of the house (between this and the Schloss
garden), with a big circular lawn in the centre, to be dotted later
with flower beds and adorned with noble plane trees, catalpas and
so on. Seclusion was to be obtained by thick shrubberies with pines
and firs at the corners. Evidently it was almost as easy for Wagner

to design a house and grounds as to shape the domestic and foreign policy of a kingdom.

As regards the theatre he had some notion, of course, of the financial difficulties ahead of him; but, as he told his Bayreuth friends, he was sustained by the depth of his artistic conviction and the consciousness of his mission, and above all by the heartening fact that he had by his side such a stalwart as Feustel. "Had I not found you", he wrote to him, "you with all your qualities of mind and character, I would perhaps have recoiled from facing the difficulties of my task"; and he sees the hand of Fate in Feustel being just who and what and where he is.[1] From his countrymen in general, he told Pusinelli, he does not expect much support for an idea so elevated as that of Bayreuth: their minds are too limited, too local. "But it will come about some day, if perhaps only through Russian, American and other subsidies." He had overlooked Turkey, the Sultan of which set an example to some of the German crowned heads. "The German Emperor", Liszt wrote to Princess Wittgenstein in November, 1872,

> "the Grand Duchess Hélène [of Russia], Madame Meyendorff and your daughter have benevolently subscribed for Patronatscheine; also the Sultan, to the extent of 3,000 thalers. But so far the German Empress, their Royal Highnesses of Weimar,[2] Queen Olga of Württemberg and many of their august cousins of both sexes have refrained, not without exhibiting some ill-will towards the scheme itself."

In a passage in a letter to Pusinelli that was omitted from the official issue of his correspondence, Wagner, in February, had asked his old Dresden friend, who was Court Physician to Prince George of Saxony, to see what help he could get for him from the royal house of Wettin. Pusinelli broached the matter with the Minister Aglarni, who replied thus on the 30th March:

> "In reply to your letter of today, I inform you herewith that I have conversed with Prince George regarding the Wagner performances in Bayreuth, and of course I have been obliged to hear in reply, 'How can I subscribe to such an undertaking?' In spite of my suggesting that we must not expect atonement [for his sins of 1849] from the man since he affords us through his works so much endless enjoyment, I dared

---

[1] Wagner's letters to Feustel, Muncker and others of his Bayreuth helpers are collected in RWBB.

[2] This seems to conflict with 'Wagner's assurance to Pusinelli in the preceding February that the Grand Duke of Weimar had already subscribed.

not come forward again with a plea for a subscription to a share. I hoped, however, to have an opportunity perhaps later to return to the matter. This has not occurred so far. Should you find the Prince in a good humour some time, then I would advise you really to make an attempt. We have time after time been enthusiastic over Wagner's music, but I believe (*entre nous soit dit*) that 'Peter's Pence' will be supported before Wagner will!" [3]

So that after nearly a quarter of a century Wagner, for the Saxon Court, was simply the indocile Royal Kapellmeister who had sinned against it in 1849. He was still expected to humiliate himself publicly, to "make atonement", before he could be graciously taken back into the fold.

2

Nor were Wagner's troubles with Munich over. In March, Düfflipp made another application for the score of *Siegfried*, accompanied by a plain reminder that the work was the King's property under the agreement of 1864. For Wagner there was now no way of escape except by a flat untruth. So far he had only *implied* that the score was not complete: now he says so in black and white. At the moment, he wrote to Düfflipp on the 27th, he was engaged, in circumstances of great difficulty, in sketching out the last act of the *Götterdämmerung*. When this was finished, however, he would proceed to the scoring of "the whole of the remainder, including the final part of *Siegfried*", at such times as his sorely damaged health would permit. [4] It would then be his highest pride to send his Majesty the autograph score. The contract of 1864 for the sale of the *Ring*, he continues, had been drawn up at the suggestion of the then Court Secretary Hofmann, as merely "a form for tranquillising public opinion". Since that time, however, the King had graciously assured

---

[3] RWAP, p. 245.
[4] See his letter to Düfflipp in RWLD, pp. 330–2. Relations between Wagner and the King were more strained at this time than they had ever been since the *Rhinegold* days of 1869. On the 14th March Wagner had told Düfflipp that he was doubtful whether he ought to invite Ludwig to the ceremony of the laying of the foundation-stone of the theatre. The Court Secretary replied on the 25th that such an invitation was "not desired". He had seen the King, he said: "I was told that the extremely disagreeable sentiment evoked by your refusal of the orchestral score of *Siegfried* still persists, and that this dis-harmony can be removed only by the fulfilment of his Majesty's wish". Wagner replied in a very irritable tone: it is "highly unjust", he says, to say he is "refusing" the score: "this score does not exist, at any rate in a complete form".

him that it was completely inoperative; and Wagner can only express his regret that it should be brought up again now, and that he has to remind Düfflipp of the King's express assurance to him that his sole concern had been to relieve him of all worldly cares and set him free to devote his life to his art. But all this is not only mendacity — for the score of *Siegfried,* as we have seen, had been completed as long ago as February, 1871 — but chicanery. It was technically true that Ludwig's central purpose in 1864 had been to secure Wagner's livelihood, and so enable him to concentrate on the *Ring,* through the medium of a legal formality that would satisfy his ministers and not give occasion for public criticism. But it is also true that it had been understood on both sides that the work was to be produced in Munich. Wagner himself, in the "programme" he drew up less than a month after his first meeting with the King, had set down the *Ring* for performance in the Munich Court Theatre in 1867/8; and it was because he had been so filled with enthusiasm by that prospect that he had decided to suspend work on the *Meistersinger* in order to complete the tetralogy.[5] Ludwig had performed his part in the compact with not only the most scrupulous fidelity to its letter but the utmost generosity as regards the spirit of it. It was Wagner who took advantage of a tacit understanding — based, however, on certain definitely implied conditions — to evade carrying out his own part in the compact as soon as it became inconvenient for him; and the circumstances that had brought about that inconvenience had been entirely of his own creation. He could make out a superficially plausible case for himself by pleading that the King had always been at one with him in desiring that his works should be produced "in accordance with his intentions". What he refrained from recalling, but the King could not be expected to forget, was that at the back of the minds of both of them in 1864 and 1865 had been that this meant "in Munich". Until the circumstances had arisen that sprang an uncrossable gulf between himself and Munich there had never been a suggestion on his part that he had ever meant, by "a production according to my intentions", "a production far away from Munich in a theatre of my own".

---

[5] See Vol. III, pp. 228–9.

THE LIFE OF RICHARD WAGNER

3

For a time the course of events was anything but smooth. In February Ludwig had "caused it to be intimated to Wagner", Du Moulin tells us, that it had been brought to his notice that the cost of Bayreuth would greatly exceed the estimate of 300,000 thalers, that he was displeased at the talk in the Bayreuth papers about Wagner's domestic luxury, and that he had a "right by purchase" to the score of *Siegfried*. Thereupon Cosima begged Richard to abandon his plan for his new home and cancel the purchase of the site. "He said, however, 'the *Siegfried* score is not completed,[6] and I know the source of these allegations, of which I have heard nothing'." He plunged into one of his moods of exasperated defiance: he would demand an explanation of the Bayreuthers, and, if it were unsatisfactory, give up the whole theatre scheme, "for", says Cosima, "we cannot hold on if the King himself works against us." He talked of selling the copyright of the *Ring* outright to Schott, washing his hands of Bayreuth, and retiring with Cosima to Italy. That petulant mood, of course, did not last long; the Bayreuth idea was by this time too much part and parcel of his being for him to be capable of abandoning it, and as regards his livelihood he could now feel tolerably safe apart from the King. It was at this time, indeed, that he signed a contract placing the whole of his business affairs in the hands of a firm of Mainz agents, Voltz and Batz, with whom, by the way, he was to have a good deal of trouble during the coming years, for Wagner was one of those men who seem to attract trouble as a tall tree attracts the lightning, without anyone being able to say definitely whether it is the lightning's fault or the tree's.

But the latest breeze from Munich blew over as so many others had done. Elsewhere the Vereine seemed to be shaping fairly well, and Wagner was too much occupied with Wotan-like visions of the future to worry over-much about the Fasolts and Fafners of the present. He might declaim to Cosima about abandoning Bayreuth; but all the same he was hard at work at this very time on the draft of the speech he was to make at the laying of the foundation-stone

---

[6] Cosima must have known perfectly well that this was untrue. Wagner, of course, could always pretend that the score was not really "completed", in the sense that he might still change his mind about a bit of orchestration here or there. There are hints of some casuistry of this kind later when he was cornered over the delivery of the score.

of the theatre, while Cosima was wrestling with the problem, no less grave, of the new dress she should wear on the great occasion. And all the while there kept coming from this town or that news of help for the Bayreuth scheme which, if not decisive in itself, meant at any rate a little more towards the sum required. The Budapest Philharmonic, for instance, under Richter, gave a concert for Bayreuth that netted about 1,000 gulden.

4

In the belief that he would be able to hold his first festival in 1873, and would consequently be rehearsing in Bayreuth in the summer of 1872, Wagner had engaged rooms at the Fantaisie [7] for himself and his large establishment for some weeks onward from April of that year. As soon as it became manifest that operations could not begin until 1874 at the earliest he calmly countermanded the requisition, and seems to have been surprised and hurt when the proprietor, one Riederer, protested vigorously against this free-and-easy way of doing business; but in the end he saw the matter from the hotel-keeper's point of view and agreed to make the Fantaisie his headquarters from the 1st May.

His fifty-ninth birthday, the 22nd May, had been fixed as the date for the laying of the foundation-stone of the theatre; and the ceremony was to be rounded off by a performance of the Ninth Symphony in the old opera house. He said his last sad good-bye to his dear Triebschen on the 22nd April; travelling by way of Munich and Darmstadt, he was in Bayreuth two days later. In Darmstadt he had a conference with Brandt; and it was apparently on the latter's urging that he asked the Leipzig architect Otto Brückwald to take charge of the theatre plan in place of the Berlin Neumann, who had shown himself too dilatory.

On the 25th Nietzsche paid his last visit to Triebschen. He found Cosima in the final stage of packing, the dismantled house wrapped in gloom, the children silent, the servants weeping, the dog too miserable to eat. The piano happened to be still there, and Nietzsche tried to ease his own and Cosima's heart with an improvisation. For him, as for the others, it was the end of a marvellous chapter. He had

---

[7] A hotel adjoining the Fantaisie Schloss and park, which in Wagner's time belonged to Duke Alexander of Württemberg.

been to Triebschen twenty-three times in the last three years; his days there, in spite of all the cross-currents swirling confusedly in the obscure depths of him, had been the happiest he had ever known or was ever to know, golden days which he could never recall in the poisoned later years without a catch in the throat. "What they mean for me!", he wrote to Gersdorff on the 1st May. "What would I have been without them? I am happy to have fixed that Triebschen world for myself in my book [*The Birth of Tragedy*]". And in the *Ecce Homo* of 1888, written long after he had severed the last intellectual link between himself and Wagner, he speaks of his "intimate relationship with Richard Wagner" as

> "that of all the recreations of my life which has refreshed me by far the most profoundly and heartily. . . . All my relations with other human beings I surrender without a pang; but at no price would I have the days at Triebschen, those days of confidence, of cheerfulness, of sublime incidents, of *profound* moments, blotted from my life. What other people may have experienced with Wagner I do not know; but no cloud ever floated over *our* sky."

That, of course, is a slight exaggeration: some of the less pleasant details of his experiences at Triebschen had faded in the golden haze and the diminished perspective of reminiscence. But his letters of all periods are proof enough of what Wagner had meant to him at that time and what his own spirit owed to Wagner. Writing to Peter Gast a couple of months after Wagner's death in 1883 his mind went back once more to the divine days in the house by the Lake, especially the time when *Siegfried* was being completed. "At that time we loved each other and hoped everything *for each other*: it was truly a profound love, without a single *arrière-pensée*." [8] He had, in truth, learned more from Wagner than he was ever willing to admit in public, for he was never greatly given to acknowledging his intellectual debts to forerunners. [9]

Cosima and the family joined Wagner at the Fantaisie on the 30th, the day after the first sod had been turned on the theatre site. [10]

---

[8] NGB, IV, 156–7.

[9] In his private unburthenings to Gast he could afford to exhibit the imperfection of his knowledge of music and of musical aesthetic, and hint at how much of what he did understand of them he had learned in Triebschen. See, for instance, his letters of the 2nd April, 1883 and 19th November, 1886, in NGB, IV, 148, 269.

[10] Writing in 1886, Richard Pohl (RWJK, p. 82) said that "Triebschen is an entail, and so, unfortunately, cannot be sold. Wagner wanted at first to make the little

After a conference with Brandt and Brückwald the pair went on the 6th May to Vienna, where Wagner was to conduct, on the 12th, a concert under the auspices of the local Wagner-Verein for the benefit of the Patronat fund. Once more the coming of the most talked-about man in Europe after Bismarck turned the town upside down. The concert hall was packed with an audience that had cheerfully paid unprecedented prices for their seats. The programme was more or less on the now familiar lines, the main features of it being the Eroica symphony, Wotan's Abschied und Feuerzauber, and the first performance anywhere of the now familiar *"Tannhäuser* Overture and New Venusberg Music" — i.e., the amalgamation at a certain point of the old overture with the new ballet music written for the Paris production of 1861. In the usual speech afterwards, and again at the banquet that followed, Wagner enlarged once more on the theme of the national character of his work. It goes without saying that the leading musical critics of the city distinguished themselves by the fatuity and the malice of their remarks on the concert. Hanslick sagely opined that if all operas were to be composed in the style of *Tristan* their audiences would soon be in the lunatic asylum, whither they would be followed by the conductors and the orchestral players if these made a habit of the Wagnerian elasticity of tempi. Speidel, unable to deny the enthusiasm of the audience, drew attention to the remarkable fact that Wagner was obviously older than when he was last in Vienna, his hair greyer, his body thinner, while "his features betrayed more markedly than ever the doctrinaire, the pedant, the Saxon schoolmaster". But even the Hanslicks and the Speidels were perhaps beginning to feel that it would be prudent to hedge a little: in their less unintelligent moments they may have had an uncomfortable premonition of the sorry fate in store for them — to be forgotten

---

property his own, but could not: consequently there seems no hope of acquiring this classical spot . . . and maintaining it intact for posterity."

In 1899 the property came into the hands of the German-American opera singer Minnie Hauk and her husband Baron von Hesse-Wartegg, who altered the house a good deal from what it had been in Wagner's time. After the singer's death in 1929 a movement was set on foot in Lucerne to acquire the property for the town. The entail having been legally set aside, Triebschen was bought towards the end of 1931 for 350,000 francs, and converted into a Richard Wagner museum at a further first cost of some 150,000 francs. The interior of the house was reconstructed to correspond, as far as possible, with its appearance in Wagner's time, as described in Cosima's letter of the autumn of 1866 to the King.

for their own sakes and preserved for all time merely as poor dead flies in the Wagnerian amber.[11]

5

Cosima and Wagner were back again in the Fantaisie on the 14th, Richter with them. On the 20th and 21st four rehearsals for the concert of the 22nd were held. The streets of little Bayreuth were already becoming crowded with enthusiasts from all parts of Europe, among them Madame Mouchanoff, Nietzsche, Gersdorff, Rohde, Cornelius, Porges, Countess Schleinitz, Countess Dönhoff and Malwida von Meysenbug. The ceremonies of the 22nd began with the laying of the foundation-stone of the theatre at eleven in the morning. Bayreuth seems to have jumped at this first grand opportunity to show its visitors what it could do in the way of vile weather and what it could not do in the way of providing amenities for the faithful. Conveyances being scarce, many devotees had to trudge to the hill on foot, through a rain that had been coming down pitilessly since eight o'clock. On the hill itself the clay was ankle-deep, so that those who had been fortunate enough to obtain carriages preferred to watch the proceedings under shelter of these. Naturally the open-air ceremony was cut down to the indispensable minimum. A military band played the *Huldigungsmarsch* and the stone was duly lowered into its place, along with a metal casket containing a telegram from the King —

"From the depth of my soul I send you, dearest Friend, my warmest and sincerest congratulations on this day that is so significant for all Germany. May blessing and good fortune attend the great undertaking during the coming year. Today I am more than ever one with you in spirit",

— and a neatly-turned quatrain of Wagner's own:

> Hier schliess' ich ein Geheimnis ein,
> Da ruh' es viele hundert Jahr':
> So lange es verwahrt der Stein,
> Macht es der Welt sich offenbar.

("Here I enclose a secret: here may it repose many a hundred years. So long as the stone preserves it, so long will it manifest itself

---

[11] Summaries of the Press criticisms will be found in BWSW, p. 83 ff.

to the world"). He struck three blows with the hammer, said "Be blessed, my stone, stand long and hold firm!", and turned away, deathly pale, with tears in his eyes. Other hammer-blows followed, from Feustel and the other Bayreuth stalwarts, the architect, a number of patrons, and the singer Niemann, whose gigantic stature gave the spectators the impression of some god of the sagas laying about him with his hammer.

The remainder of the ceremony had to be transferred to the old theatre, whither Wagner drove through the still pelting rain with Nietzsche and one or two other intimates. "He was silent", says Nietzsche in a memorable passage in his *Richard Wagner in Bayreuth,*

"turning inward on himself a look which it is beyond the power of words to describe. . . . We know that in moments of supreme danger or at decisive turning-points in their lives men see their whole life's experience concentrated into one swift inner vision, and have an intensified perception of all that is recent and all that is most remote. What must Alexander the Great have seen in that moment when he caused Asia and Europe to be drunk out of the same cup? But the spectacle before Wagner's inward eye that day — how he became what he is, what he will be — that is something which we who are nearest to him can realise to some degree as we gaze back; and only outwards from that look of his is it possible for us, for our own part, to comprehend his great deed, and, by the help of that comprehension, to stand security for the fruitfulness of it."

Wagner and his personal party entered the theatre at mid-day. On the stage was the choir, made up of contingents from various towns, the orchestra, which had come from all parts at his invitation for nothing more than the players' expenses, and the quartet of singers — Marie Lehmann (a sister of the more famous Lilli), Wagner's niece Johanna Jachmann-Wagner, Niemann and Betz. In the boxes that had once been adorned by the eighteenth century Markgrave and his pompous little court sat an audience representing everything that was best in Germany in the matter of personal devotion to Wagner and belief in the greatness of his ideal. He rose and delivered the speech that had been intended for the actual stone-laying; hence the references in it to the building that was to rise on the hill, a building of modest material and simple construction, he said, but planned as no other had ever been to bring home to the audience the full meaning of what it would see and hear.

If his venture was to succeed it would have to be, could only be, through the re-birth of the true German spirit, in which he still placed his faith, despite many disappointments. The undertaking had been described in many quarters as "a National Theatre in Bayreuth". But it was not that, for there was as yet no German nation and no German theatre in his sense of the words: what was about to come into being in Bayreuth was simply the realisation of "the thought of a single individual" and of those who had loved and understood him, a thought that some day might bring into being the real, the prouder theatre of the German Folk.[12]

His address over, the choir sang the "Wacht auf!" chorus from the *Meistersinger*, Feustel called for a "Hoch!" for the King of Bavaria and another for the Kaiser, and singers, players and spectators left the theatre to refresh themselves for the great deed of the day, the performance of the Ninth Symphony. They reassembled at five o'clock. The proceedings began with the inevitable *Kaisermarsch*, with, of course, the choral ending, which was sung with great fervour. There had been an awkward moment or two at one of the rehearsals of the Symphony when Johanna Wagner, true to the traditions of her species, showed an imperfect acquaintance with the contralto part: Wagner had to call on one of the ladies of the choir to set her on the right path. But at the performance all went well; under Wagner's direction the familiar work seemed to everyone to yield up its whole secret for the first time. When it was over the tension relaxed: there were celebrations of Joy in other senses than those of Schiller and Beethoven in the Sonne and Reichsadler and Goldener Anker Hotels, where Wagner went round from group to group with well-chosen words of thanks and encouragement, and toasts were drunk to the King of Bavaria, the town of Bayreuth and the German spirit.

6

It was midnight before he could drive back to the Fantaisie, exhausted, but proud and happy, no doubt, as he had never been in all his life before. Soon after eight o'clock the next morning he was at a meeting of the Patrons and the heads of the Vereine, discussing in detail the plans for the festival of 1874. One point on which he

---

[12] The speech is given in full in RWGS, IX, 326 ff.

laid special stress was the necessity for keeping the tickets out of the hands of the professional speculators: the festival audience was to be not a mob of rich sensation-hunters but a forgathering of enthusiasts animated by his own ideal. Within a few hours of the end of the meeting the visitors had almost all departed their several ways. Bayreuth relapsed into its old-world slumber; and Wagner could take a sorely-needed rest before setting out on the next stage of his pilgrimage, the quest for singers.

Two great figures whose lives had been inseparably interwoven with his for many years had been absent from all these solemn ceremonials and rejoicings. Bülow, for obvious reasons, could not be there; but Wagner had done his best to bring Liszt to Bayreuth. He broke the long silence between them with a letter of the 18th May to Liszt, who was at that time in Weimar. He had drifted back into the nomad life of his youth, wandering about restlessly from one friend to another in one country and another. It was not merely that he found the company of his Carolyne, now in Rome and more deeply immersed than ever in religious mysticism, a trifle oppressive, but that he could not do without the adoration of young and pretty female devotees and the flattering society of the titled ones of this world. He still had a soft spot in his heart for quiet little Weimar and its Grand Duke, and was probably more really comfortable and happy there than in any of the larger towns of Germany or Italy. The Olga Janini affair, which had taken so awkward a final turn for him, was now closed,[13] and he had come under the strong hand of the beautiful Baroness Olga von Meyendorff, by all accounts a haughty young lady who would brook no infringement of her proprietary rights in him. Princess Wittgenstein, who knew how neglectful he was, when left to himself, of his health and the most ordinary comforts, asked his and her old friend Adelheid von Schorn to mother him unobtrusively during his stay in Weimar; and it is to Adelheid that we are indebted for certain interesting details about the relations between Wagner and Liszt at this time.

Wagner's letter of the 18th runs thus:

"My great and dear Friend — Cosima maintains that you would not come even if I were to invite you. We should have to endure that, as we have had to endure so many things! But I cannot forbear to invite you. And what is it I cry to you when I say 'Come'? You came into

[13] The full story of this piquant episode in Liszt's life is told in NML, Chapter IX.

my life as the greatest man whom I could ever address as an intimate friend; you gradually went apart from me, perhaps because I had become less close to you than you were to me. In place of you there came to me the re-incarnation of your inmost being, and completed my longing to know you very close to me. So you live in full beauty before me and in me, and we are one beyond the grave itself. You were the first to ennoble me by his love; to a second, higher life am I now wedded in *her*, and can accomplish what I should never have been able to accomplish alone. Thus you could become everything to me, while I could remain so little to you: how immeasurably greater is my gain!

"If I now say to you 'Come', I thereby say to you 'Come to yourself!' For it is yourself that you will find. Blessings and love to you, whatever decision you may come to! — Your old friend,

"Richard".

It could not have been merely the fear of offending his violently anti-Wagnerian Carolyne that kept Liszt from accepting the invitation, for he went to Bayreuth not long after this. Apparently the old wound dealt him by Wagner and Cosima still pained him, and he had been particularly grieved by the prospect of his daughter changing her faith; and while he would have been glad to talk these and other matters over with them he may well have felt that the best time for that was not during the turmoil of the ceremonies in Bayreuth. Fräulein von Schorn, who was in the closest touch with him at this time, thought, however, that had Wagner's letter reached him a day earlier he would have accepted the invitation, so great was his longing to see his daughter and his friend again. Adelheid had intended to travel to Bayreuth with a contingent of choral singers from Weimar; but these were found to be unnecessary, Wagner having been able to get as many as he wanted from other towns.[14] But Liszt pressed her to go for all that, for his sake as well as her own. He gave her a letter for Cosima; his reply to Wagner he entrusted to Baroness Meyendorff.

Wagner took Liszt's failure to appear in ill part, and, as usual when crossed, behaved badly. On the evening of the 21st there was a small party of intimates at the Fantaisie, which Adelheid attended in company with Malwida von Meysenbug. "Wagner entered", she says,

---

[14] She sang in the chorus, however. It was composed, she says, rather of "soloists" than of "choristers". The orchestra of more than a hundred contained the pick of German players, with Wilhelmj as leader.

"when the guests were already assembled. Having greeted some of his acquaintances he suddenly confronted me, gave me his hand, and said, 'And whom have we here?' One of the bystanders replied, 'Fräulein von Schorn, from Weimar'. He let go of my hand, turned on his heel, and walked away. It was not an agreeable situation; I did not know whether I ought to leave or stay. But the next moment the explanation dawned on me: the trouble was not my innocent self but Liszt. Wagner was aware that I had brought Cosima a letter from her father, and imagined this to be the answer to his invitation: he had been deeply offended at Liszt's not having come, and I had to pay for it. . . . Wagner had to take Fräulein von Meysenbug and myself in to dinner. The table was a long one: he sat at the narrow end, with us two on either side of him on the long sides. He took care during the whole meal not only not to speak to me but even to look at me. I was so guiltless in the matter of Liszt's absence that I could not take Wagner's bad treatment of me very much to heart; rather was I amused at this small-mindedness on the part of the great man."

Liszt's reply was handed to him by Baroness Meyendorff the next day, during the interval at the concert. "She was treated even worse than I had been", says Adelheid.[15] On the strength of Cosima's diary Du Moulin reports that

"her father's letter was very beautiful, but the lady, unfortunately, very disagreeable. And so the one person of all who ought to have been at Bayreuth was absent, being represented by a lady who claimed for herself, as it were, ambassadorial rights, and delayed the outer reconciliation still further by her reports of supposed slights."

At this time there was no love lost between Cosima and the Baroness, who seems to have treated her *de haut en bas;* later, however, she seems to have recognised Cosima's great qualities in handsome fashion. It could only have been the fact that "the spy", as Cosima called her at that time, was the bearer of Liszt's letter that soured Wagner's temper. It ran thus:

"Dear, noble Friend — I have been too deeply moved by your letter to be able to thank you in words; but I hope from the bottom of my heart that every shadow, every consideration that keeps me fettered far away will disappear, and that we shall soon meet again. When that happens, you will see clearly for yourself how inseparable my soul remains from both of you, how in my inmost being I live again your 'second' higher life, in which you will accomplish what would have

---

[15] Her story is given in SZM, p. 212 ff.

been impossible for you alone. This is God's grace to me: God's blessing be with you both, as my whole love is."

And in a postscript:

"It goes against the grain with me to send these lines through the post. They will be handed to you on the 22nd May by a lady who has been for several years acquainted with my thoughts and feelings." [16]

---

[16] There are some small differences between the text of the letters as given in the *Briefwechsel zwischen Wagner und Liszt* and in the sixth volume of *Franz Liszts Briefe*.

CHAPTER XVIII

POLEMICS IN 1872

1

MEANWHILE THINGS had been going anything but well with Nietzsche's idealistic effort to identify the work of Wagner and the cause of Bayreuth with the essence of Greek tragedy in what he regarded as its best days. *The Birth of Tragedy out of the Spirit of Music* was having a very rough crossing on its maiden voyage. The book fell between a number of stools. The musician pure and simple would wonder what Aeschylus and Sophocles and Archilochus and Socrates and Apollo and Dionysus were doing in the operatic galley. The average metaphysician would not be at home in either philology or music. The specialist in Greek antiquity would keep asking himself what connection there could possibly be between his own science and the Schopenhauerian philosophy on one side and the Wagnerian aesthetic on the other. The common herd of literary reviewers would not know what to make of so unusual a book, while the specialist journals would sniff at its reckless apriorism.[1] Both the Nietzschean and the Wagnerian devotees of today are scandalised at the lukewarm reception given the book by the Press; yet it was all perfectly natural. Rohde tried to place an article on it in the *Literarisches Centralblatt*: it was declined there, but ultimately found a home in the issue of the *Norddeutsche Allgemeine Zeitung* of the 26th May.[2] Nietzsche's other professional colleagues for the most part either maintained a diplomatic silence towards the book both in public and in private or were frankly scornful of it. We shall see later what were the reactions of the great Ritschl, Nietzsche's master at Bonn and Leipzig, to whose

---

[1] Nietzsche himself, in a letter of the 23rd November, 1871 to Rohde, said he feared that "the philologists would not read the work because of its music, the musicians because of its philology, the philosophers because of its music and philology." In this he was wrong. The book was read by all and sundry; the trouble was that none of them could accept its facts or its conclusions as a whole.

[2] It can be read today in the second volume of Rohde's *Kleine Schriften* (1901), pp. 340–351.

glowing recommendation the young man had owed his professorship at Basel.

No one, however, was prepared for the storm that broke over Nietzsche's head on the 1st June, when there appeared a savage frontal attack on the book by another budding philologist, Ulrich von Wilamowitz-Möllendorff, who only a few years before had been sitting on the benches of the Pforta school with Nietzsche. The "Zukunftsphilologie" in the title of his pamphlet [3] was a jape at the "Zukunftsmusik" of which Wagner was supposed in some quarters to be the quack apostle. Wilamowitz laid about him with all the gay abandon of cocksure youth. He threw text after text, authority after authority at Nietzsche's head, drew his attention to all sorts of things he had either not known or had overlooked, differed from him as to the application of this text or that, and generally raked him fore and aft with a machine gun fire that never stopped for a moment. Though much of the shooting missed the target by a mile, and was obviously prompted more by a schoolboy delight in throwing things in general than by a disinterested desire to establish the truth about anything in particular, he scored enough small debating points to do Nietzsche much harm. The tone of the brochure was ill-mannered, Wilamowitz joining up in this respect with the main line of tradition of German controversy between rival scholars; and in his eagerness to confute everything that Nietzsche had said he exposed himself in turn to cross-fire from several points.

As Nietzsche was reluctant to plunge into what was sure to be an acrimonious wrangle, Rohde, though by nature the least polemical of men, chivalrously undertook his defence in a pamphlet of his own which appeared in the following autumn. [4] In this he in turn tripped Wilamowitz up on several points of scholastic fact. It goes without saying that the enemy countered vigorously a few months later with another brochure. [5] By that time the controversy had degenerated into nothing much better than a canine free-for-all; and it calls for more patience than most students possess today to go back to it and try to discover, in this chaos of snapping teeth and

---

[3] WMZP.

[4] RA. The manufactured title of it, *Afterphilologie*, was a riposte in kind to his adversary's coinage of *Zukunftsphilologie*.

Nietzsche, in a letter of the 16th July (NGB, p. 335 ff), supplied Rohde with a quantity of ammunition to be used against Wilamowitz.

[5] WMZZS.

angry yelps and snarls, what it really was that the little animals were rending each other over.[6]

One unpleasant after-effect of this war of words was that Nietzsche found himself, before long, losing some of his pupils at Basel and, for the moment, acquiring few new ones. Parents sent their sons to Basel to train for the career of philologist, not to be suckled on a frothy mixture of Wagnerism and Schopenhauerism: and while it is true that Nietzsche had no intention of infusing these elements into his university teaching, the academic world could be pardoned for being reluctant to take the risk. In the circumstances it was natural that Greek scholars who were asked to recommend a teacher for some budding philologist or other should suggest a professor in some other town who, they would feel, could be more implicitly trusted to stick to his last than seemed to be the case with their gifted young colleague at Basel. Rohde's own professional advancement appeared likely, for a time, to be prejudiced by his having publicly thrown in his lot with Nietzsche.

2

Wagner did not improve matters for either Nietzsche or himself by entering the lists. In one of the November issues of the *Musikalisches Wochenblatt* there appeared under his signature an *Open Letter to Friedrich Nietzsche, Professor of Classical Philology at the University of Basel*. He had just read, it appeared, Wilamowitz's pamphlet, and he felt it was high time that a really authoritative word was spoken not only on the subject of Greek tragedy but on that of academic philology in general. He began with a modest tribute to his own qualifications to speak that decisive word. True, he could boast of no Greek now; but never since German education began could there have been a boy more attracted to classical antiquity than he had been at the Dresden Kreuzschule, that is to say, from about his ninth to his fourteenth year! So ardently had he

---

[6] Wilamowitz developed into one of the most distinguished Greek scholars of his epoch. Charles Andler, who apparently knew him personally, tells us that "when one questions the great Hellenist about it [his controversy with Nietzsche and Rohde] today, he does not hesitate to describe it as a sin of his youth." (ANVP, II, 291, *note*). Andler himself calls the *Zukunftsphilologie* "brutal". It is amusing to note that Rohde, for his part, spoke of his own brochure in later life as "a youthful folly". The editor of his *Kleine Schriften* evidently did not think it worth reprinting in 1901.

devoted himself to Greek, indeed, that he had almost neglected his Latin. His enthusiasm for Hellas had so deeply impressed his master, Dr. Sillig — "who, I hope, is still living" — that he actually urged young Richard to adopt philology as his profession.[7] But alas, the passion for Greek had been killed in him by the unintelligent methods of his teachers in the two Leipzig schools he had attended from his fourteenth to his eighteenth years: "something had been suppressed in me by a fatally wrong discipline".

In the course of his life, he went on to say, he had come upon musicians of all sorts who knew Greek very well but could not apply it to their own art, whereas he, "hampered" as he was in his "access to the antique" by his ignorance of the language, had been able to shape for himself out of the spirit of antiquity an ideal art-world of his own. The inference, he claimed, was obvious: the German teachers of Greek have no more understanding of the true antique spirit than German teachers of French have of French history and culture, while he, "unhampered" by mere specialist learning, is qualified to speak with full authority on all these subjects. Professional philologists, it appears, are "of no use to anyone but themselves". The crying need of German culture is for some scholar such as Nietzsche to step boldly out of the professorial ranks, scrap the tiresome apparatus of original texts, footnotes and so on, and let daylight in on the true inwardness of the classical world.

Nietzsche, he goes on to say, had accomplished the beneficent deed which *he* had long been waiting for; he had

> "spoken not to his colleagues but to us. . . . This time we are given the text but no notes — from the mountain heights we looked down upon the broad plains, undisturbed by the scuffling of the peasants in the tavern down below."

Of these "scuffling peasants" his readers had a pretty specimen in Dr. Ulrich von Wilamowitz-Möllendorff, who, in his handling of his native tongue, seems to a purist like Richard Wagner "little better than a Berlin street-loafer of the old days staggering from beer to gin." Wagner really despairs of German scholarship when he looks round him at the men of learning; and he exhorts Nietzsche to "step out from a vicious circle" and set things right with "a creative hand".

---

[7] Wagner ran no risk of a correction on this point. Sillig had died in 1855.

From first to last the Letter is the bluster of an incorrigible amateur who lacks even enough familiarity with the subject he is dog-
matising about to be aware of the extent of his own ignorance of
it. Problems of such baffling complexity as the origins of Greek
tragedy and the relations of it to the "Greek soul" are not to be
solved by the easy process of constructing a theory out of one's inner
consciousness with an imperfect knowledge of the historical and
other facts, and then professing to look down one's nose from supernal heights upon the patient collectors and sifters and debaters of
those facts as merely so many stupid louts engaged in a tavern
brawl. Whatever harm had been done to Nietzsche in academic
circles by the attack of Wilamowitz must have been a flea-bite compared to the damage done him by Wagner's maladroit champion-
ship.

3

The scholars' opinion of *The Birth of Tragedy* had been expressed
once for all by Ritschl. No one admired and liked the brilliant young
Graecist more than he did. No one was so sincerely anxious as he
was to help his former pupil to carve out a great career for himself.
But the speculative hot-air of *The Birth of Tragedy* had been more
than he could stand. The book had reached him on the last day of
1871. For a whole month Nietzsche had waited impatiently for his
verdict on it. On the 30th January, unable to contain himself any
longer, he wrote to his old master expressing his pained astonishment at not having heard from him. The tone as well as the substance of the letter must have deepened Ritschl's concern. Of all
books, complained Nietzsche, this of his was the least deserving of
being smothered in silence. For it was a kind of "manifesto". It was
"rich in hope for our understanding of antiquity, rich in hope for
the German nature,[8] even if a certain number of individuals would
have to go down before this." It had been his chief aim to "take possession of the younger generation of philologists", and he would
regard it as a "scandalous sign" if he failed in this.

He was unwise to appeal on grounds such as these for a verdict
from Ritschl, for in the old scholar's eyes he was merely worsening an already bad enough case. Ritschl wrote him very frankly on

---

[8] Once more we see how purely German in its application the book was intended
to be.

the 14th February. Underneath his ironic protestations that he is too old now to begin taking a new view of life and learning, the tone of quiet contempt for Nietzsche's main thesis is unmistakable. The gist of his letter is that historical problems must be settled along historical lines; that Ritschl cannot persuade himself that the world is going to be "redeemed" by any system of philosophy whatever; that he cannot agree to call the natural decline of an epoch or a culture "suicide"; [9] that for his own part he does not intend, at the age of sixty-five, to waste his time and energy in a study of the Schopenhauerian philosophy merely in order to check Nietzsche's fanciful deductions from it — in plain words, that for him a historical-philological subject is a matter pure and simple of historical and philological facts and of conclusions drawn from these, vaporous metaphysical theories of the nature of the universe having no *droit de cité* in that territory. He fears that if the mass of unripe young students follow Nietzsche's lead they will be betrayed into an undervaluation of exact knowledge without acquiring in compensation anything of any value in the sphere of art; and — which must have been the most unkindest cut of all — that while poetry will not be at all benefited by a procedure such as that of Nietzsche the doors of philology will be flung wide open to every sort of dilettantism. [10]

4

Ritschl's finger had lighted unerringly on every weak spot in Nietzsche's book, and most unmercifully on the weakest spot of all, its dilettante handling of the complex, but for all that concrete, problem of the actual origins of Greek tragedy. And Ritschl's views, we may rest assured, were those of practically every Greek scholar who had dipped into the book. [11]

Nietzsche did not reply to Ritschl's letter until the 6th April, and then only in a few words tacked on to talk about other matters. One suspects that in his heart of hearts he must have found the criticisms unanswerable, though his inordinate self-esteem would not allow him to admit this outright. He naïvely pleaded that what he had

[9] The reference is to Nietzsche's theory that Greek civilisation had committed suicide under the "rationalising" influence of Socrates and Euripides.

[10] Ritschl's letter will be found in NGB, III, 104–143.

[11] As, indeed, they are the views of every Greek specialist today: hardly one of them who is concerned solely with the historical problem seems to regard *The Birth of Tragedy* as even worth mentioning as a contribution to the subject.

been driving at would become clearer to Ritschl after he had read the essay he had in hand on *The Future of our Educational Institutions:* anyhow, he ventured to flatter himself, it would be decades yet before the wretched philologists would be capable of understanding a book "so esoteric and in the loftiest sense scientific" as *The Birth of Tragedy.* A few weeks after the publication of the book he had told Gersdorff that he confidently expected it to live through the centuries, "for certain eternal things are said in it for the first time." Today it is read less for its own sake or for any light it throws on its subject as a whole than for Nietzsche's sake and the light it throws on his relations with Wagner and on his own intellectual evolution. Had he not lived to become, as the creator of Zarathustra and the philosopher of the Will to Power, a world-figure of the front rank, *The Birth of Tragedy* would long ago have faded into the darkness that now envelops the bulk of the Wagner-literature of the nineteenth century.

He must be given credit, of course, for his perception that the "Greek mind" had a darker element in it that had been overlooked by the typical Graecists of the eighteenth and early nineteenth centuries, such as Winckelmann and Goethe. His mistake was in linking this up with mostly irrelevant modern phenomena such as Schopenhauerism and Wagnerism. And even as regards the really great feature of the book — the insistence on the significance of the "Dionysian" element both for the Greeks and for the modern world — he had been anticipated by Heine.[12]

Nietzsche's book went quite soon into a second edition: but its success seems to have been for the most part among the Wagnerians. Liszt, Bülow, Schuré, Mathilde Maier, Countess Schleinitz, Malwida von Meysenbug and others of the faithful wrote to congratulate the author on it, but not one of these enthusiasts could be regarded as an authority on Greek origins. Ritschl was right: the doors had been flung wide open to the dilettanti.[13] Wagner's *Open Letter* must have

---

[12] See, on this point, the brilliant study of Heine in E. M. Butler's *The Tyranny of Greece over Germany* (1935), especially pp. 294 ff. Mrs. Butler puts it that "there was very little for Nietzsche to add to this impressive description [i.e. of Dionysus]. He had only to expand, elaborate and analyse three or four pages by the master-magician Heinrich Heine . . . Dionysus, who came late into Greece, came late into Germany too. Heine ushered him in and then left it to Friedrich Nietzsche to see that he got his rights."

[13] Nietzsche's correspondence with Rohde and Ritschl about the book will be found in NGB, Vols. II and III.

supplied the final demonstration of the dangers ahead if the amateurs were to be allowed to claim that difficult questions of scholarship could be settled by them over the heads of the scholars.

5

Pace both the Wagnerians and the Nietzscheans, the philologists were fully justified in their distrust of Nietzsche's airy intuitional method of explaining "the Greek mind". What was basically a matter of scholarship and reasoning had been taken out of its true sphere and made a mere weapon in the strife of contemporary German philosophical, cultural and aesthetic parties. Every German who disliked the culture of his fellow-Germans grasped at *The Birth of Tragedy* as a stick with which to belabour his opponents. Peter Gast, the third-rate composer Nietzsche's laudation of whom has covered him with eternal ridicule, lets us see just why the book made the impression it did on people like himself.[14] "The most secret impulses of culture seemed to be unveiled for us", he wrote in 1908;

> "and when Nietzsche described the Apollonian and Dionysian art-powers as finally succumbing to the utilitarian-rationalistic tendency represented by Socrates, we understood why it is almost impossible for great art to shoot forth and flourish under the dominion of our own culture of erudition and intellect. . . . The *Birth of Tragedy* is a colossal protest of the artistic and heroic man against the will-weakening, instinct-destroying consequences of our Alexandrine culture. . . . Our culture annihilates nature in man: but culture should heighten human nature through restraint." [15]

People have every right to feel that way about the world around them if they are so inclined: what they are not entitled to do is what Gast and Nietzsche and Wagner did, to read back their own contemporary prepossessions and prejudices into ancient Greek life and thought and then claim that the gods of Greece are uttering oracles

---

[14] Gast, whose real name was Heinrich Köselitz, was at that time studying, he tells us, counterpoint and composition under E. F. Richter in Leipzig. "We [i.e., people like himself] felt that no one before had ever seen [as Nietzsche had] into the very depths of the Greek soul." Having already read Schopenhauer and Wagner, they felt they possessed "many of the modern prerequisites for understanding the book." As Gast was eighteen in 1872, the extent of his specialist acquaintance with "the Greek soul" may be imagined.

[15] Gast's Foreword to Vol. IV of NGB, p. xv ff.

through them. That, as Ritschl rightly contended, was dilettantism pure and simple, whether it came from an excellent Greek scholar like Nietzsche or a mere self-complacent amateur like Wagner.

Not the least interesting feature of the case is the uncomfortable suspicion evidently felt not only by loyal friends such as Rohde but by Nietzsche himself that *The Birth of Tragedy* really was, at bottom, just high-flying fancy masquerading as logical demonstration. Rohde recognised all along that to a large extent the book was basically just "poetry", that would appeal or not to the reader according to his willingness or reluctance to poetise the past and the present along the same lines as the author, which meant, in the final resort, whether he accepted or rejected the Schopenhauer-Wagner philosophy and aesthetic. Rohde confessed to a fear that the effect of the book on the ordinary non-mystical reader might be the opposite to what its author had intended. Like Nietzsche, he himself was inclined just then to see all life and art, and ancient Greece, and the present and future of German culture through Wagner's eyes under the intoxicating influence of Wagner's music and out of respect for Wagner's ideal of art. "I have come back from Bayreuth", he had written to Nietzsche after his return from the ceremony of the laying of the foundation-stone of the theatre in May,

> "with the feeling that we have left our *home* behind us there, and that it is a moral obligation on my part to stand by your side as a brother-in-arms, with my smaller strength, in the fight for this highest of all good things." [16]

As a scholar he was well enough aware that the central thesis of *The Birth of Tragedy* lacked substantiation, but he thought the "spirit" of it would be a force for good.[17] He was always conscious of what he called Nietzsche's two natures — the poet and musician in him at odds with the scholar and the thinker, — and he wondered uneasily when, if ever, the two would become harmoniously one.

---

[16] NGB, II, 316.

[17] Rohde's biographer Crusius surmises that his enthusiasm for the "Dionysian" was in large part the product of some experiences of his during a holiday in Italy; the southern sunlight, the southern colour, the freedom of the southern mind from the German "moralic" virus had the same effect on him as they had later on Nietzsche and as they have had before and since on many another visitor from the thicker-blooded north. See CER, pp. 39–40.

Nietzsche himself, in calmer and wiser moments, came to recognise that *The Birth of Tragedy* was more poetry than fact. In a projected Foreword which he discarded when the book went to press, he gave free expression to what Seillière calls the pathological division of his personality that accounts for so many of his oscillations of opinion.[18] "I wish expressly to advise readers of my earlier writings", he wrote,

"that I have abandoned the metaphysical-artistic views which in essence dominate there: they are agreeable but untenable. Any man who allows himself to speak prematurely in public is generally compelled to contradict himself in public."

True enough, as every thinker or artist who lives long enough to outgrow his callow youth is only too well aware: by "speaking in public prematurely" with a *Rienzi* a Wagner is "compelled to contradict himself in public" with a *Tristan* and then a *Parsifal*. And Nietzsche, in his Foreword of 1886 — he calls it "An Attempt at Self-Criticism" — to a new edition of *The Birth of Tragedy*, admitted that even in his own eyes the book no longer looked as good as it had done in 1872, and that the original impulse at the back of it had been not so much to investigate the problem of the origin of Greek tragedy for its own sake and truth's sake as to justify the ways of Wagner and Schopenhauer to men, and to find, by hook or by crook, ammunition to fire at the detested German culture of the years following the founding of the Reich. He admits now that the book was more dogmatic than reasoned, "very convinced and therefore elevating itself above the necessity of demonstration, distrustful even of the *propriety* of demonstration", that it was a sort of "music", "a book for initiates" who, like himself in those days, were "baptised with the name of Music", and that he would have done better.to have said what he had to say "as a poet"; that he had "obscured and spoiled" his "Dionysian presentiments" with "Schopenhauerian formulae", and "ruined the grand Hellenic problem by the admixture of the most modern things." In saying which, and a great deal more to the same effect, he was justifying all the coolness and suspicion his book had met with in 1872. And Wagner's

---

[18] SNWR, p. 81.

intervention damaged not only Nietzsche but himself: the musician's bombastic tone, his claim to be a law-giver in yet another domain in which he had no specialist knowledge, certainly did nothing to correct the impression of him already current, unfortunately, in many German circles, as a Cagliostro whose self-assurance knew no bounds, a megalomaniac who had to have a theatre of his own because those already existing were not good enough for *his* "operas".

As for Nietzsche, it cannot be too strongly stressed that during the late 'sixties and early 'seventies his whole thinking was at the mercy of the musical — that is to say the Wagnerian — side of his being. As early as the summer of 1868 he had told Frau Ritschl that he hoped one day to find

> "some philological matter that can be treated musically; and then I will stammer like a baby and pile up images, like a barbarian lost in dreams in the presence of an antique Venus-head. . . ." [19]

Curt Wachsmuth, the editor of his correspondence with Ritschl, rightly remarks that

> "this looks like the first dawning of the ideas sketched in his Basel lecture of January, 1870 [on *The Greek Music Drama*] and then worked out *in extenso* in *The Birth of Tragedy* of 1871."

The latter book is of interest today chiefly because it shows its author fumbling his way half-blindly towards his Zarathustra *via* his Dionysus; and his own "Attempt at a Self-Criticism" in 1886, with its terminal quotation from what he calls "that Dionysian demon Zarathustra", is at once a summary of all that is poetically attractive in the book and a demonstration of all that is intellectually wrong with it.

7

Another little controversy in which Wagner imprudently involved himself about this time must also have done him considerable harm in quarters not too kindly disposed towards him.

Weissheimer had at last succeeded in getting his *Theodor Körner* produced in Munich, and the Augsburg *Allgemeine Zeitung* of the 31st May had not only described it as showing the Wagnerian influence but had hinted that it owed its acceptance by the Munich The-

---

[19] NGB, III, 52.

atre to Wagner's favour. This Wagner irritably denied in a letter to the paper: his "protection", he said, had indeed been sought for this "work of a former acquaintance", but had been refused by him in 1868 because of "the very dubious quality of the work".

Weissheimer replied to this in an Open Letter in the issue of the 8th June. He disclosed that Wagner had first of all written to him privately at the beginning of the month, asking him to contradict the statement that *he* had had anything to do with the acceptance of *Körner* by the Munich management. This, said Weissheimer, he had been prepared to do at once; but before he could take up his pen he had found in the paper a communication of the same date from Wagner, in which he had not only forestalled Weissheimer's reply but had been rude to the author of the *Allgemeine Zeitung* paragraph, who happened to be completely unknown to Weissheimer. With all this, however, he would not have concerned himself in the least had not Wagner gone further and tried to discredit the success his opera had had. "You have the audacity", he continued,

> "to speak of 1868! After having been unceasingly active for your cause in word, in print, and at the conductor's desk, and after having come to your assistance [20] in the most critical moments of your life, as can be proved by some five-and-twenty of your letters, this 'former young acquaintance of yours' approached you in 1868 with the completed score of *Körner*. Your first word to him was, 'Is your *Körner* really so urgent?', and I soon became aware that so far as you were concerned there was no urgency. You persistently refused to acquaint yourself with the score; and after seven weeks I quitted Munich without your having seen a note of it. And now, without the smallest knowledge even today of my work, you say you repudiate it 'because of its very dubious quality'. . . . You have been in too much of a hurry, as is evident, indeed, from the style, or, to be more precise, the no-style, of your 'cor-

---

[20] Wagner had laid the young man's purse under contribution. Wagner's bad temper in 1872 may not have been uninfluenced by the fact that in 1869 Weissheimer had asked him to return the money he had borrowed. This has recently come to light in some letters of his to Weissheimer offered for sale by the Berlin firm of D. Solomon in 1932. On the 5th August, 1869 we find Wagner angrily protesting against the world's notion that he is "swimming in good fortune": all he is managing to do, it appears, is to "maintain a decent standard of living" and "fulfil his serious obligations". He has been astonished and hurt at Weissheimer's inconsiderate reminder of this ancient debt. At the moment he can send him only thirty louisdor. The balance he will remit at Christmas, if Weissheimer will let him know the full amount, with interest, and his address at that time — "through a third person". The letter was printed, apparently in full, in the *Berliner Tageblatt* of the 28th January, 1932.

rection'. Do not do that again, and cease setting about a man who has done you no harm, and who, in spite of the 'very dubious quality' of your character, will continue to admire your real genius."

The wretched wrangle went on for a fortnight, to the great delight of the scandal-loving Müncheners.[21]

Wagner's next step could have been foreseen. Having put himself in a false position and exposed himself to a damaging rejoinder, he broke out into the usual lamentations over the wickedness of the world towards him. Was it not monstrous that he should be held up in the composition of his *Götterdämmerung* by annoyances of this kind? And when he found the *Allgemeine Zeitung* letters being reprinted not only all over Germany but actually in the *Bayreuther Tageblatt* his self-pity knew no bounds. He asked Feustel, who was personally acquainted with the editor of the Bayreuth paper, to tell the reprobate that henceforth the name of Richard Wagner should be left entirely out of his columns except when it was a matter of a simple report of his activities in the town. If in the future the editor should be anxious to print the truth, the whole truth and nothing but the truth about any matter concerning him — "this Weissheimer incident", for example — all he has to do is to take his inspiration direct from *him*. And when the local editor still declined to toe the line Wagner was angrier than ever at "so wicked a spirit *in loco*" being allowed to rear its head in *his* Bayreuth.

8

It is always a relief to turn from the more paltry to the greater elements in his make-up. There is nothing more heroic in the history of art than his long fight against terrific odds for the ideal he had now set before himself. Every detail of the complicated Bayreuth business had to pass through his hands for many years; and one wonders how ever he found time and strength to conduct the immense correspondence imposed on him, and at the same time to work without haste, without the smallest slackening of mental control, at the exacting score of the *Götterdämmerung*. But these days of endless labour, these sleepless nights, these racking cares about the finance of the great undertaking to which he had pledged himself were al-

[21] RLW, II, 130–1. For the course of events in connection with *Theodor Körner* in 1868 see *supra*, p. 136ff.

ready telling on him. It was about this time that he confided to Cosima his fears that his heart was damaged. The most dread enemy of all was creeping up to the gates of the citadel in the dark. Wagner had, in fact, signed his own death warrant in going to Bayreuth, though his resilient temperament and his indomitable will were able to postpone execution of the sentence for a few years yet.

With the re-opening of the German operatic season he intended to set out on a tour of the theatres in search of likely singers for the *Ring*. Two or three of the rôles he had already been able to cast — that of Siegmund, for instance, which Niemann came to study with him in the Fantaisie in August. But as regards the majority of the *Ring* parts he was as yet quite uncertain; and as he had had practically no first-hand acquaintance with the German theatres, apart from that of Munich, for a good many years, and in a matter of this kind he could rely on no one's judgment but his own, there was nothing for it but to go and spy out the land for himself. Before setting out, however, he had the satisfaction of restoring his relations with Liszt to something like their old footing.

One of his reasons for throwing out fresh feelers may have been Cosima's decision to become a Protestant, a step which she knew would cause her father pain. Be that as it may, late in August Wagner took the advice of good friends like Countess Dönhoff and Madame Mouchanoff, who had been working hard to bring about a rapprochement, to write and ask Liszt if a visit from him would be welcome. Liszt's reply was that he and Cosima could always count on something more than a mere "friendly reception" from him. And so on the 2nd September the pair set out on a three-days' visit to Weimar. There could never have been any doubt that Liszt's heart was with his remarkable daughter and the man towards whose towering genius his loyalty had never faltered. But his spirit had sagged pitifully during the last few years. He could regain the captaincy of his soul as against neither his Princess in Rome, nor the latest feminine influence, that of the masterful young Baroness Meyendorff, nor the tobacco and alcohol on which he had come more and more to rely to numb the pain that the world and his own divided nature had inflicted on him. When Cosima saw him again she was saddened by his "spiritual lassitude", his long fits of silence: even when he tried to make music for them at the piano it sometimes "wouldn't go", as she sorrowfully expressed it.[22] She parted from him again on the 6th September sick and sad at heart; and on the way back to Bayreuth she had to endure in consequence an outburst of "jealous ill-temper", as she describes it in her diary, on Wagner's part, who, in his illimitable need of her, could not bear the thought that a particle of her affection should be expended on anyone but himself.

"Cosima", Liszt wrote to the Princess after his visitors had left,

"is truly *ma terrible fille,* as I once called her, an extraordinary woman, of high merit, raised high above ordinary standards of judgment, and fully worthy of the admiration she inspires in all who know her, commencing with her first husband, Bülow! She has devoted herself absolutely and enthusiastically to Wagner, as Senta did to the Flying Dutchman; and she will be his salvation, for he listens to her and follows her like a clairvoyant."

Six weeks later Liszt was in Bayreuth. Wagner by this time had left the Fantaisie and taken up winter quarters in Wölfel's house in the Dammallee, No. 7; and there Liszt stayed with him from the 15th October to the 21st. He seems to have been rather more cheerful than he had been in Weimar, no doubt because he was unaccompanied and unencumbered. He viewed the site for the theatre and that for Wagner's new house; he played Bach and *Tristan* and his own *Christus,* and was deeply moved when Wagner read him the sketch for *Parsifal:* "it is impregnated with the purest Christian mysticism", he wrote to the Princess. But the tragedy of his later life, his loss of elasticity, his homelessness and loneliness in spite of his never-ceasing migrations from one hospitable hearth to another, were once more all too visible to Cosima. In an expansive moment he talked of settling in Bayreuth, but all three knew in their

---

[22] A satirical portrait of Liszt as he appeared about this time in none too sympathetic or understanding eyes will be found in the novel of Catulle Mendès, *Le Roi Vierge,* to which reference has been made in Chapter II. As I have pointed out elsewhere, the modern legend of the saint-in-a-stained-glass-window Liszt was the creation in part of Princess Wittgenstein, operating through his biographer Lina Ramann, in part of his young piano pupils of the last years of all, who were conscious of how much they owed to his kindness and felt an almost religious love and pity for the pathetic ruin he had manifestly become. To the ordinary spectator of the 1870's he appeared very much as we see him in Mendès's pages, a faintly comic blend of the incomparable pianist, the would-be composer, the Don Juan in a cassock, the womanchaser and the women-chased. Few realised the profound inner tragedy of the tired and disillusioned and self-divided man.

hearts that this would never be. "He is weary, weary", Cosima wrote in her diary. But the closer she and her father drew together in spirit again the more jealous Wagner became. On the eve of her formal reception — on the 31st October — into the Protestant Church he began, she says, to talk about Liszt once more, and in such violent terms that she was struck dumb. "I must indeed have been neglectful in some way or other", she confided humbly to her diary,

"for it to be possible for Richard to continue to be so jealous. But it does not seem to me to be right for him to fly out so violently at me as he does time after time. . . . I could almost wish, for peace' sake, that my father might never come again. I do not do so, because I hope I shall be more fortunate and more tactful in future!"

Richard's increasing load of care left him with no capacity for pity for anyone but himself: even of Cosima's devotion to the children he was sometimes morbidly resentful.

9

The pair set out on their grand tour on the 10th November. It took them to Würzburg, Frankfort, Darmstadt, Mannheim, Stuttgart — where Nietzsche joined them for a couple of days — Karlsruhe, Mainz, Bonn, Magdeburg, Dessau and Leipzig. They returned to Bayreuth on the 15th December, where they found the work on the great building making good progress, thanks to the mild weather that winter.

On the whole the round of the theatres had proved disappointing: Wagner had found sadly little intelligence anywhere. If it happened to be a work of his own that he heard, he hardly knew whether to be angrier at what was left out or at the maltreatment of what was left in. At Karlsruhe, for instance, in the second act of *Tannhäuser* the Knights on one side of the Hall and the Ladies on the other rose *en masse* at one point and reversed their positions on the stage, for all the world, as he said, like the *chassé croisé* of the contredanse. Nor were things in general any better where the works of other composers were concerned. At Cologne the Queen of Night fulminated in the broadest daylight. Occasionally he would come upon a singer who showed some notion of dramatic characterisation or a conductor who had an inkling of the right tempi; but for the most part everything annoyed him to such an extent that he left the theatre in a rage long before the performance had ended or shortly after it had begun. In one place he would find a promising voice allied with the rudiments of a dramatic style, elsewhere a voice without style or style without voice. The bulk of the conductors and producers he thought hopelessly incompetent. Hardly anywhere did he find the smallest perception of the fundamental difference between his own music-drama and "opera". The majority of the German singers had even yet not grasped the vital point that *his* musical-dramatic texture was a continuous one. Their acting powers being too undeveloped for the task thus set them, all they could do was to concentrate on what he called the "effective operatic bits", forcing these out of the picture, coming down to the footlights in prima donna style to hurl their best notes at the heads of the audience, basking in the applause, and letting dramatic verisimilitude and coherence go hang. And the audiences were as Bœotian as the performers; for them too the prima donna and the tenor in their spots of theatrical high-light were practically the only things that really mattered. The only performance he could really praise was one of Gluck's *Orfeo and Euridice* in tiny Dessau.[23]

The tour had been interspersed with the regulation banquets and speeches, but these were no consolation to him for the disappointment and exasperation and fatigue he had undergone. On the whole what left the deepest impression on him was the few hours he spent in Magdeburg. He had not seen that town of his sorrow since 1836. It had hardly changed outwardly since then, and he must have wandered through its well-remembered streets like a phantom Doppelgänger. He showed Cosima the theatre, still in its old form, in which *Das Liebesverbot* had been given its solitary performance; the podium from which he used to conduct, after the manner of those days, in a sky-blue swallow-tailed coat with wrist-ruffles; the street in which Minna had lived; the hotel where he had had an embarrassing meeting with his creditors. How far afield he had gone during the last six-and-thirty years! Riga, London, Paris, Dresden, Zürich, London and Paris again, Biebrich, Vienna, Munich, Triebschen — always in pursuit of an ideal of art and home that

[23] The full story of his experiences is given in an article entitled *A Glance at the German Operatic Stage of Today*, which appeared in the *Musikalisches Wochenblatt* in January, 1873. RWGS, IX, 264 ff.

ever evaded him. And now, in yet another town strange to him, he was fighting desperately to realise his vision in a Germany that denied him both the money and the human material he needed not for his own ends but for the service of art and the glory of his native land.

10

And, as had so often been the case with him in moments of spiritual crisis, and particularly, as we have seen, in the Paris days of 1860/1,[24] the more his lot threw him into the throng of men the more devastating became the sense of his inner loneliness. On this subject he poured out his soul to the King in a letter of the 7th October. He seemed to himself, he said, only a ghost moving about in the crowd among whom his life-course now lay — not a man of flesh and blood like other men but simply the incarnation of an idea, the fulfiller of a destiny imposed on him from birth. He has passed beyond the environment of his earlier years: the people now about his path belong to a fresh generation in which he has no personal roots.

> "Everything is changed: even Germany I hardly recognise any longer. When I travel about to inspect the personnel of the various theatres, with an eye to the choice of singers for our stage festival, everything appears to me just a phantasm of the imagination."

In Bayreuth especially everyone is friendly, even affectionate, towards him; yet he has the feeling that all this has come to him too late, or would have done so had he not won for himself, in this his sixtieth year, his sole consolations, Cosima and his home. He throws out a strong hint that it would be an added solace to him to see his generous benefactor again; but to this the King makes no response. In August he had sent Ludwig not only the fourth and fifth volume of his Collected Writings but a copy, accompanied by a dedicatory poem, of the Orchestral Sketch of the third act of the *Götterdämmerung*. The King thanked him, through Düfflipp, for his gifts, and assured him that it would have been a pleasure to receive him on his birthday (the 25th August) but for the fact that he was spending it at Hohenschwangau with his mother. The young man may perhaps have been slightly displeased to find that not

---

[24] See Vol. III, pp. 79–80.

only was he being fobbed off with the mere Orchestral Sketch but even this, with the exception of a few pages, was not in Wagner's own handwriting.

It may have been the uncomfortable consciousness that all was not going ideally well between them that made Wagner write again in December, describing his emotion on finding himself, during his recent tour of Germany, once more in the hotel in Stuttgart where, in May, 1864, Pfistermeister had brought the message from the King that had altered the whole course of his life. He is distressed, he continues, at the thought that, busy as he is with the preparations for his Bayreuth festival, he cannot send the King, as his Christmas gift this year, "the final working-out of the lately-composed sections of my big work", by which he means the third act of *Siegfried* and the score of the *Götterdämmerung* — thus repeating the fiction that *Siegfried* was not complete in every respect and ready for performance. It was perhaps because Ludwig had a strong suspicion that this was merely fiction that, so far as we know, he did not reply to Wagner's letter.

CHAPTER XIX

DIFFICULTIES IN BAYREUTH

1

To the casual observer all might seem to be going well enough with the plan for the theatre. Thus Liszt could inform the Grand Duke Carl Alexander of Saxe-Weimar that, audacious as Wagner's enterprise might appear, it had every chance of succeeding, and that when it did,

> "Germany will realise the honour of it, and pay just tribute to the transcendent genius of Wagner as poet, musician and dramaturge, and to his long and tenacious efforts to raise dramatic art from the low level to which the old theatrical routine has reduced it."

Mme Mouchanoff could assure her daughter that "Bayreuth is like a new Mecca: every German musician prays towards it." But Wagner himself could cherish no such rosy illusions. He knew that all the prayers and paeans in the world would be of no avail unless the money came forward better than it had been doing. His opinion of the Germans was that they were "bad", while the princes he described to Pusinelli as "very, very bad". In Stuttgart, in November, 1872, he had been approached by Hofrat Hemsen, reader to the King of Württemberg, who told him that his royal master was "well inclined" towards his undertaking. Repeating this to Feustel, Wagner hoped that "something would come of this". But when, in September of the following year, he wrote to Hemsen hinting that the German princes might do something to help him to realise a plan of so noble a national purpose as this, his cry fell on deaf ears. The name of the King of Württemberg does not appear in the register of subscribers for Patronatscheine. The non-German Sultan of Turkey, as we have seen, took ten Scheine, and the anything-but-German Khedive of Egypt sent a handsome donation of £500 sterling. But the German princes, with few exceptions, justified the worst that Wagner had been goaded into saying about them. Nor was he more successful with Bismarck, to whom, in June, 1873, he

sent his recently published brochure regarding the Bayreuth theatre, and asked, not for money, but only for an attitude of sympathy
towards his truly German ideal. He received no answer of any kind.

The financial state of affairs in 1872 may be guessed at from the
fact that the six Patronatscheine taken by the Grand Duke of Mecklenburg towards the end of January, 1873 figure in the register as
Nos. 250–255. By the following April, says Glasenapp, hardly
200 of the 1,300 Scheine needed to set Bayreuth on its feet had been
subscribed for.[1] Feustel was beginning to be decidedly worried about
finance. The Bayreuth town council had not only presented Wagner
with the site for his theatre but pledged itself to give him every
possible assistance in achieving his ideal. But Bayreuth seems to
have been the one town in Germany that was free of municipal debt,
thanks largely to the wise administration of its affairs by such men
as Feustel and Muncker; and these gentlemen's probity, no less
than their business caution, shrank from the thought of entering officially into large commitments with builders, machinists, designers
and so forth without seeing their way clear to meeting their liabili-
ties punctually. And so Feustel, early in 1873, suggested that Wagner should conduct a series of concerts in various towns in aid of the
fund for Bayreuth, for wherever Wagner went he aroused the utmost
personal enthusiasm, new Vereine sprang into being, and occasionally fresh subscriptions were not merely promised but received.
But Wagner was appalled at the prospect thus opened out before
him. It would need, he said, some two hundred concerts to contribute anything substantial towards the large sum required, and the
strain on his already deteriorating health would be serious. There
appeared to be no help for it, however; either he set out to raise in
this way enough to warrant the placing of the most essential orders
for the next few months or operations on the theatre would have to
be suspended.

2

On the 12th January he went to Dresden, to take preliminary
soundings there. The only net results of the three days he spent in
the town were the usual compliments and serenades, a few fresh

---

[1] This seems, on the surface, inconsistent with the 250–255 just mentioned. The
explanation may be that the certificates were not formally entered in the register
until the cash for them had been received.

recruits for the local Verein, a performance of *Rienzi* so plenti-
fully cut that he grimly compared the work to a plucked hen,[2] and
a banquet, with the customary speeches on the customary themes,
on the Brühl Terrace on the 14th. The next day he left for Berlin,
where, on the 17th, he gave a reading of the *Götterdämmerung* in
Count Schleinitz's quarters in the Hausministerium, before a select
audience that included Prince George of Prussia, Field-Marshal
Moltke, the Crown Prince of Württemberg, various ambassadors and
members of the Prussian aristocracy, Professor Helmholtz, the
economist-politician Delbrück, and Bismarck's crony Lothar Bu-
cher. Wagner prefaced the reading with an exposition of his views
on music-drama as distinguished from opera, and touched on the
significance of his Nibelung work for German culture. He was
rewarded with promises of subscriptions for twenty Patronatscheine,
and the prospects of a concert were discussed.

On the 18th he was in Hamburg, a town without, as yet, a Wagner-
Verein. Here there were more serenades, more laurel wreaths, more
banquets, and a performance of the *Meistersinger* that gave him little pleasure. He conducted a concert on the 21st and another on the
23rd: the net return of the two was only some 3,600 thalers, but a
Verein was formed, and Wagner made some new friends in the
town.

At Schwerin, on the 26th, he was heartened by an excellent performance of the *Flying Dutchman* under Aloys Schmitt. The title-
rôle was taken by Karl Hill, a baritone who had attracted Wagner's
attention at Frankfort some ten years earlier. Wagner seems to
have decided, after this Schwerin performance of his, to cast him
as Alberich for the Bayreuth *Ring*.[3]

From Schwerin he went, on the 27th, to Berlin. The President of
the local Wagner-Verein had tried to obtain the Opera House for
a concert to be conducted by Wagner; but the Intendant, Hülsen,
had refused the request, on the ground that it was not the practice to
let the Royal Opera House for private purposes. The concert was
given on the 4th February in a smaller locale, the Berlin Concert
Hall, the orchestra being for the most part that of the Opera. The

[2] He left after the fourth act and spent the rest of the evening with the Wesendonks.
[3] In a letter of the 22nd August, 1875 to King Ludwig he speaks of Hill's "demonic
passion" as marking him out especially for the part of the sombre Alberich as the
foil to the "Licht-Alberich, Wotan". Hill died insane in 1893.

Emperor and Empress were present, and the net proceeds seem to have amounted to about 8,000 thalers. Efforts were made to bring about an integral production of *Lohengrin* under Wagner. As against this, Hülsen offered a performance — but with the usual cuts — for the benefit of Bayreuth. This was not agreeable to Wagner, and after some weeks' debate the idea was abandoned.

Berlin was anything but reluctant to hear Wagner, but its interest in him was largely commercial. A new-rich class had sprung up, prepared to pay high prices for whatever it wanted, and an epoch of prima donna worship had set in, to the great profit of the Opera. Wagner was welcome enough as a box office draw, but of his high aims there was little understanding either in official circles or among the general public. He could probably have had his "Wagner Theatre" in Berlin without much difficulty, but only as one star turn among others. We shall see later how Hülsen comported himself as a business man towards the new situation brought about by the successful establishment of Bayreuth.

It was an exhausted and temporarily disheartened Wagner that returned to Bayreuth on the 6th February. Nowhere in the whole Reich, he now knew, was he likely to meet with less real understanding of his aims than in Berlin. One proof of this was an article that caught his eye in a new edition of Brockhaus's Konversationslexikon, in which the public was calmly informed that it had been the hope of his influential Berlin friends to instal him at the Opera as successor to Meyerbeer, and that, this scheme having failed, he had "turned back with renewed love to Bavaria". Wagner protested against this perversion of the truth, not merely on its own account but because it appeared in a publication of his own brother-in-law, who, he thought, should have known him better.

3

One beneficial result of the collapse of his hopes of guiding and governing Bavaria through King Ludwig, and all Germany through Bavaria, was that he mostly kept away from practical politics during the last ten or eleven years of his life. Now and then in his last phase of all, when his mind had taken a fresh mystical turn and at the same time he had come to be regarded in some quarters as a seer gifted with supernal wisdom, the mantic mood would take possession of him once more, and he would descend from his Sinai with a fresh set of tables of the law in his hands. But in the main the writings of his last period are on subjects about which he was peculiarly qualified to speak — subjects directly concerned with music in general and his own practice in particular. In the summer, autumn and winter of 1872 there had appeared the luminous articles on *Actors and Singers, On the Name Music-Drama, A Letter to an Actor*, and *A Glance at the German Operatic Stage of Today*. These were followed in April, 1873 by some articles in the *Musikalisches Wochenblatt* on *The Rendering of Beethoven's Ninth Symphony* that remain today the starting-point for all discussion of the technical problems of performance that confront us in the master's last works.[4]

Nietzsche, accompanied by Rohde, spent his Easter holidays of 1873, from the 7th to the 12th April, in Bayreuth. He brought with him some new manuscripts of his own, one of them being a composition for piano, four hands, which Wagner indulgently played with him. Though Nietzsche had not realised it at the time, Wagner had been very angry with him for not having spent the New Year with him. Unaware of this at the time, Nietzsche sent Cosima, as a belated Christmas present, the manuscripts of what he called "Five Forewords to Five Unwritten Books", bearing the titles "The Pathos of Truth", "The Future of our Educational Institutions", "The Greek State", "The Relation of Schopenhauer's Philosophy to a German Culture", and "The Homeric Contest". He received no acknowledgment of them at the time, but attached no significance to the silence when he learned that Cosima and Wagner had set out on their trip to northern Germany. Far from taking offence, indeed, and undeterred by the obloquy that his adherence to Wagner had already brought on him, he plunged into the fray again in his idol's defence in a letter that appeared in the *Musikalisches Wochenblatt* of the 17th January (1873). It was motivated primarily by his resentment of Dr. Puschmann's notorious book demonstrating that Wagner was insane — which had been published in the preceding autumn [5] — and of a recent article by Alfred Dove in a German

---

[4] The essay on *State and Religion*, which appeared for the first time in 1873 in the eighth volume of Wagner's Collected Writings, was a public imprint of the paper written for King Ludwig's private instruction in July, 1864. For a summary of it see Vol. III of the present Life, p. 263.

[5] See the present Life, III, 564. Another so-called psychiatrist had treated Scho-

weekly journal. (The title of the first of the "Forewords" mentioned above has reference to Dove's article).[6]

A letter of Cosima's in February explained satisfactorily the various reasons for the delay in acknowledging the manuscripts; but Nietzsche was pained to learn from it that Wagner had been seriously offended with him for quite a while. "God knows", he sighed, "how I come to offend the Meister so often! Each time I wonder at it afresh and simply can't make out just what the cause of it has been." But manifestly it worried him, for he goes on to say:

> "Do tell me what *you* think about these repeated offences. I really cannot imagine how anybody could be more faithful — in all essentials — to Wagner, or more profoundly devoted to him, than I am: if I *could* imagine it, I would show myself even more so. But, if only to be so faithful in the higher sense, I must preserve my freedom in small subsidiary matters and in a sort of necessary 'sanitary' (so to speak) abstention from frequent personal intercourse with him. Of course one must not say a word about this, but one feels it, and it makes one despair when it brings in its train vexations, suspicions and reticences." [7]

4

Already, perhaps, the radical intellectual re-orientation that was preparing within him was showing itself in some barely definable way in his talk and his letters, and Wagner was subconsciously sensitive to it. More light on the psychology of the pair is thrown by a letter of a year later to the same correspondent. Evidently Nietzsche's daemon was once more whispering to him, "Keep away from Bayreuth, where your intellectual independence is in danger!" He excuses himself to Gersdorff for doing so on the ground that Wagner and Cosima are too fully occupied with their own grave affairs to receive visitors, while he himself has his hands full with the third of his *Thoughts out of Season*. Why does Gersdorff, he asks, try almost by threats to induce him to go to Bayreuth? "One would think", he complains,

---

penhauer from the same standpoint. See Nietzsche's indignant letter to Rohde of November, 1872, in NGB, II, 366.

[6] The letter to the *Wochenblatt* is given in FNWN, p. 139 ff. It has been omitted from the English version of that book.

[7] Letter of the 24th February, 1873 to Gersdorff, NGB, I, 235–6. Gersdorff, who had been in Bayreuth at the years'-end, had told Nietzsche how bitterly Wagner had resented his absence.

"that I would not go there of my own free will; and yet in the past year I have been there twice, and twice in the year before that. . . . You and I know that Wagner's nature is strongly inclined to mistrust; but it had not occurred to me that it would be a good thing to provoke this mistrust. And finally, remember that I have duties towards myself that are very difficult to fulfil, my health being as poor as it is." [8]

Evidently some, if not all, of the materials for the later rupture were already beginning to assemble within him, though he himself was not clearly aware of it yet, and the spark that was to set off the explosive mass was not to come until a few years later. What made the situation so peculiarly dangerous was the fact that Nietzsche's nature was an exact copy of Wagner's where the supposed obligations of friendship were concerned. He could no more endure independence of mind in his friends than the older man could, with the consequence that he lost almost all of them as time went on. A typical instance is his intolerant attitude towards his old Leipzig fellow-student Romundt — later his colleague in Basel — when the latter felt drawn towards Catholicism. As Bernouilli puts it, Nietzsche does not come out of that matter well: his despotic conception of friendship reduced his colleague — who was of the same age as himself — almost to the rank of a mere "creature".

"Already we see the first step towards the demand that later was to endanger all his other friendships. His friends must think as he thought . . . apparently no friend of his was to go his own way; to enjoy Nietzsche's friendship he was under an obligation to follow in his footsteps." [9]

We may recall also Nietzsche's ruffianly treatment of the high-minded Malwida von Meysenbug in 1888. Her good breeding, no less than her sense of what was due to so great an artist as Wagner, had made her protest against the coarseness of the attack on him in *Der Fall Wagner*. Nietzsche's letter to her in reply reveals the arrogant Prussian always latent in him. "These are not matters", he bellowed back at the fine-fibred old lady,

"on which I permit any contradiction. Where questions of decadence are concerned I am the highest tribunal at present on earth; the men of today, with their miserable degeneration of instinct, ought to regard themselves as fortunate in having some one to tell them the plain truth about obscure things."

---

[8] To Gersdorff, 4th July, 1874; NGB, I, 279–80.
[9] BON, I, 107.

Wagner had known how to induce belief in himself: that went along with his genius. But his was a "lying genius", "whereas I have the honour to be the reverse of this, a genius of truth." He followed this up a few days later with another letter, from the draft of which, found among his papers after his death, his sister gives us a few extracts. He had sent Malwida *Der Fall Wagner*, he said, because he wanted to prove to her once again that she had never understood so much as a word or a wish of his. Like Wagner and all the rest of the world, she was wholly lacking in the ability to distinguish between the true and the false.

> "You are an extreme instance of this, you who have been in error your whole life long about almost everyone, even about Wagner, and all the more about a rather more difficult case — myself. Have you *no* comprehension of my *mission?* Of what is meant by 'the transvaluation of all values'?" [10]

Make all allowances for the fact that the Nietzsche of the last year or so of his sane life was a man broken by suffering, soured by disappointment, and undermined bodily and mentally by drugs and disease; the fact remains that all these things are answerable only for the crudeness of tone in the letters. [11] The substance of them comes from the very substance of Nietzsche himself as he had been from the first, a man as unable to tolerate opposition as Wagner was. A clash between two such temperaments was inevitable sooner or later.

5

However, in the spring of 1873 his heart was still wholly with Wagner, whatever subtle changes, of which he himself was far from

---

[10] NGB, III, 648 ff.

[11] We have another sample of this in his letter of the 21st May, 1887 to Rohde, à *propos* of some remarks of the latter about Taine. The great French thinker had recently been doing valuable propaganda work for Nietzsche, who consequently resented his friend's criticism of him. "No, my old friend Rohde", he wrote to him (NGB, II, 580), "I permit no one to speak as disrespectfully of M. Taine" — this from the man who indulged himself in the vulgarest disrespect towards Wagner and everyone else whose ideas did not commend themselves to him! — "as you do in your letter; least of all, indeed, you, since it is against all decency to behave in this way towards a man whom you know *I* esteem highly. Indulge yourself, if you like, to your heart's content in nonsensical talk about myself: that lies in the *natura rerum* — I have never complained about it, or expected anything different." But a thinker like Taine is another matter altogether: he admired Friedrich Nietzsche, therefore not a word must be said against him.

fully conscious as yet, might be going on in his mind. Bayreuth had succeeded Triebschen as his spiritual home. He was deeply moved, he wrote to Gersdorff on the 5th April, at the thought that in a couple of days he would be there once more.

> "Every step will be rich in memories of last year: I still regard those days as the happiest of my life. There was something in the air which I had never felt anywhere else, something quite indescribable but filled with hope. . . . I hope my visit will set right the bad results of my not having gone there at Christmas, and from the bottom of my heart I thank you for your plain and forcible exhortation."

Wagner's depression in face of the financial difficulties now crowding upon him and threatening the very existence of the festival theatre called forth everything that was generous in the younger man's nature. In a letter to Nietzsche of the preceding October Wagner had sorrowfully confessed that he was coming to understand less and less the world around him, and even Germany itself. "More and more", he wrote,

> "I am coming to feel that I know my contemporary world less and less. Perhaps it is all to the good if one is creating for posterity. . . . More and more I ponder over 'What is German?', and my latest studies in this field have landed me in a singular scepticism, with the curious feeling that 'being German' is a purely metaphysical concept."

The trouble was that it was anything but a metaphysical world with which he had to do. But the fighter in him squared up unflinchingly to the conflict.

> "The thing is to see and yet not to see. If one gives up hope, one can perhaps escape despair also. In the end one feels that the only way a man can achieve consciousness of himself is to separate himself definitely from the whole contemporary world by out-and-out war on its vileness. For my part I have arrived at the point where I do not intend to mince my words in any quarter: and should the Empress Augusta come my way she would get it straight from me. Something *must* come of it all, for one thing is certain — any sort of compromise is simply not to be thought of. The only thing to do when one is cordially hated is to make oneself feared."

Brave words, but not practically helpful: neither being hated nor being feared was likely to bring a single fresh thaler into the Bayreuth treasury. Things were going far from well with the theatre project. The Vereine were well-intentioned but not always very

comprehending. Some of them deducted "expenses" before handing over their contributions to Feustel. A few individuals thought
that by joining a Verein they were providing in advance their travelling expenses to the festival; others that they were merely staking
out a claim to seats, payment for which could be made when the
time arrived. Other people gave their names as Patrons but saw no
immediate necessity to send in their subscription. Wagner's personal enemies and those of his art stopped at nothing, fair or foul,
that might prejudice the public against the undertaking: one of the
stories most gleefully set going was that he was using the funds subscribed by his dupes for the theatre to build a splendid mansion for
himself in Bayreuth. The commercial crisis perturbing Germany
just then — the aftermath of the war — was everywhere being
made an excuse for tightening the purse-strings. Altogether it was
becoming plainer every month that unless money came in more
quickly and in larger sums the enterprise would have to be abandoned.

Nietzsche had come away from Bayreuth in April as sad and
angry over it all as Wagner and Cosima were. His "holy rage", as
he described it in a letter to Rohde on his return to Basel, found immediate vent in the first of the *Thoughts out of Season:* feeling that
he must "vomit lava", he chose as his victim the venerable David
Strauss, whose once-famous book *Der alte und der neue Glaube,*
published a few months earlier, had already run into three or four
editions, and whom Nietzsche now held up to ridicule as the incarnation of the newest species of German philistine. Nietzsche's essay
was the direct outcome of his experiences in Bayreuth. "My brother's visit to Bayreuth", says Frau Förster-Nietzsche, "had not fulfilled his happy expectations, nor, in some respects, those of Wagner." According to her, the latter was far from pleased to find that
the professor had brought with him, as his latest literary effort, only
an essay on "Philosophy during the Tragic Age of the Greeks",
instead of something bearing more directly on himself and Bayreuth. That is perhaps putting it a trifle crudely; but we can easily
imagine that Wagner, exhausted and disillusioned after his concert
tour, was hardly in the most receptive mood imaginable for anything
of that sort, while Nietzsche, already feeling the first stirrings within
him of something that was ultimately to carry him far away from
Bayreuth and from Wagner, would be more sensitive than usual to

a drop in the temperature of their personal intercourse. But there cannot be the least doubt that he was still convinced of the greatness of Wagner's mission and of his own duty to help him to accomplish it.

On her return home after the tour in January and February Cosima had poured out the bitterness of her heart in a letter to Wagner's young nephew Clemens Brockhaus. The sacrifice of time and strength, she said, had been virtually useless. Wagner had lamented that even among those who flocked to his concerts and were willing to become Patrons there was small understanding of his real aim: he felt more lonely than ever in a world that was daily sinking deeper and deeper into a complacent materialism of which Strauss's book was the symbol. "Often I ask myself", said Cosima, "which will prove the greater, his own force or that of the world around him." Manifestly she and Wagner had opened their souls on these lines to Nietzsche when he visited them in April, for in his notebooks we find jottings such as these:

> "There is something comical in the fact that Wagner cannot persuade the Germans to take the theatre seriously: they remain cold and easy-going, while he gets angry, as if the salvation of the Germans depended on it. And especially just at present they believe they have more serious things to occupy them, and they find only amusement in the fanaticism that makes a man take art so earnestly".
>
> "Wagner is not a reformer, for so far everything remains just as it was of old. In Germany everyone takes his own affairs seriously, and is amused at anyone who claims to be the only one who takes things seriously".
>
> "Effect of the financial crisis".
>
> "General uncertainty of the political situation".
>
> "The significance that Wagner attaches to art does not fit in with our social and industrial affairs".
>
> "The importance which Wagner attaches to art is not German".

These and many other jottings are dated by Nietzsche's editor January, 1874, and associated with the draft of the fourth of the *Thoughts out of Season*, the *Richard Wagner in Bayreuth*. But as these were the very thoughts that were filling Wagner and Cosima with peculiar bitterness in the spring of 1873, we can hardly doubt that Nietzsche's jottings are echoes of what he had heard in the house in the Dammallee during his visit there.

6

Cosima tried to remove Wagner's depression by an especially elaborate celebration of his birthday in May. As this involved the co-operation of a number of Bayreuthers the preparations for it necessarily became the talk of the little town; but Cosima, who did nothing by halves, managed to keep Richard in the dark about them by having special copies of the local papers printed for his use, from which everything relating to the coming events was deleted. On the morning of the 22nd a group of musicians from Würzburg, concealed in the garden of the Dammallee house, awakened him with the strains of the "Wacht auf" chorus from the *Meistersinger*. In the evening he was taken to the old theatre, where, in presence of a large audience, he was given his second surprise — a performance of the Concert Overture he had written in 1831. This he had so completely forgotten that after it had got fairly going he asked Cosima who was the composer of it. She smiled but made no reply. Then he began to speculate about it: it could not be by Beethoven, he said, or by Bellini: and it was only gradually that the truth of the matter dawned on him. Next came the central event of the day, a performance, made possible by the fact that the dramatic company of one Herr Wittmann was occupying the theatre just then, of Geyer's serio-comedy *Der bethlehemitische Kindermord*.[12] This was followed by performances by Alexander Kummer, a son of the Karl Kummer who had been the Court Theatre oboist in Wagner's Dresden days, of the *Albumblatt* of 1861 and the *Träume* from the five Mathilde Wesendonk songs.

Then came the greatest surprise of all. The reader will remember that in Magdeburg, in 1835, Wagner had set to music a New Year's cantata by one Schmale, the local theatre regisseur, entitled *Beim Antritt des neuen Jahres*, his contribution consisting of an overture, two interludes and two choruses.[13] Peter Cornelius, at Cosima's instigation, had supplied a new text for the work, basing it on a remark of Wagner's, in the Munich period, to the effect that as a young man he had been impressed by the painter Genelli, whom he had met at the house of one of his brothers-in-law. On this foundation Cornelius had constructed a scene in which the artist, by means of his

---

12 See Vol. I, p. 27 ff.
13 See Vol. I, p. 176.

own pictures, turns the vague thoughts of the youth in the direction necessary for his budding genius to take — that of the music drama. To this naïve product Cornelius gave the title of *Künstlerweihe*, describing it, in a letter to his friend Reinhold Köhler, as a "rhymed novel": [14] the poem and music were accompanied by tableaux vivants of Genelli pictures. The poem was spoken by Wagner's niece Franziska, whose husband, Alexander Ritter, had brought with him from Würzburg a contingent of musicians to reinforce the local performers. The stage management was in the hands of Karl Brandt's son Fritz. Cosima had done things thoroughly, and Wagner was deeply moved by it all. [15]

Seven days later, on the 29th May, he and Cosima went to Weimar to hear the first complete performance of *Christus*, under Liszt's direction. They were not wholly in tune with the work, liking neither its aromatic sensuousness nor the touch of the sophisticated in its religious outlook. It was not "German" enough for either of them. Wagner, who had been taken to Weimar rather against his will, showed "tact", we are informed, towards his father-in-law's work: "Richard", we learn from Cosima's diary, "passed through every phase of transport to downright revolt, arriving finally at the profoundest, most affectionate fair-mindedness". He could never quite reconcile himself to what he called the priestly element in Liszt's church music, the aroma of incense it exhaled. Felix Mottl used to tell a piquant story of an experience of his own during one of the Bayreuth festivals. Wagner and Liszt had left the dinner table, leaving Cosima and Mottl at their coffee. Suddenly Wagner came back, red in the face and obviously very angry. "This old humbug", he said, "absolutely insists on playing me his latest Ave Maria: I really can't stand any more!" Cosima reproved him gently: "How can you let yourself be provoked into saying such things again?

---

[14] Extracts from it are given in CPC, II, 206 ff.

[15] How seriously he took the domestic celebrations of his birthday may be gathered from a story he himself told Albert Gutmann in later years. "The other day that dreadful man Sch. . . . . . came here [Wahnfried]. I happened to open the door myself. I started back in terror. I said to him, 'Good God, have I got to see this face!' The tasteless fellow had come in bright yellow shoes. Of course my wife had to ask him to stay to lunch, on his stepfather's account. There he showed himself in a still more offensive light. It was my birthday. My good Siegfried was making a speech about me that was really moving. But Sch. . . . . . never stopped eating. He said to my wife, 'I like this asparagus; give me some more of it'. What a glutton! I can't stand gluttons!" This Sch. . . . . . was evidently Standhartner's stepson Gustav Schönaich. He had done Wagner many a service in days gone by.

Haven't you always had the highest opinion of Papa? Didn't you say only a little while ago that he had inaugurated a new epoch in art?" "Yes", replied Wagner: "in fingering!" [16]

7

He needed all the small consolations that Cosima could bring him, for things were not going at all well with the Bayreuth scheme. To the King, in June, he put a brave face on the matter. The building was progressing,[17] nothing could surpass the affection the Bayreuthers showed him,[18] the interest in his venture was world-wide, the artists were eager to co-operate, Feustel and Muncker were a tower of strength, and he hoped before long to settle down in the new home with which the King's generosity had provided him. Ludwig's reply was full of the old protestations of love and admiration for him and Cosima; it ended with the hope that Wagner had not forgotten his plans for *Parsifal*. But as the weeks went on, Wagner became less and less able to burke the plain issue: either he must obtain more money, and quickly, or the Bayreuth undertaking was doomed. To maintain his friends' interest in it he prepared a brochure setting forth the nature of his scheme, giving an account of the proceedings at the laying of the foundation-stone, and ending with a description of the building, with its new devices, such as the second proscenium and the sunken orchestra, for increasing the dramatic illusion. Six architectural plans and elevations were added to make these latter points clearer. The document [19] is a masterpiece of lucid exposition. The faithful were to be invited to Bayreuth in the autumn to see the design taking practicable shape: they would go away, it was hoped, encouraged to persevere with him to the end.

He now believed that if things went well he would be able to start rehearsals in 1874 and give his festival in 1875. But in spite

---

[16] GAWM, p. 126.

[17] The *Hebefeier* — the celebration of the reaching of the highest point of a building, with speeches, music and junketings for the workmen — took place on the 2nd August, 1873. Liszt was present.

[18] Perhaps he generalised too liberally from a few experiences. Kietz, who was in Bayreuth in the summer of 1873, says that at that time the majority of the inhabitants were distant and suspicious because of the reports about him that had come from Dresden and Munich. "I myself", says Kietz, "often heard him discussed in my hotel by natives and strangers in a harsh, unfriendly way." KW, p. 148.

[19] It is reprinted in RWGS, Vol. IX.

of every economy the funds in hand would not go much further than completing the shell of the building. Orders for the expensive new machinery and scenery could not be placed unless a large sum could be raised immediately. The Vereine could do little more than they had already done; even fresh concerts, from which Wagner shrank because of the drain they would be on his strength and the interruption they would cause in his creative work, would not bring in anything like the amount required. The situation by midsummer, 1873 was this: of the 3/400,000 thalers needed, only 130,000 had been subscribed, after the most intensive efforts — which manifestly could not be repeated on the same scale — on the part of Wagner's most influential social supporters and the various Vereine, plus the money he himself had raised by concerts. There was nothing for it now but a big loan. For this an unimpeachable guarantee would be required; and the only possible guarantor was the King.

To Ludwig, therefore, he opened out his heart in August. He confessed now that in front of the world he had to put a braver face on the matter than the facts warranted; enemies and the indifferent were waiting all too eagerly for a public admission on his part that the undertaking had come up against insuperable difficulties. The German princes, he said, were either lukewarm or niggardly. The richer nobility had no German soul left in them; they preferred to spend their money on "Jewish or Jesuit undertakings". The plutocrats of the Bourse would help him only if he would transfer his theatre to Berlin or Vienna, in which case a million would be placed at his disposal. Feustel never lost heart, never had the smallest doubt that if only the performances could take place the receipts would be more than adequate to cover all the expenditure. But the vital thing is the machinery, the orders for which must be placed at once. Feustel, he says, is convinced that all that is required is a guarantee which, in essence, would be purely formal. Only to King Ludwig can Wagner look for such a guarantee; so he asks that Düfflipp shall be sent to Bayreuth to make himself acquainted with all the details of the matter.

8

On the 9th September Wagner raised the question again in a letter to Düfflipp, in which he repeats that the proposed guarantee will be, in his opinion and Feustel's, no more than a formality, in view of the monies bound to come in in respect of Patronatscheine. Without the guarantee he simply cannot proceed with the building; and he asks Düfflipp to hear what Feustel, who will be in Munich shortly, has to say about it all, and to give him the King's decision. The answer came a fortnight later, evidently after the Court Secretary had conferred with the King. His Majesty, he said, could not comply with Wagner's request,

"remembering, no doubt, your previous declaration, when the 25,000 thalers designed for the Bayreuth theatre undertaking were sent to you personally, that you were certain you would not have to call on the King for any further material participation".[20]

Düfflipp had since then laid Feustel's written explanation before his Majesty, and had received the reply that nothing could be done, though the King had listened to him with the greatest interest. To Feustel himself Düfflipp had explained that the King, deeply involved in his own building plans, was averse to doing anything that might frustrate or delay these. Two months later, on the 21st November, the Cabinet Secretary, Eisenhart, wrote to Düfflipp:

"His Majesty desires to know whether you have written to Herr Richard Wagner about the matter mentioned, and made it absolutely clear to him that he cannot count on any moral or pecuniary assistance in connection with his undertaking".

For Ludwig's hands were full enough with his own grandiose schemes. Wagner had been confident enough that he could carry his own plan through in his own way; and this being so, the King was justified in feeling that he was under no moral obligation to take any more of the burden of it on his shoulders.

9

The circular to the subscribers had been sent out at the end of August. Although meant for them alone, it soon found its way into the papers; and by a misreading of some portions of it the impression got about that Wagner contemplated turning the undertaking

---

[20] Ludwig appears to have forgotten that while the 25,000 thalers had first of all been given to Wagner for the theatre, he himself had later agreed that they should go to provide for Wagner's new home.

into a sort of limited company. Heckel felt called upon to warn him solemnly against such a course; and Wagner had to assure him with equal solemnity that nothing of the sort had ever entered his mind. Then Heckel himself suggested a new strategy — a public Appeal for Bayreuth to be issued by the Mannheim Wagnerverein, and subscription forms to be displayed in all the German book and music shops. He himself would undertake all the routine work in connection with this; and in order to shame the public into doing the right thing the Appeal was to disclose, as Heckel put it, "the humiliating fact" that Chicago and London had both offered to put up a Wagner theatre according to the composer's plans. Wagner wisely discountenanced this last suggestion: in view of the offers he had had from Berlin and Vienna, he pointed out, it could not be truly said that no German capital would have given him what he wanted — under certain unacceptable conditions; the crux of the matter had been his own insistence on a "neutral spot" like Bayreuth. "Cities like Chicago and so on could perhaps be found in Germany as well — but not the *German public*". As for the plan for subscription lists, he thought it would be better if this were launched by "a consortium of influential people from *various* German centres". And if a manifesto were to be issued, he would suggest Nietzsche as the writer of it.

Thereupon Heckel wrote to Nietzsche, who undertook to indite an "Appeal to the German Nation". He drafted it in the third week of October; it was to be submitted to the consideration of the delegates who were to assemble at Bayreuth at the end of the month to see the progress that had been made with the theatre — Wagner thought the sight would encourage them, — and to decide upon a future course of action.

Frau Förster-Nietzsche tells us that her brother drafted the Appeal only "after much hesitation". If that be true, the hesitation may have been due to the fact that he had already contemplated something of the kind on his own initiative but had not quite seen how to go about it. He sent Rohde a sketch for it. Stress was to be laid on the importance of the Bayreuth plan; on the disgrace to the German nation involved in regarding an undertaking that called for the utmost self-sacrifice from all concerned as the mere adventure of a charlatan; on the fact that in France, England or Italy an artist who had done so much for native art as Wagner had done could certainly count on support for a scheme to give the nation a theatre worthy of it; and so on. That Nietzsche himself was none too sanguine about the success of such an Appeal is suggested by the rather worried tone of the letter in which he asked for any help that Rohde might be able to give him.

Rohde had even more doubts about the matter than his friend had. He shrank from trying to make the aims and ideals of a man like Wagner comprehensible to the multitude; and what made it all the more difficult was his presentiment that the results would be small. He saw at a glance that Nietzsche had adopted the wrong tone in his Appeal. While the believers needed no converting, the doubters and the lukewarm were not likely to be won over by Nietzsche's indignant, accusatory way of addressing them, justified as this might be. The day might come, said Rohde, when, if the undertaking failed, people like himself and Nietzsche could pour out all the bitterness of their hearts. But the task of the moment, and a difficult enough task it would be, was to *persuade* the canaille.

> "You will understand me, dear friend, when I say frankly that your *Mahnruf*[21] strikes me as a kick — a thousand times deserved — administered to the *kakoi* rather than as an enticement to the cur crouching behind the stove, whom, after all, you have to have in mind if you decide on a step of this sort."

He leaves the document to the judgment of the delegates; if they approve of it, there is nothing in it to which he would refuse his own signature. But all the same he doubts whether it will have any effect.

The "Mahnruf" was a remarkable document, noble in its idealism, eloquent in its indignant plain-speaking, its angry defiance of German philistinism, its calling down upon the Germans the contemptuous verdict of the civilised world if they allowed the work that had been begun on the hill at Bayreuth to crumble to ruin. But Rohde was right in his view of the probable effect of it. It was too unconciliatory; the vehemence of it would cause an agreeable rise of temperature in the believers, but was unlikely to persuade anyone who had so far shown no disposition to be persuaded.[22]

With all these worries and fatigues Wagner was unable to make

---

[21] Warning, exhortation, admonition: the term is stronger than "Anruf" (call, appeal, summons). If a "Mahnruf" was Nietzsche's idea it was not precisely tactful.
[22] It will be found in full in FNWN, pp. 172-6.

as much progress with the scoring of the *Götterdämmerung* as he would have liked. Nor was his domestic situation wholly free from care. Cosima was perturbed at the expense he was blithely running into in connection with his new house; and at the end of September we find him asking Schott, as a favour, to pay him at once the 10,000 francs due to him on the delivery of the *Götterdämmerung* score. The good Schott obliged by return of post.

10

In August Wagner had been gratified by the decision of Malwida von Meysenbug to make her home in Bayreuth for the rest of her life: he could never have about him too many of the devoted souls who looked to him for salvation. But the raw climate of Bayreuth, after her long residence in Florence, was more than Malwida's delicate constitution could stand; before the end of the first winter she was driven back to Italy again. Other visitors of that summer were Schuré, Wagner's old friend Gustav Kietz, and Anton Bruckner. Kietz spent some weeks in Bayreuth, during which he made busts of Wagner and Cosima — not without some difficulty in the former case, for the Meister, who detested nothing so much as being at rest for three minutes at a time, had a disconcerting habit of singing and making impish grimaces, so that each time Kietz raised his eyes from his modelling he found a different face before him.[23] It was while Kietz was in Bayreuth that Bruckner arrived there. He had come to ask Wagner to allow him to dedicate one of his symphonies to him. After careful and non-committal consideration of the scores — for he was incapable of mere conventional politeness in matters of this kind — Wagner accepted the No. 3. Bruckner had come straight from a cure at Karlsbad, where he had drunk nothing but the waters. In spite of his protests Wagner insisted on his draining one large glass after another of a heady beer. The next day the poor man came to Kietz in great trouble. The beer having gone to his head, he could not remember which of the two symphonies, the No. 2 or the No. 3, the Meister had chosen: "Oh, the beer, the dreadful beer!" he moaned. Kietz had been too busy with his modelling to pay much attention to the talk of the two musicians; but some references to D minor and a trumpet had stuck

---

[23] His lively account of these days will be found in KW, Part IV.

in his memory because he thought it was Beethoven's Ninth that they were discussing. He mentioned this to the simple soul from Vienna, who jumped up and embraced him: it was his own D minor symphony — the No. 3 — about which Wagner had been talking. Thus far Kietz in a contemporary letter to his wife. It looks, however, as if Bruckner's mind was still not quite at rest, for a couple of days later he sent a note to Wagner — "Symfonie in D moll, wo die Trompete das Thema beginnt. A Bruckner"; at the foot of which Wagner scribbled "Ja! Ja! Herzlichen Gruss! Richard Wagner." [24]

It was during this summer of 1873 that the first of Nietzsche's *Thoughts out of Season*, the *David Strauss, Confessor and Author*, was published; and so blind was Wagner still to everything in the young man that was not the reflection of his own mentality that he could write him, after reading the *David Strauss*, "I swear to you, by God, that I look upon you as the only person who knows what I am driving at!"; though a further remark of his in the same letter (of the 21st September) — "I repeat what I said recently to my own intimates, that I foresee the time when I shall have to defend your book against yourself" — suggests a suspicion on his part that Nietzsche's mind was making a somewhat erratic swerve away from its real interests.

After the King's unwillingness to guarantee a loan for Bayreuth the situation looked black indeed. A meeting of Patrons and Verein delegates was called for the 31st October: it was sparsely attended, many of the people most likely to be interested having apparently not seen the public notice. The Bayreuth weather behaved in characteristically malignant fashion; the day before and the day after were wonderfully fine, but on the day itself it rained heavily, and the delegates saw the theatre under the worst conditions imaginable; Nietzsche had a new hat ruined. The ceremony of inspection over, the faithful went to the town hall, where Nietzsche's "Mahnruf" was read. It was applauded but rejected, much, it is said, to Wagner's annoyance. Nietzsche having declined to recast it, his suggestion that Professor Adolf Stern, of Dresden, should be commissioned to draft a new Appeal was adopted, together with Heckel's proposal

---

[24] A facsimile of the document is given in BFF, 1938, p. 36. For Bruckner, Wagner was always the greatest of masters; while Wagner, for his part, could declare as late as 1882 that Bruckner was the only living composer who "reached out to Beethoven".

that the book and music sellers should be asked to display sub-scription forms.

A day or so later there was another meeting at Feustel's house, at which Stern's Appeal was read and approved; from a letter of Nietzsche's to Gersdorff we gather that his own "Mahnruf" was to be held in reserve and launched later, with an imposing array of signatories, in case Stern's "optimistically coloured" Appeal did not achieve its end. To Rohde he wrote: "To be frank, Wagner, Frau Wagner and I are more convinced of the efficacy of my 'Mahn-ruf'; it seems to us only a matter of time for it alone to become nec-essary."

The Appeal was duly sent to the German book and music dealers, 3,946 of them in all. Not one of them took the slightest notice of it on his own account, but a few students in Göttingen put their names down for some half-dozen thalers. Heckel also sent a circular to eighty-one German theatres, asking them to prove their interest in German art by giving performances for the benefit of Bayreuth. Three refused; the other seventy-eight ignored the suggestion.

CHAPTER XX

THE KING TO THE RESCUE

1

O N THE 19th November Wagner wrote to Heckel, "Tomorrow I am going to Munich, to see if there is still any hope of an intervention on the part of the King." The "still" calls for elucidation; and, in general, this is the best place for a connected account of the events that led up to Ludwig's rescue of Wagner and Bayreuth.

We have seen that in August and September Wagner had put out some feelers to the King, who, however, had rejected the suggestion of a guarantee intended to provide the funds for completing the equipment of the theatre, repayment to be made out of the proceeds of the performances. Apart from Ludwig's lapse of memory in connection with the 25,000 thalers he had already given Wagner, it has been widely assumed that he was momentarily prejudiced against Wagner on account of the notorious Dahn affair. Felix Dahn, the story ran, had published a volume of poems among which was an ode to the King which he asked Wagner to set to music; and Ludwig had been mortally offended by the latter's refusal. The incident, however, was not quite as was at one time thought. The rumour of the King's displeasure was certainly current, and, as is so often the case in affairs of this kind, the person most directly concerned was the last to hear of it. Feustel had been told the story in Munich and had passed it on to Heckel; but apparently it was not until later that he ventured to mention it to Wagner.

Fresh light has been thrown on the affair by the recent publication of Wagner's letter of the 9th January, 1874, the King's reply of the 25th, and a further letter of Wagner's to Düfflipp of the 10th.[1] Evidently Wagner's friends had at last given him a hint of what was being said in Munich circles; so Wagner explains to Ludwig that some time ago Dahn had sent him, along with his new volume

---

[1] Not the 10th January, *1875*, the date given in KLRWB, III, 27, *note*.

of poems — which Wagner lacked the leisure to read at the time, — an ode to the King which, the poet had said, he had reason to believe his Majesty would like Wagner to set to music.[2] That Dahn should want him to compose music to one of his poems, he told the King, had not surprised him; and the story that Ludwig had expressed the wish that he should do so he had taken as merely one more illustration of the world's ignorance of the true relations between them. Had he had any doubts in that connection, Wagner would have written to the King and asked, if he really desired something to be written expressly for him, to be allowed to supply, as was Wagner's habit, his own text; in any case it would have been impossible for him to cast into music such un-German lines as these of Dahn, with their imitation of the antique metres. He had apparently told Dahn all this at the time and then dismissed the matter from his mind as of no real importance; and he asked the King, in case the latter should have been misled by anything that Dahn had written to him on the subject, to reassure him about it.

"I can well understand", was Ludwig's reply,

> "that you did not feel inclined to compose Dahn's verses, and you were quite right. In the summer I received him in audience, when he expressed the wish that you might set his verses to music. Not wishing to say anything unwelcome to him, I expressed myself as for rather than against the idea. *Voilà tout.* Do not think me so petty as to be angry with you for refusing: thank God your genius is intended for higher things than setting fulsome poems to music!"

The one-time belief that Ludwig had refused to guarantee a Bayreuth fund out of pique over the Dahn affair probably arose from the coincidence that it was just about the time when the matter was cleared up between himself and Wagner that the King changed his mind with regard to the theatre.

---

[2] The old theory that the ode was the "Macte senex Imperator" can no longer be maintained. See on this point Max Koch's argument in MKRW, III, 464–5. Koch's own theory that the poem in question was not the "Macte senex Imperator", as Heckel, Glasenapp and others thought, but an opera text, *Der Fremdling* — which was set to music later by the tenor Heinrich Vogl and performed in Munich in 1899 — will not hold water. Wagner's letter of the 9th January to the King makes it clear that the poem in question was an *ode*, and that it did not form part of the published volume of poems but had merely accompanied it.

2

On the 16th January, 1874 Wagner had turned in desperation to another quarter for help. To Heckel he addressed a letter which was to be passed on to the Grand Duke of Baden's Cabinet Chief, together with a petition from Heckel himself for an audience. Wagner explained the situation in which the theatre undertaking now found itself: 100,000 thalers had been collected from "the more immediate friends of my art", but this no more than sufficed for the building itself; now he needed an advance — to be repaid ultimately out of the receipts from the festival — in order to commission the stage machinery and decorations. "Lately I approached my exalted benefactor, the King of Bavaria, with regard to such a guarantee; but for reasons not clear to me his Majesty refused." So Wagner's thoughts turn to the new Reich for help — not *via* the Reichstag deputies, of whose capacity in a matter of art he has a poor opinion, but through the Kaiser himself. He suggests that the production of his *Ring* (in 1876) shall be in the nature of a festival in celebration of the peace of 1871; and to this end he hopes that the Grand Duke of Baden, together, perhaps, with three or four other notabilities, will lay the case before the Kaiser and ask for a subsidy for the Bayreuth undertaking.

The reply was to the effect that the Grand Duke regretted he could not pass the suggestion on, as in view of the many weighty problems confronting the Reich just then it could hardly hope to succeed. The letter of the Cabinet Secretariat to Heckel was dated the 1st February. Only a week later Wagner could write jubilantly to his faithful henchman in Mannheim, "The thing is settled with his Majesty; the undertaking in which you play so splendidly serious a part is assured." The Fates had followed their normal technique with him; after amusing themselves by bringing him within a hair's-breadth of total wreck they had decided to pilot his buffeted ship into port.

At the very time when Wagner's letter to Heckel was under consideration in Mannheim the King had turned full face to him again. Precisely what had wrought the sudden change in him we do not know; but the surmise may be permitted that he had heard through diplomatic channels of Wagner's last despairing appeal to the

Kaiser and of the evasive answer to be given to it,[3] and had realised that the moment had come to cut through all personal piques and misunderstandings and do the splendid, decisive, historic thing. "From the depths of my heart", he wrote to Wagner on the 25th January,

> "I beg you to forgive me for my long delay in writing to you. . . Do not be angry with me on that account, dearest Friend. It is my consolation that you know me and can have no doubt that my true and genuine friendship for you and my enthusiasm for your divine, incomparable works are so deeply implanted in my soul that it would be lunacy to believe in any decline of my ardour for you and your great undertaking. No, No and again No! It shall not end thus! Help must be given! Our plan must not fail. Parcival knows his mission and will do everything that lies in his power. . . . Do not despair, but make me happy at once with a letter."

It will be seen that the King stressed once more the point that has been so often insisted on in the present biography. It is *"our* plan" that must not be allowed to fail — the old plan of a co-operation of King and artist for the regeneration of German culture.

He goes on to make the rueful confession that his own finances are in anything but brilliant condition just now. He was being held up, indeed, in his own building schemes by shortness of money, and it was a sign of his true nobility that at this very time he should add to his responsibilities that of securing the finances of Bayreuth. Had he not intervened when he did, the Bayreuth theatre might have remained for all time the mere shell it was then; for Wagner's friends could do no more than they had done, the German public was mostly indifferent, and Wagner himself, with the abortive appeal for the support of the Reich, had played·his last big card — and lost. To Heckel he wrote on the 9th February, "I *knew* that it would all be in vain" — i.e. the appeal through the Grand Duke of Baden; and he adds, with an ironic side-glance at the talk even then current about the "madness" of King Ludwig, "My cause requires a 'wise fool'; but who is foolish nowadays?" It was indeed the "mad

---

[3] About a fortnight had elapsed between the receipt of Wagner's letter by Heckel and the reply of the Grand Duke's Secretary. It is tolerably certain that during that time soundings were made in Berlin, and that both there and in Mannheim it had been felt that it would be impolitic to intervene. Wagner was regarded as, in a sense, the special property of the King of Bavaria; and the latter's sensitiveness and his dislike and suspicion of the pushful Hohenzollerns were known to everyone in Berlin.

King of Bavaria" who saved the greatest of all monuments to German art and culture from crashing in ruins.

3

It must have been immediately upon the receipt of Heckel's gloomy news that Wagner had written once more, on the 3rd February, at great length to the King. He reminded him of their ten-years' association in the cause of German art, during which, and to the end of which, Ludwig alone among the princes had understood him and helped him: he alone had sustained, through bitter trials, the artist's faith in the German spirit. The princes had no feeling for what is good and great, while the Folk, without the right leaders, are blind. The 100,000 thalers so far raised for his theatre have been the result mainly of the efforts of his friends, for the *German nation* has contributed little. In grave and dignified words he tells his benefactor of his heartbreak not only over the *Ring* but over all he has done; for what now does it all come. to, what is left to him but hopeless resignation in the face of his failure to fire the German soul? Now, thanks to the King's encouraging letter, he sees the possibility of carrying his plan through: that letter has confirmed him in his old belief that in the German world it is only the King — the ideal King — who can lead the Folk into the right path because he is the incarnation of all that is best in them, mute, willless, directionless as they are without guidance from above.

The matter now passed into the hands of the King's business advisers, and on the 26th February (1874) a contract was signed between the Court Secretariat and the Committee of Management of the Richard Wagner Theatre — Wagner, Käfferlein, Feustel and Muncker. Its clauses may be condensed thus:

I.   The Theatre Committee requires 100,000 thalers to provide (a) the requisite scenery, (b) the gas installation, (c) the fitting up of the interior.

II.   This sum will be advanced to the Committee for those purposes by the King's Kabinettskasse,[4] repayment to be made within a year and a half. (The Committee, it will be remembered, had been sure that, given the necessary loan, the building could be completed in

---

[4] I.e., his personal funds.

1874 and the performances take place in the summer of 1875. The receipts from these were to be ear-marked for the liquidation of the loan).

III.   From the time of the signing of the contract until the whole advance is paid off, all monies received in respect of Patronat-scheine are to be allocated to the Kabinettskasse.

IV.   Until the complete repayment of the loan, the scenery, machinery, gas equipment and internal fittings are to be the property of the Court Secretariat.

V.   Half the proceeds of any concerts given by Wagner for the benefit of the theatre are to be at the free disposition of the Bayreuth Committee, the other half to go towards repayment of the loan.

VI.   The Committee pledges itself to furnish to the Court Secretariat (a) copies of contracts made for the lighting, decorations and machinery, and (b) monthly statements of payments made to the contractors in respect of these.

As will be seen, it was an agreement in due legal form between one group of business men and another.

Perhaps within a very short time of the signing of the agreement the Court Secretariat began to suspect that the Bayreuth Committee's estimate of future possibilities had been over-optimistic; for on the 20th April the King ordered his Secretariat to give the Committee formal notice that this would have to be his last intervention on behalf of the theatre — that in no circumstances could he listen to any further demands, from whatever quarter they might come.

4

On the 23rd August Wagner poured out once more his gratitude to the man who alone, for ten years, had made it possible for him to realise his life's ideal in spite of the indifference of his fellow-countrymen towards it. The King was in Paris at that time. As soon as possible after his return he wrote to Wagner (on the 19th September) in the old cordial vein, congratulating him on having at last been able to occupy his new home, rejoicing that the preparations for the festival were going on so well, and asking to be kept constantly informed about it all.

On the 1st October Wagner reports progress to his benefactor.

Thanks to the loan, he had been able to place the necessary orders in connection with the theatre in April, and preliminary negotiations with his singers had begun. It had become evident, however, that, for a variety of reasons, the work could not be completed by the following summer, so that the opening festival would have to be postponed to 1876. He had discovered at last the right artist for the scenery — the Viennese painter Joseph Hoffmann, who had submitted sketches for the whole tetralogy of which Wagner warmly approved. But Hoffmann, who was new to this kind of work, had no suitable studio for it and no assistants; consequently, through the mediation of Karl Brandt, it had been arranged that the practical realisation of the designs should be entrusted to the brothers Max and Gotthold Brückner, of the Coburg Court Theatre, for whom a studio was to be erected in Bayreuth. Wagner's contract with them provided for the delivery of everything necessary by the 1st May, 1876. Preliminary rehearsals with the singers were to start in July, 1875 and extend through August. (Already, as will be seen, the foundations of the agreement with the Court Secretariat had been undermined through no fault on Wagner's and the Committee's part but over-optimism: liquidation of the King's loan by the summer of 1875 out of the receipts from the performances was now out of the question).

The final rehearsals and the festival itself, Wagner went on to say, were to take place in June, July and August, 1876. The general routine of the performances was already settled — commencement at four o'clock, the second act at six, the third at eight, the spectators to refresh themselves during the intervals in the gardens and the adjacent countryside and be summoned again by the trombones from the terrace of the theatre. Wagner's experiences so far with the singers, he says, have been most encouraging; all have declared it to be a point of honour with them to keep themselves free for the festival, even at the sacrifice of fees for "guest" performances elsewhere.[5] His orchestra he will select from the best of the players in the opera houses that close down for three months each summer.

---

[5] The names he gives the King are not in every case those of the singers who appeared in 1876. He would have liked, for instance, the Swedish Christine Nilsson for his Sieglinde. She was so enthusiastic for Wagner that she offered herself without any fee, he tells the King. But she had not sung in German before; moreover her husband, a Frenchman, was afraid she could never appear in Paris again if she took part in these German festival performances.

His tone is less assured when he touches on the financial side of his undertaking. The King's vigorous intervention has encouraged his friends and brought in some new well-wishers: a number of Berlin painters, for instance, have agreed, on the instigation of Countess Schleinitz, to an auction of their pictures for the benefit of Bayreuth. But he confesses that for the funds still needed he must rely on the sales of tickets to the richer public when the dates of the performances are finally announced. In the circumstances he is compelled to ask the King for permission to make immediate use, for the most necessary purposes of the theatre building, of the whole of the monies received for Patronatscheine.

The suggestion appears not to have found favour in the eyes of either the King or his Secretariat. Ludwig himself was perhaps a little chilled for the moment at the news that the work he so longed to see, and for which he had made so many sacrifices, could not be given before the summer of 1876. It may possibly have been unfortunate also that in this same letter Wagner raised once more the question of his allowance. He had settled down in his new house in the preceding April. He wishes, he says, the King could see it, if only to satisfy himself of the falsity of the reports in the Press of the luxury of it. The utmost economy has been practised in its construction; but even so it could not have been achieved but for the new copyright law and the royalties it guaranteed him, and his heirs for thirty years after his death. But at the moment he is rather hard pressed; consequently he would be grateful if his benefactor would confer a new favour on him.

It will be recalled that on the 2nd March, 1869 the King had granted him a loan of 10,000 florins, to be redeemed by monthly deductions of 166 florins 40 kreuzer from his pension. These repayments had been made regularly until the end of August, 1871, when Ludwig, at Wagner's request, ordered them to be suspended for the whole of 1871 and 1872, the sum already paid by Wagner in respect of the former of these years to be returned to him. The redemption was to commence again in 1873, though now at the lower rate of 100 gulden a month. By October, 1872 Wagner's difficulties had so increased that he had to ask for a further suspension of payments: the request was granted, his allowance being paid him in full through 1873 and 1874. The unredeemed portion of the loan in October, 1873 was therefore 6,500 florins. Wagner now asks that the arrangement for remission of the monthly payments shall be again extended; as he points out to the King, when the liability was originally contracted and the deductions from his pension were first made he had not foreseen that he would have the felicity of a large family to care for.

On the 23rd October Düfflipp sent Wagner the King's reply. Exemption from the monthly repayments was to continue to the end of 1875. His Majesty regretted, however, that he could not consent to any modification of Clause III of the contract of the previous 26th February with the Bayreuth Theatre Committee, for the Kabinettskasse, having heavy and unceasing demands upon it in connection with the King's own building plans, absolutely could not dispense with the promised reimbursements in respect of monies received for Patronatscheine. "I am expressly to inform you", Düfflipp concluded,

"that you are not to see any ill-will in this. It is simply and solely that circumstances compel him to withhold his consent; and he would therefore take it ill if the matter were brought up again."

5

Wagner's calm proposal that a vital clause of the agreement with the King should be set aside the moment it became inconvenient to him to observe it could hardly have met with the approval of business men like Feustel and Muncker, to whom a contract was a contract. His verbose and fumbling reply of the 24th October to Düfflipp suggests that he too was conscious that he had gone a little too far, though he had still not quite lost belief in his power to work on the King's emotions. He must have been misunderstood, he says, if his letter to Ludwig had given the impression that he wanted an amendment of Clause III. What he had meant was simply that an "exact elucidation" of it was desirable — though what there was obscure about it could not have been apparent to anyone but himself. If, he contends, the meaning of it is that the King's loan, the date of the redemption of which was to be August, 1875, and the purpose of which was to provide for the full construction and the fitting up of the theatre, is to ensure the giving of the festival in 1876, it is manifest that this end-result can only be attained if "the necessary work in other directions can proceed without interruption, for otherwise, even if the stage-fittings made possible by the royal loan be guaranteed, the performances would still be impossible if all other needs are not also provided for. It is these additional essential works that we now have to consider. We found that the surrounding land will have to be properly laid out if the theatre is to be made accessible in 1876. As we could not cover the cost of this out of the royal loan, I have resolved, in spite of my great repugnance to such a step, to give concerts this winter in Pesth and Vienna, in order to raise entirely by my own private efforts the money necessary for this work on the terrain."

Therefore it seems to him and his advisers that while (a) the loan is to be applied simply and solely to the purposes set forth in the agreement, and, as stipulated there, the machinery, fittings and so on thus acquired are to be the property of the Court Secretariat until the loan is redeemed, yet (b) the help afforded by the loan will utterly fail to achieve its object if the current receipts from other quarters are not to be disposed of "in the sense of making the performances in 1876 possible"; consequently (c) his considered view is that *besides* the work done in virtue of the loan the other necessary preliminary works must *also* be carried out — of course with all conceivable economy — without drawing on the funds provided by the loan, the repayment of the specific advance being postponed until the object of his Majesty's intervention — the giving of the performances in 1876 — is fully secured. If Düfflipp should now tell him that he has been wrong in this assumption, that the loan of 100,000 thalers was not intended unconditionally to achieve an undertaking the like of which Germany has never seen before, then he must admit that he has been sadly in error and that it will be better for his peace of mind if he gives up trying to finish what has been begun. But if his original assumption as to the King's intentions be correct, he reiterates his conviction that the 100,000 thalers will be repaid to the Kabinettskasse on the 30th August, 1876 down to the last heller and pfennig, for the business direction of the undertaking is in good hands.

Wagner's need of the occasional receipts from Patronatscheine for the immediate purposes of his theatre must have been dire, for in spite of Düfflipp's warning that the King was reluctant to hear of the matter again he seems to have kept recurring to it through the following year. In September, 1875 we find him once more pressing Düfflipp for a decision in his favour. Unless, he says, he has permission to devote the proceeds of the first 600 Scheine to the most necessary ends, such as the completion of the fabric, the fitting up of the auditorium and the making of the costumes, the festival will have to be called off for 1876, which means that, in spite of the brilliant success of the rehearsals of that summer, public confidence will be undermined and the sacrifices of all of them will be in vain. Evidently the theatre had arrived at its most critical moment. But, as usual, the King could not find it in his heart to fail him in the hour of need, though his own financial difficulties were increasing at this time. On the 27th September he ordered that Clause III should be so amended that out of each Schein (520 florins) after the 426th the Court Secretariat was to receive 315 florins, the balance to be retained by the Theatre Committee. The King added to this rescript the words,

"When informing the Richard Wagner Theatre Committee of this it is to be further stressed that I am not disposed to make any more concessions in the matter and consequently must not be importuned about it again."

6

But on the 1st January, 1876 Wagner had once more to tell Düfflipp that without a further credit the final preliminary work for the festival of the summer of that year could not be carried through. Düfflipp's reply of the 12th, in which he promised to send Wagner's letter on to Hohenschwangau, shows how serious the King's own position was just then:

"The contents of it [6] have grieved me greatly, and I would gladly reach out a helping hand to you if I could. But unfortunately the abyss yawning in front of us is widening each day, and in the end it will engulf everything. The last request of your Administrative Committee I had to leave unconsidered for four weeks, as there was no money in the department. In the end it was only by selling bonds at a loss that I could raise funds to send the remittance to Bayreuth".

The King himself, in fact, was already heading for bankruptcy. Wagner was in a situation hardly less desperate. His Committee, he told Düfflipp on the 19th January, had recently estimated that

---

[6] Wagner's letter had made it clear that he and his Committee were overwhelmed with anxieties.

preparations for the festival that year would have to be suspended unless they could obtain somewhere a credit of 25/50,000 thalers. As a last resort they had made an appeal to the Kaiser for help. He had favourably commended the matter to Bismarck, who had replied that in view of his own ignorance in matters of that kind he could do no more than refer it to the Reichstag for discussion. It seemed likely, said Wagner, that a grant would be made, but only after a public debate, which would bring all sorts of annoyances in its train. His own impulse was to terminate negotiations in that quarter and begin giving concerts again. But he asks Düfflipp to lay the case once more before the King and find out whether he approves of the Committee making the necessary formal petition to the Reichstag. If he disapproves, Wagner will of course not follow up that line; but in that case there will be nothing for it but to abandon the idea of holding the festival that year, as it will be simply impossible to complete the necessary preliminary work.[7]

To this the King seems to have made no reply. Wagner was consequently forced back on the Berlin plan once more; he resolved to go there in March to take further soundings, for anything would be better than the public confession of failure involved in the postponement or abandonment of the festival.

In his letter of the 1st October, 1874 he had told the King that the Kaiser and a number of other German rulers would attend the festival, not because they had any understanding of its real significance but more or less because they would regard it as the proper thing to do. Accordingly he has erected at the back of the auditorium a "Princes' Gallery", holding about a hundred people and with an entrance of its own. This gallery is to be at the sole disposal of Ludwig whenever he chooses to see a performance; and Wagner asks whether the King will honour him with his presence at the festival or be deterred by his well-known objection to the company of his fellow-monarchs in any theatre. Wagner proposes to ensure his privacy by giving in the first week of August (1876) a performance — really a final rehearsal — of the whole tetralogy for him alone, no one else being admitted to the theatre on those evenings. Ludwig replied on the 7th March (1875). He is rejoiced

---

[7] Bismarck's unwillingness to involve the Kaiser in the Bayreuth matter had once more been due to his fear that, as he put it later to Poschinger, if Berlin assisted Wagner the King of Bavaria "would think we were poaching on his preserves".

at Wagner's suggestion, he says, which will save him from having to do the honours to

> "tasteless princely colleagues and transplant to Bayreuth the dull, venal Court life that is as hateful to me as ever, and that will embitter the artistic delight to which I am looking forward so ardently".

But he asks that *three* complete performances of this private kind shall be given him, so inappeasable is his desire to sink himself in Wagner's godlike art, to console himself for his years of weary waiting for the *Ring*. Wagner accepts the suggestion with enthusiasm; for him the King's wish is law.

It must have been as evident to him, however, as it is to us that the matter might not turn out in practice as easy as it looked on paper. There was no knowing whether, when the time came, Ludwig would really abandon his beloved mountain solitude, or, supposing him to do so, precisely when he would find it both convenient and possible to spend so many days in Bayreuth. There was a risk of the theatre being disorganised or even totally immobilised at certain times, and thereby, of course, much-needed receipts from public performances being lost. These and other practical considerations were no doubt in Wagner's mind when, on the 22nd February, 1876, while the question of the Berlin subsidy was still on the carpet, he asked Düfflipp to be good enough to give him as definite an idea as possible of what his Majesty's intentions were. The front row of seats in the new gallery, he says, is intended for royal personages. Behind them is a gangway, and behind this again, on a slightly higher level, seats for the Court attendants. He is now faced with the problem of allocating all these seats for the various performances, and he would like to know the King's wishes as to the places he desires to be reserved for his own use. Ludwig having already placed the Bayreuth Schloss at the disposal of royal visitors to the festival, Wagner further asks now for assistance in making the delicate necessary arrangements for them and their attendants. He gives Düfflipp a list of the potentates among his Patrons; it includes the Kaiser, Prince George of Prussia, the Grand Dukes of Mecklenburg, Baden and Sachsen-Weimar, the Dukes of Dessau and Altenburg, and possibly the Duke of Meiningen. The Sultan of Turkey and the Khedive of Egypt will probably not be there in person, but a number of minor German notabilities — non-reigning Princes like Hohenlohe, Radziwill, Metternich and so on — are sure to attend, though no doubt the Duke of Württemberg will accommodate these at his Fantaisie estate. He concludes by asking for the loan of a horse from the King's stables to play the responsible part of Grane; he has been advised not to hire a circus horse, as these animals are inclined to start dancing as soon as they hear music.

From all this it looks as if he contemplated the King's attendances at the festival coinciding with those of some of the other princes: in any case it was obviously impossible for him to leave all these ticklish problems to be settled offhand when the time came. Perhaps the thought of the prospect before him appalled the privacy-loving King, for no answer seems to have been returned to Wagner's letter.

7

The general rehearsals for the festival were planned to begin in the summer of 1876. They would involve Wagner in an expense of more than 2,000 marks a day for the singers and orchestra alone; so it is not surprising that on the 25th May he had once more pointed out to Düfflipp the impossibility of his carrying on to the end unless the King waived his right to the allocation of the receipts from Patronatscheine to the liquidation of the loan: otherwise, he says,

> "we shall not have a pfennig in hand to pay the players and singers, who are due here on the 1st of June, and there will be nothing for it but to announce the abandonment of the festival".

All he needs is a remission of the repayments for two or three months at the most, at the end of which time he will be in a position to extinguish the whole loan. (Naturally, as the time for the performances approached, the applications for seats would increase in number). The King must have realised the intolerable burden of work and worry that now lay upon Wagner; and at the beginning of June Düfflipp was commissioned to assure him that he could rely on being able to carry his great undertaking through. On the 16th the Secretary asked the Committee for a statement as to how the loan would be repaid in the event of his Majesty granting the request for a moratorium. The advances made by the Kabinettskasse between the 23rd May, 1874 and June, 1876 amounted to 216,152 marks (about 70,000 thalers). On the 29th June Düfflipp could inform Wagner that the King was willing to forego repayments on account of the loan until 800 Patronatscheine had been sold. At considerable inconvenience to himself, he had saved Bayreuth.

Throughout all this time the personal relations between Wagner and Ludwig were of the friendliest kind. In December, 1873 the Maximilian Order for Art and Science was once more offered to Wagner,[8] and this time he accepted it, not because he attached any value to things of that sort but because he had no plausible excuse for declining it. The King shared his opinion on these matters: "Rest assured", he wrote him, "that only when I learned that an Order would not be offensive to you did I act on the suggestion of the Capitular, for well I know how superior you are to such things".

8

Wagner had entered into possession of his handsome new home on the 28th April, 1874, and in his letters to the King he was happy to satisfy his protector's inexhaustible appetite for details of his private life. He had sought for a name for the house that would symbolise his having found a refuge, at last, from the illusions of the world. He found it in "Wahnfried"; [9] and unable, as usual, to refrain from breaking into verse on a great occasion, he had had engraved across the portal the lines

Hier, wo mein Wähnen Frieden fand —
WAHNFRIED
Sei dieses Haus von mir benannt.

(Here where my illusion found peace, be this house named by me Peace from Illusion).[10] It is Wotan taking the stage; we would hardly be surprised to hear some day a trombone concealed in a nearby shrubbery give out the Spear motive. A sgraffito panel over

---

[8] On an earlier offer (in 1864), which Wagner had declined, see Vol. III, p. 316–7.

[9] "Peace from Wahn". "Wahn" is generally untranslatable by a single English word: it means something of "illusion", of "error", of "madness", and other things.

[10] Apparently the lines were jibed at by the ribald. Lilli Lehmann speaks of them (LMW, p. 211) as "the much-derided inscription" — a dark saying into the meaning of which one had to be initiated.

the lintel — the work of a Dresden painter, Robert Krausse, but Wagner's own design — is allegorical. It had better be described in his own words to the King. It represents "the Art-Work of the Future".

> "In the centre is the Germanic mythos. As we [Cosima and himself] wanted characteristic physiognomies, we decided here on the head of Ludwig Schnorr. From either side Wotan's ravens are flying towards him, and he reveals the legend to two female figures, one of them, resembling Schröder-Devrient, representing antique tragedy, while the other, with Cosima's head and mien, represents Music: a little boy, armed like Siegfried, and with my son's head, stands by her side and looks up to his mother happily and bravely."

In front of the main entrance was a railed enclosure destined to be occupied later by a bust of the King. With regard to this he handled his generous benefactor very skilfully. The granite base was already there, he says, but difficulties have arisen in connection with the bust. He wants it to be in bronze, and in view of the dimensions of the house and the setting generally it will of course have to be twice life-size. Zumbusch, the sculptor, had told him that marble would be cheaper and easier, since a bronze casting would necessitate a new model, which would take time and cost much money. But because of the inclemency of the Bayreuth weather a marble would have to be boxed-in with wood for some six months of the year; and Wagner's heart bleeds at the very thought of that. In his perplexity he can only stare sadly at the empty place and wonder what he ought to do. The technique worked to perfection; the King had a bronze bust made and sent it to Wagner as a present.

Inside the house, he tells the King, everything has been planned so as to obtain a large drawing-room, opening out on to the garden at the back, which is the admiration of all who have seen it. Here are his books, pictures, memorials, presents and precious documents of all kinds; his piano; his big writing-desk and a smaller one for Cosima. A well-planned hall contains the marble busts of himself and others: along the frieze runs a Scandinavian snake-motive which frames Echter's pictures of the Nibelung's Ring, copied from frescoes in the Munich Residenz. This hall gives entrance to "the modest dining-room".

After breakfasting with Cosima, he tells the King, at ten o'clock he goes down to the drawing-room, where, if business allows, he works until one. The children join him at lunch, which is generally a merry affair, little Siegfried being particularly bright. Coffee is taken in the garden. He runs his eye over the Bayreuth *Tagblatt* — the only newspaper he allows in the house, — and discusses art, philosophy or life with Cosima. Then a short rest, after which he goes to the drawing-room, where he and Cosima deal with their correspondence. He regards it as one of his lucky days when there is no bad news from the outer world, when the post has brought him nothing worse to cope with than the usual poems sent him with the request that he shall set them to music, essays on the philosophy of art which he is to read and pass on to the King of Bavaria, or requests from English and American art-lovers for his autograph — requests which he has learned by experience to ignore. In the afternoon, all going well, he takes a walk, or drives with the children to the Eremitage or the Fantaisie, or perhaps pays a visit to his theatre — though as a rule he has to keep away from this by reason of the daily crowd of sightseers from near and far. At seven o'clock, a light meal with the children. At eight, he and Cosima settle down to reading in the drawing-room, unless visitors drop in, in which case the evening is given up to talk and music-making. On these occasions he entertains what has come to be known locally as "the Nibelung Chançellery" — a little group of devotees who correct his proofs, copy parts, and so on, and whom he is training to be his coaches and conductors of the future. They consist, he says, of a Saxon [Hermann Zumpe], a Hungarian [Anton Seidl, whose facial resemblance to Liszt, by the way, was a subject of frequent comment by our fathers], a Russian [Joseph Rubinstein], and a Macedonian [Demetrius Lalas].[11]

Had it not been for his cares in connection with the theatre his life would have been quite an agreeable one. He must have missed the majestic Swiss scenery; but he had a new country to explore on his walks and drives, while there was always privacy for him

---

[11] The last-named seems to have dropped out of musical history. Seidl, who died in 1898 at the age of forty-eight, had a distinguished career as a Wagner conductor. Both he and Rubinstein will come into our story again later. Zumpe (1850–1903) served as Kapellmeister at various German theatres, including that of Munich. A small volume of his reminiscences, diaries and letters, with a foreword by Ernst von Possart, was published in 1905. His experiences in Bayreuth between 1873 and 1875 are told in Chapter II of this.

Franz Fischer, Felix Mottl and one or two others also functioned in the Kanzlei at various times.

in the great garden of the Neues Schloss, into which the King had given him permission to make a little gateway from his own garden at the rear of the house. His most serious trouble, apart from the finances of the theatre, was the Bayreuth climate, to which he could never adapt himself, and which in the long run was to drive him out of the town for a considerable part of each year.

CHAPTER XXI

SPADEWORK IN 1874

1

WE CAN now take up the general narrative again at the point at which it had to be interrupted in order to tell to the end the story of the King's rescue of Bayreuth.

The year 1874 made several gaps in the circle of Wagner's older friends and acquaintances. His servant of former years, Franz Mrazeck, died in Munich in January. He was followed in February by Wagner's sister Luise Brockhaus, in May by Franz Schott and Mme Mouchanoff-Kalergis, in October by Peter Cornelius, Heinrich Wolfram (the husband of Wagner's sister Klara), and Albert Wagner, the oldest member of the family. (Klara Wolfram died in the following March). Mme Mouchanoff and Cornelius, like Frau Julie Ritter, Uhlig, Baudelaire, Rossini, Auber, Halévy, Berlioz, and many others who had watched the struggles of Wagner's early and middle periods with varying degrees of sympathy or detachment, did not live to see his final resounding triumph.

He had been right when he told King Ludwig that a new generation had sprung up that looked to him for leadership. The Hillers and the Dorns and others of that type, though still alive and as busy as ever, were now no more than symbols of a German musical world that had almost passed away. Wagner's present friends, coadjutors and devotees were mostly young people for whom he was the central orb of a new and glorious system. The King was twenty-nine; Bülow, the oldest of them all, but still young, was forty-four; Nietzsche was thirty. Some of the older singers, such as Niemann (forty-three), Betz (thirty-nine), and Karl Hill (forty-three) were finding a new youth in Wagner's art; while all over Germany there was springing up a younger generation of singers devoted to him and destined to rise to fame on his shoulders. In 1874 Vogl and his wife, the former Therese Thoma, were twenty-nine; Marianne Brandt was thirty-three; Amalie Materna twenty-nine; Eugen Gura thirty-two; Lilli Lehmann twenty-six; Georg Unger thirty-seven; Hedwig Reicher-Kindermann twenty-one; Theodor Reichmann (the first Amfortas) twenty-five; Hermann Winkelmann (the first Parsifal) twenty-five; Heinrich Gudehus twenty-nine; Therese Malten nineteen. Side by side with these was growing up a type of conductor very different from the plodding time-beaters of Wagner's early and middle years — Richter (thirty-one in 1874), Seidl (twenty-four), Hermann Levi (thirty-five), Zumpe (twenty-four); while in the middle and further distance new waves of conducting talent were preparing to form — Mahler was fourteen in 1874, Karl Muck fifteen, Richard Strauss ten, Mottl eighteen, Nikisch nineteen, — along with a fresh supply of great Wagnerian singers and producers. From 1876 onwards for many years there emanated from Bayreuth a force that was to change the face not only of musical creation but of musical performance. Wagner had already achieved the greatest sum of transformation that has ever been accomplished by one man in the whole history of music; even the composers in this country or that whose strong personalities managed to assert themselves against his influence later, or even consciously to rebel against it, owed more of their vitality than their pride would sometimes allow them to admit to Wagner's puissant loins.

2

His thoughts during 1874 were not so exclusively concentrated on his theatre that he could not spare a little time for the pleasing business of the embellishment of his fine new house. His own financial situation was obviously worsening for the time being; but he left the worrying about that to Cosima. As usual, his fertile brain soon lighted upon a new expedient for raising money. From Schotts he could wheedle no more now in respect of the still unfinished *Ring*. But on the 23rd January, 1874 he sprang a fresh surprise on his much-enduring publisher. "I need 10,000 gulden", he wrote,

"to complete my house and garden. If you will advance me this sum at once in respect of compositions to be delivered later, I will pledge myself to supply you, from half-year to half-year, with six large orchestral works in all, each of the dimensions and the importance of a big overture, the first of them to be delivered by the end of the present year at the latest."

The *Götterdämmerung*, he says, will be finished during the coming summer; then he will have leisure to work out some sketches that have occupied him for some time past. This sort of composition will give him more pleasure than to go on writing operas merely for the theatres to botch, whereas his purely orchestral works have always gone well. As a basis of payment for these new works he suggests the contract Peters had offered him for a new work after the success they had had with the *Kaisermarsch:* they were willing to give him 1,000 thalers for such a work, and he has no doubt he could easily persuade this rival firm to pay him in advance for six compositions of the sort. In a word, "thanks to my rapidly growing vogue I have a noose round your neck, my worthy publisher, and if you don't pay up handsomely and at once it will be drawn tight by your competitor Peters and myself". Then comes a moving appeal to Schott's better nature: "If this proposal of mine, this wish, this prayer is somewhat out of the common, it is Franz Schott to whom I make it, and after all it is Richard Wagner who is doing so".

Schott's reply has not been published, but we gather from Wagner's letters that he had not exactly warmed to the suggestion in its entirety, though "in essentials", as Wagner puts it later, he was not unwilling to consider it. The vital points are that Wagner needs money and his value in the market is rising. He suggests an agreement that in consideration of an immediate payment of 10,000 florins in respect of future new works and of proceeds from the sale of the *Ring* libretto, he, Richard Wagner, shall deliver to Schotts henceforth each and every new work from his pen. He had presumably forgotten that already on the 17th January, 1862, when offering Schotts the score of the *Meistersinger*, he had formally undertaken not to sell any of his existing *or future* works to any other publisher without first giving Schotts the opportunity of acquiring them. This he had confirmed in a further letter of the 12th July of the same year;

"I do not regard the advances you made to me as relating only to the publication and the theatrical management of my latest work, the *Meistersinger,* but stand pledged not to allow anything of mine to be printed without having first offered it to you, so that until my debt to you is extinguished I recognise you as the sole legitimate proprietor of all my works, now complete, already in hand, or yet to be delivered".

Notwithstanding all this, he had sold the score of the popular and profitable *Kaisermarsch* to Peters in the early part of 1871. Schott had evidently protested when he became aware of it, for on the 13th April of that year we find Wagner airily dismissing the matter as of no real importance. Peters, he said, had spontaneously offered him some time ago 1,500 marks for a March if he cared to write one; and he had decided to do so when he and his wife needed money for their projected tour of Germany.

"I know, most esteemed one, that I am still indebted to you for advances, so that I could not have expected you to pay cash down on this occasion. So I jumped at [Peters'] offer, which really came most opportunely. I thought you would take it ill of me, but after all would forgive me. And so — apologies!"

The ever-forgiving Schott made a new contract with him in February, 1874, under which he was to receive a fresh advance of 10,000 florins against future works, with the proviso that until the debt was redeemed Schott was to acquire any such work at twenty per cent less than any other publisher might offer: if, however, the price offered by the latter should be regarded by Schott as excessive, and a work consequently be declined by him, Wagner was to apply the sum received from the other publisher to the extinguishing of his debt to Schott. And having thus gaily disposed of the difficulty of the moment, the Micawber of Bayreuth could breathe freely again.

That he intended to write the orchestral works of which he spoke is beyond question; his mind was occupied with many plans of this kind just then and all through the following years. But he never wrote one of them; the only work of the new category which Schotts ever received from him — and that was in 1877 — was the *Siegfried Idyll,* which had been written in 1870.

3

In February the second of Nietzsche's *Thoughts out of Season,* — *The Utility and Harmfulness of History* — was published. Wagner seems to have been inwardly cool towards it, as it was in no way concerned with him and his work. Elisabeth will have it that already her brother had his doubts about Wagner; but the fact remains that he was still, at this time, convinced of the necessity for

Bayreuth and grieved by Wagner's difficulties. On the 11th February, after commiserating with Malwida von Meysenbug on her sufferings under the Bayreuth climate, he goes on to say,

"One distress we have in common, one which hardly anyone else can feel so strongly — our distress over Bayreuth. For alas, our hopes were too great! I tried first of all not to think any more about the trouble there; then, this proving impossible, during the last few weeks I have been thinking hard about it, searching out rigorously all the reasons why the undertaking is standing still, perhaps, indeed, foundering".

There is no suggestion here of waning belief in Wagner; Nietzsche's distress is occasioned purely and simply by the fact that Bayreuth seems likely to crash because of the drying up of funds; Wagner's hopes, and the hopes of Nietzsche himself and all the others, had been based on fallacious trust in German culture and the German spirit. Four days after this letter we find Nietzsche telling Rohde that according to an announcement in the Mannheim paper that acts as Heckel's mouthpiece, the festival is now positively assured. "If so, then the miracle has happened! Let us go on hoping!" He had begun, he said, to search out in the coolest way possible the reasons for the undertaking having miscarried; in doing this he has "learned much", and believes he now understands Wagner much better than he had formerly done. He manifestly has in mind his essay *Richard Wagner in Bayreuth,* which was published in the following year. At that we shall glance in due course; meanwhile his final words to Rohde should be noted — if the report be true and the "miracle" has really happened, they two will be happy and hold a festival of their own. Here again there is no hint of any "doubts" about Wagner or about the value of Bayreuth and the necessity for it.

It is evident, however, that the aloofness he detected in Wagner's and Cosima's letters acknowledging the second of the *Thoughts out of Season* had hurt him, and not unlikely that his pride took offence at the tone of patronage in Cosima's letter and her criticisms of his style; as he said later, if Cosima, who after all was not a German, was so anxious to improve the style of German writers she might do worse than make a beginning with that of Richard. It is notable that in a letter of the following April to Gersdorff he makes it clear that he is thoroughly discontented with himself and what he is doing, and resentful of outer constraints on what he is conscious of as new developments within him.

"I long for nothing more than a little freedom, a little of the genuine breath of life; and I revolt against the unspeakable servitude to which I am subject. There can be no question of real productivity so long as one feels so unfree, so full of suffering and the sense of being weighed down by embarrassments. Shall I ever be able to achieve this? I doubt it more and more. . ."

He was becoming increasingly out of tune with his Basel environment and his professional routine.[1] But there can be little doubt that a minor conflict was already beginning within him with respect to Wagner. It was not, as the older Nietzscheans would have had us believe, that he had thought out the whole intellectual and aesthetic matter afresh and come to the reasoned though as yet tentative conclusion that Wagner was not all he had taken him to be. The trouble was simply and solely the counterpart of Wagner's trouble with regard to him. For the now developing "positivist" side of Nietzsche's thinking Wagner had no use, because it had no bearing on his own life-ends. Nietzsche, for his part, being what he was, could come to no other conclusion than that if Wagner did not alter the whole orientation of his thought when *he* changed his, then Wagner must be a besotted self-illusionist, and everything for which he stood a danger to German culture. To go his own new way quietly and let Wagner go his was impossible to one so arrogantly self-centred as himself. A complete breach between the two men some time or other was therefore a certainty.

4

But while the younger man, as yet rather unsure of himself, fretted himself over his unsureness and was only too prone to visit the consequences of it on others, the older and harder one, his metal tempered in many a fire, never doubting himself for a moment, pressed on unceasingly with the whole strength of his tyrannic nature .towards his clearly-seen goal. The summer of 1874 was mainly devoted to preludial studies for the festival of two years

---

[1] See, on this point, his letter of the winter of 1873–4 (NGB, I, 263 ff) to the musician Carl Fuchs, who thought of settling in Basel as a teacher. Nietzsche says that he and Professor Overbeck have often thought of fleeing from it all into some corner of the world where they can be free to live and to think. Rohde, again, confesses to Nietzsche his own disheartenment over everything, his uncertainty as to his direction, his feeling that he is alone in the world, without friends, without consolations.

later. As early as the preceding March he had settled down in earnest to the problem of choosing his cast. With regard to the women he was still very uncertain; and as to the men, he had more or less definitely decided only on four — Betz as Wotan, Niemann as Siegmund, Hill as Alberich, and Emil Scaria, of Vienna, as Hagen. With some of these he was to have trouble from time to time, for they were old enough on the one hand to have acquired theatrical habits of which he found it hard to break them, and on the other hand to have won great popularity in their own theatres in virtue of these very habits, so that their pride jibbed at the suggestion that they had anything to learn, even from a Wagner. Scaria, who was thirty-six in 1874, was naturally gifted, but both his musical and his general education left much to be desired. He came to Bayreuth towards the end of June bubbling over with enthusiasm, but Wagner soon discovered that as yet he had not even read the text of the *Ring*! He was at once taken in hand by Richter, who spent two months in Bayreuth, helping Wagner in testing and coaching such of the singers as presented themselves that summer.

The best impression was made by Hill, who, apart from the fact that he seemed to have been created by nature for the part of Alberich, appears to have been a man of some culture. Of Betz and Niemann Wagner felt that he could be reasonably sure when they had had some instruction from him. Scaria had the right voice for Hagen and much of the temperament for the part. So far, then, all was reasonably well. But the Siegfried and the Brynhilde were yet to be found. For the former, Wagner first of all had in view Franz Diener, a young Heldentenor of twenty-five, whose shortcomings, however, soon became manifest. Then Richter thought he had discovered the right man in one Franz Glatz, a young Hungarian jurist who had the presence for the part, a powerful voice of much promise, and something of the culture Wagner so much desired in his singers. The fact that he had had no stage experience was if anything in his favour, for at least he would have no conventional theatrical tricks to unlearn. But the hopes built on him soon foundered: his vocal method proved too faulty to be capable of reformation within any reasonable time, and it was tolerably clear that he would not last out a long series of rehearsals and performances. Therese Vogl had been chosen for Sieglinde, but Wagner seems to have had at this time no thought of using her husband even for the part of Loge,

[429]

which he was destined to take in the end. For his Loge Wagner had in mind in 1874 George Unger, of Mannheim, who, however, became, *faute de mieux,* the first Siegfried — incidental evidence of the difficulty Wagner had for a long time in casting that important rôle. His distress with regard to the equally important Brynhilde, who has to carry so much of the tetralogy on her shoulders from the *Valkyrie* onwards, was ended when Amalie Materna came to Bayreuth in July. She was a member of the Vienna company, and had been recommended to Wagner by her colleague Scaria. A round of "guest" performances in Germany and London that summer made it impossible for Wagner, who as yet knew nothing of her except by hearsay, to see her on the stage; and for some days after her arrival in Bayreuth she was so hoarse that she could not sing for him. But when she did so he realised at once that he had found his Brynhilde.

In general, though some progress was made in 1874, much was still uncertain. Still, a beginning had been made; Wagner and his assistants had given a few of the leading singers instruction enough to provide them with material to work upon during the twelve months that were to intervene before they would come together again in Bayreuth. For the rest he could only hope that by the summer of 1875, when the real work of tuition would begin, most at any rate of his problems of casting would have solved themselves. But he had no intention of being rushed. Reputations meant nothing to him; either the right new singers would have to drop into his lap from heaven or he would take some of the older ones to pieces and rebuild them on his own lines. One of the singers who called on him in August, 1874 was Marianne Brandt, of Berlin, who was destined to sing Kundry in some of the *Parsifal* performances of 1882. She had a European fame; but Wagner seems to have been only mildly impressed when she sang him some selections from the rôle of Ortrud. It is she to whom he refers, without naming her, in a passage near the end of his *Retrospect of the Stage-Festivals of 1876.*[2] According to him, this "very talented singer, whom my tuition in several rôles of my operas in years gone by had helped to great renown", had "declined to co-operate in our festival" on the ground that in an environment such as that of the Berlin Opera House "one

---

[2] RWGS, X, 116–7. The article was first published in the *Bayreuther Blätter* of December, 1878.

becomes so bad". It may have been so, though we suspect that Wagner's main object when penning that sentence was to administer a slap in the face to Hülsen. But the basic truth seems to have been that she had been offered the rôle of Waltraute and had deemed so "small" a part rather beneath her dignity. From a letter of hers of August, 1874 to Liszt we gather that she did not greatly care for a "narrative" part like this; she felt that her strength lay in dramatic changes of passion. But Wagner had no use for singers who wanted to be just their usual selves in the *Ring*.

Nor was it only the singers who caused him anxiety. Not only did occasional small differences of opinion arise between him and his stage craftsmen but these gentry began to develop differences between themselves in which he necessarily became involved. It had been arranged, it will be remembered, that the execution of Joseph Hoffmann's designs for the scenery should be entrusted to the brothers Brückner, of Coburg, who had the necessary facilities and experience for work of that kind. But in the autumn of 1874 trouble arose between the artist and the painters, with Brandt, apparently, taking the side of the latter. It took some time to appease the rival parties. In the end, Hoffmann surrendered, for a cash consideration, his claim to "inspect" the Brückners' work; but while the trouble lasted it meant yet another strain on Wagner's sorely taxed time and strength.

In spite of all difficulties and delays, however, his great undertaking was making sure if slow progress during the summer and autumn of 1874; and in December the costumes were commissioned of Professor Carl Emil Doepler of Berlin. A letter of the 17th December to Doepler shows Wagner to have been not quite clear in his own mind how the many problems of attiring his gods and heroes were to be solved, though of one thing he was certain — he did not want anything on the semi-classical, pseudo-Germanic lines adopted by the painters Cornelius and Schnorr in their illustrations of the *Nibelungenlied*.[3] The problem was obviously one, in the main, for archaeologists who had specialised in the Teutonic Middle Ages.

---

[3] Wagner's very interesting letter to Doepler will be found in RWBA, II, 335–6. Doepler's coloured designs, forty-one in all, were issued in an album at some later date — *Der Ring des Nibelungen, Figurinen erfunden und gezeichnet von Prof. Carl Emil Doepler, mit Text von Clara Steinitz.* (Berlin, n.d.; but as the publication is dedicated to Kaiser Wilhelm II the date cannot be earlier than 1888).

Looking far ahead, as usual, and, as usual where matters of theatrical practice were concerned, not only willing but anxious to learn from anyone whose experience and competence transcended his own in a specialised technical field, Wagner saw that certain episodes of the *Ring,* and more particularly that of the swimming Rhine Maidens, would call for the co-operation of an expert in stage movements; and his experiences at little Dessau in December, 1872 had brought to light the very man he needed. Though the Dessau theatre had only modest vocal and orchestral resources at its disposal its performance of *Orfeo* had been outstandingly good, thanks in part to the intelligence of the Director Normann but even more to his coadjutor Richard Fricke, who, after a successful career as a dancer, had become ballet-master in Dessau. Wagner had at once marked him out for co-operation in the *Ring* performances. In August, 1874 he asked for his help in the working-out of a complete plan for "the choregraphic realisation of the first scene of the *Rhinegold*" in terms of the machinery designed by Brandt: for this purpose he would require him in Bayreuth for the whole of the July and August of the following year. Fricke accepted the invitation, and at once began a thorough study of the *Ring* scores.

For a long time to come, Wagner's whole energies had to go into the preparations for his festival and the completion of the *Götterdämmerung.* He could no doubt have dispensed very well with the visit paid him by Nietzsche in August, a visit that was marked by an unpleasant scene between them that has passed into history. Nietzsche was obviously in poor condition physically and mentally, more fretted than ever by his lack of harmony with his Basel environment, and in general in one of those moods when the most saintly among us can find no better way of relieving his tension than by getting at cross-purposes with whoever happens to be nearest him. He incensed Wagner at the outset by saying that he found no pleasure now in the German language, preferring to express himself in Latin. But worse was to come. He had brought with him the piano score of Brahms's *Triumphlied* — a celebration, by eight-part choir, baritone solo and orchestra, of the German victories of 1870/1. Elisabeth's story of what followed is rather disingenuous. In one breath she tells us that Nietzsche had brought the score with him "apparently in the naive belief that it would please Wagner"; in the next, that "on further consideration" it seemed to her that "this red-bound volume was a sort of experimental object". One does not need to be a very profound psychologist to see that the latter is the genuine explanation: Nietzsche simply wanted the gratification of annoying Wagner. The latter, he knew, had no great opinion of Brahms [4] as a composer, and he had good reasons for disliking him as a man.[5] Elisabeth's account of the affair in later years, on the alleged authority of Wagner himself, ran thus:

> "Your brother laid the red book on the piano, and every time I came down to the drawing-room the red object stared at me — it literally exasperated me as the red rag does the bull. I saw quite clearly that what Nietzsche was saying to me was, 'You see, here is someone else who can write good music!'. Well, one evening I let myself go in good earnest".

He laughed heartily at the recollection of it, Elisabeth adds. In reply to her question how Nietzsche had taken his outburst, Wagner is said to have replied,

> "He said nothing, but simply blushed and looked at me with modest dignity. I would give a hundred thousand marks here and now for a demeanour such as Nietzsche's — always distinguished, always dignified. That kind of thing is invaluable in this world".[6]

6

That is quite possible; always, when he looked back on his outbursts of temper, Wagner could take a humorous view of himself. But there are plentiful grounds for our saying today that if Nietzsche could describe the official biographies of Wagner as "*fable convenue* or worse", Elisabeth's biography of her brother often falls into the same dubious category, — more especially in her thoroughly disingenuous handling of the causes that led, or at any rate contributed, to Nietzsche's mental collapse in January, 1889. The more she tries to veil the fact that he had taken the Brahms score to Bayreuth with the deliberate intention of trying Wagner's

---

[4] Whose first symphony did not appear until 1877.

[5] See, in Vol. III, pp. 471–2, the story of the trouble Wagner had had with him over the score of the Venusberg music.

[6] She adds that when she told this story to her brother he remarked, "Ah, on that occasion Wagner was not great."

temper the clearer that intention reveals itself to us. In her *second* account of the episode (in *Wagner und Nietzsche zur Zeit ihrer Freundschaft*) she tells us that her brother took the Brahms score with him

> "not suspecting, as I believed at that time, that Wagner might possibly take it in the wrong way. Later, however, I found among my brother's papers the following note: 'The tyrant tolerates no other individuality beside his own and that of his intimates. The danger for Wagner is great if he does not recognise Brahms etc., and the Jews'."

Well and good; but it would have been more honest of Elisabeth to disclose something she conceals, that this private jotting of Nietzsche's dates from *the earlier part of 1874:* it occurs among his sketches for his *Richard Wagner in Bayreuth*, together with sundry others in the same vein, such as:

> "Wagner's is a ruling nature, only then in its element, only then assured, moderate and firm: hindrances to this propensity make him immoderate, eccentric, refractory". ". . . Thirdly, he insulted the Jews, who today own most of the money and of the Press. When he did this he had no occasion for it; later it was revenge". " 'False omnipotence' develops something 'tyrannical' in Wagner. The feeling that he is without *heirs;* consequently he tries to give the utmost possible breadth to his reformatory idea, and as it were propagate himself by adoption. Striving for legitimacy".

(Then follows the passage about Brahms and the Jews quoted by Elisabeth.)

It seems clear, then, that Nietzsche had been brooding discontentedly over the subject of Wagner's "tyrannical" nature and his dislike of Brahms for some time before he went to Bayreuth in August. We need not take with absolute literalness the editorial rubric — "Aus dem Januar 1874" — at the head of the posthumously published jottings relating to the *Richard Wagner in Bayreuth*. There are nearly seventy of them; and though they may have been begun in January there is no reason to suppose that they *all* relate to that month.[7] As Elisabeth had been living in Basel with

---

[7] The extracts from his note-books — some of them running to considerable length — number more than 2,000. The arrangement of them in groups with such descriptive titles as "The Greeks", "The Philosopher", "Richard Wagner", "Music, Art, Literature", "Women, Marriage", "Nietzsche on himself", and so on is the work of his editors. The printed order of them is consequently no precise clue to the date of any one of them.

him since the April of 1874, it is a fair assumption that he had often discussed Wagner with her. The Basel performance of the *Triumphlied* (under Brahms himself) took place not "in the spring", as she says, but on the 9th June; and, as we now know, Nietzsche's note-books were packed by that time with memoranda that show how far he had diverged by now from Wagner. Correlating all the facts, and Elisabeth's comments on them, it seems evident that not only was the Nietzsche who went to Wahnfried in August already, to some extent, secretly inimical to Wagner, but he had deliberately inflicted the *Triumphlied* on him to observe his reactions and, he hoped, to find them confirming his private speculations as to Wagner's "tyrannical" nature where other composers were concerned. Elisabeth unwittingly gives her case away when she says it has "*since* occurred to her" that the red-bound score was "a sort of experimental object". That was precisely what it was, and no doubt she was as well aware of the fact all the time as her brother was.

As an experiment it lacked science, for anyone less tactless and femininely malicious than Nietzsche would have realised in advance that the composer who was just then devoting his whole imaginative energy to the completion of the colossal *Götterdämmerung* was not likely to behave normally when one of the poorest works of a composer whom he disliked so sincerely as he did Brahms was made to stare him in the face every time he entered his drawing-room. In periods of great imaginative tension a creative artist instinctively resorts for mental change to a type of art or literature at the furthest remove from his own of the moment; so it is not surprising to discover from Cosima's diary that Wagner was taking particular pleasure at this time in such things as Boïeldieu's *La Dame blanche* and Isouard's charming little *Cendrillon*. It was very thick-fingered of Nietzsche to insist, as he did, on going through a work which Wagner could only regard, as he seems to have done in his fury of the moment, as "Handel, Mendelssohn and Schumann swaddled in leather".[8]

---

[8] This is the characterisation of the *Triumphlied* in Cosima's diary.

The harassed state of Wagner's nerves during these months of ceaseless work and worry is best shown by the deplorable incident that occurred at Triebschen on the 21st November. That day should have been the greatest one in Cosima's life, for it saw the completion of the work for which she had sacrificed so much and borne so much obloquy. On that day Wagner wrote the last note of the *Götterdämmerung* orchestral score. The stupendous *Ring* was really finished, after twenty-six years of preoccupation with it: even his death before it was produced could not silence it now. And it was on this day of all days that he came nearest to breaking Cosima's heart.

He had completed the score, apparently, a day or two in advance of his expectations. Towards midday on the 21st he called to Cosima, asking her to bring him the newspapers. Unaware that the last note had been written, believing he had sent for her, as he sometimes did, because he was overwrought and needed a few moments' relaxation, and anxious not to add to his nervous tension by speaking of his work, she handed him a letter that had just arrived from Liszt, relating to a projected meeting of them all in Pesth. Later she encountered Richard as he was leaving his room to go in to lunch. He asked her what reply she proposed to send to her father. She told him, but, she says, intentionally kept her eyes averted from his manuscript so as not to vex him. (Apparently he was one of those people who dislike their work being looked over until it is finished.) But at this he took offence: his score, he said bitterly, was complete, "but when a letter comes from your father all sympathy for me disappears". Hurt as she was, she remained silent during the meal; but when it was over and he renewed his "bitter complaints" she burst into tears and fled to her diary for the easing of her heart.

"And so", she wrote,

"I have been robbed of this supreme joy, but not through the smallest stirring of bad feeling in me. The fact that I have dedicated my life in suffering to this work has not won me the right to celebrate its completion in joy. So I celebrate it in pain, consecrate the noble, wonderful work with my tears, and thank the eternal God who has laid on me the burden of expiating this completion by my sorrow. To whom can I tell this sorrow, to whom voice my lamentation? With Richard I can only keep silence. I confide it to these pages; may they teach my Siegfried to cherish no anger, no hatred, but only infinite pity for that most pitiful of creatures, man. . . . May all my sufferings find atonement in this unutterable one! The children saw me weeping and wept with me, but they were soon comforted. Richard went to his room with a last bitter word. I sought out some *Tristan* chords on the piano, but every theme was too sadly piercing for my mood. I can only sink back into myself, pray, and worship. . . Hail to thee, great day of achievement, day of fulfilment! If it is the lot of genius to end its flight so high, what is there for a wretched woman to do? Only to suffer in love and ecstasy."

But his anger, as was usual with him, soon died down. She had hardly closed her diary when he came to her, took her in his arms, and said that the cause of their sufferings was that they loved each other too passionately. And so, the next day, they celebrated the completion of the mighty work.

His contrition was most fully expressed, perhaps, in a tiny composition performed in Wahnfried in honour of Cosima's birthday (the 25th December) of that year. For the Christmas Day of 1873 he had set to music a few playful lines of his own — a "Kinder-Katechismus zu Kosel's Geburtstag", as he described them — in praise of Cosima; these were sung by the children to a piano accompaniment:

Solo: Sagt mir, Kinder, was blüht am Maitag?
Chorus: Die Rose, die Rose, die Ros' im Mai.
Solo: Kinder, wisst ihr auch was blüht in der Weihnacht?
Chorus: Die Kose- die Kose- die kosende Mama, die Co-si-ma!
Solo: Verwelkte auch die Maitagsrose, neu erblüht sie in der
    Weihnacht Schoosse.
Chorus: Ros' im Mai, kos' im Mai, allerliebste, allerschönste
    Co-si-ma!

For the fête of Christmas, 1874 Wagner scored the little piece for a small orchestra (strings, flute, oboe, 2 clarinets, 2 horns and bassoon), and had it performed again in Wahnfried by the children and a body of players from Hof. This time, however, he added a postlude based on the final bars of the *Götterdämmerung* — the motive of "Redemption by Love".[9]

---

[9] The score, with a facsimile of Wagner's manuscript, was published by Schotts in 1937.

CHAPTER XXII

BAYREUTH IN 1875

1

TODAY WE can see nothing in that letter of Liszt's to justify Wagner's irritation, which probably arose from its indirectly reminding him that he was more or less pledged to participation with Liszt in a concert; the reminder of anything so distasteful to him as concert-giving had had the misfortune to arrive at the worst time imaginable. But the year 1874 moved to its end in quiet happiness for them both, Cosima secretly searching for the lost manuscript of the symphony of Wagner's youth,[1] he already plunging deep into his *Parsifal* subject. As he brooded upon this, the old desire came upon him to lose himself in the delights of creation and forget his troubles with the pestilent outer world: "I wish", he said to Cosima, "we were finished with all this nonsense, and I could get down to *Parsifal*." But his responsibilities and worries with regard to Bayreuth were unending. At the beginning of December he had to go to Coburg to see Brandt and the brothers Brückner: there he had at any rate the satisfaction of seeing how well the full-scale realisation of some of the *Ring* scenery was shaping in the studio. But a musical farce to which he was taken amused him so little that he left the theatre before it was more than half over. At Leipzig, which he reached on the 20th, he saw a performance of *Jessonda* that brought him his first acquaintance with Eugen Gura, a young baritone who was later to become closely associated with his work. His experiences that evening led him to respond to an invitation of the editor of the *Musikalisches Wochenblatt* to write something for the new year's number of the paper. His article on *An Operatic Performance in Leipzig* [2] begins with some gaily ironic remarks about musical journals, their writers and their readers — he knew of no good reason for the existence of any one of the

---

[1] See Vol. I, Chapter V.
[2] RWGS, X, 9–10.

three, — and goes on to a discussion of the failings of German opera in general as shown in Spohr's work (for which he had a great liking), and more particularly in the performance of it which he had just heard. It must have been a remarkable one in some respects: perhaps only in a German opera house of that epoch could the spectator have been rejoiced by the spectacle of "a young Brahmin with a blond moustache and whiskers". But Wagner speaks in high praise of the Tristan d'Acunha of Gura, "a tragic embodiment of the most moving simplicity". "There was no doubt about it", he adds; "everything in the impersonation was pure and noble." Presumably he had already marked Gura out for a part in the *Ring*. (He sang Gunther in 1876).

Early in the new year the score of Liszt's latest work, *The Bells of Strassburg*, arrived at Wahnfried. Wagner and Cosima found it "a curious work, very effectively put together, but so alien to us!" Richter and his lately-acquired young wife came to spend a few days with them, and already Cosima's intuition fastened on one or two of his shortcomings; she felt that in spite of the closeness of their association there was no real affinity between him and them, that he was infected with the characteristic Viennese levity; and she recorded in her diary "the decided impression that in future Richter will take other paths".[3] Her resentment against him was occasioned mainly by the irresponsible way in which he had handled a scheme for Wagner concerts in Vienna and Pesth. The essence of the whole plan had been that, partly for economy's sake, partly to spare Wagner unnecessary fatigue, the same programme should be given in both towns, and the preliminary rehearsals, not only in Pesth but in Vienna, be taken by Richter. But he had chosen to get married at the time most inconvenient for Wagner and for the concerts, and when it came to the point he could not obtain further leave from Pesth to take the Vienna rehearsals. Liszt, for his part, had no desire to appear in the Austrian capital that winter. Wagner had hoped that the Bayreuth fund would profit to the extent of

---

[3] There is abundant testimony that Richter never won Wagner's full commendation as a conductor: for one thing his rhythm was too four-square. Julius Hey, who was almost daily with Wagner during the rehearsals of 1875, tells us that "for Wagner, Bülow was and remained the incomparable master of the baton, the model conductor in the highest sense of the term." At Munich he had achieved marvels in the way of drawing sensitive phrasing and a song-like delivery from the orchestra not only in Wagner's works but in French and Italian opera. See HRWV, p. 141. In later years Wagner thought most highly of Seidl.

10,000 gulden from Vienna and 5,000 from Pesth; in the end he had to be content with less than this.

He and Cosima left Bayreuth on the 20th February. During their absence the children were looked after by Nietzsche's sister.[4] She had arrived in Wahnfried early in the month, and consequently saw a good deal of Wagner and Cosima before they left. She has left us a picture of a sorely worried Wagner, seething with anger against his fellow-Germans, and sometimes, in his more overwrought moments, flying out even at Cosima without the smallest provocation. "I often used to marvel", says Elisabeth, "at her meekness under these unjustifiable outbursts of temper. On the whole it must be admitted that to be the wife of a genius is a hard task." Like so many other people, she was lost in admiration of Cosima's combination of charm and breeding and unbending strength of will.

2

The enforced defection of Richter so far as Vienna was concerned threw, of course, extra work on Wagner. He arrived there on the 21st, was received in state by the local Wagner Verein, and took up his quarters with the faithful Standhartner. He made several new acquaintances and renewed some old ones, among the latter Princess Sayn-Wittgenstein's daughter Marie (now Princess Hohenlohe), whom he had not seen since the Zürich days, and his former patroness in Paris, Pauline Metternich. He also met again, at the house of the painter Makart, his old friend Semper, now domiciled in Vienna, and aged and broken by a lifetime of vexations and disappointments. The rehearsals for the concert began on the 24th; the orchestra was that of the Opera, augmented to 108 players. The programme consisted entirely of his own works — the *Kaisermarsch*; the Norns Scene as a purely orchestral piece without the voices; the episode of Siegfried's parting from Brynhilde, followed by the Rhine Journey; the scene of Siegfried's death,

---

[4] This was at Cosima's request. According to Elisabeth, Wagner told Nietzsche, about this time, that in the event of his death he wanted him to act as Siegfried's guardian and educator. It was largely for this reason that Nietzsche urged his sister to accept the invitation. A stay in Wahnfried, he said, would be "a high school" for her. "When I think of the multifarious duties I may have in the future as regards Wagner's family, it seems to me *most important* that *you* shall be thoroughly at home there."

with the Funeral March; and the bulk of the final scene of the *Götterdämmerung*. He was satisfied with Materna, though obviously she still had much to learn. But as regards the tenor Glatz he was quite disillusioned; there could be no question now of his ever being able to sing Siegfried at Bayreuth. The concert, which was given on the 1st March, ended with a demonstration of enthusiasm by the great audience that surpassed everything of the kind in Wagner's previous experience of Vienna.

On the 6th he went to Pesth, where he had only the final rehearsal to take for the concert of the 10th, Richter having done the preliminary work. Earlier local estimates of the likely profit — and it has to be remembered that Wagner was coming only at the suggestion of the Pesth Wagner Verein, and that if the proceeds for Bayreuth were not to be substantial there was no reason why he should waste his time and strength over the affair — had had to be modified. The choir for *The Bells of Strassburg* would mean an extra expense, besides immobilising a large number of otherwise saleable seats. When Liszt heard of this he generously suggested that his cantata should be withdrawn and the Emperor concerto of Beethoven substituted for it, he himself undertaking the solo part with his "old ten fingers", as he put it. But the sacrifice was not accepted, and the programme consisted of the Liszt work; the concerto; the Forging Songs from *Siegfried;* the scene of Siegfried's death (with Glatz as singer); and Wotan's Farewell, sung by Herr Lang, the leading baritone of the Pesth theatre, who also took the solo part in *The Bells*. Liszt conducted his own work and Richter the concerto, in which the "old ten fingers" wrought marvels of delicacy and fire.

Two days later Wagner was in Vienna again, where, at his own desire, the previous concert was repeated at lowered prices for the benefit of the less affluent music lovers; this time, however, Glatz was replaced by Labatt. On the 15th Wagner and Cosima left for Bayreuth. The two Vienna concerts seem to have brought in about 9,000 and 4,000 gulden respectively, that in Pesth about 1,300 gulden.

On the 5th, Wagner had written to Düfflipp offering to perform the *Götterdämmerung* excerpts privately for King Ludwig in the Residenz Theatre, but was told that the King could not accept the offer until after Easter. Probably it was made only in order that

Wagner might have an excuse for visiting Munich, where he had a double object in view — to hear the Vogls in *Tristan* and decide what use, if any, he could make of them for the *Ring*, and to get an audience of the King. Ludwig perhaps guessed what his basic purpose was and had no desire to come under his personal spell just then, fearing a new appeal to his generosity for the benefit of Bayreuth. After his return to Bayreuth Wagner urged Hermann Levi to arrange a Munich performance of *Tristan* for him not later than the 6th April; but Levi was instructed by Düfflipp to inform him that "as his Majesty is continually unwell, and it would be too painful to him to have to miss a performance of *Tristan*, he wishes this to be postponed to the 10th May." Wagner's plans thus came to nothing; by the month of May his hands were more than full with other matters.

3

Although the preliminary rehearsals for the *Ring* were to take place that summer, and the contracts with the orchestral players had been sent out months before, Wagner had as yet hardly more than touched the perimeter of his problem of casting the parts: as he complained to the King in April, while in any other nation a creative artist would find his human material ready to his hand, he had to make his out of the rawest material — to say nothing of all the administrative work thrown upon him. So that he had barely recovered from the fatigue of his Austrian journey when he had to set out on a fresh tour through Germany, partly in order to raise more money by concert-giving but mainly to find singers for his festival. He left Bayreuth on the 9th April for an itinerary that included Hanover, Leipzig, Brunswick and Berlin. In Hanover he saw a performance of *Lohengrin* in which the Elsa, Fräulein Weckerlin, pleased him to the extent that he could offer her the small part of Gutrune.

At a banquet given him by the local Künstlerverein the Hanover Theatre Intendant, Hans von Bronsart, an old and faithful friend of Bülow's and the confidant in days gone by of all his troubles over Wagner and Cosima, was conspicuous by his absence. He declined the invitation to the banquet on the simple ground that "he was Bülow's friend". "I will attend with enthusiasm any time", he wrote to Bülow, "a celebration in honour of the greatest composer of our day, if only he adorns it by his personal absence." Bülow implored him to reconsider his decision, not for Wagner's but for Bayreuth's sake, but Bronsart was implacable.

At a poor performance of *Tannhäuser* at Brunswick Wagner thought the Tannhäuser, Hermann Schrötter, not without promise if he could be cured of the bad routine-tricks of so many of the German singers of that time. For a while he thought of him as a possible Siegfried; but this hope proved as illusory as so many others. He went so far as to offer Schrötter the part (on the 23rd April), and a week or so after sent Joseph Rubinstein to Leipzig to coach him in it. But a fortnight later the singer wrote him that he would have to withdraw from the agreement, as his Intendant, Herr von Rudolphi, had taken it ill that it had been entered into without *his* having been consulted.

On the 24th and 25th Wagner conducted two concerts in Berlin. The programmes were on the same lines as those of the recent concerts in Vienna, but this time he had an adequate tenor in Niemann: the soprano, as before, was Materna. The net profit was some 6,000 thalers, the Berlin Wagner Verein having shouldered the expenses, which amounted to 1,800 thalers, for which, however, it was given six Patronatscheine. After a few days at home he was off again to Vienna, where, on the 6th May, he gave a third concert; this time the programme contained Hagen's Watch by the Rhine, sung by Scaria, in place of the *Kaisermarsch*. The tenor was once more Labatt, while Materna, of course, sang in the *Siegfried* and *Götterdämmerung* excerpts. All in all Wagner had by now raised about 40,000 florins for Bayreuth by his own exhausting exertions. And still his sleepless nights were haunted by the spectre of bankruptcy; at this very time he contemplated handing back to the town the land in front of the theatre terrace, for the money that would have to be spent on its development would be needed to meet the expenses of the summer's rehearsals. We see him, indeed, at this time almost breaking under his financial and administrative burdens, and begging Feustel to be allowed to concentrate on the most necessary work of teaching the singers and orchestra their business; minor problems such as the accommodation of the visitors to the festival, he thought, should be taken entirely off his hands by the Bayreuthers, who, after all, would find his great undertaking not unprofitable to them.

By the time he was back in Wahnfried again, on the 10th May, he was no further than he had ever been towards the final solution of his Siegfried problem. And entangled with this was another. For his Sieglinde he wanted Therese Vogl, but he was doubtful whether her consent would not be dependent on his engaging her husband also as Siegfried. This he could not see his way to do; the most he had in mind for Vogl was Loge. There was the possibility, then, if the Vogls took offence, of his having to look around for another Sieglinde. For Siegfried, Heckel had recommended Ferdinand Jäger, but the suggestion found no favour in Wagner's eyes. A young tenor of the Mannheim Opera, Georg Unger, had been well spoken of by Heckel and Richter; but his career so far had been undistinguished, and Wagner, as late as the spring of 1875, could see in him, at most, only a possible Loge, though his build and presence made him almost the ideal Siegfried. In the end it was Unger who played the part in the festival of 1876, but not before Wagner had gone to infinite trouble with him and been beset by constant doubts as to his capacity.

4

Wagner's carefully drawn up plan of campaign for the summer of 1875 was as follows: during the whole of July, piano rehearsals with his singers; during the first half of August, "reading-through" rehearsals for the orchestra, in which the singers would take part; then a week of practice at the more difficult stage situations, especially that of the swimming Rhine Maidens. He would be his own stage manager throughout; he needed only the help of Richard Fricke for episodes such as that just mentioned — an experienced choregraphist whose job it would be to translate Wagner's intentions into practice, giving plastic shape to the singers' evolutions in the apparatus devised by Brandt. He wanted Fricke to come to Bayreuth as soon as possible and attend as many piano rehearsals as he could, and thus acquire a sure sense of the "tempi" of the machinery as determining the choreographic pattern he would have to work out during the next twelve months. Wagner wanted his help also in the dynamic handling of the chorus of Gibichungs in the second and third acts of the *Götterdämmerung*. Fricke was further to keep himself completely free of all other duties for the whole three months of June, July and August in the following year. He arrived in Bayreuth on the 20th July and remained there until the end of August (1875), during which he was in daily consultation with Wagner. He kept a diary of all that was said and done in connection with his work both during those six weeks and throughout the summer of 1876; his book [5] is consequently one of the most valuable documents we possess for the understanding of Wagner's stage ideals and his methods of realising them.

The singers so far engaged arrived in Bayreuth at various times during the summer of 1875 — Materna, Niemann, Scaria, Betz, Eilers from Coburg (who was to play Fasolt), Reichenberg from Stettin (Fafner), Lilli Lehmann, her sister Marie and Fräulein Lammert from Berlin (the Rhine Maidens), Frau Jaïde from Darmstadt (Erda, and Waltraute in the *Götterdämmerung*), Gura from Leipzig (Gunther), the two Vogls from Munich,[6] Hill from Schwerin (Alberich), Marie Haupt from Cassel (Freia), Schlosser from Munich (Mime), Niering from Darmstadt (Donner and Hunding), Frau Sadler-Grün from Coburg (Fricka), Weiss from Breslau (Froh),[7] together with Richter, Brandt and Doepler, the designer of the costumes. Hülsen also came, partly to ask Wagner to conduct the projected first Berlin performance of *Tristan*, partly to inspect the theatre that by now was the talk of all Germany. He was present when, on the 24th July, a trial was made of the scenery for the opening scenes of the *Rhinegold* and the *Valkyrie*. In connection with the former, Wagner expressed the desire to hear how his music would sound in the theatre. The two Lehmanns and Fräulein Lammert accordingly clambered on to the stage from the auditorium and sang the Rhine Maidens' trio, Alberich joining in from the wings. These were the first strains heard in the building; and everyone was delighted with its acoustics. The orchestra was heard there for the first time on the afternoon of the 2nd August. As Wagner entered the theatre that day he was given an ovation by the personnel, and Betz sang Wotan's opening monologue:

---

[5] FBDJ.

[6] Vogl was in no very good temper. *He* already knew the Siegfried music, he told Wagner, and he was confident that Unger would not be able to master it in time to be of any use at the orchestral rehearsals.

[7] It was Unger, however, who sang Froh in 1876.

'Tis ended, the everlasting work!
On mountain peak
see! the gods' abode:
stately soar
its glittering walls!
As in dreams 'twas designed,
as my will did direct,
strong and fair
stands it in sight:
fortress peerless and proud!

Wagner, deeply moved, thanked them all in a few heartfelt words.

The orchestra numbered 115, with 64 strings. It was made up of the best players from several German opera houses, with no less a personage than August Wilhelmj as leader.[8] All the theatre rehearsals, both then and in 1876, conformed to much the same pattern: Richter conducted, while Wagner, sitting with the score in front of him on a desk lit by a petroleum lamp, occasionally gave instructions to both players and singers. He was enchanted with the success of his sunken orchestral pit, with the violins and violas nearest the conductor and the audience, the double basses flanking the violas, and the 'cellos, harps, flutes, oboes and cor anglais beyond the main string group; then, in the further middle distance, the clarinets, bass clarinet, bassoons and part of the horns; and at the back, underneath the stage, the remaining horns, trumpets, contrabassoons, trombones and drums. The blend was exquisite, while the heavy brass had a mellowness not attained till then in any theatre or concert hall.[9] The orchestral rehearsals went on from the

---

[8] The players took no fee, being content to receive simply their travelling and maintenance expenses. Some of the singers showed the same friendly spirit.

[9] Wolfgang Golther (*Bayreuth*, Berlin, 1904, p. 72) reproduces a design by Marette (1775) that anticipated in essentials the Bayreuth plan; the invisible orchestra descends stepwise to a space beneath the stage, which thus acts "almost like a soundingboard".

The desirability of removing everything from the spectators' sight that might militate against the stage illusion must have occurred to many people from the earliest days of opera. Goethe, in *Wilhelm Meister*, had suggested an invisible orchestra in the concert room also, so that listeners would not be distracted by the motions of the conductor and the players. In a chapter on a "Projet d'un nouveau théâtre" in his *Mémoires ou Essais sur la Musique* (Paris, 1789, Vol. III, p. 30 ff), Grétry recommended a sloping amphitheatrical auditorium holding no more than 1,000 people, with uniformity of seating (no boxes) and an invisible orchestra, separated by "a wall of hard stone from the stage, so that the sound may strike back into the auditorium".

1st to the 12th August, at a systematic rate of one act per day. The primary purpose of them was simply to give the players a broad idea of the tetralogy as a whole: details would be filled in during the rehearsals of the following year. On the 13th Wagner gave a garden party at Wahnfried for the whole of the opera personnel and a few close friends, about 150 people in all. Some enterprising Jack Sheppard among them profited by the occasion to pocket a few of the irreplaceable souvenirs lying about the drawing-room, including the sole existing example of a medal symbolising the Schopenhauerian philosophy.

5

On the whole it was a harmonious brotherhood that set sleepy little Bayreuth buzzing and gaping during those three months of 1875. Vast numbers of sausages were eaten and vast quantities of beer were drunk, with an occasional resort to more civilised liquors. The power of Wagner's personality, the passion of his idealism, and his unique grasp of every problem of opera production lifted all the singers above themselves for the time being. Most of the solo rehearsals took place at Wahnfried, with Joseph Rubinstein or one of the other members of the "Kanzlei" at the piano. In the evenings there were parties at the house, at which Liszt, who had arrived in Bayreuth at the end of July, would often play. In general the relations between Wagner and his singers were excellent. But occasionally one of them would become temperamental; and then a fresh weight of care would fall upon his already overloaded shoulders.

His greatest trouble, now as so often in the past and again in the future, was with the arrogant, surly Niemann. The tenor arrived on the 28th July in one of the atrabiliar moods so frequent with him. A large company had assembled at the station to greet him. "When he appeared", says Kietz, whose letters to his wife from Bayreuth give us many sidelights on the town at this time, "he behaved anything but amiably." He greeted Kietz, but took no notice of any of the others with the exception of the Vogls. "He inveighed loudly against having had to leave beautiful Baden-Baden for this cold, dreary hole, and it was not long before his inconsiderate manner spread gloom over Bayreuth." Kietz soon found himself excluded from the rehearsals in Wahnfried because Niemann would not have anyone present when he was singing. On the 1st August Kietz recorded that "everyone is in a very serious mood because of the sudden departure of Niemann, whose behaviour had provoked much displeasure." That evening Liszt played some Beethoven at Wahnfried. "Wagner was very quiet; one could see that he was suffering." Later, as the company was breaking up, he spoke regretfully of the vexatious episodes that had ended in Niemann's departure: "Niemann", he said sadly, "is the only one who has not grasped the seriousness of our undertaking." "It would be a great loss", adds Kietz, "if a substitute has to be found for Niemann, for his whole appearance as well as his voice and his acting fit him wonderfully for Siegmund." But the philosophical Richter consoled him: "Don't worry", he said; "Niemann will be here for the performance."

The trouble had long been brewing. Knowing the morose, irritable nature of the man with whom he had to deal, Wagner always handled him with particular care and showed him much trustful friendship; he had confided to him all his troubles with regard to the casting of some of the parts in the *Ring,* and relied largely on his estimate of this singer or that. But Niemann took it as a grievance that Wagner should consistently look elsewhere than to him — admittedly the first tenor in Germany just then — for his Siegfried. Wagner's reasons were clear enough: he wanted someone younger-looking for his favourite hero, and he disliked the idea of any two leading parts being taken by the same singer on successive nights, because of the loss of illusion this would involve. Niemann's vanity, again, rebelled at the assumption that *he* needed to go to Bayreuth and be coached from the roots upwards like the rest of them. He had evidently been brooding over his grievances while at Baden-Baden, for on the 21st July he informed Wagner by telegram that he had not studied the *Götterdämmerung* because he understood that he would not be wanted in it. As the only possible rôle for him in that opera was Siegfried, it is evident enough what was in his mind. All through that summer Wagner was doubtful whether Unger would prove equal to the part; and in June he seems to have feared that even if he could make a Siegfried in *Siegfried* out of him he could not rely on him to shoulder the *Götterdämmerung* part also.

6

Niemann had not been many hours in Bayreuth before he injected his poison into it. Julius Hey, the Munich singing teacher who, at Wagner's request, had undertaken the vocal improvement of Unger, has left us a contemporary account of all that happened. Either because Niemann was imperfectly acquainted with his part, or because his self-esteem resented his being put through the same mill as the others, or — a consideration which, in fairness to him, must be taken into account — because he could catch and strike fire from a dramatic part only when he was on the stage,[10] he showed up badly at the rehearsal of the first act of the *Valkyrie* at Wahnfried. As to his general competence there could be no question. He had, Hey tells us, the presence for Siegmund, an impressive voice, and great power of plastic movement and of facial expression. But the voice — by all accounts of a baritonish quality — had been none too thoroughly schooled: Hey regretted that Niemann could not have been taken in hand by Wagner ten years earlier, after the death of Schnorr. Mentally and temperamentally ill at ease, the tenor played nervous pranks with the tempi and the rhythm, so that Wagner had more than once to stop and correct him. At last, conscious that he was cutting a bad figure and feeling that he must vent his ill temper on someone, the huge bully went up to the little Rubinstein, who had been accompanying faultlessly at the piano, seized him by the shoulders, and shook him angrily. Wagner was for once at a loss what to do or say. Deeply hurt, after one disapproving look at Niemann he sat silent for a while, his eyes fastened on his own score; then he said quietly, "Let us continue, please." Niemann's outburst had relieved his tension; he resumed the duet with Frau Vogl, and now sang better; but everyone was glad when the rehearsal came to an end.

The company then went into the garden — all except poor Rubinstein, who took his leave. Wagner, having by now recovered his equanimity, turned upon his guests all the familiar and famous charm: he was always at his best when relaxing among his artists. To Hey he made excuses for Niemann, the real grounds for whose bad temper — his not having been chosen for Siegfried — he well

---

[10] It was for this reason, says Hey, that he was never at his best in the concert hall.

knew, and he was confident that all would go well when the tenor could feel himself really inside the skin of the character on the stage. He even saw Niemann's angularities and tempestuosities as assets for his Siegmund; better all this, he told Hey, than the "self-satisfied, pomaded, salon tenor-type" that was his particular abhorrence.

Meanwhile Niemann, still smouldering inwardly, found it difficult to tune in with the rest of the gay company, which included Liszt, Cosima and Countess Dönhoff. He sat down at a corner of the table of Frau Jaïde (the Erda) and a few of the other singers, but sulkily declined any refreshments. At last the spoiled child deigned to take a piece of ham which Frau Jaïde sportively reached out to him across the table on her fork. The ice having been broken, he in turn took something from her plate with his own fork, thanked her, and left the company. Cosima, who had seen this from afar and been annoyed by it, went into the house, saying a few words en route to her factotum Schnappauf. The latter took a message to Frau Jaïde, who at once followed her into the house. She returned a few minutes later, strode in her best grand opera style to her table, and said excitedly, "I am going! What I have just been through I will tell you at Angermann's." [11] The horrifying story of Cosima's reprimand was duly told to her colleagues later. Niemann took such offence at it that he swore that, like Frau Jaïde, he would shake the dust of Bayreuth off his feet. This no doubt encouraged some of the others; and a meeting was called for the following morning to discuss the situation. On the way to Wahnfried the next afternoon Hey fell in with Richter and a few others, all of them looking grave. It appeared that at mid-day Niemann had let himself go with Cosima, thrown up the part of Siegmund, and definitely refused to have anything more to do with Bayreuth. Betz had sided with his Berlin colleague and was also threatening to depart. That evening, at Wahnfried, even Liszt's playing could not dispel the clouds that had settled upon the place. "We were too happy!" was Wagner's resigned comment upon it all as he said good-night to Hey. Niemann had been only three days in Bayreuth; but during that time he had managed to spoil the whole atmosphere of the place.

A letter of the 16th August to Betz, which the latter was to pass on

---

[11] The famous Bayreuth hostelry at which singers and players used to foregather.

to the aggrieved tenor, shows Wagner, uncertain as he still was about Unger, half-resolved now to entrust both Siegfrieds, as well as Siegmund, to Niemann. A few weeks later the singer was in Bayreuth again; but he did not call on Wagner, though he assured him, through Betz, that he would take part in the festival. It was not until October that Wagner resumed direct communication with him.

7

Wagner's main preoccupation that summer, however, was with Unger. The young Mannheim tenor, who was even more gigantic than Niemann, answered well enough in some ways to Wagner's stage ideal of his Siegfried. But his vocal method was faulty, and through lack of artistic individuality he had reached his thirty-eighth year without making any great name for himself. Wagner, however, appears to have sensed a latent something in him; and in characteristically thorough fashion he set himself to draw it out. He persuaded Hey, who had his confidence as a teacher of singing, to get leave from the Munich Music School and spend some weeks in Bayreuth, overhauling Unger's vocal method from the foundations upward. He induced the tenor to break his connection with the Mannheim theatre — where he would be sure to forget, during the coming twelve months, all he had learned at Wahnfried and fall back into the pitiful old operatic routine, — and devote himself entirely for a whole year to his Bayreuth task, studying vocal technique with Hey in Munich and miming with Wagner. (To make this possible, of course, Wagner had to pay him a compensatory allowance). Nor was this all. Wagner did not merely take him to pieces and reconstruct him as an actor, teaching him a new art of dramatic inflection, of gesture, of movement. He took him to pieces also as a human being. He saw that the rather sluggish mentality of the man was at war with the rôle chosen for him — that of the natural, healthy, unsophisticated boy cutting like a shaft of sunlight through the world of black guile and grey care that had sprung from the conflict for power between Wotan and the Nibelungs and the curse laid by Alberich upon the gold. So Wagner worked to make Unger not only fictively but actually one with the character of Siegfried, transforming his attitude towards life, modulating his whole temperament from the minor to the major. It was uphill work,

[451]

and often it must have seemed in vain. But Wagner persevered, and so, to his credit, did the tenor. He sang both Siegfrieds in 1876, and, if not rising to the full height of Wagner's ideal, probably came nearer to it than any other German tenor could have done just then.

On the 22nd August Wagner gave King Ludwig a *résumé* of his work with the singers that summer. He is pleased with their zeal, he says, and, in the main, content with his choice of them. His one real difficulty is over his Siegfried: he is still doubtful about Unger, and fears he may have to allot the part to Niemann, whom it would not suit. The latter's Siegmund, however, will undoubtedly be the greatest achievement of his career. Materna is the one woman, at present, who can shoulder the terrific task of Brynhilde; her vocal endurance is inexhaustible, she looks the part, and her expression is "sympathetic". He has definitely given Sieglinde to Frau Vogl, as Fräulein Weckerlin's voice had proved "insufficiently energetic" for the part; she will now play Gutrune. Hill, Scaria, Vogl and all the others receive their special word of praise. The sisters Lehmann and Fräulein Lammert will make an incomparable trio of Rhine Maidens; while his three Norns will be singers of the first order — Frau Sadler-Grün (his Fricka), Frau Vogl and a certain Fräulein Preiss from Brunswick (who, however, did not appear in 1876). Even in the chorus of Gibichungs in the second act of the *Götter-dämmerung* there will be several players of principal parts, such as the Fasolt (Eilers), the Fafner (Reichenberg), the Donner and Hunding (Niering), and the Froh (Herrlich). Thanks to the refusal of the orchestral players to accept anything beyond their expenses, the summer's rehearsals have cost him no more than 12,000 marks for a total personnel of 140. This amount he had himself covered by his recent concert-giving; and the festival now seems assured for the following year. The stage equipment is complete; the gas installation is well in hand; but there is much to be done at the auditorium, and the costumes have still to come. Finance is still his most urgent problem. The undertaking will even now be crippled if his Committee has to observe strictly the obligation entered into with regard to the Patronatscheine; so he begs the King to allow him to retain the receipts from these until the 600th certificate is reached. As we have seen, Ludwig gave a command to this effect on the 25th September; and Wagner could now look forward to the festival year with more confidence than ever before.

8

The pages of Hey and Fricke should be read by all who want to understand what Wagner required of his singers and actors. There used to be much talk, a generation or so ago, about the so-called *Sprechgesang* — a term apparently designed to make more acceptable to us the canine sounds emitted by some Wagnerian singers who had never learned how to sing; a more cynical name for it in those days was "the Bayreuth bark". But nothing could be further from Wagner's intentions than this method of hurling masses of craggy consonants at the suffering listener without any regard to either beauty of tone or accuracy of pitch. Wagner's musical ear was much too fine to enable him to endure ugly sounds either from the orchestra or from the human throat. No man of his epoch was more sensitive to sheer beauty of melodic delivery. The very life of a work, he always insisted, was in its melody: his constant complaint against players of the last Beethoven quartets in particular was that they had not "sought out the melody", or, having unearthed it, could not make it *sing*. A priori, therefore, it would be the height of absurdity to suppose that in his own works he favoured mere incisiveness of declamation at the expense of beauty of sound, a mere "speaking through the tones".

Quite the contrary. His first demand was for a *bel canto*. But it would have to be a German, not an Italian *bel canto*, for his music was German, not Italian, and it was through the German language, not the Italian, that his singers had to convey the meaning of what they were saying. His views on this matter are still of international application. Italian opera singing is what it is, in its beauties as in its limitations, in virtue of not only the traditional nature of Italian melody but the peculiarity of the Italian language and the physiology of the Italian throat. In every country, every day, we are confronted with pathetic demonstrations of the folly of singers of other nations trying to imitate what they call "the Italian production": the only result of it all is to brand them as unfruitful hybrids. Their native language itself, to say nothing of the cultural heredity underlying what is being sung, is an insuperable obstacle to their transplanting the Italian tone, the Italian vowels, the Italian accents, inflections and phrasings into music the whole life of which is bound up with the genius of another tongue: no singer with a grain of culture could persuade himself that we can ever shape a stanza of Shakespeare or Tennyson or Goethe or Leconte de Lisle in song as we would one of Metastasio or Boïto. Not even the most intelligent of singers can surmount these national obstacles, as anyone of the English-speaking race can easily convince himself by listening to a first-rate foreign artist singing the music of the listener's own land in the listener's own language. When the most accomplished German Lieder singer attempts Purcell, for example, even if the speech-accent be as near impeccable as makes no matter, the *music* itself somehow suffers a fatal change in English ears. The melodic phrases do not slip from the tongue with the shape an English singer would unconsciously give them. Purcell or Elgar, in these circumstances, becomes, for English listeners, merely inferior Heine-Schumann; just as in the parallel Italian case it becomes, at its best, bad Verdi or Puccini.

Wagner's complaint against the German singers of his early and middle years was twofold: they tried, with often ludicrous results, to produce Italian sounds from an organ so physiologically recalcitrant to them as a German throat, and, as a result of regularly singing inept German translations of popular Italian or French operas, they had come to lose all sense not only of the specific virtues of their native speech but of the significance of words in general in opera. The translation meaning nothing to them, they had come to regard the words — all and any words — as merely a conventional apparatus for "putting themselves across" to the audience *via* the music. And in this delusion they had been aided and abetted even by some of the best German composers, who, intent only on writing a melody that should curve agreeably on its own account, would often give the same line now one set of verbal stresses, now another. Weber, for instance, first of all makes his heroine say "Was ist mein Leben gegen *dies*en Augenblick" and in the very next breath "Was ist mein Leben gegen diesen *Augen*blick"; careless of the fact that "What is my life against *this* moment" — which is what Euryanthe is really trying to impress on us — is not at all the same thing dramatically as "What is my life against this *moment*."

The average German opera singer of Wagner's epoch must have seemed, to Wagner's eyes and ears, to have floated himself into popularity by very much the same methods as those of the Dashwood children in *Sense and Sensibility*, who had gained their uncle's affections "by such attractions as are by no means unusual in children of two or three years old: an imperfect articulation, an earnest desire of having their own way, many cunning tricks, and a great deal of noise" — a naive technique of endearment still practised with great success by some of our most highly-paid operatic tenors on the more gullible members of their audience. What Wagner wanted was first of all beauty of tone; next, so perfect a vocal technique that the singer would never have to resort, even in the most difficult passages, to anything but pure singing; then a feeling for the quality of words *as* words, the varying build and weight and ring and rhythm of them; then the ability to bring out the verbal-dramatic point of a sentence not at the expense of the melodic-dramatic essence of the music but in the most intimate collaboration with this, the two strands of meaning being so blended as to be inseparable; then an art of gesture, pose and movement as complete, as flexible as the accompanying arts of singing and declamation; and finally a power of imaginative absorption in the character and in the drama as a whole, and of re-creation of these from the inside in terms of the actor's own physique and temperament, that should make the whole opera seem to spring into life as the inspired improvisation of the moment. What he could never endure was the application to one work or one situation of a formula for "effect" which the artist had found useful in another, and had accordingly standardised. He always insisted that these standard recipes were bad art, whether in a singer or in a conductor: he was especially scornful, as has already been pointed out, of the conductors who, at this point or that of a work, turn on to it their favourite recipe for excitement, or tenderness, or grace, for "working-up", for an "effective" pianissimo or crescendo or accelerando, or whatever it is they plume themselves upon as *their* specialty. The scope for nuance, he held in theory and proved in practice in his own conducting, was infinite; but it all ought to grow naturally out of the special nature of the composer and the work in hand, animating the surface of the work from the inside, not being merely plastered on it from the outside. He made the same demands upon his singers: if they could not create a character from the inside they would never do so by applying trick-formulae to it from without.

When once they knew and understood their part vocally and musically, his further training was devoted to helping them to realise the dramatic conception in terms of gesture and action. Here again he would have no conventional recipes; a leap or a blow, a gesture of pity or scorn, by a character in one situation would be inapplicable to another character in the same situation or a different one. He himself found all this easy enough, with his born genius as a mime, and a mime, moreover, playing in a work that had been created by himself and was filled with his own imagination in every fibre of its being. There was not a movement of hand or arm or eye or the whole body which he could not illustrate for each singer in each moment of the drama. He did not insist on a slavish reproduction of the model he had given; what he wanted was a translation of it into the singer's own bodily idiom. One day, for instance, after he had shown Niemann how he should move in a certain situation, the tenor protested that while this was easy enough for Wagner it was impossible for a man of *his* bulk. This Wagner at once admitted; and he left it to the singer to discover how best he could achieve the desired end in terms of his own physical structure. During the rehearsals of 1876 he created a little confusion occasionally among his singers by prescribing today a movement or a gesture different from the one he had illustrated for them yesterday. Fricke attributes this changeableness to forgetfulness due to fatigue. In part it may have been so; but it is not improbable also that it came from the inexhaustible plasticity of his own imagination: he was far too good a mime to imagine that there is only one way of translating a given mental state into a bodily motion.

But with whatever difficulties he confronted his actors from time to time there was never an occasion on which they did not recognise his unique gifts both as actor and as producer. It was in the rehearsals of 1875 and 1876, even more than in the performances of the latter year, that the foundations were laid of the new art of operatic representation.

CHAPTER XXIII

PREPARING FOR THE FESTIVAL

1

A WEEK'S HOLIDAY in Teplitz, from the 12th to the 19th September, was all the relaxation Wagner could allow himself in 1875. From then until the accomplishment of his festival in the following summer he had hardly a day's rest from labour or respite from care.

Both he and Julius Hey were still rather doubtful whether Unger would prove equal to the task allotted him. A final test was made of him in the theatre in September in the difficult third act of *Siegfried.* The tenor, who seems to have done cheerfully everything required of him, acquitted himself in a manner that surprised them both; even the exacting Hey was astonished at the improvement in his voice. Wagner's mind was at once made up: Unger should be his Siegfried, on condition that he cancelled his engagement with Düsseldorf, settled in Munich for some months to continue his vocal studies under Hey, and then went to Bayreuth to be coached by Wagner in the details of his acting. The necessary arrangements were at once made with Scherbarth, the Düsseldorf opera director.

For his Christmas gift that year Wagner sent the King the first three volumes of *Mein Leben,* the last of which brought the record of his life down to the production of *Tannhäuser* in Paris in 1861.[1] Ludwig, who remembered that Wagner had told him in 1865 that the autobiography would end with their first meeting in May, 1864, the remainder of the story of his life being left to Cosima to complete, begged him to carry his own work down at least to the production of the *Ring* in 1876. This, however, was never done, for obvious reasons.

Already he could foresee a fresh crop of difficulties ahead of him in connection with the financing of Bayreuth. The receipts from

---

[1] The fourth and final volume was not printed until 1881. See the present Life, Vol. II, p. 157 *note.*

Patronatscheine seemed to have dried up; as late as February of the following year only 490 had been subscribed for out of the 1,300 on which he and his helpers had latterly based their calculations. So in the autumn of 1875 we find him once more reduced to petitioning the Kaiser for help, apparently to the extent of 30,000 thalers. The Kaiser himself seems to have been in favour of granting the petition; but the President of the Imperial Exchequer (Delbrück) was against it on purely financial grounds, while the Minister for Culture, Herr Falk, was a jurist with no interests outside the law. The Exchequer department advised Wagner to make an application to the Reichstag. His contemptuous reply was that he had had it in his mind to appeal only to the grace of the Kaiser and the discernment of the Chancellor (Bismarck), not to the opinions of the Herren Deputies. The letter of the 15th October from the Exchequer, suggesting recourse to the Reichstag, had been addressed to the "Highwellborn Professor Richard Wagner, Bayreuth".

2

His opinion of his fellow-countrymen at this time was anything but flattering to them; but although the vast majority of them declined to dip into their pockets to help Bayreuth his vogue as an opera composer had never been so great as it was now. Munich, among other cities, did its best to induce him to give a concert there, or at any rate to conduct a performance of *Tristan;* and Hermann Levi,[2] when making this request, could assure him that during the ten years that had elapsed since he left the town a new musical generation had sprung up that was whole-heartedly for him, such opposition as now existed being confined to a few of the older people who could not or would not forget the past. His reply to all this was that he had no desire to go on repeating fragments from the *Ring* in the concert room, that to conduct a performance of *Tristan* would be beyond his physical capacity, and that while he never doubted the affection of the Müncheners as a whole for him the place was peopled by too many "ghosts" with whom he had no desire to resume acquaintance.

In other quarters his necessities in connection with his festival were taken advantage of to subject him to a species of veiled black-

---

[2] He had been Count Kapellmeister at Munich since 1872.

mail — "Either do what we ask of you, or you cannot count on our good will when the time comes for us to grant leave of absence to the singers you want for Bayreuth." Franz Jauner, the Vienna Opera director, with such valuable cards as Materna and Scaria up his sleeve, coerced him in this way into collaborating in some performances of *Tannhäuser* and *Lohengrin,* though Wagner refused to conduct any of them, or even to countenance them unless the now standardised cuts were restored. He spent six weary weeks in Vienna, from the last day of October until the 16th December. There were the usual scenes of wild enthusiasm and the usual compulsory speech-making on his part. One sentence in his speech after the first *Tannhäuser* performance (on the 22nd November) gave great offence in some quarters and was gleefully seized upon by the hostile portion of the Press to stir up bad blood. He had reminded the audience that it was in Vienna, some fifteen years ago, that he had first heard his *Lohengrin* and realised the affection of the local public for him: the memory of all this, he added, now encouraged him to bring his works still closer to them "to the extent that the forces available permit".[3] The next morning the Press hounds were baying delightedly at his heels: this was arrogance, they said, impudence, ingratitude. Thereupon Wagner called the singers together on the morning of the second *Tannhäuser* performance (the 25th November) and cast the charges from him, though he admitted that the phrase that had given such offence had been "improvised on the spur of the moment". The truth was that though he could honestly praise the singers for the brave efforts they were making on his behalf he was incapable of flattering them beyond their deserts. He had already expressed his gratitude, he said, in a letter to Jauner which the latter could send to the Press if the personnel so desired. But if he did so Wagner would at once leave the town, since he would regard such a wish on their part as evidence of a lack of confidence in him. With the Press he himself would have nothing to do: "I despise the Press", he said — a statement which the journalists, when it reached their ears, converted into "I hate the Press".

---

[3] The Tannhäuser was the Swede Labatt, of whom Wagner never had a very high opinion. Materna was the Venus: she had undertaken the rôle at Wagner's wish, and was apparently not at her best in it. The various performances were conducted by Richter, who had recently succeeded Dessoff as assistant Kapellmeister at the Vienna Opera.

Lohengrin was given on the 15th December. The one feature of the performance that Wagner could sincerely praise was the singing of the chorus. "Don't shout", he had admonished them at rehearsal; "sing as beautifully as you can, as if every one of you was a soloist"; and they had taken him at his word. (To show his gratitude to them he returned to Vienna in March to conduct a performance of *Lohengrin* for their benefit. This was the solitary occasion in his whole life when he conducted this work of his. It was then that the *mot* went round Vienna that "there was more temperament in the sixty-three-years old Meister than in the thirty-six-years old apprentice [Richter]." With the leading singers he was less pleased, apart from the Ortrud (Materna) and the King (Scaria). To the Elsa (Frau Kupfer) he addressed the point-blank query "Are you musical?", no doubt in a tone that left no doubt as to what his own answer to the question would be; while the Lohengrin (Georg Müller) made him wonder, as he put it to Hey, why on earth he had allotted the leading intellectual parts in all his works to tenors. What he really thought of the Vienna solo personnel is clear from a passage in his letter of the 26th January, 1876 to King Ludwig:

> "I achieved miracles there, but with a trouble to which I could hardly bring myself to go through again! Wretched singers with huge salaries, who openly said I was there to ruin them, because I pointed out to them the bad habits into which they had fallen without endowing them with the strength to shake them off for ever! They admitted I was right, but asked me what use this sudden re-baptism would be to them, seeing that they would be bound to revert to the old belief again!"

Among the minor personnel of the Vienna Opera at that time was a young tenor, Angelo Neumann, who was already quietly preparing himself for what he felt to be his real career, that of an impresario. He studied Wagner's methods at rehearsal with particular care, and has left us a record of them in the early pages of his memoirs.[4] In the following year he became part-director of the Leipzig Theatre. The story of his signal services to Wagner in later years will be told in due course. His considered opinion in 1907 was that Wagner was not only the greatest dramatist of all time but the greatest stage-manager and the greatest actor. "Today", he wrote, "after more than thirty years [since the Vienna performances of 1875], I have an imperishable memory of certain demonstrations of his marvel-

---

[4] NERW.

lous gift of expression as a mime. I have never since been able to see a performance of *Tannhäuser* or *Lohengrin* without seeing him again as he was in this scene or that."

Hanslick and Speidel once more showed themselves at their most contemptible in their treatment of him during his autumn visit to Vienna, but the majority of the critics were with him. It was at these performances of *Tannhäuser* that the opera was given for the first time in the definitive revised version, the new Venusberg music not following upon the complete Dresden overture, as it had done in Paris, but being dovetailed into it in the fashion now familiar to concert- and opera-goers. The general verdict seems to have been that the new matter and the old came from different mental worlds and did not blend; and it may have been as much for this reason as from mere conservatism that soon after he had left Vienna the Opera reverted to the overture in its original form, which, there and everywhere, was one of the public's favourite pieces. He left the Austrian capital with the melancholy conviction that even yet it had no real understanding of his ideal.

3

Still questing for singers, he attended, while he was in Vienna, performances of various works for most of which he probably had no great liking, among them *Carmen*, Gounod's *Romeo and Juliet*, Goldmark's *Queen of Sheba*, Verdi's *Requiem* [5] and Meyerbeer's *L'Africaine:* with this last he was so disgusted that he left at the end of the first act. He went also to one of Hellmesberger's chamber concerts at which Brahms played the piano part in his own new C minor quartet: probably a greater attraction for Wagner was the opportunity of hearing Mozart's E flat quartet and, above all, the great A minor of Beethoven.

Most of his free evenings he spent with old friends or recent acquaintances such as Standhartner, Semper, the painter Makart, Bruckner, and — always a favourite composer of his — Johann Strauss. Hellmesberger tried to persuade him to pay a diplomatic visit of quasi-inspection to the Marchesi singing classes at the Conservatoire, but this he bluntly refused to do. It would take more than that, he told Hey, to rid "these out-and-out Italians" of their

---

[5] Under Richter. Verdi had heard *Tannhäuser* in Vienna in the preceding June.

prejudice against his music: Madame Marchesi in particular had distinguished herself by declaring his operas "unsingable", the ruin of the human voice, and so on.

One meeting of those days has passed into history. The fifteen-years-old Hugo Wolf, already a fanatical Wagnerian *in posse*, had waited four hours in the queue for a place in the fourth gallery at the first performance of *Tannhäuser*. On the morning of the 11th December, as Wagner was on his way to a *Lohengrin* rehearsal, the boy "accosted him very respectfully", as Hugo put it in a letter to his father, in the vestibule of the Imperial Hotel. Wagner "looked hard" at him for a few seconds and then passed on. By running at top speed Hugo managed to get to the Opera before the great man's cab arrived there.

> "I saluted him again, and would have opened the door for him; but before I could do so the driver jumped down quickly and opened it himself. Then Wagner said something to the driver: I think it was about me."

The boy had already made friends with the manager of the hotel; through him he scraped acquaintance with Wagner's valet and Cosima's maid, and on the afternoon of the 12th the latter seems to have smuggled him into Wagner's apartment a quarter of an hour or so before the Meister came in from a Philharmonic concert, accompanied by Cosima, Goldmark and others. "I saluted Cosima very respectfully", Hugo tells his father. "She did not however think it worth while to bestow even a look on me: she is indeed known everywhere as an extremely haughty and self-important lady." He was presented by the maid to Wagner, who took him into his sitting-room. Hugo began to tell him how greatly he would value his opinion on some of his compositions. Wagner interrupted him with the remark that he had "far too little time just now"; he could not even keep pace with his correspondence.

> "When I begged the Meister to tell me if I would ever come to anything he said: 'When I was as young as you are now, no one could say from my compositions whether I would go far in music. You must at least play me your compositions on the piano; but I have no time at present. When you are more mature and have written larger works and I am in Vienna again you can show me your compositions. It's no use; I can give no opinion'. . . Thereupon I went away, deeply moved and impressed by the Meister."

Obviously Wagner could say and do no more in the circumstances. But had they met again before his death in 1883 he might have been persuaded to look at Wolf's D minor quartet (1879–80) and such songs as the *Morgenthau* of 1877, the *Die Spinnerin* of 1878, and the *Wiegenlied im Sommer* and *Wiegenlied im Winter* of 1882; and these, one imagines, would have been enough to convince him of the genius of the boy.[6]

4

It was on the night of the 2nd March (1876) that Wagner conducted *Lohengrin* for the benefit of the Opera chorus. The next evening they showed their gratitude by singing the "Wacht auf" chorus from the *Meistersinger* for him in the waiting-room of the railway station before he entrained for Berlin. He was touched by their devotion; but it was a weary, disillusioned Wagner who waved farewell to them from his carriage window, and a Wagner whom Vienna had seen for the last time. He never forgot the bitterness of those weeks of exhausting but fruitless effort, and, above all, the venom that the more despicable section of the Press had spat at him. More than three years later he told Jauner that he had left Vienna that night firmly resolved never to set foot again in the town

> "where every scurvy cur can fall with impunity on a man like myself and void his foulness on me. . . No, no! Greet State Councillor Hanslick and Herr Speidel for me, and all the rest of the rag-tag and bob-tail. I'm not angry with them, since they make money in Vienna by their trade, and the public seems to prefer them to me. And so, my blessing!"

Henceforth he wanted nothing to do with any theatre but his own. Perhaps in the end he had achieved only one real reform by all his labours and sufferings in Vienna: he had managed to persuade the tenor to play Lohengrin without the full beard that had been customary until then.[7]

---

[6] In 1890 Wolf gave his friend Friedrich Hofmann an expanded version of the story of the meeting in 1875. According to this, Wagner had glanced at the manuscripts in Hugo's hand and said in a friendly manner, "*Piano* music? I don't understand that at all. If ever you write songs, then come and see me." When Wolf remarked that he was "not yet an independent" Wagner replied "quite familiarly, as friend to friend", "Well, I also was not independent at one time. Look at my *Rienzi;* there are some poor things in that!"

Wolf attended a performance of *Parsifal* in 1882, when he tried, but unsuccessfully, to get an introduction through Materna.

[7] GAWM, p. 121.

Apparently the German tenors of that day were too much attached to their beards to part with them for stage purposes. Niemann's photographs show him well-bearded as Tannhäuser, Siegmund and Tristan. Schnorr, with his profuse fungus, looks a fearsome Lohengrin and Tristan according to our notions. Unger was a bearded Siegfried at Bayreuth in 1876, Tichatschek always a bearded Tannhäuser, Vogl a bearded Tristan and even Loge. In some cases the beard justified itself: Niemann, for instance, still looks very impressive as Siegmund. But there the growth was in keeping with the supposed age and the general hard-bitten character of the hero. It was a very different matter when Walther von Stolzing appeared with a beard: Nachbaur, judging by the photograph we have of him as Walther, must have looked rather like a portly middle-aged Nuremberger who had amassed a fortune in the grocery business. Yet Nachbaur was only thirty-three when he "created" the part of Walther at Munich in 1868. What makes the problem still more intriguing is the fact that in the figurine for Walther made by the Munich stage designer, Franz Seitz, the character is depicted clean-shaven.

The general abolition of the tenor beard seems to date from the post-Wagner days. In the 1882 performances of *Parsifal*, under Wagner himself, Gudehus was luxuriantly bearded; but in the following year one of the Parsifals (apparently Winkelmann) was clean-shaved. When the *Ring* was revived at Bayreuth in 1896 Burgstaller was a beardless Siegfried. No doubt by that time the European eye had become more sensitive in these matters.

Perhaps the tide was beginning to flow in the direction of facial chastity even in Wagner's later years. Niemann is reported as saying in 1882 that to sing Parsifal he would cut off, for the Meister's sake, not merely his beard but his nose. But even the minor sacrifice of the two was not demanded of him. Wagner would never have approved of a Parsifal of fifty-one.

5

He had gone to Berlin to supervise a production of *Tristan* there. After another fortnight of tiring work for him at rehearsals the opera was given on the 20th March, under Eckert, with Niemann as Tristan, Betz as Marke, Frau von Voggenhuber as Isolde, and Marianne Brandt as Brangaene. Niemann seems not to have been quite in his best voice, and in any case the difficult second act did not suit him. He was superb, however, in the third.

This was the first performance of *Tristan* in Berlin, and Hülsen deserves some credit for having brought it about,[8] for neither he himself nor the local musicians as a whole were warmly disposed towards Wagner. Hülsen, indeed, had in years gone by been decidedly unfriendly towards him, largely, perhaps, because of his prejudice against the "revolutionary" of 1849. But although convinced to the last that Wagner had taken the wrong path in his later works he respected his stubborn idealism and behaved honourably towards him as an official. On his own initiative he had persuaded the King of Prussia to set aside the contract of 1843, under which Wagner, in accordance with the practice of those days, had sold the Berlin performing rights of *The Flying Dutchman* outright for some 300 thalers, and to grant him a seven per cent royalty on all performances *from the first* — after, of course, the original lump sum had been covered. Hülsen told the King that he regarded himself as morally bound to take this course, in view of "the composer's genius, his anything but care-free position, and the considerable material profit" the Berlin Opera had derived from his works. There had been fifteen performances of *The Flying Dutchman* since 1844, the gross receipts from which had been 16,217 thalers. On these, Wagner was granted a royalty of seven per cent; so that in December, 1874 he received from Hülsen the welcome sum of more than 818 thalers (some 1135 thalers less the first lump payment of 316 thalers).

In February, 1876 Hülsen sent the Kaiser an official document that certainly does his memory credit. In the coming summer, he said, the first production of the *Ring* would take place in Bayreuth.

"Although . . . I cannot follow Wagner's aims to their ultimate consequences, no one, and least of all the director of a theatre, can deny the truly notable services of this composer as musical-dramatic creator. As a matter of fact, some of the operas of his earlier period are at present so popular that performances of them almost invariably mean a sold-out house. It must be further recognised that Wagner works for the achievement of the Bayreuth festivals with a rare, indeed amazing perseverance, and makes considerable sacrifices for this undertaking,

---

[8] It has to be borne in mind, of course, that a powerful Court clique was working for Wagner in Berlin.

which can be regarded as, so to speak, the coping-stone of his whole artistic effort."

Hülsen is not himself convinced that Bayreuth is "of truly national significance", as the Wagnerians contend, for only a small part of the nation will be able to benefit by it. But the undertaking is of so great importance for the development of opera that he, for his part, believes it ought to be carried through; it will at any rate decide whether Wagner's latest works, which the composer himself looks upon as the culmination of his art, will meet with general understanding and sympathy and set younger composers on a new path. And so, as the Bayreuth scheme is notoriously in need of money, he asks the Kaiser to decree that the net receipts from the coming first performance of *Tristan* in Berlin shall be given to the festival fund. Apparently he estimated the amount in advance at some 6,000 marks; but thanks to the packed house and the increased prices that were willingly paid, Bayreuth benefited to the extent of nearly 14,000 marks.[9]

Relations between Hülsen and Wagner were more cordial at this time than they had ever been. Wagner not only occupied the Intendant's box during the *Tristan* performance but dined at his house, while both of them, on another occasion, were guests at a dinner party given by Niemann and Betz. But Hülsen still seems to have made no attempt to conceal his opinion that *"Tannhäuser* and *Lohengrin* will endure, but *Tristan* and the *Ring* will probably be forgotten in fifty years."[10] Seven performances of *Tristan* in all were given in March, April and May of 1876, and two more followed in the winter. Then it disappeared from the repertory for four years. In spite of the inveterate hostility of most of the Berlin Press towards Wagner and Bayreuth, the work had had an undeniable success; so that the main explanation of its being shelved for so long must presumably be sought in the Intendant's antipathy to it.

6

After his return to Bayreuth, the whole of Wagner's energy was necessarily turned upon the preparations for the *Ring* rehearsals and performances. Troubles soon began to descend upon him in bat-

---

[9] KGSB, pp. 91–2.
[10] Thus Kapp. Glasenapp makes it "fifteen years".

talions. The auditorium of the theatre was still far from being ready. Several of the German theatre directors having already made up their minds that the only practicable and popular section of the *Ring* would prove to be the *Valkyrie*, Wagner was already being pestered with requests for permission to produce this one work — requests which he angrily refused. Jauner in particular soon began to put the screw on him. As the price for leave of absence for Materna he demanded the right not only to give the opera without fee but to produce *Tristan* with the inadequate Müller, whereas Wagner insisted on Unger being engaged.

The Bayreuth rehearsals were timed to begin in May; and early in April Wagner received the shattering news that he would have to find a new Sieglinde and a new Norn, as Frau Vogl was expecting a confinement in August. Giving Wagner this unpleasant news, Vogl humorously apologised for Loge's not having followed Alberich's example and cursed love. Wagner not only took his disappointment philosophically but offered to be godfather to the coming child, which he hoped would turn out to be a genuine Volsung. There followed an anxious four weeks' search for a new Sieglinde. Frau von Voggenhuber was at first willing to take the part, but soon found that her engagements would not allow her to do so.[11] Wagner's next choice was Marianne Brandt, but Lilli Lehmann and one or two others of the lady's Berlin colleagues reminded him of her lack of beauty: Niemann, it was feared, would find it impossible to give of his best as Siegmund with such a Sieglinde. Wagner did not agree: the lady, he rather tartly replied, had at any rate a slender figure, beauty was not so important on the stage as off it, the perspective of the Bayreuth theatre would count for a good deal, and in any case an artist like Niemann could surely so far lose himself in the dramatic illusion as not to be put out of his stride by intrusive reality. Garrick and Kean, he pointed out, with only a beer-jug in their arms, could send a thrill of horror through the spectators as the supposed father made to throw the supposed child into the river. Whether Fräulein Brandt was really so plain that Niemann was not reassured even by the analogy of the beer-jug we do not know; but Wagner evidently pursued the matter no further.[12]

---

[11] One of these "engagements", apparently, was of the same domestic order as Frau Vogl's.

[12] See Wagner's letter of the 26th April to Lilli Lehmann, in LMW, p. 223.

Hey now suggested one of the singers at the Munich Opera, Josefine Scheffzky, a lady who occupies a tiny corner in King Ludwig biography. The King seems to have admired her voice so much that he frequently had her sing to him in private; but as she made indiscreet use of the privileges accorded her, on the one hand giving him her unsought opinions regarding his entourage, on the other hand gossiping about him to her associates, she soon fell from grace. The story goes that the King, who could not endure ill-looking people near him, preferred to have her sing concealed in one or other of the bushes of the Winter Garden of the Residenz.[13] She came to Bayreuth early in May and was at once engaged by Wagner, presumably on the strength of her voice alone, for in the matter of feminine beauty she seems to have been no improvement on the Brandt. Time was running short, however, and Wagner was in no position just then to be over-fastidious. Lilli Lehmann, who in general was an excellent judge of singers and actors, obviously had a poor opinion of her. "She was large, powerful, and had a strong voice", she writes, "but possessed neither the poetry nor the intelligence to express in the very least what, as a matter of fact, she did not even feel, to say nothing of the insufficiencies of her technique."

7

Wagner now had his cast virtually complete with the exception of his Hagen. Scaria had begun to make trouble for him in the preceding January, when he suddenly sprang a demand on Wagner for a fee of 7,500 marks for the month of August (i.e. for the final rehearsals and performances), plus 250 marks for each day he would spend in Bayreuth in July.[14] The thing was impossible, if only for the reason that if Scaria insisted on placing *his* co-operation on a strictly professional footing there would be discontent and perhaps revolt among the other singers, most of whom were making a sacrifice of one kind or another for Bayreuth and art. So Scaria now faded out of the picture, and with him the First Norn, who, presumably at the instigation of her Vienna colleague, also threw

---

[13] For further information about her see BLKB, pp. 431–3.
[14] Scaria was heavily in debt: Wagner had received a legal writ of attachment of his Bayreuth "honorarium" for the benefit of his creditors.

up her part. For Hagen Wagner had to fall back on a certain Kögl, of Hamburg.

Singers, conductors, machinists and others arrived in detachments from the end of April onwards. Finance was an ever-present problem. The auditorium was still incomplete; even at the third full rehearsal of the whole work, which began on the 29th July, only the first four rows were properly numbered, the remainder being merely chalked. Fricke was often in despair, doubting whether this or that singer would be equal to his part, or this or that stage apparatus be in working order in time. With everyone's nerves at full stretch contradictory orders were sometimes given, and there was more than one unpleasant scene. The 26th July Fricke describes as the most painful of his life. He, Wagner and Karl Brandt were at loggerheads over the difficult final scene of the *Götterdämmerung;* they separated in ill humour, and the next day the honest Fricke laid his case before Wagner in a long letter. He was between three fires, he said: he could do nothing to realise Wagner's intentions if Brandt and Doepler stuck obstinately to their plan for the construction of the Hall of the Gibichungs and the arrangement of the bier. Fricke did not like the way in which the pillars of the Hall collapsed — it was a mere ordinary small-theatre effect, he contended, — he disapproved of the way in which the earlier episode of the Rhine Maidens was handled — they should be lowered a foot, — the whole final scene was impossible on the present lines, and so on. Apparently Brandt would tolerate no interference with the mechanism he had designed, while within the rigid frame of that mechanism Fricke could not manoeuvre his human masses properly; and even Wagner's authority was insufficient to smooth the difficulties out. If he had any time during those anxious weeks to turn his thoughts back to the Munich *Rhinegold* and *Valkyrie* days of 1869 and 1870 he must have recognised, one imagines, that the scenic shortcomings of those productions could be accounted for on quite other grounds than ill-will on the part of Perfall and the others towards him personally. Even in this long-desired theatre of his own, with ample time at his disposal and with every thread of the production in his hands from start to finish, things were constantly going wrong at rehearsal, and some of his problems remained finally unsolved even in performance.

8

It was one thing for him to construct this colossal drama of land and water and cavern and cloud, of gods and heroes and giants and dwarfs, in his own imagination: it was quite another thing to realise it all in terms of steel and wood and stone and canvas, the small four-square of a stage, and the physical and mental capacity of merely human actors. All sorts of unexpected difficulties, trifling in themselves and most of them ultimately capable of being overcome or by-passed, but time-wasting and temper-trying when they first reared their heads, sprang up when his inner vision came to be translated into theatrical reality. It was easy enough to see, in imagination, Alberich disappearing in a magic cloud of vapour; but when the vapour became a physical fact the steam penetrated to the recesses of the orchestral pit, so that the harpists could not keep their instruments in tune. The orchestra further complained of the intolerable draught: Wagner went down and found their complaint justified, but could say no more than "I composed the opera, and now I have to shut the windows as well!"

The Rhine Maidens' swimming machines were thoroughly tried out for the first time on the 30th May,[15] with three local gymnasts to impersonate the swimmers. Each of them had to recline in a sort of long cradle the supporting undershaft of which ran down below the scenes to a trolley on three wheels. The cradle could be lowered or raised and propelled backwards and forwards; a "steersman" ran the trolley to and fro across the ground, while three conductors — Seidl for Woglinde, Fischer for Wellgunde, Mottl for Flosshilde — controlled the evolutions of the Rhine Maidens in accordance with the music for each part.[16]

Four days later, the sisters Lehmann and Fräulein Lammert having meanwhile arrived, the time for the supreme test had come. The three ladies watched the perilous machines going up and down with their passengers in them, and were horrified. Lilli at once declared that for no man, for nothing on earth, would she deliver

---

[15] It was at this rehearsal that the idea came to Wagner to have Wotan, at the words "Thus greet I the fort", snatch up a sword which Fafner had rejected from the Hoard — a sword that had been forged by Alberich for use against the giants and the gods.

[16] A drawing of the apparatus, and another showing how it was operated in the depths of the stage, will be found in JRW, pp. 218, 219.

herself up to such a device of the devil: she had just risen from a sick-bed and still suffered from dizziness. The other two daughters of the waves remained mute. Fricke tried to cajole them. "Courage, Fräulein Marie", he said, "just try it, and I wager that your fears will vanish and you will feel nothing but the joy of swimming." A ladder was hoisted, and Marie Lehmann, with many an "Ach" and "Oh" and squeals and squeaks was assisted into it by Brandt and Fricke. They buckled her in fast and the maiden voyage began. Soon the terror vanished from her face; she began to find the gyrations quite delightful. Lilli next tried it, then Fräulein Lammert; and soon all three were not only careering in the depth of the Rhine like happy children born to the sport but singing divinely. A load was lifted from Wagner's heart: the success of the opening scene was assured, though poor Hill had many an anxious moment to go through before he could feel safe in his clamberings up the rocks, and, above all, in Alberich's final plunge into the depths. He was a constitutionally nervous man, and his sufferings, says Fricke, were indescribable. "Wagner's magical influence over him is tremendous; he has got the terrified man to do something which no Intendant or regisseur could have wrung from him." Fricke, for his part, gave Hill the soothing assurance that "with Brandt's machinery it is a positive pleasure to do the plunge; you are practically in Abraham's bosom." One day, no doubt to encourage Hill, it had been arranged that a bottle of champagne, baptised "the Rhinegold", should be placed on the highest point of the rock: with this in his hand he was to make the plunge. But the plan did not work: it was found impossible to put the bottle in place, so Fricke had to present it to Alberich after he had made his leap. However, from that day Hill showed no more signs of terror.

9

It goes without saying that in so temperamental an army as these singers and players and machinists and designers there was an occasional little revolt. As the days went by and Wagner became either more exhausted or more inventive he grew more contradictory in his instructions, till sometimes the actors did not know what to do. One day he discovered that he could not endure Eilers appearing as Hunding the day after he had died as Fasolt: he now thought of giving the part of Hunding to Kögl, who was not coming up to expectations as Hagen. A day or two later he decided to entrust Hunding to Niering (the Donner). Eilers, who had heard from some of his colleagues what was in the wind, of course took offence, talked of going back to Coburg, and was only brought to see reason by Fricke. Another day there was trouble with the excellent Materna, through no fault of the lady's own. She was singing with the utmost ardour in the second act of the *Götterdämmerung* when Wagner halted her, none too gently, and asked her to go back to a certain point. She was chilled, could not recapture the former fire, grew nervous and made some mistakes; whereupon Richter took her to task for not knowing her part. The poor woman made her way home in tears.

There was one model member of the company with whom Wagner had no trouble from first to last, one artist by the grace of God who did cheerfully and with the highest competence whatever was demanded of him, who never felt a single pang of jealousy of his colleagues, never considered himself slighted or underpaid, never whined, never stormed, never sulked, never threatened to throw up his part and return to the place from which he had come. This was the gifted horse who played Grane. He was nine years old, says Fricke, and gentle as a lamb, accepting guidance from any hand that might be suspected to have a piece of sugar concealed in it. He never lost his nerve in the most trying situations, accompanying Brynhilde without a tremor over the steepest and rockiest of stage mountains. It is sad to have to record that in the end he was excluded from one of his best scenes — the moving episode in the *Valkyrie* in which he had to stand near the wings while Brynhilde forewarned Siegmund that he would be slain in the coming fight with Hunding — simply because Wagner was afraid he would steal the act from Niemann and Materna. For he drew all eyes to himself, kept the spectators wondering what effect from his extensive repertory he would produce next, and so, in Wagner's opinion, was likely to detract from the impressiveness of what the mere human hero and the Valkyrie had to say to each other.

On the 4th August a miniature storm broke out among the minor personnel. The builders of the theatre had presented Wagner with a large slab of black marble, which was intended to contain, in the style of an ordinary play-bill, the titles of the operas, the names of the characters and of the leading artists, and so on, and was to be placed on the front of the building, immediately over the spot marking the situation of the foundation stone. Wagner had it engraved accordingly, adding the names of Richter, Brandt, Hoffmann, the Brückner brothers, Doepler and Fricke. There was no room for anything more. But the orchestra, the Vassals and all the other general components of the production took such offence at the omission of *their* names that the tablet had to be covered up for the duration of the festival.

10

Scaria's defection had thrown a fresh load upon Wagner's already overburdened shoulders. The new Hagen, Kögl, was tried on the 25th June. He had an exceptionally good voice, but proved dull-witted; his memory, too, was very faulty. At first Wagner used to be angry with him on this account, attributing his mistakes to lack of study of his part; but it turned out later that he was suffering from a nervous malady over which he had no control. Wagner rapidly made up his mind about him, and on the 12th July wrote to Scaria in friendly fashion, tactfully regretting that the singer's financial difficulties had made the sacrifice originally contemplated impossible for him. Next year, Wagner hoped, the situation at Bayreuth would be very different. For the present, even if every seat were sold they would do no more than cover the bare costs of the festival. In 1877, however, the greater part of the receipts will be available for the singers, and for that year he can offer Scaria 12–15,000 marks for the four weeks from mid-July to mid-August. He hoped Scaria would now find it possible to come to Bayreuth on the 22nd or 23rd July and remain until the end of August, for an honorarium of 100 marks a day to cover his expenses, while in the event of all seats being sold he would receive a further indemnity of 3,000 marks. To this appeal Scaria seems to have returned no reply; so on the 15th a trial was made of Gustav Siehr, of Wiesbaden, in the part of Hagen. As usual, the Fates rallied handsomely to Wagner's side when things were beginning to look really black for him. Siehr mastered the rôle in a couple of weeks, and proved, in voice, bearing and acting, everything he could have desired his Hagen to be.[17]

11

How Wagner managed to keep his difficult team together and keep driving it on towards his goal in spite of all their bickerings is a mystery. In July it was Brandt's turn to give trouble. He had started by treating Fricke *de haut en bas*, but this attitude he had modified as time went on and he saw that the little ballet-master from Dessau really understood his business. Fricke describes him and his father as undoubtedly the most competent men in their own line he had ever met with. But the younger Brandt, he says, had been spoiled by success and had an offensive manner. Almost on the eve of the festival he took umbrage at an omission on the part of an unofficial printer to give him his proper title, and threatened to leave Bayreuth. Then trouble arose between him and Doepler over the latter's costumes, and Wagner had to bear the crossfire of both men. And all this while he was racked with anxiety as to whether the whole of the scenery and machines would be ready and in good working order in time for the festival.

The dragon was a source of endless worry to him and to Fricke. The monster had been ordered from London, no firm in Germany, apparently, being equal to the construction of anything so saga-like. For one reason and another it was sent to Bayreuth in sections, and even these were late in arriving. "The dragon has not yet arrived", Fricke writes mournfully on the 29th June; "it is coming from England, and one section of it, the tail, is swimming the Channel." Three weeks later he records that the tail has arrived; it suggests that the complete beast will be huge, but as yet there are no signs of the front part. The tail, it appears, is capable of a sort of caterpillar motion, and the bristles on it are a foot long. England also had the credit of providing the big snake into which Alberich changes himself for Mime's benefit. Fricke calls it "a masterpiece of fancy and machinery: it opens its mouth wide, rolls its eyes horribly, and the

[17] Erich Engel (ERWL, p. 526) gives a play-bill for the festival that may mislead the unwary reader. According to this, the Hagen was Kögl. The explanation is that the play-bill is a reproduction of an advertisement inserted in the Cologne *Nachrichten* by the local Wagner Verein. As Scheffzky, not Frau Vogl, is correctly named in it as the Sieglinde, it must seemingly have been drawn up in Bayreuth some time between the early days of May, when Scheffzky was engaged, and the second week of July, when Siehr was substituted for Kögl.

body is covered with bright scales." As for the Fafner dragon, the middle portion followed the tail in a few weeks, but the head was still lacking when a full rehearsal of *Siegfried* was held on the 2nd August. At last the head came, but minus the neck. That, indeed, never arrived; two years and a half later Wagner could write that it was "still lying lost in one of the stations between London and Bayreuth".[18] At the performance the head and body had to be joined together as best they could, with the unfortunate result that unsympathetic critics found the dragon a subject for merriment. It had cost Wagner £500; and after seeing it in action with the rather awkward Siegfried, Fricke came to the regretful conclusion that the duel was a spectacle for little children only.[19]

Only a man of inexhaustible energy and superhuman courage could have carried the burden of those months without breaking down. But the strain was visibly telling on Wagner, and a little incident on the 2nd July indicates that his fretted nerves were getting out of hand. At Christmas of the preceding year he had been asked by a Committee in New York to write a March [20] in celebration of

---

[18] It was later said to have been sent in error to Beirut in Syria. That is not at all improbable; was there not a notorious European statesman who, at the Versailles Conference, imagined Cilicia to be only another spelling of Silesia?

[19] In the *Daily Telegraph* of the 12th July, 1930 Mr. W. Courthope Forman, a brother of the Alfred Forman who translated the *Ring* into English in 1877, gave some amusing details, from old family documents, of what he called the "stage fauna" for the drama. Wagner's English agents were Alfred Forman and Edward Dannreuther, who placed the orders with a well-known maker of pantomime "props", Richard Keene, of Milton Street, Wandsworth. These orders included, besides the dragon, "a car with a yoke of rams for Fricka in the *Valkyrie*, a bear, a magpie and an ousel for *Siegfried*, and sacrificial beasts and a pair of ravens for the *Götterdämmerung*". As the date fixed for the performances drew nearer the most urgent messages were sent from Dannreuther in Bayreuth to Forman in London: for example, on the 25th July — "For heaven's sake have the bear sent off before the last part of the dragon; *Siegfried* is to be rehearsed again next week. The King will be here, and Wagner will be in despair if the bear is wanting. Car has arrived. Rams still missing, body of Fafner ditto." To which Forman replied: "Case with Fafner's legs left last Saturday; case with the remainder of body to go tonight or tomorrow; bear tomorrow or Friday; Fafner's head Saturday or Monday".

The body of the dragon arrived in August, but not the head, though this had been despatched to Ostend on the 5th or 6th. "Wire about head to all stations after Cologne", Dannreuther telegraphed frantically to London. At last the head arrived, but without an important part of the neck; so that poor Fafner was rather handicapped when he sallied forth from his cave to give combat to Siegfried on the 16th.

[20] Now generally referred to as the *Centennial March*. He himself never laboured under the delusion that it was one of his finest works. He is reported to have said later that the best thing about it was the 5,000 dollars he received for it.

The mysterious psychology of the creative genius is well illustrated by the fact that while he was working at the March one day there came to him the theme of the chorus — "Komm, holder Knabe" — of the Flower Maidens in *Parsifal*.

[475]

the centenary of the United States' Declaration of Independence. This he had finished in the following February; and on the 2nd July (Gluck's birthday) a performance of it in the Bayreuth theatre had been arranged for his benefit. When he took up his position at the conductor's desk at eleven that morning he found that Richter was still rehearsing elsewhere with the brass. After waiting a while, Wagner became angry, threw down the baton, and walked out, saying that it was no pleasure to him to rehearse with tired-out players. "He was terribly excited", says Fricke, "talked about lack of respect, and even used the quite unjustified word 'intrigue'." Richter's mild plea that he had to rehearse or he would never be ready left Wagner unmoved; and it was only after Feustel and Wilhelmj had exercised their diplomacy on him that he consented to return to the orchestra. The incident, trifling in itself, is interesting as showing how prone he was to see "intrigue" in the most innocent frustration of his wishes. It gives us a standard by which to measure the justice of some of his accusations of "intrigue" against Pfistermeister and Perfall and the rest of them in the Munich days.

CHAPTER XXIV

THE FESTIVAL AND AFTER

1

WAGNER'S ENEMIES had done, and were to continue to do, every-thing in their power to strangle Bayreuth in its birth. There was no baseness to which they were not prepared to stoop. The Press particularly distinguished itself: any incident calculated to dam-age the undertaking was gleefully reported everywhere, while if the facts did not exist they were invented. An anonymous Catholic pamphlet circulated among the Bavarian peasants prophesied the destruction of the festival theatre by fire, and described in highly-coloured detail the fearful end of the audience which a moment be-fore had been revelling in "sinful sounds". A few cases of typhus among the soldiers of the Bayreuth garrison were multiplied to such an extent by the Vienna and Munich papers that not only did the enquiry for Patronatscheine cease immediately but the theatre Com-mittee was bombarded with enquiries from nervous prospective visitors about the "epidemic". The defection of Scaria was gleefully magnified into an irreparable disaster for the *Ring*. Although Wagner's Committee had announced three cycles of the work, the Press publicised a fictitious decision on their part to give only two, because of "insurmountable difficulties"; the natural result was a falling off in applications for tickets for the third cycle. And, as a matter of course, the voice of the professional deadhead was heard everywhere in the land: as Fricke put it, everyone who happened to have drunk a glass of wine with Wagner twenty years ago thought he was entitled to see at least one performance free. The Commit-tee particularly insisted on not following the usual practice of the German theatres and admitting all and sundry to rehearsals, mainly because Wagner was sometimes outspoken in his criticism of the singers, and the Press would have been only too delighted to feed its readers with spicy reports of "scenes" between him and them. In the theatre his outbursts were taken, for the most part, philosophically: everyone saw the intolerable strain he was undergoing, and few grudged him the relief of an occasional explosion.

The casting of the *Ring* at the festival of 1876 was as follows:

Singer	Rhinegold	Valkyrie	Siegfried	Götterdäm-merung
Betz	Wotan	Wotan	Wanderer	
Gura	Donner			Gunther
Unger	Froh		Siegfried	Siegfried
Vogl	Loge			
Hill	Alberich		Alberich	Alberich
Schlosser	Mime		Mime	
Eilers	Fasolt			
Reichenberg	Fafner		Fafner	
Sadler-Grün	Fricka	Fricka		3rd Norn
Marie Haupt	Freia	Gerhilde	Wood-Bird	
Jaïde	Erda	Waltraute	Erda	Waltraute
Lilli Lehmann	Woglinde	Helmwige		Woglinde
Marie Lehmann	Wellgunde	Ortlinde		Wellgunde
Marie Lammert	Flosshilde	Rossweisse		Flosshilde
Niemann		Siegmund		
Niering		Hunding		
Scheffzky		Sieglinde		2nd Norn
Materna		Brynhilde	Brynhilde	Brynhilde
Antonie Amann		Siegrune		
Reicher-Kindermann		Grimgerde		
Johanna Wagner		Schwertleite		1st Norn
Siehr				Hagen
Weckerlin				Gutrune

It will be remembered that the King had expressed the desire to hear the *Ring* in privacy. This wish of his was gratified on the 6th, 7th, 8th and 9th August, in the shape of a "general rehearsal" that was a performance in everything but name. He had point-blank refused to have his pleasure spoiled by any of the publicity attached to his office. He wanted, he told Wagner, no ovations from the populace, no dinners, no audiences, no visits from people of rank:

> "I detest all this kind of thing from the depths of my being. I am coming simply to feast myself enthusiastically on your great work, to refresh myself in heart and soul, not to be gaped at by the inquisitive and offer myself up as an ovation-sacrifice."

The town, of course, was beflagged for the occasion, and the royal waiting-room at the station richly decorated for his arrival. But the King outwitted the sensation-hunters; he came, accompanied only by Count Holnstein (his Master of the Horse) and an aide-de-camp by a train that reached Bayreuth at one in the morning of the

6th. He had the train stopped near the Rollwenzel — the famous hostelry, midway between the town and the Eremitage, in which Jean Paul Richter used to do his work. There Wagner and a royal carriage from the Eremitage were awaiting him. It was the first time the King and the artist had seen each other since the *Meistersinger* night of June, 1868. They had much to talk about, and it was not until half-past three that Wagner was able to return to Wahnfried.

Ludwig did not visit him there, much as he longed to do so; he knew that the house was beset each day by a curious crowd. The *Rhinegold* performance was fixed for seven o'clock on the evening of the 6th, and long before that hour the theatre and the route to it from the town were packed with hopeful spectators from near and far. But again they were disappointed: the King, accompanied by Wagner, drove by a roundabout route from the Eremitage through the Bürgerreuth, thus by-passing the town. He was conducted to the royal box by Wagner, who sat by his side during the performance. Later Cosima and the five children were summoned to him, and the latter presented him with a wreath. This was practically all he permitted in the way of ceremonial during the whole of his visit; but after the *Rhinegold* rehearsal he drove back to the Eremitage, though in a closed carriage, through the crowded streets of the brilliantly lighted town; [1] and the next morning he consented to receive Bürgermeister Muncker and two other local notabilities.

The general rehearsal had gone well, even Wagner being unaware of a little harmless deception practised on him. In order to give Hill a few moments' rest, the more agile Fricke, made up to

[1] According to Glasenapp it was on Wagner's respectful advice that he did this. Walther von Rummel, the son-in-law and biographer of Friedrich von Ziegler, the King's Cabinet Secretary, would have us believe that it was Ziegler who took it upon himself to order the procession through the town, "contrary to the express wish and command of the King". That is frankly incredible on the face of it. Ziegler seems to have been answerable for a story which has attained a wide circulation, of what happened when the King alighted from the train on his arrival at Rollwenzel. "Ziegler", says Böhm, "frequently told the story, which is repeated by his son-in-law, that Wagner had annoyed the King by seating himself by his side in the carriage without being invited: although he never gave Wagner a hint of his astonishment at this, he remembered against him for some time this breach of Court etiquette." (BLKB, p. 340). But Ziegler was not with the King on that occasion: Ludwig was accompanied only by the Master of the Horse, Count von Holnstein, and an aide-de-camp, Major von Stauffenberg. It was on Ludwig's *second* visit to Bayreuth, for the third cycle of the *Ring*, that Ziegler accompanied his royal master. The incident *may* have occurred then; but if the Cabinet Secretary's memory could be so untrustworthy as to dates we cannot have perfect confidence in it as to facts.

look like him as Alberich, took over the pursuit of the Rhine Maidens over the rocks for some twenty-four bars before the Nibelung's despairing cry of "Could I but seize one!" In the dim lighting of the scene no one noticed the substitution. For the *Valkyrie* (on the 7th) and the other performances (on the 8th and 9th) Wagner persuaded the King to allow the house, for acoustical reasons, to be occupied by an audience made up of holders of Patronatscheine and others: owing to the darkness and the shape of the theatre he was in no danger of any intrusion on his dearly-loved privacy.[2] The *Valkyrie* went off well; *Siegfried* also, in spite of the fact that the still headless dragon had to be heard but not seen. But Fricke's heart was heavy within him after the *Götterdämmerung*. The final scene worked out no better than it had done before: "I fear", Fricke wrote in his diary, "that all the beauties of the earlier parts will be ruined by the ending." It must be remembered, however, that Fricke saw the performance not from the house but from the wings, where, no doubt, things looked worse than they really were.

2

The reader will recall that the poem of *Siegfried's Death* had been written in 1848, but that Wagner had altered the closing scene considerably in the following years,[3] even making changes in it (in 1856) after it had been privately printed in 1853. In the imprint of the final text of the *Götterdämmerung* in the sixth volume of his Complete Works (1872), he drew a line across the page at the point at which the Vassals bring Brynhilde her horse,[4] and underneath the line inserted this note: "Before the poem was worked out in music the following verses also were allotted at this place to Brynhilde . . .", then he quotes thirty lines, commencing with

Ihr, blühenden Lebens	You, blossoming life's
bleibend Geschlecht:	abiding abode,
was ich nun euch melde,	of my words be mindful,
merket es wohl!	mark what they mean!

and concluding with

---

[2] As was only to be expected, many people had sold their admission cards for the *Valkyrie* at high prices: consequently free admission was cancelled for *Siegfried*, a uniform price of twenty marks being charged.

[3] For details see Vol. II, p. 347 ff.

[4] See RWGS, VI, 254–6.

Nicht Gut, nicht Gold,	Not goods, nor gold,
noch göttliche Pracht;	nor greatness of gods;
nicht Haus, nicht Hof,	not house, nor land,
noch herrischer Prunk;	nor lordly life;
nicht trüber Verträge	not burdensome bargains'
trügender Bund,	treacherous bands,
nicht heuchelnder Sitte	not wont with the lying
hartes Gesetz:	weight of its law;
selig in Lust und Leid	happy, in luck or need,
lässt — die Liebe nur sein.	holds you nothing but love.

He continues thus:

"In these verses the poet had endeavoured in advance to express sententiously the musical effect of the drama. But in the course of the long interruptions that delayed the realisation of the poem in music he was impelled to cast the final stanzas of farewell into another form, more correspondent to that effect. He appends these lines herewith";

and he quotes twenty lines, beginning with

Führ' ich nun nicht mehr	Fare I now no more
Nach Walhall's Feste,	to Walhall's fastness,
wisst ihr, wohin ich fahre?	where is the rest I ride to?

and ending

Trauender Liebe	Suffering love's
tiefstes Leiden	most sunken sorrow
Schloss die Augen mir auf:	widely opened my eyes;
enden sah ich die Welt.	wither saw I the world.[5]

"It became finally evident to the composer", continues Wagner, "that these lines would have to be omitted from the actual representation, the sense of them being fully expressed in the drama as realised in music."

Some of the lines in question had always been particular favourites of the King; and when he discovered that they were not to figure in the final composition of the *Götterdämmerung* he could not refrain from voicing his regret to Wagner (in September, 1874). In the following April he asked him to set to music, for his sake, the passage beginning "Verging wie Hauch der Götter Geschlecht" and ending "Selig in Lust und Leid lässt die Liebe nur sein". This is perhaps one indication among others that he was not quite so un-

---

[5] Alfred Forman's translation.

musical as he is alleged to have been; but he showed some innocence in practical theatrical matters when he further asked that
the setting of "these words, so significant, so full of truth, this noble
evangel of Love which Brynhilde bequeaths to the world before
leaving it", should be incorporated in the performances he was to
hear at Bayreuth. Wagner, in his letter of the 6th April, 1874, promised that his wishes should be complied with. To dovetail the passage into a public performance would have been a difficult matter.
But Wagner did actually set it to music, though apparently not until
the performances attended by the King during his first visit to Bayreuth were over. He sent him, through Düfflipp, the scrap of manuscript as a birthday gift on the 21st August.[6]

3

Ludwig left Bayreuth immediately after the *Götterdämmerung*
rehearsal on the 9th August; and from Hohenschwangau his love
and gratitude welled out to "the artist by the grace of God" who had
come to this earth "to purify, bless and redeem it", "the god-man
who in truth cannot fail nor err". "Fortunate century", he cried
prophetically, "that saw this spirit arise in its midst! How future
generations will envy those to whom fell the incomparable happiness
of being your contemporaries." He longed now to see the *Ring* a

---

[6] A facsimile of Wagner's draft of the setting, which runs to only thirty-three bars
for voice and piano, is given in KLRWB, III, 88. He has managed to work in references to the Vengeance motive, the Treaty motive, and, at the end, the World Hoard
motive. The final fair copy, made for the King by Wagner himself, seems to have
disappeared; but the Wahnfried archives contain the pencil sketch and the first fair
copy. See BFF, 1936, p. 110.

We know now that there was an earlier case of a reverse kind, in which Wagner
scrapped some words *after* they had been set to music. Until recently it was supposed that *Lohengrin* in its first form was represented by a draft which differs in
certain respects from the text as we now have it. But in an article on *Die Urgestalt des
"Lohengrin"* in the *Bayreuther Festspielführer* for 1936 (consequently too late for me
to be able to make use of it in the earlier volumes of the present Life) Dr. Otto
Strobel published for the first time what is evidently the sketch which Wagner tells
us, in *Mein Leben*, he dashed off in wild excitement in Marienbad in the summer of
1845. In this, at the point in the third act at which Lohengrin prays for a sign from
heaven for Elsa's sake, the Swan sings softly "Leb' wohl, du wilde Wasserfluth, die
mich so weit getragen hat; leb' wohl, du Welle blank und rein, durch die mein weiss
Gefieder glitt: am Ufer harrt mein Schwesterlein, das soll von mir getröstet sein."
This was not only carried over into the later poem but actually set to music, and then,
on riper reflection, discarded. In August, 1853 Wagner wrote out the words and music
as a contribution to the album of Lydia Steche, at that time a member of the Leipzig
opera company.

second time, though that would involve his visiting Bayreuth when other crowned heads were there. He begged Wagner, however, to have him protected from their unwelcome society by a partition, and to ensure their being kept away from him by gendarmes, if necessary, during the intervals. In the preceding December he had had to sit through a Munich performance of *Lohengrin* in the company of his mother, the Archduchess Elisabeth, and the latter's children. "It was horrible", he said;

> "and in proportion as the *Ring* surpasses *Lohengrin* will my torture be increased if I have to be with people with whom I shall have to exchange chatter." "I envy", he went on indignantly, "the mere curiosity-seeking princes who will attend the first two cycles only because they regard it as their duty to do so. Is there a single one among them who has longed for thirteen years, as I have done, to live to see these festival days, a single one who, from his youth onwards, has clung to you, as I have done, in unshakeable friendship and fidelity, with an enthusiasm that has never faltered and never will?"

Wagner agreed with him; he had just had to sacrifice part of a rehearsal, he said, because the theatre company wanted to welcome the Kaiser at the station, and it would have given offence if he were not at their head.[7] The Kaiser had greeted him with the congratulations to be expected on the achievement of his festival, which he regarded as a "national" matter. "It was well meant", says Wagner, "but I saw only the irony of it: what has the 'nation' to do with my work and its realisation?" He promises the King the desired immunity at the third cycle; in any case, he says, the curiosity of the other princes will have been satisfied by the first two, and they will all have departed. But he ventured to give the young man some friendly advice — to show himself to the people who adored him and knew how great had been his services to Wagner's cause, and to bestow honours on some of those who had been most helpful to him, such as Heckel, Brandt, Wilhelmj, Richter, Niemann and Betz. Niemann and Betz, he said, besides having been the best of all his performers, had from the first declined any remuneration, and had promised to try to infuse into the others the same self-sacrificing spirit. But on the main point the King would not yield; he would

---

[7] The Kaiser, with various other German royalties, descended on Bayreuth for the first cycle of performances. He was able to see only the *Rhinegold* on the 13th August and the *Valkyrie* on the 14th before going off to the military manoeuvres at Babelsberg.

attend the third cycle, he telegraphed Wagner on the 26th, only on condition that, as before, there was to be nothing whatever in the shape of an ovation.

He left Berg the same day for Bayreuth, where he attended the third series of performances, which lasted from the 27th to the 30th. At the conclusion of the *Götterdämmerung* he appeared in the front of his box and joined with the excited audience in applauding Wagner as he came before the curtain. Wagner spoke quietly and gravely. The festival of that year was over, he said; whether it would be repeated he did not know. It had been embarked upon in trust in the German spirit and completed for the glory of the King of Bavaria, who had been not only a benefactor and protector to him but a co-creator of his work. He hoped it would not be re-garded as arrogance on his part if he said that the festival had been a step towards an independent German art;[8] time would show whether it were so or not. The King drove from the theatre to the Eremitage, and then, after a short rest, to the Rollwenzel station, where he entered his train. The avenue from the Eremitage to the Rollwenzel was packed with spectators who insisted on demon-strating their loyalty. In their cheers, perhaps, the lonely misan-thrope may have detected a note of recognition of all he had done for Wagner and for German art and their gratitude to him for it; and that thought may have brought him some consolation for all he had suffered through Wagner and for Wagner's sake. His last words were exchanged with the artist through the carriage window. More than four years were to elapse before they saw each other again.

4

What were Wagner's thoughts when he left the theatre on the night of the 30th? Equally compounded, one imagines, of triumph and care. He had brought into port the great argosy he had begun to plan more than a quarter of a century earlier, after a voyage of

---

[8] This remark of his, implying that until then Germany had lacked an art, gave great offence in some quarters. "It was not to everyone's taste", wrote Saint-Saëns, who attended the performances of 1876, he being at that time an ardent Wagnerite; "but his admirers have long known that his tactlessness is on a par with his talent, and they do not attach any importance to his utterances. If I were to report what he has said about a highly placed personage of the Imperial Court [Bismarck?] there would be an exchange of diplomatic notes between France and Germany." *Harmonie et Mélodie*, p. 97.

unexampled difficulties and dangers. He had accomplished the greatest feat in the whole history of artistic endeavour; whatever happened now, nothing could alter the fact that his theatre stood there on the hill, a model and a challenge to future generations, and that he had given his nation the first great lesson in that German style which he held to be vital for the salvation of the German theatre and of German culture as a whole. But he must have been racked by two anxieties — Would his theatre ever reopen, or would it remain for all time a monument to baffled hopes and frustrated idealism? Would the lesson in style sink in, or soon be forgotten?

As regards the former care, even in his most depressed moments after the festival of 1876 he could hardly have imagined that the theatre would open its doors to his art only once more in his lifetime, after an interval of six years, and that the day was not far distant when he would say bitterly to Cosima, "Every stone in that building is red with my blood and yours!" Far behind him now were the naive days when he could believe that all he had to do was to obtain a few thousand francs from some rich well-wisher, erect a temporary theatre, "invite" singers and players and audiences from near and far, give his great work, and then turn his back on it and them with a noble gesture. His vision had been translated into a reality more magnificent than anything he had ever seen in his dreams; but the translation into reality had meant also translation into the hard-cash values of the world, and what that signified he was soon to discover. As regards the artistic results of it all, though he could praise his collaborators in all sincerity at the moment, the halo soon faded from many of them.

Letters to Lilli Lehmann, Siehr, Wilhelmj and Materna in the early days of September contain cordial praise of these people's efforts; and no doubt similar letters were written to some of the others. But already on the 9th of that month, we learn from Cosima's diary, during a long talk about their experiences during the festival, Wagner swore that he "would have no more of those matadors Betz and Niemann". Betz, continues Cosima, "was so furious at not being allowed to take a call that he came to treat his task with positive contempt." Brandt had not come up to Wagner's expectations, while "Richter was not sure of a single tempo. Misery! Agitation! Richard very sad; says he wishes he were dead." The prime causes of this despair seem to have been Betz and Niemann, who

apparently had not behaved very well towards the end of the festival. For the performances which he still hoped would be possible
in 1877 Wagner was now contemplating Siehr as his Wotan in
place of Betz; and it is interesting to find him telling Siehr, who
was a genuine bass, while Betz was more of a baritone, that it was
never a baritone voice that he had had in his mind when writing the
part but a true bass, though with a wide register: occasional high
notes could be altered, he added. To Hill, on the 23rd September, he
wrote that he could not rely on Niemann again if the tenor were to
learn that Unger, after a year's further study, was to play Siegfried
again in 1877; consequently Wagner had in view Anton Schott,
Hill's colleague in Schwerin, for his next Siegmund, while Fräulein
Hofmeister, of Frankfort, would replace Scheffzky as Sieglinde.
No doubt there had been a good deal of bickering and heartburning
everywhere when the tension of the performances relaxed; and
Wagner was mercilessly critical both of failures to rise to the full
height of his ideal and of lapses in loyalty to himself.

5

By November, 1878, when he came to write his *Retrospect of the
Stage Festivals of 1876*, he could see the festival at a sufficient distance to allow him to do his chief collaborators justice in the public
eye. But a few weeks after that, in a private letter to the King, the
long-smouldering fire burst out again, fanned into flame by the bitter
consciousness that all his work in 1875 and 1876 might as well not
have been done for all the permanent influence it was likely to have
on German art. One man of letters he has lately found, he says, who
grasps the significance of his ideal and is willing to devote his life
to it — Hans von Wolzogen. But for the musician and the dramatist who could be trusted to maintain and continue his ideal in practice he still searches in vain.

"I do not know any conductor whom I could trust to perform my music
in the right way, or any actor-singer of whom I could expect a proper
realisation of my dramatic figures unless I myself had taught him
everything bar by bar, phrase by phrase. The German capacity for
bungling in every sphere of art is unique; every compromise I have
allowed myself with it from time to time merely reduced me to the
condition in which [you] found me on the evening of the last perform-

ance of the *Götterdämmerung* in Bayreuth, when in my seat behind you I started convulsively again and again, so that the Dearest One asked me sympathetically what was wrong with me. It would have been too humiliating just then to confess what had driven me to such despair — to explain that what horrified me was the discovery that my conductor [Richter] — whom nevertheless I regard as the best I know — often could not maintain the right tempo even when it had been achieved, simply because he was incapable of understanding *why* it should be thus and not otherwise." [9]

That was his tragedy. He could never meet with executive artists of the same calibre as himself, a single actor or conductor or singer who could give his characters and his verbal and musical phrases the life with which his imagination had endowed them. Many of his performers were willing enough to learn from him. But it was always a sheer matter of passing his own high current through them while he had them before him under his personal spell: within a week of leaving him and going back to the routine of their own theatres they reverted to what God had made them from the beginning. His case was unique in the history of art — a simple fact which the armchair aestheticians have mostly failed to notice. Most opera composers are creators more or less in the abstract, giving their interpreters a kind of scenario of emotion which it is their function to fill out in practice in terms of a school-craft of which they are supposed to be masters but of which the composer has only a generalised notion. But Wagner was a far better conductor than any of his conductors, a far better actor than any of his actors, a far better singer than any of his singers in everything but tone. Each of his characters, each of his situations, had been created by the simultaneous functioning within him of a composer's imagination, a dramatist's, a conductor's, a scenic designer's, a singer's, a mime's. Such a combination had never existed in a single individual before; it has never happened since, and in all probability will never happen again. None of his interpreters had anything like his volcanic intensity of feeling in any one of the spheres upon which his art touched: no single one of them ever came within measurable distance of living with the same intensity in every one of those spheres. And so he was doomed to perpetual disappointment where

---

[9] We may take it that Cosima was voicing Wagner's opinion when she criticised Richter's tempi in her diary: "he sticks too close to his four-in-a-bar", she says. Wagner preferred a more flexible rhythmic line.

the performance of his works was concerned; the best that his interpreters could give him was no more than an approximation to his
ideal.

6

Yet he was generous enough in his recognition of whatever it was
that they could give him, for he was too consummate a practician
himself not to know how hard some of them had striven, under his
goading, to make themselves for the time being what he desired them
to be. Many of us have asked ourselves how the *Ring* performances
of 1876 would compare with those of the opera houses of today. The
answer probably is that, all in all, the best of today would not be
able to bear comparison with them. When all allowances have been
made for certain advances in stagecraft since Wagner's day, and
for an occasional first-rate mind at the conductor's desk or on the
stage, it still remains probable that Wagner would not have passed
for public consumption a single one of the performances to which
we are accustomed. However good one or other of these may be in
parts, they are decidedly not good as a whole; they perhaps correspond, broadly speaking, to those performances of his operas in
German theatres that made Wagner despair of ever getting an adequate representation of any of his works except in a theatre of his
own.

In his public *Retrospect*, written in the latter part of 1878, he
distributed his praise generously but discriminatingly. He now
regretted, he said, not having accepted Niemann's offer to take the
Siegfried of the *Götterdämmerung*, thus allowing the less practised
player of the part to concentrate on the youthful Siegfried of the
earlier opera. His "predilection for a certain dramatic realism" —
i.e., his fear of a break in the illusion if the same hero were played
by different people on successive nights — had made him reject
Niemann's suggestion; the result being that "after his great exertions on the preceding day the singer of Siegfried [10] had not sufficient energy remaining for the part of the hero in the final tragedy."
But he praises unreservedly Betz's Wotan, Niemann's Siegmund,
Hill's Alberich, and Siehr's Hagen. These are the only singers he
mentions by name, his plea for merely commending the others in

---

[10] Nowhere in the *Retrospect* does he mention Unger by name.

general terms being that, as in the case of the marble tablet, space was lacking for any more names. The omission of Unger's name must have been due to some disappointment with him; but we perhaps must not take that omission too seriously when we find Wagner also failing to mention any of his women singers by name, though he makes it clear that he was delighted with Materna's final scene and with the exquisite singing of the Rhine Maidens' trio by the sisters Lehmann and Fräulein Lammert.

He, of course, was surveying the whole production from the supreme heights of his ideal. If we want to find a measuring-rod for the performances of 1876 and those of a later day we should perhaps see them all through the eyes of Lilli Lehmann. That great artist lived until 1929, and her memoirs were published in 1920, when she was seventy-two. She had lived to play herself the principal female characters in every Wagner opera except the *Meistersinger*, and to hear at their best most of the leading Wagner singers of the second and third generations, such as Van Rooy, Rosa Sucher, Jean and Edouard de Reszke, Van Dyck, Burgstaller, Scheidemantel, Gudehus, Therese Malten, Reichmann, Winkelmann, Anna Bahr-Mildenburg, Carl Perron, Luise Reuss-Belce and Schmedes. She was a first-rate judge both of singing and of acting, and her verdicts in general can probably be relied upon. In her opinion Niemann was not merely Siegmund but *the* Siegmund, Wagner's Siegmund:

> "never since have I heard or seen a Siegmund to compare with him; all the rest of them — they can resent what I am saying or not, as they please — may as well let themselves be buried. His intellectual power, his physical impressiveness, his incomparable expression were superb beyond words. . . . This Siegmund was unique; [11] it will no more return than another Wagner will."

"Vogl's Loge", she continues, "has never since been equalled: he was born for the part." She has high praise for Hill's Alberich, for Gura's "really magnificent" Gunther, and for Schlosser's "excellent" Mime; and while apparently feeling that Materna had not fully mastered the Wagnerian style at that time she testifies that she had the immense vocal resources required for the three Brynhildes. All in all, then, we may perhaps sum up that the 1876 performances

---

[11] Of Niemann's Tristan she says that it "was certainly the most sublime thing that has ever been achieved in the sphere of music drama".

were equal at their least good to the average good of today, and, at their best, better than the present-day best.[12]

To the strain on Wagner of rehearsals and performances during these summer months of 1876 had been added that of the almost daily or nightly reception of friends and casual visitors. Nearly everyone, from Liszt onwards, who had played a part in his life was in the town at one time or another. Even Bülow had been invited; and Du Moulin, presumably on the evidence of Cosima's diary, assures us that at an earlier period he had been offered the musical directorship. Bülow had all along intended, for reasons that can easily be understood, to keep away from the festival, grievously as the decision to do so pained him. He had diplomatically planned to be too fully occupied in America to be able to respond to a call from Bayreuth; but his health had broken down during an American concert tour, and now he was at Godesberg, with his health, as it seemed at the time, irretrievably ruined. But virtually all the other surviving old friends of Wagner were there to share in his triumph and feel with him in his anxieties and sufferings.[13] One man alone tore across the general harmony with a shrill discord — Nietzsche. That summer of 1876 marked the beginning of the end of the friendship between the two men.

---

[12] Saint-Saëns' comments on some of the singers are interesting. He thought Unger more a baritone than a tenor, his high A's and even G's being colourless and of faulty intonation. He thought most highly of all of Schlosser's Mime and Materna's Brynhilde. But both the Siegmund and the Siegfried he found better to look at than to hear. Time, he said, had devoured Niemann's high notes since he had sung Tannhäuser in Paris in 1861, and it was now impossible for him to sing piano or legato. Unger was "still less satisfactory", comparing badly with the tenors of the Paris Opéra, though none of these was as good an actor as either of the German tenors. Betz, "the leading German baritone", Saint-Saëns thought "an admirable singer" but a "mediocre actor". "Singers really worthy of the name are rare in Germany . . . the majority of those taking part in the *Ring* shout instead of singing." *Harmonie et Mélodie*, pp. 88–96.

[13] One unexpected caller at Wahnfried was Dom Pedro, Emperor of Brazil, who, it will be remembered, had hoped, in 1857, to induce Wagner to go to Rio de Janeiro and produce his operas there. See Vol. II, pp. 478–9, where the story is told of his registering at a Bayreuth hotel under the name of Pedro, and, on being asked to fill in his "occupation", writing "Emperor".

CHAPTER XXV

NIETZSCHE IN 1876

1

THE BREACH between them has been the subject of one of the most wrongly-written chapters in both Wagner and Nietzsche biography, thanks primarily to the misleading and disingenuous treatment of the subject in Elisabeth's Life of her brother. Her handling of it is, indeed, the most suspect feature of a biography that is open to grave suspicion at many points.

In the second week of July, 1876 Nietzsche sent Wagner the fourth of his *Thoughts out of Season,* the famous *Richard Wagner in Bayreuth.* Busy as they were with preparations for the festival, both Wagner and Cosima seem to have found time to read the long essay almost at once, Cosima sitting up half the night to do so. The next day — the 11th — she sent him a telegram of thanks for "the only refreshment and uplift" she had lately had besides the mighty impression given her by the *Ring.* On the 12th Wagner dashed off a brief letter of thanks on his own account: "Friend! Your book is prodigious! However did you learn to know me so well? Come soon and get accustomed to the impressions by means of the rehearsals." He was so delighted with the brochure, indeed, that he sent a copy of it to the King, who, in his turn, found it "extraordinarily fascinating".

In *Ecce Homo,* written in 1888, Nietzsche elaborated the complacent thesis that his earlier writings on the subject of Wagner, so far as there was any good in them, were not really about Wagner but about himself. What he had "heard" in Wagner's music in his youth and early manhood, he had now discovered, had "nothing whatsoever to do with Wagner": when he had rhapsodised about Dionysian music in those days he was describing not what he had heard, say, in *Tristan,* but merely what he had heard inside himself. And the proof of this was his *Richard Wagner in Bayreuth,* in "all the decisive psychological passages" of which *he* was "the only person concerned", so that *his* name or that of Zarathustra should be substituted for that of Wagner wherever the latter occurs.[1] Even the sympathetic and discerning Andler calls this, and rightly so, *une construction faite après coup,* and adds that "Nietzsche's insolence towards Wagner would be more blameworthy but for the fact that this construction of 1887 [really 1888] is chimerical." [2]

Cosima has been censured for imposing a "Wagner legend" on the world after the Master's death. Nietzsche set out to create his own legend during his lifetime. So far as his connection with Wagner was concerned, this legend was the product in part of a consuming vanity which in the last years of his life had become pathological, in part of an intellectual resentment — emotionally he never really managed to shake off the older man's spell — of the many debts his own mental life had owed to Wagner, as well as of the awkward position into which he had sometimes allowed himself to be betrayed in public by his devotion to him. The line he took, a line at once brazen and naive, was that whatever he now felt to be weak in his earlier writings was due to the malign influence of Wagner, while in whatever was strong in them it was about himself that he had been talking under the guise of a description of Wagner. *He,* in fact, not Wagner, had been the great man. *He* had had prophetic visions of this, that and the other: in the too generous enthusiasm of youth he had let himself be persuaded that these visions were Wagner's also, but in wiser years he had come to see that all he had done was to catch a faint reflection of his own world-shaking thoughts in Wagner's faded eyes. This was the Nietzsche legend that he was bent on creating for posterity. The dutiful Elisabeth took it over from him and embroidered it. Everything she has to say about her brother's relations with Wagner is directed by it and coloured by it; and to consolidate it she has no scruple either in presenting the facts in the way most propitious to it or in making it appear as if experiences and reflections that only occurred to her later, under the influence of the legend, were contemporary with the events she is describing.

---

[1] Wagner himself, he continues, had a notion of this truth: "he did not recognise himself in the essay". This is in flat contradiction to Wagner's letter of the 12th July. Pierre Lasserre (*Les Idées de Nietzsche sur la Musique,* p. 171) also finds Nietzsche's statement "peu compatible" with Wagner's letter.

[2] ANVP, III, 335 *note.*

2

Neither her own nor her brother's reading of what happened in 1876 can be accepted at its face value now. Taking her cue from him, she argues that at that time, as on more than one previous occasion, Nietzsche, out of sheer loyalty to Wagner, had written about him for the public in terms that were an exaggeration, or even a contradiction, of what he really thought. In proof of this she draws our attention to the jottings in Nietzsche's note books of 1874 and 1875 that served to some extent as sketches for *Richard Wagner in Bayreuth*.[3] But in these jottings there is nothing whatever to support Nietzsche's later assertion that in the "decisive moments" of *Richard Wagner in Bayreuth* the portrait he is painting is not that of Wagner but that of Nietzsche-Zarathustra.[4] It is quite true that much of what he has to say by way of analysis of the man Wagner can be seen to bear upon his own later dramatisation of himself, for the two men were fundamentally alike in several respects. But the reading, in *Richard Wagner in Bayreuth,* of Wagner's nature and character as moulded by his ideal and his struggle against the world is too penetratingly accurate in most respects not to rank as a painting from life. It is demanding too much of our credulity to ask us to believe that Nietzsche set out to make a portrait of himself and then found that it answered faithfully at point after point to the man called Richard Wagner.

Nor do the historical facts lend the smallest support to the *construction faite après coup.* Elisabeth's thesis is that in a gush of grateful emotion in 1875 her brother "strung together all his sentiments of the last sixteen years or so", and then "the sorrowfully-departing disciple wrote his second letter of farewell, *Richard Wagner in Bayreuth*"; that he worked at it from August to October, 1875, was dissatisfied with it, and laid it aside because of "some conflict within him". The impression it is sought to convey to the reader is that in his heart of hearts the super-critical Nietzsche had already parted company from Wagner, and the *Richard Wagner in Bayreuth* was a desperate attempt to do the older man a last gener-

---

[3] They will be found in NW, X, 397–425.
[4] "Most German critics", Mr. A. H. J. Knight comments, "seemed to be convinced, and almost touched, by this explanation, which to my mind appears a little disingenuous." *Some Aspects of the Life and Work of Nietzsche,* p. 75.

ous service by painting him not as the younger one saw him then but as he had seen him in days gone by.

Now nothing is more certain than that in 1875 Nietzsche was still heart and soul with Wagner in all essentials. In June of that year he was looking forward to attending the rehearsals at Bayreuth with Rohde and Gersdorff.[5] But his health broke down completely that summer; his doctor forbade him the excitement of Bayreuth, and in July he went to Steinabad to recuperate. Before leaving he wrote to Rohde urging him to "come to Bayreuth: I will do all I can to be fit for Bayreuth by August, which I am not at the moment." [6] To Gersdorff he laments that his doctor has forbidden him Bayreuth, but he hopes to be there next year.[7] To the musician Carl Fuchs he cries, "Just imagine, the doctors will not allow me to go to Bayreuth this summer! What a command like that means!" [8] To Gersdorff (still from Basel), on the 7th July, the cry goes up again, "I am of your opinion as regards Bayreuth. It's no use; I can't endure to be away from it. Let's wait a little; I shall be able to find some way." [9] The voice is not precisely that of "a sorrowfully-departing disciple" who is "a disciple no longer". His letters from Steinabad show him fretting over his inability to be at the rehearsals. When he gets a letter from one of his friends who has gone to Bayreuth, he tells Overbeck, he experiences a kind of convulsion for half-an-hour; he feels as if he must leap up, cast everything from him, and hasten to join him there. On his walks he hears in imagination something of the "flowing gold" of the *Ring* orchestration, and is filled with a sense of infinite loss.

"My sole consolation is the thought that you [plural] are there; it might have come about that none of us had gone, and then we would hardly know what happiness could await us there";

and he begs Overbeck to tell him how it has all sounded.[10] On the 1st August he assures Rohde that for more than three-quarters of each day he is in Bayreuth in spirit, haunting the place like a ghost. He asks his friend for details of what is going on there: as for

[5] Letter of the 15th June to Overbeck, in NBO, pp. 28–9.
[6] NGB, II, 501.
[7] NGB, I, 323.
[8] NGB, I, 324.
[9] NGB, I, 327.
[10] NBO, pp. 39–40.

himself, he conducts whole sections of the music on his walks, for he knows it by heart. Rohde is to greet Wagner most fervently for him.[11] It is a grief to him that he cannot be in Bayreuth, he tells Carl Fuchs, but he rejoices to think that his friends Gersdorff, Overbeck and Rohde are there, though each letter he receives from these more fortunate ones makes him miserable.[12] He is oppressed by the fear that next year and the one after that he may be unable to attend the festivals, as he is likely to get only a few days' leave from his duties in Basel, though he hopes it may turn out that he will be free for the whole of August.[13] And in December of 1875 he can tell Gersdorff that he regards it as a piece of good fortune that he (Nietzsche) has had such "educators" as Schopenhauer and Wagner.[14]

3

As for the essay *Richard Wagner in Bayreuth*, Peter Gast's testimony is at variance with the tendentious suggestions of Elisabeth. She would have us believe that when her brother read her the first eight of the ultimate eleven sections of the essay in the autumn of 1875, and she expressed her delight with them and asked why he did not continue them, he replied sadly, "Ah, Lisbeth, if only I could!" [15] According to her, he had had his doubts since January 1874 not only about Wagner's value "for the future of the human soul" but even about "the purely artistic worth" of his work; there was a bitter struggle going on within him between his love for Wagner and his honesty towards himself. Elisabeth even goes to the

---

[11] NGB, II, 505.
[12] NGB, I, 347.
[13] NGB, I, 353–4.
[14] NGB, I, 361.
[15] There are far too many occasions on which Elisabeth conveniently "remembers" a little remark of her brother's that comes in pat to confirm whatever she happens to be asserting at the moment. In 1907 she laid down the admirable principle — for others — that "only those reminiscences of Nietzsche are really trustworthy that are based on letters and diaries contemporary with the event". Few of her own "recollections" of what her brother "said" to her comply with this condition. The story of what Nietzsche said to her in 1875, "Ah, Lisbeth, if only I could!" did not appear in the *Leben* of 1897. We meet with it for the first time in 1905, in Elisabeth's comments on her brother's letters to Malwida von Meysenbug (NGB, III, 515) — thirty years after the alleged event. In the *Leben* and *Der junge Nietzsche* another story is told — how, in June, 1874, he said to her, "O, Lisbeth, we all have our worm gnawing at us; I too": the said worm being his reluctance, from sheer love of Wagner, to say publicly what he really thought of him.

length of trying to make out that her brother's longing to meet
Malwida von Meysenbug had for its "mysterious background" the
hope that in her company he would find himself strengthened in his
old feeling for Wagner! [16] Furthermore, we are told, it was simply
in his joy at being granted a year's leave of absence from the Basel
University (from October, 1876 to October, 1877) that he "cast a
glance again at his unfinished essay and resolved to complete it and
send it to Wagner as a birthday gift". [17]

We have a more trustworthy account of the matter from Peter
Gast. The latter, as a young man of twenty-one, had gone to Basel
in the October of 1875 to sit at the feet of the admired author of
The Birth of Tragedy. Towards the end of April, 1876 Nietzsche
allowed him to take the unfinished manuscript of *Richard Wagner
in Bayreuth* to his lodgings. Gast read it with increasing enthusiasm; and when returning it to its author he could not refrain from
expressing his regret that it would remain no more than a torso.
At this point, were Elisabeth's suggestions correct, we should have
expected Nietszche to have given him at least a hint of the "struggle"
going on within him, of his doubts whether, in view of his present
disorientation from Wagner, he could honestly commit himself to
saying in public what he himself no longer wholly believed in private. But Nietzsche said nothing of the sort; what he did say was
that he regarded the essay as too personal for publication. "A few
days later" he told Gast that after reading through his essay again
it had occurred to him that it might give Wagner some pleasure to
receive it for his birthday on the 22nd May. [18] Gast made a copy of
it for that purpose; and then Nietzsche's own interest in his work
increased to such an extent that he sent the manuscript to the
printers; he added the final three sections in June, and the book was

---

[16] NGB, III, 514–5.

[17] NGB, III, 520.

[18] This is at variance with Elisabeth's account of the matter, which, again, is at
variance with itself. In the *Leben* and *Der junge Nietzsche* she tells us that what
prompted Nietzsche to send the then existing portion of the manuscript of *Richard
Wagner in Bayreuth* to the printer in May, 1876, and then go to Badenweiler for a few
days in June to complete it, was an up-surge of the old love within him after receiving
Wagner's warm letter of the 23rd May, written in reply to Nietzsche's letter of good
wishes for his birthday (the 22nd). But in her later elucidation of the letters to
Malwida her story is that it was the joyous prospect of a year's leave from the University that made him look again at his unfinished essay, give it to Gast to copy, and,
stimulated by the latter's admiration of it, decide to have it printed as his contribution to the festival of the coming summer.

published in early July of that year as a "Festschrift" for the Bayreuth festival.[19]

4

The general story of 1875 is repeated when we come to the summer of 1876. Once more Nietzsche is consumed with longing to go to Bayreuth, and once more he chafes at the thought that he may be frustrated. His health had steadily deteriorated. Already in June, 1875 he had told Gersdorff that he had been through a very bad time and had perhaps an even worse one before him. Troubles with his stomach, violent headaches lasting for days, vomiting for hours at a time in spite of the fact that he had eaten nothing, immense exhaustion, inability of his eyes to bear the light, these are some of the items in his catalogue of woes.[20] Six months later his condition had grown so much worse that he looked back on the Christmas just over as the most painful of his whole life. One day, feeling himself on the verge of collapse, he had had no doubt that he was suffering from a serious affection of the brain — that this, indeed, was the cause of all his other troubles; he recalled gloomily that his father had died of brain fever at thirty-six, and feared that his own life-course would be even shorter. As for going to Bayreuth, he says, it is still the same old story — either he should not [for reasons of health], or he cannot [for reasons connected with his University duties].[21] In May, 1876 he is still so grievously unwell that he is planning to ask for a year's academic leave from the following October and spend the winter with Malwida in Italy. On the 21st July he tells Gersdorff that his health from day to day is pitiable: what will be the end of it all? he asks. But he is glad to find that his essay has "legitimised itself" in Wahnfried; both Wagner and Cosima have praised it.[22] His letters to Rohde tell the same general story. His health has improved in some respects, he tells his friend on the 16th May, though his eyes still fail him; and he is summoning up all his strength for a month

---

[19] Gast's story will be found in his Foreword to Vol. IV of NGB, p. xxiii ff. He makes it clear that it was Nietzsche himself who told him in the first place that he had an incomplete essay on Wagner in his drawer.

[20] NGB, I, 322.

[21] NGB, I, 363–4.

[22] NGB, I, 381.

in Bayreuth.[23] By July his health has worsened again, but he *must* win through until and during Bayreuth, whither he means to go on the 10th August.[24] Nowhere is there a passage in these contemporary documents to support Elisabeth's thesis.

5

Let us now examine the Elisabethan legend more specifically in connection with the events of the summer of 1876.

Nietzsche became insane in January, 1889, and died, without recovering his reason, on the 25th August, 1900. His sister was the first in the field with a full-scale biography of him: she published the first volume of *Das Leben Friedrich Nietzsche's* in 1895, and the second and third volumes in 1897 and 1904 respectively. Later she recast this work into the form familiar to most present-day students of Nietzsche biography, the earlier *Leben* being now out of print and not generally accessible: *Der junge Nietzsche* appeared in 1912, *Der einsame Nietzsche* in 1914.[25] Publication of the collected edition of Nietzsche's letters began in 1900; the fifth volume, containing his letters to his mother and sister, did not appear until 1909. Nietzsche was thus presented to the world in the first place as seen through Elisabeth's eyes, the reader being vouchsafed only such extracts from his correspondence as she chose to supply for her own purposes, and having, for the most part, no independent check either upon their accuracy or upon her method of linking them up. Moreover, the autobiographical *Ecce Homo*, in which Nietzsche had worked assiduously at the establishment of his own legend of his intellectual development, his friendships, and his partings from friends, and which can now be seen to have played a con-

---

[23] NGB, II, 520. A passage in Mr. Knight's valuable book (*Some Aspects of the Life and Work of Nietzsche*, p. 30) is typical of the mistaken notions current as to Nietzsche's intellectual attitude towards Wagner at this time. "*Richard Wagner in Bayreuth*", says Mr. Knight, "was written rather against Nietzsche's will — that is perhaps why it is such an unmixed encomium — and when, after avoiding his friend for some time, the philosopher *allowed himself to be fetched* [italics mine] to the opening performances at Bayreuth, the reaction was completed."

[24] NGB, II, 529. The explanation of the "10th August" is that he had heard that no one would be admitted to the *rehearsals;* therefore he planned to be present at the first *public cycle*, which would begin on the 13th of that month. As a matter of fact he went to Bayreuth in the last week of July, having learned that the rehearsals would be open to him after all.

[25] English translations 1912 and 1915.

siderable part in Elisabeth's interpretation of this or that episode in his earlier life, was not disclosed to the world until 1908.[26] She thus had a long clear start in her set purpose of imposing the legend upon the literary world before her readers were in a position to check her facts, her interpretation of them, her manner of presenting them, by the full text of the contemporary documents of Nietzsche's middle years. We shall find ample reason, as our investigation proceeds, to doubt not only her competence but her probity as a biographer of her brother. The English-speaking reader who does not understand German is at a particular disadvantage: for whereas a score of books in his own language, based on *The Young Nietzsche,* have dinned into him unceasingly Elisabeth's version of Nietzsche's rupture with Bayreuth in the summer of 1876, his letters to her during that period are known to him only from the manipulated extracts given by her.

6

Our first task, then, is to examine critically the text and dating of his Bayreuth letters to his sister. They are here translated complete, apart from a sentence or two that has no connection at all with the subject of our enquiry. The sentences printed in italics are the only ones she saw fit to reproduce in *Der junge Nietzsche.*[27]

---

[26] The title-page of the first edition bears no date. The unpublished manuscript of *Ecce Homo* had been in Elisabeth's sole possession all this time. In that book Nietzsche re-writes the story of his intellectual development and his relations with Wagner and others in accordance with his own conception of himself in his last years of sanity; and it was from this fascinating but misleading manuscript that Elisabeth took her cue again and again when writing of her brother's earlier years: there are no less than twenty-four citations from it in the second volume of the *Leben* (1897). She assured her readers in the third volume of the *Leben* (p. 891 *note*) that "*Ecce Homo* consists of a series of autobiographical sketches, the first half of which is filled with the happy mood of those golden autumn days [1888]. Later a strange exasperated note is heard, which here and there has a suggestion of the morbid, though there is not a single personal attack. For the rest, the present volume [i.e., volumes II and III of the *Leben*] contains [in quotations] all of it that is absolutely necessary to an understanding of Friedrich Nietzsche." No one today would accept that as an adequate, or even truthful, description of *Ecce Homo.*

[27] Our references will generally be to this work, because it is the one most likely to be in the hands of the English reader. The earlier *Leben* will be referred to whenever that becomes necessary to complete the argument.

1st Letter

Bayreuth, Tuesday, 1 August 1876.
I have almost regretted it! For up to the present it has been pitiable.
From Sunday midday to Monday night headaches; today exhaustion;
I just can't write.
*I was at the rehearsal on Monday. It did not please me at all and I
had to leave.* Everything fixed up at Giessel's.[28] I have moved in, but I
am spending the day at Fräulein Meysenbug's, where there is a fine
cool garden; and there I shall take my midday meal until you come
and set up *our* establishment. . . .
It is frantically sultry here. Just had a storm.
Never on a journey have I been better attended to than this time, my
good sister; victuals admirable. The night in Heidelberg, as [the
train] did not go any further.
Hearty greetings from Olga [Malwida's adopted daughter, Olga
Herzen, who had become Mme Gabriel Monod] and Fräulein von
Meysenbug. *Everyone eagerly expecting you.*
Hurry, hurry, my good Lama! [29]

2nd Letter

Bayreuth, 4 August 1876.
Friday morning.
*Things are better now: for the last three days I have not had to
look after myself, for I spend my time at Fräulein von Meysenbug's; I
am in the garden first thing in the morning, drink milk, bathe in the
stream, and eat only what agrees with me. Meanwhile I have seen and
heard the whole Götterdämmerung. It is a good thing to get familiar
with it; now I am in my element. . . .*[30]
*The King is coming tonight. He has wired that he is delighted with
my essay.*[31] *The Schurés are also coming today. The Wagners and the
children have often asked after you. . . . My health has taken a good
turn: I am much more cheerful. . . .*
Besides members of the Committee I have seen Frau von Schleinitz,
Porges, Baligand, Lallas [Lalas], Heckel, Richter. *I must be very care-*

---

[28] Where he and (later) Elisabeth were to lodge.
[29] Nietzsche's pet name for his sister.
[30] "My" is underlined in the Correspondence and in the extract given from the
letter in *The Young Nietzsche*, but not in the *Leben*. In the English version of the
former book the "whole" before "*Götterdämmerung*" is omitted; yet, as we shall see
later, it is important.
[31] I.e., *Richard Wagner in Bayreuth*. Nietzsche must have heard this from Wagner, who had received the King's telegram on the 21st July. See KLRWB, III, 81.

ful, however, and I decline all invitations, including those of the Wagners. Wagner thinks I make myself scarce.

Entry to the general rehearsals is still not certain; however, make your arrangements as if it were. . . .

3rd Letter

Bayreuth, 5 August 1876.
Saturday morning.

I realise that it isn't going well with me! Unceasing headaches, though not of the worst kind, and weakness. Yesterday I was able to listen to the *Valkyrie* only in the dark: seeing was quite impossible! *I long to get away; it is too irrational for me to stay. I shudder at the prospect of each of these long art-evenings; yet I do not keep away.*

In this distress I suggest that you arrange with some good friends for the second cycle of performances [20–23rd August]. You could all live together in the Giessel apartments, which, on the terms on which we have them, are the cheapest in Bayreuth: you should see the prices elsewhere!

This time you must see and hear for me as well. *I have had quite enough.*

Nor shall I be at the first performance [public cycle], *but somewhere else, only not here, where it is nothing but a torture to me.*

Perhaps you will send a few lines to X, and offer him my seat for the first performance [cycle]; or someone else, anyone you like.

Forgive me for all the distress you are once more having over me. I will go away into the Fichtelberg or somewhere.

Just wire the time of your arrival to Fräulein von Meysenbug.

Of course you will have the entrée to the general rehearsal [of the whole cycle]; that is arranged.

4th Letter

Klingenbrunn, Sunday [6 August 1876] [32]
You are in Bayreuth, I hope, and finding good people there to look after you now that I have vanished from the place.

I see clearly that I cannot [33] *hold out there; indeed, we ought to have known that in advance. Just recall how circumspectly I have had to live during the last few years. I feel so jaded and exhausted by my short stay there that I shall have difficulty in getting over it. I have had*

---

[32] The "6 August 1876" is in square brackets in Elisabeth's text, implying that it is an editorial addition.

[33] *Nicht* is underlined.

a bad day in bed here; persistent headaches as at certain times in Basel. *This place is very pleasant; dense woods and mountain air as in the Jura. I will stay here perhaps ten days, but will not return via Bayreuth, for I shall not have enough money for that.*

There follow some instructions as to lodgings. Then he continues thus:

So we shall probably not see each other again this year.[34] *How things turn out! I have to summon up all my self-command to bear the enormous disappointment of this summer. I will not see even my friends; everything now is poison and harm [Schaden] to me."*

---

[34] As he was planning to go to Italy for a year in October, and Elisabeth would be returning to her mother in Naumburg after hearing the *Ring*.

CHAPTER XXVI

ELISABETH'S FALSE WITNESS

1

LET US now do first of all what one or other of the countless writers on this subject who have merely echoed Elisabeth surely might have done long ago — test the trustworthiness of these letters, as presented to us in the Correspondence, purely by their internal evidence. The first thing that will strike the critical reader is the number of gaps in the citations from the letters in the biography; even the fact that there *are* omissions is sometimes concealed from him there.[1] With the presumable reasons for these omissions we shall deal later. Our first task is to examine the editorial dating of the letters, for it stands to reason that if the dating is not correct the whole picture she has painted of Nietzsche in Bayreuth is a falsification. And there cannot be the smallest doubt that the letters, as presented to us by Elisabeth, are a complex of *suppressio veri* and *suggestio falsi*.

The central purpose of our preliminary investigation being to discover exactly when Nietzsche went to Bayreuth, how long he remained there, and how much of the *Ring* he had heard before, unable to endure his physical sufferings any longer, he fled to Klingenbrunn, the reader will find it helpful to have before him a time-table of the rehearsals and performances.

---

[1] Elisabeth's treatment of the third letter may be taken as typical of her method. "His violent effort to pull himself together had lasted only a few days", she says. "He wrote: 'I long to get away'," etc. By omitting what precedes "I long to get away" she concealed from her readers the vital fact that Nietzsche longed to get away because his headaches and his bad eyes made sitting in the theatre a torture to him. The English translator of *Der junge Nietzsche*, apparently with the Elisabethan thesis at the back of his mind that Nietzsche fled from the town because of his disillusionment as regards the art of Wagner, makes matters worse by rendering the passage thus: "His violent effort to be his old self in regard to Wagner's work had thus only lasted a few days." In the German original there is nothing whatever corresponding to "in regard to Wagner's work ".

2

The plan for the whole three summer months of 1876 had been drawn up by Wagner long in advance, and it was adhered to with only a trifling alteration or two necessitated by some little difficulty of the moment. After the preliminary detail work, sectional rehearsals began in the theatre on the 3rd June and lasted until the 12th July: these were sometimes for the singers alone, with piano accompaniment, sometimes for the wind, sometimes for the full orchestra, and sometimes for singers and orchestra combined. With this sequence, which was known as the first rehearsal-cycle, we are not concerned. Then came the

Second rehearsal-cycle, which ran from the 14th to the 26th July, one-half of the *Rhinegold* being taken on the 14th, the other half on the 15th, the *Valkyrie*, one act per day, on the 17th, 18th and 19th, *Siegfried* in the same fashion on the 20th, 21st and 22nd, and the *Götterdämmerung* on the 24th, 25th and 26th. (The 16th and 23rd were rest-days). These rehearsals were not in costume, though with scenery and "props". Next came the

Third rehearsal-cycle, from the 29th July to the 4th August, at a rate of a whole opera per working-day (i.e. on the 29th, 31st, 2nd and 4th). These were practically straight runs-through, with occasional interruptions by Wagner. Then came the

General rehearsal (the one attended by the King), which ran, at the rate of a whole opera each day, from the 6th to the 9th. Finally there were the three

Performance-cycles — the festival proper, open to Patrons and the general public — on (1) the 13th, 14th, 16th and 17th August, (2) the 20th–23rd, (3) the 27th–30th. In what follows, the second rehearsal-cycle will be referred to, for brevity's sake, as RC 2, the third as RC 3, the general rehearsal as GR, and the first performance-cycle as PC 1.

3

Let us now examine the internal evidence for Elisabeth's dating of the four letters, noting, *en passant*, that she does not provide us with a single definite date in the whole of the relevant chapters in *Der junge Nietzsche* and the *Leben*.

1. The correct date of the first letter is not, as Elisabeth would

have us believe, Tuesday the 1st August but the preceding Tuesday, the 25th July. She tells us in the *Leben* (1895) that her brother left Basel for Bayreuth "in the middle of July". This she repeats in *Der junge Nietzsche*, apparently forgetting, or not wishing to remember, that in her "explanations" of Nietzsche's letters to Malwida [2] she had altered it to "towards the end of July". This latter date is the correct one. Glasenapp tells us that Nietzsche arrived in Bayreuth on the 24th July, that Count and Countess Schleinitz came on the 16th, Heckel a few days later, the Russian Princess Bariatinsky on the 23rd,[3] Edward Dannreuther, Nietzsche and others on the 24th, and "shortly afterwards" the Schurés and the Monods. This tallies absolutely with a passage in Mr. W. Courthope Forman's article in the *Daily Telegraph:* [4] "About the middle of July Dannreuther received a letter from Bayreuth saying 'Come as soon as you can' . . . Later Dannreuther departed for Bayreuth". "On the 25th July", continues Mr. Forman, "Dannreuther wrote [to Keene in London], 'For heaven's sake have the bear sent off before the last part of the dragon; *Siegfried* is to be rehearsed again next week. The King will be here, and Wagner will be in despair if the bear is wanting. Car has arrived. Rams still missing' ", etc. Obviously all this was written after a talk with Wagner immediately after his arrival in Bayreuth on the preceding day. Let us note also that Nietzsche's last letter from Basel is one to Gersdorff dated the 21st July.

It being established, then, that Nietzsche arrived in Bayreuth on Monday the 24th, we naturally ask ourselves, when Elisabeth dates what she describes as "the first news from Bayreuth" (thereupon quoting fragments from our first letter) the "1st August", whether it is conceivable that a man in Nietzsche's deplorable state of health would have let a whole week pass without letting an anxious sister — who, moreover, would be keen to have all the news from Bayreuth — know that he was safely there. The letter is visibly, in every line, the kind of thing a man dashes off home at the earliest possible moment after a journey. The writer sends news of the weather; he

---

[2] In NGB, III, 525.

[3] Later he says that Wagner made a "return call" on this lady at her hotel on the 26th. He adds that this and other details of Wagner's activities at this time are "not based on his own experiences", by which he means that he has taken the facts from Cosima's diary, which she had placed at his complete disposal in 1895.

[4] See *supra*, p. 475.

had had to change trains at Heidelberg; the food had been good en
route; he has been to Giessel's and arranged about his lodgings; he
has seen Malwida, who sends greetings; and so forth. Moreover, he
was "at the rehearsal on Monday". If Nietzsche were really writing on the 1st August, this could only refer to the rehearsal of the
Valkyrie (in RC 3) on Monday, the 31st July. On this point there
will be something to be said later: meanwhile we may ask how it
comes about that, having gone to Bayreuth, according to Elisabeth,
in the middle or latter part of July, expressly to be present at the
rehearsals, he makes no mention of any of these until the 1st August,
and then refers to only one of them — the *second* opera of the cycle
"on Monday". On the internal evidence alone this first letter can be
seen to belong to Tuesday, the 25th July, and the rehearsal which
Nietzsche says he heard "on Monday" was the non-costume one of
the *first act only* of the *Götterdämmerung* (in RC 2) on the afternoon of the day of his arrival, the 24th.

4

2. With these simple facts in our minds, the misleading character of Elisabeth's detached quotations from the letter at once becomes evident. "I almost regret having come!", Nietzsche is made
to say in the English translation of it in *The Young Nietzsche*. "For
up to the present everything [*sic*] has been pitiable. On Monday I
attended the rehearsal: it did not please me at all; and I had to
leave." There is no warrant for the "everything"; it apparently
owes its appearance in the English version to the fact that Elisabeth
has been clever enough to force the card she wanted on her readers
and her translators.[5] By falsifying (in the Correspondence) the

---

[5] French as well as English: Daniel Halévy, for instance, renders the passage
thus: "Je regrette presque d'être venu; jusqu'à present tout est miserable." (*La vie
de Frédéric Nietzsche*, 4th ed. 1909, p. 187). Halévy's English translator renders this
"up till now, everything is wretched," which the reader, as a matter of course in
view of the Elisabethan context, takes to mean "everything connected with the rehearsals." Halévy, again under the influence of Elisabeth, goes on to attribute
Nietzsche's discontent to his exasperation with Bayreuth and its motley crowd.
He was evidently unaware that at the time of writing his first letter Nietzsche could
have seen practically nothing of all this; he had gone to Giessel's immediately on
his arrival in the town, and then straight to the rehearsal. Elisabeth, by presenting
her own tendentious theory of the matter and quoting only so much from Nietzsche's
at that time unpublished letter as suited her purpose, had succeeded, in *Das Leben*,
in giving her readers an entirely false notion of what had happened.

date of the letter, by omitting most of the text and arbitrarily joining up two sentences that are not connected in the letter itself, she
makes her garbled citation read like first-hand confirmation of the
thesis she has been steadily hammering into the reader's head —
that when her brother went to Bayreuth he had already weighed
Wagner's art in the balance and found it wanting. Falling into the
trap, the translators convert Nietzsche's simple "up to the present
it has been pitiable" into the more comprehensive "everything" —
i.e., all his experiences in Bayreuth — "has been pitiable". We
have only to read the letter in full, with our eyes unclouded by Elisabeth's chicanery, to see that what has been "pitiable" so far has
simply been Nietzsche's health.[6] He has had an incessant headache
from mid-day Sunday to Monday night; that is to say, from about
the time he parted from her in Basel on Sunday, the 23rd, to bed-
time on the night of his first day (Monday the 24th) in Bayreuth.

3. A more scrupulous presentation of the simple facts would
also have made it clear to the reader that at the time of writing to
Elisabeth on the Tuesday all that Nietzsche had heard of the *Ring*
was part of the non-costume run-through of the first act of the *Götterdämmerung* on the 24th. For, as has just been pointed out, if we
accept the date of "1st August" for the letter, then the rehearsal
which he says he had heard "on Monday" could only have been that
of the *Valkyrie* on the 31st July. But in that case why should Nietzsche, having, as Elisabeth says, left Basel in the middle or towards the end of July "for the rehearsals", omit, in his first letter
home, all mention of the previous rehearsals he had gone to Bayreuth expressly to hear — of the *Götterdämmerung*, act by act, on
the 24th, 25th and 26th, and of the *Rhinegold* on the 29th? Are we
not driven to conclude that up to the time of writing Nietzsche had
attended only one rehearsal, that of the 24th? And even this first act
of *Götterdämmerung* he had not heard to the end owing to his headache![7]

---

[6] The German is "Denn bis jetzt war's jämmerlich". The expression corresponds
with a passage in his letter of three days earlier to Gersdorff — "Gesundheit von Tag
zu Tag jammervoll" ("Health from day to day pitiable").

[7] It is because the Nietzsche biographers and commentators have failed to un-
earth this simple fact that the best of them consistently misrepresent what had
happened. Thus Charles Andler (ANVP, II, 447) tells us that "Nietzsche arrived
enfeebled and hopeless. . . . He saw the end of the third cycle of rehearsals, and at
first [*sic*] was silent about his feelings. Then [*sic*] he wrote to his sister in Basel: 'I

4. In his second letter, of "Friday morning, 4 August", he says that things have been going better with him for the last three days, thanks to his pleasant life at Malwida's, and that "meanwhile", i.e., on Elisabeth's chronology, between the 1st and 4th, he had heard "the whole *Götterdämmerung*" — which of course would imply that he had also heard the *Rhinegold*, *Valkyrie* and *Siegfried*. Does this passage, the reader may perhaps ask, refer to the rehearsal of the *Götterdämmerung* in RC 3? That is impossible, because that rehearsal did not take place until the evening of the 4th, and Nietzsche is alleged to be writing to his sister on the *morning* of that day. Obviously when he says he has "now seen and heard the whole *Götterdämmerung*" he means the completion of the set of one-act-per-day rehearsals (in RC 2) of the 24th, 25th and 26th July. That is why he uses the otherwise meaningless word "whole." On these grounds alone, then, we should feel entitled to give the second letter (of "Friday morning") an earlier date than "4 August" — a date nearer that of Nietzsche's first letter, that of the 25th July. But there are two other reasons for being sceptical as to the "4 August". With one of these we shall deal later. Meanwhile we will only comment that from the 25th July to the 4th August is ten days; and it is frankly incredible that Nietzsche would have let so long a period go by without giving his sister any further news of himself, of the people he had met in Bayreuth, or of what he had seen and heard of the *Ring*, than was contained in his first hurried letter. We would feel justified a priori in saying that there must have been other letters during that time, and asking what had become of them. But there is no need to take quite so poor a view of Nietzsche's quality as a correspondent; as we shall shortly see, the true date of this letter of the "4 August", or at all events of this part of it — assuming "Friday" to be in the original — is Friday the 28th July, three days after the true date of Nietzsche's first letter. For the second time we have found Elisabeth post-dating a letter by a whole week.

5. In the third letter of the official Correspondence, which is

---

have almost regretted. . . .'" Nietzsche had *not* heard "the third cycle of the rehearsals" (which extended from the 29th July to the 4th August) or any of it at the time when he wrote "I have almost regretted. . . ." He had heard only part of the first act of the *Götterdämmerung* in RC 2. Andler's interval between "at first" and "then" is entirely fictitious.

there dated "Saturday morning, 5 August", Nietzsche says that "yesterday" he had heard the *Valkyrie*. But writing on the 5th he could not possibly have done so "yesterday", for the simple reason that the rehearsal on Friday, the 4th, was not of the *Valkyrie* but of the *Götterdämmerung* in RC 3. The *Valkyrie* rehearsal of that cycle had taken place on Monday, the 31st July; and the work did not appear again in rehearsal until Monday, the 7th August, in the GR series attended by the King. By that time, as we know, Nietzsche was in Klingenbrunn. Manifestly this sentence, at any rate, of the letter of "Saturday, 5 August" was written on Tuesday, the 1st.

Further suspicions as to the "5 August" are aroused when we find Nietzsche, at the end of this letter, asking Elisabeth to wire to Malwida the time of her arrival in Bayreuth, as she will not find him there when she comes. Now after receiving word from him, in his second letter, that she was to proceed on the assumption that she would be admitted to the GR on the 6–9th August,[8] Elisabeth evidently made preparations for her own departure from Basel. She tells us that she arrived "on the day before the first general rehearsal" — i.e., on Saturday, the 5th — by which time "Fritz had already left". So that if her dating of the "5 August" were correct we should be presented with the curious spectacle of Nietzsche writing his instructions (as regards wiring to Malwida) on the very day she was leaving Basel, perhaps at the very time she was in the train! At the end of this letter of the alleged 5th, after the lines about telegraphing to Malwida, he tells her that "of course you will have the entrée to the general rehearsal: that is arranged". This vital information, on which depended her final decision to come in time for the beginning of the GR on the 6th, he entrusts, according to her, to a letter written on the very day of her departure; and, more remarkable still, that letter arrived in Basel, some 250 miles away, before she left there, for she herself informs us that she "received the news that Fritz no longer wished to remain in Bayreuth" on "the morning of my departure". Manifestly the third letter, like the

---

[8] She would have the entrée to the *performance*-cycle in virtue of her holding of a Patronatschein. What she had all along been eager to do was to attend the GR also — a point on which her brother set her mind at rest as soon as possible (in his second letter). She herself tells us that she was one of the very few people smuggled into the first two rows of seats on the *Rhinegold* evening of the GR cycle when the King was there. The reader will recall that on the other three evenings Ludwig had consented to the theatre being filled for acoustical reasons.

first and the second, has been wrongly dated in the published Correspondence.

6

The final proof that the letter of the "5th August" was written on the 1st is afforded by a letter of Overbeck's of the 2nd (from Basel) to Nietzsche.[9] "The latest news", he says, "has strengthened the belief I have always held in secret, that Bayreuth agrees with you." (His informant, of course, was Elisabeth). "Today I saw your sister again: she has now made arrangements to go to you on Saturday" (the 5th). As we have seen, the reference in the letter of the "5th August" to "yesterday's" rehearsal of the *Valkyrie* (actually the 31st July) indicates that it was written on the 1st August. Our first impulse is to assume that this letter had already reached Elisabeth when she met Overbeck on the 2nd. But on second thoughts we must reject this supposition. Had the letter been in her hands by that time she would certainly have told Overbeck that far from Bayreuth agreeing with her brother his health had taken so bad a turn that he had decided to flee from the town. It is clear that on the 2nd August the last letter she had had from Nietzsche was that of the 28th July, wrongly dated by her the "4th August". It was in this letter that he had given her the assurance that she could count on admission to the rehearsals, whereupon, as Overbeck says, she made arrangements to leave Basel on the 5th (or more probably the night of the 4th), so as to be in Bayreuth in time for GR 1 on the 6th. The letter (our third) of the pseudo-5th, which she would have us believe reached her on the morning of the day it was written — the letter of the 1st in which he told her of the alarming turn for the worse in his health — must have arrived in Basel *after* she had encountered Overbeck on the 2nd. She tries to make out that when she arrived in Bayreuth on the 5th and found that her brother "had already left" she was "greatly upset", for she "felt certain that something great and grievous had decided him"; consequently she spent "a whole morning" (presumably that of the 6th) weeping at Fräulein von Meysenbug's. Had she dated the letter of the "5th August" correctly, and had she given the reader of her biography the full text of that letter, instead of quoting from it only the passage beginning "I long to get away", plus a couple of later sentences detached from

---

[9] NBO, p. 47.

their context, he would have seen that she knew perfectly well, at least two days before her departure from Basel, *why* her brother had left Bayreuth, and that his reasons for doing so had been reasons purely and simply of health, not of a revolt of the superior artist and thinker in him against Wagner's mind and work.

Nor is this all. She arrived in Bayreuth on the 5th. Let us, for argument's sake, take it that she did so early enough in the day for it to be possible for her to spend the "whole morning" weeping at Malwida's, though it is more probable that she left Basel on the night of the 4th (by the same train that Nietzsche had taken) and arrived in the early afternoon of the 5th, and the morning given up to tears was that of the 6th. Whichever way we decide to look at it it does not affect her own statement that *on the 6th* she received her brother's letter from Klingenbrunn commencing "You are in Bayreuth, I hope": that is to say, the letter reached her on the day on which, according to her, it was written!

6. Let us now glance at the final letter, that from "Klingenbrunn, Sunday", with the confessedly editorial elucidation of "6 August". "When I reached Bayreuth on the day [Saturday, the 5th] before the first general rehearsal", Elisabeth informs us, "Fritz had already left". If, then, the letter of the "5th", in which Nietzsche announces his intention of leaving Bayreuth, be correctly dated, he could not have fled *earlier* than that date. Now in the Klingenbrunn letter he says he will stay there "perhaps ten days"; and Elisabeth informs us, in fact, that her brother "spent about ten days wandering about the woods of Klingenbrunn", but returned to Bayreuth, contrary to his intention when leaving there, "on the day before the beginning of the first [performance] cycle." That is to say, he returned on the 12th; so that if Nietzsche had quitted the town on either the 5th or 6th he could have been in Klingenbrunn a week at most. We shall see later that "about ten days" is correct: for the moment we need only note that this fact throws further doubt on the dating of the third letter.

One further point, small in itself but illuminative of Elisabeth's methods, may be noted in connection with the fourth letter. The version of the document which she gave the reader both in the *Leben* and in *Der junge Nietzsche* was this: "I will stay here perhaps ten days, but will not return [to Basel] *via* Bayreuth." After all that had gone before, the innocent reader would naturally see in this an

[511]

expression on Nietzsche's part of so consuming a disgust with Wagner and Bayreuth that he could not bear the thought of returning there — which is just what Elisabeth wanted him to see. The concluding portion of Nietzsche's sentence — "for I shall not have enough money for that" — was deliberately concealed from him. Why omit those few words, unless the object was to convey a totally wrong notion of what had been in Nietzsche's mind at the time of writing? The reason he himself gave her for deciding not to return to Bayreuth for the performances was simply that he doubted at that time whether his funds would run to a further stay there.

7

1. So far we have been concerned only with the text itself of the letters and the editorial dating of them. Now let us see what further light is thrown on our problem by external evidence.

In the second letter, of "Friday morning, 4 August", Nietzsche says in one sentence that "the King is coming tonight", and in another that "the Schurés are also coming today." The former statement at once raises an obvious difficulty, for the King arrived not on the night of the 4th but on the night of the 5th.[10] One's first surmise would be that the letter, or at least this part of it, should have been dated by Elisabeth not the 4th but the 5th, for with the town agog with the great news, and all Bayreuth beflagging itself on the 5th to give the King a loyal reception, Nietzsche could hardly make a mistake on that point. It might alternately be suggested that a false rumour of Ludwig's arrival might have got about on the 4th, and that it was on the strength of this that Nietzsche told his sister on the "4th" that "the King is coming today". Postponing consideration of these points for a moment, let us first look at Nietzsche's further statement that "the Schurés are also coming today." Our existing doubts as to the dating of this letter of the "4th" would be strengthened if we knew that the Schurés had been in Bayreuth for some days before then; and this proves to have been the case.

We know definitely when and whom Wagner entertained at Wahnfried during the period of the rehearsals and performances. He was able, for obvious reasons, to do so formally to any great extent only on the "off" afternoons and evenings, when he had not been ex-

---

[10] Actually in the early hours of the 6th.

hausted by his work in the theatre; and we know precisely which days those were. Sometimes he would give a small dinner party, while on the wholly free Thursday evenings during the rehearsal period, the 27th July and the 3rd and 10th August, he "received" on a large scale. Now Glasenapp tells us, on the evidence of Cosima's diary, that on Saturday the 29th July there was "a small French dinner" at Wahnfried, the guests being "the Schurés, the Monods, Malwida, etc." Recalling that Glasenapp had already told us that Nietzsche arrived in Bayreuth on the 24th, and "the Schurés from Paris and Professor Monod and his wife shortly after", this all fits in with our argument that the correct date of the letter of "Friday morning, the 4th", in which Nietzsche says that "the Schurés are also coming today", is Friday, the 28th July.[11]

But how does our revised dating of the letter fit in with Nietzsche's information that "the King is coming today", seeing that Ludwig arrived on the night of the 5th August? By two curious pieces of good luck we are helped out of that difficulty by Fricke and Dannreuther. From Fricke's diary we learn that the King had actually been expected, in the third week of July, to attend the *RC 3 series which began on the 29th July;* and this would involve his arriving *on the 28th.*[12] In Dannreuther's letter of the 25th July we read that *"Siegfried* is to be rehearsed again next week. The King will be here, and Wagner will be in despair if the bear is wanting." Now a *Siegfried* rehearsal "next week" would mean the 2nd August, following on the *Valkyrie* on the 31st July and the *Rhinegold* on the 29th; and this, as has been said above, would have meant Ludwig's arrival on the night of the 28th.

Perhaps it was the sentence in Nietzsche's letter "the King is coming today" that led Elisabeth, in 1909, to date the letter "Friday 4th August". She would remember that the King was present at the General Rehearsals which she attended. These began on the 6th. Unaware, then, that there had been a previous "false alarm" as to Ludwig's coming on the 28th July, she assumed that her brother's "Friday" meant Friday the 4th August.[13]

---

[11] Arriving then, Schuré would be in time for the RC 3 series, which began on the 29th.

[12] FBDJ, p. 123.

[13] This takes it for granted, by the way, that his letter really bore the heading "Friday". It is to be hoped that some day some one who can get access to these letters will tell us precisely which are Nietzsche's datings and which Elisabeth's.

We have thus three guides to the correct dating of the letter of "Friday morning, 4 August". (A) Nietzsche's remark about having "meanwhile heard the whole *Götterdämmerung*" obviously refers to the completion of the one-act-per-day rehearsals of the 24th, 25th and 26th July, and must therefore have been made on the 27th or 28th; for if it were made, as Elisabeth implies, on the 4th August, we cannot understand, in the first place, his not adding that he has also heard the rehearsals of the *Rhinegold* on the 29th July, of the *Valkyrie* on the 31st, and of *Siegfried* on the 2nd August; and in the second place, his having heard by the morning of the 4th a performance of the *Götterdämmerung* which did not take place until the evening of that day! (B) His remark that "the Schurés are coming today" can relate only to somewhere about the 28th July, having regard to the fact that the Schurés were at dinner at Wahnfried on the 29th. (C) The Schurés having arrived on or before the 28th, and the King also being expected "today", this "expectation", in the light of the clue afforded by Fricke and Dannreuther, can in its turn relate only to the 28th. Beyond question, Elisabeth has given the letter of the "4th August" a date later by a week than its true one.

8

2. Glasenapp records a reception at Wahnfried at which, he tells us, Schuré first made Nietzsche's acquaintance. That evening Wagner, it appears, was perturbed by the young man's gloomy and obstinate silence — he did not utter a word, says Glasenapp, during several hours. The date of that reception must have been either Thursday, the 27th — Thursdays, as has been said, were the evenings on which Wagner received on a large scale — or Friday, the 28th, which happened also to be a rest-day in the theatre before RC 3 began on the 29th. In spite, then, of the slight dubiety as between the 27th and 28th in our conjectural dating of the letter of the "4 August", it remains clear that the true date of it can only be either the one or the other.[14]

3. The only other mention of Nietzsche in Glasenapp's record of these days is in connection with a reception at Wahnfried on Thursday, the 3rd August, following a small dinner party at which only

---

[14] After the experiences we have had of Elisabeth's fallibility in the matter of the days of the month, we cannot trust her implicitly even as regards days of the week.

Liszt — who had arrived in the town on the 1st — Count and Countess Schleinitz, Count and Countess Danckelmann and Baroness von Meyendorff were present.[15] Glasenapp's very detailed list of the guests at the reception includes, besides members of the dinner party, Malwida, Wagner's niece Johanna and her husband Alfred Jachmann, Richter and his wife, the Eckerts, the Schurés, several of the performers, Klindworth, Leopold Damrosch, Brassin, Servais, Schäffer, Hans von Wolzogen, "and a young pupil of Nietzsche's, Brenner . . . but not Nietzsche himself, who, because of distressing headaches, had left Bayreuth for Franconian Switzerland." Andler asserts that

> "Glasenapp is in error when he says that Nietzsche was absent from Bayreuth on the 3rd: Nietzsche excused himself because he was unwell, but did not leave Bayreuth until three days later, remaining away from the 6th to the 13th August." [16]

Here we have a cardinal example of the confusion in Nietzsche biography wrought by Elisabeth and by Nietzsche himself. Andler is relying too trustfully on a passage in *Ecce Homo* in which Nietzsche says that "in the middle [of the festival] I very suddenly left the place for a few weeks . . . excusing myself to Wagner simply by means of a fatalistic telegram." Even in this account of the matter, an account, as we shall see later, rich in mis-statements of Nietzsche's own, there is nothing whatever to indicate that he did not leave Bayreuth until the 6th August. As early as the 1st he was telling his sister that in consequence of headaches and eye troubles and exhaustion he was longing to be away. Is it not probable that he went away, as Glasenapp implies, on the 2nd or 3rd, telegraphing his excuses to Wagner either before he left Bayreuth or just after his arrival in Klingenbrunn? As has been pointed out already,

---

[15] These "dinners" were much earlier in the day than the term would suggest to modern readers. Glasenapp tells us that between the "dinner" and the evening reception on the 3rd August there was a scenery rehearsal at the theatre. Fricke's diary confirms this, and so helps us to define the date still more positively; he says that this Thursday, the 3rd August, ought to have been a rest-day, but at his request the troublesome final scene of the *Götterdämmerung*, which was a constant anxiety to him, was run through once more. He adds, "Just greeted Dr. Fr. Liszt and Frau von Meyendorff in the theatre." This fixes the date beyond question. And the exact fixing of it is important, as will appear later.

[16] ANVP, II, 449, *note*. He gets the "6th," of course, from Elisabeth's dating of the letter. But he has overlooked her statement that she arrived in Bayreuth on the 5th, by which time "Fritz had already left".

Elisabeth gives "ten days" as the period of his absence; and he himself says, in his letter of the 6th, that he will be in Klingenbrunn "perhaps ten days". The wording of the letter suggests that it was written a day or so after his arrival there; he has "had a bad day here", confined to his bed. And as we know that he was back in Bayreuth on the 12th, does it not all point once more to the fact that he had left Bayreuth on the 2nd or 3rd? [17]

---

[17] It is a minor matter that Andler should tell his readers that Nietzsche had *left the rehearsal* in suffering *on the 1st*. That is the date wrongly given to his letter of the 25th July in the Correspondence: the rehearsal in question had been on the 24th.

CHAPTER XXVII

THE REALITIES OF THE MATTER

1

WHY DID Elisabeth first of all, in the biography of her brother, tell the story of the summer of 1876 in the misleading way she did, avoiding anything so precise as dates, withholding every passage in Nietzsche's letters that might have raised doubts in the reader's mind as to the complete truth of her story, and then, when the time came to publish his Correspondence, suppress some of his letters to her [1] — an operation she could perform without much fear of detection, seeing that these documents had all been in her sole possession for some thirty years, — and mis-date most of those she decided to submit to the world's inspection? The theory of simple bungling must in general be ruled out; two years before she published her brother's letters to her Glasenapp had brought out his fifth volume, from which she could easily have derived sufficient facts and dates to enable her to date the documents more correctly had she wished to do so. Her purpose from the beginning had been to mislead the public in Nietzsche's favour; to conceal from it the simple facts that he had been a pitifully distempered man during the whole of his short stay in Bayreuth, and that when he had fled from the place he had heard no more of the *Ring* than (a) a non-costume rehearsal of the *Götterdämmerung,* one act at a time, (b) presumably the *Rhinegold,* and (c) a rehearsal of the *Valkyrie* at which his eyes had been such a torture to him that he had not dared to look at the stage; [2] and to establish the legend that he had

---

[1] We are justified in suspecting this. It is most unlikely, for instance, that Nietzsche communicated with her only once between the time when he left Bayreuth on the 3rd(?) August and the 12th, when he reappeared in Bayreuth; he must at least have told her that he intended to return, and why.

[2] We may reasonably doubt whether he saw the rehearsal of *Siegfried* on the 2nd. He was not at the reception on the 3rd, having "left the town", as Glasenapp says. On the 1st he had told Elisabeth that after hearing the *Valkyrie* (on the 31st July) his bad eyes, his headache and his exhaustion made him "long to be away" and that it would be "crazy" of him to remain any longer in Bayreuth, that he had "had enough" and that she must do the rest of the "hearing and seeing" for him. Is it likely, then, that in spite of all this he had gone to *Siegfried* on the 2nd?

given the *Ring* and Wagner a fair trial and found them both wanting in the high qualities *he* demanded from music and the drama.
It would never have done to let the impression get about that her
brother had left Bayreuth in a fit of pique — excusable to a great
extent by the physical sufferings he was undergoing — fled to
Klingenbrunn, there begun to self-justify his pettish flight by com-
mitting to his note-books resentful reflections on Wagner and his
art, and then in after years, having realised that his behaviour in
Bayreuth presented him in anything but a dignified light, had begun
to weave a legend of his own about it all and to impose that legend
on others. And to establish that legend he no more balked at un-
veracity than his sister did later.

2

One proof of this seemingly harsh verdict is afforded by a letter
of his to Mathilde Maier written two years after the Bayreuth episode.

The editor of Wagner's letters to Mathilde Maier prints at the
end of the volume the draft of a long letter of hers to Nietzsche; [3]
it is undated, but the tenor of it suggests that it was to this letter that
Nietzsche was replying on the 15th July, 1878. Mathilde, like many
other people, had been puzzled and perturbed by the change in Nietzsche evidenced by the *Human, All-too Human* of 1878; and Nietzsche sets himself to account for and justify the change. This letter
of his was used by Elisabeth for the first time in *Der einsame Nietzsche:*

> "It cannot be helped: I am bound to cause all my friends distress,
> simply by declaring at last how I freed myself from distress. Two
> things were making me more and more ill, and in the end had almost
> estranged me from my good temperament and my capacities — the
> metaphysical clouding of all that is true and simple, the struggle *with*
> reason *against* reason, which [i.e., the struggle] would fain see a
> wonder and a prodigy in everything; and the corresponding baroque
> art of over-tension and glorified unrestraint, by which I mean the art
> of Wagner."

Now, he continues, he is living in a "pure mountain air" of thought;
and he assures Mathilde that if only *she* could pass through a crisis

---

[3] RWMM, p. 273 ff.

and undergo a change of the same kind she would long for an experience such as his.

> "During the Bayreuth summer [of 1876] I became fully conscious of this. After the first performances, which I attended, I fled to the mountains; and there, in a small village in the woods, I made the first sketch — about a quarter of the whole — for my book *Human All-too Human,* which at that time was to bear the title of *The Ploughshare.* Then, at my sister's request,[4] I returned to Bayreuth, and now was sufficiently composed inwardly to endure the difficult-to-endure, and to remain *silent* before everyone."

3

Of the final part of our quotation all that appears in *The Lonely Nietzsche* is "during the Bayreuth summer I became quite conscious of this, and fled after the first performances". That statement, as we now know, is untrue. Nietzsche had heard none of the first *performances,* but only a few of the *rehearsals,*[5] which could have given him only an imperfect idea of the totality of the *Ring* even had he been in a normal state of health at the time. As the reader is aware, there is not a single sentence, not a single fragment of a sen-

---

[4] This is at variance with Elisabeth's explanation of the matter in *Das Leben* and again in *Der junge Nietzsche.* "I cannot be quite sure now", she says there, "what it was that induced him to return, as a new and changed being, to Bayreuth on the day before the beginning of the first cycle. If I remember rightly what he told me later [!] it seems as if even in Klingenbrunn he had not been able to convince himself that everything was at an end for him in Bayreuth. It was longing that drove him back, longing for the Dionysian music which he had formerly heard in Wagner's works: he would so willingly have submitted to the working of the old magic on him!"

This is obviously one more *construction faite après coup.* We are inclined to place more faith in Nietzsche's own simple statement in 1878 — that he had returned at his sister's request. In any case, it is evident that letters must have been exchanged between the brother and the sister during the ten days when Nietzsche was in Klingenbrunn. Why have these been withheld from us?

In her edition of the Correspondence Elisabeth says that Fritz returned "because meanwhile he had recovered rapidly". By 1915, when she was writing *Wagner und Nietzsche zur Zeit ihrer Freundschaft,* she seems to have remembered the passage quoted above from the letter of 1878 to Mathilde Maier; so now she tells us that "he returned, he said, on my account", but with the embroidery that it was probably because he wanted to put the impressions he had derived from the rehearsals to another test and see if they were final.

[5] There can be no question as to his prevarication. His own words are: "Ich flüchtete nach den ersten Aufführungen, denen ich beiwohnte, fort in's Gebirge". But what he had heard by the time of his flight were not *Aufführungen* (performances) but only *Proben* (rehearsals): he was as fully aware as the rest of us of the distinction between a rehearsal and a performance, and always preserves it verbally in his letters of 1876.

tence, in his Bayreuth letters to Elisabeth to suggest that he fled from the town because he had at last realised the badness of Wagner's art: his contemporary story was simply of incessant headaches, suffering eyes, and inability to face the prospect of any more of those long evenings in the theatre. It is true that he says that the first rehearsal he heard (that of the first act of the *Götterdämmerung*) "did not please me, and I had to come out". But what had displeased him was not Wagner's work but the rehearsal.[6] Would even a perfect rehearsal, however, have been likely to "please" a man in the throes of a headache which, at the time of Nietzsche's writing to his sister, had lasted some thirty-six hours, and had left him in such a state of misery and exhaustion that he could hardly guide his pen? But it would never have done for Elisabeth to let the world know the commonplace human reason for her brother's turning his back on Bayreuth: it had to be represented as the revolt of a superior artistic nature against an imposture of which it had too long been the innocent victim.[7]

4

Even Elisabeth confesses that "had a kind Providence watched over my brother's friendship with Wagner it would have prevented him from going to Bayreuth", though she characteristically tries to make out that he had gone there "in the same way that Luther had gone to Rome", hoping to confirm his faith but, as events turned out, only to lose it. What she refrained from telling her readers in 1897, and what they could not have discovered for themselves until the Correspondence was published in 1909, was that the Nietzsche who had gone to Bayreuth was an incurably distempered man, seeing everything through jaundiced eyes and inclined to get at cross-purposes with everything and everyone. Even when Elisabeth finds him,

---

[6] He was probably even less "pleased" at the rehearsal of the third act on the 26th July, when there was an angry scene between Wagner, Fricke and Brandt over the failure of the episode of the substitution of a lay figure for the corpse of Siegfried to work satisfactorily. See Fricke's long account in FBDJ, pp. 125–129.

[7] Alfred Baeumler, for instance, assures us that Nietzsche, "the absolutely genuine man", saw through "the fraudulent, the unheroic, the enervating in that Wagnerian orchestral tone which Overbeck, to [Nietzsche's] joy, had once described as 'flowing gold'"; that the philosopher "turned away from an art which, by exasperating the nerves, cripples the Will to Action, and was the opposite of what he had promised" [in *Richard Wagner in Bayreuth*]. All this is mere fancy.

in his second letter, saying that things are now going better with him, and that he is glad to have heard the whole of the *Götterdäm-merung*, as a result of which he is now "in his element", she has to insert a fresh comment designed to prevent us from reading into his own admission of better health, and consequently a better frame of mind, the correlative admission that his moods were at the mercy of his health. Running true to form, she assures us that

> "later on (!) he explained this spirited letter by saying that at that time he had made a mighty effort to summon up all his spiritual strength and tried to transplant himself back into his former senti-ments."

There is not a line in his first and second letters to lend the smallest support to this suggestion *faite après coup*.

His work at the construction of the Nietzsche-Wagner legend went on through the following years and reached its completion in *Ecce Homo,* the manuscript of which, let us always bear in mind, was in Elisabeth's sole possession all the while that she was writing Nietzsche-biography in terms of the legend.[8] In *Ecce Homo* he still kept up the fiction he had tried to foist on Mathilde Maier ten years earlier. His story now is that

> "in the middle [of the festival] [9] I very sudenly left the place for a few weeks, despite the fact that a charming Parisian lady sought to console me; I excused myself to Wagner simply by means of a fatalistic telegram. In Klingenbrunn, a secluded spot in the woods in the Böhm-erwald, I carried my melancholy and my contempt for Germans about with me like an illness",[10]

and there he jotted down his *Ploughshare* reflections. This is a tissue of misrepresentations. Nietzsche did *not* leave Bayreuth in the mid-dle of the festival, but about the 3rd August, a good ten days before

---

[8] Peter Gast appears to have made a copy of the manuscript, but no one else had read it.

Ecce Homo had been written between the 14th October and the 4th November, 1888: only a few minor changes were made in it in the following weeks. Nietzsche sent it to his publisher Naumann, and the printing was begun. But he kept changing his mind as to whether to issue *Ecce Homo* before *Nietzsche contra Wagner* or vice versa; consequently the setting-up had not been completed when he collapsed on the 3rd January, 1889. The work was brought out for the first time, with a *Nachwort* by Raoul Richter, in 1908: (the issue bears no date). The edition was limited to 1250 copies.

[9] The English translation has "in the middle of the *festivities*". The German is simply "mitten drin": "festival" has to be supplied from Nietzsche's earlier ref-erence to the "first Bayreuth Festspiele".

[10] NEC, pp. 77–78.

the festival began. He was not in Klingenbrunn for a few weeks, but only for ten days. The "charming Parisian lady" who "sought to console him" was a certain Mme Louise Ott, with whom he seems to have fallen in love, and with whom he corresponded occasionally afterwards. But they had not met by the time that he suddenly packed his trunks and left Bayreuth, excusing himself to Wagner by telegram; he did not make Mme Ott's acquaintance until *after* he had returned to the town on the 12th August for the first performance-cycle of the 13–16th.[11] What conclusion are we to come to as a result of all this misstatement — that Nietzsche had a most untrustworthy memory, that he was deliberately falsifying the facts, or that he was one of those people who tell so often a story which they want other people to believe that they end by believing it themselves? The reader may make his choice, according to the degree of his charity or his cynicism.[12] One sometimes wonders whether Nietzsche's was not a woman's personality that had somehow become incarnated in a male body. There is so much that is characteristically feminine about his naïve faith in his "intuitions", his weathercock veerings, his petty spitefulness when his vanity was hurt, and that recklessness of statement, and hardihood in sticking to a demonstrably false statement once made, that so often invalidates for judge and jury the swearings on oath of a woman in the witness box.

5

From the mass of evidence we now possess with regard to Nietzsche's behaviour in 1876 and his subsequent enmity to Wagner we may draw three conclusions by way of explanation of it all.

---

[11] He even conceals from us, in *Ecce Homo*, the fact that he had returned to Bayreuth from Klingenbrunn and attended a whole cycle of the *Ring*: to admit that would have spoiled the picture of his sudden and final disillusionment over Wagner and his Spartan severance from him. Even Elisabeth is constrained, as we have seen, to suppose that he came back because he doubted, after all, whether "everything was really at an end for him in Bayreuth", because of his "longing" for the old Dionysian magic of Wagner's music.

[12] This was not the only case in which Nietzsche bore false witness. In December, 1888 he told the musician Carl Fuchs that he was not to take seriously the remarks about Bizet in *The Case of Wagner*. Bizet, he said, did not come into consideration at all; he had merely used him against Wagner as an "ironic antithesis". This is in flat contradiction to his letters to Gast and others, in which he had sung Bizet's praises at the top of his voice. He evidently did not foresee the publication of his letters, and still less that of his rapturous marginal comments in the piano score of *Carmen*. These have been published in book form by Hugo Daffner — *Friedrich Nietzsches Randglossen zu Bizets Carmen* (Regensburg, n. d.).

In the first place, Nietzsche was a lamentably sick man between the time he left Basel and the time he fled to Klingenbrunn. Most of the German Nietzscheans pooh-pooh this simple way of accounting for what happened; they prefer to see it all in grandiose terms of the imitation "Dionysianism" of the shoddy artist Wagner and the veritable "Dionysianism" of the greater artist and thinker Nietzsche, in terms of the coming to grips in deadly combat of two irreconcilable worlds of the spirit, the one bogged in a decaying past, the other reaching out triumphantly to the future. That procedure has two attractions: it follows the easy lead of Nietzsche and his sister, and it affords glorious opportunities for that fanciful reconstruction of the actual and the sham-profound philosophising in which a certain species of the German intellect has always revelled.

A law in logic, which forbids us to resort to a remote explanation of anything when a simple one that will solve our problem lies nearer to hand, may be invoked in the present instance. The philosopher — nay, even the saint — is not wholly composed of undiluted spirit going through its evolutions, its permutations and combinations, in an insulated world of pure ideas. The spirit is tied to a body, and is often at the mercy of the malaise of that body. It is an agreeable diversion of the poetising or philosophising faculty in us to regard a great historical figure as simply an apparatus for producing poetry or philosophy, every factor in the problem of the whole man that does not bear on that idealised conception of him being excluded by us, in the way that the mathematician, to arrive at his own symmetrical constructions, excludes material realities and operates within a closed circle of purely conceptual relations of line and number. But all simplifications of this sort are liable to break down when reality pokes its head into the business. A problem posed high in the air begins to look rather different when it is brought down to earth. There is nothing to be said a priori against the poets of every age treating Helen of Troy as a symbol, the purest essence of the beauty towards which the heart of poetic man incessantly yearns. But the symbol, the essence, has been arrived at only by a long historical process of condensation and abstraction, at the cost, to some extent, of the commonplace everyday facts. We may be fairly sure that there were days when Menelaus must have found Helen very trying. She would not be feeling and looking her best, her temper would not be at its sweetest; and if on one of those days we had happened to enter the royal house and begun to rave about the divine qualities of ladies with faces that could launch a thousand ships and burn the topless towers of Ilium, Menelaus would probably have replied tartly that poetry is one thing and reality another, and that *we* were lucky in not having to live with the lady in question on the days when she was neither poetical in herself nor calculated to kindle poetry in others.

6

Nietzsche had every right to be proud of the "pessimism of courage" that enabled him during the last decade of his sanity to preserve his intellectual life intact in spite of the sufferings of his body. The victory over the wretched body was all the more magnificent because the sufferings were such as few men can have had to endure for so long. But we shall miss the clue to several things in his life if we fail to take into account the influence of his bodily condition on his mind in more than one crisis; and in that summer in Bayreuth he was obviously suffering so atrociously that calm objectivity of judgment was not to be expected of him.[13] This is not to imply that his sudden revolt against Bayreuth was the result purely and simply of his bodily malaise. That would be as superficial a reading of his case as the counter-dogma of the German Nietzscheans that his illness at that time had no influence at all on his moods, his revolt against what he had previously admired being purely intellectual. All that need be contended is that his bodily condition, though in the long run only one factor among several, was at the moment the decisive factor. No one knew better than himself that he had long over-exercised his mind at the expense of his body, and a body subject to grievous congenital disabilities at that. In the August of 1875

---

[13] "One must be really sound to be open to artistic impressions", Cosima wrote to Houston Stewart Chamberlain in 1902. "I almost believe that the whole miserable Nietzsche affair arose from the fact that in 1876 he was tortured by the most frantic headaches." WHSC, p. 638.

The artful Elisabeth, knowing that everyone who had come into contact with her brother in Bayreuth at that time had put this interpretation on his conduct, resorts to her usual tactics. "I cannot say", she remarks in her summing-up in the *Leben* and *Der junge Nietzsche*, "that Fritz was suffering bodily during those weeks in Bayreuth. He even had very few headaches; but in order to excuse himself for appearing so seldom at Wagner's house we often made use of the plea of illness." Yet in the first couple of letters he wrote her after his return to Basel it is once more the old pitiful story of headaches and eye troubles!

he had written to his mother, "It appears that for six years I have been sorely overtaxed in Basel and am now paying the penalty. Why does one become a professor at twenty-four!" He had lived the intellectual life too intensively and exclusively not to be exceptionally vulnerable to the first shock that the material world might deal him; and the Fates had ordained that that shock should be administered to him in Bayreuth — not by Wagner's art, but by Bayreuth itself.

7

His mistake in 1876, he said later, was that he had gone to Bayreuth with an ideal, and found instead the crudest reality. And there spoke the professor who had lived so entirely among his books that he had a very imperfect notion of what the actual world of men is like. It is clear from everything that he and Elisabeth have to say on the subject of Bayreuth that he had been shocked and angered to find that the visitors there did not correspond at all to the conception he had pre-formed of them in his study. "Without a doubt", the professor ignorant of the world had forecast in *Richard Wagner in Bayreuth*,

> "in Bayreuth even the spectator is a spectacle worth seeing. . . All who take part in the Bayreuth festival will seem like men out of season: they have their home elsewhere than in the present age, and find elsewhere both their explanation and their justification. . . As for us, the disciples of this revived art, we shall have the time and the will for thoughtfulness, profound and holy thoughtfulness."

He went to Bayreuth in this state of childlike professorial innocence, found the town and the people looking and behaving quite differently from what he had prefigured to himself in his study, and, in his anger at being unable to accommodate himself to their mundane ways, condemned them both out of hand. He found, as Elisabeth, following his lead, piously stresses in *Der junge Nietzsche*, not a communion of initiates and anchorites of art, caught up from earth into the skies, but a "herd" in which "the few idealists like ourselves" were lost. Most of the herd seemed to Elisabeth and her brother to be there only because they had 900 marks to spend on the luxury of the three cycles. Some of the German males had the bad taste to be corpulent. Some of the women had the still worse taste to be wearing smart frocks and jewels.

"And these, alas!" cries the outraged Elisabeth, "were the spectators who were supposed to be strangers to their age!" — that supposition, however, having existed nowhere but in the mind of a recluse as ignorant of the world as Nietzsche was at that time. "It was the same crowd that one can see at any first night at the theatre." The professor of classical philology put his nose into Angermann's tavern one night, no doubt expecting to find in those hallowed halls, the regular resort of the singers and players and the enthusiasts of the Wagner Vereine, a cenacle of white-robed devotees, putting into practice the Pythagorean regimen of silence and purification, musing raptly upon what they had heard that evening in the theatre and preparing themselves for the spiritual repast of the following day. He found instead a roaring, ranting, disputatious crowd of enthusiasts and cavillers. And instead of the expected "profound and holy thoughtfulness" he came upon an odour of beer, tobacco smoke and sausage-fed human flesh that drove him out into the blessed freshness of the night again.

8

But what did the poor man expect? Was he so ignorant of human nature as not to know that a comfortable bank balance and an appreciation of good food and tobacco and well-cut clothes and jewels can go perfectly well in practice, in normal beings, with the keenest sensibility to the spiritualities of art? What would he have said could he have gone behind the scenes in the Bayreuth or any other theatre and found the singers at their usual occupations in such places, Parsifal, for instance, deep in a game of cards or draughts while waiting for his cue to return to the stage and bemoan his fruitless quest of the Grail? Phenomena of this kind are simply humanity's way of relaxing from one supreme mental tension and preparing for another; and only a man pathetically ignorant of human psychology expects the artist to be off the stage, or behind the stage, the ideal figure he is playing on it. And worst of all, perhaps, was the fact that whenever Nietzsche called at Wahnfried he found the drawing-room full of all sorts of people, and the conversation running on all sorts of themes far remote from the Dionysian origin of tragedy and the future of German culture, with Cosima practising her consummate art as a hostess and Wagner passing from one individual or group to another with a rough-and-ready joke on his lips. "It was as if I had been dreaming", cried the poor man in *Ecce Homo*.

"Where was I? I recognised nothing; I scarcely recognised Wagner. In vain I called up my reminiscences. Triebschen — a remote island of blessed spirits: not the shadow of a resemblance!"

As if cosmopolitan Bayreuth were or could be a retreat of the spirit like little Triebschen; as if Wagner could convert his vision of the stupendous *Ring* into reality in the theatre without having to mingle with the miscellaneous crowd that the festival had gathered together, or Cosima having to entertain some of them! "Poor Wagner!" cries Nietzsche. "Where had he arrived? If at least he had gone into a herd of swine! But among Germans!" And so, unable, as he says, to endure the dreadful spectacle any longer, the sick, gauche, unworldly young recluse from Basel suddenly packed his trunk and left, merely excusing himself to Wagner by means of a telegram.

9

He had fled, as we gather from his letter to Mathilde Maier and from his later *plaidoyers,* not merely to Klingenbrunn but to the Greeks — those Greeks who now and henceforth stood, in his eyes, for everything that Wagner had promised to be but failed. But how, we may perhaps be permitted to ask, would this same Nietzsche have behaved if, instead of envisaging his beloved and admired Greeks in the pathos of distance bestowed on them by more than twenty intervening centuries, he had been in Athens some year in the month of Elaphebolion, a studious young Greek from Corinth who had been privileged to visit Euripides occasionally and discuss the problems of tragedy, myth, ritual and religion with the great artist, and who now, for the first time, was to attend one of the famous festivals?

What would he have found? Assuredly not the ideal spectator dreamt of in *Richard Wagner in Bayreuth.* He would have found the streets of Athens and the Attic equivalent of Angermann's filled with an excited, noisy, garrulous crowd, not all the members of which, perhaps, were strictly sober. In the theatre he would have found, of course, Sophocles and Agathon and Socrates and perhaps the young Aristophanes; but also the wild Alcibiades, and the crafty demagogic Cleon, and the disgusting Cleisthenes, and the Sausage-seller and the Lamp-seller and other specimens of "the mutable rank-scented many". Among the spectators would have been all the types described with such refined distaste by Plato, Alciphron, Theophrastus and others — the hired parasites who formed a claque to applaud what the more intelligent members of the audience were hissing; the irresponsible young bucks who hissed noble lines for the sheer fun of the thing; the simple souls who munched their sausages and olives during the performance of a tragedy, very much in the way that the German Hausfrau used to get on with her knitting during *Fidelio* or *Don Giovanni;* the over-gorged and under-intellectualised philistine who slept through the finest passages of a play; the nuisance who whistled his own accompaniment to the melodies; the religious bigots who made a disturbance when some remark or other in a play offended their pious susceptibilities; the muddled reasoners who had clamoured for a military generalship for Sophocles merely on the strength of some fine political sentiments expressed by him in the *Antigone.*

And if in the evening our supposititious young Corinthian had called on Euripides and found his idol behaving diplomatically to a miscellaneous crowd of admirers and flatterers, would he not, especially if he had been suffering agonies from headache and eyestrain all through the festival, have sent a message to the poet declining an invitation to his next reception, fled to Delphi or somewhere, and there filled his tablets with bitter reflections on the poet and his devotees and the Hellenes in general? And yet, and yet! these strangely composite audiences, by universal assent, had in the mass a perception of dramatic values and a sensitiveness to poetic beauty far above anything that the best of modern civilisations can show. They no doubt justified, at their worst, all that their critics had to say with a contemptuous curl of the lip about them. Yet it was they who, by and large, bent the knee to an art which they knew to be higher than themselves, who singled out the best of the scores of plays that were put before them, and placed Aeschylus and Sophocles and Euripides on the pedestals from which all the fluctuations in European taste since then have failed to dislodge them. But Nietzsche could see the Athenians in the mellowing, idealising perspective of the centuries, while his contemporary Bayreuthers were too close to him, too real. Moreover, they were mostly Germans, and nothing in this world did the distempered man hate so much as his fellow-countrymen.

The strangest thing of all, however, is the inability of the present-day Nietzscheans to see the situation of 1876 and the decade following any more clearly than Nietzsche did. We find Alfred Baeumler, for instance, writing thus in 1932:

> "At the first Bayreuth festival in the summer of 1876 the Germany of Bismarck came for the first time into view on the field of culture. The Kaiser of the new Reich was present, and people believed they were assisting at an event that was to be the starting-point of a wonderful national future. Actually it was the reflection of a present that bore within it the germ of decay. The reality was a State that had been slowly hollowed out by trade and industry, a commercial condition that choked every virile will to guidance and mastery. Civic security was the watchword, and a culture calling itself learned gave its blessing to this security."

People went about looking for "salvation from the workaday", "forgetfulness of existence".

> "The paralysed sought safety in the intoxication of art and a philosophy of sublime flight from the world. 'World-redeeming love' as against 'power' — that was the philosophy of *The Nibelung's Ring*. For Nietzsche to have been conscious of the falsehood of this state of affairs and of this art, and for him to have given immediate and lively expression to this perception, marks him out as the exemplary man of the epoch — nay, as a political figure." [14]

What all this typical Nietzschean rhodomontade has to do with the merits of the *Ring* as a work of art, which was all that the Bayreuth audiences were thinking about in 1876 and is all that matters today, is not clear. In any case it was not about things of this sort that the prophetic soul of Nietzsche was thinking, but purely and simply whether his health and his eyes could stand any more evenings in the theatre, or any more well-fed and well-dressed Germans about him, when he packed up his bag in the first days of August and fled to Klingenbrunn. And as for the relative values of a system of "virile" German real-politics and an art that helps us to turn our back for a few hours on disgusting reality, the spectacle of the world during the last few years is perhaps sufficient comment

---

[14] *Nietzsche in seinen Briefen und Berichten der Zeitgenossen*, pp. 188–189.

on that matter. Even some Germans may possibly be reflecting by now that they might have been happier under a Wagnerian philosophy of "world-redeeming love" than under one of "power". Could fifty Wagners have led the nation into worse disasters than one Nietzsche has done? "When today", Baeumler wrote in 1937,

> "we see the German youth marching under the sign of the swastika, our minds go back to Nietzsche's *Thoughts out of Season*, in which this youth was invoked for the first time. Our highest hope today is that the State shall now stand open to it. And when we call out to this youth 'Heil Hitler!' we greet at the same time, with the same cry, Friedrich Nietzsche." [15]

10

First of all, then, we must attribute Nietzsche's sudden revulsion against Bayreuth in 1876 to a fit of atrabiliar exasperation, occasioned by resentment against the mere human beings he saw all round him, and inability, in his lamentable state of health, to see the motley throng around him for just what it mostly was. And *pace* Elisabeth, who will not admit for a moment the possibility of such a thing, it is clear enough from the records that his pride was wounded by his feeling of his own relative insignificance in Bayreuth. Lou Andreas-Salomé, the gifted woman to whom he was at one time strongly attracted, but from whom, as a matter of course, he parted in time as he did from virtually every one of his friends, summed him up accurately enough when she said that

> "he had never lived outside himself; his whole life was so profoundly inward that it was only in conversation and in the ideas of his writings that he revealed himself." [16]

The Bayreuth of actuality was something very different from the ideal picture he had painted of it in the seclusion of his study, and therefore, having committed the offence of being different from Nietzsche, it had no right to exist. In the miscellaneous throng at Wahnfried he was silent, self-absorbed, morose. Schuré has left us [17] a penetrating study of him as he saw him in those days and during

---

[15] Essay on *Nietzsche und der Nationalsozialismus*, in *Studien zur deutschen Geistesgeschichte* (Berlin, 1937), p. 294.

[16] Lou Andreas-Salomé, *Friedrich Nietzsche in seinen Werken* (1894), p. 5.

[17] In an article *L'individualisme et l'anarchie en littérature, Friedrich Nietzsche et sa philosophie*, in the *Revue des deux Mondes*, 15 August, 1895, pp. 775–805.

the later week when Nietzsche returned for the first performance-cycle.

"When talking to him I was struck by the superiority of his mind and the strangeness of his physiognomy. A broad forehead, short hair brushed back, the high cheek-bones of the Slav. The heavy drooping moustache and the bold cut of the features would have led you to take him for a cavalry officer, had it not been for an indefinable something of timidity and at the same time haughtiness in his address. The cautious meditative manner was that of a philosopher. Nothing could have been more deceptive than the seeming calm of his expression. The fixed eye betrayed the dolorous travail of his thought: it was the eye at once of an acute observer and a fanatical visionary. This double character gave him a touch of the unquiet and the disquieting, all the more because he seemed constantly to be riveted to one single point. In moments of effusion his gaze softened, but then it would become hostile again. His whole manner had the distant air, the veiled disdain that often characterises the aristocrats of thought. . . 'His look was turned inwards', as Frau Salome says: 'his eyes reflected his interior impressions; his gaze seemed directed far away towards unexplored regions of the human soul. In an animated conversation a piercing flash would sometimes come into his eyes, but in his sombre moments loneliness spoke out of them with an expression at once mournful and menacing, as if coming from uncanny depths'.[18]

"During the general rehearsals and the first three performances Nietzsche seemed sad and depressed.[19] He was already suffering from the beginning of the cerebral disorder that was to overwhelm him later, but suffering still more from a profound and unexpressed melancholy. In Wagner's presence he was timid, embarrassed, almost invariably silent. Wagner, launched upon that colossal enterprise of his in which he had to manage thirty-five principal personages . . . to say nothing of the chorus, the machinery and the orchestra, enjoyed, like a *young* Wotan in spite of his sixty-three years, the legitimate triumph of having created a world and set it in motion. During the few hours of relaxation permitted him by his labours of Hercules he gave rein to the whimsical gaiety, the exuberant humour that was, so to speak, the foam of his genius. Having to infuse his own soul, his own thought into these creatures of flesh and blood, compelled to maintain in equilibrium all

---

[18] The citation is from Lou Andreas-Salomé's book, p. 12.

[19] Schuré's memory, after nineteen years, was not accurate as to what Nietzsche had heard in 1876, if by "the first three performances" he meant the three cycles and not merely three evenings of one cycle. Nietzsche had returned from Klingenbrunn for the first performance-cycle. Elisabeth tells us that she and her brother "gave up our seats for the second cycle to relatives." The third cycle he could not have attended, for it ran from the 27th to the 30th August, and on the 29th we find him writing to his sister from Basel. Nor did he hear the "general rehearsals" of the 6th–9th, for he was in Klingenbrunn all that time.

the amours-propres, the rivalries and the petty passions of this regi-
ment of actors and actresses, he became himself regisseur and actor.[20]
A subtle charmer and subduer of souls, he achieved his ends by a
blend of the violent and the caressing, of animal rage and sincerest
tenderness, never losing sight of his goal. Living in this tempest which
he himself invoked, and controlling it, he could give only a casual attention to his disciples and admirers. In the face of the prodigies of art
that he was accomplishing under our eyes each day, every one of us
felt, not Mime's sentiments, of course, but Mime's amazement as he
watched Siegfried re-forging the fragments of his father's sword . . .
Did Nietzsche's pride suffer from this inferiority? Was his exacerbated
sensibility wounded by certain rough familiarities on the Master's
part? Did the captious moralist in him revolt against certain inevitable
contrasts between the human nature of a great man and his genius?
Was he reluctant to admit that a creator of this scope, achieving a
miracle in art that had been pronounced impossible by the whole
world, can see his best friends only as the instruments of his work, particularly in the moment when he is fighting his way towards its achievement against the winds and the waves?"

11

Schuré goes on to describe the earlier relations between the two
men, with Nietzsche

"figuring to himself the reformation of Germany as a sort of school of
philosophy, aesthetic and morals, with Schopenhauer as the revered
ancestor, Wagner as the artist and workman, but himself as the prophet
and supreme legislator",

and to ask whether, perhaps, "this dream of the Schopenhauerian
philosopher" could find its real counterpart in "the whirlpool-like
Valhalla of Bayreuth, with its impetuous and masterful Wotan."

"The author of *The Birth of Tragedy* disappeared like everyone else
in the apotheosis of the Master, who, not taking much notice of him or
chaffing him a little, seriously hurt and vexed at seeing his disciple
so morose and not understanding why, seemed to be calling to him in
the words of Loge to the Rhine Maidens as the gods take their rainbow way to Valhalla:

---

[20] Curiously enough, Nietzsche himself had said very much the same thing:
"Deep-thinking men appear like actors in their intercourse with other people, because they have always to feign a surface before they can make themselves understood." (*Menschliches, Allzumenschliches*, II, Section I, No. 232).

Ye in the water!
why wail ye to us?
Hear what Wotan doth will!
Gleams no more
on you maidens the gold;
in the gods' recovered glory
bask ye henceforth in bliss!"

Schuré then describes Nietzsche's "lack of enthusiasm" during
the rehearsals and performances.

"When we left together,[21] not a criticism escaped him, not a word of
censure, but he showed the resigned sadness of a beaten man. I still
remember the air of lassitude and disillusionment with which he spoke
of the Master's coming work. 'He told me that he wanted to re-read
universal history before writing the poem of his *Parsifal!*' he said,
with an ironical indulgence in his smile and his accent, as if to say,
'See the illusions of these poets and musicians, who want to take the
universe up into their phantasmagoria and succeed only in putting
themselves into them!'"

The world has too long taken too seriously Nietzsche's fulminations against Wagner's attitude towards art and the cosmos in the
last few years of his life. Wagner himself had more sense than to
take the young man as seriously as he took himself; who, he no
doubt asked himself, as we ask ourselves today, was this young professor from Basel that he should give marching orders to all the
creative minds of Europe?

12

The second main reason for Nietzsche's turning away from Wagner just at that time was that his whole system of philosophy — as
far as we can speak of a "system" in connection with so unsystematic a thinker — was just then undergoing one of its fundamental
changes of direction. He was embarking on what is called his positive phase. With that phase in itself we have no concern here. He
was perfectly entitled to turn his back on his philosophic past whenever he liked; what he was not entitled to do was to assume, with
his usual vanity, that he had only to announce the new tables of the

---

[21] This evidently means "when we left Bayreuth together": we learn from
Nietzsche's first letter to his sister after his return to Basel that they had travelled
thither in company. Schuré had therefore had ample opportunity for studying him
at close quarters.

law from the heights of his own Sinai for it to be the duty of everyone else in Europe to accept the revelation and fall in under his
banner. His attitude was always that of Leconte de Lisle — "Il n'y a
de vrai que ce que je dis et dans l'instant où je le dis."

The third reason for Nietzsche's "apostasy", as the Wagnerians
called it, concerns us more closely, for it has to do with his attitude
towards music in general and Wagner's music in particular. It is
evident enough now that round about 1876 a change was going on
in his musical constitution the full results of which did not become
apparent until some years later. Scattered about in his note books
are many intuitions with regard to music and the drama that deserve
the most respectful consideration; for it was in the very nature of
his genius to flash a light for a moment upon some aspect or other
of almost every subject he touched upon. But his intuitions in the
sphere of music never get beyond this first stage: he could strike a
spark, but he could not light a lamp, still less keep it going for long.

Looking back, as we are now able to do, upon his whole record,
not only his published books but his note books and his letters, we
see that he was never really capable of grasping an art like that of
Wagner in its totality, or, indeed, music of any kind that showed any
complexity of thinking or intricacy of organisation. He had been
swept off his feet in his impressionable youth by the passion of
Wagner's music, especially *Tristan*. But his limited musical faculty
was unequal to the task of holding all that had been forced into it
under that high pressure; and the time came when, by sheer reple-
tion and exhaustion, his whole nature rebelled against the strain.
His natal bias, it soon became evident, was towards the simple in
music; [22] and as the bulk of his intellectual energy became mobi-

---

[22] One of the most exquisitely fatuous passages in *Der junge Nietzsche* is that in
which Elisabeth describes herself and her brother encountering Wagner one morning in 1876 when he was leaving Wahnfried. "I cannot recall precisely what Wagner
said" — she was not always so modest, by the way, about her memory of conversations of twenty years or so earlier — "but suddenly my brother's eye brightened,
and with an expression of the tensest expectation he seemed to hang on the Meister's
lips. Did he believe that Wagner was going to say, 'Ah, my friend, the whole festival
is nothing more nor less than a farce, it is not what we two had dreamed and longed
it to be; even my music ought to have been something quite different. I will return
to simplicity and melody! . . .' But if that was what Wagner's first words had led
him to expect, what followed showed him how mistaken he had been; and the happy
gleam faded from my brother's eyes. No! Wagner was no longer young enough to
take sides against himself."

We recall Isidor von Reutter's assurance that Schnorr's spirit had told her that

lised, as it did during the last ten years of his sane life, for the great assault on all current philosophies and political ideologies, he had less and less of it to spare for music. He could not do without music, but now he asked from it only refreshment for a restlessly straining and tired mind. His ludicrous infatuation with Peter Gast's simple-minded art was due to the fact that it soothed him without making any demands on a mind exhausted by incessant thinking and depressed by ill health and the heartbreaking sense of isolation. In 1880 he cured his "profound melancholy in Stresa" by "singing and whistling" Gast's melodies; and, it goes without saying, he at once raised his own appetite, his own capacity, or lack of capacity, to the dignity of a norm for music and for all mankind. He made the truly remarkable discovery that

> "whatever is good in music must be capable of being whistled; but the Germans have never been able to sing and therefore drag their pianos about with them — hence their lust for harmony".

He wants only "comic music", of the type which, seemingly, his adored Peter, and his Peter alone among the Germans, can supply to perfection. He hears *Carmen* in November, 1881, and at once decides that his own ideal of "comic opera" has been achieved.[23] The French, it appears, are

> "on a better path than the Germans in dramatic music; they have a great advantage over the Germans in one vital point — with them, passion is not so drawn out (as, for example, all passions with Wagner)."

And as *Carmen* seems to him to be at the opposite pole from Wagner, it becomes as a matter of course, for him, "the best opera in existence".

13

Later he takes up, for a while, with the now forgotten August Bungert, whom he had met in Genoa in 1883. Bungert's *Die Studenten von Salamanca*, it seems, is "written in a new style — big

Wagner "ought to make smaller demands on the human voice, and write more songs, so that he will become popular and make everything easier." But in the Isidor von Reutter case this sort of thing is unkindly regarded as a proof, not that she was Europe's most consummate aesthetician, but that she was a half-wit.

[23] "A genuine French comic opera talent, not at all disorientated by Wagner, but a true pupil of Hector Berlioz." (!)

definite symphonic forms". The great Bungert's taste had formerly been for "the ultra-romantic" and the "last" Beethoven; but he has outgrown all that. He is now anti-Germanic and pro-Hellenic, and is going to lead a new development in German music. But even Bungert seems after a while to be a trifle too Germanic for the German-hating Nietzsche, who desires in music the "melody" that is so lacking in Wagner. Then, in a moment of candour unusual with him, he confesses that he is

"an ignoramus in matters musical: all my memories of it are ten to twenty years old, and at that time I was a different being from what I am now, or rather, at that time I was not yet 'myself' ".

He recalls how Wagner used to try to show him, in Triebschen, wherein the greatness of Beethoven's last quartets resided. (It is plain enough to the musical reader of Nietzsche's works how much of whatever permanent value there is in his discussion of music in his earlier works is the echo of conversations in Triebschen). His recollection of the last quartets [24] is that

"on the whole they are unclear and freakish music; though here and there, it is true, the heavens open as they do nowhere else. I used to say, 'These are assertions without proofs', this is 'set' but not composed".

Manifestly the real Beethoven was as beyond his limited musical capacity as the real Wagner was. And he feels (in 1883) that it is time for him to turn from music of this puzzling kind to the simpler art of Haydn's quartets.

Eighteen months later he hears the overture to Gast's *Der Löwe von Venedig* in Zürich, and blesses the composer for it:

"may it be the symbol of your course through the world — it was so daring, so virile, so witty, so gallant, so entirely after my own heart, full of clear sky and assuredly full also of — the future."

And once more, as so often in the past and the future, he will suffer no contradiction: *his* august approval is all that is necessary to establish the value of Peter's music. Mottl, it appears, has not been enthusiastic over Gast's scores. But they have been Nietzsche's joy and consolation for years; "and I stick to it that where your music is concerned it is *I* who am right, not Herr Mottl". What stands in the way of the universal acceptance of this wonderful Gastian music

[24] He had been present at some of the performances of these in Triebschen.

is "Wagnerism and the coarsening and loutishness that has taken possession of Germany since the founding of the Reich". In 1886 he tells the composer that "at the moment I lack an aesthetic *in puncto musicae*; I have a taste — for instance, for Pietro Gast — but no grounds, no logic, no imperative for this taste" — a piece of self-criticism which he would have done well to extend to others of his judgments *in puncto musicae*. The taste for Wagner, now at its zenith, will in ten years, he opines, have made way for other needs; and then the "glorious music" of Peter Gast will meet with the recognition that is its due.[25]

For music should be "cheerful", going lightly on its feet, putting poor serious things such as politics, Bismarckism, Wagnerism, socialism and Christianity in their proper place. Nietzsche himself has by this time become "antitheatrical, antidramatic"; therefore it follows as a matter of course that music has been "ruined by considerations and conventions of drama"; and therefore, incidentally, Wagner's art is bad art. Proof of this is superfluous: people like himself and Gast have no need of a "musical aesthetic": the strength and quality of their impressions are sufficient: they must not be pressed for proofs. And as the months slip by, the naïveté of his taste in music becomes more and more clearly defined. He is enchanted by Offenbach, three of whose operettas he has heard in Nice. And how fortunate Offenbach is in his librettists: these texts "are probably the only service opera has ever done to poetry". A little later it is the turn of Lalo's *Le Roi d'Ys* — which owes its success to its "lovely melodies" — of *La Belle Hélène,* and of Audran's *La Mascotte* to enjoy the favour of this exacting critic, Europe's law-giver in musical aesthetic: "this music, never common, with so many pretty, witty little melodies, is altogether in the idyllic vein now indispensable to me in the evening". His true love now is operetta music — French, however, not German: even Johann Strauss's *Der Zigeunerbaron* he finds detestable. Indeed, he

---

[25] Gast's opera was first performed, under its original title of *Die heimliche Ehe*, in Danzig in 1891, and again in Chemnitz in 1933, without exactly setting the musical world on fire. It would have infuriated Nietzsche to read in the *Westsächsische Zeitung* of the 13th February of the latter year — the fiftieth anniversary of the death of the Wagner whose vogue he imagined to be at its "zenith" in 1886 — that Gast's work would have stood a better chance had it been given a month earlier, for in February it had been crushed by the immediate proximity of the Wagner-week in Chemnitz. See Friedrich Götz, *Peter Gast, der Mensch, der Künstler, der Gelehrte* (1934), p. 29.

can find no higher praise for his booklet *The Case of Wagner* than
to say it is itself "operetta music".

14

This was the supreme authority that was now putting Wagner in
his place as a composer, an authority from which there could be
no appeal. Bülow, like Mottl and all the other conductors, had not
been impressed by the Gast scores sent to them; so in October, 1888
the arbiter of European taste writes to his Peter:

> "Bülow has not replied with regard to *Der Löwe*. He will be sorry
> for it. For it was *I* who had written him a rude and entirely justifiable
> letter so as to finish with him once for all. I gave him to understand
> that 'the first mind of the epoch had expressed a wish in the matter':
> I allow myself to speak like that now."

And this was the half-crazed frame of mind in which he spat out
the venomous nonsense of *The Case of Wagner*.[26]

As he drew nearer to the final catastrophe his judgments on music
and musicians became wilder but no whit less dogmatic. At a concert in Turin in December, 1888 he lighted, after the *Egmont* overture and a March by Schubert, on "an absolutely divine, profound
inspiration", after the fourth bar of which he was dissolved in
tears. It was a piece for strings, he told Gast, by "a composer named
Rossaro, who died in Turin in 1870: music, I swear to you, of the
very first rank". Then came Goldmark's *Sakuntala* overture, which
our oracle finds "a hundred times better than anything of Wagner's", Bizet's *Roma,* which excites his admiration, and a piece by
Vilbac that was "the last word in delicacy of invention and of
sound". His last discovery of all in Turin seems to have been a
Spanish operetta that put even Rossini and Offenbach in the shade.
The time had been when *La belle Hélène,* which followed the Spanish masterpiece, had stood for him for all that is best in witty buf-
foonery; but now — the old story! — he had been unable to sit it
through.[27]

---

[26] In his blind hatred of everyone and everything Wagnerian at this period he
even thought of introducing the venerable Malwida, who had never injured a human
being in all her life and had shown Nietzsche infinite kindness, into the pages of
Ecce Homo, where she was to perform a parody of Kundry's "laugh".

[27] All the above citations are from his correspondence with Gast, NGB, IV.

Evidently it was basically a mind of the utmost simplicity where music was concerned. For a brief period the tremendous emotional impact of *Tristan*, the *Meistersinger* and the *Ring* had set a fire raging in the youthful Nietzsche. But his musical arteries were unable to stand for long so high a blood pressure; and when the reaction came the world was treated to the edifying spectacle of the pint-pot capacity railing peevishly at the impermissible magnitude of quarts — for that, in the last resort, is all that Nietzsche's objurgations of the musician Wagner amount to today.

CHAPTER XXVIII

THE LOAD OF CARE

1

EVEN BEFORE the festival of 1876 was over Wagner had learned from Feustel that the financial result was a deficit. But of the magnitude of that deficit he seems to have been blissfully unaware at the time, and so he took it almost as a matter of course that the performances would be renewed and improved upon in the following year. He still had great hopes for Unger, whom he persuaded, for a subsidy of 12,000 marks, to spend another twelve months, from the 1st October onwards, studying with Hey in Munich and qualifying himself not only for Siegfried but for Tristan and Tannhäuser. From his parting advice to the tenor when the festival was over we realise once more how thorough were his methods, how exacting were the demands he made on his interpreters. He warned Unger that a mere improvement in his vocal technique would not be enough; wholly different timbres, springing spontaneously from a wholly different mentality of the moment, were required, for example, for the third act of *Tristan* and the third of the *Meistersinger*. Furthermore, Hey was to promote Unger's education in other arts besides music; the tenor was to frequent the Munich galleries and there acquire a sense of the variety and beauty of plastic and mimetic pose.

But this optimistic mood was not to last long. No sooner was he free of the nervous tension of the last few months than the mere slackening of the strings began to tell on his health. He could still talk hopefully of a new and better festival next year, with the churlish Betz out of it; but even when giving this news to Lilli Lehmann on the 7th September he added, "But on the whole I must not occupy myself too much with the future, for there is enough of a load on my soul."

As usual, it was to the King alone that he could reveal all that was in his heart. The festival had been an unquestionable outward success, he wrote to him on the 11th; but within himself he feels that he and his work and his ideal have no home in the world of the present. He plans to give three cycles of the *Ring* in 1877, to show at least, under better conditions as regards the singers and the scenic apparatus, how it should be performed. For this reason he will not grant other theatres the right to produce the work, though several of them have offered him high prices for it. At Bayreuth, he thinks, the worst is over so far as finance is concerned: the main capital expenditure in connection with the theatre being done with, it should now be possible to meet current expenses each year out of receipts, lowering the price of seats, attracting larger audiences, and enabling him to pay his singers adequately. But for the present his one desire is to relax and forget. He means to spend the winter in Italy, hoping to return next May with health so far restored that he can devote himself in July and August to a second and better series of performances.

He left Bayreuth with his whole family on the 14th, on an itinerary that took him by slow stages through Munich, Verona, Venice (where he stayed from the 20th to the 27th, revisiting his haunts of the *Tristan* days), Bologna (where, on the 27th, he was given a civic welcome as an honorary burgess of the town), Naples (where he spent a week, from the 29th September to the 5th October), and finally to Sorrento. There he remained until the 7th November, when continued bad weather drove him back first to Naples, then to Rome, where he remained nearly a month. Here he met for the first time Comte Arthur Gobineau — the author of a now famous but at that time entirely neglected work, *Inégalité des races humaines* [1] — with whom a close friendship was to develop in later years. Wagner made the acquaintance also in Rome of Liszt's pupil Sgambati, in some of whose chamber music he showed a certain interest. His own creative faculty, too, began to stir within him under the influence of the Italian light and colour. The time was not yet ripe for him to commence formal work on the music of *Parsifal*, though we may be sure that this was shaping itself in his mind coincidently with the drafting of the drama. But we learn from Cosima's diary that he actually began in Sorrento "a symphony of mourning for those who had fallen in the war", based on a theme

---

[1] In four volumes, 1853–1855. The English volume entitled *The Inequality of Human Races* (1915) is a translation of Gobineau's first book only.

already associated in his mind with *Romeo and Juliet*.[2] He saw, he told Cosima, "the biers being brought one after another into a hall, so that the individual grief was always being lost in the general suffering. Afterwards would come the song of triumph." [3]

The heavy expenses of the tour were defrayed out of the fee he had received for the American *Centennial March*. He would have been happy enough in Italy, where almost every day brought a new delight to his eyes, a new refreshment to his soul, had not Bayreuth pursued him wherever he went, embittering his days and hagriding his sleepless nights. For he learned from a now frightened Feustel that the deficit amounted to some 120,000 marks, an estimate that was to be increased by another 30,000 marks before many weeks had gone by; and it appeared that Wagner was expected either to find this sum himself or at least to point out to others a way of raising it.

A loan, he told Feustel, would be difficult to negotiate; it was one thing to raise money for an undertaking in good going order that gave every promise of succeeding, and quite another to get it for an undertaking that was now, thanks to the malice of a large portion of the Press, under suspicion of having been a failure. But obviously an appeal of some sort there would have to be,[4] and for a time Wagner was optimistic enough to believe that there was still enough of the old German idealism left for Bayreuth to be saved. His first thought was to appeal again to the Kaiser, who had been liberal with his distribution of orders to the singers; would he not do something now for Bayreuth itself — not for Wagner personally, for he wanted nothing for himself, but for the cause of German art? Would not the Reichstag, at a hint from above, support the festival theatre as a national institution?

But he soon realised that there was no hope of any unaided understanding of his ideal on the part of either the Kaiser or Bismarck or the Parliamentary deputies. So towards the end of October he turned to King Ludwig with a suggestion that *he*, as the guardian of the interests of German culture, should instruct the Bavarian Embassy in Berlin to have the matter raised in the Reichstag. The

---

[2] No doubt as a result of the day or two he had spent in Verona in October.
[3] MECW, I, 777–8.
[4] Not more than half of the 1,300 Patronatscheine on which the Committee had counted had been taken up.

proposition to be submitted was that the Imperial Government should take over the festival theatre and all its accessories at cost, including the overhanging debt, and assign it as a national property to the magistrate of Bayreuth, who would be under obligation to give, in accordance with the purposes of the founder, yearly festivals on the model of those of 1876. The expenses of these would be defrayed by the sale each year of 1,000 seats, plus a yearly subsidy of 100,000 marks by the Reich, in return for which the latter would have the right to allot the remaining 5–600 seats gratis to Germans unable to pay for them, thus conferring a genuinely "national" character on the institution.

These, Wagner told the King, were the broad lines upon which the proposition might be put forward. "It has only one defect, namely, that I would have to entrust its accomplishment to the Reich." It would be vastly better, he said, if Bavaria and its King were to undertake it alone; better for the misunderstood and slighted German spirit than any "constitutional" patronage, especially through the medium of the musical and theatrical schools, with what he called their rabble of hidebound professional bunglers, place-seekers and journalistic scribblers. To this suggestion of Wagner's, however, the King was not in a position to respond.

2

It was about this time that Wagner and Nietzsche met again — for the last time. Nietzsche had gone, accompanied by a fellow-philosopher, Dr. Paul Rée, to Sorrento, where he stayed for some time as Mâlwida's guest at the Villa Rubinacci. His sojourn in the place coincided in time with that of Wagner, and the two groups saw each other frequently, though Wagner conceived a prejudice against the Jewish Rée and objected to meeting him oftener than was necessary. At a hint from Malwida, who knew Wagner's anxieties in connection with the theatre debt, Nietzsche avoided the subject of Bayreuth; but on the last evening they spent together, during a walk along the coast, Wagner began to speak of the thing that now lay nearest to his heart, his *Parsifal*. It was clear that he had turned Christian; and as Nietzsche was now definitely anti-Christian, this was, of course, an unforgivable offence on Wagner's part. His reversion — more emotional than intellectual — to a faith that he had long ago abandoned need not be taken too seriously: had Nietzsche been a finer-fingered psychologist than he was he would have seen that Wagner was not writing *Parsifal* because he had turned Christian but that the artist in him had become Christian-minded largely because of his growing absorption in *Parsifal*. And not only did the new world of emotion generated in him by the nature of the subject turn his thoughts in the direction of Christianity, as the religion traditionally associated in a thousand ways with that order of emotion, but, most curious phenomenon of all, it led to a partial repetition in another form of the Mathilde Wesendonk episode: he now "fell in love" with Judith Gautier, as we shall see shortly.

And as for Nietzsche, though the positivist in him revolted angrily against the subject of *Parsifal,* and though in his last days he was possessed by a fanatical hatred of Wagner, the emotionalist in him was dissolved in tears by the sheer beauty of the Prelude when he heard it for the first time in Monte-Carlo in January, 1887. "When I see you again", he wrote to Peter Gast,

"I will tell you exactly what I then *understood*. Putting aside all ir-relevant questions (to what end such music *can* or *should* serve?), and speaking from a purely aesthetic point of view, has Wagner ever written anything *better?* The supreme psychological perception and precision as regards what had to be said, expressed, *communicated* here, the extreme of concision and directness of form, every nuance of feeling conveyed epigrammatically; a clarity of musical description that reminds us of a shield of consummate workmanship; and finally an extraordinary sublimity of feeling, something experienced in the very depths of music, that does Wagner the highest honour; a synthesis of conditions which to many people — even 'higher minds' — will seem incompatible, of strict coherence, of 'loftiness' in the most start-ling sense of the word, of a cognisance and a penetration of vision that cuts through the soul as with a knife, of sympathy with what is seen and shown forth. We get something comparable to it in Dante, but nowhere else. Has any painter ever depicted so sorrowful a look of love as Wagner does in the final accents of his prelude?" [5]

A whole month later he wrote in the same strain to his sister about the *Parsifal* prelude:

"I cannot think of it without feeling violently shaken, so elevated was I by it, so deeply moved. It was as if some one were speaking to me

[5] NGB, IV, 277–8.

again, after many years, about the problems that disturb me — naturally not supplying the answers *I* would give, but the Christian answer, which, after all, has, been the answer of stronger souls than the last two centuries of our era have produced. When listening to this music one lays Protestantism aside as a misunderstanding — and also, I will not deny it, *other really good* music, which I have at other times heard and loved, seems, as against this, a misunderstanding!" [6]

But the Nietzsche who had come to regard himself as the heir of the ages, the sole saviour of European civilisation, forgot all this, and all the implications of it, when he settled down, in the spring of 1888, to write his venomous and fatuous *The Case of Wagner*. It was sufficient for him then that Wagner had "sunk at the foot of the Cross" just when *he* had turned his back on that symbol; that of itself was enough to mark Wagner out as a destroyer of civilisation as Nietzsche now understood the term. He censured *Parsifal*, Elisabeth tells us, as "a change of front". An objection to a procedure of that sort in another man on the part of one who changed his own front as often as a chimney-cowl in a variable wind is truly amusing. But when Nietzsche, again according to Elisabeth, "could regard this sudden change [7] only as an attempt to come to terms with the ruling powers in Germany, who had become pious — his sole object being success", he became simply contemptible. Never in his life did Wagner trim the sails of his artistic thinking to catch the wind of a German "success"; and in the case of his last opera he tried in advance to rule out all fear of success as the world understands it, all complaisance towards the mentality of the "ruling powers" and hope of favours from them, by insisting that the work should never be publicly performed anywhere but at Bayreuth. We need take Elisabeth's highly-coloured picture of the scene between the two men at their last meeting in Sorrento no more seriously than we do many another attempt of hers to make us see her brother not as he actually was at any given moment but as he liked to see himself, and wished others to see him, in after years. We shall be on safer ground if we take the whole Sorrento episode as just another illustration of the shrewish intolerance in Nietzsche that made it hard for him to credit anyone who happened to think differently

---

[6] NGB, V, ii, 710–711.
[7] As a matter of fact it was anything but "sudden": the transformation had been taking place in Wagner for some time.

from him with either intelligence or sincerity. Wagner had done no more than he himself had done — in obedience to an irresistible inner urge he had let the categorical imperative of his today cancel out his yesterday. But what was a laudable process in Nietzsche was an offence in anyone else. Wagner-Parsifal, in the jargon of the Nietzscheans, was "saying No to life", while *he* was now the sole representative left on earth of the Wagner-Siegfried who had once "said Yea to life". That antithetic abracadabra is as empty of meaning for the world today as is the jargon of the mediaeval schoolmen wrangling over the purely verbal distinctions of scholastic theology.

3

Both Wagner and Cosima seem by this time to have taken Nietzsche's measure as a thinker and to have decided to worry no further about him. For them he would not be the idealised semi-mythical figure which the disseminators of the Nietzsche legend succeeded for a whole generation in imposing on the world, but simply a young man of extraordinary gifts with a flaw somewhere in his intellectual make-up that made it impossible for him to remain of the same way of thinking on any subject for any length of time. They had had too many opportunities of studying him at the closest quarters not to be well aware of the extent to which his judgments and his actions were determined by his mood and his health of the moment. Wagner probably dismissed him from now onwards from serious consideration; with his own creative work to be completed, and with the grievous burden of Bayreuth on his shoulders, he would have neither time nor inclination to perturb himself over an ill-balanced young former devotee who was now obviously in the sulks and expected his petulancies to be taken more seriously than they deserved. But Cosima was observing Nietzsche critically; and by a fortunate chance the pages of Du Moulin have preserved for us a letter of hers to Malwida that is invaluable as a contemporary record of how the young man looked in her eyes just then. The letter belongs to a slightly later date — after their return to Bayreuth — but it is obviously her sober summing-up of Nietzsche after her recent experiences of him in Bayreuth and Sorrento. She and Malwida had been reading a play by Wagner's former friend Karl Ritter, of which Cosima did not think much, but about which, apparently, Nietzsche had been enthusiastic. At the same time, one gathers, he had been disparaging Shakespeare and Calderon — as, indeed, he was to disparage one great mind after another during his chameleon intellectual life. Cosima's comments on him are perhaps the most penetrating piece of psychology that ever came from her pen.

"Nietzsche's delight [in Ritter's play]" she wrote to Malwida,

"shows once more how poor his judgment is. I believe there is in Nietzsche a dark productive substratum of which he himself is unconscious: it is from this that whatever is significant in him springs, but then it alarms him, whereas all he thinks and says, which is brilliantly lit up, is actually of no great value. It is the tellurian element in him that is of importance; the solar element is insignificant, and rendered even alarming and unedifying by its conflict with the tellurian. His verdict on Shakespeare reminded me of a friend — only sixteen years of age, it is true — who maintained that people could not seriously admire Homer; or of Raff, who said of Beethoven's C minor symphony, 'Between ourselves, I shouldn't care to have written it'; or of the French attaché who burst into loud laughter when I spoke of the great poets of the thirteenth century. I can well understand your impatience at the way in which the Spaniards are dismissed by so raw a critic . . . 'Great thoughts come from the heart', says Vauvenargues, a dictum which may be applied to Nietzsche, for his great thoughts assuredly come to him not from his brain, but from what? Who can say?" [8]

Evidently Cosima saw him very much as we have come to see him now, as a lame reasoner but a brilliant intuitionist with a superb style, a philosopher with

> One foot in sea and one on shore,
> To one thing constant never.

Nietzsche, true to the principle of never admitting a fault but making a virtue of it, dignified his vacillations by describing them as a "perpetual renewal of himself". It is an easy and agreeable process, and one to which every individual has an indefeasible right. The trouble only begins when the sloughing snake reviles all the other ophidians for not casting their skins at the precise moment when his has become an inconvenience to him.

---

[8] MECW, I, 794 ff.

4

As the year 1876 drew to its close Wagner began to despair of finding a solution of his Bayreuth problem. Feustel was thoroughly scared, while his son-in-law Adolf von Gross, a man of fine intelligence and unshakeable steadfastness, who in later years, after Wagner's death, was to be a tower of strength to Cosima, had not yet come into the foreground of the picture. Heckel was courageous enough but not always practical. He held that the citizens of Bayreuth ought to shoulder part of the deficit, leaving the remainder to be raised by Wagner's friends; and it had to be pointed out to him that when the town granted the site it had been understood that it should bear no responsibility for the financing of the theatre. Heckel was opposed to the idea of Wagner sending out a circular appeal for public help; he thought that the composer's friends should set out to raise the amount required privately. He suggested giving four cycles, instead of three, in 1877, the whole receipts from the first — for which voluntary supplemental payments should be invited — to be devoted to liquidating the debt. Wagner's realistic reply was that the creditors would not wait that long. He pointed out, too, a basic self-contradiction in the plan: in one breath Heckel was urging him not to make a public appeal — on the grounds that in the first place this would advertise the desperate condition of the undertaking, and in the second place Germany was just then in such bad shape financially that the response would probably be small, — and in the next breath pressing him to plunge into a new festival and to appeal for large voluntary donations for seats.

If his health improved, he said, he would see what could be done with regard to a festival in 1878. But at the moment he was very tired of it all. He had embarked upon Bayreuth in the hope that "the German spirit" would support him. Now he would have to assume that it would not; and his disillusionment was so complete that he thought of handing over the whole theatre to some impresario or other, or perhaps the Munich Court Theatre. He had dared the first festival, he told Feustel, in order to show that his ideal goal *could* be reached. But the only result so far had been to land him in a morass of debts and worries; and he simply could not go on reproducing the same soul-racking situation for himself year after year. He is compelled now, he said, to look squarely in the face the possibility that there may never be another festival: if the present deficit cannot be covered soon there will be nothing for it but to declare the undertaking bankrupt, turn over to the King what is legally his, dispose of the remainder to the highest bidder, and apply the money towards discharging the other debts. He himself was willing to sell Wahnfried for the benefit of the creditors and give Feustel authority to apply his private income to the liquidation of the debt. Furthermore, Cosima would hand over to the creditors a legacy of 40,000 francs from the estate of her mother, who had died in March, 1876.

5

So it went on, with everyone distracted and no one able to suggest a practicable way out. There were a few gifts of money from friends and well-wishers, but these came nowhere near meeting the deficit. The Vereine declaimed and fussed about but could obviously do little more than they had done in the first place, for the majority of the members were people of small influence and only moderate means. On his way from Italy Wagner saw Düfflipp in Munich on the 18th December, when he learned that the King was set against the idea of approaching the Reichstag. Wagner now did his best to have the Bayreuth theatre taken over and run by the Munich Intendanz. As he pointed out to Düfflipp, it would prove a first-rate investment for some capitalist or other, who, however, would be sure to place considerations of profit before those of art. It would be much better, he thought, for the Bavarian Government to take over the festivals, employing, for the most part, the Munich personnel. Two days later he was home again in Wahnfried, with his health hardly any better than when he had left, and the problem of the theatre still unsolved. But even yet his indomitable spirit would not accept defeat. In the early part of January we find him telling Standhartner that he still hopes to be able to continue the festivals, though on a new plan: the sensation-hunting crowd and the croaking journalists are to have no part in them, no one being admitted but the members of the reorganised Vereine, who are to take 1,000 tickets for each cycle at 100 marks each, while a certain number of seats are to be allotted free to students. This scheme was to prove as illusory as all the others.

On the 22nd January (1877) Düfflipp arrived at Wahnfried to

discuss the situation with Wagner, Feustel, Muncker and Gross. But he had no concrete suggestions to make, for the state of the King's personal finances did not permit him to come to Wagner's rescue, while the Bayreuth Committee was no doubt reminded of the Cabinet's legal position as a kind of debenture holder under the agreement of 1875. Nothing whatever came of the conference, and on the following day Wagner confessed his depression and hopelessness to the King. He saw now, he said, that he had been a fool to create his great work "in reliance on the German spirit;" "and I must atone for my presumption by retiring with my wife into utter poverty." To Heckel, on the 11th February, he wrote that his faith in the German public was at an end. "What we accomplished last year was a miracle, and will remain so as long as anyone remembers it. But beyond that we cannot go: this we must recognise." A festival in 1877 is now entirely out of the question; meanwhile it falls to him to cover the deficit, and to this end he is contemplating giving some concerts in England.

6

Meanwhile there had been a new development.

The reader will remember that one of the minor singers in the Vienna company at the time Wagner was producing *Lohengrin* there in 1875 was a certain Angelo Neumann, a young man of thirty-eight whose heart was set on becoming an impresario. This ambition had been realised in May of the following year, when he became joint manager of the Leipzig theatre with one Dr. August Förster, who had formerly been connected with the Vienna Hofburg Theatre. In the face of much opposition from various quarters in the town he opened his campaign with a production of *Lohengrin* — under a new conductor, Josef Sucher, in whom he had great faith — that was the prelude to a liveliness in the Leipzig opera house such as it had never known before. In the summer of 1876 it was arranged between the two colleagues that Förster should attend the first cycle of the *Ring* and Neumann the second. But Förster was so prejudiced against the work by some of the more rabid critics whom he met at Bayreuth that on his return he pronounced it to be quite impossible elsewhere, except, perhaps, so far as the *Valkyrie* was concerned. Neumann, with his hands full at the mo-

ment with the affairs of his own theatre, thereupon gave up the
idea of going to Bayreuth. But by the merest accident he met at
supper a man who had just returned from the festival, who told
him that while it was not within his capacity to say whether the *Ring*
were possible or not it wås at least Neumann's duty as an opera
director to see it; whereupon he handed him a ticket for the second
cycle. That was at eleven o'clock at night; and it was characteristic
of Neumann that an hour later he was in the last train of the day
to Bayreuth. He saw the second cycle through, was profoundly impressed, and now had only one idea in his head — to reproduce
the whole colossal work in Leipzig, be the difficulties and dangers
what they might. He put his plan before Liszt, who passed it on to
Wagner; and Neumann was given an appointment at Wahnfried at
nine the next morning. Wagner was still in his bedroom. Liszt sent
a note up to him, and the servant brought a hasty line or two in
reply: "I can't come down, because I am in my shirt. I've considered
Neumann's plan, but still cling to my idea of repeating the *Ring* in
Bayreuth next year."

Neumann, however, seems to have had his private doubts whether
that would prove possible; and on his return to Leipzig he prevailed
upon his co-director, on the 27th August, to lay before Wagner a
formal proposal, "in case you should decide not to repeat the festival
for the present", to allow the *Ring* to be given in Leipzig with the
Bayreuth machinery and decorations. Förster offered Wagner a ten
per cent royalty on the gross receipts, with a substantial prepayment
as soon as the contract was signed. Wagner thanked him heartily
for his friendly interest, but declined the proposition. "My work is
not yet complete", he wrote: "the first performances have shown me
that much could be improved upon. So give me time to produce it
again next year here in Bayreuth in carefully corrected style." The
matter therefore lapsed.[9]

7

By the end of January, 1877 Wagner had every reason to doubt
whether a second festival would be possible that year; and as he
was anxious to find a post for Unger where the tenor could devote

[9] The documents relating to the negotiations with Neumann and Förster are in
NERW, pp. 18–51.

himself mainly to the Wagner repertory and prove that he had profited by what he had learned in Bayreuth, he suggested, of his own
accord, that Förster should engage Unger for the Leipzig Opera, in
which case, he told Sucher, "I am ready to enter, if Dr. Förster still
so desires, into negotiations with him as regards permission to give
my *Ring*." In a second letter, which is lost, he appears to have said
definitely that there would be no Bayreuth festival in 1877. So towards the end of February Förster wrote him again, agreeing to the
engagement of Unger if Wagner would guarantee his all-round competence in the Wagner rôles, and repeating the proposal as to the
Ring in Leipzig made in his letter of the preceding August. Wagner, in reply, vouched for his tenor — who, if he still had much to
learn, was commendably anxious to improve himself — but could
give Förster no definite assurance as regarded the *Ring*. The legal
rights in it, he said, were vested in the King of Bavaria, who might
soon take upon himself the responsibility of its production. In that
case Wagner's original intention of reserving the work for Bayreuth
for three years would call for modification; and if he were to hand
it over to the German theatres, Leipzig should be the first to receive
permission to give it. Thereupon Förster went to Wahnfried, and in
March a contract was signed under which the Leipzig Town Theatre
was to have the sole north German rights in the *Ring* for two years;
the south German rights being vested in Munich (whose property
the work actually was), and the Austrian in Vienna, which seemed
to be keen about acquiring it. Then, when the affair appeared to be
virtually settled, the difficulties began.

Wagner had been politely reminded, via Düfflipp and Feustel,
that under the agreement of 1864 the theatrical rights of the *Ring*
had been assigned by him to the King. So we find him, in April,
1877, asking that the ancient Munich agreement shall be regarded
as a dead letter. He repeats his old contention that the contract had
been merely a legal façade to cover the King's support of him during the years that were to follow its signing. From this view of the
matter Ludwig himself would probably have been the last to dissent. But certain rights under the agreement had been legally vested
in the Munich Court Theatre, and those rights neither the Intendanz
nor the King's financial advisers were willing to renounce. Wagner
stressed the point that of his own free will he had conferred on the
Munich Theatre the performing rights in all his works; and from

the many productions of them by the theatre during the last thirteen years — productions highly profitable to the institution — he had not drawn any royalties. But now that the King has declined the suggestion that he shall assume the care of the festivals in Bayreuth, it has become necessary, for various reasons, for Wagner to be at liberty to negotiate with the German theatres with regard to the *Ring*. For one thing, by hiring out the Bayreuth scenery and apparatus he could raise something towards paying off the debt on the theatre; for another, it was time for him, at the age of sixty-four, to think of making some provision for his large family.

Of the three front-line theatres desirous, as we have seen, of producing the *Ring*, Leipzig seemed the one most likely to act first. But it proposed to use much of the Bayreuth material; and if it did, obviously this would be unavailable for Munich until Leipzig had finished with it; yet manifestly Munich had the first call upon it so far as *Siegfried* and the *Götterdämmerung* were concerned. (The machinery and décor for the *Rhinegold* and the *Valkyrie* productions of 1869 and 1870, of course, it already had. The intention of the management was first of all to perform the last two sections, and then take the tetralogy into its repertory as a whole). As regards Leipzig and Vienna, then, it was now largely a question of taking care that neither of them produced *Siegfried* and the *Götterdämmerung* before Munich had done so. Wagner had to press Düfflipp to come to some definite arrangement about it all without delay, for Förster could not be kept in suspense indefinitely; as it was, he seemed to be hesitating as to the engagement of Unger at Leipzig before the sum total of his projected rights was legally assured.

8

Wagner, in fact, was in a most difficult position. Just then he needed Richter for the coming concerts in London; and the Vienna Intendanz, seeing its strategic advantage, made no scruple of putting the thumb-screw on him — either he agreed at once to letting Vienna have the *Ring*, or he would not get Richter. So Wagner had to yield, stipulating, however, that Vienna should not produce the *Rhinegold* before the end of 1877 and the *Valkyrie* before the end of 1878 — for Leipzig was impatient to get to work immediately. As regarded Munich, Düfflipp pointed out to him that the real difficulty was not the agreement of 1864 but that of February, 1874, which the King and his Cabinet could not see their way to regard as non-existent. Under that agreement, 216,152 marks in all had been advanced to Bayreuth, and the whole of this debt was still owing. Düfflipp quite reasonably urged that the abandonment of the idea of a festival in Bayreuth in 1877 or 1878 meant that a certain sum which might have become available for partial liquidation of the debt to the Treasury could no longer be counted on. Moreover, the unique attractiveness of Bayreuth would largely disappear if other theatres were to take up the *Ring*; as Düfflipp put it, even supposing Förster to accept the responsibility of running the festivals, under a changed régime it would be impossible for Bayreuth to charge the high prices of 1876, so that the surplus likely to become available for paying off the debt would be smaller than Wagner seemed to imagine. The great pull of Bayreuth had been, and always would be, that the world in general would have to decide between hearing the *Ring* there or not hearing it at all.

Düfflipp was especially anxious to hear from Wagner what prospect there was of Clause IV of the agreement of February, 1874 not becoming a mere scrap of paper — the clause under which "the decorations, machinery, gas installation and internal fittings" of the Bayreuth theatre were pledged to the Court Secretariat as security for a loan of 100,000 thalers. For the resources of the Kabinetskasse, Düfflipp goes on to say, are so strained by the building operations of the King that the failure of Bayreuth to meet its obligations to Munich will have serious results for the Treasury in the coming years. As for poor Düfflipp himself, his one longing is for the day when he can lay down his office and be free of all these responsibilities and cares. Meanwhile he is delighted to have Wagner's assurance that he regards his works as being at the disposal of the Munich Court Theatre for all time, without honoraria or royalties; and he ventures to express the hope that that undertaking on the composer's part will forthwith be put on paper in due legal form.

By the end of April the situation was one of complete deadlock. The King and the Court Secretariat were unable to promise help of any kind. Wagner was resolved not to embark on another festival unless and until the General Patronatsverein was in a position to guarantee the financing of it. His only chance of paying off the huge debt lay in his selling the *Ring* to the German theatres; but as Munich had the first moral and legal claim to the complete work the other theatres negotiating for it were likely to be kept in suspense indefinitely. Wagner suggested a combine of the Munich, Leipzig and Vienna theatres with the object of continuing the festivals, with himself as artistic adviser; but obviously neither of the three institutions concerned could be expected to put its best endeavours into a scheme of that kind.

This, then, was the general situation at the time when Wagner plunged into the unlucky London adventure.

9

An ambitious young firm of London concert agents, Hodge and Essex, had conceived, in conjunction with Wilhelmj and the violinist Hermann Francke,[10] the idea of twenty concerts to be given in the Albert Hall, under Wagner, in the summer of 1877. On paper the prospects were rosy enough; the Albert Hall held some 10,000 people, and Wagner's enormous prestige could surely be counted upon to fill it. A profit of £500 on each concert was dangled before his eyes. But in the end the agents decided to give only six concerts in fourteen days, for which Wagner was promised £1,500 — subject, of course, to that amount being earned. Several of his friends, and in addition the American impresario Ullmann, who managed Bülow's concert affairs, warned him, through Liszt, against the undertaking. So did Bülow, who, a couple of years before, had lost some £1,500, the reward for a year of almost suicidal hard work, through the dishonesty of an English agent. But even the £1,500 promised by Hodge and Essex would go some way towards paying off the Bayreuth debt; and so, abandoned as he seemed to be by his own countrymen, Wagner imprudently closed with the offer. Richter was engaged to conduct, with Seidl and Fischer as his assistants, and eight singers — Materna, Frau Sadler-Grün, Fräulein Waibel,

---

[10] In his article on Wagner in *Grove's Dictionary* Edward Dannreuther says that contrary to the impression conveyed in the Glasenapp Life he himself "had *nothing whatsoever* to do with the planning of the [London] 'festival' nor with the business arrangements. All he did was to attend to the completion of the orchestra with regard to the 'extra' wind instruments, and at Wagner's request to conduct the preliminary rehearsals." But from four unpublished letters from Wagner to Dannreuther, copies of which lie before me, it is clear that the latter had been of service in various small ways, as he was almost the only person in London in April, 1877 to whom Wagner could write in German.

Fräulein Exter, Hill, Schlosser, Unger, and Chaudon (of Vienna) — were engaged at what, for those days, were high fees: [11] Materna was to receive £600, Hill £500, Unger £100, Sadler-Grün £200, Schlosser £150, Chaudon £100, and Weibel and Exter £50 each, while Richter was to be paid £100 and the other two conductors £60 each.

The contract was signed on the 15th March. Wagner arrived in London, with Cosima, on the 1st May, and the first full rehearsal, with Richter as conductor and Wilhelmj as leader of the orchestra, took place three days later. Throughout the five weeks of their stay in London Wagner and Cosima were the guests of Edward Dannreuther at his Bayswater house in the secluded Orme Square (No. 12), from which it was a pleasant walk across Kensington Gardens to the Albert Hall. He kept to himself as much as he could, but was necessarily dragged into a number of social and public engagements. He met George Eliot [12] and George Henry Lewes, Brown-

---

[11] The fees to Materna and Hill, however, were based on the original assumption of *twenty* concerts. This is clear from a letter of Wagner's to his niece Johanna's husband Alfred Jachmann, published for the first time in 1927, which seems to have been unknown to Glasenapp. It now appears that as Hodge did not know German and Wagner could not write in English, Jachmann volunteered towards the end of February to go to London and take soundings in all possible quarters. He met Hodge on the 3rd March, discovered that the agent's capital was inadequate for so ambitious a scheme, and arranged that only six concerts should be given. It was on the basis of Jachmann's report that Wagner signed the contract on the 15th: one of the conditions of it was that Dannreuther should take the preliminary rehearsals, as Richter knew no English.

Both Materna and Hill, before Wagner approached them, had made arrangements for tours in May and June that would have brought them in a large sum of money. The 12,000 marks in the one case and the 10,000 in the other were therefore intended to compensate them for giving up these engagements, and were based on the supposition that there would be twenty concerts in London during those two months. When the number was reduced to six Wagner had to fulfil his obligations to the singers: but he was given to understand in London that the six concerts would yield as much profit to Hodge and Essex as the twenty originally planned. See JKJ, pp. 90–96.

[12] She and Lewes seem to have been accompanied at the concerts by Herbert Spencer. It is amusing to see the philosopher (in *An Autobiography*, II, 297–9) trying his best to pass Wagner's complex art through the milling machinery of his own severely logical mind.

Glasenapp says that Wagner met Edward Burne-Jones at George Eliot's house, but apparently this is a mistake. Lady [Georgiana] Burne-Jones, the painter's widow, says that one day George Eliot took Cosima to the artist's studio, and the two met again two or three times afterwards, but that "Wagner was too much engrossed by work to accompany his wife to the Grange: polite messages were exchanged between him and Edward, but they did not meet. We went to several of his concerts, and even to a morning rehearsal of one at the Albert Hall, which was an extraordinary thing for Edward to do. . . He did not, as a rule, love Wagner's

ing, Rudolf Lehmann, Herkomer (who painted a well-known portrait of him), and other notabilities of the world of art and letters, was photographed by Elliott and Fry, saw again his old friends Sainton and Lüders, with whom he exchanged reminiscences of the Philharmonic concerts of 1855, went the round of the picture galleries, looked in occasionally at a theatre, was dined and wined and toasted in public and in private, and, on the 17th May, was received at Windsor by the Queen and Prince Leopold.

The orchestra, as befitted the locale, was a large one, consisting of 48 violins, 15 violas, 20 'cellos, 22 basses,[13] 28 wood wind, 8 horns, 5 trumpets, 5 trombones, 5 tubas, 7 harps and 6 percussion.[14] The concerts took place on the 7th, 9th, 12th, 14th, 16th and 19th May: the 12th and the 19th were Saturday afternoons. Wagner himself was to conduct the first part of each concert, Richter the second: Wagner, in his wretched state of health, "scarcely did himself justice", as Francis Hueffer, who was at that time the musical critic of the *Times*, expressed it.[15] The programmes were designed to outline the operatic development of the composer from *Rienzi* to the *Ring*, the *Kaisermarsch* being added at the first concert, the *Huldigungsmarsch* at the fourth, and the *Centennial March* at the sixth. At the fourth, Unger showed the first signs of a hoarseness that was to pursue him to the end. As he did not feel equal to Siegfried's Forging Songs, and Hill, who might have repeated Wotan's Abschied in their stead, had by that time gone home, the Ride of the Valkyries was played a second time, and the scene of Siegfried's farewell to Brynhilde attempted. In this, however, only Materna was audible, the tenor not having a good note left in his voice. That same night word came from Hill that he too had developed hoarseness; so the programmes of the last two concerts had to be modified. Still, the artistic and social success of the undertaking was beyond question: the huge hall was reasonably well occupied, the audiences were wildly enthusiastic, and several members of the royal family, in-

---

music"; but when he heard a concert performance of *Parsifal* in the Albert Hall in 1884 he realised, to his delight, that Wagner had struck in music the "Celtic" vein of the Grail legend which he himself was trying to express in some of his paintings. See *Memorials of Edward Burne-Jones*, by G. B.-J., edition of 1912, II, 43, 79.

[13] The famous Albert Hall echo must have had immense fun with these.

[14] Glasenapp manages to make the total 170.

[15] *Half a Century of Music in England* (1889), p. 72. Wagner's ignorance of English made things difficult at rehearsal for both himself and the players.

cluding the Prince of Wales and the Duke of Edinburgh, graced some of the concerts with their presence.

But on the material side there was another story to tell. Not only had Hodge and Essex under-estimated the costs of the affair but they had plunged into it with insufficient capital; and, incredible as it sounds, they did not even know that though the Albert Hall contains some 10,000 seats, something like a third of these are private property; the owners can either occupy the seats themselves without payment, sell them on their own account, or simply leave them vacant, as they choose. (Apparently the empty chairs at each concert were mostly those of owners who neither came themselves nor disposed of their seats). After the third concert it was plainly evident that the agents' promises to Wagner could not be kept. On the 13th May he had to confess to Feustel that he ought to have had more sense than to go to London, which he had done not so much because he had believed that a financial success was possible but because he wanted to demonstrate to the German friends of his cause that it "was neither laziness nor love of ease" that had made him ask them to look about for some way of covering the Bayreuth deficit. He now urged Feustel to send out at once an appeal from the Executive Council for subscriptions; he himself would head the list with 3,000 marks. Should this appeal fail, he says, he has finished with Germany: he will accept an offer from Ullmann for a tour in America, sell Wahnfried, and turn his back for ever on his native land.

10

By this time it had become evident that the venture would not of itself even cover expenses. Wagner, who had advanced money to part-pay the singers out of his own pocket, had now to ask Feustel to send him a personal remittance. Feustel, worrying only about the situation in Bayreuth, seems to have thought that Wagner's troubles in London were being exaggerated. Wagner had to speak plainly to him; he needed the London money there and then for his artists, he said, in order that he might not appear as a bankrupt. By now he had practically had to take over the gamble on his own account; and in an attempt to save the situation two more concerts were given on the 28th and 29th May. All he received from Hodge and Essex in the end was something over £700. This sum he sent

on the 3rd June to Feustel for the benefit of the more pressing of
the Bayreuth creditors, his total personal contribution to the debt
thus amounting to about 10,000 marks; and he had the satisfaction
of being able to say that not a single person concerned in the concerts had lost a penny through him.[16] As for himself, after five weeks
of work and worry he was poorer to the extent of £1,200. A number
of his London admirers, with Dannreuther, Hueffer and Lord Lind-
say at their head, raised a subscription of £561, which Dannreuther
brought to him in Bayreuth in August. But as it was offered not to
the Bayreuth cause but to himself personally, as an expression of
gratitude for the pleasure he had given the donors by the London
concerts, he courteously but firmly declined to accept it. To Ludwig
Schemann, later in the year, he expressed his indignation at the
current view that he had gone to London as an "impresario": *"that
at least"*, he said, "I hope I shall be spared by posterity." [17]

His cares in connection with Bayreuth had pursued him even to
London. On the 23rd May he learned from Düfflipp that Munich
intended to produce *Siegfried* in 1877, the *Götterdämmerung* in
1878, and after that the whole *Ring*. Should Bayreuth decide to
hold another festival, Munich would give it all the assistance possible; and Perfall was willing to co-operate with Vienna and Leipzig in any way that Wagner might desire. But, he was told, it would
be inadvisable to dispose of "even the smallest part" of the Bayreuth apparatus to Leipzig; it would be better to hand it over, against
a suitable reimbursement, to Munich, whence it could always be
transferred to Bayreuth if it should happen to be needed for a
festival. Evidently the Munich Intendanz feared an indefinite postponement of its own plans if the machinery and decorations for
Siegfried and the *Götterdämmerung* were to pass temporarily into
the custody of another theatre. But even this difficulty might have
been overcome had not Wagner's relations with Förster gradually
taken a turn that was to end in a complete breach between them.

On the 25th April — i.e., before going to London — Wagner, in

---

[16] Hueffer (p. 76) says that "a sum of £700 was eventually remitted to Bayreuth.
But this Wagner did not expect when he left London, and the last words he uttered
standing at the carriage window as the train steamed out of Victoria Station were,
'All is lost except honour!'" Wagner's letter of the 3rd June to Feustel, however,
places it beyond question that he received the £700 *before* he left London.

[17] SERW, p. 37. Wagner's letter of thanks and refusal to his London friends will
be found in Hueffer, pp. 77–9.

a long letter to Förster, had tried to place the negotiations on a definite footing. His main points were these:

1. He would prefer to assign the *Ring* rights to a theatre that would engage Unger, so that he might feel fairly confident that the leading tenor rôles would be interpreted in accordance with his intentions.

2. He would release Förster from any obligation to take either the finance or the management of a future festival in Bayreuth on his own shoulders. The Vereine seemed to be bestirring themselves, and if they could provide him with an audience it would be Wagner's duty to superintend the productions, leaving administrative details to his Committee.

3. He has given Leipzig and Vienna the exclusive German production rights of the *Ring*, apart from Munich, and it is understood that in return the three theatres are to place their best artistic forces at his disposal for any Bayreuth festival that may be decided upon — when the Vereine feel strong enough to assume the financial responsibility for it, — and the theatres are further to have delegates of their own on the administrative Committee. The Bayreuth performances are to take place at some time in the summer that will be agreeable to all three theatres; that is to say, the festivals will be so planned that the absence of this singer or that will not hamper any of the theatres in the arrangement of its own repertory for those weeks.

4. Förster is to have the right to produce the *Ring* so long as he remains director of the Leipzig theatre, or, alternatively, for a term of years not to exceed six.

5. Wagner will press the Munich Intendanz to hurry on with the productions of *Siegfried* and the *Götterdämmerung*, so that Leipzig also can give these works by the end of 1878. Vienna is likely to proceed more slowly.

6. For the granting of this special privilege to the Leipzig theatre, Förster is to pay him 10,000 marks on the signing of the contract.

7. Wagner's royalties are to be ten per cent on the gross receipts for each performance, subscription seats included.

8. Munich has a lien on the Bayreuth apparatus as security for a debt of more than 200,000 marks. He has suggested to the Intendanz that it shall use the Bayreuth material for its own production of the

Ring. But as it already has that for the *Rhinegold* and the *Valkyrie*, it may prefer a cash settlement; in which case Förster, no doubt, will be agreeable to taking over the whole of the Bayreuth material and making his own arrangements with Munich as regards payment for it.

9. Wagner has a pressing debt of 4,000 marks to settle in Leipzig; and perhaps Förster, having decided to carry the thing through, will oblige him with this amount at once.

11

Förster replied that he still regarded his agreement of the preceding August with Wagner as definite. Wagner's latest letter, however, has changed the aspect of the situation at one or two vital points. The priority of Munich means, in effect, that he cannot produce the last two sections of the *Ring* before the end of 1878. For all that, he is ready to abide by the original agreement, the terms of which he now proceeds to *préciser:*

1. No other theatres besides those of Munich and Vienna are to have the *Ring* until a full year after the Leipzig production.

2. Though Munich has the first claim to *Siegfried* and the *Götterdämmerung*, Leipzig is to be at liberty to give these two works at the end of 1878 whether Munich has produced them or not.

3. Förster agrees to an advance of 10,000 marks in respect of royalties, with a first payment of 4,000 marks at once. A further payment of 3,000 marks will be made on the 1st July, and the final 3,000 on the day after the first performance of the *Rhinegold*.

4. The contract becomes null and void on the day when Förster ceases to be director of the Leipzig theatre, and all rights then revert to the composer or his heirs.

5. Förster agrees to Wagner's suggestion as to co-operation with Munich and Vienna in the event of a resumption of the festivals in Bayreuth; also to the steps Wagner proposes to take with regard to the stage material. He asks only for a speedy decision, as in case of a failure to come to an understanding with Munich in the matter he will have to make other arrangements without delay. He has no hopes of a business success, for the Leipzig theatre lacks the resources of some of the larger theatres; but he recognises that the honour Wagner has done him will give his theatre an exceptional

standing in Germany. Neumann's later comment on it all was that Förster, who was an honourable man, was secretly less keen now than he had been originally. His cautious temperament had warned him from the first against so vast an undertaking, but he had been temporarily infected by Neumann's enthusiasm; afterwards he had been to some extent influenced by Wagner's and Neumann's enemies, and had begun to have his doubts.

For a while, however, matters seemed to be proceeding satisfactorily. Then a serious misunderstanding developed as to the interpretation of the clause relating to the cash transactions. Förster's view was that the first 10,000 marks were to be regarded as an advance on royalties, while Wagner looked upon it as a fee; otherwise, he said, if his royalties are to be earmarked to pay off the "advance", it will be a long time before he receives any actual royalties. This had not been in his mind when making the arrangement with Förster. He had conferred a great advantage on the Leipzig theatre, he said, by giving it the exclusive north German rights in the *Ring*; for Hamburg, Hanover, Cologne and Frankfort had all been anxious to give the work, and presumably their terms, in their totality, would have brought him in more than those of Leipzig alone could do. He therefore regards the 10,000 marks not as an advance in respect of royalties but as "compensation" for the surrender of these advantages, a surrender that would benefit Leipzig, for obviously the exclusive performances there would attract visitors from all the other north German towns.

Though this did not quite correspond to what had been in Förster's mind when he concluded the agreement of August, 1876, he was willing, he said, to make it easier for Wagner to benefit by royalty payments before the amount of the advance of 10,000 marks had been earned. He accordingly suggested a new arrangement: the advance was to stand, but of the ten per cent royalties six per cent should go towards the liquidation of the advance, the remaining four per cent being paid to Wagner after each performance.[18] This letter reached Wagner while he was in London; and on the 10th May he sent Förster a letter that was hardly calculated to give the machinery the oiling it so badly needed, having regard to the quantity of grit now in the wheels. He gave Förster the choice between

[18] Förster had already paid to one Steckner, in Leipzig, the 4,000 marks mentioned by Wagner in an earlier letter.

(a) 10,000 marks as "premium", plus ten per cent of the gross receipts, or (b) a continuing royalty of ten per cent, along with an advance of 4,000 marks (i.e., the sum already paid by Förster), on which five per cent interest was to run until the principal was extinguished. In addition, there was to be no further obligation on Wagner's part as to conferring exclusive rights for any period of time, while the Leipzig theatre would be bound to produce *Siegfried* and the *Götterdämmerung* within the time agreed upon. If these conditions were not acceptable, Förster could withdraw entirely, in which case Wagner would refund him the 4,000 marks at once. Förster was further to regard himself as released from his contract with Unger.

According to Neumann, Förster had already taken fright, and so a pretext for cancelling the contract was not unwelcome to him. His reply was that he regarded Wagner's later conditions as contrary to the clear legal meaning of the original contract. The question now arises, would it be expedient for him to insist on his indubitable rights and press for the fulfilment of the contract?

> "My answer to this question is: No, it would not be expedient. If you could give a definite acceptance of a definite offer, and then, under cover of having imperfectly understood one paragraph of the contract, try to upset the contract, naturally it occurs to me that before long you might feel moved to change your views again. This uncertainty gives me an uncomfortable feeling, which indeed would not diminish my enthusiasm for your work, but would cloud the pleasantness of our personal relations, add to the difficulties of my production of the work, and endanger the success of the undertaking."

He therefore gives Wagner back his word and asks for the immediate return of the 4,000 marks, as well as the contract with Unger.

Wagner replied to this on the 17th May, still from London.[19] He wrote in conciliatory terms. No doubt there had been misunderstandings on both sides, he said. But it would be distasteful to him now to sever the connection with Leipzig that had made so great a sensation in the Press, and to have to enter into public explanations

---

[19] Neumann calls the letter "a model not only of clear logic but of noble-minded self-denial." He tells us that he did everything in his power to bring Förster round to his own way of thinking, but his colleague by this time had really taken fright.

The prime cause of the trouble, however, seems to have been the divergent interpretation of the financial clause. Förster had intended the 10,000 marks to be an *advance* on royalties, while Wagner had taken it to mean a capital payment independent of royalties.

with regard to it all; so "if you have no other grounds for refusing, I beg you to send me, for my signature, the contract in legal form, corresponding to your last offer." But Förster was not to be won over. He took, or professed to take, the view that Wagner's heart was no longer really in the matter as Förster had first conceived it, and so he too, he says, must be forgiven if he puts artistic considerations aside and looks at it all from the purely business point of view. He has the highest respect for Wagner's genius, but he feels that the composer has misrepresented his intentions; and while not presuming to criticise him,

> "I have the impression that I am confronted by not only an artistic individuality but a business one of so strongly marked a kind that I cannot promise myself a successful end to my relations with it."

Much as it pains him to do so, he suggests ending the matter quietly now, to avoid a rougher ending later. After that, of course, there could be no question of the negotiations being renewed.

Neumann was deeply grieved at this collapse of all his hopes. But he was as incapable as Wagner was of accepting defeat; and before six months were over he had solved the problem of the *Ring* in a way entirely his own.

CHAPTER XXIX

BAYREUTH SAVED

1

O N THE 4th June Wagner left London for Ems, where he and Cosima were joined by the children. There, in a villa with a fairly quiet garden, he stayed for four weeks, vainly trying to restore his weary mind and broken body.[1] Through Feustel he made another payment to stave off the more clamant creditors, this making a total backing for Bayreuth so far, out of his own funds and those of Cosima, of some 50,000 marks. He was now thoroughly disillusioned with regard to everything. He saw clearly, he said, that it was not the *Ring* that had been condemned, but — Bayreuth.

> "My work will be given everywhere, and will attract numerous spectators, but — no one will come to Bayreuth . . . I can blame the place only in so far as it was I who chose it. And yet I had a great idea in so doing; I had it in mind to create, with the support of the nation, something absolutely new and independent in a place which should become significant just through this creation — a kind of art-Washington. I had too good an opinion of our higher society. Partly for my sake, partly out of curiosity, they sacrificed themselves for once to the immense inconvenience of Bayreuth, but they drew back in horror before the notion of doing it again. Hence the attitude of aloofness everywhere towards the position I am in."

A very important firm in London, he continued, had approached him with an offer to repeat the festival there during the coming season with the whole of the Bayreuth apparatus; he had only to say the word and a theatre would be built for him in Leipzig; while Würzburg and Nuremberg were willing to repeat the Bayreuth performances, which in themselves had been so successful. As for Bayreuth, it would never be what he wanted it to be until he could realise his old plan for a musical-dramatic School there. This scheme occupied his mind for a long time. But in the end it came

---

[1] It was precisely this time that his enemies in Vienna thought appropriate for the malicious publication of the "Putzmacherin" letters in the *Neue Freie Presse*.

to nothing: his world-vogue now was greater than that of any other opera composer in the whole history of music, but the one thing he could not do was to get his fellow-countrymen to share his belief in Bayreuth. He was the sole person who had not profited a penny, and had never had any desire to profit, by the festival of 1876; and now it was upon his shoulders that the whole burden of that disastrous year rested. And this was the man whom Nietzsche, in his petty resentment and mean egoism, accused of pandering, for the sake of "success," to the taste of the German public of the post-war years! The more we learn of what was really going on in Wagner's soul at that time the more contemptible a figure does Nietzsche cut at the bar of history.

The King was horrified to hear that Wagner was reduced to thinking of selling Wahnfried and settling in America. "I implore you", he wrote,

> "to give up this frightful idea: it would be an indelible stain on all Germany if it allowed your great spirit to abandon it rather than make some sacrifice in order to retain the Fatherland's greatest genius. For myself, the grief would be so overwhelming as to poison, nay, destroy for ever, my joy in life."

Wagner, in his reply, poured out all the bitterness that was in his heart. His exertions on behalf of Bayreuth during the last few years, he said, had proved very expensive for him, for not only had he made nothing personally out of his many concerts but he had paid his own expenses everywhere; and now the Bayreuth deficit was engulfing not only the residue of his own savings but Cosima's small capital. If only to make some provision for his large family he would have to leave the Germany that had turned its back on him in his hour of need and make his home in America. No one understands his ideal of the theatre: no one will help him to found the long-desired School, though the ignorant politicians and "their parasites the pseudo-artists" keep on founding or maintaining Conservatoires here, there and everywhere.

> "What became of the Munich Music School? What I did for that, and into the hands of what kind of people has it now fallen! Even in Würzburg a Royal School of Music has just been founded: as if we hadn't 'musicians' enough already! Yet when *I* say openly what I long for, who listens to *me?* It should be the affair of the princes, who ought to stand above the miserable coteries of their Ministers. I have ap-

proached them all: and the only response has been obtuseness. *One* alone listened to me. He helped me until now — now, when I am succumbing!"

He asks if he may have an audience next month in Munich, so that he may try, for the last time, to induce Ludwig and the art institutions of his kingdom to unite to save "the Bayreuth idea" for the honour of the German spirit and the eternal glory of his royal benefactor. And he sends Ludwig a fair copy,[2] made by Cosima, of the poem of *Parsifal*, with the significant inscription in his own handwriting on the last sheet of the manuscript, " 'Erlösung dem Erlöser'! R.W."

2

The King's reply of the 14th July is wholly taken up with his rapture over the receipt of the poem and his longing for the day when he can hear the music; evidently he had turned over to Düfflipp the painful business of dealing with the more material side of Wagner's letter. On the 20th July Wagner went to Munich to try to find out how matters now stood. When he was told by Düfflipp that the King had given him no definite instructions with regard to Munich, Bayreuth and the *Ring*, Wagner, in the words of the Secretary's report to his royal master,

"looked astonished and aghast: he fell back in his chair, drew his hand across his brow, and said in a tone of profoundest emotion, 'Ah! Now I know where I am! So I have nothing more to hope for! And yet the King's last letters were so cordial and kind that I thought the old days had come back again!' "

He put the financial position frankly before Düfflipp. The receipts in respect of the Patronatscheine in 1876 had been disappointing, and the cost of the building, its equipment and the performances had exceeded the estimates. About 149,000 marks were still owing to contractors and workmen, in addition to the debt of 216,000 marks to the Bavarian Kabinetskasse. The London concerts had brought in only 15,000 marks. Cosima's inheritance had supplied another 32,000, so that some 102,000 were still owing to the contractors and others, some of whom were demanding immediate payment under threat of legal proceedings.

---

[2] Still in the Munich archives.

Wagner, continued Düfflipp, was in a cleft stick: it was impossible, in these circumstances, for him personally to embark on another festival, yet to let the performances lapse would damage not only his cause but the town of Bayreuth, which had made many sacrifices for him. Realising the gravity of the situation, Düfflipp suggested that Perfall, with whom he had already discussed the possibility of helpful action on the part of the Munich Intendanz, should be called in to conference. He had difficulty in persuading Wagner to meet Perfall personally; but in the end the two men came together, and, apparently, buried the hatchet. The most likely ways of liquidating the outstanding debt of 102,000 marks were discussed: as regards the liability to the Kabinetskasse, Düfflipp told the King, there seemed to be no way of clearing this off except by Munich utilising for its own performances as much as possible of the Bayreuth stage material.

Perfall's report and proposals were sent to the King on the 24th July: they ran thus:

> "Wagner desires a repetition of the *Ring* in Bayreuth for the following reasons: (1) to wipe out the remaining deficit on last year's festival; (2) respect for Bayreuth is increasing. The cheapest way to run the performances would be by means of the Munich vocal and orchestral personnel: this would rehearse from the coming winter to the June of 1878, and then, with a few reinforcements from other theatres, migrate to Bayreuth for the festival. Wagner and Düfflipp agreed."

But the King would not assent to this; he preferred, he said, the earlier plan, under which the festival of 1878 would be given in Munich.

A few weeks later Perfall summarised the situation as he now saw it. As soon as the King's decision became publicly known, he told Düfflipp, the hands of the opponents of Bayreuth would be strengthened, and the idea of repeating the performances there would have to be abandoned. If the King had in mind a private Munich performance of the *Ring* for himself, this would necessarily have to be followed by a public production. In that case Perfall did not think that much of the Bayreuth apparatus would prove serviceable in Munich, having regard to the differences between the two stages. If Ludwig will be satisfied with the existing Munich décor — and indeed there will not be time, by the spring of 1878, for a new one to be prepared — a saving of 10,000 to 12,000 marks can be effected, which will go far towards providing the scenery and costumes for *Siegfried* and the *Götterdämmerung*. All in all, Perfall thought, the best plan would be to give up the Bayreuth idea and concentrate on a public production of the whole tetralogy in Munich in the summer of 1878, the expenses to be met, in part, by reducing the number of those private performances for which the King had already shown such a partiality.

3

For refuge against all these troubles Wagner was now turning more and more towards his *Parsifal*, which he longed, he told the King on the 23rd August, to complete as his "final victory over life".

> "No external consideration impels me to this, for it goes without saying that this 'Stage-*dedication*-festival' will not be handed over to our well-looked-after Court and Town theatres. Only a few will hear the work, and its final destiny will be to please him who once graciously awakened in me the sleeping germ of it."

Once more, this was the suffering artist, estranged from the world, whom Nietzsche, in his currish malice, accused of pandering to the religious prepossessions of the ruling powers in Germany! On the contrary, it was precisely because of the peculiar nature of the *Parsifal* subject that he deliberately planned to exclude from the hearing of the work everyone who could not share his view of it as a "stage-dedication-drama" — that is to say, ninety-nine per cent of his fellow-Germans. He was writing it, he told Cosima, solely for her: he had lost all belief in the "German spirit": the new work would be "pure and simple nonsense in the midst of our contemporary interests".

Hülsen's attitude towards the appeal for help was no doubt typical of that of the directors of the German theatres as a whole. He counselled the Kaiser against it, on the grounds that the Bayreuth undertaking represented "only a particular specialty of musical development", whereas it was the duty of an Intendant to be "impartial" and "objective" in his furtherance of the various ends of art. He did not exclude, however, the possibility of something good coming out of the projected Music School at Bayreuth under the aegis of one so gifted and energetic as Wagner. But so lukewarm a recommendation was not likely to quicken the sluggish pulse of the powers that were in Berlin: and accordingly support of this newest plan of Wagner's was refused.[3] What the German governments in general thought of him at that time was incidentally shown during the prosecution of a certain Count Harry Arnim for having said in a political article that "next to Wagner, Bismarck is the greatest man living today". This not unhandsome tribute to the Chancellor was held to be legally punishable as an "insult" to Bismarck, "since Richard Wagner is universally regarded as a man suffering from megalomania".

Düfflipp, unable to extract a definite decision from the King, appears to have maintained silence towards Wagner for several weeks after the composer's departure from Munich. So on the 19th September Wagner wrote to him again, saying that he could only surmise that insurmountable obstacles blocked the way of the plan they had discussed at their last meeting. He had no longer any hope for a production of the *Ring* in 1878 in Bayreuth by the Munich forces; and with that hope, of course, vanished the possibility of the deficit being met. He could trust now, he said, only to a Munich production of the work for some alleviation of his financial burden. For himself, in his sixty-fifth year he could not face again single-handed the labours and disappointments of a Bayreuth festival — with the whole of the financial and administrative work falling on his shoulders, and at the end of it all the disheartening conviction that as soon as his singers and players got back to their homes they would forget all he had taught them at such murderous cost to himself.

As the festival of 1876 faded more and more into a mere memory, indeed, he became increasingly critical of the defects of the performances. His dominant idea now was to establish in Bayreuth the Music School in which musical-dramatic interpretation should be taught from the foundations upwards; with the forces thus trained for him he planned, in a moment of super-optimism, to give model performances of all his works during the next few years. The first two years of study would be devoted to the education of conductors, singers and players; then the *Flying Dutchman*, *Tannhäuser* and *Lohengrin* would be given in 1880, *Tristan* and the *Meistersinger* in 1881, the *Ring* in 1882, and *Parsifal* in 1883. This was the

[3] KGSB, p. 92.

scheme he put before a meeting of some twenty delegates from the Vereine in Bayreuth on the 15th September, at the conclusion of which the statutes of a new Patronatverein were drawn up. One of the delegates was Ludwig Schemann, the future apostle of Gobineau, who met Wagner on this occasion for the first time. He saw a good deal of him then and in the following years, and he records a fact that always struck him — the great difference between Wagner's manner in a small circle of people who really understood him and were devoted to him and his manner in more miscellaneous gatherings. The remark throws a good deal of light on the summer of 1876, when, as Schuré observed, he had to handle diplomatically the motley crowd that surged in and out of Wahnfried, and Nietzsche took pettish offence at not finding him on those occasions the Sarastro whom he had known at Triebschen. To the delegates he read the poem of *Parsifal* — a thing he would never have dreamed of doing at one of Cosima's crowded receptions; and Schemann adds his testimony to that of many people who, year after year, were moved by Wagner's incomparable reading of his own works almost beyond anything they felt afterwards in the theatre. Schemann particularly remembered twenty-five years later the effect of Amfortas's lament in Wagner's sorrowfully ecstatic rendering of it; never again, he says, did he experience a comparable emotion except on one occasion when Karl Hill sang the scene in private.[4]

4

At the open session, held on the stage of the theatre, Wagner addressed the delegates for half an hour before he read out his detailed plan for the School.[5] Franz Muncker managed to take the speech down in shorthand, in spite of the fact that Wagner spoke very rapidly.

He made it clear that it was only through stress of circumstances that he had abandoned his primary intention of giving the festival of 1876 before the Patrons only and thrown it open to the public. But this concession of his had placed the festival in a false light, and exposed him and his Committee to the charge of aiming at a financial success of the ordinary kind; while the reports of the Press,

---

[4] SERW, p. 16 ff.
[5] This will be found in RWGS, X, 16–18.

which had attended only the first cycle, had discouraged people from attending the second. Even the majority of his Patrons did not grasp his real aim: the general feeling among them was, "The thing has been done; it has been a great success; the Kaiser and the princes have honoured Wagner with their presence: what more does the man want?" Whereas his sole thought, then and after, had been how to rescue the undertaking from this falsifying atmosphere and restore it to its original purity of conception.

When the amount of the deficit became known, he continued, everyone had failed him. In November, 1876 he had sent out a printed statement of the case to the Patrons: the only practical result of it all was that "Herr Plüddemann's aunt in Coblentz" sent him 100 marks. The Munich authorities had jibbed at taking over the Bayreuth theatre, on the ground that it would cost them much more to run than it had cost him, for *he* could always count on a good deal of free co-operation on the part of his artists: moreover, as the festivals would be held during the summer months, the Intendanz would be in the peculiar position, so far as singers and players from the Munich theatre were concerned, of having to pay them twice over during their holidays, which would be very expensive. The Reichstag, and even the Vereine, having proved unhelpful, his Committee had fancied the plan of public admission to the festivals by ticket — which would mean that speculators in such things would at once get busy, as they had done in 1876 in Bayreuth itself, even complimentary passes having been advertised in the local *Tagblatt* for sale at high prices! Every scheme suggested, however, had foundered on some rock or other, and in the end *he* had had to try to save the sinking ship by his own efforts. To pay off the most pressing creditors he had had to raise a personal loan of 32,000 marks at five per cent interest.[6] The London concerts had brought in something more; and that was virtually all. The Munich Intendanz had offered to shoulder the deficit if he would allow the *Ring* to be given there with the Bayreuth décor. But, said Wagner, much of the Bayreuth scenery and machinery could not be adapted to any other stage. Such of it as could be moved was already the property of King Ludwig so long as the loan granted by the Kabinetskasse remained unliquidated. As for granting Munich the right to perform the *Ring*, that right was already the King's in virtue of the agreement of 1864;

[6] This was evidently in connection with Cosima's legacy from her mother.

it had only been through his Majesty's good will, indeed, that he had been able to give the work in Bayreuth.

In all, the King had advancced some 200,000 marks towards the cost of the theatre, and the greater part of the burden of the huge deficit on the festival of 1876 now lay on Wagner's shoulders. They had accomplished much: they owned the building, they had proved the necessity of such a theatre in such a place, and they had shown that a production of the *Ring* was feasible. But beyond this, a second festival would mean their starting all over again from the beginning. He could not "invite" a second time the co-operation of his artists. Though it went against the grain with him, he had listened to his Committee's suggestion for discharging the debt of the first festival by giving a second on purely business lines, and he had authorised them to approach the singers of 1876. Many of them were willing to come again, for this time they would be properly paid, and they had suggested "not bad" figures for their honoraria. But others had declined a second festival, on the ground that their unfriendly Intendants would not grant them the same privilege in the matter of absence as in 1876. In view of all these difficulties and risks Wagner must be excused from "playing the impresario" again. His ideal still was to create an art and found a style of a type impossible in the wretched ordinary German theatre; and the road to that goal lay through the projected new Music School. So he asked the delegates to say frankly whether they would be content to work slowly and patiently with him along that line, or whether they merely wanted to troop to Bayreuth every now and then "to see something extraordinary". If the latter, then it would be better for him and for them to part company at once.[7]

5

The formal plan put before the delegates was designed to train performers not only for Wagner's works but for "all good dramatic works of distinctively German masters"; the Bayreuth course would consist first of all of an education in "the proper mental conception" of each work and "the higher mode of rendering it". There was also to be a school for higher pianists, who, under Wagner's own guidance, would study the great German instrumental works

---

[7] Muncker's report of the speech will be found in RWJK, 1886, pp. 200–208.

with a view to becoming conductors. If possible, in the third quarter of 1878 an orchestra was to be got together to study both purely instrumental delivery — particularly quartet style — and the accompanying of dramatic singers; and there would be lectures designed to foster an understanding of the true "German style" necessary for the performance of German music.

But this scheme, like so many others of his, foundered on the rock of his compatriots' indifference to his lofty ideal. The Press and the majority of the professional musicians were against him. The theatres were interested in him only commercially, as the greatest box-office attraction of the day. Several of them wanted only the *Valkyrie;* others were willing to undertake the whole *Ring,* but made the usual maddening stipulation that the *Valkyrie* should be played first.[8] Of his larger aims no one seemed to have any understanding; and so, by the end of the year, he was forced to abandon the idea of the School, the financial minimum for the founding of it not having been forthcoming. On the 8th December he announced to the Patrons and the members of the Vereine a sort of "compensation" for the failure of the School plan — the founding of a journal, the *Bayreuther Blätter,* that should serve as a mouthpiece for himself and those who thought and felt with him.

It was the realisation of an idea that had obsessed him for many years. He found an editor after his own heart in Hans von Wolzogen, a young man of twenty-nine in 1877 whose private means enabled him to settle permanently in Bayreuth and devote his life to the cause of Wagner.[9] The new magazine, the first number of which appeared in February, 1878, was intended to be free of the usual publishing interests and of dependence on advertisements or public

---

[8] Jauner had virtually blackmailed him, in the end, into allowing the *Valkyrie* to be given in Vienna on the 5th March (1877), the price for the concession being Materna. Towards the end of the month Jauner sent Richter to Wahnfried to negotiate for the remainder of the *Ring.* Richter took with him 20,000 marks as first part-payment for the rights. Liszt, who was staying in Wahnfried at the time, tells us that Wagner rejected the proposal and the money categorically.

A few days later Jauner tried blackmail again. Learning that Richter was indispensable to Wagner for the London concerts, he did his best to barter his Kapellmeister for the *Ring* rights, and apparently only changed his tone when Wagner told Richter that, if Jauner persisted in behaving like this, he himself would inform Prince Hohenlohe (Marie Wittgenstein's husband) that Vienna would *never* get permission to give the *Ring* so long as Jauner remained director of the Court Theatre. (See RWHR, p. 155). After that, thanks in part to Standhartner's diplomacy, relations with Vienna became more friendly.

[9] He died, at the age of ninety, in 1938.

sales. Wagner introduced it with an article in which he poured out his contempt for the Press and the public of the big cities. Salvation, he held, could come only from the tiny towns that represented the real Germany, and from a nucleus of right-minded people who would turn their backs disdainfully on the State theatres, the High Schools of Music, and the concert halls and other places in which bad style had become traditional. And at the end of his article he announced *Parsifal* for the summer of 1880, "in circumstances similar to those of the first *Ring* — only this time, make no mistake about it, solely *among ourselves!*" To the King, at the year's end, he wrote:

> "I have no more hopes for that 'German spirit' in which I placed my trust when I penned the dedication of my *Ring*. I have had my experience, and — I am silent. I build no hope either on Pommern or on the Mark Brandenburg, or on any other province of this curious German Reich: I no longer build any hope even on the Margraviate of Bayreuth. I simply conclude a peace with the world, the first clause of which runs, 'Leave me in quiet'!"

All he asks is to be left alone to cherish the consolatory illusion of his *Parsifal*.

6

Meanwhile they had been doing some hard thinking in Munich. Wagner's idea in handing over the Bayreuth *Ring* to the Intendanz had been that something might be spared from the takings for the liquidation of the Bayreuth debt. But, as Düfflipp told the King in October, it was doubtful whether that would be possible unless the whole of the Bayreuth apparatus, scenery and costumes could be utilised in Munich, as otherwise they would have to face an expenditure of not less than 120,000 marks, for the covering of which they would have to look to the receipts. Still, there was a manifest desire on the part of the Intendanz to help Wagner in some way or other. Its first approach to him had not been conspicuously generous. In November (1877) Feustel saw Perfall in Munich, when the Intendant suggested the payment to Wagner of a royalty of one per cent on the Court Theatre performances of his works. This Feustel declined, in part, no doubt, because he thought it niggardly — for the Theatre had done very well out of Wagner — but laying most stress on the argument that it would mean little in relation to the large Bayreuth debt, and the creditors were threatening to take action at the end of the year if their claims were not met by then. But Feustel saw clearly enough that it was only by way of royalties that the problem would ever be solved; and on the 15th January (1878) he laid the whole case before Cosima and suggested that she should write direct to the King. Of the debt of 147,851 marks, he said, 49,823 had now been paid off, leaving a balance of 98,028 marks (exclusive of overdue interest). It would be impossible, he said, for him to stave off legal proceedings much longer.

"I see only one way of avoiding a catastrophe — for the Munich Court Theatre to grant your husband a royalty on his works for, say, ten years, with a total of 10,000 marks per annum. By this means a capital would be acquired which, with the addition of the amount received from the sale of the restaurant, would liquidate everything."

On the 16th, evidently at Feustel's verbal suggestion, Cosima, unknown to Wagner, wrote to Ludwig, enclosing Feustel's letter and entreating him to give it his favourable consideration.[10] The final decisive step appears to have been taken by Perfall, who, in a memorandum of the 25th to the King, pointed out that for many years the Munich Theatre had profited handsomely by Wagner's works without the composer himself having benefited financially. He therefore suggested that Wagner should receive a royalty of ten per cent on the gross receipts from all future performances of his works until the Bayreuth deficit — now estimated, he says, at 98,634 marks — should be completely covered, and that Wagner should agree to *Parsifal* being produced either in Bayreuth with the Munich singers and orchestra or with that personnel in Munich itself.

At the commencement of 1878 Düfflipp's health necessitated his laying down an office which he had discharged for so many years with such scrupulous regard for the King's and the country's interests and such sympathy and patience where Wagner was concerned.[11] He was succeeded by Ludwig von Bürkel, the government assessor to the Department of Police. Glasenapp is warm in his praise of this gentleman's "admiration of Wagner's art and person", this "able and adroit, good and faithful man who was equally un-

---

[10] The two letters will be found in KLRWB, IV, 217–8.

[11] He seems to have tendered his resignation in October, 1877. Apparently one of his reasons for resigning was that he could not conscientiously acquiesce in a course of action on the King's part that was bringing him nearer every year to bankruptcy. See BLKB, pp. 353, 594–595.

derstanding of and equally devoted to both parties" [the King and Wagner]. The modern historians of Bavaria, however, see him in a rather different light. According to Böhm, Bürkel did not share his predecessor's scruples where the balancing of the royal finances was concerned,

> "and did not shrink either from the incurring of fresh debts or from drawing upon the trust fund left by King Max II, thus opening out new sources of revenue for a short time, after the exhaustion of which he retired, covered with orders and titles, leaving the Treasury marching with giant strides towards ruin. The sources tapped in this way naturally facilitated a more generous support of the Bayreuth undertaking, without Wagner incurring any of the blame laid, both when the crash came and earlier, by Düfflipp, a part of the Liberal Press, and all true friends of the King and the monarchy, on this new adviser of the crown."

7

The remainder of the story of the Bayreuth debt can be briefly told. The King's letters show his affection and admiration for Wagner to have been as warm as ever. But as it was utterly beyond his power to help him financially out of his own resources, the only means of salvation was the one indicated by Perfall. On the 31st March (1878) an agreement was signed, at the instance of the King, between the Intendanz and the Court Secretariat of the first part and Wagner and the Bayreuth Committee of the second part, the clauses of which may be summarised as follows:

I. The Committee certifies that the outstanding debt in respect of the festival of 1876 amounts to 98,634 marks, 65 pfennigs.

II. The Committee will raise ready cash to repay this by contracting a loan at $4\frac{1}{2}$ (or at most 5) per cent interest, with repayment of the principal in regular instalments.

III. The King decrees that 10 per cent of the gross receipts from all performances of Wagner's operas in the Munich Court Theatre from the 1st January, 1878 shall be devoted to discharging the loan.

IV. Wagner gives the Intendanz the assurance, accepted on its behalf by the Court Secretariat, that he long ago conveyed to his Majesty the right to produce all his works in the Court Theatre without payment, and recognises that the concession made in Clause III is a wholly voluntary one on the King's part, without any legal obligation.

V. On his Majesty's behalf the assurance is given that the royalties referred to in Clause III will be paid until the debt is completely liquidated, and that until this object is achieved the payments made by the Intendanz shall not be less than 6,000 marks per annum. When the debt referred to in Clause I is fully paid off, future royalties shall be devoted to repaying the King's advance of 214,000 marks.

VI. At Wagner's request, the assurance is given on behalf of his Majesty that if, after the repayment of the deficit mentioned in Clause I, the yearly stipend of 8,000 florins (13,715 marks) now payable to him should be suspended, the legal royalties on the performance of his operas secured him by the Reich enactment of the 11th June, 1870 shall accrue to him or his heirs.

VII. Wagner and the Committee undertake that they will try to dismantle and sell the two restaurants near the Bayreuth theatre as soon as possible, the proceeds to go towards the liquidation of the loan referred to in Clause II; and the Court Secretariat is to be kept fully informed with regard to the sale and supplied with the relative vouchers.

VIII. Wagner contracts with the Intendanz that the first performance of his *Parsifal* in Bayreuth shall be given with the orchestra, the singers and the artistic personnel of the Court Theatre, which Theatre shall afterwards have unrestricted right to produce the work without any further obligation as regards royalties than that set forth in Clause III.

IX. For *Parsifal,* Wagner shall be at liberty to supplement the Munich forces from outside quarters as he may think fit, and to keep his promises with regard to the first production of the work already made to the members of the Wagner Vereine.

X. All expenses for the *Parsifal* rehearsals and performances in Bayreuth, together with the cost of maintenance of the building, fire insurance, etc. until 1880 [12] shall be defrayed out of the funds in hand for those purposes.

XI. The Court Secretariat will guarantee to the granters of the loan referred to in Clause II that the royalties set forth in Clauses III and V will be duly paid to them until the whole loan is discharged.

---

[12] The projected year for the first performance.

Glasenapp gives Feustel, Muncker and Bürkel the whole credit for this agreement of the 31st March. It is difficult to say what hand, if any, Bürkel had in the discussions that culminated in the agreement. It is certain that the new Court Secretary was well-disposed towards Wagner from the start — perhaps because he saw that friendliness to him would be a sure passport to the King's favour. Glasenapp implies that it was Cosima's letter of the 16th January to the King that turned the scales. Perfall's memorandum to Ludwig of the 25th January, however, contains no suggestion of any pressure from above. On the contrary, it says that "after ripe reflection", following on Feustel's appeal for help in the preceding December, Perfall had come to the conclusion that Wagner *should* be helped, and accordingly, having regard to the profits the Theatre had made out of the composer's works, he "recommends" the payment to him of a royalty of ten per cent on future performances. It was not until the 27th — i.e., after the receipt of Perfall's memorandum — that the King replied to Cosima, saying that immediately after receiving her letter he had communicated with his Court Secretary, who would at once proceed, with Feustel and Perfall, to arrange for the liquidation of the Bayreuth debt in the manner suggested. Glasenapp, of course, would be none too willing to give Perfall any credit for good intentions where Wagner was concerned.

8

This, then, was the sharply realistic ending to Wagner's dream in 1850 of "the German spirit" voluntarily "co-operating" with him in the achievement of his ideal! In the strictest sense of the words, it was he who paid for conferring Bayreuth on a frigid and largely hostile German world.[13] But at any rate, thanks to the only man who really understood him — the "mad" King of Bavaria — he could now sleep at night unracked by cares of all kinds, and devote what remained of his health to the completion of his *Parsifal*. It was with a heart full of gratitude that he wrote to Feustel on the 3rd February,

[13] It would be interesting to know exactly how much would have accrued to Wagner between the date of the agreement of 1864 and the year 1878 had he received royalties on all the performances of his works in Munich during those fourteen years. Perhaps, if we knew all the facts, it would turn out that he had fully earned his "stipend".

"For today, dear friend, I wish to express my glad thanks to *you* for the extraordinary patience, wisdom and energy you have displayed in dealing with my sorry position as regards the Bayreuth deficit; although it is the King's noble friendship for me that has achieved the result, it is to your efforts that I owe the successful accomplishment of it. This satisfactory turn is all the more agreeable to me as fundamentally it is owing to the expected success of my own work that we are now provided with the means to stand up against the dreadful material results of the year 1876. That is honourable . . . The chief gain is that now I shall be able to devote myself to new creation with the equanimity without which the good spirits take flight from us queer 'geniuses' ".[14]

The agreement of the 31st March, 1878 was obviously a business document designed to cover, as business documents should, all possible contingencies. There was never any real fear that the King would permit a public performance of *Parsifal* in Munich: he had too much respect for Wagner's wishes for that. But after Wagner's death he gave orders (in September, 1883), for the work to be produced three times for him alone in the Court Theatre in the spring of 1884. (He had not attended the Bayreuth performances of 1882). He had hoped to hear it with the Bayreuth cast, but when the time came Materna, Scaria and Winkelmann broke their contracts with Munich for the sake of more profitable engagements in America. For the rest, the three performances, which took place on the 3rd, 5th and 7th May, 1884, were given mainly with the Bayreuth forces. Levi conducted, and Fritz Brandt (son of Karl Brandt) and others of the Bayreuth personnel were in charge of the scenic arrangements. The Bayreuth scenery and apparatus were borrowed. Further private performances followed on the 5th and 7th November, 1884 and the 26th, 27th and 29th April, 1885; these were mainly entrusted to the Munich forces. (The King died in June, 1886). The cost of the performances in May 1884 was 67,735 marks; that of the November performances of the same year 100,887 marks.

In an article, *Schatullen-Geheimnisse Wahnfrieds*, in the *Rheinisch-Westfälische Zeitung* of the 3rd September, 1933, Josef M. Jurinek gave the authentic figures from the Wahnfried account-books of the theatre royalties earned by the Wagner operas during the thirty years from 1883 (the year of the composer's death) to

---

[14] The documents relating to the long negotiations with Munich will be found in RLW, II, 161–183.

the centenary of his birth, 1913. The figures testify to Wagner's enormous popularity and his financial value to the opera houses of the world, more particularly when it is taken into account that, as Jurinek says,

> "eleven of the largest German Court (or State) Theatres paid, in general, no royalties on Wagner's older works, as the Master had surrendered his scores to these theatres in return for a first and final payment of 10 louisdor. Furthermore, many of the theatres paid a royalty of only three per cent."

The royalties received from 1883–1913 totalled 6,120,193 marks. The figures for Munich for 1892, 1893, 1894 and 1895 are apparently not available, but are estimated at 175,000 marks. The grand total from Munich alone is 590,000 marks. On the whole, the town did very well out of Wagner.

It may be added, for the benefit of the malicious-minded, that the Wagner family has never profited by a pfennig from the Bayreuth festivals. The receipts have been handed over to the Festival Fund; the expenses have been borne privately. "I know", said Jurinek, "the total amount expended up to 1914, but am pledged to silence with regard to it, as Wahnfried 'does not wish to make a parade of sacrifices'."

CHAPTER XXX

THE BREACH WITH NIETZSCHE

1

FROM 1877 onwards all was going well with the *Ring* so far as the German theatres were concerned. Schwerin, a town of no great size, gave the *Valkyrie* with enormous success in January, 1878, special trains bringing in enthusiasts from many places in the neighbourhood, including Berlin. For a long time Wagner was plagued by requests for the *Valkyrie,* either alone or as a preliminary to a complete *Ring.* With Schwerin, as with Vienna, he had had to give way on this point, for there also he was powerless in the hands of the blackmailers, the Schwerin theatre having demanded the *Valkyrie* as the price for Hill's release for the London concerts of 1877; whereupon other opera houses, not knowing the special circumstances, assumed that they were entitled to a similar concession. Vienna, after some twenty-five performances of the *Valkyrie,* ventured upon the *Rhinegold* towards the end of January, 1878, but did not achieve the *Götterdämmerung* until February of the following year. Weimar, Cologne, Mannheim, Brunswick and Hamburg made intrepid nibbles at this or that section of the work in 1878 and 1879. Munich produced *Siegfried,* with a new décor by Jank and Döll, on the 10th June, 1878, the *Götterdämmerung* following on the 15th September; both works were conducted by Hermann Levi. The whole *Ring* was given in Munich in November of that year, and repeated in May, 1879 and later. Some private performances were also given for King Ludwig; and it was in one of these that Ferdinand Jäger, a young tenor who was to be closely associated in after years not only with the Wagner works but with the songs of Hugo Wolf, appeared as Siegfried.

In January, 1878 the irrepressible Neumann had turned up once more at Wahnfried, and gone away with a contract in his pocket for a production of the *Ring* in Leipzig, the *Rhinegold* and *Valkyrie* to be given on the 28th and 29th April, *Siegfried* and the *Götter-*

dämmerung on the 21st and 22nd September. Wagner, who had soon seen that Neumann, a rare combination of the idealist and the practician, was a man to be relied upon, became so docile in his tactful hands as to write down the contract from his dictation: it provided for a ten per cent royalty on the takings, with an advance of 10,000 marks, to be paid in three instalments between the date of the signing of the contract and the 1st April, 1879, and liquidated by a deduction of half the royalties as they fell due until the whole pre-payment was covered. The agreement was carried out by Neumann down to the last detail, each section of the work being produced on the precise date specified, with Sucher as conductor. He had assembled a company that brought to light more than one young artist who was later to achieve fame, among them Joseph Lederer (Siegmund), Marie Widl (Brynhilde), Julius Lieban (the incomparable Bayreuth Mime of later years), and a young man who had been playing among the second violins at Vienna, and whom Neumann, on the recommendation of Otto Dessoff, took on first of all as chorus master. His name was Artur Nikisch.

To the *Ring* rehearsals Wagner sent Richter and Seidl to spy out the land. They went prepared to curse, but remained to pray: "Magnificent!" Richter wired to Wagner; "Neumann has done marvellously!" For the *Siegfried* and *Götterdämmerung* performances Wagner tried to induce Neumann to substitute Seidl for Sucher as conductor; but to this he could not consent, nor was it possible for him to engage Jäger as Siegfried, as the composer had suggested. Unger, towards whom Wagner had cooled a good deal since his experiences with him in London, sang Siegfried in the final sections of the tetralogy in Leipzig. Seidl, in whom Wagner, as he told Förster, had now more confidence than in any other conductor, obtained an appointment in Vienna, where, however, for some reason or other he was not a success. Later he became closely associated with Neumann, who summed him up, when writing his memoirs, as "one of the most highly gifted of Wagner conductors".[1]

2

"The battle of Leipzig", as Wagner gaily called it, having been thus brilliantly won, Neumann now planned to repeat his *Ring* per-

---

[1] In the English edition this becomes "the most wonderful of Wagner conductors".

formances at the Berlin Opera. Wagner approved of the project, but, having no faith in the Berlin authorities, made it a condition that the performances should be given with the Leipzig orchestra. "I assure you", he wrote to Neumann, "that in no circumstances short of a complete transformation in Berlin, the general director-ship [Hülsen] included, will I entrust my *Nibelungen* to the Prussian Royal Opera." Neumann foresaw that both in Berlin and in Leipzig objections would be raised to the employment of the Leipzig orchestra, but he loyally pledged himself not to run counter to Wagner's wishes in any way. For the time being, consequently, the project came to nothing.

Neumann then thought of the Viktoria Theatre as the best locale for his ambitious Berlin venture, in which, in May, 1881, Materna was to be the Brynhilde, Therese Vogl the Sieglinde, Vogl the Loge and Siegmund, Jäger the Siegfried, and Otto Schelper the Wotan and Hagen; the orchestra, under Seidl, would be a combination of the Leipzig and the Meiningen forces. Neumann, as a matter of courtesy, informed Hülsen of this scheme, and received the reply that although Hülsen still regarded the *Valkyrie* as the only feasible section of the *Ring*, he had allowed himself to be convinced by Neumann's arguments: "if I cannot hinder the production of the *Nibelungen* in Berlin, I would prefer it to be in my theatre rather than in the Viktoria." After a long conference with Neumann he promised to lay the "sublime plan" before the Kaiser, without whose sanction nothing further could be done. This sanction was obtained; but meanwhile, apparently, Hülsen had begun to have his doubts as to the "technical details" — "the more I think about the matter, the less I believe it possible to get a technical production worthy of the Royal Opera House."

Thereupon Neumann went to Bayreuth to acquaint Wagner with the newest developments. Wagner at first refused to have anything to do with the Royal Opera, but was won over in the end by Cosima and Neumann, the latter assuring him that he also would decline to work with Berlin unless he were convinced that the production would be in accordance with Wagner's wishes. On the 30th November (1880) he put his case frankly and uncompromisingly before Hülsen. He wanted to be sure that, in view of the Director's notorious coolness towards the *Ring*, and other forces in the Opera House being known to be ill-disposed towards Wagner, he could count on

sufficient enthusiasm inside the theatre if difficulties arose: if Hülsen thought these would prove insurmountable he was to say so
candidly then and there. Hülsen's reply was to the effect that while he
could not guarantee "enthusiasm" on his own part he would do his
best, though after what Brandt had told him he was doubtful about
the possibility of the solution of the technical problems of the *Ring*
on the Berlin stage. But reading between the lines, he continued, it
seemed to him that Neumann wished to withdraw his offer because
Wagner was set on the performances taking place in the Viktoria
Theatre. (This, of course, was not the case now). On the 5th December Neumann inspected the Royal Opera stage with his Leipzig
machinist and came to the conclusion that all would be well there.
Then a fresh difficulty arose; he had to insist on both rehearsals
and performances being conducted by Seidl, but this, it appeared,
would have been contrary to the regulation prohibiting the Opera
orchestra from playing under anyone but a Kapellmeister with a
royal appointment. This little problem was solved, however, by
Seidl being given, with the Kaiser's consent, a Berlin engagement
for three months.

Then Hülsen threw fresh grit into the machinery. He proposed,
he said, to wire to Wagner that it was settled that the *Ring* should
be produced with a combination of the Berlin and Leipzig orchestras under Seidl, *provided Hülsen were granted the right to give the
'Valkyrie' alone later*. Knowing Wagner as he did, Neumann warned
the Director against this step: Wagner would not vouchsafe a reply,
he told him, for the request was equivalent to saying to him, "Your
Rhinegold, Siegfried and *Götterdämmerung* are worthless". "He
must reply", said Hülsen; "it would be rude of him not to." But at
their next meeting he had to confess that Neumann had been right:
"the fellow hasn't replied. I shall have to inform his Majesty." On
the 9th December a telegram reached Neumann from Berlin —
"Certain insurmountable obstacles in the way of our plan. Definite
decision Monday"; this was followed on the 11th by another —
"Regret to say I must withdraw irrevocably. Forgive me, but it can't
be helped." A request on Neumann's part for a personal talk was
bluntly refused; and in a following letter Hülsen explained that the
Kaiser had agreed with him that "the question of the conductor"
and "the unbecoming behaviour of the composer" had between them
"turned the scale". Hülsen had been further annoyed by some "dis-

reputable sheet" or other having given the affair an unpleasant publicity, perhaps on the strength of gossip it had picked up at the
Landvogt restaurant.

That is the story as told by Neumann in his memoirs. Recently
some fresh light has been thrown on the matter.[2] It appears that
there had been a cabal against the scheme among the leading singers of the Opera. On the 9th December a circular signed by Betz,
Lilli Lehmann, Mathilde Mallinger, Niemann and the basso buffo
August Fricke had been distributed among the company, inviting
them to a meeting at Betz's house on the 11th to discuss the implied
insult to them all in this plan to give the *Ring* in Berlin with "forces
from outside", and to consider what means they could devise to
ward off a "calamity" of that sort. After the meeting a letter was
sent to Hülsen informing him of the "shattering effect" on the signatories to it of the news that the *Ring* was to be given in May, 1881
under Neumann's direction, with singers imported from Munich
and other towns, some of the local singers, the Royal Opera orchestra and chorus, and Seidl as conductor. This portentous document
was signed by Marianne Brandt, Lilli Lehmann, Minna Lammert,
Mathilde Mallinger, Wilma von Voggenhuber, Betz, Niemann,
Fricke and fifteen others.[3]

Hülsen, in his reply, opined that the decision of the Kaiser and
himself with regard to the *Ring* production would not have had so
shattering an effect on the Berlin singers but for the gossip current
in certain beer houses frequented by the male members of the company, gossip reprinted, with embellishments, in some irresponsible
sheets for the delectation of the scandal-hungry public. Though he
was under no obligation, he said, to account to the Opera personnel
for his way of directing the theatre, he would tell them frankly the
facts of the case. For his own part he regarded a production of the
Ring in its entirety as a pre-requisite step towards getting the composer's permission to give the *Valkyrie*, "which in my opinion is
the only section of the tetralogy likely to maintain its place in the
repertory". As for the present plan, it was his conviction that it
could not be carried through without some reinforcement of the
local personnel; and as for the décor, that was a matter not within

---

[2] In an article by A. Laszlo, Betz's son-in-law, on *Die geplanten Aufführungen des
Nibelungenringes auf der Berliner Kgl. Opernbühne*, in the *Signale* of the 28th May,
1930.

[3] Lilli Lehmann is discreetly silent about this matter in her memoirs.

the competence of the malcontents. He had not been pleased, however, with Wagner's insistence on the engagement of Seidl, nor with the composer's "unbecoming conduct" in not replying to his enquiry regarding the *Valkyrie;* so after taking all the circumstances into consideration he had come to the conclusion that the *Ring* production was "impossible", and had advised the Kaiser accordingly. From the remainder of his letter it is fairly clear that while Hülsen resented the singers' attempt to dictate to him he was secretly glad that they had given him so plausible an excuse for closing down on the negotiations with Neumann.[4]

Ten years earlier an incident like this would have fretted and embittered Wagner; but now, preoccupied with *Parsifal* as he was, he could take it all calmly. He remained mostly undisturbed also by another and more serious matter — his final breach with Nietzsche, which occurred in the summer of 1878.

3

In *Ecce Homo* Nietzsche paints a heroic picture of the breach as he chose to see it some years later. He tells us, in his usual grandiloquent style, that when *Human, All-too Human* was published he sent two copies to Bayreuth.

"Thanks to a miracle of intelligence on the part of Chance, there reached me simultaneously a fine copy of the *Parsifal* text, with an inscription from Wagner — 'To his dear Friend Friedrich Nietzsche, from Richard Wagner, Higher Ecclesiastical Councillor'. In this crossing of the two books I seemed to hear an ominous note. Did it not sound as if two swords had crossed? At all events we both felt it to be so, for each of us remained silent. At about this time the first *Bayreuther Blätter* appeared: then I understood *for what* it had become high time. Incredible! Wagner had turned pious."

The harmless banter of the "Ecclesiastical Councillor" was lost on him; the flippancy of it, the suggestion that Wagner was poking fun at him — at him, Friedrich Nietzsche! — was an outrage.

[4] Betz, of course — "the matador", as Wagner called him — could not let the opportunity go by to bellow back at Hülsen that his personal honour had been outraged by the suggestion that *he* frequented beer houses, and that he would not have his private life criticised by anyone, even the Herr Director himself. His letter of the 17th December reminds us curiously of that of the 1st September, 1869 to Perfall à propos of the Munich *Rhinegold*. The man was evidently an arrogant, ill-tempered bully, bursting with a sense of his own importance, and always looking about him for a grievance and a pretext for throwing his weight about.

But there was no "crossing of swords". The *Parsifal* poem was sent to Nietzsche in the last days of 1877: *Human, All-too Human* was not published until May, 1878; so that the swords missed each other by a matter of more than four months.[5] As usual, Nietzsche is quite untrustworthy as regards his facts, owing to his habit of melo-dramatising himself and Wagner in his later years and casting him-self for the star rôle. In 1878 his reactions were not at all those with which he credited — or discredited — himself ten years later, as is shown by his letter of the 4th January (1878) to his friend Seydlitz. In this he discussed the lately arrived *Parsifal* poem quite objectively, even if his excursion into prophecy was far from happy. Its Christianism, he said, was alien to him as a lover of the Greek spirit; and on that matter, of course, he had every right to his own point of view. He blundered badly, however, as to the practicability of the opera.

> "Much that is bearable by the inner eye", he opined, "will hardly be tolerable in performance: think of our actors praying, trembling, with ecstatically straining throats. The interior of the Castle of the Grail *cannot* be effective on the stage, any more than the wounded swan. All these fine inventions belong to the epic, and, as I have said, are for the inner eye. The language reads like a translation from a foreign tongue. But tne situations and the enchainment of them — is not all this poetry of the highest kind? Is it not a last challenge to music?" [6]

Plainly he was not so rabidly prejudiced at that time against the work as he became later. Nor is there anything here of the tone that makes most of his public references to Wagner in the latest years so offensive. Much as he disliked the religious milieu of the opera, in 1878 he could at all events make an effort to see it in the terms that alone really matter, those of an aim set and an aim achieved in art. And if for the most part he failed in this, it was an honest and not in the least discreditable failure. Bülow went astray in somewhat similar fashion when, in his letter to Cosima thanking her for a presentation copy of the poem, he jibbed at the words with

[5] Constrained to admit this, Frau Förster-Nietzsche pleads that possibly her brother had confused the date of the despatch of his book to Wagner with the date of his sending part of the manuscript to the publisher. "In general his memory for facts was defective, which accounts for many errors. His mind was continually occupied with such momentous problems that actual events did not impress them-selves on it." Well and good; but she never had any hesitation in relying on this faulty memory of his whenever it suited her purpose to do so.

[6] NGB, I, 421.

which the stage action of the first act closes, the words in which the disappointed Gurnemanz roughly dismisses the long-mute Parsifal:

> Thou art no·more than a fool!
> Hie thee hence, get thee gone from us!
> Take this from Gurnemanz:
> leave thou our swans for the future alone,
> and seek thyself, gander, a goose.

To no one in the theatre today does it occur to smile when he hears those last two lines: the verbal homeliness of them is spiritually transfigured, as Cosima rightly noted in her diary after receiving Bülow's letter, by the music that follows them — the soft, heart-searching throb of the wistful "Pity" theme from the mystic heights of the hall. It was impossible, of course, for Bülow or Nietzsche or anyone else to realise years in advance how the music of the opera would again and again achieve a conviction which the mere reader of the poem might judge to be a priori impossible.

4

Only Nietzsche is to blame for the unpleasant portrait he un-wittingly paints of himself in the last writings of his devoted to Wagner. His behaviour in 1878 had been dignified and delicate. Though he could have no doubt by now that his way and Wagner's must henceforth diverge, he still loved the older man and respected his idealism and his towering genius too much to be vulgarly dis-courteous to him. He parted from him, indeed, with a great deal of regret at its being inevitable, for his own conscience' sake, that he should have to alienate him by his scientific freethinking. For Wag-ner, too, the feeling that the idyll of love, friendship and confidence that had begun at Triebschen was now at an end was at first very painful. One day he could say angrily to Cosima, "It is no great honour to me that this man has praised me" — a sentiment to which posterity has given its cordial assent, — but on the morrow she would find him grieving over what he regarded as Nietzsche's "de-fection", over the gradual narrowing of the always small circle in which he felt he was understood, and in which he could bestow affec-tion and have it returned; and Cosima has testified that for a while this "defection" tortured him even in his dreams.

At first he could not bring himself to read the book through, though he seems to have done so a little later. We can see now that in more than one quarter the suspicion was already forming, among the people who stood nearest to Nietzsche, that all was not well with him mentally. In June, 1878, soon after the arrival of *Human, All-too Human,* Wagner received a visit from Dr. Otto Eiser, a Frankfort physician whom Nietzsche had recently consulted with benefit to himself; and from a letter of mid-June from Cosima to Malwida von Meysenbug it is clear that Eiser had told Wagner that he regarded *Human, All-too Human* as "marking the beginning of mental derangement". That, of course, does not of itself make sense for us now: there was nothing wrong with Nietzsche's intellectual apparatus when he was writing that book. But Eiser, though perhaps not to be accepted as an authority in matters of philosophy, may well have been speaking with some assurance from his purely professional observation of his patient: he had seen him at close quarters, had perhaps received certain confidences, and from one or two physical symptoms may have prognosed already the collapse of some ten years later. There can be no doubt that more than one of Nietzsche's closest friends was tormented in the late 1870's by the fear that some evil was threatening him. This is evident enough from a letter of Wagner's of the 24th May, 1878 to Nietzsche's Basel colleague Professor Franz Overbeck — obviously in reply to some anxious comments by the latter:

> "From your cursory hints I gather that our old friend keeps himself aloof from you also. Some startling changes have assuredly taken place in him; and those of us who have had the opportunity to observe him for years in his psychical convulsions would almost be justified in saying that a long-threatened but not unexpected catastrophe has come upon him." [7]

---

[7] BBW, 1909, No 1. The words "long-threatened but not unexpected catastrophe" are significant. Elisabeth's frantic efforts to mislead her readers as to the basic cause of her brother's collapse in 1888 deceive few people today. It seems probable that several of his friends, Wagner among them, suspected, if they did not actually know, the disease from which he was suffering. In this connection a letter of Houston Stewart Chamberlain's to Cosima of the 11th August, 1900 (WHSC, p. 602) has a curious interest. Chamberlain tells her of an old friend of his, the musician Adolf Ruthardt, who saw a great deal of Nietzsche in Sils-Maria in the summer of 1885. "The man will certainly go insane, if he is not so already", he told Chamberlain afterwards; and he made some "confidential communications" about what he called the "secret" of Nietzsche's life. The medical reader who is interested in the subject will find the records of the Jena clinic in which Nietzsche was placed in 1889 in the journal *Die medizinische Welt* for the 4th October, 1930, No. 40, pp. 1452–4.

Yet, knowing all this as he did, it was Wagner who gave the now strained threads of their friendship the final trifling twist that snapped them. In the April, June and August numbers of the *Bayreuther Blätter* there appeared three articles on *Public and Popularity* which, though unsigned, were manifestly from his pen.[8] The first two, which have no connection with Nietzsche, are packed with the soundest sense with regard to the subject indicated by the title. But in the third article he diverged into one of his usual rambling criticisms of the academic public, the universities and the professors; and à propos of these last he made merry at the expense of those of them who, mixing up aesthetics with the newest theories of the physical sciences, delude themselves that they are thereby on the way to achieving "an as yet illimitable progress in the art of criticising all things human and non-human". It is evident enough today that in this and one or two other passages Wagner was sniping at the author of *Human, All-too Human*. But as it is hardly to be supposed that the average subscriber to the *Blätter* would be well versed in Nietzsche's barely three-months-old book, the gibes were in all probability intended only for Wagner's private gratification and the young man's private annoyance.

5

As to the latter we have Elisabeth's testimony. She describes Wagner's third article as containing "a string of very angry attacks on my brother, which were in no way mitigated by the fact that he was not mentioned by name." That seems to us now a rather exaggerated description of the article; still, there was enough in it to sever the last link of Nietzsche's personal attachment to Wagner. Looking back on it all in the light of everything we now know about him, it is a fair presumption that what hurt him most was a passage in which Wagner laid an unkind finger on what Nietzsche knew, and knew that his friends knew, was his most vulnerable spot — his seemingly irresponsible changefulness. These newest philosophers and philologists, said Wagner derisively, seem to have derived from their experiments in physical science

---

[8] RWGS, Vol. X.

"a profound authority for a quite peculiar scepticism that enables them to maintain themselves in a state of continual self-gyration, now turning their backs on accepted opinions, now returning to them in some confusion, — which seems to assure them their meet and proper share in the eternal general progress . . . Every German professor is bound at some time or other to have written a book that made him famous; [9] but as it is not given to everyone to discover an out-and-out novelty, in order to make the necessary sensation the man has naturally to resort to representing a forerunner's views as fundamentally false, a course all the more effective in proportion to the significance of the author he is now deriding, and to the plentiful misunderstanding that author has met with."

This would strike home: there must have been many a conversation between the two men during which Wagner had shown some exasperation at Nietzsche's inability to remain of the same opinion on any subject for very long, and his sublime certainty that his latest revelation from on high was the last word of wisdom that could be spoken on a given subject.

The position had become hopeless. Each of the two men was constitutionally incapable of seeing any matter from any standpoint but his own; each was convinced that the destiny of European culture lay in his hands. And Cosima could not have improved matters by her contemptuously patronising letter to Elisabeth after a complete reading of *Human, All-too Human*. Elisabeth is justified in saying that this letter "betrayed not the smallest understanding either of the book or of the quality of the author". More Catholic than the Pope, as was the way with her where Wagner was concerned, Cosima could see nothing in it all but a "betrayal"; she conjectured that Nietzsche had "gone over to a well-fortified enemy camp", and hoped that "the author's treachery would bear him good fruit". Elisabeth is probably right, again, in her surmise that these were not so much Wagner's opinions as those of "some infuriated Wagnerians", with just a little added venom of Cosima's own. Clearly things had come to such a pass that it was not only inevitable that the two friends should part but better that they should do so.

Nietzsche at first preserved his poise. A couple of months before Wagner's article appeared — shortly, indeed, after his own book had been published, — he had written to Peter Gast,

---

[9] The reference is obviously to *The Birth of Tragedy*.

"In Bayreuth my book is under a sort of ban; indeed, the author himself seems to have come under the big excommunication.[10] They are trying to keep my friends but drop me: I hear a good deal of what is going on behind my back and being planned against me. Wagner has missed a fine opportunity to show greatness of character. I must not let that warp my judgment either of him or of myself." [11]

Even in September, after the appearance of the third *Blätter* article, he could write philosophically to Gast that he "put Wagner's polemic in the category of the all-too-human". It was only later, when his normal good breeding had broken down under drugs and disease and suffering of all kinds, when his spirit was hopelessly poisoned by the evidence, growing in volume every day, that it was Wagner, not he, who was yoking all Europe to his triumphal chariot, that he lapsed from this lofty philosophical tone into the hobbledehoy ruffianism of *The Case of Wagner*.

6

This is perhaps the best place to tell the remainder of the Wagner-Nietzsche story.

The final decade of Nietzsche's sane life is of the highest importance in his evolution as a philosopher, but it has the minimum bearing on Wagner biography. Those last ten years present us with a Nietzsche of whom we can never be sure, at any given moment, whether he will sing like a poet, philosophize like a sage, prophesy like a seer, snarl like a cur, or bray like an ass. It is the animal analogies that mostly spring to the mind when we look at him in his last morbidly anti-Wagnerian years. For a long time, in his heart of hearts, he could not shake off the spell of Wagner's powerful, and, for all its angularities, fascinating personality. "For my part", he wrote to Gast in August, 1880, "I suffer atrociously when I am deprived of sympathy", — in which respect, as in so many others, he closely resembled Wagner.

"Nothing can compensate me, for example, for the fact that during these last years I have lost the sympathy of Wagner. How often I dream of him, and always of the intimacy of our one-time meetings! Never

[10] Apparently his publisher Schmeitzner, who also issued the *Bayreuther Blätter*, had repeated to him something that had been said about him and his book at Wahnfried.

[11] NGB, IV, 7.

did an ill word pass between us — nor in my dreams, — but many a merry and heartening one; and with no one else, perhaps, have I laughed so much as with him. Now that is all over; and what boots it that in many things I am right as against him! As if that could blot out the memory of this lost sympathy!" [12]

But Wagner, during these final years, committed two offences unforgivable in Nietzsche's eyes: he calmly went his own way as artist, thinker and dreamer regardless of Nietzsche's philosophical and musical mutations, and, worse still, he had the whole world listening to him, whereas Nietzsche's was a solitary voice crying in the wilderness. His own intellectual past had faded from his memory to such an extent, he told Gast in the spring of 1881, that when he turned over the pages of one of his earlier books he seemed to be listening to some story of old travel-adventures that he had forgotten. [13] And because his own imperious genius was driving him relentlessly towards new formulations he simply could not understand why the rest of the world did not at once place the same value on these as he did: as he saw it, it was "leaving him in the lurch". [14] In 1882 he thought he had "said his last word" on Schopenhauer and Wagner: he had had to make it clear how his earlier views of them had changed, "for after all I am a *teacher*, and it is incumbent on me to show in what respects I have become another" [15] — a duty and a right which, of course, one would not deny him or any other thinker. But for some time yet his drift from Wagner preserved the dignity of a purely intellectual alienation; as yet he could not bring himself to speak with personal rancour of the man to whom he owed so much. [16] The situation changed with Wagner's death in

---

[12] NGB, IV, 35–36.

[13] NGB, IV, 56.

[14] "There were moments, indeed whole periods, in my life — for instance, the year 1878 — when a word of hearty encouragement, an acquiescent hand-pressure, would have been the greatest refreshment of all to me; and it was just then that everyone left me in the lurch." NGB, IV, 71. It never occurred to him that, as Wagner saw the matter, it was Nietzsche who was leaving *him* in the lurch.

[15] NGB, IV, 116.

[16] Elisabeth would have us believe that her brother, "in spite of his youth, had exercised great influence on Wagner, and could have exercised more." So, it appears, she "had often been told": "this is evident in the third act of *Siegfried*, which is so much superior to the others[!]. Wagner himself assured me more than once that it was his acquaintance with my brother that inspired him to write this music." This is Elisabeth's highest flight into the preposterous.

Nietzsche called at Triebschen for the first time on the 15th May, 1869. He was not received, but, he tells us, from the inside of the house he heard Wagner playing

1883. Nietzsche sorrowed over it, but at the same time felt, as he told Gast, that it had freed his hands considerably.

"It was hard to have to be, for six years, the opponent of the man one had honoured most: I am not made of coarse enough stuff for that. Ultimately it was the ageing Wagner against whom I had to defend myself; as for the real Wagner, I myself will be to a great extent his heir, as I have often maintained against Malwida. Last summer I realised that he had robbed me of all the people worth working upon in Germany, and had begun to drag them into the confused hostility of his old age." [17]

7

No: the stuff of him was not yet coarse enough for him to forget how he and Wagner had loved each other, and what he owed intellectually to the older man. For a little while still after Wagner's death the emotional side of him, at any rate, turned back with a nostalgic heart-ache to the Hesperidean Triebschen days. But as the years went on the coarser strain in him got more and more the upper hand. Intellectual loneliness, Promethean sufferings, disappointment at his failure to draw all men after him, rage at Wagner's triumph, combined to poison his spirit. [18] By the beginning of

some chords which he recognised later as those accompanying the words "Verwundet hat mich der mich erweckt". By the 15th, then, Wagner had got that far with his composition, if not further. In the Breitkopf edition of the opera the third act commences on page 255. The "Verwundet" passage occurs on page 340, and the remainder of the score occupies only 25 pages. Did Nietzsche, perhaps, "inspire" these? If so, he must have been a very remarkable young man indeed. As we have seen, several of these 25 pages are based on a quartet sketched for Cosima in 1864. Apart from all that, it is sufficient to point out that Nietzsche entered Triebschen for the first time on the 17th May, when he spent the afternoon there. His next visit lasted from the afternoon of the 5th June to the morning of the 7th. By that time the third act must have been well advanced, for Wagner finished the Composition Sketch on the 14th. To speak, then, of Nietzsche having "inspired" the "third act" (no less!), thereby contributing to its "superiority" to the others, is to talk the most outrageous nonsense.

We need have no hesitation in saying that never in his life did Wagner "assure" Elisabeth that his acquaintance with her brother had played even the smallest part in the "inspiration" of the third act. He was not given to silly talk of that kind about his work. Like another historical character, Elisabeth was too much given to relying on her imagination for her facts. And this is the biography that has been accepted as gospel by two generations of docile Nietzscheans!

[17] NGB, IV, 135–6.

[18] Rohde and Nietzsche met in Leipzig in the spring of 1886, after a long separation. Rohde was shocked at the change in the friend of his youth. "An indescribable atmosphere of strangeness enveloped him, something that struck me at the time as eerie", he wrote to Overbeck in June: Nietzsche seemed, he said, to have come from a land inhabited by no one but himself. CER, p. 150.

the fatal year 1888 he could confess to Peter Gast that his condition now was one of "chronic touchiness", inclining him to "a kind of revenge that isn't precisely beautiful, a sort of excess of harshness. Witness my latest work." [19]

His fury against Wagner increased as he managed to persuade himself that the triumphant "old robber" was cheating him out of his rightful dominion. The note of personal venom becomes shriller as the months go on. He had honourable scruples, at one time, as to the justifiability of including in *The Case of Wagner* so purely personal, indeed confidential, a matter as the now notorious footnote on the composer's possibly Jewish origin: [20] then he decided to retain it because he felt that any weapon, however dirty, was good enough to use against Wagner,[21] the man whom he had come to hate as he hated nothing else on earth. He describes his lamentable pasquinade as his "declaration of war" on Wagner. In his morbid self-esteem he could see only one thing now — that Wagner's enormous vogue stood in the way of the world's acceptance of *him* as its prophet, saviour and Führer. Already in 1887 he had assured Malwida that his "mission" was so stupendous that he felt he must turn his back on the rest of mankind, that now he cannot endure even the odour of humanity. A few weeks later, when he has finished *The Case of Wagner*, he vomits for the hundredth time his hatred and contempt for the Germans, who regard him as fit only for the madhouse; and what especially blocks the path of their understanding of him is "the Bayreuth cretinism". "The old seducer Wagner robs me, even after his death, of the few people on whom I might work": he is gratified, however, to discover that a handful of *illuminés*, such as Georg Brandes and certain Americans, regard him as "the most independent mind in Europe and the *only* German writer".

---

[19] Letter of the 1st February, 1888, NGB, IV, 352.

[20] He doubted also, he told Gast in August, whether he had not gone too far "not as regards the things themselves but as regards speaking out about them". For a while, when reading the proofs, he even thought of deleting the passage.

[21] To Gast, 18th August, NGB, IV, 398: "As regards the footnote, I have decided to retain it in its entirety, except for a more cautious nuancing of the question [of Wagner's racial origin. This suggests that in its original phrasing the note had taken the form of a positive assertion of Jewish parentage, whereas in the published work all that Nietzsche does is to put the slyly insinuating question, 'Was Wagner a German at all? There are grounds for asking this.'] I am returning, in a sort of Epilogue, with all possible emphasis, to Wagner's falsity; consequently any suggestion in this regard will be valuable." To this mean pass had he come.

Fresh light on his state of mind in the last few weeks of his sane life is shed by an undated letter of his (as yet unpublished) offered for sale in Mr. Otto Haas's Catalogue No. 19 (January, 1944).[22] "He wants to be known in England", runs the summary. "His next works, ready for print, are to be published simultaneously in English, French and German. 'The horned-beast race of Germans . . . is utterly alien to me: they will confiscate my books and employ other police measures. My task — one of the greatest that a man could take on himself — is to *exterminate* Christianity: America, England and France necessary' ". The *Götzendämmerung* (*Twilight of the Idols*), which he desires to have translated into English, is "anti-German and anti-Christian par excellence, so it should have a great effect on the English . . . I am not a man, I am dynamite." But the anti-German quality of the work is to be a bait for not only the English but the French, who, he had assured Taine, "will perceive in it the deep sympathy for them which they deserve: every one of my instincts has declared war on Germany."

Manifestly his soul was at that time a boiling cauldron of hatred of his fellow-countrymen for not having accepted him as their mentor; and for their failure to do so the "old robber", the "old seducer" Wagner, he held, was principally to blame.

---

[22] It is addressed, according to the description in the Catalogue, to a lady whom he wants to translate into English an article on him by Peter Gast. The lady in question can only be Miss Helen Zimmern, whom Nietzsche had met in Switzerland, and who had done good work in making German thinkers known in England. Mr. Haas opines that the date of the letter is "late fall 1888". A reference in it to Taine, however, proves that it cannot have been written before the middle of December.

CHAPTER XXXI

WORK AT *PARSIFAL*

1

WAGNER'S relative equanimity in the face of such unpleasant affairs as that of Nietzsche and that of the Berlin *Ring* was typical of his attitude towards life in general during the years immediately following the settlement of the problem of the Bayreuth debt. This had been his greatest anxiety for a long while; with it finally out of the way the man of sixty-five, his heart toughened by suffering and his spirit tempered by philosophy, found little difficulty in casting up his last account with the outside world. His moments of fury with it were fleeting: for the most part his mood now was one of a disillusionment and a sorrow too deep for the kind of anger that used to flame so volcanically from him at the slightest frustration in days gone by.

The new German State he had already written off as a total loss where culture was concerned. He had no faith left in the Germans, he had told the King in the December of 1877. The German spirit as represented by the Reich, he wrote him a few months later, was well on the way towards barbarism. The process had begun, it appears, in 1866, when the ancient links between the princes and their Folk had been disrupted not from without, by foreign conquest, but from within, by a shoddy Hohenzollern King. "This new Germany disgusts me. This a Kaiserdom? A Berlin as capital of the Reich!" And of course he still saw the Jews as one of the main forces at work in the disintegration of the true German spirit. During a visit of Ludwig Schemann to Wahnfried Wagner worked himself into a paroxysm over Bismarck's tolerance towards the Jews; the poor German peasant, he said, would soon be without a yard of soil on which to eat his breakfast. So inflamed did he become by his own eloquence, says Schemann, that at the end of his tirade he had to rush out into the winter night to cool down in the sympathetic company of his Newfoundland dog.

[598]

Now and then the King would try to console him. Ludwig hated the Prussians as sincerely as he did, but, as he quietly pointed out, they did not constitute the whole of Germany. He exhorted him not to lose faith in the real German spirit, which might fail for a time to recognise its greatest men but remained unshakeably true to them once it had taken them to its heart. The best of the Germans, he said, were already on Wagner's side; the rest were not worth worrying about.

Wagner's views on the new German political and commercial world found expression in a lively article entitled *Shall we hope?*, which appeared in the *Bayreuther Blätter* for May, 1879.[1] The "barbaric State", with its materialistic delusions, its crude slogans, its wretched journalism, could do nothing to further art, he contended; great art could come only from great men working in harmony with the spirit of their race. That he himself had not abandoned hope, he went on to say, he had proved by his completing his *Parsifal* within the last few days. But he made it clear that "hope", in the larger sense of the word, could be justified only by the infusion of a new spirit into German culture. Bismarck was not big enough for the task laid on him by destiny. As for Germany in general, he wrote to Konstantin Frantz, he was convinced, by historical analogies, that by the middle of the next millennium it would have relapsed into barbarism.[2] The salvation of the world could lie only in Christianity. But *his* Christianity was not the official one of the churches: had religion depended upon these for its being it would have crashed in ruin long ago. Wherever the Church had had power it had wrought as much evil as the State; the Inquisition, for instance, had either destroyed or banished many of the best minds of France, Italy and Spain. His own Christianity was undogmatic, non-sectarian, non-official, a religion of the heart, based on pity and the renunciation of the Will, and having at its centre the mystically-aureoled name of Jesus: the Christianity, in short, of his own *Parsifal*. He was sorely troubled about the poor and the oppressed and about the fate of the smaller nations, confronted as they were

---

[1] RWGS, Vol. X.

[2] He had expressed the same opinion in *Public and Popularity:* taking two thousand years as "the period covered by the great historical cultures in their evolution out of barbarism and back to it again", he estimated that our present civilisation would come to an end about the middle of the twentieth century. He does not appear to have been far out in his reckoning.

by a Germany that was making militarism and commercialism its gods. "To conquer new provinces", he cried prophetically,

"without ever considering how they are to be won over! Never to ask oneself how Holland, Switzerland and so forth are to be converted into friends! Only the army! [3] . . . It is not the Jews we have to complain about, for each organism tries to further its own interests. Is is *we*, the State, who are to blame, for permitting these encroachments. The Bourse, again, which was originally a free and good institution, what have we allowed it to develop into!"

But if he had a poor opinion of his fellow-countrymen as he saw them living and working around him, he had not lost his naïve belief in the innate superiority of the German "blood" to all others, and its God-given mission to set the tone of the whole world's culture. This becomes most clearly evident, perhaps, in the quasi-autobiography that appeared in the *North American Review* in 1879 under the title *The Work and Mission of my Life,* and was afterwards re-issued, "translated back into German", as *Richard Wagners Lebens-Bericht* in 1884.[4] Intended originally, perhaps, to appeal particularly to the German element in the United States, it opens with a complacent laudation of the German breed for the enduring benefits it has conferred on the institutions and the culture of every foreign country into which it has infiltrated. The English, the French, the Normans, the Lombards, the Andalusians have all profited by this infiltration; especially England, where German culture has remained "the specific culture of the British Folk-spirit, after the Frenchified society of the Norman nobility had exercised nearly a thousand years of domination over the Saxon people of England". (It will be seen that he knew no more about England and the English than about many another subject upon which he dog-

---

[3] To the King he wrote in September, 1881, "I must devote my last energies to preventing — but God knows how! — my little Siegfried from one day being a soldier and falling a victim to some stupid bullet in one of the wretched wars brought on us by Prussian politics. " But he had forgotten that he had done as much as any man of his epoch to make the German mind excessively and dangerously self-conscious. Saint-Saëns saw the case clearly enough as early as 1885. "What German music brings us ", he wrote, "is not solely music but also German ideas, the German soul." It had been a different matter when the German soul was that of a Goethe or a Schiller; but Sachs's address to the Nurembergers in the final scene of the *Meistersinger* is "the cry of pangermanism and war on the Latin races." *Harmonie et Mélodie*, pp. 312–314.

[4] The text seems to have been the work of Hans von Wolzogen. It is not included in the official edition of Wagner's Prose Works.

matised with all the fantastic assurance of the born amateur). And it appears that it is "the genuine German spirit" that is now civilising North America, thanks to the emigration there not only of Britons — basically German — but of Germans straight from the fatherland itself. It is upon this German spirit that the future of America depends. The wonderful thing about the German race, it appears, is its unique gift for producing "the quite special German *great man*", a product to which the other nations aspire in vain. "Just recall these great German philosophers, poets and musicians, the like of which are not to be met with in any non-German breed since the decay of Hellas!" Unappreciated as these supermen were by their own countrymen, they have spread the German influence far beyond Germany's borders, because "the fundamental affinity of the German blood" declares itself in all the nations. "And so the ideal power of the *German spirit* is revealed perpetually as a truly *international* power, and wins back for the mother-Folk the esteem and honour of the nations." And much more to the same effect.

It is all pathetically naïve, and it has a peculiarly foolish ring today. It is the old German belief, rearing its head once more, in the qualities of "blood" — a sadly over-rated fluid; while as to the German belief that the Teutons are God's own leaders and pre-servers of culture it is doubtful whether that proposition would command whole-hearted acceptance anywhere today, even in Tokyo. The consoling feature of all this typically German wool-gathering is that, heaven be thanked, the special intuitions that go to the making of great art are not dependent upon the degree of the great artist's intelligence in any other sphere than his own; and if the indulgence in sham-intellectual maunderings of this sort helped Wagner in any way to write the *Ring* and the *Meistersinger* and *Parsifal,* and to keep the flag of his spirit flying gallantly at the mast in spite of contrary winds or no wind at all from the German world around him, it did all that could have been asked of it, and enough to make us look upon it with a tolerant eye.

2

Whatever the state of Wagner's intellect may have been at this time, however, his heart was in the right place, as was proved by the energy with which he threw himself into the campaign against vivi-

section, some of the sickening horrors of which were just then beginning to be public knowledge. It was in the summer of 1879 that
he became acquainted with the activities of one Ernst von Weber, the
founder-president of the Dresden Society for the Protection of Animals. So great now was Wagner's influence in Germany that the anti-
vivisectionists made a special appeal to him to rally to their cause.
He did so in an *Open Letter to Herr Ernst von Weber, author of
'The Torture-chambers of Science'*,[5] which appeared originally in
the *Bayreuther Blätter* for October, 1879, and afterwards as a
pamphlet some three thousand copies of which were printed at
Wagner's expense. It is an eloquent pleading of the cause of suffering animals that cannot plead their own. In one passage in it Wagner is obviously side-glancing at *Human, All-too Human*, where
Nietzsche had taken the plausible but far from original line that
pity is only a sublimated form of egoism and an enfeeblement of
the soul. Wagner, basing himself on Schopenhauer, argues that pity
is "the only true foundation of morality", that it is by its very nature
something other than a sort of "calculation of utility", something
philosophically more fundamental than the mere "regret", tinged
with satisfaction at our own escape, that one feels when misfortune
overtakes another. Knowing Wagner's views on these matters as well
as he did from private conversations, Nietzsche must have had him
in his mind when he was writing certain sections of his book; and
Wagner must have found a correspondent pleasure in publicly de-
nouncing his "positivism".

But in general the ugly, evil outer world made little impact on
him during these years. The *Parsifal* subject had now taken full
possession of him, and, as always, he found supreme happiness in
pouring forth his energy in creation. "I have often told you", he
wrote to the King,

> "that a work is a joy to me while I am writing it, my misery beginning
> only when it is finished, a misery for which no external success, how-
> ever great, is any compensation."

He was cocooned all this while in a curious inner world of his own,
a world in which the only veritable realities for him were his operatic characters, their psychology, their environment, a world the
crying need of which was "redemption". He and Cosima, we learn

[5] RWGS, Vol. X.

from the latter's diary, came more and more to see the most esoteric "connecting links" between *Parsifal* and the *Ring*.

> "Just as at an earlier time they had seen Titurel as, in a sense, the heir of Wotan, so now they recognised similarities between the nature of Wotan and that of Kundry. Each of these longed for redemption yet revolted against the bringer of it — Kundry in the scene with Parsifal, Wotan in that with Siegfried."

Titurel was for Wagner a Wotan who had attained redemption through denial of the world. Balzac's absorption in his characters to the point of talking about them as if they were actual beings whom you might run into any moment at the corner of the street seems almost impersonal detachment when we watch Wagner at work. For him, Wotan, Siegfried, Titurel, Amfortas, Kundry were not stage fictions, puppets to be posed and manipulated according to the requirements of art, but cosmic entities interwrought with each other in all sorts of strange ways. He analysed the characters of Alberich and Klingsor as he might have done those of two contemporary politicians of the baser sort. "For the former", he told Cosima,

> "he had at one time the fullest sympathy: in the scene with the Rhine Maidens he had stood, so to speak, for the longing of the Ugly for the Beautiful. In the case of Klingsor such sympathy was impossible. In Alberich's demoniacal character, his greed and fury, we saw the naïveté of a pre-Christian world, whereas Klingsor was the incarnation of the characteristic evil that brought Christianity into the world. Klingsor does not *believe* in the good, in which respect he is the analogue of the Jesuits: herein is his power, but at the same time his ruin, for there remains only *One* throughout the aeons."

Phrased in that way, all this does not seem very lucid. But the psychic depths of the great artistic creators are a mysterious underworld of which at present we know too little. What to the ordinary observer seem pure phantasms of the imagination are to the creator of them realities of a superior order, living their own life according to their own inner laws, influencing each other, contending for mastery with each other, mating to produce beings like or unlike themselves. Wagner himself, in the eighteen-fifties, had been astonished to find one day that, without his having done any conscious thinking about the matter, the philosophy on which he had based his first conception of the *Ring* had changed from optimism to pessimism; and when he came to turn the *Meistersinger* sketch of 1845 into poetry more than fifteen years later another and quite different Hans Sachs from the one originally conceived came into being as his pen flew over the paper.[6] In most great artists the process of creation goes on so entirely in the subconscious depths that even the existence of these subtle transmutations can remain long unsuspected by us later spectators of the finished product, and, when at last we get a faint intuition of them, it is only by a long and ardent absorption in the soul of the artist that we can trace them out from work to work, however imperfectly. No one has yet succeeded, for example, in showing how the central force of Beethoven's nature, the impulse to a dionysiac Joy, fought its long fight for realisation in one work after another until it won its conclusive victory in the posthumous quartets: in essence the impulse had from the beginning been the same, but how many false starts he had had to make, into how many byways he had had to plunge and then, leaving them only half-explored, retrace his steps, before his spirit fully found itself, by a divine instinct, in the rapturous melismas of the slow movements of the last quartets! This world of the imagination functions in ways of its own so deep below the surface-consciousness that its phenomena are not expressible in terms of the verbal language, an imperfect one at best, of that consciousness.

3

Nothing could be further from the truth than the belief entertained in some quarters that *Parsifal*[7] is a "senile" work. Into no other work of his had Wagner ever put such severely critical thinking. He knew well that he was engaged on the creation of a musical world undreamed of till then not merely by others but by himself — Kundry, for instance, he regarded as the most "original" of all his female characters, — and his fundamental technical problem, upon which he brought to bear the whole maturity of his powers and his experience, was how to realise this strange world in an idiom purely its own. He had no lack of "ideas": rather was he embarrassed at times by a superabundance of them, ideas not only for *Parsifal* but for instrumental works with a new content and in a new

---

[6] On this latter point see Vol. III, p. 157.
[7] Wagner finally decided on the spelling "Parsifal", as against "Parcival" or "Parzifal", in February, 1877.

style. His surface preoccupation in connection with *Parsifal* was
mainly with problems of harmony and orchestration, with refining
his ceaselessly developing harmonic sense to ideal conformity with
the spiritual poignancies of his subject, and endowing this strange
new world of his with an orchestral colour and texture entirely its
own. The colour, he told Cosima, he wanted to be at the furthest
remove imaginable from the scoring of the *Ring:* it must have the
softness and the shimmer of silk, must be like "cloud-layers that
keep separating and combining again".

He was particularly conscious of the difficulties confronting him
in the composition of the prelude to the third act. This music, he
saw, called for a new harmonic weaving: the spiritual gloom and
tension would have to be unbroken, yet within them there would have
to be nuance after nuance. The form, again, could not be pre-im-
posed; it would have to be born out of the inner logic of the moods.
As he put it to Cosima, "My preludes have to be *elementarisch*
[going down to fundamentals], not dramatic, like the *Leonora*
overture, for then the drama itself would be superfluous." And the
sombre world into which that prelude was taking him kindled once
more in him, by sheer reaction, the old desire to write symphonies,
cheerful, pleasant works that would not fly too high —

"a return to the original form of the symphony, in one movement, with
an andante middle section. After Beethoven no more four-movement
symphonies are possible; everything in them seems to me just an
imitation — when a big scherzo is attempted, for instance."

His own symphonies would be "symphonic dialogues", a theme and
counter-theme conversing with each other.

4

One of the most curious characteristics of his complex nature
came to the surface again during the *Parsifal* period. It was almost
simultaneously with his commencing work at the opera that he began a new correspondence with Judith Gautier. There had evidently
been an emotional episode between them in her lodgings in Bayreuth during the festival of 1876, when the weary man, strained beyond endurance by the cares and labours of his great undertaking,
had fallen sobbing on the breast of the beautiful young Judith, and

she had consoled him. He reminds her of this in a letter of 1877: [8]
he calls it

> "the most exquisite intoxication, the highest pride, of my life, the last
> gift of the gods, whose will it was that I should not break down under
> the misery of the delusive glory of the *Nibelungen* performances."

There are many expressions of "love" in the letters; but the core of
the correspondence is the orders for fine fabrics and perfumes and
bath salts to be sent him from Paris. As always when he was about
to absorb himself in creation, he needed to insulate himself as much
as possible from the unpleasant outer world. It had been so in Dresden, again in Zürich, again in Vienna, and again in Munich; and
his way of doing it was by way of soft hangings and shimmering
satins and ravishing odours.[9] As formerly with the Vienna Putzmacherin he gives Judith the most minute instructions as to all these:
Paris, the luxury centre of the world, was to place all its resources
at his disposal. The perfumes had to be extra-strong, he explained,
because his sense of smell was weak. "Do not think badly of me",
he wrote her towards the end of 1877;

> "at my age one can indulge oneself in childish things. I have three
> years' work at *Parsifal* before me, and nothing must tear me away
> from the sweet peace of creative isolation."

And again later: "I am weary, and desire nothing but the solitude
of work".

Now and then he creates the illusion in the reader, as he probably
did in Judith, that he was "in love" with her, as when he writes,

> "Why in heaven's name did I not find you in my Paris days, after the
> failure of *Tannhäuser?* Were you too young at that time? We will be
> silent. But let us love!"

But all this is for the most part Wagnerian "literature", a parallel to
his former self-delusion that he was "in love with" Mathilde Wesendonk. What he was really in love with was in the earlier case his
Tristan, in the latter his *Parsifal;* it was merely that from the im-
mensity of his artistic passion something flowed over to the mere
woman and glorified her in his eyes. That Cosima knew about it all
and did not take it too seriously is fairly manifest. It is true that

---

[8] RWJG, p. 145.
[9] On this point see Vol. II, pp. 407–8, 559–60, and elsewhere.

there was a superficial air of secrecy about the whole matter: Judith
was to have her consignments addressed not to Wagner at Wahnfried but to his factotum the local barber Schnappauf. That, however, admits of the easiest of explanations. After the malicious publication of the Putzmacherin letters it was mere ordinary prudence
on his part not to have parcels addressed to the famous Richard
Wagner bearing the labels of Paris furnishers and costumiers and
perfume manufacturers whose names were household words all over
Europe. Malicious tongues would soon have been set wagging, and
it would have been only a matter of time for the journalists to be at
their foul work again: consigned to a Bayreuth hair-dresser the parcels would arouse no comment anywhere.

And just as Mathilde Wesendonk had been faded out when
Tristan was off his hands, so as soon as he had fairly settled himself
in the mood he needed for *Parsifal* he had no further illusions about
Judith or use for her. In February, 1878 we find him blandly telling
her that he has asked Cosima to

> "take charge of the commissions with which I have plagued you for so
> long . . . Furthermore, I have just now so much unpleasant business
> on my hands . . . that I can no longer find the necessary leisure to
> get on with the composition of *Parsifal*. Be indulgent with me! It will
> all be over soon, and then I shall find once more the lovely moments
> of leisure in which to talk to you about myself . . . Be nice to Cosima:
> write her fully; then I will hear all about it. Love me always: thus you
> will often see me before you, and one of these days we shall see each
> other in the flesh again."

That, apparently, was the last of his letters to the fair Judith. She
had served her turn, done her little work for *his* work; with *Parsifal*
fairly launched he had no further use for the intoxication he had
associated with her for a few brief months.

5

From the beginning it had been his desire that *Parsifal* should be
given nowhere but in Bayreuth, and before an audience of Patrons
only. For this purpose a Patronatverein had been founded, and a
production planned for 1880. But already in the summer of 1879
it had become clear that this date could not be adhered to, and the
usual difficulties began to mount up. Wagner's wish was that the
subscribers' money should be returned to them if they so desired.

But at the same time his Bayreuth Committee began to be worried over the Munich contract of March, 1878 for the liquidation of the debt to the King. Under Clause 4 of that agreement Wagner had granted the Court Theatre the right to produce all his works, including those at that time in hand; this meant, of course, *Parsifal*. Clause 8 had provided for the employment of the Munich personnel for the Bayreuth production, after which the Court Theatre was to have the unconditional right to repeat it in Munich; while under Clause 10 the receipts from the Bayreuth performances were to go towards covering the costs of production and the upkeep of the festival theatre. Manifestly the Bayreuth production and the consequently ensuing performances in Munich were vital factors in the liquidation of the debt, so it is not to be wondered at that the Committee was perturbed by the implications of a postponement of the festival. Just about that time, too, the rumour was current all over Germany that the King was contemplating resigning his throne; and the bare hint of this was disturbing the bankers who had negotiated the loan, for there was no forecasting what the attitude of a Government of politicians pure and simple, notoriously unfriendly to Wagner, would be towards Bayreuth.

It was with all this in his mind that he wrote to the King on the 7th July, 1879, begging for his intervention. An actual production of *Parsifal*, he argued, was only a subsidiary, not a decisive part of the agreement of March, 1878, the vital point of that being his undertaking not to grant any other theatre the right to give the work before the Munich Court Theatre. His Committee had therefore come to the conclusion that it would be as well to have an "elucidation" of the contract, to the effect that the date of the Bayreuth production was to be left entirely at Wagner's discretion. One difficulty, he says, is piling up on another. *Parsifal* is something so new in conception and detail that he is certain to have more than the normal trouble with singers, designers, machinists and the rest of them; and in any case he is unwilling at the moment to pledge himself to anything unless he is sure of a Patronat fund so substantial that the interest on it will guarantee "model" productions every three years or so; and these are to be before the Patronatverein members only, the public being excluded.

The King was wholly sympathetic: on the 10th July he instructed Bürkel to inform Feustel that he "had no objection to the postponement of the work to a date considered suitable by the Meister Richard Wagner", and was agreeable to that fact being made public and to the appropriate addition being made to the contract of 1878 should the Committee think that necessary. To Wagner himself he sent an affectionate letter in his own handwriting, which appears to be lost. In his reply (on the 25th August) Wagner tells him once more of his anxieties in connection with his new work. His stupendous efforts for the *Ring* in 1876, he says, have had as their final result nothing more, nothing better, than the abandonment of it to the theatres as an ordinary repertory piece: how then can he face without the bitterest foreboding the prospect before his *Parsifal?* What would please him best would be to complete it for his own artistic satisfaction, then seal the score with seven seals and leave the production to his son when he shall be of an age and an experience for it. All that holds him back from such a course is the knowledge how ardently the King desires to hear the work.

A production, he continues, will assuredly bring him one wound after another. He already foresees that for purely financial reasons the one or two performances before the Patrons will have to be followed by others before the public at large, with all the degradations of himself and his art that these will bring in their train — the merely curious crowd, the gaping sensation-hunters, the stupid, malicious journalists, and all the rest of the rabble. Why cannot the production take place for his royal benefactor alone:

> "it would be an outrage like the profanation of the Eleusinian mysteries to hand this work over to the theatre public of our towns, with its usual late-coming and early-going, its chatter, its boredom, and all the rest of it."

With the ordinary theatre he wants nothing more to do. For his interpreters he does not know where to look: a Fräulein Ihle, of Hamburg, has been suggested to him as a possible Kundry,[10] but he can think of no one capable of playing Parsifal:

> "never again can I embark on manufacturing such a simulacrum as in my desperation I tried to do in the case of Siegfried, when I knocked that Herr Unger into some sort of shape at the cost of my health."

Yet Siegfried is relatively easy for a tenor, given the voice and the build and a certain amount of stage experience. Parsifal will be a

---

[10] The musical encyclopaedias seem to have no knowledge of this lady.

different matter altogether. Lately Ferdinand Jäger, with his splendid voice, imposing figure and capable acting, has developed into quite a good Siegfried. But Wagner will never be able to make a Parsifal of him; and for Parsifal a *pis aller* such as he had put up with in the case of Siegfried simply will not do.

Not only would he not bind himself now to a production even in 1881 but he shrank more and more, as time went on, from a production anywhere. Out of tune with the German world as he was — the failure of his attempts to move the authorities to forbid vivisection was a grief that brought him many a sleepless night, — he could not endure the thought of *Parsifal* some day going into the repertory in the Munich or any other theatre; and there were times when the desperate man could think of no other way of averting a catastrophe of that kind than by denying the work even to Bayreuth. But that, of course, would be impossible, if only for the reason that the King's heart was set on hearing the work he had looked forward to so eagerly for so long. He was haunted, again, by the fear that financial needs would one day force his or his legatees' hands with regard to *Parsifal* as they had done in the case of the *Ring*, for his household expenses were now heavy, and there was his large family to be provided for after his death. In 1877 he had had to sell to Schotts a number of odds and ends from earlier years, including the *Album Sonata* he had written for Mathilde Wesendonk in 1853. These he could surrender without a pang; but it was an unspeakable grief to both him and Cosima to have to sell Schotts the score of the *Siegfried Idyll*. Only his wretched health held him back from undertaking an American tour in 1881, the sole purpose of which would have been to raise money enough to place him and his family above any possible temptation to deliver *Parsifal* up to the theatres. His dubious position as regarded the international copyright of his new work gave him much anxious thought; but he planned to guard himself against the piracy of foreign theatres by publishing only a piano score.[11]

---

[11] The unauthorised and morally indefensible production of *Parsifal* in New York in December, 1903 was only made possible by Schotts having been imprudent enough to publish a miniature score. The melancholy story is told in full in MECW, Vol. II, Chapter XIX.

6

In the early days of January, 1880 Wagner and his family were in Munich en route to Italy; and Cosima broached to Bürkel a plan for a Bayreuth "protectorate" with the King at its head, or, in case of his declining, the Grand Duke of Mecklenburg. To this there would hardly have been any objection on Ludwig's part. But Hans von Wolzogen and another Bayreuth henchman, Friedrich Schön, went rather further on their own responsibility: they put before Bürkel a scheme for a "protectorate of the German princes" from the Kaiser downwards, which, in their opinion, promised better financial results. Bürkel put this plan before the King and received an emphatic snub: Ludwig rightly refused to entertain the idea of being merely among those present in a company of princes who so far had shown neither understanding of Wagner's ideal nor willingness to make pecuniary sacrifices for it. So Muncker, on behalf of the Bayreuth Administrative Committee, had to assure Bürkel that "some of our much too zealous Wagnerians, among them Herr von Wolzogen", had been acting without the Committee's sanction, or indeed its knowledge. Wagner himself took the Committee's view of the matter: he would not hear of the protectorate being offered to the Kaiser unless Ludwig himself desired this. The King, through Bürkel, left Cosima in no doubt as to his opposition to the whole plan: an undertaking such as that of Bayreuth, he held, begun in Bavaria and doing its great work there, should have as its protector the King of Bavaria alone. And so, the necessary formalities having been gone through by the Committee, the King, in February, 1881, formally assumed the rôle of "protector of performances of Wagner works in Bayreuth".

All this, however, meant merely the removal of a minor annoyance from Wagner's path. It left untouched his central problem, that of saving *Parsifal* from the commercial theatres. We can hardly doubt that had he been unable to solve this problem in any other way he would have gone to the extreme length of withholding the work even from Bayreuth, for a production there would mean that the Munich Intendanz would at once exercise its legal rights, and after that the descent of *Parsifal* to the German theatres *en masse* would have been practically certain. From this torturing dilemma Wagner was ultimately rescued, as he had been so often before in his direst difficulties, by the sympathetic understanding and the generosity of the young King.

Wagner brought up the question once more in September, 1880. It had been a great grief to him, he told his benefactor, to have to part with the *Ring,* for the reasons that on the one hand he had been unable to raise a sustentation fund sufficient to guarantee periodical performances of it in Bayreuth, while on the other hand his need to provide for the future of his family had compelled him to sell the performing rights to one German theatre after another. The thought of *Parsifal* meeting the same fate was a perpetual torment to him. The very subject of the work, he insisted, ought to bar it from the ordinary theatre:

"how, indeed, can a drama in which the sublimest mysteries of the Christian faith are shown upon the stage be produced in theatres such as ours, before such audiences as ours, as part of an operatic repertory such as ours? I could have no ground of complaint against our Church authorities if they were to protest, as they would be fully entitled to do, against a stage representation of the holiest mysteries complacently sandwiched between the frivolity of yesterday and the frivolity of tomorrow, before a public attracted to it solely by frivolity. It was in the full consciousness of this that I gave *Parsifal* the description of a 'stage-*dedication*-play'. I must have for it therefore a dedicated stage, and this can only be my theatre in Bayreuth. There alone should *Parsifal* ever be performed. Never must it be put before the public in any other theatre whatever as an amusement; and my whole energies are devoted to finding out by what means I can secure this destiny for it."

Somehow, he goes on to say, he will bring about a production in 1882, though how the money is to be raised he does not at present know. On one point, however, his mind is made up: the King having turned a deaf ear to his appeals that a change shall be made in the Intendanz of the Munich Theatre, he, for his part, will in no circumstances accept the co-operation of Perfall in the first production of the work in Bayreuth. The reader may be reminded again that under Clause 8 of the contract of 1878 the first production of *Parsifal* in Bayreuth was to be with "the orchestra, the singers and the artistic personnel of the Munich Court Theatre, which shall afterwards have the unrestricted right to produce the work . . ." The first part of this clause had manifestly been designed by the Munich authorities to bring into operation the second part as a matter of course: what would be, in effect, a Munich production in Bayreuth could easily have been transferred afterwards to Munich.[12]

As always, the King was at once sympathetic and resolute. He would make no change in the Intendanz at the behest of Wagner; but he realised what a thorn in Wagner's flesh the thought of *Parsifal* descending to the ordinary theatres was, and he would relieve him of any further anxiety on that score. By a decisive stroke of his pen on the 15th October he annulled Clause 8 and all the consequences that might result from it. "For the furtherance of the great aims of the Meister Richard Wagner", he wrote,

"I decree that the orchestra and the chorus of my Court Theatre shall be at the disposal of the Bayreuth undertaking for two months in each year from 1882 onwards: my General Intendant Baron von Perfall and my Court Secretary von Bürkel (as head of the Court- and Cabinet-Treasury), are to come to an agreement with the Patronatverein in Bayreuth for the choice of these months in conformity with the requirements of the Munich Theatre and with regard to the settlement of the costs, and they are to report to me thereon. I further decree that all previous contracts with regard to the production of the stage-dedication-festival-play *Parsifal* are hereby annulled".

This was the end of the matter.

To Wagner himself, nine days later, he wrote:

"Your project for spending six months in America does not commend itself to me, since the fatigue this would involve would be detrimental to you. But I am wholly in accord with you that *Parsifal*, your solemn stage-dedication-festival-play, shall be given only in Bayreuth, and never be desecrated by contact with any profane stage."

Thus once more it was "the mad King of Bavaria" who had saved Bayreuth and its ideal. Justly could Bürkel say, when forwarding the royal rescript to the Patronatverein, "Thus the wishes of the Meister are fully met, and an example of readiness for sacrifice set to the other art-loving monarchs which, it is to be hoped, will find many imitators."

Wagner had begun work on the composition in August, 1877, after leaving Ems. The Prelude was fully sketched by the 26th September, on which date he played it on the piano to Cosima. (He

---

[12] It is true that under Clause 9 Wagner was to be at liberty to supplement the Munich forces from outside as he might think fit, by which was meant that if Munich had no adequate Parsifal or Kundry he could engage one from elsewhere. But obviously Munich in its turn could engage these people as "guests".

made a slight alteration in it in 1881). The O.S.[13] of Act I was finished on the 31st January, 1878,[14] that of Act II on the 11th October of the same year, and that of Act III on the 26th April, 1879. After that, for reasons of health, he gave himself a long rest before taking up his work again. On the 7th August, 1879 he began ruling the bar lines for the whole of the F.O.S., on scoring-paper of thirty staves to the page, a plan made possible only by the completeness of his vision of every detail of the work. The actual F.O.S. was begun on the 23rd August, 1879. The sorry state of his health made it necessary for him to spend the greater part of 1880 in Italy; and it was not until his return to Bayreuth in mid-November of that year that he was able to take up the scoring again (on the 23rd). The F.O.S. of Act I was finished on the 25th April, 1881. Act II occupied him from the 6th June to the 19th October. Act III was begun in Palermo on the 5th November, 1881, and completed, also in Palermo, on the 13th January, 1882.

The final page of the score bears the misleading date of the 25th December, 1881. The explanation is that Wagner had promised Cosima to present her with the finished work by that date — her birthday. His bad health making that impossible, he resorted, in order not to disappoint her of her dual Christmas and birthday gift, to the harmless little fiction of writing out the last page of all, with a dedication to her, leaving a few blank pages to be filled in later.

---

[13] O.S. = Orchestral Sketch: F.O.S. = Full Orchestral Score.

[14] On Christmas Day 1878 he brought the Meiningen orchestra to Wahnfried and conducted two performances of the Prelude, the first, in the morning, for Cosima alone, the second, in the evening before some sixty guests.

CHAPTER XXXII

IN SEARCH OF HEALTH

1

IN THE TWO LAST preceding chapters we have thrice had to disrupt the strict sequence of events in order to present in connected form the full stories of (a) Neumann's first attempt to give the *Ring* in Berlin, which ended in failure in December, 1880, (b) the breach with Nietzsche in 1878 and its ultimate consequences for both men, (c) Wagner's work at *Parsifal* and his struggle to safeguard the work from the theatres, a struggle terminated in October, 1880 by King Ludwig's renunciation of Munich's rights in the matter. We have therefore to pick up again a number of chronological threads that had perforce to be dropped or tangled for the time being.

Throughout 1878, 1879 and 1880, as we have seen, Wagner's main preoccupation was with the composition and scoring of his *Parsifal*. He seems to have had an inner conviction that this not only would but should be his last work for the stage. Now and then, it is true, he would talk of taking up *Die Sieger* when *Parsifal* was off his hands. But the subject must already have lost most of its one-time hold on him; once he spoke of completing the poem and leaving it to his son to compose the music if he liked — a passing fantasy which we need not take very seriously. All the evidence goes to show that had his health survived the last inroads made on it by the *Parsifal* production of 1882 he would have found an outlet for his still considerable musical energy in symphonies and quartets.

His prose works of the years now under consideration were devoted, for the most part, either to reflections on music drama in general and his own in particular, or to attempts to save the German cultural world from what he held to be its Gadarean plunge into a sea of materialism and militarism. To the former category belong the treatises *On Poetry and Composition* (*Bayreuther Blätter*, July, 1879), *On Opera Poetry and Composition in Particular* (*Blätter*, September, 1879), and *On the Application of Music to the Drama*

(November, 1879).¹ In these admirable works we have the ripest fruits of a lifetime of experience in his own special sphere of art and reflection upon it. In the second category are *Religion and Art* (*Blätter*, October, 1880), and its supplements *What boots this Knowledge* (December, 1880), *Know Thyself* (February–March, 1881), and *Herodom and Christianity* (September, 1881).² In these Wagner is once more at the favourite Teutonic game of weaving purely verbal fantasies and then hunting for facts that may be supposed to give them a concrete backing.

The keynote to *Religion and Art* is given in the quotation from a letter of Schiller to Goethe prefixed to the essay —

"In the Christian religion I find an intrinsic predisposition to the highest and noblest, while its various manifestations in life appear to me so repulsive and insipid simply because these are only abortive representations of that highest",

— and in Wagner's own opening words —

"One may say that where religion becomes artificial it behoves art to rescue the quintessence of religion by apprehending the figurative value of the mystical symbols which religion would have us believe in their literal sense, and by revealing the hidden depths of the truth of these symbols by means of an ideal representation."

He goes on to describe the development of humanity in his usual *a priori* way. The human race, it appears, has been in a state of progressive degeneration for thousands of years, and that for many reasons: for one thing it has been eating the wrong food, for another, it has lacked the guidance of the Schopenhauerian philosophy. The Will to Live must complete itself in the Will to Redeem; and in some way not made quite clear to us this is to be accomplished by a return to the principle of pure Christianity *via* music. Everything in the world today is rotten — politics, property, gold, credit, and, above all, Jewry and all it stands for. Blood-crossings have led to the nobler races being tainted by the ignoble. There is no virtue in, no hope for, any but a "pure" race, of which the German could be the shining exemplar if it would only rid itself of the Jews and follow the path of true redemption pointed out by Richard Wagner of Bayreuth. He had been appalled by the "levity", the "frivolity", of the so-called statesmen who, in 1871, had decreed "the equalisation

¹ Reprinted in RWGS, Vol. X, pp. 137–151, 152–175, and 176–193 respectively.
² RWGS, X, pp. 211–285.

of the rights of all German citizens, without regard to differences of 'confession'." This "conferment of full right upon the Jews to regard themselves in every conceivable respect as Germans" seems to Wagner on a par with the rule in Mexico that the possession of a blanket authorises a black to consider himself a white.

The Germans, of course, are by nature the flower of humankind: to fulfil their great destiny they have only to restore their sullied racial purity, or at all events to achieve "a real re-birth of racial feeling". The true German, when he "feels his breath quitting him under the pressure of an alien civilisation", should refresh himself at the ever-living, ever-fresh waters of the German language: by so doing he will be able

"always to draw from the pristine fount of our own nature, which makes us feel ourselves no longer merely a race, a variety of man, but one of mankind's primal stocks".

This it is that has enabled Germany to produce "the great men and spiritual heroes" it has done. What matter if "the builders of foreign fatherless civilisations are incapable of understanding and prizing" these great men and spiritual heroes? We Germans can do it, and that is enough. But are we Germans in our turn incapable of understanding and prizing the great spirits of other civilisations? By no means:

"with our clarity of gaze, filled full as we are with the deeds and the gifts of our forefathers, we are able to estimate these others rightly and value them according to the spirit of pure humanity indwelling in our souls",

— in other words, according to the degree of their conformity with German and Wagnerian notions of what constitutes the spirit of pure humanity.

Consideration of the true inwardness of the Schopenhauerian doctrine of the Will, with its implications as regards suffering and pity, conducts Wagner to the remarkable conclusion that "the degeneration of the human race has come about through its departure from its natural food", i.e. the fruits of the earth. True, only about a third of mankind is addicted to the abominable practice of flesh-eating, but that third, unfortunately, is "the degenerate but ruling portion". Does an objector timidly suggest that a flesh diet is a necessity in the cold northern climates? Wagner is ready for him.

"What is to prevent our carrying out a rationally conducted migration of these peoples to those quarters of the globe whose enormous fertility is sufficient to maintain the entire present population of the earth, as is claimed for the South American peninsula itself?"

Why not rescue those rich tracts from "the English traders" and put them to better use? As for "these northern lands of ours, which are alleged to cry out imperatively for flesh-foods", they could be reserved for "the hunters of boars and big game".

2

In all essentials, it will be seen, he was in 1880 just where he had been when sketching the *Meistersinger* in 1845. Germany and Europe had changed politically and socially as far as externals were concerned, but, as Wagner saw the matter, they remained internally rotten: at bottom his complaint from the beginning had been the eternal one of the artist and idealist unable to adapt himself to a world shaped and run by non-artists. His nature was too uncompromising for him to be able, as wiser men have done, to dismiss the world with all its ugliness and rottenness with a contemptuous shrug of the shoulders and get on with his own job and find release and consolation in it: as George Meredith has put it:

> But, as you will! we'll sit contentedly,
> And eat our pot of honey on the grave.

The imperious strain in him would not allow Wagner to seek this simple way out; in everything, he must convince and coerce or fight and go under. Nietzsche, in the years of cooler reflection that followed the publication of *The Birth of Tragedy,* came round to the opinion of those of his friends who had told him at the time that he would have done better not to present his thesis argumentatively but to make a poem of it. And Wagner, we now feel, would have been wiser if, instead of trying to swing the world round to his sociological point of view by means of lame arguments from unsubstantiated premises, he had simply hugged his pet delusions all the more closely to his breast and made music out of them. That is what he had done in the "Wahn! Wahn!" monologue that constitutes the nodal point of the *Meistersinger:* the wrongness and pitifulness of things is far more convincingly demonstrated there, in terms of poetry and music, than in all the angry and confused writings of

[618]

his revolutionary period. And once more, round about 1880, it is in the music of *Parsifal*, not in his articles in the *Bayreuther Blätter*, that he sings the supreme song of love and pity for this lamentably ill-constructed universe.

But in a world that obstinately refused to accept him as its leader and prophet there was always one enclave where his lightest word was law, a sort of private Sinai of his own. In Wahnfried he could be sure every evening of an audience that hung reverently upon his lips and allowed him to do virtually all the talking. Much of his talk at these gatherings has been preserved for us by Wolzogen [3] and in the diaries of Cosima. His comments on music, made mostly by way of elucidation of some favourite work of his, are still of great interest, even if some of them throw rather less light on the work or the composer under discussion than on his own musical constitution. In his lucubrations on other matters — poetry, tragedy, fiction, history, politics and so on — we find him today less impressive than his acolytes at Wahnfried did. Judging from the specimens that have come down to us, little of what he had to say about literature rose much above the level of earnest dilettantism. Even the faithful Wolzogen seems to have had his doubts, when writing his reminiscences, as to the quality of much of this talk of Wagner's when submitted to the cold test of print. "What one tries to reproduce of his talk by an effort of the memory", he says, "can never be more than an artificial patchwork in our ordinary literary idiom". The really impressive thing at the time, it appears, was not so much Wagner's words as the fire of his conviction, and, of course, the incomparable art of his delivery.[4] We can well believe it: we remember Wagner's own story of how Garrick, with only a beer-jug in his hand to represent this, that or the other, could thrill his listeners to their very marrow.[5] But alas, the Garrick of Bayreuth, with his wonderfully modulated voice, his flashing eye, his plastic pose, his power of self-projection, is dead and gone; what is preserved for us in the pages

---

[3] In WEW.

[4] Berthold Kellermann, who was present at many of these Wahnfried gatherings, speaks of the "wonderful expressiveness" of Wagner's readings; and it is interesting to learn that when reading aloud he lost every trace of his Saxon accent. See KEK, p. 90.

Kellermann, at that time a young man of twenty-five, had gone to Wahnfried in 1878, on Liszt's recommendation, to take Seidl's place as copyist and to superintend the musical education of Siegfried, Daniela and Blandine.

[5] See *supra*, p. 467.

of Wolzogen and Cosima is for the most part only the beer-jug, which, truth to tell, is of itself hardly distinguishable from any other utensil of its humble kind.

Glasenapp, we can now see, drew copiously upon Cosima's diaries for his excerpts from Wagner's talk on these occasions. She seems to have recorded piously almost everything the oracle said, her intention being to provide Siegfried with all the material necessary for the authentic biography of his father which she trusted he would one day write, — the word "authentic", of course, being taken in the sense it had for herself and Richard.[6] For his musical appreciation lectures he had generally the assistance of Joseph Rubinstein or Kellermann at the piano, though he himself would sometimes play the illustrations.[7] And when he was in the professorial mood he demanded regular attendance and concentrated listening on the part of his classes. On one occasion poor Kellermann offended him mortally by absenting himself from one of his expositions of Bach's fugues. In vain did the young man plead that he had had to practise for a coming concert: Wagner made it clear to him that he had sinned almost beyond hope of forgiveness, and "it was a long time", says the grieved Glasenapp, "before they could get down to the 'Forty-eight' that day."

3

Wagner's outbursts of temper on the smallest provocation at this time were excusable by the poor state of his health. He was really well and happy only when working at *Parsifal:* as soon as he left that ideal world behind him he was made sadly conscious of a ceaselessly active mind weighed down by an ailing body. The festival of 1876 and the anxieties of the following years had left their permanent mark on him; and now the climate of Bayreuth began to take a hand in the game. Persistently bad weather throughout 1879 not

---

[6] "For our son's benefit", Wagner told the King in October, 1879, "she keeps an exceptionally precise diary, in which she records each day my health, my work, my conversation, and so forth".

Cosima's diaries occupy twenty-one quarto note-books. The entries begin in January, 1869 and end on the 12th February, 1883, the night before Wagner's death.

[7] His capacities as a pianist have perhaps been underestimated. Every writer on this subject quotes Wagner's own confession that "in my whole life I have never learned to play the piano properly". But it is constantly overlooked that when he penned this sentence in 1842 his "whole life" meant nothing more than his first twenty-nine years. On Wagner's playing see KEK, p. 90.

only depressed him but, by depriving him of exercise, brought on rheumatism, chronic catarrh of the stomach, and even, in time, a return of his old enemy erysipelas. He suffered much from insomnia and from cramp in the chest: "If only my heart isn't affected!" he would sometimes say anxiously to Cosima. The doctors were reassuring but unhelpful; again and again they declared him to be organically quite sound, but their treatment made him no better. Visits from old friends such as Klindworth, Liszt and Malwida were an occasional consolation, and for regular company there were Wolzogen and Rubinstein and other disciples. In October, 1879 there was added to their number Heinrich von Stein, a young aristocrat of fine nature and solid culture — "slim and blond, like one of Schiller's young men" was how Wagner described him to the King, — who had come to Wahnfried, of his own free will, to superintend the education of Siegfried.[8] And all the while Cosima was watching over the ailing man with a devotion that never slackened, and heartening him with those harmless little solemnities that gave him such pleasure on his birthdays and at Christmas. On the 22nd May, 1878, for example, she staged for his benefit a little play written for the occasion by Wolzogen and acted by the children, who had been rehearsing it in secret since the beginning of the year. The theatre properties were drawn upon for some of the costumes. Daniela played Erda, and Eva, Blandine and Isolde the Three Norns; and all took part in some marvellous tableaux with their brother, the music being drawn from Wagner's works, and the action including the strewing of flowers round the bust of the Meister.[9]

---

[8] He was one of Malwida's protégés. He was only twenty-two when he arrived in Bayreuth. A year or two later he became a teacher at the universities of Halle and Berlin. His promising life was cut short in June, 1887.

[9] A full description of the ceremonial will be found in Glasenapp's sixth volume, pp. 102–106. We learn from Cosima's diary that at ten in the morning Wagner was brought down from his room to admire a little tableau of the ten-years-old Siegfried, "dressed like father Geyer and with his hair arranged like his". Why the "father" Geyer? So again in the letter of the 28th May in which Wagner gave the King a description of the tableau: "On the easel in the centre of the hall was a new portrait of my wife by Lenbach, a work of extraordinary perfection and beauty. . . . In front of it stood my son Siegfried, in black velvet and with blond curls, looking absolutely like the young Van Dyck: he was supposed to represent, in a significant new-birth, my father Ludwig Geyer . . . giving the final touches to the painting." Once more, why, unless Wagner meant it literally, the "mein *Vater* Ludwig Geyer" — it would surely have been just as easy for him to write "mein Stiefvater" — and why the "in bedeutungsvoller Wiedergeburt"?

What must have been another pleasant experience for Wagner was to find Bülow rallying to his side in the violent controversy that broke out in Germany after the attack on Schumann in the *Bayreuther Blätter,* an article which, though it bore the signature of Joseph Rubinstein, obviously represented the views of Wagner. It gave great offence in many quarters: Julius Kniese of Frankfort, who was later to become one of the stalwarts of the Bayreuth festivals, cancelled his subscription to the *Blätter,* and many other protests reached Wahnfried. Bülow, however, sent Rubinstein a telegram consisting of the one word "Bravissimo!" [10]

4

By the summer of 1879 Wagner's health had deteriorated to such an extent under Bayreuth conditions that it became almost a matter of life or death for him to escape from them for a considerable time. He decided to spend the coming winter in Italy; and in September, after long negotiations in connection with two houses at Posilipo, near Naples, the Villa Maraval and the handsome and superbly situated Villa Angri, he took the latter for six months from January, 1880 at the high rent of 1040 lire a month. On the last day of the old year he and his family left Bayreuth for Munich, where he spent an evening with Lenbach, Bürkel and Levi. The family party set out for Italy on the 3rd January. According to Sebastian Röckl they travelled in a salon-coach placed at their disposal by the King. This, however, is incorrect; in his first letter to Ludwig from Posilipo, Wagner, after describing the deplorable state of his health that winter and his present exhaustion, says that "at a cost far exceeding my means I obtained a so-called salon-coach, that made it unnecessary for us to change between Munich and Naples." He arrived on the 4th to find Gersdorff awaiting him at the station.

Wagner promptly went down with erysipelas, which confined him to his room for the first fortnight or so. He was so enchanted with Naples and its environment, with its walks, and with the views over land and sea that he promised himself a speedy recovery from all

---

[10] He may have been set against Schumann by the prejudice of Clara and the Leipzig Schumannians against himself. He certainly had no liking for Joseph Rubinstein, partly because he was a Jew, partly because he was so closely associated with Wagner. In his letters he refers to him as "the false Rubinstein" — the genuine one being Anton, — or "the false Demetrius".

his ills. But once more his luck was out. Vesuvius, it is true, rose courteously to the occasion and staged a magnificent show for his benefit all through the spring. But as a whole the winter was the coldest in Neapolitan memory, and both his mind and his body were slow to recover what they had lost in Bayreuth during the past three or four years. Friends soon began to gather round him. Gersdorff had to leave Naples in mid-January, but almost immediately afterwards Stein arrived, soon to be followed by a new acquaintance for Wagner — Paul von Joukowsky, a rich young Russian painter of amiable nature and agreeable manners, who had a studio not far from the Villa Angri. He spoke German as his mother tongue. Apparently he had met Cosima at some time or other in Munich; but though he had attended the festival of 1876 he had not ventured to call at Wahnfried.

He immediately succumbed to Wagner's fascination, and remained to the end his devoted and intelligent admirer. Wagner swept him off his feet. "No one who has not known Wagner in the intimacy of his home", he wrote in after years,[11]

> "can have any idea of the goodness of his nature, his childlike lovableness. Frau Wagner was right when she compared him to the child with the orb whom St. Christopher carries across the stream: he was a child in spirit, with a whole world within him."

It was an ideal family life to which Joukowsky was now admitted as an intimate: Cosima, with never a thought for herself, living only to guard Wagner against annoyance of any kind and fortify him for his work, father and children brimming over with love for each other. Characteristically enough, Wagner had hardly known the young man five minutes before he was giving him his views on Russia and her problems:

> "I know how Russia can be helped", he said, "but no one asks me for my opinion. The Tsar should set fire to St. Petersburg with his own hand, transfer his residence first of all to Odessa, and then go to Constantinople. That is the only way to show what there is in the Slav race. But to do that would need a stout fellow, and that sort isn't made any more."

---

[11] His reminiscences do not seem to have been published. Glasenapp had access to the manuscript.

Whether Joukowsky was impressed by this specimen of Wagner's political wisdom or not we do not know; but his own artistic soul he now gave entirely, as so many others had done, into Wagner's keeping. It was soon settled that the gifted young Russian should design the scenery for *Parsifal*, and from July onwards he made his home in the Villa Angri for the closer interchange of ideas on that matter. The sky was not always cloudless. Wagner was fretted and excitable; "for all the childlike goodness of his genius", said Joukowsky,

> "one sometimes had the feeling that one was living at the foot of a volcano, so easily was he excited. A single unpremeditated remark would be sufficient to work him up into the most passionate rage or plunge him into the profoundest indignation."

Joukowsky, an artist pure and simple, had seemingly never troubled to read any of Wagner's prose writings. This was a constant source of annoyance to the philosopher and prophet, who complained that he was always having to start at the beginning with one person after another. One day Joukowsky stirred up a storm by an innocent reference to the "hissing" of *Tannhäuser* in Paris in 1861. "It was not the French", Wagner shouted at him, "but the German Jews!" But Joukowsky's quiet good breeding and his respect for Wagner's towering genius as an artist combined to see them both safely through tempests of this sort.

5

Wagner remained in Italy some eleven months. He explored the Naples neighbourhood thoroughly. He visited Perugia, where he received a gratifyingly cordial welcome; it was only later that he discovered that it was as the successor of the great Morlacchi (a native of Perugia) in the Dresden Kapellmeistership that he was. known there. In May he made an excursion to Amalfi with Joukowsky, and on a nearby height, in ancient but fallen Ravello, which was still rich in reminders of the Arab occupation, he lighted upon a scene that must have compensated him for many disappointments in Italy. At the Moorish Palazzo Rufalo (or Ruffali), occupied by an Englishman, Mr. Neville Read, he found the realisation of his dream of Klingsor's castle and garden. "Here", he wrote to the King, "we came upon some splendid suggestions for Klingsor's magic garden: Joukowsky at once made some sketches for the second act of *Parsifal*." And in the visitors' book he wrote, "Richard Wagner, with wife and family. Klingsor's magic garden is found! 26 May, 1880. R.W."

"We have decided", he told the king, "that Joukowsky shall execute detailed designs not only for the scenery and costumes of *Parsifal* but for all my operas; and as they will be done in exact accordance with my instructions we may hope to bequeath something really serviceable to posterity."

Visitors came and went — Stein, Rubinstein, who used to soothe Wagner with Strauss waltzes, Plüddemann, Sgambati, the painter Böcklin, Humperdinck, Malwida, Liszt and others. Differing in this respect from the average host, he was not only glad at the coming of his guests but grieved at their departing. In his pathetic need of companionship and sympathy he could never understand why those who were necessary to him should ever leave him at the call of other duties, other personal ties. He was vexed with Liszt for not settling down permanently with him, instead of going year in and year out on his nomad's round of Rome, Weimar and Pesth. When Malwida told him that her pleasant stay with him would have to come to an end he broke out into passionate reproaches of her for what Glasenapp calls "her lack of perfect oneness with him and his", and bemoaned the strange and lamentable fact that "people always had their abodes and their actions determined by other considerations": they should belong to him wholly. "On another occasion", continues Glasenapp, "he reproached her passionately for the feigned affairs that were enticing her away from him; she ought to remain with him and let these other people come to her, instead of her going to them."

With the Italian theatres he had little to do; for Italian operas in general he had no great appetite, and Italian performances of the works he liked, such as *Il Barbiere*, displeased him by their lack of "style" and "good tradition". A highly successful production of *Lohengrin* in Rome on the 3rd April brought on him a deluge of congratulatory addresses, letters and telegrams; but he could not be persuaded to attend a performance, though he was sufficiently impressed by the reports that reached him to think once more, as he had often done in the past, of training an Italian company in *Tristan*. On the invitation of the authorities he paid one or two visits to the Naples Conservatoire; but the bad style of the students in an operetta by one of them which they performed for his benefit wrung from him some candid comments later in a letter to the president of the institution, the Duke of Bagnara. He regretted, he said, to see so much good material being largely misdirected. For among these students he found in embryo everything that had disgusted him his whole life long in the German opera houses — indifference to the drama of opera, concern only for "effective" high notes and the applause of the audience. For models they should be set to work at things like *Figaro*, the two *Iphigenias* and Spontini's *Vestale;* for in art, as in life, there are good manners and bad, and the only way to make the former instinctive is to keep the impressionable young from contact with the latter. The advice was too frank, perhaps, to be acceptable.

With the outer world all this time he had as little to do as possible. Every time he left his luxurious house he was cut to the heart by the contrast between a land so lovely and poverty so dire. He was thoroughly out of tune with the world as he saw it, utterly at a loss to understand it: he saw nothing but degeneration everywhere, and no way out of it all except by some process of universal re-birth that was more of a mystical faith with him than a practical proposition. In the summer of this year he refused to sign a monster petition to the Reichstag — organised by the rabid antisemite Dr. Bernhard Förster, who later became the husband of Elisabeth Nietzsche, — against the Jews and their increasing power in Germany. The reason he gave for his refusal was that after the failure of the petition against vivisection he had sworn never again to sign any of these documents. But it is just possible that he may have felt he could not in ordinary decency take the field so openly against the Jews when one representative of the race, Rubinstein, was an inmate of his own household, another, Neumann, was organising a touring Wagner Theatre that would mean large receipts for the composer of the *Ring*, and a third, Hermann Levi, was attracting all Munich to his performances of the Wagner operas.

6

As was always the case with him, Wagner was finding it difficult to bring his expenditure into harmony with his receipts. His only certain income, as he himself pointed out, was his pension from

King Ludwig: his royalties from the theatres were now substantial, but he had no guarantee that they would continue indefinitely: and he was engaged on his last opera, which, however, he had no intention of selling to the theatres, while the receipts from the Bayreuth production were mortgaged to Munich. He had a large family to educate and provide for after his death. His Italian holiday was very expensive, partly because of the need for a good deal of self-indulgence in the frail state of his health, partly because of his passion — more than a passion, a necessity of his being — for surrounding himself with friends: even his normal household consisted of ten or eleven people, among them two governesses, one Italian, one English.[12]

We have seen him, in his first letter to the King after his arrival in Posilipo, delicately hinting that the salon-coach he had engaged in Munich had been a bit of a drain on his resources. And sure enough the young King's love, which by now had taken on a new tinge, the old romantic fervour having merged into a kind of reverential tenderness for the ageing but still indomitable idealist, proved equal to the occasion. On the 16th June, 1880 he wrote to Bürkel,

> "In order to enable the Meister Richard Wagner to prolong the stay in Italy that is essential for his health, I grant him for the five months June to October of the present year a rent allowance of 5,200 lire in all, to be paid by my Kabinettskasse in monthly amounts of 1,000 lire (in October 1,200 lire) to his credit with the banker Feustel in Bayreuth";

and when communicating this decision to Cosima the Court Secretary was instructed to add that "the mention of the month of October as terminal date does not imply any pressure on the Meister and his family with regard to their return to chilly Germany." The warm-hearted young man, whose alienation from a political world about which he no longer had any illusions was just then entering on its fateful final phase, no doubt felt himself fully recompensed by the arrival of the fourth volume of *Mein Leben* in August, and by the growing hope that a production of *Parsifal* would be possible by the summer of 1882 at the latest.

For all its beauty and the mental stimulus it gave him, Posilipo brought Wagner no real improvement in his bodily health; so in

---

[12] A Miss Parry.

the third week of August he and the family removed to the Villa
Torre Fiorentina, some twenty minutes' drive from Siena, where
he remained until the 4th October. Liszt, who spent nine days there
with him, described the house, in a letter to the Princess Wittgenstein, as a "habitation princière". He thought the rent for the place
— 800 lire a month — "pas excessif"; but as Wagner still had the
Villa Angri on his hands for two months his expenses must have
been heavy.

He found Liszt, of whom he saw a good deal off and on during
the next two-years-and-a-half, very much improved as a human
being. He had learned a good deal by sad experience, and he had
developed some sense of humour. Wagner had only one fault to
find with him, but that was a grave one: Liszt showed no enthusiasm
for the readings and expositions that were the very breath of Wagner's being; he preferred a game of whist in bright young, and, if
possible, titled company in which he was certain of affectionate admiration. During his stay at the Torre Fiorentina he played through
most of the third act of *Parsifal*, Wagner taking the singing parts,
and a number of his own works. It was on one of the latter occasions, according to his own later account, that at a certain moment
in the third act of *Parsifal* Wagner said to him jestingly, "I stole
that from you". It was a little while before Liszt discovered that he
was referring to his *Die Glocken des Strassburger Münsters*, a composition of about 1869–70 which Liszt had almost forgotten.

The Siena sojourn conferred one enduring benefit on Wagner
— the interior of the Cathedral so impressed Joukowsky that he
made some sketches of it that were afterwards incorporated in the
stage setting of the Grail scene in *Parsifal*. Wagner's health still
showing few signs of improvement, as soon as his lease of the Torre
Fiorentina expired he removed (on the 4th October) to Venice:
there he stayed nearly a month, making his headquarters first in
the Hotel Danieli, then in the Palazzo Contarini. It was here in
Venice that his real friendship with Count Gobineau began; it was
only now, seemingly, that Wagner realised the intellectual stature
of the richly cultivated and many-sided Frenchman: he read *La
Renaissance* and other works of his with great delight and began the
serious study of the *Inégalité des races humaines*, rejoicing to find
in it what he imagined to be a scientific confirmation of his own
theorisings about race, blood and degeneration.

Bad weather generally pursued him wherever he went, and Venice failed, as Posilipo and Siena had done, to effect any real improvement in his health. He left there on the 30th October for Munich, where he remained for more than a fortnight, mainly because he wanted Cosima and the children to hear some of his works in the Court Theatre, a desire which the King and the Intendanz were delighted to gratify so far as the exigencies of the repertory allowed. On the 1st November he heard Beethoven's Mass in D at an Odeon concert under Levi, on the 4th the *Flying Dutchman* — after which he declared his intention of re-casting the work in a single act, — on the 7th *Tristan*, when he received a great ovation from the audience, and on the 10th *Lohengrin*. This last was a private performance, at which Wagner sat with the King in the royal box. It was destined to be their last meeting.

On the 11th Wagner went to the *Magic Flute* — an especial favourite of his, — and on the following afternoon he gratified the King's hunger for *Parsifal* by running through the prelude with the Opera orchestra; and for Ludwig's guidance he wrote the now famous "programme note" in which he described the prelude as being based on the three themes of "Love", "Faith" and "Hope?".[13] The listeners consisted only of the King, Cosima and a few specially favoured friends, of whom Lenbach was one. The painter's account of the occasion has passed into history. The main points of it are these. The King, to Wagner's visible annoyance, was late. Wagner kept looking impatiently first at the royal box, then at his watch. At last Ludwig arrived, listened to the prelude with rapt attention, and then asked for a repetition. Wagner, though feeling this to be a "profanation", complied, but became really angry when the King now asked for the *Lohengrin* prelude, so that he might compare the two. Exasperated beyond endurance, Wagner turned over the baton to Levi and walked away. Afterwards he entertained a few friends, Lenbach among them, at dinner. For a little while he was amiable enough; then he broke out into a denunciation of the King, who, like all the great ones of this world, thought only of himself — "King or Kaiser, they are all alike!" He next fell foul of Lenbach

[13] The note of interrogation is Wagner's own. The analysis will be found in RWGS, XII, 347.

for speaking well of Bismarck. That outburst over, he left the room with flaming cheeks. Lenbach, feeling himself insulted, asked for his coat and hat and had to be placated by Cosima. Wagner returned after a little while in the best of humours and was charming towards them all.

Glasenapp is sceptical, perhaps with good reason, as to some of the details of the story, which comes to us at second hand, Lenbach having told it at a later date to Heinrich von Poschinger, who, at a later date still, printed it in his book *Bausteine zur Bismarck-Pyramide*.[14] Lenbach is no doubt right as regards what happened at the hotel; Wagner did not like his political opinions, and that the two men quarrelled over Bismarck is extremely probable. But Lenbach's story of Wagner's feelings and behaviour at the rehearsal should perhaps be taken with a grain of salt. That Levi, not the composer, conducted the *Lohengrin* prelude is certain; but may it not simply have been that Wagner, feeling unwell, or being unable to attune himself to *Lohengrin* the moment after he had lived through the emotion of *Parsifal,* had called the Kapellmeister to the conductor's desk as a matter of course? For there is not the smallest trace in the letters that passed between him and the King during the next few days of either a sense of bad behaviour on the one side, calling for explanation and apology, or of offence taken on the other. Had there been anything of that kind in the minds of either of them Wagner would surely have made some reference to it in his grateful letter of the 14th; while in the King's ardent reply of the 17th from Hohenschwangau he thanks Wagner warmly for having "personally" conducted the *Parsifal* prelude, but makes no reference at all to the other performance.

Nor is there any hint of a contretemps in the King's diary. In spite of the atrocious "editing" of that document by Edir Grein, the entries give us all the information we need. As Grein has printed it, the entry for this date runs thus:

Am 12 Nachmittag 2 mal das wunderbar herrliche vom Schöpfer selbst dirigirte Vorspiel zu Parsifal gehört! Tief bedeutungsvoll.

Auch das Vorspiel zu Lohengrin Abends mit Ihm "aus dem Stegreif" beigewohnt, sehr gelungene Vorstellung. Ich habe immer sagen hören, dass zwischen einem Fürsten u. einem Untergebenen keine Freundschaft möglich ist . . .

---

[14] Berlin, 1904, pp. 122–7.

As it stands, the sense of this is as follows:

> On the 12th (afternoon) the marvellously glorious prelude to *Parsifal* twice, conducted by the composer himself. Profoundly significant.
>
> Also attended with Him in the evening the prelude to *Lohengrin* "aus dem Stegreif". Very successful performance. I have often heard it said that a friendship between a monarch and a subject is impossible . . .

Grein has muddled both the uninformed reader and himself by failing to notice that "Also the prelude to *Lohengrin*" should be joined to the preceding German sentence, that a full stop should follow "*Lohengrin*", and that "Abends" ("in the evening") begins a new sentence dealing with an entirely different matter. The true sense of what the King wrote is this: "in the afternoon of the 12th heard the *Parsifal* prelude twice under the composer. Also the prelude to *Lohengrin*. In the evening went with Him to a performance of *Aus dem Stegreif.*" The casual reader can hardly be expected to know that "aus dem Stegreif" has not here its everyday meaning of "impromptu" but is the title of a play by Hermann von Schmid of which the King was rather fond; and that "Him" does not mean Richard Wagner but the equerry Richard Hornig, who had for a long time enjoyed the special favour and confidence of the lonely and mistrustful King.[15]

It would appear, then, that Lenbach was making a great deal of fuss about nothing, and drawing largely on his imagination in the process. There had been no display of temper and bad manners on Wagner's part towards the King; all he had done was to hand over the baton to Levi for the *Lohengrin* prelude as a simple matter of routine, and the King himself saw nothing more in it than that.

On the 17th November Wagner was back again in Bayreuth, obviously not much better for his Italian holiday: he had hardly settled down in Wahnfried before he was attacked by the cramp in his chest that used to distress him so much. The usual annoyances at once began, among them a demand from Voltz and Batz for 100,000 marks as the price of their releasing him from a business agreement

---

[15] More than one reader with only a superficial second-hand acquaintance with the diary has expressed to me his astonishment that on the day after hearing the *Parsifal* prelude Ludwig should have taken Wagner to a performance of *Aïda*, and that Wagner should have allowed himself to be taken. But in the entry immediately following the passages quoted above, and reading "Saturday the 13th, with him at the opera *Aïda*", "him" again means Hornig.

which, in his opinion, they had carried out far from efficiently. Another source of exasperation was Lina Ramann's official biography of Liszt, the first volume of which — obviously inspired by Princess Wittgenstein, — arrived about this time. Knowing Liszt, the Princess and the Countess d'Agoult as they did, both Wagner and Cosima must have seen at once the falsity of much of the book. Du Moulin's comments on it, and on the reception it had in Wahnfried, may be based to some extent on Cosima's diary, or they may be his own, in which latter case he has achieved a sprightliness and force of characterisation rather uncommon with him. "The good Ramann", he writes,

> "reminds us of nothing so much as a metal-worker who has been cast into prison and forced to coin false money in his cell. The Princess Wittgenstein was the mistress, and she supplied the metal: this was genuine, but the die that gave it its stamp was false." [16]

However, Wagner soon felt sufficiently recovered to take up the scoring of *Parsifal* again. The super-refinement of his self-critical sense at this time made him for a while so dissatisfied with the work that he talked of re-writing it; but in the end he concentrated on the thing nearest to his heart just then, — making the orchestration the perfect counterpart of the subtlety of musical thinking and novel dramatic characterisation in the opera. Sometimes he would complain that for the right fixation of his inner vision in colour he would need instruments not yet invented; in the absence of these, he drew new delicacies of blend from those at his disposal. Joukowsky came and made his permanent quarters in the Reichsadler Hotel and settled down to real work at the *Parsifal* designs: that for the magic garden was re-made seven times before Wagner was satisfied with it. Difficult as the work was, said Joukowsky in after years, this was the happiest time of his life: "I forgot fatherland, family, everything that had formerly been dearest to me, to sink myself wholly in the contemplation of this unique spirit." Stein also came for a time and was agreeable company for Wagner, even though he occasionally made the mistake of arguing with him. Finally, Wagner found a melancholy pleasure in reading his old letters to Uhlig, copies of which Cosima had succeeded in obtaining from the Uhlig family: he rose from the perusal of them with a

---

[16] MECW, I, 925.

mournful sense, he said, of how greatly he had needed love in the Dresden and Zürich days, and how little of it had been granted him.

At Christmas the King sent him a small model of Hohenschwangau in gold, to serve as a paper-weight, and an exquisite little Renaissance cabinet of ebony inlaid with silver. On the day itself the family regaled him with a tableau designed by Joukowsky in the style of the old Italian religious painters: Daniela, as Mary, knelt in adoration before the youthful Jesus (Siegfried working at a carpenter's bench); behind the Virgin stood Joseph (a Neapolitan boy named Peppino, whom Joukowsky had adopted); and three angels made a consort of music — Blandine with a lute, Eva with a flute, and Isolde with a viol, — while from the small house-organ came the strains of the chorale with which the *Meistersinger* opens. At Wagner's request Joukowsky afterwards made a painting of the tableau. Cosima's Christmas gift was the manuscript of the piano arrangement of Beethoven's Ninth Symphony which Wagner had made in 1830, at the age of seventeen: he had presented it in 1849 to Uhlig, from whose heirs Cosima had managed to acquire it.

In his last letter of 1880 to the King, Wagner said that his one desire now was for health and a long life devoted to useful work. He had decided, he continued, to spend at least the six winter months of each year in Italy, in Venice for choice; for the real attractions for him in Italy were the cloudless sky and the mild air, the dying vegetation, however, being something he disliked seeing; and in Venice, between the blue sky and the blue sea, he would not be conscious of this. The summers he would spend in Bayreuth, where he held out to the King the promise of something that might attract him thither.

CHAPTER XXXIII

TROUBLE WITH BULOW
AND OTHERS

1

ALTHOUGH the orchestration of *Parsifal* was still far from finished, it was by now taken as a matter of course that the opera
would be produced in 1882, and the year 1881 was largely spent in
preparations of all kinds for it — discussions with Brandt and the
brothers Brückner with regard to the scenery and the stage apparatus, search for the singers of the two principal parts, and so on.
All this had the usual effect of lowering Wagner's health, souring
his temper, and making him curse the Fates for having made him
an opera composer, that most unfortunate species of artistic creator, whose work can be brought into full being only with the co-
operation of a multitude of other people, some of them not ideally
intelligent: as Wagner expressed it to the King, "when the composer has finished the work and it is off his hands it becomes the
devil's property". Once, in a moment of double exasperation over
the abominable Bayreuth weather and the *Parsifal* problem, he
growled, "If only the wind would blow the cursed theatre down!
I certainly wouldn't put it up again!" In January he had to drop
his scoring to discuss a few of the major difficulties of the inscenation with Brandt, whom, in spite of the memory of how troublesome
he had often been in 1876, he recognised as the one man in Germany who could solve all his technical problems for him. But it
chilled him to have to come down to earth to translate his visions
into the mechanics of the theatre. Klingsor's spear, for example, was
one thing as Wagner bent over his score, absorbed in the legend,
and quite another when it became a matter of projecting it across
the garden and leaving it suspended in the air over Parsifal's
head. When they went through the Transformation Music in the first
act together Brandt declared that it still allowed him too little time
for the working of the complicated stage apparatus; so Wagner

[634]

had to set to and write music enough to occupy two or three minutes more. "Now I suppose I shall have to compose by the yardstick", he grumbled.

For his chief singers he hardly knew as yet where to turn. For his Parsifal, he told the King in March, he could not think of a single tenor who would come anywhere near his ideal: "these people are all pitiable — they have a bit of voice, they are monstrously over-paid, and they are utterly talentless, lazy and vain". Jäger seemed to possess the negative virtue of having fewer disqualifications for the part than most of them, but the King did not greatly care for him. Wagner, however, thought he would have to make do with him, though in the end he would probably double the casting of the part; at any rate, he said, Jäger's Parsifal would be better than Unger's Siegfried. Materna might do for Kundry, but in this case also he would no doubt look round for a double. The other rôles were easier, while Lilli Lehmann had undertaken to train the Flower Maidens.

For his conductor Wagner was committed to Levi, by reason not only of his competence and devotion but also of his position as Kapellmeister in Munich. But it never ceased to rankle in him that the man was a Jew; and so, when Levi was at Wahnfried in January, he tried with the best intentions, but not very tactfully, to persuade him to submit to baptism, though how that operation would have improved Levi's conducting is not clear. Levi, the son of a Rabbi, did not take kindly to the idea. In June Wagner was guilty of a further gaucherie that almost ended in a breach between them. Levi had gone for a walk in the town and returned to Wahnfried ten minutes after the regular time for luncheon. Wagner met him watch in hand, reproved him before the whole family for his unpunctuality, and ended by saying, "Now let us go in to lunch. But no: first of all read the letter I have left on your bedroom table." "I went up to my room", says Levi,

"and found there an anonymous letter from Munich, in which the most offensive reflections were made on my character and on my relations with Wahnfried, and the Meister was conjured to preserve the purity of his work by not allowing it to be conducted by a Jew."

Levi held that it would have been more tactful of Wagner to have put the letter in the fire and kept silence about it; but Wagner justified himself by the sophistical plea that had he done so its poison would have remained at work in him, whereas by disclosing the letter to Levi he had saved himself from that danger. Levi, however, remained unappeased, and after leaving Wahnfried he wrote from Bamberg, on the 29th June, asking Wagner to release him from the obligation to conduct *Parsifal*. Wagner wired him to return at once so that the unfortunate affair might be put in order. Apparently Levi refused, for on the 1st July Wagner sent him a letter that was exquisitely typical of his inability to see anything from any point of view but his own. As he saw the matter, it was Levi who was in the wrong.

> "With all due deference to your feelings, you don't make things easy for yourself or us. It is precisely your gloomy way of looking at things that weighs upon our intercourse with you . . . In heaven's name come back at once and get to know us as we really are . . ." [1]

2

The story as thus told by Glasenapp, however, is incomplete. The anonymous letter, we now know, not only insulted Levi as a Jew but accused him of intimate relations with Cosima, — a fact which, paradoxically enough, made Wagner feel that he *must* retain him as his conductor, for only by so doing, he held, could he give the anonymous writer the lie. These facts we learn from a letter of Julius Kniese of the 17th July, 1883 to his wife.[2] Apparently Kniese derived his information (in 1883) from Bürkel, who must have had it from Levi. The truth of his account of the matter has recently been established beyond question by the publication of Cosima's letter of the 1st July, 1881 to Daniela. On the preceding 29th June, she says, there had been an unpleasant incident at Wahnfried,

> "an anonymous letter to Papa, in which such a scandalous accusation was made against poor Levi in connection with me that he could not contain himself and went away abruptly." [3]

Cosima, it will be observed, says nothing to Daniela about the conducting of *Parsifal* by a Jew; evidently the real source of the trouble at Wahnfried had been the reference to Cosima; and with

[1] RWSK, pp. 326-7.
[2] *Der Kampf zweier Welten um das Bayreuther Erbe: Julius Knieses Tagebuchblätter aus dem Jahre 1883, herausgegeben von Julie Kniese* (Leipzig, 1931), pp. 95-6.
[3] CWBD, p. 215.

this disclosure Wagner's thick-fingeredness in showing the letter to Levi becomes all the more surprising.[4]

The storm blew over, as so many others of a similar kind in Wagner's life had done, the occasional crudity of his manners being unable to alienate for long the people who revered him as an artist. But Levi had still many a bitter moment to go through in Bayreuth and out of it on account of his origin and his faith. Wagner's desire to placate him is understandable: the King, who was free of anti-semite prejudice, would have taken a serious view of the matter had Levi been goaded into refusing to be associated with *Parsifal*, for it was Ludwig who was making a production in Bayreuth possible, and moreover he had set his heart on having that production transferred later to Munich for his private pleasure. So in his letter of the 19th September to the King we find Wagner saying he believes he can repose full confidence in Levi's "extraordinary zeal and almost passionate devotion", for which reason he does all he can to "calm him down with regard to his Judaism".

> "Notwithstanding that many amazing complaints reach me as to this most Christian of works being conducted by a Jewish Kapellmeister, and that Levi himself is embarrassed and perplexed by it all, I hold firmly to this one fact, that my gracious King has generously and magnanimously granted me his orchestra and chorus as the only effective way of achieving an exceptional production of an unusual work, and consequently I accept gratefully the heads of this musical organisation . . . without asking whether this man is a Jew, this other a Christian." [5]

To this the King replied in his customary calm way in his affectionate letter of the 11th October:

> "I am glad, dear Friend, that in connection with the production of your great and holy work you make no distinction between Christian

---

[4] Levi tells us that immediately after an awkward luncheon he packed his bag and went off to Bamberg without saying good-bye to Wagner. Glasenapp questions his chronology, maintaining that he did not leave Wahnfried until the next day. Cosima's letter would appear to confirm Levi's account; but on whichever day he left it is clear that he did so in anger and disgust at Wagner's tactlessness.

Du Moulin, like Glasenapp, omits all reference to the part Cosima's name played in the letter.

[5] This, as Dr. Strobel points out, is at variance with the facts. Alexander Ritter told Kniese that Wagner had informed the Munich Intendanz that he did not want Levi, preferring to nominate a conductor of his own choice for *Parsifal*, and had been told in reply that he could not have the Munich orchestra without the Munich Kapellmeister. (Kniese, p. 17).

and Jew. There is nothing so nauseous, so unedifying, as disputes of
this sort: at bottom all men are brothers, whatever their confessional
differences."

But this tolerance was too much for Wagner. In his next letter
he exhibits the fanaticism and the sophistry of the German anti·
semite of all epochs. It is obvious to us of today that, with a combina·
tion of malice and ill-breeding which people of most other nationali·
ties find it hard to understand, he lost no opportunity, year in and
year out, of fretting the life out of his Jewish friends and collaborators about their Judaism. Joseph Rubinstein had gone to him in
1872 in a desperate effort to escape, by means of Wagner's art, from
the misery of a soul divided against itself and suffering under the
insults levelled at his race. A more tactful man than Wagner would
have seen the wisdom, to say nothing of the delicacy, of barring
the subject for ever from their conversations. Instead of doing that,
he harped to Rubinstein's face, as he did to Levi's, on the supposed
inferiority and vileness of his condition; and then it was they, of
course, who were responsible for the tortures they went through.
Rubinstein and Levi, he now self-righteously informs the King, have
been a great trouble to him. "These unfortunates", it appears, lack
the basis of that Christian education that gives "the rest of us" a
sense of oneness in spite of all our differences; and as a consequence they suffer such agonies of soul that often they contemplate
suicide. He had had to "exercise great patience" with them; indeed,
"if it is a question of humanity towards the Jews, I can confidently
claim credit on that score."

He cannot even give the Jews of his own circle with one hand
what is theirs by right without taking it from them with the other.
He cannot deny the magnitude of the services done him by Neumann, who, he says, "regards it as his mission to force the musical
world to recognise me". His explanation of this, however, is that
the Jews, thanks to their experience as dealers in, and appraisers
of, pictures, jewellery and furniture, have acquired an instinct for
the genuine and permanently valuable thing which the Germans
have so completely lost that they let the Jews fob them off with the
bogus! As for King Ludwig, Wagner can only surmise that he is so
tolerant towards the Jews because he has had nothing to do with
them: "for you they are only a conception, for us they are an
experience". He himself has associated in friendly, compassionate

and sympathetic wise with several of these people; but this magnanimity on his part cannot blind him to the fact that the Jewish race is

> "the born enemy of pure humanity and everything that is noble in it:
> it is certain that we Germans will go under before them, and perhaps
> I am the last German who knew how to stand up as an art-loving man
> against the Judaism that is already getting control of everything."

To this charming specimen of Hitlerism *avant la lettre* the King
made no reply.

3

At Wahnfried life had resumed its usual course after the return
from Italy. "Guests came and guests departed", as Sieglinde says,
and there was the customary houseful of people associated in one
way or another with Wagner's work. They must have been a difficult team to drive, so different from one another were they in temperament. We perhaps do Wagner some injustice when we so often
draw attention to his irritability and bad manners. He could be
trying enough, of course, as when he resented Joukowsky's taking
a fortnight's holiday from Bayreuth.[6] In July Heinrich Porges had
the temerity to differ from him during dinner on the subject of
Schelling: Wagner was so angry that he walked out of the room
when coffee was being served. But he himself must have had many
provocations from the people who were in and out of his house all
day long. On this matter we have been enlightened lately by the
publication of Cosima's letters to her eldest daughter Daniela, who,
fortunately for the Wagner biographer, was often away from home
and so had to be kept supplied with the latest news from Wahnfried,
in wise and charming letters that show Cosima at her best. Thanks
to these, we can see the ordinary round of life in Wahnfried very
much as it must have been from day to day. One comes to the conclusion that they all saw more of each other than was good for them,
and that their tempers and their behaviour sometimes suffered in
consequence. The main source of trouble was the unhappy, sensitive, brooding Rubinstein, who made up for the restraint imposed

---

[6] "He never liked it", says Glasenapp, "when the few people whom he regarded
as belonging to him went away from him. So he was annoyed by this brief absence
of his young friend, who had attached himself so closely to him: when he saw the
roses blooming in the garden he would have liked to show them to Joukowsky, who
was so susceptible to beauty; and so, as he himself said, half his own enjoyment of
them was destroyed."

on him by his reverence for Wagner's art by a considerable amount of rudeness towards some of the others — even, at times, to Cosima herself. A soul so sadly riven within itself needs solitude rather than society if it is not to be always showing its worst side. The tragedy was that without the powerful magnetic attraction of Wagner he would have had nothing whatever to help him to attain even an approximate and fluctuating stability.

He had introduced himself to Wagner in February, 1872 in a letter from Kharkov in which he lamented the disabilities and dangers to which his race was subject in the Germany of that epoch. He had not only contemplated suicide but attempted it, he said.[7] So he had decided to write to Wagner, who perhaps could help him, though not, he hoped, out of simple pity, not out of the mere desire to save him from suicide.

> "Could I not be useful to you in connection with the production of your *Nibelungen?* I think I comprehend the work, even if not entirely. So I hope for help from you, help I urgently need. My parents are rich and would supply me with the means to go to you."

Whereupon Wagner had invited him to Triebschen, treated him kindly, and afterwards taken him with him to Bayreuth, which he made his home, off and on, until Wagner's death.

It was his dog-like devotion to Wagner that made him at times intractable. He appears to have kept himself rather aloof from the other disciples, resenting, perhaps, their having any share with him in the man whose art was the centre-pin of his own unhappy being. He would not even accept the general instructions which Wagner had occasionally to issue to his "Nibelungen Chancellery"; whatever Wagner desired of him had to be communicated to him personally. In 1881, as Cosima's letters to Daniela indicate, he was more than normally difficult. He seems to have taken a dislike to the gentle Joukowsky and was often rude to him, and then to Cosima when she tried to pour oil on the troubled waters. "Malvolio Rubinstein" is her humorous description of him on one occasion. When she wants to commend him for good behaviour she does so by saying that he has been "very human", evidently a condition so rare

---

[7] He took his own life not long after Wagner's death — in September, 1884 — in Lucerne, having apparently gone there, after many fruitless attempts to accommodate himself to the ways of the world, to live once more in some sort of association with the spirit of Wagner.

with him as to call for comment. One day, because Kniese had been at Wahnfried and it came out that he had protested publicly against Rubinstein's article on Schumann, the young man almost cut Cosima in the street.

Joukowsky, for his part, was often ill and an anxiety to Wagner, and about this time he seems to have run into debt, perhaps as a result of his having given up his ordinary work to devote himself wholly to the *Parsifal* designs: in October the Patronatverein made him a payment of 4,000 marks for his sketches, which could hardly be called excessive. With one thing and another, Cosima's and Wagner's happiest moments were late at night when everyone had gone and they could relax from the strain of holding the balance between so many temperaments, so many susceptibilities. One thing is clear, that but for Cosima, with her self-control, her tact, her philosophical acceptance of the facts of human frailty, life at Wahnfried could not have endured an average week without an upheaval. And no one knew this better than the ailing Wagner, and it deepened his sense of gratitude towards her and dependence on her. It may have been at her suggestion that he acquired a billiard table, on which, she assured Daniela, "Stein plays well, Papa excellently".

4

In the spring of 1881 Wagner appears to have been irritated, and not without some justification, by an act of Bülow's that has been consistently misrepresented in the biographies. The accepted legend is that Bayreuth benefited to the extent of 40,000 marks as the result of a series of recitals given by Bülow for the benefit of the cause. The story is correct in all particulars, except that Bülow did not raise 40,000 marks in this way, and Bayreuth did not get the money. As it is desirable that Wagner biography should be cleared of as many as possible of the legends that encrust it, this one of Bülow and Bayreuth deserves detailed examination.

In a letter of the 10th September, 1880 to Hans von Wolzogen,[8] Bülow says that he has now completed the remittance to Feustel of the 40,000 marks he had set himself as his goal. His concerts, however, had realised only 28,000 marks; for the remaining 12,000

---

[8] Wagner was in Italy at the time; but in any case Bülow would not have communicated with him direct.

he has drawn on his savings. This represents, he says, "a not inconsiderable sacrifice" on his part, since he will have to replace the amount by his own exertions later. He has "anticipated" the intended full sum in this fashion for two reasons: in the first place because he hopes his action may serve as an example to "well-to-do enthusiasts", in the second place because he sees no prospect of earning 12,000 marks as a pianist for some time; for his recent appointment as Kapellmeister at Meiningen will leave him with scant leisure for touring, and in any case, after his signing Förster's petition to the Reichstag against the Jews he must expect not only an unfriendly attitude towards himself in the Press but a falling off of about fifty per cent in his audiences, for the concert public is made up of more Jews than Germans. At the end of his letter he says that if the Bayreuth School [for style] does not come into being,

"it is my wish, as you already know, that the 40,000 marks obolus shall be devoted to the erection of a statue to Wagner in Bayreuth: the Bismarck monument in Cologne cost exactly that sum".

If, however, the Committee and Wagner prefer to allot the money to any other purpose, anything they may suggest will be agreeable to him.[9]

At this point we must diverge for a moment to deal with another story that will undoubtedly develop into yet another Wagner-Bülow legend unless it is strangled in its cradle.

In a book on Bülow published in 1935 Ludwig Schemann says:

"Everyone knows that in the 1870's Bülow raised 40,000 marks for the Bayreuth sustentation fund by means of a tour as pianist. [A glance at the letter quoted above would have made it clear to Schemann that even this was not strictly true]. But it is not also known how this plan came into Bülow's mind. The facts were disclosed to me by a common friend. Bülow was standing with him one day before the Bismarck monument in Cologne. He asked, as it were casually, how much it would cost. When he was told, he flashed out, 'Wagner must have one too'. It must have been peculiarly gratifying to the always magnanimous Bülow that the money he had earned with such difficulty was used later not for a monument to the Meister but for the furthering of the splendid work, at once cultural and caritative, of Bayreuth."[10]

_____

[9] BB, VI, 28–31.
[10] SHB, pp. 46–47.

This account of "how the plan" for the concert tour "came into Bülow's mind" must be rejected as pure fiction: Schemann's inform-ant had no doubt heard of Bülow's suggestion, in his letter to Wol-zogen, that the money might be spent on a Wagner statue,[11] and his imagination and the impulse to dramatize himself had done the rest.

Bülow's letters between 1878 and 1880 place it beyond question that the Bismarck monument played no part whatever in his original plan. That monument was not unveiled until April, 1879. The idea of doing something for *Wagner and Bayreuth* had come into Bü-low's head in 1877, after he had learned that the festival of 1876 had involved the undertaking in heavy debt and the London con-certs had been a financial disaster; he was filled with rage at the indifference of the German musical world to Wagner's plight, and he resolved to do something not only to help the Bayreuth cause but to shame, if possible, his fellow-countrymen. Blended with all this, too, was a personal motive, and not at all a discreditable one, for making a telling public gesture on behalf of Bayreuth. It had been a searing grief to him not to have been able, for obvious reasons, to attend the *Ring* performances in 1876, and he hoped that by the honourable sacrifices, both of money and of personal pride, that he was now proposing to make for the Wagner cause it would be possible for him to visit Bayreuth later with his head held high. This becomes clear from a passage in a letter of his to his confidant Karl Klindworth of the 20th January, 1879:

"The day after tomorrow I play again in Berlin for Bayreuth. You, Bayreuth and Moscow have a wrong notion of the affair. It is far less a matter of the 10,000 marks — which in shabby Germany [12] will cost me more time and trouble than I thought — than of the *moral significance* of this piano-strumming of mine . . . and (egoistically) of making it possible for me to be present at *Parsifal*." [13]

---

[11] The letter had been in print since 1907.
[12] "In shabby Germany" is in English in the original.
[13] BNB, p. 60. His longing to hear *Parsifal*, which, he knew, would have to be in Bayreuth or nowhere, was intense: witness his comic rage after hearing Levi play a good deal of it to him from memory in Munich in June, 1879, and learning of the evenings at Wahnfried when Wagner used to sing the voice parts while the Jew Rubinstein accompanied at the piano and the Jew Levi listened with the manuscript score in his hands. "Why didn't your father and mine have us circumcised at the proper time?" he asks Klindworth in characteristic Bülowian fashion.

To Carl Bechstein, again, he writes, in August, 1878, that the recital he proposed to give in Berlin was "of the greatest importance" for *him*: "proceeds for Bayreuth; that is to say, not for the composer but for *Parsifal* — a moral necessity, so to speak, for me."

Bismarck's name does not occur at all in the correspondence relating to the plan until the 6th April, 1879, when Bülow tells Marie Schanzer — the lady who became his wife a few years later — that while conducting and playing in Cologne he had been present at the unveiling of the Bismarck monument. (He was a fanatical worshipper of the Chancellor).

> "On Wednesday I played again for Bayreuth: I mean to raise enough money by my Beethoven recitals for a fitting monument [14] to be erected to Wagner in his lifetime, as has been done for his fellow-giant Bismarck."

Perhaps Schemann's informant had heard of this letter also [15] and it had contributed to the manufacture of his story of the Bismarck monument having been the starting-point of Bülow's plan. But obviously the "monument" that Bülow has in mind is the firm establishment of the Bayreuth festivals and the School for style that was so dear to Wagner's heart. Bülow is giving his recitals not for a statue of Wagner but "for Bayreuth" — not the town but the institution.

When the Bismarck idea first occurred to him as an *alternative* to the festivals and the School we do not know. In his letter to Wolzogen of the 10th September, it will be recalled, he refers to his alternative suggestion of a Wagner *statue* as being already familiar to his correspondent. When had he first made that suggestion? Could it have been in February, 1880, when, taking advantage of Wagner's absence in Italy, he had given two recitals for the cause in Bayreuth itself? If so, why is there no mention of a Wagner *statue* in his letters of that time to any of his other correspondents? While in Bayreuth he had written to Klindworth telling him that the local inhabitants had turned up in surprising force at his recital, which had yielded about 800 marks net: Cologne had produced 545 marks and Munich 2,400, and he anticipates 1,000 in Frankfort: "you know that I intend to raise 40,000 marks in all". And

---

[14] Or "memorial": "Denkmal" may mean either.
[15] It was published in 1904.

as late as the 6th September, 1880 — i.e. four days before his letter to Wolzogen, — when telling Klindworth that he is still 12,000
marks short of his goal but that he is supplying them out of his
savings, there is still not a word of Bismarck, of a Wagner *statue*, or
of any other plan alternative to the original one of "Bayreuth".

One is forced to put the question plainly — was Bülow, who was
in a perpetually strained and irritable condition just then, deliberately trying to insult Wagner by his proposal of a statue? Was
it pure tactlessness on his part or a masterpiece of impish malice?
No one could have known better than he how offensive to Wagner
would be any association of his name, even in private, with that of
Bismarck; no one could have known better than he that all that
mattered to Wagner was the ideal of Bayreuth, and that he would
turn with contempt from a suggestion that he could be compensated for the failure of this by anything so paltry in comparison
as a statue; no one could have known better than he that Wagner's
gorge would rise at the thought of such a statue being paid for not
merely out of Bülow's labours but, in large part, out of his savings.
It was a foregone conclusion that he would refuse the money. Had
the writers who have enlarged on the agreeably sentimental theme
of the Bayreuth funds benefiting to the tune of 40,000 marks by the
magnanimity of Bülow taken the trouble to consult their Glasenapp
they would have discovered that no such thing happened. Feustel
and the Committee were naturally reluctant to look a gift horse
of this size in the mouth; but Wagner, as Glasenapp categorically
assures us, declined the money.[16] His statement has recently received final confirmation by the publication of Cosima's letter of
the 16th March, 1881 to Daniela, who was at that time in Berlin:

> "Papa [Wagner] is sending the 40,000 marks back [to "Deinem
> Vater", Bülow], with the request that it shall be invested for you
> [plural, meaning the Bülow children], as I have given to the theatre
> the legacy I received from my mother." [17]

The palpable snub would hardly be likely to improve Bülow's
temper, and perhaps it accounts for a good deal in his attitude towards Wagner during the negotiations over the proposed adoption
of the children.

---

[16] GRW, VI, 439. This volume appeared in 1911.
[17] CWBD, p. 171.

This awkward but unavoidable question had been under discussion at Wahnfried for some time; and about 1880 it became necessary to strive for a settlement of it with Bülow. It was the desire of both Cosima and Wagner that the latter should formally adopt the two Bülow girls, and that they should take his name. The step was manifestly in their interest. They had come to regard the Wagner house and family as their own; they were happy there, and their education and general training for life could be better looked after there than anywhere else, for Bülow, apart from the fact that his nomad life made it impossible for him to provide a real home for them anywhere, was utterly unsuited for the practical duties of parenthood. By this time he could have become little more than a dim memory to them. When Daniela, now a young woman of twenty-one, met her father in Berlin in April, 1881, it was the first time they had seen each other in twelve years; while Blandine did not see him until 1892 — twenty-five years after her migration to Triebschen with Cosima. Bülow could not deny that Cosima was an ideal mother, or that Wagner was all to them that a father could be, or that it was as well for the five children to be drawn together in every way possible; and when he saw Daniela in 1881 he realised what an excellent piece of work her mother had made of her, especially in the matter of social poise. But partly out of pride, partly out of blind resentment of ancient wrongs, he refused from first to last to fall in with the wishes of Cosima and Wagner.

When the children were all very young no explanations had been necessary: at Triebschen, Wagner had been "Vater" to them all. But as Daniela and Blandine grew up they had had to be enlightened to some extent as to the real state of affairs. Bülow now becomes, in Cosima's letters to Daniela, "Dein Vater", while Wagner is "Papa". But manifestly there were things they still did not know, things about which Cosima was understandably reluctant to go into details. Among these was the paternity of Isolde. Some queer kink in the distracted and unhappy Bülow made him persist, even in his communications to Cosmia, in affecting to consider Isolde not Wagner's child but his: "nos trois filles en commun" he calls the three elder girls in a letter of July, 1875. He insisted — vastly, we may be sure, to Wagner's annoyance — in making the same financial provision for Isolde as for the other two. It must have been he who misled Daniela on this point; and we can imagine the disturbance in the Wahnfried atmosphere when letters from her to her step-sister arrived addressed to "Fräulein Isolde von Bülow".

While thus gratuitously endowing Wagner's offspring with the name of Bülow, Hans objected violently to a formal adoption of Daniela and Blandine that would have meant their taking the name of Wagner. Even when he was in the wrong Bülow could always be intractable; but when, as in the present instance, he had a quite good case an army mule could have taken lessons from him in obstinacy. He and Cosima having failed to come to an agreement by correspondence, they met in Nuremberg in July, 1881 to see what could be done by talking. They had not seen each other for eleven years. Two painful and exhausting interviews left the problem precisely where it had been all along. "Hans with me", Cosima wrote in her diary,

> "from four o'clock to half-past six. I tried to subdue his violent accesses of emotion and to overcome his injustice towards Daniela. In vain! He asked me to stay till the following morning, as he had not succeeded in putting his proposal in the way he had wished. I consented . . . A second interview. Hans said he could not tell whether white was black or black was white. He has no star to guide him now. He was seized with a nervous twitching. We said farewell. I fetched Daniela, and would have liked to have another talk with him, but he did not desire it."

It is doubtful whether Bülow enjoyed two consecutive hours of real health and happiness in the whole course of his professional life; and in the years with which we are now concerned he was often on the verge of a breakdown. In this fretted condition he clutched at any opportunity that presented itself for venting his spleen on Wagner — not the artist but the man. No one in a rational frame of mind would have inserted that tactless sentence about a Wagner statue in a letter to Wolzogen which he must have known would have had to be placed before Wagner. That letter was dated "Bad Liebenstein, 10th September, 1880". Bülow, in a more than usually wretched state of health, had gone to Liebenstein in quest of a cure. "I have received indirectly rather bad news of Bülow's health", Liszt wrote to Princess Wittgenstein on the 7th. On the 12th — two days after the despatch of the letter to Wolzogen — he read in the papers that Hans had had a stroke that deprived him of the use of his right hand. That story turned out to be exaggerated, Liszt wrote to the Princess a few days later; but Bülow's own letters of this period show his nerves to have been in a deplorable condition, though he succeeded, as he always did, in making his weak body obey his masterful mind when it came to the practice of his art.

Perhaps we shall not go far wrong, then, if we attribute the febrile tone of his letter to Wolzogen to one of those accesses of malicious temper to which he was so subject, accesses in which he both said and did things he had cause to regret later. What is certain is that at the time of the negotiations with Cosima over the children he was in a condition of morbid irritation with Wagner. "His health is passable", Liszt writes in July, "but his temper is neither conciliatory nor indulgent. He is suffering from too much brains, too much spirit, too much study, too much work, too many tours and fatigues"; and again in September, "I saw Bülow in Meiningen. He is in a sad state physically: he is threatened with a malady of the liver, and his *moral* is hardly more satisfactory."

It had not improved his temper to be consumed with longing to see Neumann's production of the *Ring* in Berlin in May, yet to have had to keep aloof from it and its composer on personal grounds. The performances were to begin on the 5th May. Liszt and Bülow were in Berlin for a Liszt concert towards the end of April, but they both left the town a couple of days before Wagner and Cosima arrived. Bülow's letters leave us in no doubt as to his frame of mind at this time and later. Naturally the sensation-loving journals were making the most of the piquant fact that Bülow would be in Berlin just before the *Ring* began, and would presumably attend the performances. In March he angrily instructed his Berlin concert agent to correct all reports and speculations of this kind:

> "I neither wish nor feel under any obligation to visit the Viktoria Theatre; moreover I have other ambitions than to play the rôle of Lepidus in the triumvirate in which the two great masters [Liszt and Wagner] rightly have the first violin parts, to say nothing of the fact — of which you cannot be entirely ignorant — that certain private relations of mine with these great masters might give occasion for all sorts of unpleasant vomiting."

He writes to the same effect a few weeks later: he will be obliged if his agent will have it made known that he is not disposed to take any part, active or passive, in any of the Berlin celebrations in honour of "Meister Liszt and his son-in-law Meister Wagner", for "engagements elsewhere do not permit of my prolonging my stay in Berlin".

It was not long after all this that he flew at the throat of the English writer C. A. Barry for innocently asking him if he had been to the Berlin performances of the *Ring*.

> " 'No', he replied. 'Why should I hear the *Ring?* I think I know it as well as anyone else, and besides, Mr. Barry, I am surprised that you, knowing my present relations with Wagner, should allude to such a subject' . . . I tried to excuse myself by saying that I had seen it mentioned in the newspapers that he had just been in Berlin, and was curious to know whether he had taken the opportunity of witnessing a performance of the *Ring*. He burst out afresh: 'Then go to your damned newspapers; I am not an information bureau!' "

Barry surmises that it was "a cartoon of Liszt walking arm-in-arm with his two sons-in-law, which had appeared in a Berlin comic paper", that was "rankling in his recollection". [18]

---

[18] See Barry's article *Some Personal Reminiscences of Hans von Bülow*, in the London *Musician*, 1 Sept. 1897, p. 331. Barry, who knew him well and met him frequently, speaks of "his irritable temper, which made one feel oneself on the brink of a volcano with him".

CHAPTER XXXIV

ON THE WAY TO *PARSIFAL*

1

ALL THIS while the indomitable Neumann had been hard at work in not only his own interest but that of Wagner, who, as early as January, 1881, could write to him, "You have done great things for me, and procured me an income on which I myself would never have counted." Neumann planned, with Wagner's consent, to give *Tannhäuser* and *Lohengrin* in Paris in the spring of 1882. He would draw upon Paris for his orchestra and most of the chorus; but he would take with him a first-rate German cast, including the two Vogls, Anna Sachse-Hofmeister, Materna, Scaria, Gudehus, Schelper and Theodor Reichmann, with Seidl and Mottl as conductors. Knowing that in Paris a series of Wagner performances in German would be primarily a matter less of music than of politics, he prepared the ground as thoroughly as he knew how, getting introductions from the highest German quarters to Prince Hohenlohe, then German ambassador to France, the Austrian ambassador, Count Beust, and the French Minister of Foreign Affairs, Jules Ferry, as well as letters to the leading French musicians and journalists. He had an inkling of what he was up against when he went to Paris in the summer of 1881 to spy out the land. Hohenlohe was friendly, as he could hardly help being in view of the instructions he had received from Bismarck; but as Neumann was leaving the embassy he said to him,

"Don't sign any contracts just yet. I should like to take soundings in Government circles as to their feelings in a matter such as a German *Lohengrin* production. Tomorrow I am entertaining the President and the whole Ministry: I will bring the subject up over dinner and find out what they think; so wait until you hear from me."

Beust went straighter to the point: "My dear friend", he said, "I regard this project of yours as extremely dangerous; I fancy, indeed, that the French will smash up your theatre for you." What was at the back of the minds of these diplomatic realists was no doubt the feeling against Wagner in France on account of the very undiplomatic *Eine Kapitulation* of 1871.

A few days later Neumann was relieved to hear that there would be no unfriendliness towards the scheme in French high quarters. He promptly booked the Théâtre des Nations, paying a deposit of 15,000 francs, made a few other preliminary arrangements, and went back to Germany with a conviction that all was well. But on his return to Paris he found that the chauvinistic press had raised such a hullabaloo — some of the papers had published a translation of *Eine Kapitulation* — that the plan would have to be abandoned; so he let his 15,000 francs go by default. When in Munich he had heard from Vogl that the King had received a despatch from Paris advising him not to grant the tenor and his wife the desired leave for *Lohengrin*, "as it was feared that the theatre would be stormed and the lives of the German artists be in danger". Back in Paris, he discovered that the sender of this telegram had been none other than Hohenlohe. Neumann had to content himself with giving what should have been his Paris production of *Lohengrin* in Leipzig (on the 19th February, 1882), with Lederer as Lohengrin, Schelper as Telramund, Sachse-Hofmeister as Elsa, and Hedwig Reicher-Kindermann as Ortrud. This last was a young singer in her twenty-eighth year, the daughter of the Munich baritone August Kindermann. Neumann, quick to perceive her gifts, had given her a five years' engagement. She had a superb voice of great range, a magnificent presence and immense endurance; and as in addition she was an actress of genius and a first-rate musician she soon became a tower of strength to him not only in the Wagner operas but in other works of the repertory.[1]

---

[1] She died, before completing her thirtieth year of life, in June, 1883. Neumann described her twenty-four years later as "an artistic personality so great that her like is very rarely met with." "She was the greatest dramatic singer of the second half of the nineteenth century, as Schröder-Devrient had been of the first. Her Brynhilde, Erda, Fricka, Ortrud, Leonora, Eglantine and Carmen were things never even approached by any other singer, before or after her, whom I have heard in my long experience."

Weingartner, who heard her in Leipzig in his youth, described her voice nearly fifty years later as "magnificent, sumptuous, the most brilliant dramatic voice I have ever heard: its glitter, however, was not white but dark-blue, like a damascene sword-blade flashing in the summer sunlight. Her noble head was cast in a Roman mould." Of her Brynhilde he says that no one who had not seen and heard it could have any idea of its vocal and dramatic quality. Her Isolde "took one's breath away". When the shattering news came of her premature death some one in his hearing made

Another plan of Neumann's in 1880 had been to give *Tristan* in Leipzig; to this Wagner had no objection if the quality of the performance were guaranteed. But the usual difficulties arose, and it was not until the 2nd January, 1882 that Leipzig had its first hearing of the opera, with Lederer as Tristan and Hedwig Reicher-Kindermann as Isolde.

All this time, however, Neumann saw clearly that his trump card would be the *Ring*. In November, 1880 he had received the consent of Wagner to a production of the work in the Berlin Viktoria Theatre under Seidl, with Materna as Brynhilde, Therese Vogl as Sieglinde, Vogl as Loge and Siegmund, Jäger as Siegfried, and Schelper as Wotan and Hagen. He even succeeded in persuading Wagner to go to Berlin in April, 1881 to supervise some of the rehearsals. Wagner approved in general of what he saw and heard, though at first he showed ill humour when he discovered that Neumann had engaged Scaria — whom he disliked cordially just then for his behaviour in 1876 — to sing Wotan in some of the performances. But the Scaria of 1881 was a different man, and Wagner soon changed his opinion of him.

The first *Rhinegold* was given on the 5th May, followed by the *Valkyrie* on the 6th, *Siegfried* on the 8th, and the *Götterdämmerung* on the 9th. (It is interesting to learn that Wagner raised no objection to the *Rhinegold* being cut in two by an interval). Scaria sang Wotan in a style that reconciled Wagner completely to him, as he confessed in a letter to the King after his return to Bayreuth. He was pleased, too, with Vogl, despite the fact that the basic commonness of the man's nature came to the surface rather too often. A place would be found for him at Bayreuth, he said,

"for after seeing Jäger at last in *Siegfried* I recognise that he is out of the question for Bayreuth; we even had to substitute Vogl for him in the later performances."

What had happened was that Jäger, who was ill and had already shown symptoms of hoarseness, was in such bad shape at the rehearsal of *Siegfried* on the 7th that Neumann thought it advisable not to let him sing the next evening. But when Wagner heard of this he flew into a temper: "You've always had something against

___

the appropriate comment, "Wagner has summoned his Valkyrie to Valhalla!". See WL, I, 91, 94, 108, 157.

Jäger", he said; "I've noticed it before now." Solely to placate Wagner, but entirely against his better judgment, Neumann allowed him to play Siegfried on the 8th; but he was in such wretched voice that at the end of the second act a deputation of the Wagner-Verein waited on Wagner with a request that Vogl should play Siegfried in the *Götterdämmerung* on the following night. Wagner was now beside himself with rage; he went on to the stage, informed all and sundry that Jäger was "fit only to keep a tavern", and insisted on his making way for Vogl. But Neumann refused. "I warned you yesterday", he told Wagner. "Now it's too late to make a change. As Jäger has sung the part tonight he must sing it tomorrow; he won't be able to make such a mess of things then, as in the *Götterdämmerung* he is never alone on the stage." So Jäger sang again, and this time rather better, on the 9th; but the next day he left the town.

In spite of this mishap the cycle had been a great success, even Hülsen being convinced now that the complete *Ring* was a theatrical possibility. After the *Rhinegold* Wagner made a short speech from the stage, praising and thanking the performers, and another and longer speech after the *Götterdämmerung*, in which he again expressed his pleasure at finding artists who understood his intentions so well; and, with his hands in those of Neumann and Seidl, he thanked these two in particular for what they had achieved for him. He left Berlin on the 10th, having promised Neumann that he would return for the fourth cycle. It would have been better for all concerned had he not kept that promise.

2

On his return to Bayreuth he was greeted by Gobineau, who had been staying at Wahnfried with Joukowsky and the children during the absence of Wagner and Cosima in Berlin. He was Wagner's guest for some four weeks. The two men could not have been wholly harmonious, so different were they in disposition and in mental and social background. Gobineau, an aristocrat to his finger-tips, must have winced at some features of Wagner's make-up as a man. Wagner was possessed by a vague irrational optimism — the world was to be "redeemed" by a combination of Christianity, as he conceived it, and the theatre: Gobineau was sceptical, weary, disillusioned, anti-democratic, detesting the multitude, its mind, its manners and all its ways as heartily as Nietzsche or Beethoven did.[2] Each of them, however, found something in the work of the other to confirm him in his own pet beliefs. Gobineau, who returned with Wagner to Berlin for the fourth *Ring,* saw in the gods and heroes of that work the verification of his doctrine of the superiority of the Germanic race to all others, while Wagner was delighted to find in the *Inégalité des races humaines* what he imagined to be really scientific support for his own amateur generalisings on that and kindred subjects.

The essay on *Herodom and Christianity* that appeared in the September (1881) number of the *Bayreuther Blätter* was in part the outcome of his talks with Gobineau, partly of his recent reading of the *Inégalité.*[3] Here we have in its crudest form the Wagnerian dogma of degeneration and regeneration and the evils that come from the mixing of "bloods". By this time his mind had almost lost the capacity for thinking; it had hardened into a medley of a priori verbalisms which he mistook for historical facts and scientific reasoning. He now finds the cause of "the purblind lumpishness of our public spirit" to be

"a vitiation of our blood, not only by a departure from the natural food of man but above all by the degeneration brought about by the mixing of the hero-blood of the noblest races with that of one-time cannibals now trained to be the skilled business leaders of society."

By the descendants of one-time cannibals he presumably means the Jews, for virtue is found only in the "Aryan" race, of which the Germans are, or should be, the finest flower, according to Wagner. Outside his proper sphere as an artist, indeed, he was now rapidly becoming a maundering old man with a few fixed ideas, his belief in his mission as a saviour of civilisation increasing as his purely intellectual powers atrophied.[4] By 1881 there was little that mattered left in him but his music.

---

[2] "Vox populi, vox dei?" said Beethoven on one occasion: "*that* you will never get me to believe!" Cosima records Gobineau as saying that he would have no truck with "the religion of the poor, i.e. the masses, with whom a great individuality was always at odds. In this miserable world, to prefer the poor, as such, to the rich, the simple-minded to the wise, the cripple to the sound, was an error of which no Hindoo would be guilty."

[3] He had already recommended the work, which at that time was practically unknown, to his readers in the May-June number of the *Blätter*.

[4] Scientific works, with their scrupulousness in the matter of research, facts and method, merely bored him. What he liked, as Glasenapp naïvely puts it, was "a

Gobineau had travelled far and wide over the earth and seen many strange peoples and strange rites, but perhaps never anything so wonderful in its way as the birthday celebrations of which he was the privileged spectator at Wahnfried in May. Wagner gave the King a detailed description of them in his letter of the 19th June. Joukowsky's gift was a painting of his tableau of the Holy Family,[5] in which Daniela figured as the Mother, Siegfried as the Infant Jesus with the carpenter's plane, and Blandine, Isolde and Eva as the three music-making angels. The ceiling of the drawing-room was decorated with the arms of each town that boasted a Wagner-Verein: they had been obtained in secret by Cosima, and were now presented to the Meister with appropriate dramatic solemnity. The prelude was staged in the hall: Klingsor (Daniela) was sitting by his necromancer's apparatus, furious that he could not accomplish anything with it, until the Flower Maidens (Blandine, Isolde and Eva) put into his head the happy idea to produce something pretty for Wagner; whereupon the curtains opened and revealed Parsifal (Siegfried Wagner), who leaped out from a mass of roses to present his father with a watch, the gift of Cosima. It was a house, we begin to have the feeling, in which everyone was always acting, more or less. In the evening the children gave a further exhibition of their talents in a scene from a play by Lope de Vega and a Shrovetide drama by Hans Sachs. Gobineau, Wagner assured the King, "rejoiced like a child" that he had lived to see such a day.

3

True to his promise to Neumann, Wagner returned to Berlin, with Cosima, the children and Gobineau, for the last cycle of the *Ring* (May 25, 26, 28 and 29). Jäger having left and Niemann not being available, Vogl had to sing Loge, Siegmund and the two Siegfrieds in each of the last three cycles; that is to say, he was on the stage each evening, a feat of endurance only made possible, says Neumann, by his temperate habit of life.

This time Wagner came back from Berlin, he tells the King, more convinced than ever that the home of his art was Bayreuth and Bay-

hypothesis of genius"; any sort of "circumspect documentation" was repugnant to him.
[5] See *supra*, p. 633.

reuth alone. Though he and his work had been received with deliri-
ous enthusiasm he seems to have been dissatisfied with the stage
management of some portions of *Siegfried,* and it was probably with
his nerves fretted that he attended the final performance on the 29th,
at which the Kaiser himself and many leading political and social
persons were present. At the end there were many calls for Wagner,
who was looking pale and ill when the curtain rose and revealed
him surrounded by his performers. Neumann stepped forward to
deliver the speech he had prepared.[6] According to his story, he had
hardly begun his second sentence — in which, as etiquette demanded, he first thanked the royal house and then the public for
their enthusiasm and encouragement, — when Wagner turned and
left the stage. Perplexed and wounded as he was, Neumann managed to finish his speech, though acutely embarrassed at having to
address his thanks to the Meister into the wings. Wagner, meanwhile, had made his way to his box, from which he bowed his acknowledgments to the applauding house.

On the stage all was confusion and misery. Vogl, painfully conscious of an anti-climax, stood there awkwardly holding the laurel
wreath intended for Wagner, who, says Neumann, was suspected by
everyone of having yielded to one of those "unaccountable artist's
whims" to which he was known to be no stranger. That was Neumann's opinion also. He at once wrote Wagner a letter in which he
expressed his belief, in plain language, that personal relations
between them ought to cease. The next day Wagner sent first Seidl,
then Vogl to explain that what had caused him to leave the stage
had been one of those sudden cramps at the heart to which he was
subject. Neumann refused to accept that assurance. Wagner repeated the explanation in a letter in which he denied that there had
been any intention on his part to "insult" Neumann or anyone else
in public, and hoped it would not mean the ending of their personal relations. But Neumann was inappeasable: he left his card
on Cosima, but did not see Wagner, who quitted Berlin on the same
day.

Glasenapp, who could never forgive Neumann or anyone else for
the crime of being a Jew, nags at him in his usual cantankerous
fashion for his account of the affair and his interpretation of it,
without, however, essentially modifying either. No one doubts now

---

[6] It is given in full in his *Erinnerungen,* pp. 173–4.

that Wagner's explanation was, at any rate in the main, the right one. Why, then, did Neumann refuse to accept it? The only reason seems to be the one for which Glasenapp falls foul of him — his attribution of Wagner's walking off the stage to an "artist's whim". But not only Neumann but every singer on the stage, at some time or other, in Berlin, in Bayreuth or elsewhere, had seen similar exhibitions on Wagner's part in moments when his temper got out of hand and his manners suffered in consequence. What more natural, then, that, having already seen him in his tantrums at rehearsals, they should assume that this was just another of them, and feel that if he had anything against either the royal house, the public or the performances, he might have expressed it in a less wounding manner?

That this was so is implicit in Neumann's own account of the sequel. He steadily refused to accept Wagner's explanation. In the following July he was once more in Wahnfried on business: as he was leaving, Wagner gave him his solemn word that he had left the stage that night for no other reason than that he felt he would faint if he remained a moment longer. "Will you believe me now?" he asked. "But even then", says Neumann,

"I could not say 'I do'. Then he flung my hand from him passionately, clutched at his forehead, and said bitterly and reproachfully, 'Ah! that it should be so difficult to win belief!' We went in silence down the path to the gate. There we stopped: Wagner embraced me and kissed me, and we parted without another word. It was not until two years later, when the tragic news came from Venice of the Meister's sudden death from a heart attack, that I realised the tragic truth of his words."

In spite of this pitiful misunderstanding, which gave equal pain to both of them, Wagner had no intention of breaking with Neumann, who, he was well aware, was the only theatre manager in Germany to whom he could look for an assured solid income during the next few years. When Neumann left Bayreuth on the 21st July he had virtually completed a new arrangement with Wagner the exact terms of which were set forth in a formal contract in the following September. He was to have the exclusive rights in the *Ring* for Berlin, Leipzig, Dresden, Breslau, Prague, Belgium, Holland, Sweden, Norway and Denmark until the 31st December, 1886, against a royalty to the composer of ten per cent of the gross receipts. "Your pride", Wagner wrote to him, "is commensurate with my trust in you and your activities" — which does not sound as if his artistic conscience had received a mortal affront by the Berlin production of the *Ring*. The root of the trouble there had perhaps been Wagner's desire to impose on Neumann, as regisseur, Karl Brandt's son Fritz, and the inability or unwillingness of Neumann and Förster to engage him.

Hardly had this contract been signed, however, when a new and still bolder scheme came into Neumann's head, the details and outcome of which will be set forth shortly.

4

All this summer Wagner was busy with preparations for *Parsifal*. The main plan of campaign had been settled at a meeting of the local Committee on the 9th January at which Heckel, Schön and Pohl had been present. "It may be regarded as settled", the Bayreuth *Tagblatt* reported the next day, "that the *Parsifal* performances will take place in July and August next year. The price of seats, designed to cover the expenses, will be decided upon at a further session early next year.[7] The Patrons will have free admission to the first performance. . . At least eight and not more than twelve performances will be given, at intervals of two or three days. The external members of the Administrative Committee urge the pressing necessity of a great improvement in the train services to and from Bayreuth upon what they are at present." [8]

A month later the paper printed the latest news from Leipzig — the *Parsifal* cast would include singers from the Leipzig and Berlin Operas, among them Reicher-Kindermann, Lilli and Marie Lehmann, and Otto Schelper. (As it happened, none of these appeared in 1882). Detail on detail, not all of them proving accurate in the sequel, followed in the *Tagblatt* during the next few weeks. Water was to be properly laid on to the hill on which the theatre stood. The temple of the Grail would be modelled on the Siena Cathedral, but with round Romanesque instead of pointed Gothic arches, "the general effect being as if the Knights of the Grail had themselves built their sanctuary in the mountains". A box with its private en-

---

[7] It was finally fixed at thirty marks.
[8] EP, pp. 7–8. Eggert's useful book contains a number of verbatim reports of progress in the Bayreuth Press.

trance was to be constructed for King Ludwig. Marianne Brandt had come to Bayreuth to study the part of Kundry with the composer. The voice parts had been sent to the singers, and the rehearsals would run from the 2nd to the 22nd July, 1882. In the autumn of 1881 it was announced that the principal parts would be cast in duplicate or triplicate: for Kundry there would be Marianne Brandt, Materna and Therese Vogl; for Parsifal, Winkelmann, Vogl and Jäger; for Amfortas, Beck Jr. and Reichmann; for Gurnemanz, Scaria and Siehr; for Klingsor, Hill; for Titurel, Kindermann; Lilli Lehmann would lead the Flower Maidens.[9] The rehearsal time-table for the following summer was already complete down to the last detail. Two performances were now earmarked for the Patrons, and eleven for the public.

In the summer of 1881 Karl Brandt spent many weeks in Bayreuth working out the Transformation scenes and the mutations of the Magic Garden in terms of machinery and action. The King being set against "the prosaic Vogl", as he called him, Jäger had once more come into the running as Parsifal, and it was to coach him in the part that Heinrich Porges went to Bayreuth in July. But Wagner had in his mind also Winkelmann, of Vienna, who arrived in August and sang certain things to his satisfaction. In September he could outline his impressions and his general plan to the King in this fashion: Winkelmann as Parsifal, Marianne Brandt as Kundry, and in addition "Vogl and Materna, and, in case of need, poor Jäger and Frau Vogl". The doubling of the chief rôles was a matter not merely of artistic principle but of practical necessity, for Wagner saw himself committed to a large number of performances on financial grounds, the production for the benefit of the Vereine being followed by performances to which the ordinary paying public would be admitted. Amfortas, he continued, would be taken by Reichmann, Klingsor by Hill, Gurnemanz by Siehr and Scaria; the latter's Wotan in Leipzig had surprised and pleased him. Lilli Lehmann would provide and train six leading Flower Maidens with good voices and good looks; another twenty would be found by Levi.[10]

---

[9] Neither she, the Vogls nor Beck sang in 1882.
[10] Lilli Lehmann declined later to co-operate. Wagner was in Italy at the time (the spring of 1882). Lilli, in her memoirs (LMW, p. 299 ff), excuses her defection on the ground that she did not wish to meet Karl Brandt's son Fritz again.

In the early part of September Wagner had gone to Dresden to submit to the attentions of his American dentist Jenkins. He spent some eight days there and in the neighbourhood, and at the Dresden Opera, he tells the King, he found, to his surprise, a tenor, Heinrich Gudehus, and a soprano, Therese Malten (at that time only twenty-six), who struck him as likely to be the best Tristan and Isolde obtainable anywhere: [11] "it will be difficult to obtain the latter from Dresden, but I will try to get both of them for some performances of *Parsifal*". Seidl, Humperdinck and others were busy copying the score or running through the music with Wagner or one of the singers: Rubinstein, however, had forsaken Bayreuth for Italy in August, in one of those moods which he himself was no more able to account for than Wagner and Cosima were. The only other trouble — with Vogl — was of a kind not infrequent in the opera house and the concert room; the tenor made any engagement of himself at Bayreuth conditional on his wife's singing Kundry. To this Wagner would not agree, the music being quite unsuitable to Therese's voice: [12] perhaps, in view of the King's antipathy to Vogl, he was glad to have so plausible an excuse for denying himself the pleasure of his co-operation.

5

Meanwhile Neumann had hatched out a new and still bolder scheme for himself and Wagner. In September he drew up a series of propositions of which the following is the gist. A company of ten persons, with Wagner at their head, was to be formed for the production of his works. Each member was to contribute 25,000

---

[11] He had heard Malten as Senta. In Dresden he had of course revisited his old haunts, and such friends of his youth as were still living. Kietz was still there. Pusinelli was dead, but Wagner had luncheon with the widow and the family. Tichatschek was still in the town. He had been pensioned since 1872, and, thanks to a black wig, looked astonishingly youthful at seventy-four. (He outlasted Wagner by three years, dying in January, 1886).

[12] "I have been in great trouble with regard to my Kundry", he told the King in June. "None of my former singers is quite right for the part: none of them has the deep notes that are indispensable for the demonic character of this woman. Lately I have been driven to thinking of Marianne Brandt, who, indeed, is the only woman I know with the stuff in her for Kundry. . . . She has 'le diable au corps', and will do her best. Still, I will not give up Materna just yet."

After Wagner's death Marianne Brandt confessed to Ludwig Schemann that while his sudden end had shaken her, his personality, as distinct from his art, had never been "sympathetic" to her. See SLD, p. 210.

marks capital and be entitled to ten per cent of the net profits; in addition, Wagner was to have a ten per cent royalty on the gross receipts. At the end of ten years after his death his heirs were to be free to withdraw from the company and to claim the return of the original investment of 25,000 marks; while at the end of thirty years the other members, as well as the heirs, should be at liberty to make a similar claim. Should Wagner find it inconvenient to pay down 25,000 marks at once, Neumann would advance the sum to him on his note of hand. Neumann was to have the exclusive right of performance of *Parsifal* in Europe (outside Bayreuth) and America. "In my opinion", he wrote,

> "the profits of the undertaking should be so immense that I do not hesitate to calculate your income from it at at least 60/70,000 marks a year. Consequently I consider this an opportunity not to be underestimated for securing the future of your family."

To this proposal Wagner, through Cosima, made some objections on business grounds — it assured Neumann, he said, the right to assign his exclusive interests to others if he should find himself incapable of giving the contemplated performances, while no provision was made for an equivalent right on the composer's part; moreover, there was no agreement as to dates of performances or for an advance payment. He suggested some modifications to meet these quite reasonable objections: he ought not, for example, to be expected to refuse Dresden, which was capable of doing the *Ring* well, the right to perform it if Neumann, owing to the peculiarities of the local situation, were to find himself unable to produce it there for some years. At the same time, he added, money was an object of immediate concern to him, as he needed a long holiday abroad for his health; so he would view with favour a proposal on Neumann's part to make him a preliminary payment of, say, 20,000 marks in respect of the anticipated profits.

Neumann at once accepted this condition; it appears that a large sum had been placed at his disposal for the erection of a Wagner Theatre in Berlin. Wagner, in his reply, displayed no enthusiasm for the Berlin part of the scheme, though at the same time not ruling it out: he himself, he pointed out, had had an offer of a Theatre of that kind years ago, but had turned his back on it because he regarded Bayreuth as the only place for the production of his works in accordance with his ideal. In any case, all that Neumann would need would be Wagner's name and his works, not his money, while it would obviously be impossible for him (Wagner) to function as a producer of the operas simply as one member of a syndicate.

The scheme as originally submitted by Neumann had included the cession to him of the right to give *Parsifal* anywhere in Europe and America, and Cosima, in her reply, had said nothing about this but confined herself to certain purely business points. From this the reader of Neumann's book is apt to draw the conclusion that Wagner had no objection to the suggested syndicate giving *Parsifal*, notwithstanding his many asseverations to the King and others that the work was to be given nowhere but in Bayreuth. The position, it must be confessed, is far from clear. It is true that in the letter to Neumann which we are now considering Wagner says,

"*Parsifal* is to be given nowhere but in Bayreuth, for inward reasons which my noble benefactor, the King of Bavaria, so thoroughly understood that he even waived a [public] repetition of the Bayreuth production in the Munich Theatre. This being so, how could I dispose of *Parsifal* in the way you suggest? Never can or will I allow it to be produced in any other theatre."

But then comes a curious proviso —

"unless a genuine Wagner Theatre were founded, a stage-*dedication*-theatre, which should travel about and so spread throughout the world just what, until then, I had fostered in all its fulness and purity in *my* theatre in Bayreuth. If we are to adhere with unshakeable consistency to this idea in connection with your undertaking, the time may come when I will hand over *Parsifal* not to any Court or Town Theatre but to the Touring Wagner Theatre alone."

Apparently what he meant was that while the opera would for the present be given only in Bayreuth, because only there could he ensure it being given under conditions that would preserve its peculiar character as a religious drama, he might have no objection later to a similar production in a touring Theatre devoted to the same aim and animated by the same ideal as Bayreuth, — but only to some such theatre. The question, however, was to arise again between him and Neumann before long.

6

All this while his health was worsening. To the King he could write philosophically in September that age had brought him more wisdom than of old in the conduct of his life.

"When I merely contemplate my position I ought to be satisfied with my life, for when I reflect how high was the goal I had set myself I see that I have been more successful than many another. To be sure, external matters should now be made easier for me, as my weariness makes my burdens harder to bear: I could now comport myself more calmly in the face of strong opposition than my temperament would have allowed me to do in my earlier days",

— thanks, he adds, to the devotion of his friends and helpers. But his ailing body was slowly but surely dragging him down. "Unfortunately", he told the King,

"not a day passes without my being gravely disturbed by a trouble that has been with me for the last five years, recurring with ever greater frequency, and now, after another year in this refractory climate, plaguing me almost without intermission. It is a nervous disorder, taking the form of a chronic cramp in the chest; it has its root in abdominal disturbances, and is at its worst in this everlastingly raw and inclement air."

The perplexed doctors, unable to find anything definitely wrong with him organically, could only fall back helplessly on the standard medical prescription of a change of air. He had an intense longing for the south: his thoughts ran incessantly upon Italy, Greece, Seville, Egypt, Madeira, anywhere where the sun was shining. By August he had drawn up the complete plan for the rehearsals and performances of the following year. This was sent to all the artists so far engaged, together with copies of their several parts; a piano score of the opera, they were told, would follow shortly, and it was impressed on them that they would be expected to arrive in Bayreuth on the appointed day note-perfect in their rôles.[13] With this off his hands, and Brandt, Joukowsky and the others now quite clear as to what they had to do, he could make his arrangements for his escape from the Bayreuth that oppressed him so sorely.

He had decided to go as far south as Palermo, influenced by the glowing accounts Rubinstein had sent him of the climate and the

---

[13] Therese Malten was definitely engaged in November.

beauty of the place. He left Bayreuth on the 1st November, breaking his journey for a few hours at Munich, where he had a talk with Levi about the preparations for *Parsifal*. From there he went in a private salon-coach to Naples, accompanied by Cosima and the children, the indispensable Schnappauf, and Siegfried's new tutor, a certain Herr Türk, from whom, however, he parted company in the following March, partly because a long and serious illness of Siegfried's made it impossible for the boy to be pestered with lessons, partly because Türk had not come up to expectations.

Wagner had left behind him a Munich inches deep in snow; on the 3rd he was in Rimini and then in Foggia, enchanted with the sight of the Adriatic and the marked change of climate: "sunlight, sunlight, warmth!" he wrote to the King, "and delightful living vegetation!" [14] Next a day in Naples, where his tired eyes could hardly bear the unaccustomed light, welcome as it was; and a night passage by boat, in glorious moonlight, to Palermo, where he found Rubinstein awaiting him, and his thirsty soul drank its fill of gardens and groves thick with orange trees. Despite a little rain, and the inevitable annoyances arising from the fact that Rubinstein was a Jew — on which he enlarged in a letter to the King, — he was now happy and fairly well, and able to make progress with the scoring of *Parsifal*. He was gratified to find, in this "luxuriant land of Greeks and Saracens", contrasting so happily with the country of his birth, which was a fit habitation "only for wolves and bears", what he took to be support for his doctrine of the world-mission of the German race; for had not this southern civilisation, as he told the King, been founded by the Normans and the Hohenstaufens, and did not the enthusiastic memory still survive in the Sicilians of the Kaiser Friedrich II and his son Manfred, whereas the French domination was remembered only as a dark passing cloud?

As invariably happened, he now thought it the bounden duty of all his friends to come at once and surround him with the domestic atmosphere he liked, and he was grievously hurt at their not complying immediately. Gobineau had to decline his invitation, his half-blinded eyes being unequal to the strong light of Palermo, "le point le plus illuminé du monde", as he described it. But Joukowsky, bringing with him an expensive present which Wagner had com-

---

[14] He had an instinctive repugnance for anything in decay. He could not even endure cut flowers in a room, Mathilde Maier tells us. See RWMM, p. 5.

missioned him to obtain as a Christmas gift for Cosima, arrived on the 23rd December and stayed a month. Wagner greeted him with tears of gratitude in his eyes: "This is as it should be", he said; "this is how people ought to behave to me!" But the year was not to end without the Fates dealing him a heavy blow. On the 27th December Karl Brandt died suddenly in his fifty-third year. His important work on *Parsifal* was so complete in all essentials that in November he had been able to show the King working models of the machinery and decorations in Munich. But his death hit Wagner hard; he had confidence in Brandt's son Fritz, but the young man was as yet almost untested by practice in Bayreuth.

Wagner had settled in luxurious quarters in the Hôtel des Palmes; but in February, weary of not only the expense but the discomfort of life in even the best hotels, he removed to an unoccupied villa in the Piazza dei Porazzi, the property of an Italian admirer, Prince Gangi, whose acquaintance he had recently made: he seems to have been quite hurt at the demand of the proprietor of the Hôtel des Palmes for compensation for the two months still remaining of the term for which he had agreed to take the rooms. The Gangi house had been built for occupation by the owner only in the summer; consequently all the living rooms were on the shady side and had no provision for heating in the winter. So Wagner had to install stoves, with a bad effect on his health after the fresh air he had been used to in the hotel. He at once caught cold, and the pains in the chest recurred. Siegfried too had been seriously ill; the boy, with his passion for architecture, had been in the habit of wandering all over Palermo and the neighbourhood, and in some insalubrious spot or other had picked up an infection which it took him several weeks to shake off.

7

Sicily was almost completely lacking in musical life, which perhaps did not greatly distress Wagner, his opinion of Italian music being what it was. His main intellectual occupation all this time was reading. He read and expounded all Shakespeare's chronicle plays to the faithful few, and his comments on them were dutifully recorded by Cosima. They do not amount to much in English eyes. He could read the bard only in German translations, which, with all respect to the authors of them, are not the same thing as Shakespeare in English. He never, indeed, seems to have had the least sensitiveness to the finer points of style, and still less to the local styles that have sprung from the genius of a language no less than from the subject matter of a work and its milieu. The fusion of "Norman" and "Saxon" speech into an organic whole in English was something he was incapable of grasping. For him, only a "pure" race — whatever that may be — can have a "pure" language: "mixed" tongues "have no value". Which marvellous conclusion leads him on to another no less wonderful. "He was disturbed", says the reverent Glasenapp,

"by the fact that a Shakespeare had been possible in the English tongue. That was an anomaly. . . It was very significant that in Shakespeare's time — for until then (up to the period of Henry VII) French had been the predominant tongue, and English only just commencing — a Shakespeare, very much as was the case with Dante, could poetise and create in this tongue that was at that time only in process of formation; but later, when the *mixtum compositum* had firmly established itself, it meant the death of poetry."

It apparently never occurred to him that, as so frequently happened with him, he was spinning a purely fanciful theory about a subject of which he knew nothing. From wild nonsense of this kind it was merely one step further to his declaration that "I prefer the worst German book to the best French: the former always evokes something sympathetic of which the latter has no inkling".

A curious product of the Palermo period has recently come to light — the so-called "Porazzi melody". On the 2nd March (1882) Cosima records that hearing Richard playing the piano she entered the room and found him noting down some music for which, he told her, he had "at last found the proper shape". On the 27th he played the fragment to her, and it "brought back the most secret incidents of her soul". On the 18th April she found a fair copy of the music on her table. What lay behind all this has been elucidated for us by Dr. Strobel.[15] On the reverse side of one of the sketches for the second act of Tristan, relating to the lovers' invocation to Night — "Wen du umfangen, wem du gelacht, wie wär' ohne

---

[15] See his article *Das "Porazzi"-Thema: über eine unveröffentlichte Melodie Richard Wagners und deren seltsamen Werdegang*, in BFF, 1934, pp. 183 ff. The page of music is now the property of Arturo Toscanini, to whom Frau Eva Chamberlain presented it in 1931. It had lain for many years in the original orchestral score of *Parsifal*.

Bangen aus dir er je erwacht?" — are jotted down eight bars of music (not used in the opera), the first seven of which coincide with those of the "Porazzi" melody. The jotting ends at that point with an "etc." The ink is brown with age; manifestly it dates from 1859, when Wagner was engaged on the second act. Deciding that it was unsuitable to *Tristan*, he did not develop the idea past the eighth bar. But that he had not forgotten it, or that the lighting upon the old page of sketches in 1882 had stirred up ancient memories in him, is shown by his brooding over it at the piano and at last rounding it off as a gift to Cosima. He struck out the eighth bar in the violet ink which he was using for the score of *Parsifal*, and, having found what Cosima describes as "the turn he desired", added a further six bars, made a fair copy of the whole, and laid this on Cosima's table.[16]

8

It was in Palermo that Wagner sat for a sketch by Renoir that has played a part in Wagner-iconography out of all proportion to its deserts. In later life the painter told Ambroise Vollard that Wagner sat for him for no longer than twenty-five minutes; but from a letter of his contemporary with the event it appears that the séance lasted ten minutes longer than this. According to his story, a friend in France had suggested that Renoir, who was in Naples at the time, should see Wagner and get permission to paint him. Renoir straightway took the boat to Palermo, but left the letter behind him. He called at the Hôtel des Palmes; but a hotel servant would not admit him, as the Meister was not receiving that day. Returning the following day with the letter he saw Joukowsky, who told him that Cosima could not see him just then, while Wagner was busy finishing the score of *Parsifal*.

Renoir explained that he had come in the hope of being allowed to paint Wagner: Joukowsky told him, with a smile, that for the last two years he himself, a painter, had been waiting in vain for an opportunity to do that. On the 14th January, his work on *Parsifal* being finished, Wagner consented to see Renoir that afternoon, though he was very tired. The conversation, which lasted for about three-quarters of an hour, seems to have consisted mostly of remarks by Wagner in bad French and embarrassed interjections by

---

[16] See the facsimile opposite page 664. "Schmachtend" means "with longing".

the painter. The next day Wagner sat for him; but towards the end of the thirty-five minutes he "lost his humour", says Renoir, "and became stiff": "I think I altered what I had done too much", he adds, though he was pleased that the sitting "wasn't too much of a farce". Still, he felt that the sketch was at any rate "a small reminder of this marvellous head". Wagner, he tells his correspondent, said, after glancing at the sketch, "I look like a Protestant clergyman". Glasenapp gives his comment on it thus: "It looks like the embryo of an angel which an epicure [17] has swallowed, mistaking it for an oyster". Evidently he did not think much of Renoir's effort: he was tired and perhaps bored towards the end of the sitting, and no one knew better than he himself and his artist friends how completely his face changed according to his health and his mood of the moment. Later Renoir made from the sketch the oil painting that now hangs in the Paris Opéra.[18]

Before Wagner left the Porazzi villa he entertained a number of his new-made friends, including Prince Gangi, Count Taska and the Prefect of Palermo, at a garden party at which he conducted a local military band in performances of the *Kaisermarsch,* the *Huldigungsmarsch* and the *Siegfried Idyll.* He became very fatigued as the concert went on, and at one stage of it, unknown to the company, he had one of his all too frequent heart attacks.

In the night of the 19th–20th March he said farewell to Palermo, moving on to Acireale, where he spent a few restful and happy

---

[17] Not "an Epicurean", as an English writer has translated the passage. Wagner's comment was probably made to Cosima and Joukowsky later. Glasenapp, by the way, gives the date of the sketch as the 15th February; it should be the 15th January.

[18] See Ambroise Vollard, *Auguste Renoir, 1841–1919* (Paris, 1920), and the same writer's *La Vie et l'oeuvre de Pierre-Auguste Renoir* (Paris, 1919). Another version of the sketch, a lithograph, is reproduced in this latter volume. Part of Renoir's letter of 1882 was quoted by Adolphe Jullien in JRW, pp. 311–312; the full text has only recently become available, in a German translation, in Hans Graber's *Impressionisten-Briefe* (Basel, 1934). Another portrait of Wagner by Renoir, in oils, is reproduced in Graber's book. Jullien gives us also (p. 157) a Renoir drawing of Wagner as he was "about 1865", made from a photograph, which might be either that of "Wagner in the 1860's" or that of 1873 (reproduced in ERWL, pp. 319, 482); more probably the latter. This Renoir drawing is in any case an unsatisfactory piece of work — more Renoir than Wagner. After seeing how he has enfeebled the face here — it is as if a soft impressionist gauze had been laid upon those imperious features, with their challenge to a hostile world — we are less surprised at the psychological misfire of the work of 1882.

Renoir, it may be added, was never more than faintly musical, though at one time he had been swept off his feet by what he calls "the passionate fluid of sound in Wagner's music".

weeks in the Grand Hôtel des Bains, with excursions to Giarre, Riposto, Taormina and Messina. On the 13th April the family set out for Naples, and on the following day for Venice, where they remained a fortnight. There Wagner looked out for a resting-place after the fatigue of the coming production of *Parsifal*. The Palazzo Loredano attracted him, but he was unable to come to an agreement with the agent about it. On the 28th, the day before his departure, he virtually decided on the mezzanine floor of the Palazzo Vendramin-Calergi. Venice brought him one disagreeable reminder of days of old. Chancing to discover in a book shop the address of Karl Ritter, who had made Venice his home for several years, he called on this former friend, but was not received; apparently Ritter's resentment of ancient wrongs, real and imaginary, was still too strong to make him wish for a reconciliation.

On the 1st May Wagner was home again in Bayreuth, to enter on his last great effort on behalf of his art — the flotation of *Parsifal*.

CHAPTER XXXV

NEARING THE GOAL

1

WHILE WAGNER was settling down to the preparations for *Parsifal* in Bayreuth, Neumann was pushing on energetically with an audacious scheme of his own. He had given up the idea of co-ordinating a Wagner Company with the recently founded Deutsches Theater in Berlin, with the composer himself as a shareholder. As his directorship of the Leipzig Opera was nearing its end, and there was a possibility that it might not be renewed, he decided in January, 1882 on a company of his own which should tour with the *Ring* from the 1st September, 1882 to the 31st May, 1883. He obtained from Wagner for that period the exclusive rights of performance of the work in all the theatres to which the concession had not already been made. "I will give thirty-six cycles in nine months", he told the composer; "according to my calculations they will bring you in at least 150,000 marks in royalties."

He had already acquired the Bayreuth stage equipment for the *Ring* for 52,000 marks — not without the usual misunderstandings, for he took the contract for "the whole of the *Nibelungen* appliances" to mean that he was acquiring not only the machinery but the lighting apparatus, whereas Wagner protested that he had never had, and could not possibly have had, any intention of ceding this, because, for one thing, 52,000 marks would be no sort of compensation for a total outfit that had cost him 150,000 and had been used for only three cycles, and for another, because the lighting installation was indispensable for all future productions in Bayreuth·and could not be replaced for less than 30,000 marks. Neumann insisted no further, though the misunderstanding was awkward for him; in a London theatre more especially he was doubtful of finding a lighting equipment adequate to so unusual a work as the *Ring*.

It was in London that he had planned to open his campaign; and thither he had gone with his Leipzig machinist in October, 1881 to inspect the stage of His Majesty's Theatre. Convinced that the work would be practicable there he made the necessary advance arrangements, and in April of the following year went once more to London with the whole of his technical staff to install the Bayreuth appliances, the opening performance being fixed for the 5th May. He was soon to realise that the London theatres, even in those days, had a lighthearted way of their own where opera was concerned. Berlioz could have given him a good deal of enlightenment on that matter, and on the general English tendency to muddle through.[1] "Under my contract with the director Mapleson", says Neumann,

> "the theatre was to be in complete working order for me, including the whole of the necessary technical and administrative personnel, heating and lighting during the rehearsals and performances, an orchestra of the numbers I had specified, a male voice chorus of about twenty-eight for the *Götterdämmerung*, and the "supers", placards and announcements — the last two being a very important and expensive factor in London. When I arrived I asked for Mapleson; I was informed that he was on an opera tour in America. I had hardly inspected the theatre and started on the preliminary arrangements when I received from the owners of the theatre, a London bank of high standing, a letter containing the surprising information that Mr. Mapleson was still in debt to the bank for his rent and consequently had no right to dispose of the theatre: if I wished to give the performances in May I must first come to an agreement with the bank as to conditions."

He sought out Mapleson's representative, who told him that the impresario was still in America, or it might be Africa, or it might be anywhere. Were the chorus and orchestra ready for him? asked Neumann. "It's doubtful". The technical and administrative staffs? "These you will have to engage yourself". So there he was — in London, with the whole of the Bayreuth apparatus, all the contracts with his singers signed, but no theatre, no orchestra, no chorus, no local technical personnel; and he was due to open in a month with the *Ring*. But Neumann was a great general, for whom difficulties existed only to be overcome. He made a financial arrangement with the bank as to the theatre. He engaged the necessary staffs. He put the placarding and advertising in hand. He telegraphed to Seidl to bring over the Laube Orchestra from Hamburg after a month's re-

---

[1] See Berlioz's humorous account of his own difficulties in London in his *Memoirs* (BMEN, Chapter LXXIV) and the *Soirées de l'orchestre*, Ninth Evening.

hearsal with it there. He engaged the chorus of the Cologne Town Theatre. And now, he fondly imagined, he had provided for everything. The poor man did not know his London. There was still something he had not reckoned with — the carpets.

> "It is well known that in the London theatres the foyers, boxes, stairs and so forth are furnished with splendid carpets and tasteful hangings. When I entered the theatre one day just before the general rehearsal I received a shock: the carpets and draperies had disappeared. When I asked what had happened I was informed that these valuable articles belonged to the furnishers and would be supplied to the theatre only for a certain payment. More negotiations, more agreements, more money to be paid out!"

But the curtains and hangings were there for the final rehearsal, and to the amazement of everyone the curtain went up on the *Rhinegold* on the day and at the hour fixed by Neumann months before — eight o'clock on the evening of the 5th May.[2]

2

Neumann had had other troubles to contend with. In spite of his warnings, Wagner had some time previously granted a concession for *Tristan* and the *Meistersinger* to Franck, the director of Drury Lane, who was working in conjunction with Pollini of the Hamburg Opera; and when Neumann arrived in London he found Franck's bills already on the hoardings. The Drury Lane performances, under Richter, were good, but the enterprise ended in dismal failure, the chorus and orchestra being left unpaid at the end of the season. Wagner had promised to attend some of Neumann's rehearsals, but in view of the delicate situation that had developed he was no doubt glad to have so excellent an excuse as his health for not keeping his word. On the same grounds he declined a doctorate offered him by Oxford University.

---

[2] Mapleson he saw only once. He turned up in the cheeriest of spirits one day, congratulated Neumann on his achievement, and invited him to lunch. Neumann had to decline the pleasure, as he was busy in the theatre: he hinted, however, that he would like to see Mapleson one day for a little business talk. The director airily agreed — "Tomorrow, day after tomorrow, any time you like". He shook hands cordially with Neumann, and with a blithe good-bye passed out of his sight for ever. "Soon after", says Neumann, "he went bankrupt, and for the £2,600 he owed me I received some eight years later a cheque for £51." Mapleson, in his entertaining reminiscences (*The Mapleson Memoirs*, 1888), maintains a discreet silence with regard to Neumann.

Even without the composer, however, Neumann was very successful with this first production of the *Ring* in London. Thanks to an
introduction from the German Crown Prince he managed to get the
Prince of Wales (afterwards King Edward VII) to attend no fewer
than eleven of the performances. The Prince had been so charmed
by the swimming Rhine Maidens that at one performance of the
Rhinegold he went behind the scenes and expressed a desire to see
the apparatus at work; but when he discovered that the occupant
of the car was not to be the pretty young Augusta Kraus but one
of the male stage hands he turned away with an impatient "What
the devil!"

Neumann's company was an excellent one, including as it did
Hedwig Reicher-Kindermann, Scaria, Schelper, the two Vogls, and
Reichmann, with Seidl as conductor. But soon Scaria was lost to
him. In the first *Valkyrie* performance he had been a magnificent
Wotan as far as the end of the second act. But in the third act he
entered from the wrong side, to the astonishment of Vogl, who had
been singing Siegmund that evening: "he crept in", says Neumann,
"timidly, shyly, as if he were being pursued, with bent shoulders
and drooping spear." Vogl, who was watching the scene with Neumann in the wings, called out, "Great heavens, Scaria has gone
mad!"

> "Imagine our horror as Scaria sang throughout the whole third act —
> the most important one in the Wotan rôle — in half-voice, transposing
> all the high notes an octave lower, all the low ones an octave higher,
> looking all the time fearfully into the wings as if some danger threat-
> ened him from there."

Neumann, who had been present on the night of Ander's mental
collapse in the Vienna Opera,[3] realised only too clearly what had
happened. The next day Scaria seemed to have no recollection of
what had occurred; though complaining of a violent headache he
ran through the Wanderer scene with Seidl at the piano. Seidl's
report on him was not reassuring; he stumbled through words and
music as if he were seeing them for the first time. He was allowed,
however, to sing in *Siegfried* on the following evening, when he forgot whole pages of the score, as if it had been to *him*, as Neumann
says, that Hagen had handed the cup of forgetfulness. It was evident now that he could not be allowed to appear again; yet still he

---

[3] See Vol. III, p. 147.

seemed to have no understanding of what had happened, and was furious with Neumann for transferring his rôles to Reichmann and Schelper. At last he was persuaded to take a vacation. Neumann did not see him again until the following August, when, to his amazement, he sang Gurnemanz in Bayreuth in magnificent style, though a special prompter had to be supplied to whisper the words to him.[4]

3

In the spring and early summer of 1882 Wagner was mostly occupied with spade-work on *Parsifal*. As there was a vague possibility of the King attending the festival special arrangements were made to ensure his privacy: not only, Wagner told him in May, would he have his own approach to the theatre but the front of the building was to be reconstructed in such a way that his box, salon and balcony would be isolated from the rest of the house, and the lighting would be so arranged that the audience would not be able to stare at him.

In April, in an *Open Letter to Hans von Wolzogen* that appeared in the *Bayreuther Blätter*, Wagner announced the end of the Patronatverein. It had become obvious that of itself it could neither finance the production of *Parsifal* in 1882 nor guarantee the continuance of the festivals in later years. Wagner would therefore be compelled to present his new work in the ordinary way to the ordinary paying public. Thanks to the demand for seats the financial success of the festival seemed to be assured,

> "so it is to be hoped that after redeeming my pledge to the Patronatverein [for two private performances before the members alone] I shall be in a position to carry on the undertaking by myself, and to repeat the Bayreuth festivals annually in the manner now dictated by necessity — by means entirely of public performances".

This change in the machinery of the festivals from a private care to a public appeal, he added, necessarily brought with it a change

---

[4] Apparently recovered, he sang with Neumann during the long tour of the company in 1882–1883, and again in Prague, where Neumann had now become director of the Deutsches Landestheater. The end came in Vienna in 1886, when in the second act of *Tannhäuser* he whispered to the Elisabeth, "What opera is it we are singing?", and had to be led from the stage. He died insane on the 22nd July of that year.

in the purpose and the scope of the *Bayreuther Blätter*: no longer a semi-private organ of the Patronatverein, it would henceforth address itself to the nation as a whole. In the following year, therefore, the sub-title of the *Blätter* — "Monthly Journal of the Bayreuth Patronatverein" — was altered to "Journal for Discussion of the Possibilities of a German Culture". The first number of the new quarterly was issued by Wolzogen shortly after Wagner's death in 1883: then a new Richard Wagner Verein was formed to further the work of Bayreuth, and this took over the *Blätter* as its official organ.

The reader will recall that Wagner's ideal had been from the first a theatre to which those who were interested in his art and his cultural ideal should have free admission. Experience had taught him that this was impracticable; but he had never given up the idea of setting aside a number of free seats for people, especially students, whose hearts were with him but who could not afford to buy tickets. In the July number of the *Blätter* there appeared an Open Letter of his to Friedrich Schön on *The Stipendiary Fund*. In this he took a rather pessimistic view both of the prospects of German music and of the future of European civilisation. He was too old now, he said, to undertake the organisation and management of a school for style even if the means for it were placed at his disposal. All he can do now in that direction is to produce his *Parsifal*. But it grieved him to think that, the financial exigencies of the public theatre being what they are, this and future festivals should be within the means only of the well-to-do. So now he suggests the forming of a fund to help the poorer enthusiasts, a fund that should be administered by a body other than the ordinary Managing Committee of the festivals. Schön at once set the ball rolling with a donation: the idea caught on, and soon after Wagner's death there came into formal being the Stipendiary Foundation which from that time to our own has done such good work.

4

Wagner had had too long an experience of the vanities and jealousies of operatic "artists" not to be aware that the doubling or trebling of the casting of the main rôles in *Parsifal* would bring a world of trouble on his head. The device was necessary, if only to provide against the possibilities of sudden illness in the company. In the Open Letter to Schön he hints that he is not unaware that the singers may not take kindly to this arrangement,

> "more especially since we have heard so much from the French and Italian theatres of the 'creation' of this rôle or that . . . By 'creation' is meant that if a singer has been the first to appear publicly in a part he has fixed the character of it once for all, and his successors have merely to imitate him . . . This has brought much evil in its train, especially when the creating has been done behind the composer's back."

It is refreshing to find the two outstanding geniuses of the operatic stage in that epoch protesting against the nonsensical theatrical jargon of "creating" a part. Some of the most vigorous passages in Verdi's letters are devoted to this absurdity. For Verdi's difficulty was the same as Wagner's, not to find singers who would "create" this or that character for him but to find performers capable of the simple feat of understanding what *he* had created and reproducing it faithfully. To the conductor Faccio the old man expressed in 1884 his ironic astonishment that in Brescia *Otello* had actually been a success without the singers who had "created" it: "I had grown so accustomed to hearing the praises of this couple sung that I had almost come to believe that it was they who had written the opera!" "I want only one creator", he told his publisher Giulio Ricordi:

> "I shall be satisfied if these people will reproduce simply and exactly what I have written. The trouble is that none of them ever do this. I often read in the papers of 'effects unimagined by the composer'! but I have never come across any of these myself. I do not admit that either singers or conductors are capable of creating: this is a notion that leads to the abyss."

And again, in the true Wagnerian vein,

> "A conductor who dares to change the tempi! I hardly think we need to have conductors and singers who can discover new effects. As far as I am concerned I swear that no one has *ever, ever* even so much as succeeded in bringing out all the effects I had intended. No one! Never, never . . . neither a singer nor a conductor."

It is a pity that Wagner and Verdi never met; they would have found themselves in hearty agreement on this and many another matter.

Wagner was tactful enough to say in his Open Letter that

"all the kindly disposed artists who are now about to gather round me with a zeal that does me honour are mainly concerned with rightly understanding the tasks I am setting before them, and achieving them under my personal guidance."

But no amount of cajolery could make some of the singers anything but the peacocks they were by nature and by habit. In particular none of them took kindly to the idea of anyone but himself or herself playing this part or that on the opening or the closing night. The Vogls had been especially troublesome. First of all Vogl was unwilling to co-operate unless his wife also was engaged: then he objected to being placed on the same level as the other tenors. On the 20th May Wagner wrote to Levi:

"I gather that with regard to the coming performances of *Parsifal* in Bayreuth Herr Vogl has informed you of the difficulties I must be prepared for if I do not unconditionally give him and his wife the precedence over the other singers. So I ask you to pass on the following considerations to the excellent artist on my behalf . . . As regards Frau Vogl, deeply as she has moved me in various portions of the rôles in which I have heard her, I thought it only prudent not to offer her the part of Kundry, which needs, to carry it through to the end, a vocal energy which I did not think I could demand of her. Consequently I entrusted the rôle in the first place to Frau Materna and Fräulein Brandt, and it was only when I got the impression that this might cause Herr Vogl some embarrassment that I left it to him to go through the part and say whether I ought to entrust it to his wife.

As Herr Vogl will have seen my public announcement that I propose to utilise various gifted singers for the many performances of *Parsifal,* when he has grasped my idea he will not be hurt if, besides his alternating with Herr Winkelmann, he finds Herr Gudehus and Herr Jäger singing Parsifal. Similarly Fräulein Malten will sing Kundry a few times; and it would be very satisfactory to me if Frau Vogl also were to appear in some of the many performances. But as against all this, Frau Materna had assumed, from the fact that I invited her first, that she would be in sole possession of the rôle; so now she stipulates, as the condition for her co-operation, for the right to the first performance, while Fräulein Brandt, who studied the Kundry part with me seven months ago to my great satisfaction, will, I confidently assume, modestly refrain from putting forward a claim to the first performance."

In view of what Levi now tells him he asks him to deliver the following message from him to Vogl:

"I must come to a decision soon; and I am prepared to cut down the number of performances so drastically that I shall be able to manage with a single cast of well-disposed and willing artists, in which case I shall have to endure with equanimity the withdrawal of those singers who are incapable of working in complete harmony with me."

Faced with this ultimatum, Vogl was driven to reply that as he foresaw that "a fourfold distribution of the principal parts" would lead to a number of complications and annoyances, and as he could not and would not separate his own name from that of his wife, he withdrew his promise to take part in the festival. As Wagner had no need at all of Therese, and could afford to dispense with Heinrich, and as he knew, moreover, that the King had not the least desire to see Vogl playing Parsifal, he could not have been greatly perturbed by this turn of events. All he did was to ask Levi to pass on the whole story to Bürkel, who, he knew, would communicate it to the King.

There followed in July a little trouble with Winkelmann. By some mistake in the rehearsal-calls Gudehus had been summoned to a scenic rehearsal in a form that may have led him to believe he was to sing in the first performance: then Winkelmann turned up in Bayreuth, threw his weight about, and Levi had to make it clear to Gudehus that he was to take the second performance and after that alternate with Winkelmann.

5

The King kept urging Wagner to compose *Die Sieger;* but in July, exhausted by his labours in the theatre, he assured Ludwig that *Parsifal* would be his last work. The devastating fatigue from which he was suffering was an admonition that he had come to the end of his bodily strength: "nothing more is to be expected of me". He was never in the least doubt that he had written his last work for the stage. It lay, indeed, in the very nature of his artistic constitution that it should be so. He was not of the order of opera composers who, having finished one opera, look round for another "subject", decide on a "libretto", and at once set to work at the music. Each one of his greater operas had been the final flowering of a seed planted in him in his youth, a seed that had to develop silently within him for years according to its own inner nature be-

fore its musical possibilities were fully manifest even to him. Without this long period of gestation it was impossible for him to create
an organism so multiplex as any of the works of his maturity. He
would know well enough, then, that whether he desired it or not
Parsifal would be his farewell to the theatre. But all through these
last years the urge to compose purely instrumental music never
left him; and he seems to have given Cosima a definite promise to
write for her a tragic pendant to the *Siegfried Idyll.*

His health was probably worse than even the friends who saw
him daily realised, worse, perhaps, than he suspected himself. Only
one person saw, by the light of pity and love, how near he was now
to his final reckoning. For a good two years before the end, Cosima
could have little doubt that the axe was laid to the root of the great
old tree; and life meant nothing to her now but delaying the fall
until at least *Parsifal* had been given to the world. Neumann and
others, when they saw Wagner in 1882, were conscious of something eerie in the atmosphere of Wahnfried; some of them said
openly to each other that they feared Wagner was not long for this
world. He was aware, in his own way, that the shadows were closing
in; and as they crept nearer he became more pathetically anxious
than ever for love and sympathy and understanding. The word
"troth", which had always meant so much to him, was now often
on his lips. He was grateful now for anything that would give his
spirit strength to hold the sword and shield that were fast becoming too heavy for the old warrior's tired arms. With profound gratitude in his heart he saw now how true to him had been more than
one man with whom his tempestuous nature and the stress of cir-
cumstance had set him at variance in days gone by. To the ageing
Liszt also had come the light and the truth. Outwardly as courteous
as ever to the half-crazy, religiously-malignant woman who had
tried to separate him from Wagner, but to whom he knew he had
once owed a great deal, within himself he had shaken off the bonds
which she and his own loyalty combined had put upon him,[5] and his
heart had gone back to where it belonged, to the artist whom he
knew, and openly proclaimed without jealousy, to be the greatest
of his century. In spite of all the differences in their temperaments
and beliefs, and all the petty fretfulness of the passing day, the two

---

[5] After his death a number of her letters to him in the last years were found still
unopened.

men were closer together now than they had been since the Weimar days of thirty years before.

Ludwig, too, Wagner now saw as he was and had been all along, the loyalest, most generous and most disinterested of friends. So in a letter to him of the 13th May he could sing the praises of Liszt and Ludwig as the two men who had most truly and abundantly given him what he had always needed most — love and fidelity. One really great man, he said, he had known in the dark days before the King came into his life as rescuer — Liszt.

> "What clouds of vapour and rubbish were spread between us — artfully, but oh, so foolishly! — from within his own circle! And how profoundly I rejoice that I never doubted him, that he, for his part, again and again cut through the web of lies, that he was the first to proclaim me to the world, and that since then it has been his joy and pride to see the fulfilment of his prophecy."

To the King also he pours out his gratitude:

> "You are right, my dear, heaven-sent Lord, to remind me so often, with pride, of the finest virtue you are conscious of possessing — fidelity. To each of my poetic conceptions you have brought your own seed of life."

On Cosima fell the major burden of these last distressful years. Richard could afford to indulge himself in the fits of peevishness and the dark discouragements arising from his heavy work and his broken health. But for Cosima there was no relief possible even of this sorry kind: she had to endure infinitely in patient silence, sustained by one thought alone, that of keeping him alive for the completion of his mission. She could read all too plainly in the faces and the guarded speech of some of her friends that they too were anxious about the Meister; and one day it cut her to the heart when an American visitor thoughtlessly remarked that Richard had aged since he saw him last. All through the period of the rehearsals he needed much sleep to restore him. "Yesterday", she wrote in her diary, "Richard fell asleep in his great dressing-room chair. I watched over him and prayed. Ah, we are both so tired, and would fain live with the children and for them alone!" And, sleepless herself in the night, she would hear him talking in his own uneasy sleep. One night he kept calling out again and again, "Adieu, children!" Italy had filled him with a deep dislike for Germany, and he could no longer stand up to the atrocious Bayreuth climate. In June and July the weather was worse than usual — grey skies, cold mist and driving rain; "he cursed Germany, he cursed Franconia, he cursed Bayreuth", and Cosima had to defend them as best she could, pleading that with all its disadvantages Bayreuth was the hearth and home of his work. And, hardest to bear of all, there were the heart spasms that would rend him almost daily and fill her soul with fear. She was never greater, never more deserving of the respect and gratitude of posterity, than in these last months of trial.

6

For the birthday of that year — the last that Wagner was to know — Gobineau had come; he was Wahnfried's guest from the 11th May to the 17th June. The King's birthday gift was a pair of black swans, to which Wagner gave the names of Parsifal and Kundry. Humperdinck, Joukowsky and the children all contributed to the celebrations. A choir of children from the neighbourhood, long coached in secret by Humperdinck, sang in moving fashion the "Faith" chorus from *Parsifal;* and there were the usual tableaux and congratulatory speeches. A pleasant surprise for Wagner was the sudden appearance on the scene of the young Count Biagio Gravina, the second son of the Sicilian Prince of Ramacca, to whom Blandine had become engaged in Palermo. In the evening a couple of young military doctors, friends of Humperdinck's, regaled the company with "Schnadahüpfln" to a guitar accompaniment. Wagner laughed till he cried, and hailed a particularly realistic representation of a peasant brawl with shouts of "An Iliad! An Iliad!" But this was too much for Gobineau, himself a mortally sick man now, and hardly in the humour for even the fictive company of the mob whom he loathed from the bottom of his patrician soul: he sat by himself in a corner of the room, growling, "C'est affreux; puéril!" The pro-Nietzschean anti-Wagnerians of the last generation tried to persuade us that Wagner and Gobineau were contrary elements that could not mix. But all the evidence goes to show that although they differed on some points they got on very well together and had the highest regard for each other. When the Frenchman left Bayreuth in June Wagner presented him with the rare first edition of Goethe's *Faust.* They never saw each other again. Gobi-

[681]

neau went off to Gastein in search of health, then to friends in the Auvergne, and finally, in October, to Italy. In Turin, on the 13th, he had a stroke when entering a railway carriage: he was removed to his hotel, where he died the same day.[6]

As the time for the *Parsifal* rehearsals drew nigh there was the usual gathering of the faithful in Bayreuth. Stein came in June, Liszt in mid-July. It had been a blow to Wagner to learn early in July that after all the King would not attend any of the performances. His motive was obvious enough: *Parsifal* meant far too much to him for him to wish to hear it under the usual annoyances inseparable from his position, the gaping, cheering crowds in the town and the theatre, the necessity for talking to people who bored him, and so forth. He preferred to wait until he could hear the work under ideal conditions in Munich, with himself as sole auditor. Wagner urged him to attend at least one performance at Bayreuth under his direction, for something of the real spirit of the work would be bound to be lost in any other theatre; but the solitude-loving King could not be persuaded. And so the last opportunity for another meeting of the two men was lost.

Before we go on to the story of the *Parsifal* festival we must take a last glance at the activities of Neumann during Wagner's lifetime and a little while after.

"If anything on this earth could astonish me", Wagner wrote to him on the 13th June, "it would be you! Heavens, what restless energy, what faith, what courage!" Neumann, his Leipzig engagement nearing its end, wound up his activities there with a series of performances of all Wagner's operas from *Rienzi* to the *Götterdämmerung*. In Prague, as director of the German National Theatre, he later carried on with the good work. But that was not all: his head was full now of his audacious scheme for a touring Wagner Theatre. In July and August he spent some time in Bayreuth, where he saw several performances of *Parsifal*. Early in August Wagner signed without debate a contract giving him all the powers he desired in connection with the *Ring*. "Then", Neumann tells us,

"came the turn of the *Parsifal* contract; it had already been agreed upon between us that if the Meister should decide to allow the work to be produced anywhere but in Bayreuth I should have the exclusive

---

[6] Cosima dedicated to his memory an *Erinnerungsbild aus Wahnfried*, which appeared anonymously in the *Bayreuther Blätter*.

rights in it for all countries. He was just about to sign the contract when he suddenly paused. He sat for some time at his desk, pen in hand, sunk in reflection. Then he turned slowly to me and said quietly, 'Neumann, I *did* promise you, and if you insist I will sign. But you would be doing me a great favour if you do not do so now. You have my word that no one but you shall have *Parsifal*'. I answered, 'Meister, if you tell me that I should be doing you a great favour, it goes without saying that your word is enough for me'. With great emphasis he replied, 'Thank you, Neumann!' He wrung my hand and kissed me; and one of the most significant episodes of my life was closed. My son was waiting for me in the arboured walk leading to the gates of the house. I told him what had happened in that memorable hour, and added, 'Karl, today, by relinquishing *Parsifal*, I have surrendered millions'. 'Father', said the seventeen-years-old boy, 'Wagner's thanks are worth more than a million'."

Neumann's *Ring* contract ran to the end of 1889. He opened his tour in Breslau on the 2nd September, with a company, under Seidl's conductorship, that included the two Vogls,[7] Unger, Reicher-Kindermann, Klafsky, Augusta Kraus, Niemann, Scaria, August Kindermann, Julius Lieban, and, when Vogl seceded, Anton Schott of Hanover. He went on to success after success with the *Ring* and Wagner concerts in town after town in Germany, Belgium, Holland, Switzerland, Italy, Hungary and Austria. In 1889 he took the *Ring* to Russia, with Karl Muck as conductor. Wagner and his heirs were indebted to Angelo Neumann for much more than a handsome income.

---

[7] For an account of his many troubles with the grasping and intractable Vogl and with his wife, who was jealous of the success of Klafsky and Reicher-Kindermann, see Chapter XVI of his memoirs.

CHAPTER XXXVI

PARSIFAL

1

ALL IN ALL, the *Parsifal* rehearsals were nothing like so difficult a matter as those of the *Ring* had been in 1876. The amount of ground to be covered was far less, while in those six years a few at any rate of the German singers had developed some understanding of the problems set them by a Wagner opera. The Parsifal and Kundry of his dreams would be hard to realise in the flesh, but apart from these two rôles the new work did not present any insuperable difficulties to singers of ordinary intelligence; Hill was a born Klingsor, and Scaria's task as Gurnemanz was relatively easy. The choruses were for the most part merely a matter of picked voices and careful rehearsal. The main trouble all along was in connection with the machinery — the two Transformation scenes, the collapse of Klingsor's castle, and the change at the end of the second act from a garden to a desert. The first of these episodes was a perpetual trouble; [1] always the music gave out before the machinery had accomplished its work. For a time Wagner took the situation philosophically, even humorously: formerly, he said, the Kapellmeisters used to pester him to shorten his operas; now people wanted him to lengthen them. But when, after many experiments, Fritz Brandt once more asked for still more music to give him time to work his ma-

---

[1] It would be interesting to know whether the idea of a transformation curtain — a succession of pictures, moving in one direction, creating in the spectator the illusion that a stationary figure in front of it is moving in the opposite direction — was entirely Wagner's own. Ludwig Börne, in a letter of January, 1831 from Paris, describes in detail an evening he spent in the Odéon Theatre watching a sort of dramatic-panoramic representation, lasting nearly six hours, of the life of Napoleon I. His escape from Elba was shown thus: "He stands with his soldiers on the deck of a man-o'-war, and the course of the ship is imitated in the most deceptive manner: the coastal scenery keeps constantly changing, from rock to rock and then to the open sea, so that the beholder gets the impression that the ship itself is in motion." Börne, *Briefe aus Paris, 1830–1831* (Hamburg, 1832), I, 188. Was a device of this kind common in Paris in the 1830's; and did Wagner, perchance, see it in use during his stay there from 1839 to 1842? It is evident from Börne's account that he himself had never seen anything of the sort in Germany.

chinery he lost his temper and swore he would wash his hands of the whole business. The situation was saved by Humperdinck, who went home, drafted a few extra bars, submitted them timorously to Wagner, and, rather to his astonishment, had them approved. They were hastily copied into the score and parts, and at the next rehearsal the timing was correct. In later years the moving curtain was manipulated more quickly, and Humperdinck's little contribution to the score was no longer required.

Wagner had worked out the time-table for the rehearsals with his usual precision. The company had to be in Bayreuth by the 1st July at the latest, note-perfect in their parts; and as the final rehearsal was fixed for the 24th there was a good three weeks in which to weld the components into an organic whole. The orchestra, mainly that of the Munich Theatre but reinforced by picked players from other towns, numbered 107.[2] Including the Knights and Squires and allowing for the double or treble casting of some of the rôles, there were 17 principal singers. The choral parts called for 6 leading and 23 subsidiary Flower Maidens, 31 Knights of the Grail, 19 voices from the middle height of the temple, and 50 children's voices in the dome.[3] The first cast of principal singers was to be Winkelmann (Parsifal), Materna (Kundry), Scaria (Gurnemanz), Hill (Klingsor), and Reichmann (Amfortas); the second cast would draw upon Gudehus, Marianne Brandt, Siehr, and Fuchs (of Munich). To these were added later Therese Malten and Jäger. Levi was the chief conductor, with Franz Fischer as second in command. There were to be sixteen performances in all, the first two for members of the Patronatverein.

With the leading singers there was no such trouble as there had often been in 1876, though each was watching the other warily, and now and then there would be symptoms of jealousy. Wagner's wise duplication of the casting made him more independent of them than he had been in the case of the *Ring;* none of them dared indulge in the luxury of "temperament" when he knew there was another

---

[2] The King had paid for the two months' use of the Munich orchestra and chorus out of his private funds. The total cost to him amounted to 50,930 marks, plus travelling expenses at the rate of 50 marks a head for 44 chorus singers and 73 players, the two conductors, and two other officials.

[3] The figures as given by Glasenapp do not agree in all respects with the official list printed in the *Tagblatt* on the 1st July, or with Wagner's enumeration in his letter of the 8th September to the King; but the deviations are unimportant.

ready and delighted to step into his shoes at a moment's notice. Materna had asked to be allowed to postpone her arrival in Bayreuth in order to visit her mother: she received a telegram informing her that no one absenting himself from the opening rehearsals would be allowed to sing in the first performance, and a second dose of the medicine was not required.

2

By mid-June the scenery had all arrived, and with the barometer set fair for a successful season the anti-Wagnerian Press thought it high time to begin its unclean work again. In 1876 it had tried to keep people from the festival by raising the scare of a typhus epidemic in Bayreuth. Now, in 1882, the Berlin *Tageblatt* announced that the performances would have to be postponed owing to an outbreak of smallpox in Franconia; and the Bayreuth authorities had to come out with an emphatic official démenti. From the Hof *Anzeiger* came a bit of trouble of another kind, emanating, apparently, from the nettled Vogl. "From Bayreuth", it said,

> "it is announced that in those Wagner circles that do not mumble devout agreement with, and blind veneration for, every ukase of the Meister, great dismay has been caused by the definitive refusal of the Vogl couple to sing, because of the brusque rejection of Frau Vogl."

Once more the Committee had to make known the real facts of the case.

Meanwhile other preparations were being pushed on energetically. Two of the grievances in 1876 had been the bad approaches to the hill and the imperfect lighting of the roads. On the 27th June the Bayreuth *Tagblatt* proudly announced that the Town Council had not only constructed a fine pavement of coal-cinders and sand and bordering stones along the main route to the theatre, but even the ditches at the side had been put in order and the paths in the fields paved. Evidently the pilgrims of 1876 had had a good deal of discomfort to put up with. There was now to be adequate lighting along the main roads. The big restaurant to the left of the theatre, seating 1,500 people, had been much improved, and diners could enjoy at that time a view over the town in the hollow that has since been lost. Little Bayreuth, in fact, with its 29,000 inhabitants, 11 breweries and 76 beerhouses, its shop windows full of "Siegfried pens" (made in England) and "Richard Wagner pens", a popular sparkling wine rejoicing in the name of "Klingsor's magic potion", and "Parcival cigars" at 56 marks per thousand, now had its feet firmly set on the modern road to progress. The one thing that nobody could improve was the weather, which seems to have been typically Bayreuthian during the first half of the festival.

The local music critic became more eloquent every day over the wonders he saw at the rehearsals. Joukowsky, he told his readers, had been responsible for the designs and the Brückner brothers for the realisation of the opening woodland scene, the interior of the castle of the Grail, the Magic Garden, and the flowery meadow of the third act. Klingsor's tower and the Transformation scenery in the first act had been done by "artists from the Preller school". The costumes had been made from Joukowsky's coloured sketches by the Frankfort firm of Plettung and Schwab, and certain of the "properties", again from Joukowsky's designs, by Bayreuth workmen.

3

Gradually the town filled with the faithful, among them Stein, Malwida von Meysenbug, Liszt and Elisabeth Nietzsche, but not her brother, though one suspects that he would have been glad enough to be there had his pride allowed him to do so without an express invitation from Wagner, which was not forthcoming. He was still a member of the Patronatverein, and as such entitled to a seat for one of the first two performances. Elisabeth had asked to be allowed to use his voucher. "I am glad", he wrote to Overbeck from Genoa on the 29th January,

> "to hear of this decision on my sister's part: I imagine all my friends will be there, including Herr Köselitz [Peter Gast]. As for myself, I have stood *too near* to Wagner for it to be possible for me to put in an appearance simply as a festival guest without a sort of 'restoration' ($\kappa\alpha\tau\acute{\alpha}\sigma\tau\alpha\sigma\iota\varsigma$ $\pi\acute{\alpha}\nu\tau\omega\nu$[4] is the ecclesiastical term). But there is no prospect of such a 'restoration', which of course would have to come from Wagner himself: nor do I even desire it. Our life-tasks diverge, and in view of this divergence a personal relationship would be possible and agreeable only if Wagner were a man of much more delicacy. . .

---

[4] "A settling of all things".

This estrangement that has come about has its advantages, which I would not be disposed to forgo for an artistic pleasure or out of pure 'good nature'." [5]

Manifestly, then, at that time he would have regarded a hearing of *Parsifal* as "an artistic pleasure"; it was mostly only personal pique that kept him away from Bayreuth. To Elisabeth, the next day, he wrote in a similar strain:

"I am very glad you are going. You will find all my friends there. But you must excuse me: I *assuredly* will not go *unless* Wagner invites me personally and treats me as the most honoured of his festival guests." [6]

On the 3rd February he further wrote, in reply to something she had said about Wagner and Bayreuth:

"Certainly the days I spent with him in Triebschen, and through him in Bayreuth (1872, *not* 1876) were the most beautiful of my life. But the all-compelling power of our tasks drove us asunder, and now we cannot draw together again; we have become too alien to each other. When I found Wagner I was indescribably happy. I had searched so long for a man higher than and superior to myself. In Wagner I thought I had found him. I was wrong. Now I can no longer compare myself with him: I belong to another order. For the rest, I have had to pay dearly for my Wagner-enthusiasm. Has not this nerve-shattering music ruined my health? And the disillusion and the parting from Wagner, did not this endanger my life? Has it not taken nearly six years to recover from this grief? No, Bayreuth is impossible for me! What I wrote you the other day was only in jest. But *you* at any rate must go to Bayreuth. It means a good deal to me." [7]

We need not take too seriously his remark that he had been jesting when he said he would go to Bayreuth only on a personal invitation from Wagner, and if he were treated as the most honoured of the guests. The letter to Overbeck, with its stress on the impossibility of his "putting in an appearance simply as a festival guest, without any sort of 'restoration' ", shows clearly enough that he would gladly have gone had Wagner made it easy for his pride to let him do so. Plainly he longed to hear *Parsifal*, rage as he might against the ruin that Wagner's music had wrought on his nerves. But Wagner could have seen no reason to humble himself to the extent of

[5] NBO, pp. 162–3.
[6] NGB, V, 476.
[7] NGB, V, 479–80.

praying him to come. His other friends, and even his other enemies, were ready to come of their own accord: why then should he regard himself as under any obligation to implore Nietzsche to do him that honour? With the memory of the young man's behaving in 1876 now like a sick spoiled child, now like a skeleton at the feast, he would probably felicitate himself on not having to go through anything of that kind this time.[8]

4

On the 22nd July there was a general rehearsal of the second and third acts with the prime cast, and on the next day another of the whole work with Gudehus, Marianne Brandt and Siehr. The final rehearsal took place on the 24th. On the following evening there was a banquet in the theatre restaurant for the personnel and the Patrons, at which Wagner spoke earnestly of his efforts in and since 1876 to establish his ideal, paid a tribute to the support given him by the King, and spoke warmly of the devotion shown him by his artists. In a second speech he toasted Liszt, who, he said, had believed in him at a time when all others had doubted.

The sixteen performances were duly given, on the 26th, 28th and 30th July and the 1st, 4th, 6th, 8th, 11th, 13th, 15th, 18th, 20th, 22nd, 25th, 27th and 29th August. At the first performance Wagner was compelled by the applauding house to speak from his box at the end of the second act and ask them not to insist on the singers taking the customary calls at that point. After the third act he had to make his views on the whole matter clear: he had no objection, he said, to the audience applauding the performers at the end of the work, and he himself went on to the stage with the intention of appearing with them. But after the lapse of a few minutes he had to explain that this was impossible, as many of them had already begun to change into their ordinary clothes. At the second performance, which, like the first, was virtually a private one, and at which he bade a kind of farewell to his Patrons, he consented to appear on

---

[8] Elisabeth tells us that when she was in Bayreuth that summer Wagner said to her, "Tell your brother that since he left me I am alone." This story does not appear in *Das Leben;* we meet with it for the first time in *Der junge Nietzsche.* Was it just another [of her *constructions faites après coup?* There is no independent evidence that by 1882 Wagner was given in the smallest degree to being sentimental about Nietzsche.

the stage in the midst of his still costumed singers. At the first public performance the procedure was adopted that developed into a Bayreuth tradition in the following years — complete silence on the part of the audience after the first act and applause after the second and the third, with the curtain rising finally on the stage-setting of the last tableau.

On the morning of the 28th Wagner met the Patrons — some five hundred in number, — for the purpose of formally dissolving the Patronatverein: it had done all of which it had been capable, but its best had been insufficient to ensure the continuance of the festivals. Henceforth Bayreuth was to be thrown open to the public, under the management of the Administrative Committee.

In view of Wagner's well-known desire that all performances should be listened to in silence it is curious to learn that at the eighth performance he himself, from his box at the back of the auditorium, applauded the Flower Maidens and gave vent to a loud "Bravo!" Did he, perhaps, think he could do so without being heard, for between himself and the spectators there were some rows of empty seats that evening? Thanks, however, to the excellent acoustics of the building he was clearly heard in the front seats, some of the occupants of which turned round angrily and hissed the unknown disturber of the peace. As he repeated his little compliment to the Flower Maidens at almost every one of the following performances, so that regular attendants came to expect it, the presumption would seem to be that he had no idea how audible he was.[9]

On the "off" days there were, as a matter of course, crowds of callers at Wahnfried, and it was these, and the receptions on Mondays and Thursdays, rather than his work at the theatre, that exhausted him and occasionally made him irritable with both his singers and his friends. Of the former he was sometimes critical: he complained, for instance, that Marianne Brandt turned Kundry's lines in the opening scene — "Should the balsam fail, Arabia holds no simple for his relief" — into "a sort of aria". It appears that she attached too much importance to the "Arabia". What was Arabia, as such, to Kundry? Wagner asked her. The name of a

---

[9] This music must have been superbly sung; as Wagner points out in his letter to the King after the festival, the leading Flower Maidens consisted of first-rate artists each of whom was used to singing Elisabeth, Elsa, Sieglinde or Brynhilde in one German opera house or another.

country, nothing more: it ought not to be thrown into high relief in that way, as if the geographical locality were of prime importance. Apparently Brandt was better in passionate moments than in those calling for simplicity and restraint. She was apt to become too "operatic" for Wagner's liking: she had style, he said, but it was a trifle too much the style of Meyerbeer, of the French school of Roger — the "harangue". And there seems to have been a little jealousy of Therese Malten on her part, as well as an occasional tiff between Winkelmann and Gudehus, and between Scaria and Siehr. Towards the end of the festival Gudehus and Malten had to go back to their ordinary duties in Dresden. For the last performance but two Wagner proposed to have Jäger as Parsifal, for the last but one Gudehus, and for the last of all Winkelmann. But Gudehus refused to return, claiming that not to have been chosen to sing on the final night was an offence to his "artistic honour".[10] In spite of these and other little troubles, however, Wagner's verdict at the end of the festival was that the performances had reached a higher level than those of 1876.

5

Some of the comments of the local critic are interesting. Scaria he praised not only for his great singing but for his perfect enunciation, which "made a text book entirely superfluous". He admired most of the other singers almost unreservedly, but had some faults to find with Jäger and Fuchs (the second Klingsor). The latter's voice he found too smooth, too lyrical, too lacking in the darker timbres one associates with Klingsor. As for Jäger, some parts of the rôle of Parsifal suited him admirably,

"especially in the third act, where it is not necessary for the hero to look so young and supple as in the first two. In the scene with the Flower Maidens in the second act the effect was marred by the almost too solid figure of the singer, in spite of his sincere endeavour to make good what was wrong in this respect by animated action and clever miming. Nor was Herr Jäger's voice quite equal to his exacting task. In its higher notes it lacks the right timbre, the clear, fluent, brilliant penetrating quality — for instance, in the cry of 'Amfortas! the wound!' after Kundry's kiss, where the effect fell short because of the

---

[10] Malten showed a better spirit; she returned to make one of the audience at the final performance.

inadequacy of the voice to express passion. He was better in the third act; but here also, in 'How fair the meadow seems today', for example, where a uniform and inwardly elevating tone is called for, the voice was not sonorous enough."

Evidently Jäger was the weak spot in the cast. But all in all it appears likely that the opera was better sung and acted in 1882 than it is as a whole today, though the modern eye would be critical of a Kundry so ample of figure as the photograph of Materna in the part shows her to have been. Marianne Brandt, in spite of her plainness, strikes one as coming physically nearer to Wagner's ideal.[11]

There had been a moving incident at the final performance on the 29th August. During the third act, realising that an indisposition from which Levi was suffering was growing worse,[12] he slipped into the orchestra, and, unknown to the audience, conducted the opera from the conclusion of the Transformation music to the end. We can imagine the delicacy of nuance he drew from an orchestra that by this time knew the work by heart and was inspired by the presence of the old Meister whom it revered. Future events gave that little episode the dignity of a symbol: it proved to be Wagner's farewell to the theatre it had cost him so much blood and tears to bring into being. The opera over, the curtain rose again as usual on the final tableau, but Wagner, desirous that his performers should receive the whole thanks of the house, could not be persuaded to appear on the stage. As the applause showed no sign of ceasing after a quarter of an hour, he addressed the company from the conductor's stand — invisible, of course, to the audience and inaudible to most of it. The last words his artists were ever to hear from him were words of gratitude and affection, and the expression of a hope that they might all meet again in the following year. The performance had ended at a little after half-past nine: it was after eleven before the audience dispersed, still without having seen Wagner.

---

[11] Wagner gave the King his general impressions of the performances in his letter of the 8th September. Ludwig, in his reply, comments on the fact that he did not mention Marianne Brandt or Jäger. The latter had no doubt been a disappointment to Wagner. The reason for his silence about Brandt was probably personal; he and she never got on very well together on the stage or off it. He seems to have had a high opinion of Malten. Brandt did not attend the garden party given by Wagner to his artists on the 28th August.

[12] Thus Glasenapp. The critic of the *Tagblatt*, in his report the next day, said that Wagner "conducted the greater part of the third act in honour of his artists". Glasenapp's explanation is more likely to be the correct one.

During the night most of the visitors to the festival departed their several ways, and the old town settled down again to its normal provincial routine. Some of the extracts given by Eggert from the local Press during the festival make amusing reading. There were many advertisements of valuable articles lost — rings, brooches, pins, bracelets, wallets, opera glasses and so forth, — and, a tribute to the general honesty of the pilgrims and the Bayreuthers, announcements, though not so many, of articles found. Thefts seem to have been comparatively few. One case, however, sent a thrill of horror through the town. No less a person than a professor of music from Vienna actually had his wallet, containing 300 marks, abstracted from the breast pocket of the coat he was wearing after the first act of one of the performances. The exquisite artistry of the feat convinced the *Tagblatt* that it would have been beyond the technique of any native of Bayreuth: "such dexterity", it said, "points to a training in one of the larger towns. Caution is therefore urgently recommended. People should go about with their coats buttoned and keep their hands on their wallets." But there were perils to life and limb as well as to the pocket in the Bayreuth of those days. One night a visitor from Nuremberg fell into a pond in the St. George quarter, and would have been drowned had he not been dragged out by some one providentially passing at the time. "This", said the *Tagblatt*, "is the pond about the danger of which so much has already been said and written; but, as usual, warnings have been without effect." The brighter side of the Bayreuth picture of those early days is seen in an announcement that visitors to the festival should not pay extortionate prices for accommodation, as the Housing Committee could direct them to good lodgings in private houses at two marks a night.

6

Various old friends of Wagner, as we have seen, had arrived during the festival. Liszt saw several performances before moving on to Weimar. Mathilde Maier came, and a number of London friends, including Dannreuther, Praeger and Cyriax. But the absence of the King was a sore grief to Wagner, and by way of birthday greeting on the 25th August he sent him by wire a reproachful quatrain:

Verschmähtest Du des Grales Labe,
Sie war mein Alles dir zur Gabe;
Sei nun der Arme nicht verachtet,
Der dir nur gönnen, nicht geben mehr kann.

Ludwig was hurt at the suggestion that he had "disdained the Grail's refreshment", and he assured Cosima that it was only indisposition that had kept him away. He had, indeed, told Wagner as early as the 17th July that he could not tear himself away from the mountains, where alone he could find health of body and peace of spirit. A few months later it must have been a bitter regret to him that by not going to Bayreuth he had thrown away the last opportunity to meet in the flesh the man to whom, as his letters show, his lonely heart was more than ever given in these last years.

On the 25th, however, Wahnfried was *en fête* for the civil marriage of Blandine and Count Gravina; the religious ceremony, Gravina being a Catholic, took place the next day.[13] Liszt, who had returned from Weimar for the wedding, had been greatly upset on the 24th by Wagner's irreverent treatment of an order conferred on him some years earlier by no less a potentate and authority in the world of art than the Bey of Tunis. Wagner, who was feeling well that evening, was in one of his mischievous schoolboy moods; and it was perhaps with the idea of poking fun at Liszt, whose reverence for orders was notorious, that he paced majestically up and down before the company with the silver star on his coat, and then pinned it to the corsage of Fräulein Horson, one of his Flower Maidens. Conduct of this kind was next door to lèse majesté in Liszt's eyes.

Financially the festival had been an unexpected success: in all, 8,200 tickets had been sold, bringing in 240,000 marks, and Wagner was already planning to give twenty performances in 1883. He had realised by now that his old idea of an art-institute of his own, supported entirely by a communion of kindred spirits, had been merely the dream of an unpractical idealist. A few weeks later, when Wolzogen suggested "Association" as an appropriate title for the new organisation which he and others hoped would arise from the ashes of the old Vereine, Wagner made it clear to him that he

---

[13] Bülow was not present at his daughter's marriage. He himself had married Marie Schanzer on the 29th July.

had finished with all that. If an "Association" developed, he wrote, it would have to be merely one of subscribers to the *Bayreuther Blätter*, the inheritors of his intellectual legacy to the world. As for Vereine for the performances of his works, he wanted to see or hear no more of them. The original Verein, he said, had been founded by Heckel "behind his back"; and it had been largely composed simply of people who wanted to get cheap admission to the *Ring*.

"Had I attached no importance to these Vereine from the beginning I could have produced the *Ring* annually from 1877 onwards before the paying public, and so spared myself the vexations I have had to endure through these Verein-dolts. The utter impotence of this Verein business was proved when it was only by the King's help that I was able to produce *Parsifal* and I could ensure a continuance of the performances only by admitting the paying public — that is to say, by a complete abandonment of the whole proud idea for which I had called the Patronat into being. In a business sense a Verein or an Association is utterly unpractical: in a theoretic-moral sense there is nothing whatever to be said for it. Imagine a board of that kind arranging and running the festivals after my death! I am now seventy years old, and I can't suggest a single person who could be trusted to give the right instructions in my own spirit to any of the participants in such performances, singers, conductors, regisseurs, machinists, scenic designers, costumiers.I know hardly one person who even shares my opinion as to what has been achieved or not achieved so that I could have confidence in him. And so — I will *not* have a committee taking charge after my death, perhaps even running *me* during my last years! Consequently neither a Verein nor — ." [14]

And to Stein, a little later, "Let us hope therefore that I myself will be able to teach and guide my people for some years yet."

7

The strain on his dwindling physical powers during the festival had been excessive. On the night of the 31st August he had a few intimates to dinner — Count and Countess Schleinitz, Stein, Joukowsky and others, — and afterwards he played to them for a long time, — the *Tristan* prelude and Liebestod and the prelude to the third act; while on the following evening he played the C sharp minor prelude of Bach and the prelude to *Parsifal*. But happy moments of this kind were rare with him now. His prevailing mood was

---

[14] The letter breaks off here.

one of profound depression. He had had more than one severe attack of asthma and cramp during the festival. In one of the early August days Scaria had been the witness of a terrifying scene. He was alone with Wagner in one of the rooms at Wahnfried. Suddenly the Meister was seized by one of his worst heart spasms; purple in the face, he sank on to the sofa and made convulsive movements with his hands as if he were fighting off an invisible enemy. The crisis passed: "I have escaped death", he said in a faint voice. It was only his courage and his desire not to dishearten his artists that kept him going in the latter stages of the festival. "He told me he longed for death", Cosima records in her diary.

> "Late in the evening I sat alone in the empty room and brooded, brooded until my overwrought brain fell asleep; and I knew, more or less, how it will be some day."

On the night of the final performance she wrote:

> "Our return home was silent and solemn. I think we can give thanks, though assuredly what we have achieved has been at a heavy cost, and we have sacrificed to it almost all our lives' comfort. To be sure, this activity is a necessity to Richard, and notwithstanding all the griefs it brings with it, the only one suited to him."

CHAPTER XXXVII

THE END IN VENICE

1

THE FESTIVAL OVER, Wagner's one thought was to escape from Bayreuth for the coming winter. On the evening of the 14th September the family left for Venice, arriving there, after a tiring journey due to the abnormal floods of that year, on the 16th. The first two days they spent in the Hôtel Europa; then they moved into the section of the Palazzo Vendramin-Calergi already reserved for them. This great 15th or 16th century building, overlooking the Grand Canal, was the property of the Duke della Grazia, who had inherited it from his mother, the Duchess de Berry. Henry Perl exaggerates somewhat when he says that Wagner and his household occupied twenty-eight of the rooms — salons, domestic offices and so forth —,[1] but for all that his lodging was imposing enough. Liszt gave the Princess Wittgenstein a description of it in a letter of the 26th November. Wagner, it appears, had secured the entresol at "the moderate price" of 6,000 francs a year: it consisted of fifteen to eighteen handsomely furnished rooms. Wagner's establishment comprised, in addition to Cosima and himself, Daniela, Isolde, Eva, Siegfried, the younger girls' governess (a Mme Corsara whom Cosima had brought from Palermo), Siegfried's tutor (Herr Hausburg), a cook, a femme de chambre and a manservant from Bayreuth, an old porter attached to the building, and two gondoliers: all in all not an excessive ménage, considering the size of the family and the number of Wagner's guests and visitors.

---

[1] PRWV, pp. 24, 25. Perl's book is not always accurate, but it has a certain value from the date of its publication, not many months after Wagner's death. He derived much of his information from Wagner's physician, Dr. Keppler. Gabriel Faure's article *La Mort de Wagner à Venice*, in *Les Rendez-vous italiens* (Paris, 1933), contains little that could not have been culled from the ordinary Wagner biographies, but he gives some interesting details of the Palazzo, over which he was shown in 1933. By then the interior had changed a good deal since 1882: in the little garden in which Wagner loved to sit there remained nothing that might have dated from that period except an ancient yew tree.

Liszt assured the Princess that as the Vendramin was so well furnished Wagner had not been put to any of the extra expense usually incurred by Northerners who rented these old Italian houses. Apparently it was not until after the date of this letter that Wagner redecorated his own room to suit his fancy, turning it into the "blue grotto" about which some sensation-hunting journalists made a great pother later: all he did was to insulate himself from the outer world, as he always loved to do, by means of soft fabrics and shimmering colours. And, as a matter of course, he indulged himself liberally in perfumes, which, as has already been pointed out, had to be strong because his lifelong habit of snuff-taking had impaired his sense of smell.[2]

2

Other friends besides Liszt came to the Vendramin from time to time — Count and Countess Schleinitz, Rubinstein, Levi, Heinrich Stein, Joukowsky, Humperdinck among them, — and he made some agreeable new acquaintances, including Alexander Wolkoff, a Russian artist and scientist, and a promising young art historian and archaeologist, Heinrich Thode, who fell in love with Daniela.[3] For the most part, we learn from Liszt, Wagner lived a very quiet life in Venice, neither paying nor receiving many visits. The town exercised its old charm on him, and he enjoyed its variegated outdoor life; but for company his own circle was enough. As always, he fretted when his friends left him or talked of doing so, — Liszt in particular. The Princess taunted Liszt with having become a

---

[2] Guy de Maupassant tells us that when he visited the Hôtel des Palmes in Palermo some years after Wagner had left there, and opened the door of a wardrobe, "a powerful and delicious perfume came from it, like the caress of a breeze blowing over a bed of roses". The proprietor informed him that it was there that Wagner used to store his linen after sprinkling it with *essence de roses*. "I drank in this breath of flowers", says Maupassant, "and I seemed to discover something of Wagner himself, of his desire, of his soul, in this trifling matter of the secret and cherished habits that go to make up the inner life of a man." (*La vie errante*, p. 87).

Friends of my own have told me that they, or relations of theirs, had had a similar experience in the Palermo hotel of the enduring vitality of the Wagnerian perfumes. I sometimes wonder whether, perchance, the proprietor, cannily aware of what his visitors had come to smell, and being reluctant, from the most disinterested business motives, to have them go away disappointed, was in the habit of renewing the scent, in the way that the custodians of historic English castles are alleged to renew periodically, for the benefit of tourists, the bloodstains on the floor of the room where the fifth earl murdered his peccant wife in the seventeenth century.

[3] They were married in 1887.

"parasite", a mere "super" in the Wagnerian drama; to which he made the calm reply that everything depends on just *where* one is a "super". And it was perhaps only the philosophical calm, amounting almost to indifferentism, that had now descended on him that could have kept the bond of affection between the two men unimpaired. Wagner did not care greatly for Liszt's latest works, and though he abstained from saying so the fact could hardly be concealed from Liszt. Even his friend's piano-playing was sometimes antipathetic to Wagner because of Liszt's notorious lack of feeling for the dramatic element in opera. And there was the eternal difference of opinion between them as to the best way of spending an evening. When company was there, Liszt's heart was set on whist, while Wagner wanted to read and expound. It was evident, said Joukowsky in his memoirs,

> "that as they grew older each of these two great men and unique friends lost more and more the capacity to understand the other's way of life. Liszt loved to have a numerous company about him: Wagner could endure only a small band of intimates. When they talked together, neither paid attention to what the other was saying: they would both speak at the same time, and this often led to the strangest quiproquos. Each was so accustomed to being the sole centre of attention that there was always a certain amount of awkwardness when they were together."

But Joukowsky was psychologist enough to see that Wagner's desire to be always talking had its roots not in vanity, as some people imagined, but in the complexity of his nature, the breadth of his culture, and the imperative necessity to rid himself of the burden of his ideas. "Whoever", he wrote,

> "has known Wagner as intimately as I have done can easily conceive how a hero-cult evolves; it is simply faith in the beings to whom the impossible is possible. His nature was demonic through and through; the powers indwelling in him possessed him utterly. His need to give artistic shape to things, his willing and wishing, his loving and hating, the ideas springing up within him, all these took complete control of him; for him, artistic creation and literary expression meant liberation from the oppressive abundance of his being. In every moment of his life he was creative; and no one who has not known him can have any conception of the breadth of the horizons his talk opened out to his listeners . . . I am convinced that it was only in Wagner's company that Nietzsche's concept of the Superman was realised. Only Michelangelo and Wagner among artists give me this impression of limitless capacity. Even in the exquisite tenderness and sensitiveness of

their nerves they were alike. In the world as it is today a man of this kind must suffer martyrdom of which only his peers could form any notion. Born to command as few other men have been, endowed with a force that could either construct or destroy, possessed with a thirst for superhuman beauty, he had to struggle for three-quarters of his life against every sort of want, ill health, distress, and the complete failure of those nearest to him to comprehend him."

Gabriel Monod, who had seen a good deal of him during the festival of 1876, characterised him in much the same way.

"On everyone who comes near him he exercises an irresistible fascination, not only by reason of his musical genius, or the originality of his intellect, or the variety of his learning, but above all by the energy of temperament and will that emanates from every fibre of him. You feel that you are in the presence of a force of nature, unleashing itself with almost reckless violence. After seeing him at close quarters, at one moment irresponsibly gay, pouring forth a torrent of jokes and laughter, at another vehement, respecting neither titles nor powers nor friendships, always letting himself be carried away by the first thing that comes into his head, you find yourself unable to be too hard upon him for his lapses of taste, of tact, of delicacy: if you are a Jew, you are inclined to forgive him his pamphlet on *Judaism in Music*, if a Frenchman, his farce on the capitulation of Paris, if you are a German, all the insults he has heaped on Germany. . . You take him as he is, full of faults — no doubt because he is full of genius — but incontestably a superior being, one of the greatest and most extraordinary men our century has produced." [4]

3

But the volcano was dying down now, though sometimes there were flashes and rumblings that gave warning of the subterranean fire that was still there. His pinched body and thinning blood cried out to him to leave everything and pitch his tent somewhere where the sun never ceased to shine. Then, in an hour when the ichor rose in his veins once more, he would feel Bayreuth drawing him back to complete his mission. He planned to give all his operas there, from the *Flying Dutchman* onwards, during the next ten years or so, by which time Siegfried would be twenty-three and able to take over from him: "only to him", he told the King in November, "can I entrust the spiritual and ethical maintenance of my work, for I can

[4] From an article by Monod in the *Moniteur universel*, quoted in JRW, pp. 310, 311.

think of no one else to whom I could depute my functions." (To Angelo Neumann he had written in the same strain in the preceding September: "With *Parsifal* stands or falls my Bayreuth achievement. And sure enough, this will perish when I die; for I know no one else who could continue it according to my intentions.") He had been depressed by the reports reaching him from all quarters of the way in which his works were being produced in the German theatres:

> "it pains me, even fills me with a sense of the futility of everything I have accomplished", he wrote to the King on the 18th November, "to abandon these works to the German nation as part of the usual opera-cobbling, when they ought to uplift and ennoble it. This means that I must keep Bayreuth in being and ensure its continuance. For the moment I cannot embark on the production of my older works there; I must wait until *Parsifal*, which I have now thrown open to the paying public, has brought in money enough to form the basis of an adequate capital fund."

So in 1883 and 1884 he proposes to give only *Parsifal*, as many times as may be possible, provided he can count once more on the generous assistance of his royal friend.[5]

But he seems to have resigned himself to creating no more. He still spoke of writing symphonies of a new kind, but apparently never got beyond the sketching stage of these. *Die Sieger* he had definitely abandoned. He read a good deal in Indian literature at this time; but the more deeply he immersed himself in it the surer became his conviction that he could not recapture the mood of *Die*

---

[5] The King replied on the 26th: "Your plan to give model performances of all your splendid works in Bayreuth rejoices me; you may remember that we discussed this matter in the *Nibelungen* year (1876). My adored Friend, it goes without saying that my orchestra is at your service as often as you may require it."

Wagner's letters of thanks to his leading singers after the performances of 1882 are interesting. He wanted practically all of them again for 1883 with the exception of Jäger, Siehr and Marianne Brandt. To Therese Malten he wrote, "I think of giving twenty performances, in which I should like you to alternate with Frau Materna, as I do not propose to invite Fräulein Brandt again." He praises Winkelmann's Parsifal, but urges him to try, under the guidance of a good teacher, to develop a smoother mezza voce. Siehr — "this mulish man", as he calls him — had evidently given him a good deal of trouble by his jealousy of Scaria; so he now asks the latter to suggest, if he can, a competent second Gurnemanz for at least four performances. Scaria, however, feared he could not be free for the whole of July and August in 1883; so Wagner in the end had to offer Siehr half of the performances, including the final one. For tenors he would rely entirely on Winkelmann and Gudehus. Kindermann he would have to give up, apparently because he was too expensive for so small a part as Titurel. See the long sequence of letters in RWSK, pp. 356–372.

Sieger. What would have attracted a composer like Meyerbeer to such a subject — its easy opportunities for "local colour" — was precisely what ended by turning him against it. Local colour for its own "effective" sake meant nothing to him. It was probably his reading, during his stay in Venice, of Oldenberg's book on the Buddha that finally parted him from the theme. There was too much in the book, he complained, about palms and lotos ponds and mango trees; the too insistent flora obscured his view of the figures and the human motives that alone interested him in drama.

4

His last public gesture to Bayreuth was an article on *The Stage-Dedication-Festival in Bayreuth, 1882,* which appeared in a double number of the *Bayreuther Blätter* for November-December, in which he spoke kindly and tactfully of his collaborators in *Parsifal.* The article is particularly valuable today for the light it throws on his artistic intentions and the manner of production he aimed at in all his works. He especially praised the Flower Maidens, not only for their faultless intonation but for discarding "that passionate accent acquired by modern singers in the opera of today, which disrupts every melodic line without distinction". He wanted, that is to say, first and foremost singing of flawless technical purity, undisfigured by the standardised recipes for "expression" which singers get into the habit of plastering indiscriminately upon a melodic line regardless of the special nature of the matter in hand.

The first thing his singers had to do was to understand thoroughly what the *dramatist* was driving at, and having grasped that, not merely to convey it in words but sing it perfectly as music; for, he continued, just as the sense of a verbal sentence is destroyed by a dropped prefix, a swallowed suffix or a scamped connecting syllable, so a musical line, by a slipshod handling of its musical particles, is turned into "merely a succession of thrusting vocal accents", which becomes more and more meaningless the more passionate the phrase is; and the result is purely nonsensical to the listener at a distance, who hears not an organic musical sentence but a series of ejaculations without connecting links. Hence his general precept that if we take care of the short notes the long ones will take care of themselves; and it was through neglect of this precept that singers in the ordinary opera house substituted for his real meaning that too easy "false pathos" of the theatre which he detested and despised. (There are far too many Wagner-singers and Wagner-conductors today who need to take lesson one in the nature of the Wagnerian verbal and musical line.) And as regards Wagnerian acting the singers have still more to learn. The last thing he wanted was the sort of routine that passes for acting in *Tristan* or the *Ring* or *Parsifal* today — "screams in operatic style", as he put it,

> "accompanied by violent motions of the arms, which the performer employs, from long habit, with such mechanical regularity that by now they have lost all meaning, and give the innocent spectator only the absurd impression of a marionette."

As for miming, he says, the rationale of this in music drama is essentially different from that of the spoken drama. The tremendous expressive power of music makes emphatic miming not merely unnecessary but baneful. Plastic movement, especially of the arms, suffices; and whereas the convention in "operatic pathos" is "to throw both arms out wide as if calling for help", it was found at the *Parsifal* rehearsals that a mere "half-lift of one arm, or even a characteristic movement of the hand or head", was sufficient to give realistic impressiveness to a heightened feeling, and an exceptionally strong emotion realising itself in a particularly powerful movement was all the more shattering in its effect when it burst out after long restraint like a long held back force of nature.

The basis of the organic continuity of music drama, he goes on to say, is the dialogue, which presents problems of its own. In the ordinary opera a duet is a more or less static affair: the singers must either both face the audience, and so "communicate to it what is intended for each other", or stand in profile to it, which makes what they are saying more or less indistinct and obscures many of their gestures. Hence, in order to avoid monotony, there had arisen the convention of making the couple cross over and change places during an orchestral intermezzo. In music drama as he conceived it, says Wagner, the problem solves itself, to some extent, by the very rapidity of the dialogic exchange:

> "we found that the heightened accents at the end of a phrase or a speech occasioned a movement on the actor's part which had only to take him about one step forward for him to have his back half-

turned to the audience and his full face to his interlocutor, as if expecting an answer; while the other needed merely to step back a trifle when he began his reply and he would be in the right position to address the former speaker — now standing in front but a little to the side of him — without himself being turned away from the audience."

In this way the stage picture was never immobilised into stock attitudes but was in constant motion correspondent with the constant variations in the purport of the dramatic action.

What follows is even more significant: what he never wanted was conventional formulae for psychological expression — the kind of thing, to give an illustration of one's own, that makes a tenor or a baritone play every debonair hero or every villain rôle in the same style, and every contralto or mezzo-soprano dip into the same little bag of feminine tricks for each seductress part, a Carmen, a Delilah, or whatever it may be. "My Flower Maidens", he says,

"grasped my meaning, and at once their delivery of the coaxing melodies took on a character of childlike naïveté . . . at the opposite pole to the sort of sensual seduction which certain people had imagined to have been my aim."

Our modern Flower Maidens and their trainers should take a note of this, and try to understand that the episode is not a "seduction scene" according to stale theatrical formulae but a psychological moment in a drama called *Parsifal*. These reflections apply also to the costumes and settings of the opera. What the theatres of today too often present us with in the scene of the Flower Maidens is precisely what Wagner barred — costumes reminiscent of the costumier's experience of "ballet or masquerade", "a certain conventional luxuriance of dress which proved absolutely unsuitable to our purpose, for this could be attained only by way of an ideal naturalness"; and the costumes should harmonise with Klingsor's garden itself, so that the living forms appear to be a natural growth from the flora of that.

5

Wagner ended with an illuminating comment on the orchestral part of the performances of 1882. No longer, he said, had the players to occupy themselves, as in the ordinary opera house, with such irrelevant considerations as "being kind to the singers"; the excellent acoustics of the Bayreuth theatre making anything of that sort unnecessary, they could give their whole minds to delicate shading and "the solving of the higher tasks" set them by the music and the drama. *Parsifal*, he concluded, had been in presentation what it had been in his conception — something which by its nearness to life yet its ideal sublimation of it enabled them all to escape, for a while, from the disgusting and disheartening burden of "this world of lying and fraud and hypocrisy and legalised murder". That, in truth, is the meaning and the magic of this last work of the old artist who had seen so much, suffered so much, in his pilgrimage through life. The "religion" of it is nothing, the beauty and the love and the pity of it everything. We feel in the presence of it as we do in that of the only other music that inhabits the same sphere — the last quartets of Beethoven: the men who can dream such music must have made up their account with time and are ripe for eternity.[6]

The artistic side of Wagner's mind was active enough to the last: it was only the decaying body that now dragged him down. And the condition of that was serious. Among the visitors to Bayreuth in the preceding summer had been Standhartner, the Viennese physician who knew Wagner's constitution well from of old. He had examined him then and had discovered that a malady of the heart of which there had been symptoms earlier had developed far. The diagnosis, however, was kept from Wagner himself, though no doubt Cosima's reticence confirmed his own suspicions. In Venice he was under the care of a resident German physician, Dr. Friedrich Keppler, who, at Perl's request, contributed to the latter's book a foreword in which he gave an exhaustive description of Wagner's malady.

"He suffered from advanced hypertrophy of the heart, especially in the right ventricle, with consequent degeneration of the cardiac tissues. There was also a fairly extensive dilation of the stomach and an inguinal hernia on the right side; this had been greatly aggravated for a long time by an unsuitable truss, so that the first thing I did was to order him a better one.

"The pains from which he suffered in the last months of his life came principally from disorders of the stomach and bowels, and particularly from advanced matorism: these occasioned — though secondarily, by direct mechanical constriction of the chest as a result of much gas in the stomach and intestines and by reflex action of the nerves of

[6] The comments on the *Parsifal* festival — *Das Bühnenweihfestspiel in Bayreuth 1882* — will be found in RWGS, X, 297–308.

the stomach and heart — painful derangements of the heart's action, leading eventually to a rupture of the right ventricle. It is self-evident that the innumerable psychical agitations to which Wagner was daily disposed by his peculiar mental constitution and disposition, his sharply defined attitude towards a number of burning questions of art, science and politics, and his remarkable social position did much to hasten his unfortunate end.

"The actual attack that resulted in his so sudden death *must* have come from such cause, but I cannot venture any surmise as to that.

"The medical treatment I gave him consisted of massage of the abdomen and the fitting of a proper truss: I avoided medicinal treatment as much as possible, since Wagner had a bad habit of taking promiscuously, and in considerable quantities, many strong medicines that had been prescribed for him by physicians whom he had previously consulted." [7]

More words than illumination, perhaps, but it gives us some idea of the nature of Wagner's malady, even if it does not suggest that his doctors, in general, were practitioners of the first order. When we read afresh the many assurances his physicians gave him, year after year, that he was organically quite sound, thus encouraging him to put a strain on himself which his heart was unable to stand, we may be pardoned the suspicion that the science of some of them was not all it might have been.

In the latter days in Bayreuth, and now more than ever in Venice, the household lay daily in the shadow of death. Cosima knew well how critical Wagner's condition was, and more than ever before she lived solely to keep him alive a little longer for his work; as she herself put it in a letter to her friend Marie von Schleinitz, her rôle was that of Aaron holding up the arms of Moses during the battle. Sometimes she and Wagner would maintain a sad silence about it all, though each knew what was in the other's mind; at other times they would be driven irresistibly to speak of the dread something that was ever lurking in the shadows around them, waiting for the opportunity to strike. For he was obviously weakening. The cramps about the heart were now more frequent. He suffered if he walked too far or too fast: if he gave rein for five minutes to his inextinguishable vitality of spirit he paid dearly for it. As a matter of course he became more irritable, wounding Cosima by his outbursts of temper, and then breaking her devoted heart by the loving

---

[7] PRWV, vi–viii.

humility of his contrition. He became pitifully dependent upon her, so that he could not bear her to leave him; yet a certain number of social calls she had to make, if only for the sake of the children. Often they found her in tears, especially after one of his irresponsible outbursts against her father. But to Richard she had always to show a calm face, even when her heart was like lead within her. Gobineau's death had been a great blow to him, for despite their occasional intellectual divergencies he had become warmly attached to that exceptionally fine spirit. But on the rare occasions when he was reminded of Nietzsche's existence — by reading a review of *Die fröhliche Wissenschaft,* and later, apparently, by the book itself — it was only to feel that their one-time friendship had been little more than a mistake. "Everything in the book that is worth anything", he said to Cosima, "is borrowed from Schopenhauer"; and the man himself was utterly "repugnant" to him now.

6

About the middle of December he was often mysteriously absent from the Palazzo. He was preparing to celebrate Cosima's birthday with a surprise — a performance of his youthful symphony of 1832. As the reader is aware, the long-lost orchestral parts of this had been discovered in Dresden a few years before, and from these Seidl had put together a score. Wagner now planned to give a private performance of the work with the orchestra of students and professors of the Venice Conservatoire, the Liceo Benedetto Marcello. Seidl, whom he wanted to rehearse it, could not come, so Wagner sent for Humperdinck from Paris. In consequence of these difficulties he had to do much of the preliminary work himself; consequently the secret leaked out, and Cosima, the children, Liszt and Joukowsky were present at the final rehearsal, in the foyer of the Teatro La Fenice, under Wagner himself, on the 22nd December. The strain proved too much for him; he had a heart attack after the first movement, could not dine with the family that evening, and slept badly. Next day, however, he seemed to have recovered his elasticity; and he was able to conduct the performance on the evening of the 24th, the audience consisting solely of the people already mentioned, Humperdinck, Count Contini, the founder and president of the Liceo, and a couple of others brought in at the last moment by Liszt.[8] Towards the end of the month Wagner sent off a long account of the affair, with some comments on the symphony itself, to the Leipzig *Musikalisches Wochenblatt*.[9]

The new year saw him still occupied with plans for the festival of the following summer. Adolf Gross had arrived with news that disturbed him. Owing to a scheme for an International Exhibition in Munich the Opera orchestra would be available for Bayreuth only for July; consequently Wagner would have to reduce the number of *Parsifal* performances to twelve. This in turn led to other complications: Scaria, for instance, protested that this new decision would upset *his* plans for the summer. Scaria's letter, however, was kept from Wagner for a while; it had been Cosima's practice for some time, indeed, to withhold from him until a more propitious moment any correspondence that might agitate him. Bayreuth was always foremost in his thoughts now; one thing he had set his heart on was a new production of *Tannhäuser*, which had by now settled down into a routine of gross misrepresentation in the German opera houses. As for *Parsifal*, it still rankled in him that the King had not gone to Bayreuth in 1882 but preferred to wait until he could hear the work in solitude in his own theatre. That, however, Wagner pointed out, might prove to be more difficult than he had thought. Some of the Bayreuth decorations, and especially the two Transformation scenes, were being remodelled in the light of the experience gained in that year, and would consequently not be available for Munich; nor did Wagner like the prospect of the work being given there without his personal supervision. So he tried his hardest,

---

[8] There had been five rehearsals, and apparently the Conservatoire authorities had profited by the occasion to put up their price for the orchestra. In BFF for 1936 (pp. 128–129) there was published for the first time a short note of the 27th December from Liszt to Wagner on the subject of "the vile sordidness and rascality of the Venice orchestra". "I think it is a mistake to yield to the demands of the canaille, in high places or low; and I have said so plainly to the responsible persons in the present matter. 1,000 francs would have been ample for your generosity". What made it worse was that Liszt, at Wagner's request, had been kind enough to play to the orchestra after the performance of the symphony.

[9] *Bericht über die Wiederaufführung eines Jugendwerkes*, in RWGS, X, 309–315. In 1887, as the reader may remember, Cosima granted the Berlin Concert Direction Hermann Wolff the exclusive right of performance of the work for one year for 50,000 marks, which she handed over to the Bayreuth Stipendiary Fund. See Vol. I, p. 102 *note*, where the date "Christmas Day" should be altered to the 24th. The story that Wagner conducted only the first two movements and Humperdinck the remainder seems also to be erroneous: Liszt, in his letter of the 28th to the Princess, says "Wagner lui-même dirigeait l'orchestre".

but in vain, to induce Ludwig to wait until the summer of 1883, when, in Bayreuth, he would give three or even more performances exclusively for him.

Literary work still occupied him to a small extent. On the 31st January he sent Stein an Open Letter intended to serve as an introduction to a volume of the young man's dramatic colloquies, modelled, one imagines, on Gobineau's *La Renaissance*.[10] His mind was running a good deal at this time on such problems as property, racial mixture, monogamy, polygamy, regeneration, and so forth; but it was not until a couple of days before his death that he began to commit his ideas to paper, and the essay was never finished.[11]

Levi came for ten days in early February to discuss the next festival and other matters, and told Wagner, no doubt to his vast amusement, that Nietzsche was trying hard to foist on him a "young Mozart" whom he had discovered — no other, of course, than Peter Gast. The Vendramin circle was narrowing a little now. Liszt, to Wagner's sorrow, had left on the 13th January for Budapest. They had seen comparatively little of each other of late: as usual, Liszt had been unable to resist the lure of titled society. "Wherever he goes", Wagner wrote mournfully to the King on the 10th January,

"he is surrounded the whole time by a crowd of acquaintances, who discover his whereabouts, hunt him up, drag him into an endless round of matinées, dinners and soirées, and consequently take him quite out of our sight, since we live remote from everything, entirely to ourselves. His latest was a dinner with Don Carlos [Pretender to the throne of Spain] and a Mexican Duke Iturbide, whom I explained as a worshipper of Fitzliputzli, and a kinsman of Itztcahuitl and Popocatapetl."

What angered Wagner was not merely that Liszt was taken away from him so often in this way, but that the notabilities who fawned upon him and wasted his time saw in him only the famous pianist, not the composer: it was his piano-playing, not his creative work, that enabled him to leave behind him a small museum of orders and decorations and gifts when he died.

Joukowsky, however, was with Wagner to the end. He should

---

[10] The Letter was published in the *Bayreuther Blätter* shortly after Wagner's death, and is reprinted in RWGS, X, 316–323. Stein's book, *Helden und Welt, Dramatische Bilder*, appeared in 1883.

[11] The fragment was published posthumously, under the title of *Über das Weibliche im Menschen*, in a volume of *Entwürfe, Gedanken, Fragmente* (1885), and later in RWGS, XII, 341–343.

have gone back to Russia for the celebration of the centenary of the birth of his father, but he would not leave Wagner; already, one gathers, he had a presentiment of disaster. For Wagner's health, though there were days when he seemed almost as well as ever, was rapidly declining. Keppler called in a local German colleague, Dr. Kapp, who made a rather vague diagnosis of "neuralgia of the stomach". Kapp having written to Wagner's Bayreuth physician, Dr. Landberg, the pair decided on massage, which was administered twice daily for a while by Keppler. For a time it seemed to do the patient good. But the cramps, on the whole, were becoming more frequent and more distressing. The doctors now prescribed valerian, which brought him some relief, and mild doses of opium were given him occasionally.

7

On the 6th February he went out, for the children's sake, to see the last night of the carnival. Perl caught sight of him there, threading his way among the masks with Daniela on his arm, and, familiar as he no doubt was with Keppler's accounts of his patient, he was astonished to see him looking so well: "his step was elastic, even youthful", he says, "his head was held high".[12] But the strain and the excitement had evidently been too much for him. He developed a cold, and spent part of the next day in bed. Once more he recovered, and, depressed by the bad weather, he planned on the 10th an excursion with Siegfried to either Verona or Bologna, which, however, did not materialise. The next day he went for a walk, but returned in ten minutes with both hands pressed to his heart. He was ill at ease and fretful, but recovered towards the evening; and when Keppler called he found the pulse quite regular. Wagner read from Fouqué's *Undine*, discussed it, and dreamed of it in the night.

On the morning of the 12th he worked at his essay on *Das Weibliche*, and at luncheon talked to Cosima at some length about his mother. In the afternoon he took a walk with Eva, and in the evening once more read to them from *Undine:* Joukowsky found him in good spirits and apparently well, and made a sketch of him reading. Wagner played with great earnestness the "Porazzi" theme and some bars of a Scherzo he was planning to write, and, after the children had retired, the music of

---

[12] PRWV, p. 110.

Tender and true
'tis but in the waters:
false and base
are those who revel above,

from the song of the Rhine Maidens as the curtain falls on the
Rhinegold. "To think that I knew it so well even at that time!" he
said to Cosima; and a little later, "They are very dear to me, these
secondary beings of the depths, these creatures full of longing".
With the record the next morning of these words of his, Cosima
closed her diary for ever.

On the 13th Joukowsky called as usual at a quarter to two for
lunch: he found Cosima at the piano, in tears, playing Schubert's
Lob der Thränen:

Nicht mit süssen Wasserflüssen zwang Prometheus unsern Leim;
Nein, mit Thränen; drum im Sehnen und im Schmerz sind wir
daheim.
Bitter schwellen diese Quellen für den erdumfang'nen Sinn,
Doch sie drängen aus den Engen in das Meer der Liebe hin.

Wagner was working in his own room: "I shall have to take care of
myself today", he had remarked to his manservant, Georg Lang,
that morning. At two o'clock he sent a message to the others that
as he was not feeling well they were to begin lunch without him.
Cosima went to see him, but he wished to be alone, as was his way
when he was at grips with his implacable foe. She left the maid,
Betty Bürkel, in the room next to Richard's. She heard him sighing
and moaning from time to time: he was sitting bent over his desk,
waiting for the anguish to pass. Suddenly his bell rang violently
twice. Betty answered it, and then broke in upon the others with
the news that the master had told her to bring "the doctor and my
wife". Cosima at once went to him. A gondola had been ordered to
take them all that afternoon to Wolkoff's house; Daniela sent off a
note of excuse to him,[13] but even yet no one seems to have suspected

---

[13] This is the story as given by Glasenapp, quoting verbatim from Joukowsky's
manuscript memoirs. According to Wolkoff himself, he waited until five o'clock, and
then, not having received any message, he went to the Vendramin, where he met
the painters Passini and Ruben, who told him they had heard a rumour that Wagner
was dead. This seems less credible than Joukowsky's account. See the *Memoirs of
Alexander Wolkoff-Mouromtzoff (A. N. Roussoff), by Himself, translated by Mrs.*

how serious Wagner's condition was. Meanwhile the maid had sent for Keppler. He arrived at three o'clock. The family and Joukowsky were sitting silent in the drawing-room when Georg, sobbing and half-fainting, came in and said "The master is dead!" He was followed by Keppler, who bade them abandon hope.

In the other room the tragedy had quickly come to its long-appointed end. Cosima had found Wagner racked by a spasm of exceptional violence; apparently a bloodvessel in the heart had been ruptured. Georg had loosened some of his clothing and eased him on to a seat, where Cosima sat down beside him and held him in her arms. While he was being moved, his watch, a gift from her, fell out of his pocket. "My watch!" he ejaculated. These were his last words. Cosima, still holding him close to her, believed he had fallen asleep; but Keppler, who had arrived a little while before, felt his pulse and found it had stopped. "We must not give up hope yet", he said: and laying Wagner on a couch he tried friction, Cosima clinging distractedly to the dead man's knees, unwilling to believe that what she had dreaded so long had really come to pass. The last glance he had turned upon her had been one of mute gratitude and love.

In the sudden desolation that had fallen on the house the faithful Joukowsky's thoughts were all for Cosima, who herself seemed at death's door, while Wagner, his last fight finished, lay on the couch in the profoundest peace his tortured spirit had ever known, his eyes closed, a gentle smile seeming to play upon the half-open mouth. All that night Cosima sat alone with the body, murmuring incoherent words of love into the deaf ears. She refused all care, all nourishment: she had lived in him and for him, and now she wanted to die with him. It was not until the late afternoon of the following day, twenty-five hours after he had died, that they succeeded in parting her from him.

8

The world was staggered by the news of Wagner's sudden death. Liszt, who was then in Budapest, at first believed it to be merely

---

Huth Jackson, London, 1928, p. 215. It is one more illustration of the difficulty of arriving at the truth regarding the smallest matter of the past, even on the evidence of the people concerned in it.

a journalistic false alarm. When he could no longer doubt he wrote to Cosima to ask if she would like him to go to her in Venice and accompany her back to Bayreuth. Through Daniela she declined his offer, for which he was not sorry. Like Cosima, he shrank from the publicity the funeral would involve, the stereotyped official condolences everywhere, the formal speeches, the musical performances and so forth. "Unless it is absolutely necessary for me to be there", he wrote to the Princess, "I prefer to keep away . . . I will see Cosima in Bayreuth in six weeks' time, in calmer mood."

When Bürkel, to whom, as to a few others, Daniela had at once telegraphed, brought the news to the King, Ludwig mastered himself with difficulty: he could only say, "Frightful! Terrible! Let me be alone." After some hours of bitter self-communion he sent for Bürkel again and broke out distractedly, "Wagner's body belongs to me. Nothing must be done without my orders as regards the transport from Venice." A few days later, when Bürkel had returned from Bayreuth and told him of the universal grief, the King said with justifiable pride, "This artist whom the whole world now mourns, it was I who was the first to understand him; it was I who rescued him for the world." That was no more than the simple truth; it was to him, and after him to Cosima, that the world was indebted for the preservation of Wagner and the completion of his life's work. They two never doubted his mission, suffered for and with him, never forsook him, never shrank from any sacrifice for him.

When the wires flashed the news of the Meister's death Bülow was at Meiningen, only half-recovered from a severe illness. By a strange coincidence, Brahms had arrived in the town on the 12th, and Bülow had pulled himself together sufficiently to greet him at the station, though he was confined to his bed the whole of the next day. It was not until the evening of the 14th that Frau von Bülow dared to break the news to him, and then only in the presence of his doctor. The next day she wrote to her mother:

"The news of Wagner's death had so shattering an effect on my husband that the atmosphere here has been one since then of the profoundest melancholy. Even I had no notion of how passionate was the love he still felt in his innermost heart for Wagner, in spite of everything. Bülow's life is so closely interwoven with the name of Wagner that, in his own words, which he brought out with great difficulty, he felt as if his own soul had died with this fiery spirit, and only a fragment of his body still wanders upon earth."

Naturally, she added, the company of Alexander Ritter had been not only welcome but a positive necessity in some of his paroxysms of grief; while the presence of Brahms brought him only painful feelings of all kinds.[14] Some days later, when he learned that Cosima's own life was in danger by her helpless abandonment to her grief and her abstinence from food, he sent her the historic telegram that was a masterpiece of kindliness and tact — "Sœur, il faut vivre."

Honest old Verdi, who never pretended, never compromised, never indulged himself in a single sentence of conventional complaisance, was cut to the heart by Wagner's death. "Sad, sad, sad!" he wrote to Giulio Ricordi on the 14th. "Frankly, when I read the news yesterday I was crushed. Let us say no more about it. A great individuality has gone, a name that will leave a powerful impress on the history of art." And reading his letter again before dispatching it, he, who rarely spoke in superlatives, crossed out the "potente", which he felt to be inadequate, and substituted for it "potentissima" — "a most powerful impress".

9

Adolf Gross and his wife had hurried to Venice as soon as they received Daniela's wire. Richter came from Vienna, a faithful Kurvenal groping to his place at the feet of the dead Tristan. While Frau Gross comforted Cosima as best she could, Adolf took on himself the heavy burden of keeping callers and inquisitive journalists from her, checking the impulses of the town authorities and others to intrude upon her grief with well-meant but unwanted official assurances of sympathy, and making arrangements for the departure. Wolkoff and others were anxious to have a death mask made by the sculptor Benvenuti, but Cosima would not hear of it: in the end Daniela, unknown to her mother, gave her consent, on condition that the mask should not go outside the family.[15] Keppler em-

---

[14] BBL, pp. 389, 390.

[15] Glasenapp's account of the matter runs thus: "'During the afternoon [of the 14th]', so we have been informed by Frau Geheimrat Thode [Daniela], 'the artists harassed me again with regard to the death mask: Passini, indeed, gave it up, but Wolkoff wounded me sorely by his insistence on my 'egoism': I had to order him sternly to be silent, and I withstood all his arguments. But when, in the evening, Dr. Keppler told me simply and quietly that I was doing wrong, and that Mama herself, to say nothing of the friends and disciples, would not thank me, I yielded

balmed the body, which was placed in a coffin ordered from Vienna: Cosima had cut off her beautiful hair, which had always been Wagner's delight, and laid it on the dead man's breast.

On the 16th the mournful cortège glided silently down the waters of the Grand Canal to the station, which Gross had prevailed upon the railway authorities, for Cosima's sake, to close for a while to the public. At two o'clock began the long slow journey to Bayreuth, Joukowsky, Gross and Richter accompanying the children, Cosima, still blind and deaf to everything in the outer world that had suddenly become a desert to her, in a small coupé alone with all that now remained of Richard Wagner. At Innsbrück they were joined by Levi and Porges. At the Bavarian frontier town of Kufstein Bürkel was awaiting them with a letter of condolence from the King, of which Daniela took charge. They arrived in Munich at three o'clock in the afternoon of the 17th; the station was filled with mourners bearing torches and bringing flowers. The train remained there an hour; and here, as elsewhere, it fell to Gross to keep, as far as was possible, all sight and sound of the crowds from Cosima. It was not until half an hour before midnight that they reached Bayreuth, where a silent throng was awaiting the last home-coming of the Meister. Cosima wished the body to be taken at once to Wahnfried, but this could not be done: it remained all night in the station under a guard of honour. At Wahnfried she missed her wedding rings, and Joukowsky went back to the station to search for them. In the end they were found on the floor of the room; they had slipped from her finger unnoticed by her, so wasted had she become after four days of virtual starvation.

At four o'clock on the afternoon of Sunday, the 18th, the last public tributes to Wagner were paid at the station. Muncker and Feustel spoke out of the abundance of their hearts, a regimental band played Siegfried's Trauermarsch, a male voice choir sang the unaccompanied chorus which Wagner had written for the home-coming of Weber's remains to Dresden in 1844, and the King's

and gave permission: I was present when the cast was made, but said nothing to Mama about it'." According to Wolkoff (p. 224), who was obviously anxious to take to himself the whole credit in the eyes of posterity for having the mask made, "Daniela's memory failed her when she told her story to Glasenapp". Of that we cannot be sure. It is evident enough from Wolkoff's own story that he had worried Daniela and Joukowsky about the death mask almost from the moment he had entered the house of mourning: the main difficulty had been all along that it was impossible to separate Cosima from the body for that purpose.

aide-de-camp, Count Pappenheim, laid a wreath on the coffin in his royal master's name. Then the long procession set out for Wahnfried through the packed, silent and half-lit streets, from every house of which flew a black flag: the coffin was on an open hearse drawn by four horses. At five o'clock it reached the house, where the public participation in the mourning ended. Only two wreaths — those of the King — lay on the coffin as it was carried through the outer gates. Snow was falling as the cortège made its way to the place in the garden where Wagner had prepared his own tomb years before. Twelve men bore the coffin there — Muncker, Feustel, Gross, Wolzogen, Seidl, Joukowsky, Wilhelmj, Porges, Levi, Richter, Standhartner and Niemann, while the four children [16] grasped the corners of the pall. It was at the graveside that the one jarring note was unwittingly struck. The address delivered by a local clergyman as he blessed the grave seems to have given offence by its conventionally and too professionally religious tone: "denominational priests", said one writer afterwards, "could not understand a spirit whose Christianity had no churchly tincture about it but was rooted solely in the personality of the Saviour and His words." [17]

One by one the friends went away in the deepening twilight, leaving only the children at the graveside, awaiting their mother. She came from Wahnfried leaning on Gross's arm; and in her presence the coffin was lowered into the vault. For a while she remained there, lost in her memories and her grief, till the children led her back to the house, the opening was walled up, and the great stone that Wagner had prepared long ago laid upon the mound. To that grave, forty-seven years later, the ashes of Cosima herself were brought.

---

[16] Blandine was not there.
[17] Richard Hofmann, quoted in GLRW, VI, 784 *note*.

NEW LIGHT ON THE
SIEGFRIED IDYLL

[See Chapter XIII]

THE "EPISODE" of bars 92–148 of the *Idyll* is a curious piece of spatchcocking that has always been something of a mystery to the listener. The key to the mystery is at last afforded by a passage in Wagner's "Brown Book" that was published for the first time in an article by Dr. Otto Strobel on *Richard Wagners "Braunes Buch"* in the *Bayreuther Festspielführer* for 1934.

The date of the entry in the "Brown Book" is "Sylvester 68–69", i.e. the last day of 1868. It consists of the melody of the episode in a slightly different form from that which it was to assume later in the *Idyll*. It runs thus:

N°. 1

and it is set to the following words:

> Schlaf, Kindchen, schlafe;
> Im Garten gehn zwei Schafe;
> Ein schwarzes und ein weisses;
> Und wenn das Kind nicht schlafen will
> So kommt das schwarz und beisst es.

(Sleep, baby, sleep. In the garden are two sheep, a black one and a white one; and if the baby doesn't go to sleep the black one will come and bite it.)

To comply with the key-necessities of the *Idyll* Wagner transposes the melody from G major (its key in the "Brown Book") to B major; he alters it at one or two points, and he completely changes the harmonic lay-out. He gives the tune to the oboe, marking it "very simply". The accompaniment is curious. It is allotted entirely to the strings, *sotto voce*, only two voices at a time, commencing with the violins:

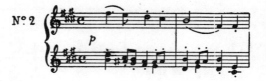

passing from one pair to another downwards, and finishing up with the 'cellos and basses growling it out in the depths:

The two accompaniment-voices run in thirds with each other almost without a break, as shown in the last two quotations.

What is the explanation of this somewhat odd section of the *Idyll* and of its peculiar harmonic and orchestral treatment? Simply this, that Wagner, in his capacity not so much of composer as of happy father, was indulging himself in a bit of playful pictorialism by way of illustration of the words of the "Brown Book" doggerel. The oboe solo gives the tune the pastoral tinge traditionally associated in music with sheep or shepherds. The almost inseparable thirds depict the two sheep walking side by side. (Continuous sequences of thirds have often been used by composers to suggest intimacy or physical inseparability: the piano part of Wolf's song "Nun wandre, Maria", for instance, is from first to last — thirty-eight bars in all — in parallel thirds, suggesting Joseph and Mary walking side by side. Handel adopts the same procedure in the closing duet between Caesar and Cleopatra in his opera *Giulio Cesare*. Numerous other examples could be cited.) The culminating realistic touch in the *Idyll* is the deep growling of the sheep as they threaten the baby (No. 3): and the listener will observe the sudden dissolution of the threat in a surge of paternal tenderness on Wagner's part.

Later there comes a slow pianissimo statement of bar 4 of the "Brown Book" tune, this time in the original key of G major and with the original harmonic substructure; the marking is "very tenderly":

N° 4

(These bars — Nos. 122–148 — have always been a particular puzzle to students of the *Idyll.*)

The episode has therefore little basic connection with the accredited hero of the *Idyll*, the baby Siegfried, who was not born when the cradle song was jotted down in the "Brown Book": the heroine of it is the little Eva, who was nearly two years old at that time.

Why Wagner permitted himself this indulgence in a naïve pictorial episode that does not explain itself to the listener in terms purely of itself, and, indeed, hardly correlates with the rest of the work, is now evident enough. The "Triebschen Idyll" — its original title — was not a "Siegfried Idyll" in the present acceptation of that term but a series of domestic confidences centring in happy Triebschen as a whole, and never intended for hearing by anyone but the family and a few intimates. It was not until 1878 that Wagner, greatly to his own distress and Cosima's, allowed the work to be published, and then only under financial duress.

BOMBASTES FURIOSO

Who dares this pair of boots displace
Must meet Bombastes face to face.

W. B. Rhodes, *Bombastes
Furioso* (1810).

I N THE NUMBER for April, 1941 of the American *Musical Quarterly*, the editor of that journal, Dr. Carl Engel, appearing once
more in his favourite rôle of Bombastes Furioso, publishes what
purports to be a review of the third volume of this biography. Dr.
Engel has so often honoured me with his disapproval of myself and
all my works that from sheer repetition I have long since ceased to
be flattered by the compliment. But latterly, thanks to a morbid
hatred of Wagner that seems to have sprung up in him because
Adolf Hitler, in his own foolish way, is a Wagner-enthusiast, Dr.
Engel finds himself moved to include the composer and myself in
one comprehensive denunciation. Having persuaded himself — and
he has never had any difficulty in persuading himself of the heaven-
sent truth of whatever his prejudices incline him to believe — that
Wagnerism and Nazism are identical in root, flower and fruit, he
now suggests that if only we realised that to give up Wagner's music
would merely be to give up "the music of Klingsor who for one
hundred years has numbed our senses with his witchcraft" and "allowed to grow up round us a garden of gorgeous flowers that at last
have revealed themselves as poisonous and death-dealing", then
"we should retaliate, then we should ban and burn every scrap of
Wagner's music and writings, and every book written about the
amazing wizard, beginning with the books of the Anglo-Wagnerian
Ernest Newman." Dr. Engel, it will be seen, is getting on: the mono-
maniac has developed into the pyromaniac.

If I have not made a practice of replying to Dr. Engel's ill-tempered comments on myself and my work during the last dozen years

---

[1] This Appendix was written in the summer of 1941, immediately after my reading the review to which I refer in it. I print it precisely as it was then, though Dr.
Engel died in 1944.

or so it is because I would as soon have thought of going round with an antiseptic cloth wiping up the slaver of a rabid dog. But I feel that I ought not to bring the present biography to a close without some exposure of the manners and the methods of this gentleman, who, on the strength of his always confident assumption of an omniscience he does not possess, seems to be accepted at his own valuation in some American circles. For this purpose — the demonstration of his passion for laying down the law on matters concerning which his ignorance is abysmal — I propose to discuss in detail just one paragraph of his review, relating to my treatment of the King Ludwig subject. I select this, rather than anything Dr. Engel has to say about Wagner, because individual temperament and emotional reaction have nothing to do with this particular matter: it is an affair purely and simply of facts. And the proof that Dr. Engel has in this case provided a perfect exposure of the bombastic ignoramus he mostly is may perhaps throw a side-light on some of his achievements in other fields.

"Appendix II" [of my third volume], he writes, "professes to deal with 'the "madness" of King Ludwig'. If anything were needed to show the author's peculiar standpoint it is these three pages of print wherein, among other wild shots, the author accuses the 'alienists' of having done 'so obligingly' the Bavarian politicians' 'dirty work' for them in 1886. Verily, one does not have to be an alienist or a psychiatrist to recognise the symptoms of Ludwig's mental malady. One has but to read the fragments of the King's own diaries, published some time between the abdication of the Wittelsbachs and the advent of Hitler, to gain an appalling glimpse into the suffering of that poor, perverted soul. Mr. Newman, with all his casuistry, cannot change the case-history of the royal patient and make him out a normal man, fit to reign over a kingdom."

The reader will kindly observe first of all the typical Engelian gambit of the first sentence of this quotation. *I* merely "profess" to deal with the subject; it is Dr. Engel who knows about it all. *My* "standpoint" is dogmatically pronounced by this oracle, without a shred of supporting evidence or argument, to be "peculiar"; for the correct standpoint we have, of course, to take up our position by the side of the omniscient Dr. Carl Engel. Now whether I am right or wrong in my reading of King Ludwig in general and his "mental malady" in particular, I can at least claim to have given as many years to the study of the subject as Dr. Engel has given minutes. For as it happens, I have been engaged for a number of years on a book on the topic, in the course of which I have familiar- ised myself with every first-hand document, wise or foolish, con- nected with it, with every published letter to and from the King, with the memoirs and correspondence of a round score of diplomats, politicians, observers, publicists and so on contemporary with the events, with all the biographies and studies of the King, in English, German, French and Italian, from the 1880's down to yesterday, with the latest German histories of Bavaria, and with the latest Ger- man treatises, based on investigation of various political archives, on the King's share in domestic and international politics during his reign. In addition I have put in a good deal of work at books and encyclopaedia articles on mental diseases, and at the numerous medical discussions of the King's case from the 1880's downwards. Whatever, then, may be the value or lack of value of the conclusions to which my study of the subject has led me, I can at any rate put in a fair claim to be acquainted with the facts of the case; and the setting of a few of these facts before the reader will suffice to dem- onstrate that Dr. Engel is the merest amateur in this matter.

Apparently the many writers who have taken the trouble to exam- ine critically the evidence for or against the King's "madness" have merely been wasting their time. It needs only an Engel, ignorant at once of the historical facts and of the literature of alienism, to give one glance at the complicated matter and decide that "one does not need to be an alienist or a psychiatrist to recognise the symp- toms of Ludwig's mental malady" — whatever, in Dr. Engel's superlative wisdom, that may have been, for he gives us no further light on that very debatable matter. To reach in five minutes the first and final truth about it all, it appears, "one has but to read the fragments of the King's own diaries, published some time between the abdication of the Wittelsbachs and the advent of Hitler". Dr. Engel's vagueness as to the date of issue of those "fragments" sug- gests no very close acquaintance with this material, which was pub- lished by Edir Grein, under the title of *Tagebuch-Aufzeichnungen von Ludwig II König von Bayern*, in 1925.

Characteristically Engelian is the confident assumption that any- one with a grain of sense who has read these "fragments" will as a matter of course take Dr. Engel's view of them.[2] Apparently he is not aware — though if he were it would not cause him to modify his dogmatism — that other writers on this subject since 1925 have read these extracts from the diaries without coming to at all the same conclusion regarding them as that of Dr. Engel. Indeed, had he read my third volume before professing to review it, instead of merely turning, as he obviously has done, to the Appendices, he would have discovered that I myself had had a good deal to say about these "fragments" in my tenth chapter.

The readers of the *Musical Quarterly* are magisterially informed that "Mr. Newman, with all his casuistry, cannot change the history of the royal patient and make him out a normal man, fit to reign over a kingdom". I will not retort that this sentence brands Dr. Engel as a casuist, for his mind is too un-subtle, his command of the finesses of the English language too slender, his methods in every matter too much those of a bull at a gate, for it ever to be possible to fasten the label of "casuist" on him. His characteristic failings are of quite another order; they arise from that combination of ignorance in the matter of facts and congenital muddle-headedness in argument of which the sentence I have just quoted is a perfect example.

It shows entire ignorance of the subject to speak of Ludwig as "the royal patient", thereby giving the unsuspecting reader the erroneous impression that the King had been the subject of medical treatment, that his "malady" had been scientifically diagnosed, and that his "case-history" had been made out in a form corresponding to the meaning of that term in medical circles. The truth is that Ludwig had never been anyone's "patient" for his "mental malady", and least of all the "patient" of the four doctors who certified his incurable derangement in 1886. Not one of these men had ever examined him in any way, ever been in his presence, ever exchanged a single word with him. With the nature of the "evidence" on which they claimed to base their findings I will deal in a moment. Here I will make only the further comment on Dr. Engel's remarks that so far from my having casuistically tried to persuade my readers that

---

[2] The "fragments", besides being most incompetently "edited" by Edir Grein (Erwin Riedinger), have obviously been selected for a purpose. Grein was severely handled, six years ago, by the Director of the Bavarian State Archives, who had access to the diaries as a whole.

Ludwig was "fit to reign over a kingdom", I have expressly said, in the eleventh line of the Appendix, that "he had, of course, become quite impossible as a king"; not, however, because he was mad, but because he would not give proper attention to what he had come to regard as the tiresome and futile business of kingship. His letters enable us to trace the whole course of his mind. The generous, romantic boy of less than nineteen who had succeeded to the throne in 1864 had believed too innocently in the goodness of man and in the possibility of the salvation of German culture by the German princes. Gradually he became disillusioned on both these points, while his shrewd common sense soon convinced him that politics was largely chicanery, and politicians, for the most part, knaves, or fools, or both. So he turned away in disgust from it all, and plunged deeper and deeper into those architectural fantasies of his that were the convulsive expression of his desire to realise himself as an artist. The result was that by 1886 not only was he on the verge of bankruptcy but a clog on the administrative machine, for he was always in the mountains, inaccessible to his ministers when they wanted to consult him, and taking slight interest in the things that interested them most. He had certainly become impossible as a king; but he was not on that account any more "mad" than is any other man who neglects a business that has become disagreeable to him in order to enjoy the things that give him pleasure.

As for my trying to "make him out a normal man", Dr. Engel is merely beating the air. No one can define a "normal" man. Normality and abnormality are definable in only a rule-of-thumb way as each the negation of the other. And so with the distinction between sanity and insanity. The two shade off into each other by a thousand imperceptible degrees, and there is no saying where one ends and the other begins. We all of us suffer, for instance, more or less, from delusions; but no psycho-chemical test can be found that will enable us to draw a dividing line between the delusions of the sane and those of the insane. We go by rule of thumb; we decide that A, who believes himself without reason to be a great military strategist, is merely peculiar, while B, who believes himself to be the great Napoleon, we declare to be insane. Alienists today frankly confess that there is no real science in matters of this kind. As one eminent recent writer has put it, "strictly speaking, insanity is really a social and legal term and not medical. . . No satisfactory definition can therefore be arrived at, since it would be necessary to define what we mean by sanity, which would involve us in equal difficulties." It is not the doctors who decide, but, as the same authority puts it, "society" that "steps in" in certain cases — when it feels that eccentricity has been carried a trifle too far, and the subject, in his own interest or in that of others, should be deprived of certain social rights. No law could interfere with a man who was ruining himself and his family by spending all his money on schemes for creating a new species by crossing animals of the most unlikely kinds; but if he were to bequeath his whole fortune to a scheme for reaching the moon by rocket, leaving his widow and children penniless, the law would certainly declare the will invalid. Medical science of itself could not prove that the one man was any more deranged than the other. It is "society" that "steps in", deciding, in a very rough-and-ready way, that the former was eccentric to the point of absurdity but not justifying legal restraint; while the eccentricity of the other had risen to such a point of absurdity that no good and much harm would be done by letting the man have his way.

The question whether King Ludwig was "normal" or "abnormal", "deranged" or "sane", is therefore one that cannot be settled *ex cathedra* by even the most scientific alienist; and in 1886 the science of psychiatry, still in its childhood, had only just been born. The four doctors grandiloquently declared the King to be "in an advanced state of paranoia, a form of mental derangement well known to alienists from experience". Modern alienists are more cautious: they deny that "paranoia" is a definite, distinguishable "form of mental derangement", and allow it no higher status than that of a convenient term. In the last resort it means nothing more than what is contained in the two Greek words that were run into one somewhere about the 1870's: the word means nothing more than "not in one's right mind", which in turn means just nothing at all in any scientific sense. The doctors who certified the King added to the "paranoia", by way of explanation to the vulgar, the word "Verrücktheit" — which, according to the dictionaries, means "mental derangement, alienation, insanity, lunacy". So that all these alleged scientists had done in pronouncing the King to be insane because he was "suffering from paranoia" was to say that he was insane because he was insane.

Dr. Engel characterises as a "wild shot" on my part my remark about the four alienists "who so obligingly did the Bavarian politicians' dirty work for them in 1886". The impression he wishes to convey is that a rank outsider like myself is presuming to criticise the honest scientific findings of four experts in their special field. But once more he only succeeds in demonstrating his own complete ignorance of the facts of the case. They are as follows.

The lengthy dossier, running to nearly twenty pages of print, containing the "evidence" of the King's insanity is tainted and flawed from start to finish. For the most part it is based on statements made by certain of Ludwig's lackeys all of whom were in the power of their official superior, one Count von Holnstein, the Master of the Horse, who had conceived a fanatical hatred of the monarch who had made him, and was now a leading spirit in the plot that was being hatched against him. These lackeys obligingly furnished domestic tittle-tattle of the sort the politicians were in quest of. They were interviewed behind the King's back. Ludwig himself was never examined by any of the signatories; there was no independent cross-examination of the witnesses, no pretence of hearing other witnesses or collecting evidence of any kind but that desired by the conspirators for their purpose. News of the plot and of the taking of "evidence" from the lackeys had filtered through to several people in the King's personal entourage. These people, men of standing and education in close present or recent association with him, were prepared to testify that they had never detected any signs of mental derangement in him; but they were either not called upon to give testimony or their offer of it was turned down. Theirs was not the sort of evidence the planners of the *Putsch* wanted.

The report of the four alienists, audaciously declaring the King to be not only insane but incapable of ever recovering his sanity! — he was not quite forty-one at the time — was signed on the 8th June, 1886. The next day a Commission, accompanied by asylum warders, set out to Hohenschwangau to arrest him. The world knows the rest of the story. The King, well aware that for their own skins' sake his jailers would never release him or allow him any communication with the outside world, chose to end his days in the Starnberg Lake on the 13th. It was naturally assumed, then and later, that the ministers took action *in consequence of* the medical report. That is an inversion of the facts: they had long been plotting action

on purely political grounds, and they wanted, and set about obtaining, a medical voucher only to give their coup d'état an appearance
of legality afterwards. Thanks to the publication in 1932 and 1934
respectively of (a) the letters to the Munich ministers from the
Bavarian ambassador in Berlin, who had been commissioned in
April to sound Bismarck with regard to the already long-planned
coup de main, (b) the contemporary jottings of the Secretary of the
Prussian Legation in Munich, who was in the counsel of the conspirators, we can now trace the evolution of the affair step by step.

The primary plan of campaign of the conspirators had been to
depose the King on the ground that his debts in connection with his
building schemes exposed him to the risk of legal action and a
declaration of bankruptcy, which would have lowered the prestige
of the monarchy. The medical dossier was merely a supporting line.
From the very beginning of the King's reign (1864) there had been
intriguers planning to depose the boy of nineteen in order to get
power into their own hands. Their technique even then was to spread
the rumour that he was insane — the convincing proof of it being
that he was infatuated with Wagner, who himself was regarded as
a dangerous lunatic by many people at that time. This rumour was
swallowed all the more credulously because there was known to be
a strain of mental instability in the royal family on the mother's
side. There had been times since 1864 when Ludwig would gladly
have resigned his office. In 1886 nothing would have induced him
to do so. Therefore he would have to be removed by force; and to
help in the accomplishment of this a medical report pronouncing
him insane would be a great help, for by a clause in the Bavarian
constitution a monarch who had been incapable for any reason of
exercising government for more than a year could be deposed.
(This accounts for the very convenient passage in the medical certificate reading "the King is incapable of exercising government,
and this incapacity will endure not merely for more than a year but
for the remainder of his life".)

In mid-April, however, Bismarck had unwittingly thrown a span-
ner into the machinery of the plot. He had suggested to the King a
simple plan for funding his debts in parliamentary form; and had
Ludwig acted energetically on it the threat of bankruptcy would
have disappeared and the ground been cut from under the conspirators' feet. We have contemporary testimony that for a while

they were in utter confusion and despair. But the King soon lost interest in the matter, and neglected to press home the order he had given to the Diet to take the matter of his finances in hand. This gave the plotters confidence, and they went on with their plan.

The "evidence" had been collected and the medical report drawn up by Gudden, at their instigation, in March. It was shown to Bismarck in confidence by the Bavarian ambassador in Berlin. He saw, of course, the object of it — to justify the coup d'état in the eyes of the country after it had been successful, — and he shrewdly pointed out a vital flaw in it. "To depose a King simply on the word of a single alienist", the ambassador reported to Munich, "seems to him a risky procedure. . . And would a report not based on a personal examination count for anything?" — to say nothing of the childish nature of some of the "evidence".[3] He advised the ministers, if they felt they *must* take action against the King, to do so in proper constitutional form through the Diet. The ambassador, however, told him that they could not follow his advice, as it "would deprive them of the tactical advantage of a fait accompli!" But they saw the wisdom of the Chancellor's warning that they would be criticised if they "deposed a monarch simply on the word of a single alienist", who, moreover, had never seen the King. So they arranged for three more signatures. A few more items were inserted in Gudden's months-old report; on the night of the 7/8th June the new document was copied out by Gudden, and on the morning of the 8th the four signed it. All of them, by the way, were functionaries the retention of whose posts would depend on the favour of the conspiring ministers after the coup d'état. One of them, replying some three years later to angry popular criticism, ingenuously pleaded that to have examined the King personally "would have necessitated postponing action"!

My criticism of the doctors and the politicians, then, far from being the "wild shot" of a mere outsider at certain good men and true, was based at every point on facts which are beyond dispute. It is Dr. Engel who, in his customary reckless fashion, is making a wild shot — the hand of impudence drawing at a venture the bow of ignorance.

I have gone into this matter at such length because this one para-

---

[3] Bismarck's contemptuous description of the report later was "rakings from the King's waste-paper basket and cupboards".

graph of Dr. Engel's provides in concentrated form a perfect sample of all the defects, congenital and acquired, of his mind — reckless irresponsibility in assertion, and a trick of imposing on the uninformed reader by the pose of knowledge far beyond the ordinary in matters of which he does not know even the rudiments. He is a case for the pathologists.

Of one grave error, it is true, he convicts me, and I must ask the reader to make the necessary correction in his copy of the third volume of this Life. The number of Wagner's Putzmacherin letters in the Library of Congress is not fifteen but fourteen.

INDEX

INDEX

[x]

INDEX